INVESTIGATIONS AT SUNSET MESA RUIN

Investigations at
SUNSET MESA RUIN

Archaeology at the Confluence of the
Santa Cruz and Rillito Rivers, Tucson, Arizona

Edited by Richard Ciolek-Torrello,
Edgar K. Huber, and Robert B. Neily

Report prepared for
the U.S. Army Corps of Engineers
Los Angeles District
Contract No. DACW09-93-D-0004
Delivery Order No. 10

Technical Series 66
Statistical Research, Inc.
Tucson, Arizona

Statistical Research Technical Series

General series editor: Jeffrey H. Altschul
Volume editor: Dale Brenneman
Production manager: Lynne Yamaguchi
Graphics manager: Cynthia Elsner
Production assistants: Karen Barber, Chester Schmidt
Cover art: Cynthia Elsner
Cover design: Lynne Yamaguchi

Published by Statistical Research, Inc.
P.O. Box 31865
Tucson, AZ 85751-1865

ISBN 1-879442-63-9

First printing: March 1999
Typeset and printed in the United States of America.
Printed on acid-free paper.

CONTENTS

LIST OF FIGURES

LIST OF TABLES

ABSTRACT

Data recovery at Sunset Mesa Ruin, AZ AA:12:10 (ASM), uncovered a segment of a single-component Rincon phase settlement dating between A.D. 1000 and 1100, as well as the remains of a turn-of-the-century adobe homestead. Excavations were confined to a 7,500-m^2 area in the northwestern corner of the site, primarily within the proposed Corps of Engineers (COE) overbank protection area along the Rillito River. The prehistoric component consisted of a discrete residential cluster of five pit houses that formed a sequential series of small courtyard groups, a midden area, 13 other pit features, and six other extramural features. A cemetery area was not identified, although two cremations discovered during the testing phase were located east of the house cluster. A second courtyard group may have been present in the heavily eroded and disturbed area immediately west of the house cluster, as suggested by the presence of two large storage vessels buried in pits. If a second courtyard group was present, the two would have constituted one of several residential precincts of this Rincon phase hamlet.

Other significant features related to the prehistoric occupation of the site included a ramada and food-storage and -preparation areas, and a segment of an irrigation canal. The ramada and food-storage and -preparation area was characterized by the presence of several reconstructible storage vessels, grinding and processing tools, masses of processed seeds, and clusters of fire-cracked rocks. This work area may have been related to the investigated courtyard group, or it might have functioned as a communal food-processing area for two or more residential groups in this and adjacent residential precincts.

A north-south-oriented, prehistoric canal segment was identified along the edge of the second terrace, on which the site was situated. The presence of this canal has implications for both the economic base of the settlement and the organization of the community. First, it suggests that the occupants irrigated their fields rather than relying on floodwater farming. Further, an evaluation of canal sediments indicated that the canal originated along the Rillito River, undoubtedly for irrigating fields on the first terrace below the site, to the west.

The historical-period components at the site consisted of a three-room adobe house constructed by Basillio Cuevas around 1893, a general surface scatter of trash related to this occupation and the subsequent Sunset Dairy dating after 1915, and more recent trash deposits related to subsequent ranch operations. Twelve historical- or modern-era extramural features also were recorded.

ACKNOWLEDGMENTS

Archaeological investigations at Sunset Mesa Ruin were sponsored by the U.S. Army Corps of Engineers, Los Angeles District, Contract No. DACW09-93-D-0004, Delivery Order No. 10. Their support is greatly appreciated. Foremost, appreciation is extended to Roderic McLean, archaeologist for the Los Angeles District, whose cooperation and assistance were instrumental in carrying out these investigations. Especially important was his concurrence in extending excavations outside of the APE, that we might be able to obtain closure on the prehistoric house cluster found at its edge. The Rillito Riverbank [P]rotection [P]roject, of which the current project is a small part, has been a cost-share project with Pima County. Linda Mayro, Pima County archaeologist, has always been extremely helpful in facilitating our research and sharing historical and archaeological information on the vicinity.

The following crew are to be commended for their efforts during August and September, 1994: Alex Benitez, Sara Fowler, Lee Lindsay, Bob Jones (crew chief), Jay Sander, and Robby Heckman. Robert B. Neily served as project director and Richard Ciolek-Torrello served as principal investigator. Particular thanks go to Sara Fowler for her organizational assistance to the project director. Thanks also go to Dan Arnit, of Innovative Excavating, Inc., for his professional backhoe services. We also are grateful to James Heidke, of Desert Archaeology, Inc., for sharing the costs for the petrographic study.

We would like to extend our appreciation to Ellen Wheller, the property owner, and Guy Parker, ranch manager, for providing access to the site and for their interest and cooperation during the fieldwork. They allowed us to extend our excavations outside of the APE onto their private land, and to cross through their dairy and pastures every day to access the site.

The processing of artifacts and samples was ably conducted under the direction of Carol Ellick, who served as laboratory director. She is also commended for coordinating the display materials for the professional information-sharing meeting and the site tour held for the COE, and for arranging for a site steward during the fieldwork. Early in the course of the excavations, we encountered problems with vandals. We are grateful to Tom Gordon, the site steward, for patrolling the site on the weekends and preventing further damage. Special thanks are extended to Robby Heckman for his enthusiasm, dedication, and diligence in conducting the ceramic analysis.

SRI support staff are to be commended for a fine, professional job in producing the final report. Dale Brenneman was the technical editor. As on so many previous occasions, Dale attacked her task with unexcelled dedication. Her meticulous and thorough review of the text, tables, illustrations, and references led to numerous technical and substantive improvements to the report. Production of the report was managed by Lynne Yamaguchi, who also laid out the entire report. She was assisted by Chester Schmidt, who coded the text and tables, and Karen Barber, who proofread and provided general support. Drafting was ably undertaken by Susan Martin, Lois Kain, and Cindy Elsner. Under the direction of Lynne, the production division has brought a high degree of professionalism and a quest for technical and aesthetic quality that has resulted in another truly stellar volume. We can only hope that its contents measure up to its appearance.

To all those associated with this project, we extend our sincere appreciation, and we apologize to any whom we may have forgotten inadvertently.

CHAPTER 1

Introduction

Robert B. Neily and Richard Ciolek-Torrello

This report presents the results of data recovery at Sunset Mesa Ruin (AZ AA:12:10 [ASM]), a Rincon phase settlement dating from A.D. 1000 to 1100, with a historical-period, turn-of-the-century homestead component. The site, which is situated near the confluence of the Santa Cruz and Rillito Rivers in the Tucson Basin (Figures 1 and 2), was excavated by Statistical Research, Inc. (SRI), at the request of the U.S. Army, Corps of Engineers (COE), in conjunction with a planned project to provide bank stabilization along the Rillito River and to construct floodwater overbank protection, staging, and recreation areas (Figure 3).

Excavations conducted within the prehistoric component of Sunset Mesa Ruin yielded five prehistoric pit houses, a ramada/food-processing and storage area, two isolated jars, 35 other extramural features, and a canal segment. The portion of Sunset Mesa Ruin investigated during both testing (Harry and Ciolek-Torrello 1992) and data recovery phases represents approximately 22 percent (18,000 m^2) of the mapped surface artifact scatter (82,200 m^2), and is located primarily within the proposed Area of Potential Effects (APE) along the terrace edge overlooking the Rillito River (Figure 4). Data recovery efforts, however, concentrated on a smaller, 7,500-m^2 area that contained buried features and deposits at the western end of the APE and adjoining areas to the south. This area represents less than 10 percent of the overall site area. Because surface artifacts are concentrated within an approximately 12,000-m^2 area along the western margin of the site, which encompasses a portion of the data recovery area, it is likely that the principal buried portion of the site is centered there. The investigated segment of Sunset Mesa Ruin, therefore, contained only a fraction of the preserved portion of a site that probably contains buried features.

The historical-period component at Sunset Mesa Ruin consisted of a three-room adobe structure, and 12 historical-period to recent trash and thermal features. These features encompassed a surface scatter sampled during testing (Harry and Ciolek-Torrello 1992), and probably constituted the entire historical-period component of the site. Limited testing was conducted during data recovery in areas adjacent to the structure and south of the APE (see Figure 4), but no additional buried historical-period features were found.

Report Organization

This report is divided into 13 chapters. The succeeding sections in this first chapter provide the historical background of the project, including a brief summary of the results of the previous survey and testing phases, and outline the research design and questions that guided excavations and subsequent analyses.

Presented in Chapter 2 is the natural environmental setting of the project. Chapter 3 provides a cultural-historical overview of the study area, highlighting recent research on Rincon phase settlements in the Tucson Basin.

Chapter 4 describes the field methods, which include backhoe trenching, mechanical stripping, and the standard procedures used in the excavation of structures and for testing extramural features, the canal and the ramada area among them. Approaches used in sampling various features for macrobotanical and pollen remains also are outlined.

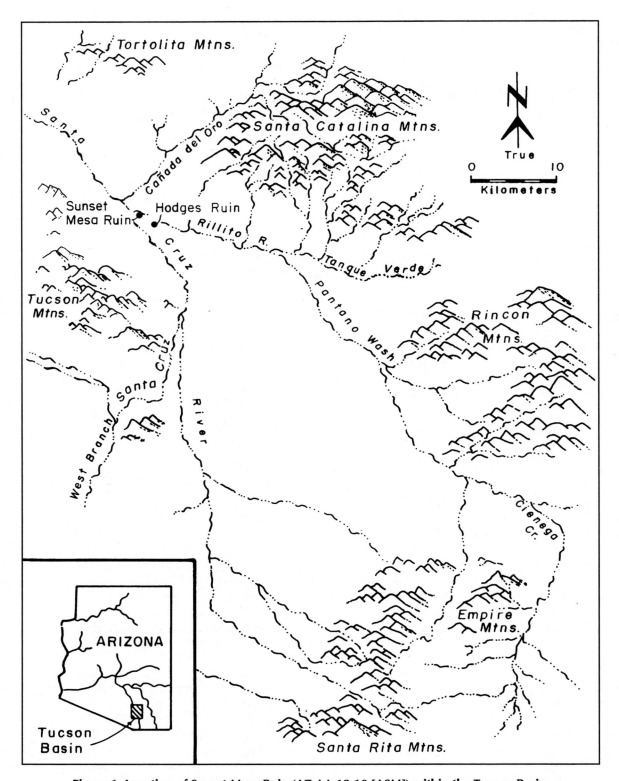

Figure 1. Location of Sunset Mesa Ruin (AZ AA:12:10 [ASM]) within the Tucson Basin.

Figure 2. Overview of Rillito River from Sunset Mesa, viewed northwest toward its confluence with the Santa Cruz River.

Chapter 5 details the various prehistoric features encountered during the excavation, beginning with each of the five pit houses and the ramada and canal features. This discussion is followed by descriptions of both the tested and untested extramural features. The chapter ends with a brief description of the historical-period adobe structure and its associated extramural features.

Results of the artifact analyses are presented in Chapters 6 through 12. These analyses include ceramics (Chapter 6), flaked and ground stone (Chapter 7), shell (Chapter 8), archaeobotanical remains (Chapter 9), pollen (Chapter 10), faunal remains (Chapter 11), and historical-period resources (Chapter 12). Analyses of ostracodes, archaeomagnetic dating, ceramic petrography, and obsidian are presented as appendixes, although relevant results of these analyses have been incorporated in the feature descriptions (Chapter 5) and the summary (Chapter 13).

The final chapter, Chapter 13, summarizes and synthesizes research at Sunset Mesa Ruin. Excavation results are assessed with regard to the specific research themes outlined in the research design presented in Chapter 1.

Previous Investigations and Project History

Sunset Mesa Ruin was first recorded by Frank Midvale (a.k.a. Mitalsky) in the late 1930s, during his independent survey of the Rillito River. He was so impressed by the site that he revisited it numerous times between 1937 and 1938, describing it as a "village of fair size" that contained some trash mounds (Arizona State Museum [ASM] site files). Midvale mentioned on the ASM site card that a map showing the locations of these surface features was in preparation. Apparently, the map never was completed, as it was not found with his other records of the site in the ASM site files (Ciolek-Torrello and Homburg 1990:46). Midvale also observed artifacts in natural exposures to a depth of 2.5 feet below the surface, and argued that deeper deposits were likely. As early as the 1930s, however, the site already had been subjected to slopewash erosion and gully erosion around its edges, which had "melted down" features, making it difficult to delineate them. Midvale

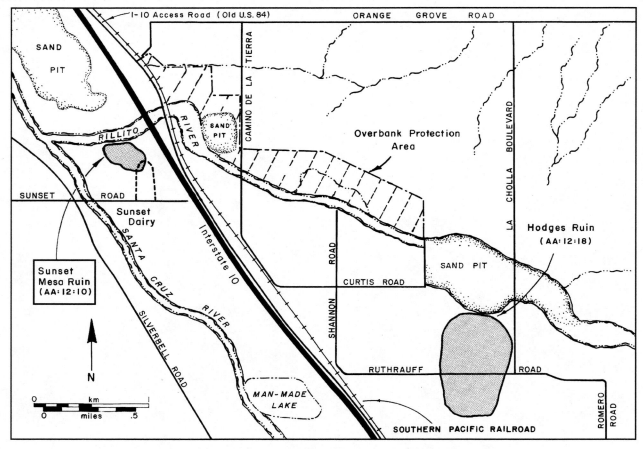

Figure 3. Sunset Mesa Ruin (AZ AA:12:10 [ASM]) and modern features at the confluence of the Santa Cruz and Rillito Rivers.

made three separate ceramic collections from the site that were curated at ASM, along with his records. These collections consist largely of sand-tempered plain ware, with relatively large numbers of Rincon Red-on-brown sherds and a few Sacaton Red-on-buff sherds, suggesting that the main occupation of the site occurred during the Sedentary period (Ciolek-Torrello and Homburg 1990:47). Trace frequencies of Casa Grande Red-on-buff, Tanque Verde Red-on-brown, and Salado Polychrome indicated that a Classic period occupation also may have been present. Finally, a few Papago Plain and Papago Red sherds suggested the presence of a protohistoric period occupation. Thus, Midvale's early research established Sunset Mesa Ruin as an important habitation site with a long occupational history.

More than 50 years passed before additional research was conducted at the site. The excavations reported in this volume represent the third and final phase of investigations conducted by SRI for the COE. During the first stage of work in 1989, SRI carried out archival research and an intensive, on-the-ground survey of the Rillito

River to identify properties potentially eligible for nomination to the National Register of Historic Places, as stipulated in Section 106 of the National Historic Preservation Act and implementing regulations (36CFR 800, COE ER 1130-2-438), that would be adversely affected by the proposed COE construction (Ciolek-Torrello and Homburg 1990). The Rillito River survey extended from the confluence of Tanque Verde Creek and Pantano Wash, which join to form the Rillito River, down to the latter's confluence with the Santa Cruz River, where Sunset Mesa Ruin is located. As a result of the survey and archival work, 21 archaeological sites were identified within a 600-foot right-of-way along each side of the river.

Sunset Mesa Ruin was recognized as perhaps the largest and most complex of these sites. Armed with copies of his records, SRI surveyors made a concerted effort to relocate the features identified by Midvale, but by 1989, no prehistoric features were evident on the surface. SRI surveyors did observe, however, a large and extremely dense artifact concentration along the heavily eroded terrace edge in the western part of the site. Although this

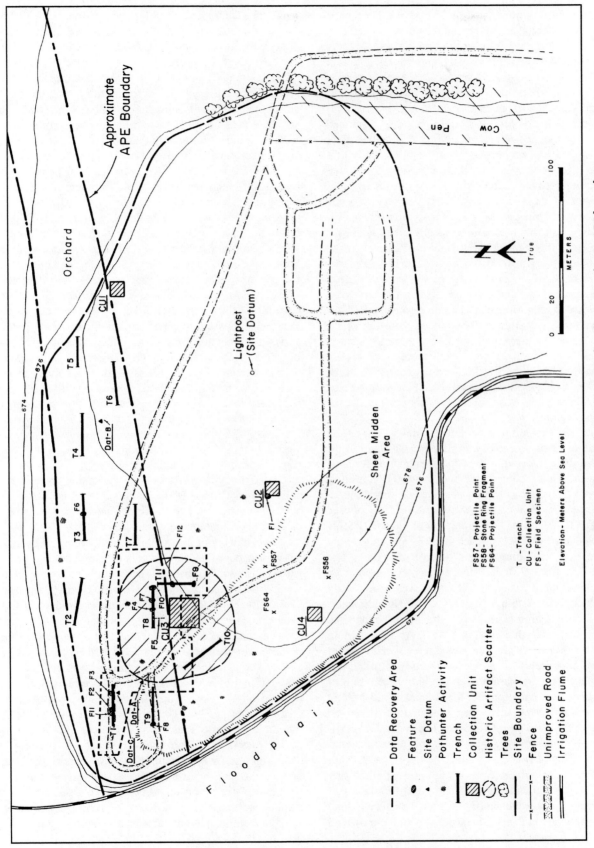

Figure 4. Plan map of Sunset Mesa Ruin (AZ AA:12:10 [ASM]) showing approximate APE boundary, testing phase trenches, collection units, and features, and area of intensive data recovery effort.

concentration was dominated by sherds and large numbers of lithic debitage, also present as lag deposits resulting from the extensive erosion were flakes, scrapers, cores, hammer stones, manos, slab and trough metates, a mortar and pestle, and shell artifacts. A great variety of lithic raw materials was observed, including basalt, rhyolite, andesite, quartz, metaquartzite, chert, and obsidian. Historical-period building materials, including fragments of an old flume, had been dumped in a large gulley at the northwest edge of the terrace in an attempt to curtail the erosion (Ciolek-Torrello and Homburg 1990:46). By contrast, artifacts were scattered in low densities over the remainder of the site, except in the vicinity of small potholes where piles of discarded sherds were found. The latter suggested that buried deposits might be found even in areas with low densities of surface artifacts.

Although portions of the site were disturbed, primarily by slope and gully erosion along the western edge of the terrace, most of the site appeared intact to the surveyors. They noted that building construction associated with the Sunset Dairy had affected the southeast portion of the site, and that another small portion had been bladed to create a target practice range, now covered with broken milk bottles. Vehicular traffic over the unsurfaced desert landscape had caused additional disturbance to the site, but this disturbance was shallow, leaving most of the site in good condition.

Based on this initial assessment, Sunset Mesa Ruin was one of eight potentially eligible sites located in the APE that were selected by the COE for National Register evaluation. This second phase in the evaluation process involved a limited testing program to locate intact subsurface cultural deposits and features within the proposed APE, and to determine the boundaries of the site. Testing was conducted in 1990 at each of the eight potentially eligible sites, including Sunset Mesa Ruin (Harry and Ciolek-Torrello 1992). The goal of the testing program was to evaluate areas of the sites that were most likely to provide information pertaining to site significance, necessitating testing portions of site areas beyond the roughly 150-foot-wide (45.7 m) APE. At Sunset Mesa Ruin, this testing program involved a reconnaissance of the site's boundaries and surface deposits, controlled surface collections, backhoe trenching, and preparation of a site map. A total of nine, approximately 25-m-long trenches was excavated in a staggered pattern within and parallel to the APE boundaries (see Figure 4). Two additional trenches were excavated in an area of artifact concentration just beyond the southern edge of the APE to determine if subsurface features were present at the site, as few were found initially within the APE. Before any of the trenches were excavated, however, artifact collections were made in 2-m-wide swaths along the projected length of each trench and additionally in four large blocks (totaling 417 m^2 in area) in portions of the site not covered by the trench collections (Harry and Ciolek-Torrello 1992:30). Following excavation of the trenches, samples of approximately 0.5 m^3 of backdirt from each trench were screened through $\frac{1}{4}$-inch wire mesh. In addition, a small area south of Trench 8 was hand stripped and screened to explore a segment of a historical-period adobe wall foundation found in this trench.

As a result of these tests, 11 prehistoric features were recorded at Sunset Mesa Ruin, including 2 possible pit houses, 2 cremations, 1 storage pit, 1 unidentified pit, and 5 roasting pits or hearths. In addition, a buried, turn-of-the-century adobe house foundation was identified along one of the backhoe trenches. The historical-period feature was associated with the Cuevas homestead, based on a historical-period map (Roskruge 1893). All but one of the features were identified in trench profiles, the exception being a roasting pit exposed on the surface. The large collection of artifacts obtained from the controlled surface collections and screened units confirmed the original survey findings that the site was occupied primarily during the Sedentary period. Almost 88 percent of the identifiable decorated pottery consists of types that can be assigned to the Rincon phase, whereas another 10 percent date to the late Rincon phase or the transitional Rincon–Tanque Verde phase (Harry and Ciolek-Torrello 1992:60). The presence of about 24 plain ware sherds, similar to those identified elsewhere as Whetstone Plain, suggested a possible prehistoric use of the site area, although typological uncertainties leave this issue unresolved. Two Papago Red sherds were recovered, along with other historical-period artifacts that place the historical-period occupation between A.D. 1880 and 1920.

The discovery of intact, buried prehistoric and historical-period deposits and features suggested that Sunset Mesa Ruin could contribute significant information about the prehistory and history of the Tucson Basin (Harry and Ciolek-Torrello 1992). Based on these findings, COE determined that the site was eligible for the National Register and, in 1994, requested that a work plan be prepared for data recovery at Sunset Mesa Ruin (Neily 1994). The plan follows the outline of work required in Stipulation 1 of a Memorandum of Agreement accepted by the Advisory Council on Historic Preservation (ACHP) on December 1, 1992. This plan was approved by COE, the State Historic Preservation Officer (SHPO), and ACHP, thus laying the groundwork for the data recovery efforts reported in this volume. The plan proposed that the bulk of the data recovery effort be concentrated in the west half of the proposed APE, where the dense surface trash deposits were exposed and the subsurface features were concentrated along the western terrace edge.

Prehistoric Research Themes

The plan of work for data recovery (Neily 1994) employed a series of prehistoric and historical-period research themes derived from historic contexts relevant to the archaeological property types identified during the testing phase (see Harry and Ciolek-Torrello 1992:128–132). The themes concerned with prehistoric property types included (1) household and community organization; (2) settlement and subsistence patterns; (3) ceramic production and exchange; (4) mortuary practices; and (5) chronology. For the most part, these themes were placed in the temporal framework of the Sedentary period (A.D. 950–1150) occupation of the Tucson Basin. Because there were ceramic indications of a Classic period temporal component, as well, Neily (1994) added to the data recovery plan a sixth theme related to the pre-Classic–Classic period transition. A seventh research theme related to the use of prehistoric irrigation in the Tucson Basin also can be addressed, based on the identification of a prehistoric canal segment during data recovery.

Household and Community Organization

Although the data recovery effort at Sunset Mesa Ruin centered on the northwestern portion of the site, it was expected that one or more organizational components of the village would be encountered. The distribution of features found during the testing phase suggested that at least two discrete clusters of habitation features were present in this portion of the site. Identifying the number, size, and configuration of associated structures and features within each cluster would provide essential information on the structure and organization of this prehistoric settlement.

Recent excavations in the Hohokam core area of the Phoenix Basin, the Tucson Basin, and surrounding regions indicate that, at least by the late Colonial period, desert communities consisted of large primary villages and smaller hamlets and farmsteads. The elemental organizational unit within each of these settlements was a well-defined courtyard group consisting of two or more houses clustered together, with their entryways opening onto a common courtyard area (Ciolek-Torrello 1988b:173; Dean 1987:256–257; Doelle et al. 1987; Elson 1986; J. Howard 1985; Huntington 1986; Neily 1990; Wilcox et al. 1981). Each of these groups was also commonly associated with extramural food-processing areas

containing roasting pits and other food-processing facilities, well-defined midden areas, and discrete cemetery areas. These formally structured courtyard groups are interpreted as the residential domain of one or more extended households or families. Some variability in the structure of households, however, has been noted in outlying regions, such as the Picacho Peak area (Ciolek-Torrello and Greenwald 1988b) and the upper Tonto Basin (Gregory 1995), where settlements were composed of more loosely structured households—at least, prior to the late Colonial period. Differences in the size and structure of courtyard groups have been interpreted as the result of various stages of household developmental cycles, in that structures were added or replaced as the household grew or changed in its residential requirements (J. Howard 1985). Variation in the composition and size of individual courtyard groups also has been linked directly to the types of subsistence activities undertaken by different household groups, the size and structure of task groups, and to different systems of land-tenure (Ciolek-Torrello 1987:72; Ciolek-Torrello et al. 1998; Huntington 1986; Klucas et al. 1998). The size, composition, and socioeconomic integration of households, therefore, hold importance for understanding the overall organization and economic structure of the settlement.

Farmsteads are isolated settlements composed of one courtyard group and one household, whereas hamlets are composed of two or more households, often arranged into clusters of spatially separated courtyard groups. Larger villages, in turn, are composed of several spatially discrete residential units, referred to as precincts or village segments, that are similar in size and composition to individual hamlets (Ciolek-Torrello 1988b; Doelle et al. 1987). Villages often are also distinguished by the presence of public facilities, such as large, central plaza areas around which courtyard groups and precincts are arranged, as well as ball courts.

The following research questions relate to household organization:

1. What type of settlement is Sunset Mesa Ruin? Is it a farmstead, hamlet, or village? Although there is no present evidence for a plaza or ball court, this issue remains to be resolved.

2. Is Sunset Mesa Ruin organized into distinct habitation components, such as courtyard groups? Can different residential precincts be distinguished? If not, how are houses arranged?

3. What types of structures are present? Are there differences in their size or function?

4. Are discrete food-processing, cemetery, and midden areas present? If so, are they associated with discrete courtyard groups, or do they reflect communal use?

5. Is there evidence for change in the size or structure of households over time?

Subsistence and Settlement

Site files from previous surveys near the confluence of the Rillito and Santa Cruz Rivers indicate the presence of numerous settlements contemporaneous with the prehistoric occupation of Sunset Mesa Ruin. These range in size from small farmsteads and hamlets to substantial villages. The differences in scale among these settlements appear to reflect not only the socioeconomic character of the individual settlements, but also the overall organization of the broader, dispersed community. Hodges Ruin (AZ AA:12:18 [ASM]), the largest settlement in the Santa Cruz–Rillito confluence area, is situated approximately two miles from Sunset Mesa Ruin (see Figure 3). The substantial size of the site, its location near the juncture of two important natural riverine corridors, and presence of a ball court suggest that Hodges Ruin represented the primary village (see Doelle 1985; Doelle et al. 1987) and the socioeconomic center of the dispersed Sedentary period community, which probably included Sunset Mesa Ruin. To what extent Sunset Mesa Ruin was economically integrated into the Hodges Ruin community represents another critical concern in understanding the organization of settlements.

Rincon phase sites in the Tucson Basin also exhibit a considerable amount of variability in subsistence patterns. The economy of larger villages consisted of diverse arrays of collected and cultivated plants, whereas smaller settlements emphasized resource collection, which, in riverine settings, included an emphasis on riparian resources. Given the location of Sunset Mesa Ruin, floodplain farming and the exploitation of available riverine resources probably accounted for the principal components of the settlement's subsistence base. The discovery of a canal during data recovery indicates that irrigation agriculture may have played an important role in the subsistence base of the settlement. The presence of storage facilities and roasting pits at the site suggested that pollen and macrofossil botanical remains would be recovered from these features, providing an opportunity to assess the subsistence practices undertaken at the site.

The research questions related to subsistence and settlement are:

1. To what extent was Sunset Mesa Ruin economically related to Hodges Ruin and other nearby contemporary settlements? What organizational or economic aspects of the settlement at Sunset Mesa Ruin reflect interaction with other settlements within the confluence region, particularly Hodges Ruin, and which suggest independence?

2. Given the riverine setting, were locally available botanical and faunal riverine resources exploited?

3. Did agricultural production constitute the principal component of the subsistence base? Which cultigens were grown?

4. Did the residents of Sunset Mesa Ruin specialize in the collection or cultivation of any species, or was the suite of resources replicated at Hodges Ruin?

Ceramic Production and Exchange

An understanding of the sources and distribution of different ceramic types has long been the primary basis for discussions of the relationships between individual settlements within a community, communities within a region, and between regions. As a result of intensive research efforts on ceramic production and the mapping of ceramic petrofacies within the Tucson Basin over the last decade, it has been possible to locate specific ceramic production areas and to determine the precise distributional patterns of specific local ceramic types to a degree unattainable elsewhere in the Southwest. On the basis of petrographic analyses of tempering materials, various modes of ceramic production and exchange have been proposed. For example, it has been argued that during the pre-Classic period, production of Rincon Red-on-brown, Rincon Polychrome, and Rincon Red pottery was limited to a few specific communities along the Santa Cruz River in the southern Tucson Basin, and this painted pottery was distributed or exchanged to other settlements and communities across the basin (Harry 1996; Wallace and Heidke 1986). By contrast, potential production locales of Classic period painted pottery appear to have been more variable (P. Fish et al. 1992).

Other studies have evaluated the distribution of nonlocal ceramics. Specifically, settlements in the northern Tucson Basin seem to have greater quantities of nonlocal Hohokam Buff Ware than do those settlements located in the southern Tucson Basin, indicating greater interaction with the Phoenix Basin to the north (Ravesloot 1989; Wallace 1987). Additionally, primary villages, such as Hodges Ruin, enjoyed greater access to Hohokam Buff Ware (Whittlesey 1986a), suggesting that these settlements represent nodes in regional exchange networks. To what extent smaller settlements within the Hodges Ruin community, such as Sunset Mesa Ruin, benefited from or shared in these exchange networks remains unclear.

Specific questions related to this research issue are:

1. Is there evidence for local production of either plain or decorated pottery at Sunset Mesa Ruin? If so, does the scale of the production reflect only local consumption?

2. Does plain or decorated pottery at Sunset Mesa Ruin derive primarily from production centers in the southern Tucson Basin? Do these patterns change over time?

3. Are nonlocal ceramics, particularly Phoenix Basin buff wares, more common than in other settlements?

4. How do these patterns in ceramic production and nonlocal ceramics compare with those at Hodges Ruin?

Mortuary Practices

The identification of two secondary cremations suggested that other burials were likely to be encountered at Sunset Mesa Ruin and that an evaluation of mortuary patterns could be made. One of the cremations was an urn burial, whereas the other was represented only by calcined bone in association with large sherds from several purposefully broken vessels. The latter burial form, rarely found in the Tucson Basin, has been identified at Hodges Ruin and possibly reflects interaction with the Hohokam of the Phoenix Basin, where it was the dominant mortuary pattern during the pre-Classic period (Greenleaf 1975:104).

Research questions related to mortuary practices are:

1. Is a discrete cemetery area present at Sunset Mesa Ruin, or are the burials scattered?

2. Are the cremations (or cemetery, if one is found) associated with a particular courtyard group, or are they part of a settlement-wide cemetery?

3. Are different mortuary patterns evident? If so, are they spatially or temporally discrete, reflecting changes in mortuary patterns or associations with different social groups, including those at Hodges Ruin?

Chronology

The primary occupation of Sunset Mesa Ruin is clearly dated to the Rincon phase, the only Sedentary period phase currently recognized in the Tucson Basin. Despite the fact that the Rincon phase is perhaps the best-known period of prehistoric occupation in the Tucson Basin, its chronological placement is not well understood, especially its early and late subphases. The presence of late

Rincon phase pottery at Sunset Mesa Ruin suggested that archaeological remains from this site can contribute to the resolution of an important chronological issue. In addition, temporal issues related to the occupation of Sunset Mesa Ruin are fundamental to the pursuit of other research themes, particularly those concerning the internal composition of the settlement, its relationship to contemporary settlements, and changes in various behavioral patterns. The discovery of diverse ceramic types and intact houses indicated a high probability for the recovery of important chronological data, such as archaeomagnetic and radiocarbon dates.

Questions related to this theme include:

1. Is an early or late Rincon phase occupation, as defined by the ceramics, present?

2. If so, does the temporal placement of these occupations based on absolute dates significantly differ from dates obtained from middle Rincon phase contexts at Sunset Mesa Ruin or elsewhere, or do they overlap?

3. Can multiple, temporally discrete occupations be distinguished at Sunset Mesa Ruin?

4. Does Sunset Mesa Ruin exhibit a settlement history similar to Hodges Ruin, or was it occupied only for a brief period?

Pre-Classic–Classic Period Transition

Although the principal occupation of Sunset Mesa Ruin appears to have occurred during the Rincon phase, diagnostic ceramics recovered during testing suggested that a Classic period occupation also might be present (Harry and Ciolek-Torrello 1992). As population density and settlement intensity increased in the Tucson Basin's riverine areas during the Colonial period, the earlier pattern of small, dispersed settlements was replaced by one of large, primary villages surrounded by smaller, subsidiary hamlets and farmsteads (Doelle 1985, 1988:283). Primary villages were distinguished by their large size and the common presence of ball courts. This hierarchically structured settlement system focusing on primary villages and ball courts reflects the expansion of the Hohokam regional system into the Tucson Basin (Wilcox 1979). The presence of the Hohokam regional system also is reflected in influences on local ceramic and architectural styles, and in mortuary ritual.

The Sedentary period was distinguished by a series of major shifts in the locations of settlements along the major drainages of the basin and into the bajada zone at the edge of the basin. Sedentary period settlements became the most ubiquitous prehistoric sites in the Tucson Basin, as this period witnessed a gradual return to small, dispersed settlements. By the late Rincon phase, many of the primary villages and their associated ball courts had been abandoned, especially in the southern part of the Tucson Basin (Doelle 1988:283; Doelle et al. 1987). The settlements of the basin apparently cut their links to the Hohokam regional system and began to develop distinctive ceramic decorative styles, architecture, and mortuary patterns (Deaver and Ciolek-Torrello 1993).

The subsequent Classic period witnessed even more substantial changes in many aspects of social organization and material culture throughout the desert regions of southern and central Arizona, as the Hohokam regional system that had dominated the region throughout the pre-Classic period completely collapsed and the area of Hohokam influence was dramatically reduced. The Tucson Basin did not escape these changes. The appearance during the late Rincon phase of surface architectural forms using adobe and jacal construction and enclosed within compounds reflected the development of new domestic organizational patterns. As in the Phoenix Basin, the platform mound appears to have replaced the ball court as the most important public architecture by the early Classic period, although these architectural features were not nearly so common as in the Phoenix Basin and other surrounding areas, such as the San Pedro valley. Platform mounds have been closely linked to the complex irrigation systems that were constructed in the Phoenix Basin, where they appear to have served as important administrative facilities in a system of hierarchically structured irrigation communities (J. Howard 1993). The absence of such complex irrigation systems in the Tucson Basin suggests that the few platform mounds found in the area played a different role in the organization of Tucson Basin communities. Many of the large villages that had grown during the Rincon phase declined in population or were abandoned, and new villages were established in different locations. By the late Classic period, many early Classic period sites—including Hodges Ruin—were abandoned, suggesting yet further community reorganization, along with population reduction and aggregation at a few sites in the Tucson Basin.

Although the transition between the pre-Classic and Classic periods is imperfectly understood, several models have been advanced to account for the drastic changes that occurred during this time. Specifically, the changes in settlement pattern between the pre-Classic and Classic periods have been correlated with environmental fluctuations (Wallace and Holmlund 1984) and a contraction of the exchange system centered in the Phoenix Basin, coupled with the development of a new, localized exchange system within the Tucson Basin and increased interaction

with eastern Arizona (Deaver and Ciolek-Torrello 1993; Doelle and Wallace 1991). Notably, both Hodges Ruin and possibly Sunset Mesa Ruin continued to be occupied into the early Classic period.

Questions that relate to the research issue of pre-Classic–Classic period transition include:

1. What was the extent and duration of the Classic period occupation at Sunset Mesa Ruin?

2. Did the size and internal structure of the settlement change?

3. Does the occupation reflect continued functional association with Hodges Ruin?

4. Are changes in production and exchange patterns evident at Sunset Mesa Ruin?

5. Is there any evidence for climatic or geomorphic changes that might have affected settlement in the area?

Irrigation Systems

At the start of the data recovery phase, the only evidence of an irrigation system at Sunset Mesa Ruin was the remnant of a concrete flume constructed during the 1930s to irrigate the approximately 35 acres of the first terrace southeast of the Santa Cruz–Rillito River confluence. Although it was anticipated that the physiographic location of Sunset Mesa Ruin was conducive to irrigation agriculture (Neily 1994:9), the discovery of a canal segment during data recovery was surprising.

In contrast to the Phoenix Basin, few prehistoric irrigation canals have been identified in the Tucson Basin (Bernard-Shaw 1988, 1989a; Bernard-Shaw and Doelle 1991; Katzer 1989a; Kinkade and Fritz 1975), and extensive irrigation systems are not expected, given the physiographic configuration of the Santa Cruz River valley. The few prehistoric canals that have been found in the Tucson Basin are small systems covering small areas and involving one or more short canal segments. Most tapped the Santa Cruz River, but some channeled water derived from springs at the foot of the mountains (Slaughter and Roberts 1996) or from runoff (Ezzo and Deaver 1998). This situation stands in sharp contrast to the Phoenix Basin, where a massive network of canal systems, characterized as the largest and most complex in the New World (Doolittle 1990), covered most of the basin and formed the socioeconomic foundation around which prehistoric communities were structured (Doyel 1981, 1991). The small scale of the previously identified irrigation canals in the Tucson Basin has led to the suggestion that local communities were not organized or integrated to the same extent as those along the Salt and Gila Rivers (Doelle and Wallace 1986; Doyel 1977b).

Specific questions related to this research issue are:

1. Did the canal at Sunset Mesa Ruin originate from the Rillito or the Santa Cruz River?

2. Was the canal contemporaneous with the occupation of Sunset Mesa Ruin? How long was it in operation?

3. What were the hydraulic characteristics of the canal? How much water did it carry? How often? And how much land could it irrigate?

4. What implications does the presence of a canal have with regard to the structure and organization of the settlement at Sunset Mesa Ruin?

Historical-Period Research Theme: Turn-of-the-Century Hispanic Homesteading

Preliminary assessment suggested that the historical-period foundation at Sunset Mesa Ruin might represent the Cuevas homestead, which was located in the general vicinity, according to the 1893 Roskruge map (Harry and Ciolek-Torrello 1992:60). Rural settlement in the Tucson Basin was hampered by the threat of Apache raiding parties until Fort Lowell was established on the Rillito River and the Apaches were settled on reservations in the 1870s. The 1880s ushered in a period of unprecedented development of farms and rural settlement beyond the confines of the Tucson townsite. Although some homesteads predate this period, most were established after this time. Excavations at a number of small, rural homesteads elsewhere in the Tucson Basin have indicated that these settlements can inform on issues of chronology, ethnic relationships, economic activities, and social differentiation (Ayres 1984; Curriden 1981; McGuire 1979).

Rancho Punta de Agua (AZ BB:13:18 [ASM]), located along the Santa Cruz River on the San Xavier Reservation, is one of the earliest known rural homesteads, occupied between 1855 and 1877. Research at this site has provided a detailed picture of rural socioeconomic patterns and indicates that the relationship between ethnicity and material culture may not be straightforward. Although the owner of the buildings at this site was a German immigrant, the architecture and other items of material culture strongly reflect Mexican influence.

McGuire (1979) has observed that the early, Euroamerican immigrants to southern Arizona often married local Mexican women and were assimilated into local Mexican culture. Several other early homesteads have been investigated along the West Branch of the Santa Cruz River and at the abandoned townsite of Los Reales on the east bank of the river (Ayres 1984:227–228). No formal reports have been prepared for these projects, however.

The Lewis-Weber site (AZ BB:13:117 [ASM]) represents a homestead founded in 1882, north of what were then the outskirts of Tucson. By the time the site was demolished in 1962, it had been absorbed by Tucson's expansion. When finally investigated by archaeologists, little remained of the early occupation. The site, however, represents the only nonurban, historical-period, post-1900 site in the Tucson area to be thoroughly investigated (Ayres 1984:228), and provides important information on late historical-period rural settlement in the area, particularly on the long-established relationship between early Euroamerican (non-Hispanic) settlers and the Tohono O'odham (Curriden 1981).

The historical-period component at Sunset Mesa Ruin has provided a rare opportunity to examine similar research issues for the Rillito–Santa Cruz River confluence area, especially with regard to Hispanic settlement. Many of the rural homesteads in the Tucson Basin were founded by immigrants from Mexico. Because very little is known concerning historical-period, rural homesteading in the Tucson Basin, particularly with regard to the Hispanic population, the historical-period component of Sunset Mesa Ruin could provide important data regarding the identity of the occupants, the time frame of the occupation, and the types of economic activities represented. Questions concerning the historical-period component at Sunset Mesa Ruin have been addressed using data from archival research and additional excavation and analyses. The following research questions are relevant:

1. Was the occupation associated with the Cuevas family? What can historical-period records and interviews tell us about the history of this family, its size and composition, its primary occupation, and economic and social standing?

2. When was the homestead founded, and when was it abandoned? Were there other occupants of the homestead?

3. What was the nature of the settlement? How was the house built? What associated structures and facilities are present?

4. What activities did the residents of the site undertake? Do these activities reflect domestic or primarily ranching or farming functions? Why was it abandoned?

5. How does the material culture found at the site reflect the ethnicity and socioeconomic status of its historical-period occupants in comparison to urban or non-Hispanic, Euroamerican rural households of the time? How did these occupants interact with the other ethnic groups in the Tucson Basin, such as the Euroamerican, Oriental, and Tohono O'odham populations?

6. Does the archaeological evidence support or contradict the archival data?

CHAPTER 2

Environmental Setting

Robert B. Neily, Jeffrey A. Homburg, and Richard Ciolek-Torrello

Sunset Mesa Ruin is located in the Santa Cruz River valley, in the northwestern portion of the Tucson Basin, in southeastern Arizona (see Figure 1). The site is situated on the second alluvial terrace, a prominent landform overlooking the Rillito River—one of the principal tributaries of the Santa Cruz River—and approximately 450 m east of the Rillito–Santa Cruz confluence (see Figure 3). Located at an elevation of 2,220 feet (677 m) above mean sea level (AMSL), the site currently lies 10 feet (3 m) above the first terrace and 20 feet (6 m) above the current Rillito River streambed.

An environmental background of the Rillito River and the confluence area has been presented previously in conjunction with the earlier phases of investigation along the Rillito, including the initial survey of the river corridor (Ciolek-Torrello and Homburg 1990) and the subsequent testing phase at Sunset Mesa Ruin (Harry and Ciolek-Torrello 1992). The following sections will present only a brief overview of the hydrology, geology, geomorphology, soils, climate, and vegetation of the confluence area.

The site is located on a largely undeveloped portion of property belonging to the Sunset Dairy, which was established in 1915 by the Knapp family (Harry and Ciolek-Torrello 1992:27). A pecan orchard covers the terrace just east of the site, and a large irrigated field is situated on the lower terrace at the site's western edge. This field was cultivated until the 1940s, when flooding and erosion damaged the irrigation system that supplied its water.

Hydrology

The Santa Cruz River, the major drainage of the Tucson Basin, has an extensive catchment area extending from the Mexican border to the Gila River, in central Arizona. The valley formed by the Santa Cruz River has been divided into four segments based on simple physiographic distinctions (Betancourt 1978:28–29). The upper Santa Cruz valley extends south from the stream's origin in the Canelo Hills to below the Mexican border, before turning back into Arizona. In the middle Santa Cruz valley, the river flows north from the border area into a broad plain between the Santa Rita and Sierrita Mountains. The Tucson Basin represents the third segment, which extends north from these mountains to the northernmost points of the Tucson and Tortolita Mountains. The final segment, the lower Santa Cruz valley, extends from this point to the river's confluence with the Gila River.

The Santa Cruz River flows north along the western edge of the Tucson Basin, near the foot of the Tucson Mountains. Historically, the river maintained a semipermanent surface flow along segments of the basin—such as near Martinez Hill, Sentinel Peak (A Mountain), and Point of the Mountain—because of the presence of igneous outcrops that formed barriers in the aquifer and created a high water table (Betancourt 1978; Doelle 1984). Several historical-period cienegas also were documented in the vicinity of San Xavier Mission and Sentinel Peak, and the vegetation along the river was characterized by dense bosques of mesquite and cottonwood trees. Beginning in the late 1880s, however, droughts and floods led to the entrenchment of the Santa Cruz River (Betancourt 1978). Subsequent erosion and increased run-off has led to continual downcutting that has lowered the water table, drained the existing cienegas, and virtually removed the floodplain riparian vegetation. At the present time, the Santa Cruz River at its confluence with the Rillito is a deeply entrenched channel. The river enters the lower Santa Cruz valley north of the Tucson Mountains, where floodwaters mingle upon inundated plains and are lost through evaporation and seepage into permeable alluvium (Betancourt 1978:28).

It is the Rillito River that is actually the dominant drainage of the Tucson Basin (Betancourt 1978:28). Along with its major tributaries, the Tanque Verde and Pantano Washes, it drains the eastern portion of the basin—including the southern flank of the Santa Catalina Mountains, the western slopes of the Tanque Verde and Rincon Mountains to the southeast, and the northern slopes of the Santa Rita and Whetstone Mountains to the south—before depositing its flow into the Santa Cruz River near Sunset Mesa (Ciolek-Torrello and Homburg 1990:7). Historical-period records indicate that the Rillito, like the Santa Cruz, was not entrenched prior to the late 1880s. A dense riparian community grew along its banks, surface water was abundant, and even beaver dams were noted along its course (Marmaduke 1983; Smith 1910). Periodic droughts and floods, beginning in 1880, led to extensive braiding of the river channel by 1941, and eventually to bank erosion and channel widening (Pearthree and Baker 1987:19–21). At the present time, however, the Rillito River, like the Santa Cruz River, is a wide, deeply entrenched channel that is usually dry throughout most of the year, receiving only a trickle of water from spring snow melt and occasionally larger quantities from the torrential flash floods that result from intense seasonal storms.

Today, the depth of groundwater varies throughout the Tucson Basin (Gregonis and Huckell 1980:7). Roughly 30 m below the surface along the Santa Cruz and Rillito Rivers, groundwater is deepest—about 75 m—in the urban area of Tucson, and shallowest—less than 8 m below the surface—along the Tanque Verde Wash and its primary tributaries (Davidson 1973).

Geology

The Tucson Basin is a deep basin (or graben) filled with as much as 3,400 m of fluvial, colluvial, lacustrine, and alluvial fan deposits (Eberly and Stanley 1978; Oppenheimer and Sumner 1980). Upland areas surrounding Sunset Mesa Ruin include the Tucson Mountains, located approximately 3 miles (4.8 km) to the west and extending to an elevation of 4,700 feet (1,433 m) AMSL, and Pusch Ridge, which rises to more than 5,000 feet (1,524 m) AMSL along the southwestern portion of the Santa Catalina Mountains, 6 miles (9.7 km) to the northwest.

The mountains bordering the Tucson Basin consist primarily of tilted blocks of Proterozoic, Cretaceous, and Tertiary rocks (Davidson 1973; Wilson et al. 1960). The Tucson Mountains, specifically Tumamoc Hill and Sentinel Peak, were likely sources for vesicular basaltic andesite. Slate and chert for flaked stone and tabular tools also would have been obtainable from this area (Eppley 1986). Rock resources for flaked, pecked, and ground stone, including igneous rocks, rhyolitic tuff, andesite, quartzite, schist, and chert, would have been available at the Santa Cruz–Rillito River confluence area and nearby washes draining the Tucson Mountains. Other raw material, such as gneiss, could have been obtained from the foothills of the Santa Catalina Mountains.

Alluvial Geomorphology and Geoarchaeology

Several geomorphic investigations have been completed in the Santa Cruz River drainage system, although no detailed studies have been conducted in the vicinity of Sunset Mesa Ruin. Because the site is located on an Holocene alluvial landform, it is instructive to review where buried cultural deposits of different ages have been identified in other alluvial settings of the Tucson Basin, and how changing geomorphic conditions affected settlement and land-use practices in those areas. Before reviewing previous geoarchaeological studies in the Tucson Basin, the Quaternary geology of the area surrounding Sunset Mesa Ruin is described.

G. E. P. Smith (1938) identified three Pleistocene terraces in the Tucson Basin, which, in order of oldest to youngest, were named the University, Cemetery, and Jaynes terraces. Mary Anne McKittrick mapped surficial Tertiary and Quaternary terraces and Holocene floodplain and channel deposits in metropolitan Tucson at a 1:24,000 scale. Mapping units for channels, terraces, piedmont deposits, and bedrock located at and near Sunset Mesa Ruin were described as follows (McKittrick 1988:25; also see Jackson 1989:4–5) (Figure 5):

cha: The most active portion of the main drainage channels. Washes commonly contain coarse- to fine-grained sand exhibiting bar-and-swale topography. The channel position is unstable and subject to rapid migration within the finer-grained floodplain deposits that include terraces 1 and 2. It is the topographically lowest unit in the map area, and is frequently too young to support dense vegetation. These areas are flooded frequently.

ch: Historically active channel deposits. The unit includes a complex of low terraces, active channels, gravel bars and floodplains The average height of the lower terraces above the active channels is about 1 m. No soil development or varnish is present. Vegetation is not well

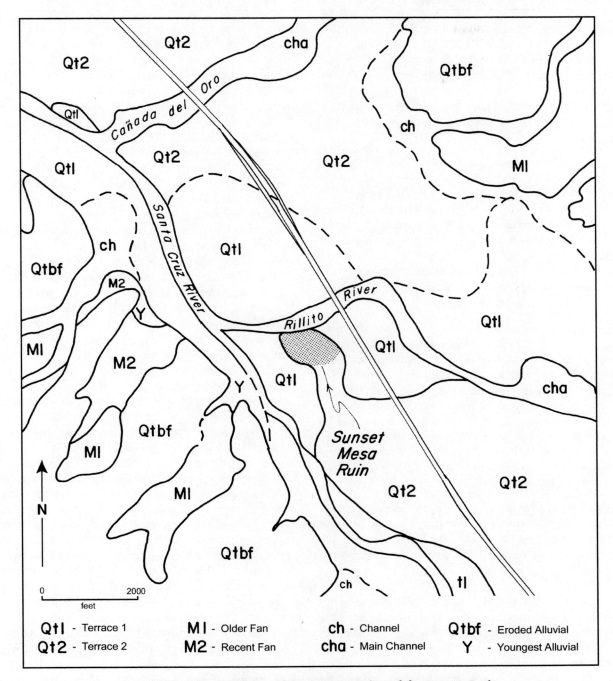

Figure 5. Landforms of the northwestern portion of the Tucson Basin.

established on these surfaces. Flooding and sediment transport are frequent, but not necessarily annual.

Qt1: The youngest and lowest terrace, and recently abandoned. Soil development is very weak to nonexistent. The terrace generally is 1–2 m above the modern stream channel and is latest Holocene to modern in age.

Qt2: Flat, well-preserved terraces associated with modern floodplains of the Santa Cruz River, Rillito River, and

Pantano Wash. These terraces lie topographically above Qt1 but below Qt3. Surfaces generally are well preserved and lack erosional modification. Soils are weakly developed (Torrifluvents). Gravelly sand dominates the sediments. Banks are unstable; recent incision and lateral erosion has left the banks standing at an angle greater than the angle of repose, often vertical. These terraces are middle to late Holocene in age.

Y: Active and recently active fans and broad, unincised channels low in the basin. Fans are incised less than 1 m. Soil is undeveloped to weakly developed (Torriorthents and Torrifluvents), showing slight increases in carbonate and clay. Surficial clasts lack varnish. Flooding occurs seasonally in broad, discontinuous, ephemeral channels. These features correlate with Qt2 and younger channel deposits.

M2: Recently abandoned alluvial fans. Streams headed in the fans are as much as 2 m deep, and interfluves are flat to slightly rounded. Soils are weakly to moderately developed (Typic Torriorthents and Typic Haplargids). Flooding and sediment transport occur on distal reaches in the larger gullies. Desert pavement is slightly developed, but discontinuous. These fans lie mainly at some distance from the mountain front, and are inset into older fans and pediments. Possibly, they correlate with Qt3 (which are late to latest Pleistocene in age).

M1: These are older alluvial fans. Soils commonly containing petrocalcic horizons and argillic horizons may or may not be present. Rounding of interfluves has occurred, creating a hummocky surface. Incision for as much as 5 m is present. Pavement is moderately developed, and varnish is more common and more developed than in M2. These fans lie close to the mountain fronts and may be associated with low pediments. Flooding is restricted to the largest gullies. Fans are isolated from active depositional and fluvial processes and correlate with Qt4 (which is middle to late Pleistocene in age).

Qtbf: This is a highly eroded gravelly alluvium that is latest Pliocene to early Pleistocene in age. The geomorphic surface is no longer preserved. Ridge and valley topography is well developed. This alluvium correlates to the Fort Lowell formation (Davidson 1973).

Jackson (1989) and McKittrick (1988) estimated the relative ages of these surfaces by measuring elevation differences between alluvial surfaces, depth of channel incision, and degree of rounding on interfluves, and by recording the stage of soil formation. Because McKittrick's surface geologic maps were prepared without the benefit of deep stratigraphic exposures and absolute dating, their efforts must be regarded as preliminary. Consequently, all of the Quaternary terraces remain poorly dated (Phil Pearthree, Arizona Geological Survey geologist, personal communication 1989). As noted previously by Haynes and Huckell (1986), the stratigraphic relationship between the terraces also is poorly documented.

Sunset Mesa Ruin is located on the Qt2 terrace. Most other archaeological sites, especially those with buried cultural deposits, also are associated with the Qt2 terrace, an extensive Holocene terrace that abuts much of the Santa Cruz River. Recent archaeological investigations at sites with buried cultural deposits have contributed greatly to our understanding of Holocene alluvial stratigraphy in the Tucson Basin. Holocene terraces (Qt1 and Qt2) are much less extensive and are lower in relative elevation than the surface of Pleistocene terraces. At Sunset Mesa Ruin, the Qt2 terrace of the Santa Cruz–Rillito River confluence (2,220 feet [677 m] AMSL) is about 6 m above the active channel of the Rillito River (2,200 feet [671 m] AMSL), and approximately 3.5 m above the Qt1 terrace (2,210 feet [673.5 m] AMSL), a landform prone to occasional flooding.

Many archaeological sites with buried deposits have been identified in late Holocene alluvial deposits of the Santa Cruz River during the last decade (Ezzo and Deaver 1998; Gregory 1999; Mabry 1990, 1993; Mabry et al. 1997). Geoarchaeological studies conducted by C. Vance Haynes and Bruce B. Huckell (1986) and Michael R. Waters (1987) over the last decade have shown that the Santa Cruz River experienced many changes during the Holocene, changes involving cyclical alluvial aggradation and channel entrenchment. Haynes and Huckell (1986) documented the alluvial record of the Santa Cruz River by recording the stratigraphy of several arroyo cuts, gravel pits, and backhoe trenches. Their study focused on Brickyard Arroyo on the San Xavier Reservation, Airport Wash in the southern Tucson Basin, and the Ina Road–Interstate 10 (I-10) area near the Santa Cruz River. Diagnostic artifacts and radiocarbon dating of natural and cultural deposits were used to date five erosional-aggradational sequences over the last 6,000 years. At least three erosional-aggradational epicycles of similar magnitude were identified as having occurred in the last 2,500 years, suggesting that the frequency of cutting and filling increased during the late Holocene. Haynes and Huckell's stratigraphic model is a valuable contribution. Particularly important are their findings that alluvium dating from 8000 to 6000 B.P., a period that corresponds to the warm and dry conditions of the Altithermal, has been removed by erosion, and that Middle and Late Archaic period sites are preserved in a buried state within younger alluvium.

A number of prehistoric charcoal concentrations were found at AZ AA:12:111 (ASM) by Haynes and Huckell (1986) at a depth of 0.3–1.5 m, in a trench dug under I-10 near Ina Road and the Santa Cruz River–Cañada del Oro confluence. Three distinct, buried cultural horizons were found separated by culturally sterile strata. The lower horizon dated to 4260 ± 140 B.P. (A-2234), four dates from the middle horizon clustered between 2700 and 2900 B.P., and the upper horizon yielded a date of 1400 ± 220 B.P. (A-3141). At the Ina Road Landfill site (AZ AA:12:130 [ASM]), located about 3 km northwest of Sunset Mesa Ruin, as many as 80 small to large hearths filled with rocks were found buried under 4 m of alluvium. Dates from charcoal in three hearths and a carbonized log ranged between 3100 and 3700 B.P. Haynes and Huckell (1986) reported a radiocarbon date of 1240 ± 210 (A-2236) obtained from charcoal found buried at a depth of 1.5 m, in a trench just north of the Rillito River and east of North First Avenue. At this same location, a weak to moderately developed paleosol was identified at a depth of 1 m. The presence of this paleosol and the radiocarbon date suggest there is a high potential for buried archaeological sites within the alluvium of the Rillito River.

Haynes and Huckell (1986) concluded that any land modification activities entailing earth-moving operations on any of the major wash floodplains may have an impact on buried sites with no surface indications. Unfortunately, it is impossible to predict exactly where these sites are buried, a problem clearly illustrated by the recent accidental discovery of the Santa Cruz Bend site (AZ AA:12:746 [ASM]), a Late Archaic period settlement of more than 200 houses, and other early settlements on the Qt2 terrace of the Santa Cruz River (Mabry et al. 1997).

Waters's (1987) investigation of the San Xavier reach of the Santa Cruz River, in the southern part of the Tucson Basin, focused on geomorphic changes that occurred during the span of Hohokam settlement, thus complementing and refining Haynes and Huckell's (1986) stratigraphic model for the late Holocene. Waters's geo-archaeological study integrated data from the San Xavier Bridge site (AZ BB:13:14 [ASM]) excavations, off-site bank exposures, and corroborative data provided by Haynes and Huckell from several other sections of the Santa Cruz River. He observed that significant environmental changes have occurred on the river, echoing Haynes and Huckell's previous assessment. Waters concluded that aggrading conditions before 8000 B.P. were followed by channel erosion and widening until about 5500 B.P., and then a return to aggradation interrupted by brief periods of channel cutting. He also considered that these major geomorphic changes were climate induced, but attributed four cut-and-fill epicycles during the last 2,500 years to other causes, including oversteepening of the floodplain in localized areas, differences in water table position relative to the channel, and human impacts.

Accompanying the geomorphic changes of the last 2,500 years were dramatic settlement shifts, with periods of alluvial aggradation coinciding with times of increased riverine settlement (Doelle 1985; Doelle et al. 1985; Effland and Rankin 1988; Waters 1987, 1988). Aggrading conditions are known to increase the carrying capacity of subsistence systems dependent on floodplain agriculture (Dean 1988). Thus, it is not surprising that settlement shifts paralleling those of the Tucson Basin have been identified in other regions of the Southwest experiencing similar geomorphic changes (e.g., Altschul and Homburg 1990; Dean et al. 1985; Euler et al. 1979; Homburg and Johnson 1991).

Based on the timing of these cut-and-fill epicycles, Waters's (1987, 1988) geomorphic model of the San Xavier reach of the Santa Cruz River bolstered William Doelle's (1985; Doelle et al. 1985) assertion that settlement changes between A.D. 300 and 1450 were related to environmental shifts on the floodplain. Waters argued that farming would have been impractical as the entrenched Santa Cruz River was slowly filling between 50 B.C. and A.D. 800. He also noted that late Pioneer period and Cañada del Oro phase settlements, dated between A.D. 600 and 800, are poorly represented by surface expressions because they are deeply buried. Floodwater farming was possible only after the river channel had filled during the later Rillito phase (A.D. 800–950) and early Rincon subphase (A.D. 950–1000), a time corresponding to intensive settlement along the Santa Cruz River. An entrenched channel began migrating upstream during the middle Rincon subphase (A.D. 1000–1100), and continued to migrate through the late Rincon subphase (A.D. 1100–1150), thus lowering agricultural productivity as floodwater farming was confined to a delta fan at the arroyo terminus. During the Tanque Verde phase (A.D. 1150–1300), channel stabilization and filling resulted in a cienega environment near Martinez Hill, creating along the cienega's margin a setting that would have been suitable to agriculture. Settlements were abandoned on the west side of the river and apparently relocated to the east side during this time. There was little change in settlement location during the Tucson phase (A.D. 1300–1450), and the cienega appears to have contracted in size as the channel refilled, thus making floodwater farming possible once again. After A.D. 1450, this portion of the Santa Cruz River became severely entrenched. Similar changes may have affected the remainder of the river and other major drainages of the Tucson Basin, which may explain the widespread abandonment of Classic period settlements at that time.

Historical-period records indicate that farming was practiced along the Santa Cruz River during the aggrading conditions that existed from at least A.D. 1696 through the 1880s. Heavy floods in 1887 and 1890, however, eroded a continuous channel more than 6 m deep through Tucson (Betancourt and Turner 1988; Cooke and Reeves 1976), undermining the sustainabilty of floodwater farming. This most recent period of erosion is still in effect today, but the main changes involve channel widening rather than downcutting. In addition to flooding, this entrenchment has been attributed to the combined effects of a lowered water table and natural climatic change (Betancourt and Turner 1988; Cooke and Reeves 1976). The current project is a part of a soil-cement revetment program that has been in progress over the decade and is aimed at keeping the channel from migrating from its present-day course.

Haynes and Huckell's (1986) and Waters's (1987) studies are noteworthy contributions, and their work has established a strong foundation for future geoarchaeological work in the Tucson Basin. Their investigations were limited to only a few subsurface exposures, however, and how well their stratigraphic units correlate to cultural deposits along other reaches of the Santa Cruz River in the Tucson Basin is unknown.

Great spatial and temporal variability characterizes alluvial geomorphic systems of the Southwest (Kottlowski et al. 1965), and because of this complexity, it is often difficult to correlate strata within the same drainage system—even over short distances, at times (Waters 1985, 1987). Dynamic geomorphic changes similar to those described by Waters for the San Xavier reach of the Santa Cruz River also must have profoundly affected the amount of arable land in other reaches of the river. Because of the time-transgressive nature of these changes over different reaches of the river and between different drainages, however, there were undoubtedly lag times. The archaeological implications of such lags and variability in the magnitude of different geomorphic processes are unknown. The numerous discoveries of Late Archaic and Early Formative period farming settlements (Ciolek-Torrello 1998; Eddy and Cooley 1985; Huckell 1995; Huckell et al. 1995; Mabry et al. 1997; Roth 1992, 1993), which presumably employed floodwater farming in or near the basin's major floodplains, demonstrate that large portions of drainages in the Tucson Basin were not entrenched when these settlements were occupied between 500 B.C. and A.D. 600. In all likelihood, the first occupants of Sunset Mesa Ruin were drawn to the confluence of the Santa Cruz and Rillito Rivers because of aggrading conditions that permitted the practice of floodwater farming, possibly in combination with irrigation. Similarly, the wide distribution of late Colonial and Sedentary period sites throughout the Tucson Basin suggests that the post-A.D. 800 aggrading conditions observed by Waters also were widespread and not limited to the San Xavier reach, where he conducted his study.

Several irrigation features have been documented recently in alluvial settings of the Tucson Basin. For example, Late Archaic period wells and Formative period canals were documented at Los Morteros (AZ AA:12:57 [ASM]) (Bernard-Shaw 1988, 1989a; Bernard-Shaw and Doelle 1991; Katzer 1989a), a village located on the Santa Cruz River floodplain at the northern end of the Tucson Mountains. More wells have been discovered at Los Pozos (AZ AA:12:91 [ASM]), a large Late Archaic period settlement along the Santa Cruz River (David A. Gregory, personal communication 1998). Small irrigation canals have been identified at a Hohokam field house

component of what is now known as the Wetlands site (AZ AA:12:90 [ASM]) (Kinkade and Fritz 1975; but see Freeman 1997), located southwest of Hodges Ruin (AZ AA:12:18 [ASM]), where the Tucson sewage treatment plant is located. Older canals have been identified at the Santa Cruz Bend site, another large Late Archaic period settlement next to I-10's Miracle Mile exit (Mabry et al. 1997). Small canals collecting run-off from alluvial fan terraces have been reported recently at the Costello-King site (AZ AA:12:503 [ASM]), an intermittently used, Late Archaic period agricultural camp located along the Santa Cruz River in the northern Tucson Basin (Ezzo and Deaver 1998), and an early Pioneer period canal has been identified at the Dairy site (AZ AA:12:285 [ASM]), northeast of the Santa Cruz River–Cañada del Oro confluence (William L. Deaver, personal communication 1996). A small, spring-fed canal also was documented at the Gibbon Springs site (AZ BB:9:50 [ASM]), a Classic period settlement in the eastern Tucson Basin (Slaughter and Roberts 1996). To this list, we can add a canal segment identified during the Sunset Mesa Ruin excavations and reported in this volume. No studies have been conducted to document the magnitude and spatial extent of prehistoric irrigation systems in the Santa Cruz River drainage system, but the mounting evidence of canals in several parts of the Tucson Basin suggests that canal irrigation held a more prominent role than has been previously thought.

Soils

The Tucson Basin is located in a zone of thermic, semiarid soils that have mean annual soil temperatures between 15 and 22° C (Figure 6) (Hendricks 1985:93). Sunset Mesa Ruin and the adjacent floodplain soil to the west have been mapped as Comoro sandy loam (Gelderman 1972: Sheet 16). A weakly developed, highly stratified alluvial soil with a high organic matter content, the Comoro series is classified in the Ustic Torrifluvents subgroup of the Entisols soil order, and the soil family is characterized as coarse-loamy, mixed, nonacid, and thermic. Entisols are distinguished from other soils by their A-C profile; that is, they lack a B horizon, an illuvial accumulation zone found in soils formed on old, stable landforms. The weak development of Comoro sandy loams is due to their relatively young age. Many of the thin bands of alluvium have been obscured or obliterated as a result of the churning effect of burrowing animals (e.g., pocket gophers, kangaroo rats, ground squirrels, and rabbits), and this destructive mixing process is responsible for translocating some artifacts.

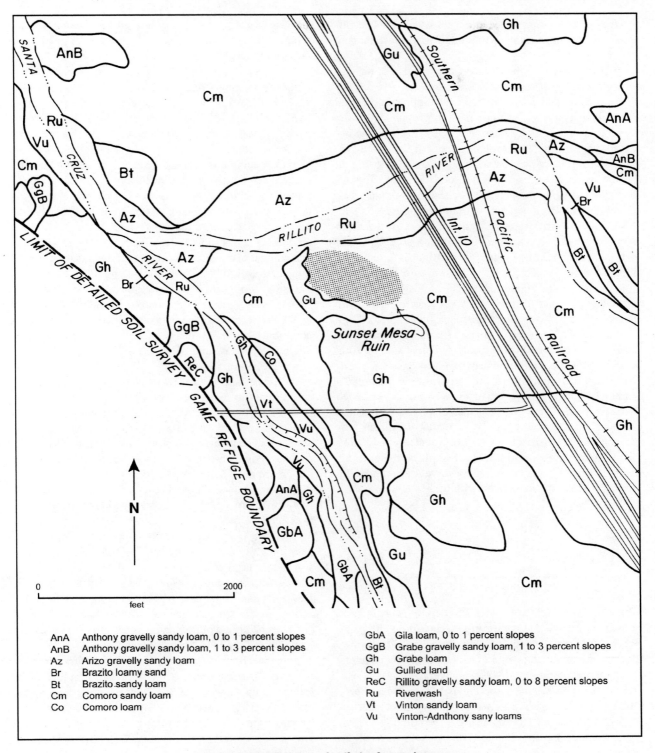

Figure 6. Distribution of soils in the project area.

AnA	Anthony gravelly sandy loam, 0 to 1 percent slopes
AnB	Anthony gravelly sandy loam, 1 to 3 percent slopes
Az	Arizo gravelly sandy loam
Br	Brazito loamy sand
Bt	Brazito sandy loam
Cm	Comoro sandy loam
Co	Comoro loam

GbA	Gila loam, 0 to 1 percent slopes
GgB	Grabe gravelly sandy loam, 1 to 3 percent slopes
Gh	Grabe loam
Gu	Gullied land
ReC	Rillito gravelly sandy loam, 0 to 8 percent slopes
Ru	Riverwash
Vt	Vinton sandy loam
Vu	Vinton-Adnthony sany loams

Based on unpublished information supplied by Don Breckenfield and Bill Svetlik from the Tucson Area Office of the Soil Conservation Service, a typical pedon of the Comoro series consists of an A1-A2-C1-C2 horizon sequence. Comoro sandy loams are found on floodplains with a slope of less than 2 percent. They are characterized by high fertility, moderately rapid permeability, moderate available water capacity, slight hazard of erosion, slow runoff, and a rooting depth in excess of 1.5 m. The Comoro soil is moderately well suited to floodwater and irrigation farming.

The dark color of the Comoro series is due to its high organic matter content. Previously, soils on alluvial terraces with organic matter contents as high were mapped as Mollisols (a soil order common in grasslands) in the Tucson area (see Gelderman 1972). Recent work, however, suggests that the organic matter is inherited primarily from the parent material, not plant additions; that is, the organic matter is washed in from upstream and deposited along with other alluvial sediments rather than being derived from vegetation that decomposed on site. Mollisols are now mapped only in areas of southern Arizona where mean annual precipitation exceeds 41 cm (16 inches), which is about 10 cm (4 inches) more than that of Sunset Mesa Ruin. Regardless of how the Comoro soil formed, it is a highly fertile soil.

A previous study of prehistoric site locations along the Rillito River demonstrated that many prehistoric village and habitation sites, especially the larger and more intensively occupied ones, are located on Comoro soils (Ciolek-Torrello and Homburg 1990:16–17). For example, much of Hodges Ruin, the largest site in the area, is situated on and near a broad area of the organic-rich Comoro sandy loam. Whether these soils were selected purposely for settlement or whether the landform was the overriding concern is uncertain. Nonetheless, Ciolek-Torrello and Homburg observed that within the portions of these Rillito River terraces they surveyed, many of the sites were strongly associated with these soils.

Climate

The climate of the Tucson Basin generally is considered a semiarid or a warm steppe climate (Hendricks 1985:36). Regional climatic conditions are characterized by long, hot summers and mild winters (see Altschul 1988; Ciolek-Torrello and Homburg 1990). The average growing season in the area is 264 days (Davis-Monthan Air Force Base n.d.), and there is a 10 percent or less chance of frost between November 10 and April 20. The combined effect of clear skies and low humidity throughout most of the year results in rapid daytime heating and nighttime cooling. Mean relative humidity at sunrise is about 50 percent, and in the afternoon is about 20 percent. Relative humidity is higher at night throughout the year. Prevailing wind directions are related to diurnal temperature patterns. Typically, gentle breezes of about 3–5 miles per hour blow from the east during the night and early morning hours,

shifting to a westerly direction in the afternoon. Average wind speed is greatest in July, at approximately 10 miles per hour.

Mean annual precipitation received by the watershed ranges from about 26.25 cm (10.5 inches) near Tucson to 93.75 cm (37.5 inches) at the highest elevations (Grove 1962, in Pearthree and Baker 1987:4–5). Precipitation occurs in two distinct seasons, summer and winter, which are separated by short, dry periods. More than half of the annual precipitation falls between July 1 and September 15 in brief, localized but heavy convective storms associated with a monsoonal weather pattern. During the monsoon season, tropical moisture from the Gulf of Mexico moves in from the south and southeast; as surface hot air masses cross mountainous terrain, they are uplifted and come into contact with cooler air, resulting in intense thunderstorms of brief duration that often are accompanied by violent displays of lightning. When these tropical air masses arrive, the relative humidity often soars to 80–90 percent. Preceding these storms, wind speeds commonly reach 50–60 miles per hour, sometimes producing great dust and sandstorms. Summer storms are erratic in nature, in both time and space. They may devastate one drainage area with flash floods, whereas an adjacent drainage may receive little or no rain at all. More than a fifth of the precipitation falls between December and March, the result of less intense but longer cyclonic storms that originate from moist, low-pressure Pacific air masses moving eastward across the continent. Winter storms are much larger but, in the long term, vary more in frequency and duration. The surrounding Santa Catalina–Rincon massif receives considerably more precipitation in the form of both rain and snow.

Major climatic shifts do not appear to have occurred over the last 4,000 years, and an essentially modern, warm, semiarid climate was established between 2000 and 3000 B.C. (Antevs 1948, 1955; Martin 1963; Van Devender and Spaulding 1979). Thus, the patterns described above are assumed to have characterized the region for the period of human occupation since at least the beginning of the Late Archaic period.

Five weather stations in the Tucson Basin provide microclimatic information for the basin (Table 1). The Experimental Farm, which provides the best proxy for the microclimate at Sunset Mesa Ruin, is located at the lowest elevation, in a riverine setting along the Rillito River that is similar to the project area. The Tucson Magnetic Observatory sits on a higher terrace between the Tanque Verde and Pantano drainages, whereas the Sabino Canyon station is perched at the highest elevation, in a deep canyon at the foot of the Santa Catalina Mountains. The microclimate at this station probably is greatly influenced by its canyon setting (Whittlesey and Harry 1990). The remaining stations are placed at intermediate elevations

Table 1. Climatological Data from Tucson Area Stations (from Sellers and Hill 1974)

Station	Elevation (feet)	Record Years	Mean Temperature (° F)			Mean No. Frost Days	Mean Precipitation (inches)	
			Daily Maximum	Daily Minimum	Annual		Annual	Snow, Sleet, Hail
Sabino Canyon	2,640	1941–1972	84.7	53.0	68.9	27	11.85	0.2
Magnetic Observatory	2,526	1934–1972	83.3	49.8	66.6	54	10.85	0.4
Experimental Farm	2,330	1949–1972	84.2	48.7	66.5	60	11.13	0.5
University of Arizona	2,400	1931–1972	84.3	52.8	68.6	27	10.73	0.6
Tucson Airport	2,584	1948–1972	82.0	54.1	68.1	20	10.98	1.6

in locations away from major drainages or mountain features that may influence the microclimate. There is little variability in precipitation or average temperatures recorded at these various stations (Sellers and Hill 1974). The Experimental Farms and Magnetic Observatory stations, however, are characterized by the lowest average daily minimum temperatures and more than twice the mean number of days with below-freezing temperatures. These two stations most closely approximate the project area's microclimate, and the data they provide suggest the prehistoric farmers of that area may have had to contend with a shorter growing season than farmers elsewhere in the Tucson Basin.

Vegetation

Sunset Mesa Ruin is situated within the Lower Sonoran Desert Life Zone, which encompasses about half of the Mexican state of Sonora and extends from the tip of Baja California northward into southern Arizona and California. The Sonoran Desert is relatively young, probably existing only for the last 10,000 years. Despite its relative youth, it is the most complex desert in North America, in terms of species diversity (Hastings and Turner 1965:10; Lowe 1964:24; Shreve and Wiggins 1964:33). This complexity is largely a function of its subtropical location, biseasonal pattern of precipitation, the intricate distribution of geologic formations and soil types, and its hydrology and topography.

Vegetation in the northeastern Tucson Basin falls primarily within the Arizona Upland division of the Sonoran Desertscrub vegetation community (Brown and Lowe 1980), which typically is found at elevations of 1,500–3,000 feet AMSL (Shreve and Wiggins 1964). The major plant communities on the higher terraces surrounding the floodplain are the creosote-bursage and palo verde–saguaro communities. A variety of cacti, including the

saguaro, are abundant in these communities. The mountains surrounding the Tucson Basin afford considerable vegetational variability and provided its prehistoric inhabitants with a wide variety of resources within a relatively short distance (Gregonis and Huckell 1980:8–10). Up through the late nineteenth century, the vegetation growing at the confluence of the Santa Cruz and Rillito Rivers was markedly different than at the present time. A desert riparian plant community, dominated by large cottonwood trees (*Populus fremontii*) and mesquite (*Prosopis juliflora*), characterized the alluvial margins of these rivers. Hackberry (*Celtis palida*), seep willow (*Baccharis glutinosa*), willow (*Salix gooddingii*), and desert willow (*Chilopsis linearis*) were probably other major constituents of the riparian community. This riparian vegetation was supported by the presence of abundant groundwater, which also would have been available for irrigation (Marmaduke 1983:17).

Historical-period land-use practices (e.g., rapid withdrawal of groundwater, grazing, wood cutting, and land clearing for urban expansion), possibly in combination with natural climatic change, have seriously degraded environments in southern Arizona. Prior to the 1850s, the region's drainages were characterized by greater surface water, cienegas, and dense stands of riparian vegetation (Hastings and Turner 1965:35–36). The Rillito and Santa Cruz Rivers were known to have maintained a continuous extent of trees and grasses, across which beaver dams were built (Smith 1910). By 1887, however, these rivers had developed wide erosional channels. As a result of continual erosion, land clearing, and a lowered water table, the riparian plant community has virtually disappeared over the last 100 years. Many of the native riparian species have been replaced by a variety of introduced, exotic species and a gradual invasion of desert scrub. Common introduced species in the riparian areas include tamarisk (*Tamarix chinensis*), Aleppo pine (*Pinus halapensis*), and Mexican palo verde (*Parkinsonia aculeata*) trees. Arizona walnut (*Juglans major*), velvet ash (*Fraxinas velutina*), and California palm (*Washingtonia fillifera*) trees commonly grow in the area today, but probably were introduced from other environmental zones of the Sonoran Desert.

At the present time, the primary native plant association represented at Sunset Mesa Ruin is best described as a creosote-bursage (*Larrea tridentata–Ambrosia* sp.) community, although some scattered mesquite and a few wolfberry (*Lycium pallidum*) and cholla (*Opuntia* sp.)

plants also are present. One introduced species, tamarisk, was probably planted along historical-period ditches constructed in conjunction with dairy operations at Sunset Mesa. Two rows of taramisk trees were located on the site immediately east of the area where data recovery took place. Below the site, desert broom (*Baccharis sarothroides*) was present, along with grasses and forbs in the old agricultural field of the first terrace.

CHAPTER 3

Previous Research and Culture History

Robert B. Neily, Richard Ciolek-Torrello, and Matthew A. Sterner

Previous Research

A considerable body of archaeological research exists for the Tucson Basin. Early excavations in the basin were first carried out during the first half of the twentieth century and concentrated on several of the major sites, such as Tanque Verde Ruin (AZ BB:14:1 [ASM]) (Haury 1928; Fraps 1935), Martinez Hill Ruin (AZ BB:13:3 [ASM]) (Gabel 1931), University Indian Ruin (AZ BB:9:33 [ASM]) (Hayden 1957), and the Zanardelli site (AZ BB:13:12 [ASM]) (Wright and Gerald 1950). Unfortunately, limited information is available on the results of this work. In 1936 and 1937, Gila Pueblo undertook controlled excavations at one of the principal sites in the basin, Hodges Ruin (AZ AA:12:18 [ASM]) (Kelly et al. 1978), situated approximately 2 miles southeast of Sunset Mesa Ruin (see Figure 3). The results from these excavations provided a basis for establishing a regional Tucson Basin chronology (Kelly et al. 1978) relative to the Hohokam chronology of the Gila-Salt Basin, as established at Snaketown (AZ U:13:1 [ASM]) (Gladwin et al. 1937).

Subsequent to this work, only a few excavations—for example, the investigation of University Indian Ruin (Hayden 1957)—were conducted in the basin until the advent of contract archaeology. Highway salvage excavations at the Punta de Agua sites (AZ BB:13:16, AZ BB:13:41, AZ BB:13:43, AZ BB:13:49, and AZ BB:13:50 [ASM]) along the Santa Cruz River in the mid-1960s (Greenleaf 1975) made a notable contribution to the understanding of late Colonial period and particularly Sedentary period village occupation. This study was also instrumental in refining the classification of Rincon Red-on-brown ceramics, resulting in the identification of several varieties believed to represent temporal subdivisions of the Rincon phase.

During the late 1970s and 1980s, numerous survey and excavation projects led to a much more detailed and comprehensive view of the region's prehistory. Notable among these projects are the Northern Tucson Basin Survey (Fish et al., ed. 1992) and the San Xavier Project (Doelle and Wallace 1986; Doelle et al. 1985), which resulted in the survey investigation of large portions of the northern and southern extremities of the basin. Large-scale and intensive excavations also were undertaken at many sites representing almost the entire span of prehistoric occupation in the region. The earliest known farming settlement in the Southwest was found at the Milagro site (AZ BB:10:46 [ASM]), located along Tanque Verde Wash in the eastern Tucson Basin. This small settlement, dated to about 800 B.C., contained small, informal pit structures, bell-shaped pits, fired clay artifacts, shell ornaments, and evidence of maize use, along with a typical late Archaic period lithic assemblage (Huckell and Huckell 1984). Late Archaic period remains also were found at the Valencia site (AZ BB:13:15 [ASM]), located along the Santa Cruz River in the southern part of the basin, together with one of the largest pre-Classic period villages in the region (Doelle 1985; Elson and Doelle 1986). In addition, excavations were undertaken nearby at the Colonial period Dakota Wash site (AZ AA:16:49 [ASM]) (Craig 1988) and the Sedentary period West Branch site (AZ AA:16:3 [ASM]) (Huntington 1986). Together with the San Xavier survey, the excavations at these three sites have provided one of the most complete occupational sequences and one of the most detailed views of prehistory in the basin (Doelle 1988; Doelle et al. 1987).

Important excavations also were undertaken along the Santa Cruz River in the northern part of the basin, in pre-Classic period components of the Lonetree (AZ AA: 12:120 [ASM]) and Redtail sites (AZ AA:12:149 [ASM]) (Bernard-Shaw 1989b, 1990), pre-Classic and Classic period components at Los Morteros (AZ AA:12:57 [ASM]) (Lange and Deaver 1989; Wallace 1995), and at a series of early Classic period sites in the Marana platform mound community (Rice 1987b). Together with the results of the Northern Tucson Basin Survey, these excavations have provided another detailed view of local prehistory complementing that in the southern part of the basin. Most notable is the identification of a distinct, local, Early Formative period phase—the Tortolita phase—equivalent to the early Pioneer period Vahki phase in the Phoenix Basin (Bernard-Shaw 1990).

The Rillito River area also has received considerable attention. Additional excavations were undertaken in pre-Classic and early Classic period components at Hodges Ruin (Layhe, ed. 1986); in pre-Classic period components at the Hardy site (AZ BB:9:14 [ASM]), near the confluence of Tanque Verde and Pantano Washes (Gregonis 1981, 1997); and in a Rincon phase settlement at the Tanque Verde Wash site (AZ BB:13:68 and AZ BB:13:146 [ASM]), in the eastern Tucson Basin (Dart and Gibb 1982; Elson 1986). Although not directly within the Tucson Basin, several projects in adjacent areas have added important information. Investigations at the Hawk's Nest (AZ AA:12:484 [ASM]), Fastimes (AZ AA:12:384 [ASM]), and Water World (AZ AA:16:94 [ASM]) sites, excavated in conjunction with Phase B of the Tucson Aqueduct Project (Czaplicki and Ravesloot 1988, 1989a, 1989b), have provided insights into late Pioneer and Colonial period communities in neighboring Avra Valley. By contrast, the Picacho Pass (AZ AA:7:7 [ASM]) and McClellan Wash (AZ AA:7:15 [ASM]) sites, excavated as part of the Tucson Aqueduct Project's Phase A (Ciolek-Torrello, ed. 1987; Ciolek-Torrello and Greenwald 1988b), and a series of sites excavated as part of the Distribution Division of the Central Arizona Project (Marmaduke and Henderson 1995) have provided a rich record of human occupation dating to the Late Archaic, Colonial, and Classic periods in the Santa Cruz Flats area, north of the Tucson Basin.

As the pace of contract archaeology and independent research has continued to expand in the 1990s, our view of human occupation in the Tucson Basin has broadened and deepened. Perhaps the most important discoveries in recent years have focused on the early pre-Hohokam occupation in the region and the development of a sedentary, agricultural lifestyle in the desert regions of the Southwest (Ciolek-Torrello 1995; Deaver and Ciolek-Torrello 1995; Huckell 1995; Wallace et al. 1995).

Several investigations have targeted Late Archaic period sites in the Tucson Basin (Ezzo and Deaver 1998; Huckell et al. 1995; Roth 1992, 1993) and in the Cienega valley, at the southeastern edge of the basin (Huckell 1995), augmenting considerably the earlier, isolated discoveries. But perhaps the most important recent investigations have been conducted at a sequence of large, Late Archaic and Early Formative period farming settlements located along the Santa Cruz River (Gregory 1999; Mabry et al. 1997). These excavations have forever altered our understanding of the development of sedentism and agricultural dependence in the Southwest and, together with excavations at the Houghton Road site (AZ BB:13:398 [ASM]) (Ciolek-Torrello 1998) in the eastern end of the basin, have led to the definition of two new phases in the chronological sequence. The Late Archaic period is now generally divided into an early San Pedro phase associated with the first small farming settlements, such as the Milagro site, and a later Cienega phase associated with the larger, more intensively occupied farming settlements, such as the Santa Cruz Bend site (AZ AA:12:746 [ASM]) (Matson 1991). The Agua Caliente phase (Ciolek-Torrello 1995) is generally accepted as the earliest phase of the Formative period, when the production and use of ceramic containers became widespread and house construction became more formal, reflecting increased sedentism.

Other periods in the prehistory of the Tucson Basin have not been neglected in the 1990s. Additional excavations were conducted at the Rincon phase settlement of the West Branch site (Altschul et al. 1996), and in early Classic period components at the 49'ers (AZ BB:14:17 [ASM]) (Deaver and Ciolek-Torrello 1993) and Gibbon Springs (AZ BB:9:50 [ASM]) sites (Slaughter and Roberts 1996) in the eastern Tucson Basin. The latter is notable for the recovery of architectural wood specimens, which provide the first tree-ring dates for the early Classic period in the Tucson Basin. Separate investigations by Desert Archaeology, Inc., and SRI have been carried out recently at different loci of the Julian Wash site (AZ BB:13:17 [ASM]), a large village located along the Santa Cruz River that dates primarily to the Colonial period. The results of these two studies have yet to be published. Also unpublished are recent excavations by SRI at Classic period components of the Badger Hole Ranch (AZ AA:12:40 [ASM]) and Dairy (AA:12:285) sites, located in the northern part of the basin. The excavations at the latter site, which exhibits a continuous occupation from the Late Archaic period, represent the only intensive study of a small Tucson phase (the last phase in the prehistoric sequence) settlement in the basin.

The 1990s are also notable for a dramatic increase in historical-period archaeological investigations. The

Table 2. Investigated Rincon Phase Sites and Components in the Tucson Basin

Site	Reference
Hodges Ruin	Kelly et al. 1978; Layhe, ed. 1986
Punta de Agua	Greenleaf 1975
Hardy	Gregonis 1981, 1997
AZ BB:13:74 (ASM)	Bradley 1980
Lonetree	Bernard-Shaw 1990
Los Morteros	Lange and Deaver 1989; Wallace 1995
AZ BB:9:54 (ASM)	Huntington 1982
West Branch	Altschul et al. 1996; Huntington 1986
Tanque Verde Wash	Dart and Gibb 1982; Elson 1986
Valencia	Doelle 1985

largest historical-period archaeological project in the region, the Tucson Urban Renewal (TUR) project, was perhaps the earliest. Much of the material from this project remains unanalyzed and unreported, although it was carried out in the early 1970s. Barnes's (1983, 1984) analysis of selected TUR materials, however, provides a cohesive theoretical framework for understanding much of Tucson's early history, from the Spanish Colonial days to the Territorial period. Jack Williams (1986, 1988, 1991) conducted investigations at sites adjacent to the San Agustín Mission and the Tucson Presidio; although the material still is not completely analyzed or synthesized, these studies provide additional insights into the Spanish Colonial and Mexican periods of occupation. Other early excavations at Rancho Punta de Agua (AZ BB:13:18 [ASM]) (McGuire 1979) and the Lewis-Weber site (Curriden 1981) provide an in-depth view of late nineteenth- and early twentieth-century rural life in the Tucson area. Small-scale excavations at the old townsite of Los Reales, northeast of San Xavier, remain unreported, as do excavations of the Elias and Angulo Ranches, lime kilns, and other features on the West Branch of the Santa Cruz River (Ayres 1984:226–227). Thus, recent studies in the downtown Tucson area represent a tremendous intensification of historical-period research and present the first comprehensive reports of urban life and material culture from the Spanish Colonial, Mexican, and American Territorial period occupations in the basin (Ayres 1990; Ciolek-Torrello and Swanson, ed. 1997; Heidke and Masse 1988; Mabry et al. 1994; Thiel 1993; Thiel and Desruisseaux 1993; Thiel et al. 1995).

Notwithstanding this considerable research, residential settlements dating to the Rincon phase and contemporary with the prehistoric occupation at Sunset Mesa Ruin are the single most common and most intensively inves-

tigated class of sites in the Tucson Basin (Table 2). The Rincon phase is probably the best understood time period in the occupational history of the region, its prehistory, material culture, and chronology having received more attention and scrutiny than any other; but despite the attention accorded this phase, many basic research issues remain a bone of contention and much is still unknown. The number of excavated sites is small in comparison to the number of known sites dating to this phase, and the sample perhaps does not fully represent the region's population of Rincon phase sites. Thus, any additional information regarding sites of this time period is welcome.

Culture Historical Background

Tucson Basin chronology has been substantially revised over the last decade as a direct result of the amount of contract archaeology undertaken across the basin. Dean (1991) has developed the most current time scale for the Formative period, whereas more recent research has led to the identification of new temporal constructs for the pre-Formative period (Figure 7). Our understanding of Tucson Basin prehistory also has benefited from the even more extensive research that has taken place recently in the Phoenix Basin and surrounding areas, which has provided greater insights into developmental trends affecting the larger desert regions of southern and central Arizona.

A brief overview of the current status of Tucson Basin prehistory is presented below. This is followed by a review of Tucson homesteading at the turn of the century.

	STAGE	PERIOD	TUCSON BASIN Dean 1991 Deaver & Ciolek-Torrello 1995 Wallace & Craig 1988	PHOENIX BASIN Cable & Doyel 1987 Dean 1991
A.D. 1900			Euroamerican	Euroamerican
A.D. 1800		HISTORICAL	Mexican	Piman
A.D. 1600			Spanish	Piman
A.D. 1500		PROTOHISTORIC	Piman	
A.D. 1400		CLASSIC	Tucson	Civano
A.D. 1300				
A.D. 1200			Tanque Verde	Soho
A.D. 1100		SEDENTARY	Late Rincon	Sacaton
A.D. 1000			Middle Rincon	
			Early Rincon	
A.D. 900		COLONIAL	Rillito	Santa Cruz
A.D. 800			Cañada del Oro	Gila Butte
A.D. 700	FORMATIVE	PIONEER/EARLY FORMATIVE	Snaketown	Snaketown
			Early Broadline	Sweetwater Estrella
A.D. 600			Tortolita	
A.D. 500				Vahki
A.D. 400				
A.D. 300			Agua Caliente	Red Mountain
A.D. 100				
100 B.C.			Cienega	?
500 B.C.	ARCHAIC	LATE ARCHAIC	San Pedro	
1000 B.C.				

Shaded area indicates precise boundary undefined.

Figure 7. Summary of chronological periods and phases in the Tucson and Phoenix Basins.

Prehistoric and Protohistoric Periods

Paleoindian Period

The Paleoindian occupation of North America, beginning around 11,500 B.P., corresponds with the final retreat of the Wisconsin glaciation at the end of the Pleistocene. This period is represented by big-game hunters who exploited a variety of now-extinct megafauna, characteristically mammoth (Haynes 1968). Although buried deposits dating to this time period have been identified in southeastern Arizona (Haury 1953; Haury et al. 1959), none have been identified in the Tucson Basin.

Surface evidence of the presence of big-game hunters, however, has been retrieved in the form of isolated Clovis projectile points. Such finds have been made from the surface of a pre-Classic period Hohokam village, the Valencia site (Doelle 1985:181), as well as from Avra Valley, located west of the Tucson Mountains. It is likely that Paleoindian deposits exist within the Tucson Basin, but such deposits undoubtedly are buried deep in alluvial sediments along the various watercourses of the basin, and would be exposed only infrequently by erosion and construction activities.

Early and Middle Archaic Periods

With the extinction of Pleistocene megafauna and a gradual trend toward warmer and drier conditions after 9000 B.C., the Archaic period is represented by a corresponding trend toward a mixed subsistence base of wild-plant collecting and small-game hunting. The Archaic period has been divided into three time periods—Early (8500–6000 B.C.), Middle (6000–1500 B.C.), and Late (1500 B.C.–A.D. 100)—based on changes in material culture and subsistence patterns (Huckell 1984b). In the Late Archaic period, however, after 1500 B.C., the arrival of maize ultimately led to the development of an agricultural subsistence strategy within well-watered riverine areas, although the Archaic subsistence base continued for populations in less arable upland areas. Huckell (1995:117) has recently suggested, therefore, that the term "Archaic" be used only with reference to a broad-spectrum, foraging subsistence base that preceded the origins of agriculture in the Southwest, and has assigned contemporary early farming settlements to the Early Agricultural period.

Little is known about the Early Archaic period, and the first definite evidence of human occupation in the region dates to the Middle Archaic period, when sites were distributed across the entire Tucson Basin. Whether the greater abundance of Middle Archaic period remains over

those from earlier periods reflects a more intensive occupation of the Tucson area or other factors is not known. Huckell (1984a:192) has suggested that the Pinto Basin projectile point style is the hallmark of this period, although its chronology is insecure. Other diagnostic styles are the Gypsum Cave and the San Jose projectile point styles (Huckell 1984a). Amargosan I and II cultural materials dating to the Middle Archaic period have been identified in the eastern fringes of the Tucson Basin (Rogers 1958; Stacy and Hayden 1975), and a Middle Archaic period occupation took place above Ventana Canyon Wash (Dart 1986; Douglas and Craig 1986) and in the Rincon Mountains (Simpson and Wells 1983, 1984). North of the Tucson Basin, small, multiple-activity and resource-processing sites assigned to this time are located in the foothills of the Picacho Mountains (Bayham et al. 1986). Projectile points dating to the Middle Archaic period are found in riverine and upland areas of the Tortolita Mountains, but intensive reuse of these areas by later populations and the erosion of early Holocene alluvial surfaces on the intervening bajada areas has made detection of Middle Archaic period sites difficult (Fish et al., ed. 1992). Base camps and specialized extractive or processing sites are present on the piedmont slopes of the Santa Rita Mountains (Huckell 1984a), and Masse (1979:149–151) reported Middle Archaic-style projectile points and tools on the lower bajada near Tumamoc Hill, in the western Tucson Basin. Few of these sites, however, have been systematically investigated (Huckell 1984b:139). The only site to receive any serious attention is a large, surface campsite (AZ AA:12:86[ASM]) located on a low terrace overlooking the floodplain, opposite the confluence of the Santa Cruz River and Cañada del Oro Wash. This site contains large amounts of tools, debitage, rock clusters, and some ground stone and shell, although much of this material probably is Late Archaic period in age (Czaplicki and Mayberry 1983:23; Huckell 1984b:139).

The distinguishing characteristic of the Middle Archaic period appears to be use of diverse microenvironments, including stabilized dune fields, bajada settings, and mountain pediment locations (Bayham et al. 1986; Dart 1986; Douglas and Craig 1986; Huckell 1984a; Rankin and Downum 1986). The only environmental zone little used was the creosote-covered, lower bajada zone (Hartmann 1981). Montane environments were most heavily exploited for hunting, whereas bajada locations appear to have been used more heavily for foraging (Dart 1986:125; Huckell 1984a). The presence of water in the form of springs or seeps may explain the concentration of sites on the upper bajada and montane zones (Huckell 1984a:238). The riverine zone does not appear to have been used intensively during this period (Huckell 1988:75; Roth 1989:152), possibly because increased aridity and erosion at this time may have made this area unsuitable for habitation (Huckell 1988:72).

A great deal of mobility is inferred for the Middle Archaic period populations of the Tucson Basin. Sites are relatively small and lack dense occupational refuse, elaborate storage facilities, and structures; special-purpose tools dominate the artifact assemblages. These data imply that small groups of hunters and collectors foraged across a wide range of environments, shifting residence seasonally as particular resources became available (Dart 1986:172–173).

Late Archaic Period

It is now generally agreed that the initial step toward the Formative lifestyle began in the Late Archaic period, nearly 3,000 years ago. Recent reevaluations of the earliest dates for maize in the Southwest have led to a complete restructuring of ideas about the development of agriculture in this region. New analyses of the earliest maize dates from such early highland sites as Bat Cave (Wills 1988), however, reveal that the earliest highland maize appeared no earlier than 1,000 B.C., bringing the age of highland maize into congruence with recent discoveries of early maize on the plateau (Matson 1991) and in the desert (Huckell 1990; Huckell and Huckell 1984). Matson (1991:207–243) has developed a new model for the evolution of maize agriculture in the Southwest based on this convergence of evidence. Following Berry (1982), he has argued that an early race of corn adapted to the warm, humid growing conditions of the Sonoran Desert spread north to the Mogollon highlands and Colorado Plateau, where drought- and frost-resistant races of maize were eventually developed.

Recent investigations have provided strong support for Matson's model, demonstrating that the earliest farming villages in the Southwest were abundant in floodplain settings in the Tucson Basin between 3000 and 2000 B.P. The Late Archaic period manifestation was substantial, with an inferred degree of residential stability, corn agriculture, and an expanded material culture inventory. These developments appear to have coincided with the onset of more moderate climatic conditions and alluviation around 4,000–3,000 years ago, which made the riverine zone a more productive habitat (Haynes and Huckell 1986). The significance of floodplain site locations to corn agriculture has been stressed and, indeed, many of the riverine sites have produced a wealth of corn pollen and carbonized corn remains, suggesting its importance in the diet (Huckell 1988). Riparian resources also increased the attractiveness of these locations. There is, however, no absolute correlation between physiographic zone and settlement function. Habitation settlements,

some of which produced evidence for corn agriculture, have been located in the riverine, bajada, and montane zones (Dart 1986; Doelle 1985; Halbirt and Henderson 1993; Hartmann 1981; Hemmings et al. 1968; Huckell 1984a; Huckell and Huckell 1984; Huckell et al. 1987; Rankin and Downum 1986; Slawson et al. 1986). Temporary camps, resource-procurement and -processing loci, and lithic quarry sites are the most common types of settlements found in the bajada and montane zones.

The riverine settlements contain pit houses, large intramural and extramural storage pits, and artifact-rich middens (Roth 1992:310, 1993:Table 1). Processing features, such as roasting pits, are abundant at these sites, and ubiquitous, copious quantities of fire-cracked rock attest to their repeated use. Although middens at many Late Archaic period sites are shallow, at some sites the depth and extent of refuse are substantial, indicating intensive and prolonged or recurrent occupation. Overlapping inhumations, multiple grave facilities, and large, circumscribed cemetery areas have been found at some sites (Eddy and Cooley 1983:22–23; Huckell 1984b:140, 1988:64). Mortuary treatment is distinguished by tightly flexed inhumations lacking grave goods, although cobbles and grinding stone fragments were occasionally used to cap graves (Dart 1986:42–46; Hemmings et al. 1968).

Late Archaic period sites are well dated by a number of radiocarbon dates from excellent contexts, which bracket the period between 3,000 and 1,700–1,800 years ago (Huckell 1988:Table 6.1). Diagnostic notched projectile point styles include those originally associated with the San Pedro stage Cochise Culture and additional, recently identified styles, such as the Cienega and Cortaro points; no Amargosan affinities have been noted (Huckell 1988:58; Roth 1989:37; Roth and Huckell 1992; Sayles and Antevs 1941:24).

The earliest known farming settlement may be the Milagro site, located along Tanque Verde Wash in the eastern Tucson Basin and dated to 800 B.C. (Huckell 1990; Huckell and Huckell 1984). Small pit structures were found at this site in association with large, extramural bell-shaped pits and a material culture inventory that included shell artifacts and fired ceramic figurines. The Matty Canyon site (AZ EE:2:10 [ASM]), along Cienega Creek in the southeastern Tucson Basin, and the nearby Los Ojitos (AZ EE:2:137 [ASM]) site are dated to the Cienega phase (500 B.C.–ca. A.D. 1) (Matson 1991:194). These sites produced abundant evidence for maize, and numerous pit houses with interior and exterior storage pits (Eddy and Cooley 1983; Huckell 1990, 1995), representing an intensification of the pattern evident at the Milagro site. The Coffee Camp (AZ AA:6:19 [ASM]) and Tator Hills (AZ AA:6:18 [ASM]) sites in the Santa Cruz Flats area, northwest of Tucson (Halbirt and

Henderson 1993), are additional sites with Cienega phase occupations in floodplain settings, although the Coffee Camp site provided no evidence for maize use.

One of the most extensive and important concentrations of Archaic period remains, AZ BB:13:6 (ASM), was located in the vicinity of the mission of San Agustín del Tucson, on the west bank of the Santa Cruz River, near the foot of Sentinel Peak. Between the summer of 1949 and April 1950, a series of salvage excavations was undertaken at the site (which came to be called the Brickyard site), about 100 m north of the mission. Slightly more than 100 burials were recovered from at least two discrete cemetery areas, with an estimated additional 50 having been destroyed prior to the salvage effort (Elson and Doelle 1987:13; Huckell 1984b:140). Four more burials were uncovered by William Wasley in 1956, while searching for the foundations of the mission buildings (Elson and Doelle 1987). None of the burials yielded any offerings to indicate age or affiliation, but the first excavations reported that the remains were in seated or tightly flexed positions, suggesting a Late Archaic period age (Huckell 1984b, 1988:65). Betancourt (1978) and Hard and Doelle (1978:14–15) have suggested, alternatively, that these were in fact protohistoric Sobaipuri or historical-period Piman burials directly associated with the mission, as flexed burial positions were also a Sobaipuri custom. The position of the later discovered burials was not reported, but Huckell (1984b:140) has suggested that those found nearer the mission were probably associated with its historical-period use. Terah Smiley found a preceramic occupation surface located beneath the burials near the mission (Elson and Doelle 1987:14). This was associated with artifacts identified by Sayles as typical of the Archaic period (Huckell 1984b, 1988:65). Much more substantial Archaic period findings were uncovered when a series of backhoe trenches was excavated along Brickyard Lane, north of Mission Lane, along the proposed realignment of Mission Road. Forty-one possible Archaic period features, including pit houses, use surfaces, and roasting pits, were identified in this area (Elson and Doelle 1987:26).

Late Archaic period pit houses also were found along the Santa Cruz River at the Wyoming Street locus of the West Branch site (Huntington 1986), the Valencia site (Doelle 1985), and the Redtail site (Bernard-Shaw 1989b). Located along Brickyard Arroyo, which enters the Santa Cruz River southeast of San Xavier, the Joe Ben site (AZ BB:13:11 [ASM]) consisted of a series of artifacts, hearths, and at least one cremation exposed in the arroyo channel about 6–8 m below the present-day ground surface (Czaplicki and Mayberry 1983:23; Huckell 1984b:139). The artifacts included diagnostic San Pedro projectile points. Radiocarbon dates from this site and stratigraphic units in similar sites located further up the arroyo indicate ages between 2000 and 4000 B.P. (Huckell 1984b, 1988:65). Other buried Archaic period habitation sites have been discovered closer to Sunset Mesa, north of the confluence of the Santa Cruz and Rillito Rivers (Huckell 1988:65–66). The Cortaro Fan site (AZ AA:12:486 [ASM]) was discovered on the terrace, about a half mile east of the Santa Cruz River (Huckell 1988; Roth 1988). Roth's excavations of pit features produced faunal remains and evidence of maize. Although no evidence of Late Archaic period occupation has been found at Sunset Mesa Ruin, materials dating to this period—in a deeply buried state—can be anticipated.

Perhaps the most important recent discoveries involve a series of Late Archaic period settlements found along the Santa Cruz River by Desert Archaeology, as part of their investigations of the I-10 corridor through Tucson. In 1994, Desert Archaeology completed at the Santa Cruz Bend site the largest and most intensive excavation effort yet conducted of an Archaic period settlement. These excavations reinforce known Late Archaic period patterns, as well as suggesting new ones. With almost 200 houses, the Santa Cruz Bend site was one of the largest Cienega phase settlements known (Mabry et al. 1997). Most of the houses were similar in size (about 3–4 m in diameter) to those at other known Archaic period settlements; however, several were much larger (about 5 m in diameter), and a large communal house measuring almost 10 m² in diameter also was present. Most of the smaller houses contained large, centrally located storage pits, which occupied much of their floor space. Intramural hearths were absent from the houses at Santa Cruz Bend, and there was little evidence for remodeling or superimposed features, suggesting a relatively short-term occupation.

Although these recent investigations have revealed a high level of maize use and the presence of large and intensively occupied floodplain settlements between 800 B.C. and A.D. 1, opinion is currently divided on whether these changes reflect the development of a sedentary, maize-dependent lifestyle at that early date or merely the intensification of the broad-based foraging-farming strategy typical of the Archaic period. Some researchers have argued that the lack of technological change, coupled with the persistence of the band type of organization, is more in concert with an elaboration of Archaic period strategies than the development of a new economic system (Ciolek-Torrello 1995, 1998; Whittlesey and Ciolek-Torrello 1996; Wills 1992).

For example, the food-processing and agricultural technologies that came to characterize maize-dependent economies in the Southwest were not employed during the Late Archaic period, whereas technologies associated with foraging strategies persisted well into what is recognized as the earliest phases of the Formative stage. Ground stone assemblages at these sites are characterized by generalized milling tools—such as basin and slab metates, mortars, stone bowls, cobble manos, and pestles—usually associated with a small-seed economy rather than the more specialized tools associated with heavy consumption of maize (Ciolek-Torrello 1995; Halbirt 1989; Leblanc 1982; Whittlesey and Ciolek-Torrello 1996; Wills 1992:158). Although ceramic technology was known to Late Archaic period people, as indicated by the fired clay figurines at the Milagro site, ceramic cooking and storage containers are notably absent from Late Archaic period site assemblages. The preparation of corn in the Archaic period probably involved roasting whole ears or employed perishable containers, and large-scale storage continued to be in underground pits. Wills (1992:159) has attributed the absence of ceramic containers to a continued pattern of high mobility that inhibited the use of fragile containers, or to a pattern of consumption in which such cultigens as maize and beans were not significant enough to warrant the use of more efficient ceramic containers for boiling or steeping, or for storage. He has expressed surprise at the apparent lack of pressure for Late Archaic period cultivators to take advantage of the unique genetic plasticity of maize and to increase its yields through phenotypic change.

Large and intensively occupied settlements were present in the Late Archaic period, but they do not represent permanent occupations. Rather, they were seasonal aggregations formed to exploit locally abundant maize crops and other riparian resources. Huckell (1990:365–370) has suggested that such sites represent base camps associated with maize cultivation, which were abandoned seasonally to allow foraging for wild plant foods and reoccupied repeatedly over periods of several hundred years. Wills (1988:477–482) has suggested that the intensive site occupations evidenced at these sites reflect their recurrent and short-term nature rather than the degree of dependence on agriculture. Houses were generally small and of relatively informal construction compared to later structures. Late Archaic period houses were circular to oval or irregular in shape, were often built in shallow, basin-shaped pits, and usually lacked hearths and entry ramps. Large storage pits were common in these small houses (Matson 1991:192). For the most part, Archaic period houses were simple shelters supported on pole frameworks covered with brush, hides, or grass (Halbirt and Copus 1993:44). Their small size, informal construction, and paucity of hearths indicate that they served primarily as storage units and secondarily as shelters. Their small size also indicates that they were not inhabited by complete households, but more likely were used by smaller task groups (Ciolek-Torrello 1995; Henderson 1992).

Whether upland camps were used by residents of permanent villages during seasonal hunting and gathering forays, or represent a distinct and overlapping settlement-subsistence system, remains to be determined. Even though some Archaic period groups became more reliant on horticulture products, it is possible that other groups maintained a traditionally Archaic pattern, using a seasonal round. Both patterns, then, might have been in effect during this time. Fluctuating environmental conditions also might have contributed to varied subsistence systems. Whalen (1971) originally described a bimodal model for Late Archaic period settlement in southeastern Arizona. This model involves the same group of people using two types of base camps, alternatively exploiting the floodplain and the bajada on a seasonal basis. Roth (1992:312, 1993) has adapted this model to the Late Archaic period in the Tucson Basin, although she has depicted the exploitation of the floodplain as more intensive than that of the bajada. It is her contention that agriculture was a fundamental component of land use in the floodplain, but could only temporarily sustain population concentrations at this early date (Roth 1992). Movement between floodplain settlements and upper bajada camp sites continued to be necessary to procure wild resources. In contrast to the intensively occupied floodplain settlements, bajada settlements were smaller, limited activity sites. Fish et al. (1988), however, have argued that the redundancy of resources in different environmental zones meant there was little need for mobility in exploiting resources in other zones.

The basic organizational unit appears to have been a fluid, composite band that regularly grouped and split apart to exploit particular resources (see Dart 1986:181). Alterations in sociopolitical structure probably accompanied the increased residential stability of the Late Archaic period, especially if population increases took place (see Dart 1986:183). The excavations at the Santa Cruz Bend site have provided us with the clearest information about Late Archaic period organization. This settlement reflected the more fluid and flexible structure Flannery (1972:25; see also Ciolek-Torrello et al. 1998) has associated with hunter-gatherer bands that form large population aggregates during periods of local resource abundance. It consisted of circular clusters of small, round houses associated with a larger house that contained abundant evidence of food processing and storage. Several of these house clusters were associated with one large, communal house. Small habitations and larger communal houses have been found at smaller Late Archaic sites, such as the Coffee Camp site, suggesting that the circular arrangement may be replicated at other contemporary farming settlements.

Recent investigations now make it clear that the first step toward a sedentary, maize-dependent way of life in the Sonoran Desert occurred during the Late Archaic period, almost 3,000 years ago. This step involved reduced residential mobility and intensive maize cultivation in large floodplain settlements. Neither maize dependence nor a fully sedentary lifestyle emerged at this time, however (Ciolek-Torrello 1995; Dart 1986:177; Huckell 1990:365–370; Whittlesey and Ciolek-Torrello 1996). According to Huckell (1988:72), the Tucson Basin was relatively well populated by people who practiced a mixed subsistence strategy of horticulture and foraging, and who occupied residential sites with pit structures, storage, and processing features on a recurrent and short-term basis.

Early Formative and Pioneer Periods

The Early Formative period, approximately A.D. 1–600 (Ciolek-Torrello 1998; Deaver and Ciolek-Torrello 1995; Whittlesey 1995), represents a broad regional pattern marked by substantive changes in subsistence and settlement, including the increased integration of agriculture into the mixed farming and foraging subsistence base, the construction of substantial pit structures—suggesting greater residential stability—and the initial production of plain ware ceramics. Settlements continued to be occupied in well-watered valley locations, such as the Square Hearth (AZ AA:12:745 [ASM]) and Stone Pipe (AZ BB: 13:425 [ASM]) sites along the lower terraces of the Santa Cruz River (Mabry et al. 1997), and the Houghton Road site along the Tanque Verde Wash (Ciolek-Torrello 1995, 1998). Current dating suggests that plain ware ceramics were introduced between 100 B.C. and A.D. 100, followed by the introduction of red wares and micaceous ceramics from the Salt-Gila basin between A.D. 400 and 500 (Deaver and Ciolek-Torrello 1995; Wallace et al. 1995).

These data run counter to earlier ideas that the Hohokam were the first sedentary farmers in the Tucson Basin, entering the Santa Cruz valley in the late Pioneer period and exploiting an empty niche along the Santa Cruz River (Doyel 1977b). Although Doyel still defended this view as late as his 1984 overview of Tucson Basin prehistory, there has been a dramatic increase in evidence suggesting a continuum of horticultural settlements along the major drainages of the Tucson Basin from the Late Archaic period to at least the early Classic period (Bernard-Shaw 1989b; Ciolek-Torrello 1998; Huckell 1988).

The transition between the Archaic and Formative period lifestyles seems to have involved the acquisition of pottery technology and more substantial architecture rather than any dramatic cultural or population changes. For many years, the earliest excavated ceramic materials in the Tucson Basin consisted of a handful of sherds and restorable vessels of Sweetwater Red-on-gray from Hodges Ruin (Kelly et al. 1978:20). The absence of associated architecture suggested a temporary or seasonal

occupation (Mayberry 1983:33). More recently, Bernard-Shaw, B. Huckell, and others in the Tucson Basin have identified remains that were part of a widespread early ceramic culture, a plain ware horizon, that fills—temporally and culturally—the large gap between the Late Archaic and Hohokam Pioneer periods. The local expression of this culture, characterized as the Agua Caliente phase, is represented by materials from El Arbolito (AZ EE:1:153 [ASM]) (Huckell et al. 1987), the Dairy site (Fish et al., ed. 1992), the Square Hearth and Stone Pipe sites (Mabry et al. 1997), and the Houghton Road site (Ciolek-Torrello 1998).

At the Houghton Road site, moderate- and large-sized pit houses dating to the period A.D. 1–400 were found in association with Late Archaic-style dart points and grinding equipment, as well as plain ware ceramics. Neckless seed jars were the dominant vessel form and red ware ceramics were present in low frequencies (Whittlesey 1998b). Apart from the dart points and a few bifaces, the flaked lithic industry was essentially Formative in character (B. Huckell 1998). The houses were characterized by a "bean" shape typical of early Mogollon house forms in southeastern Arizona and southwestern New Mexico. Also present was a large house similar in form and construction to early Mogollon communal structures (see Anyon and LeBlanc 1980). The presence of a communal structure and the scattered arrangement of other houses at this site suggest the development of a social organization less formal and involving smaller groups than the courtyard groups that characterized communities during the Colonial and Sedentary periods. The location and architecture of the Houghton Road site suggest a relatively permanent agricultural community in a riparian setting. Plant remains recovered from excavations, however, indicate a continuation of the Late Archaic period's diversified subsistence base. Such upland resources as acorns and agave are common, together with high frequencies of corn remains (L. Huckell 1998).

Recent excavations at several sites in the Tucson Basin also provide ample evidence of a substantial red ware horizon occupation that followed on the heels of the plain ware horizon culture. Perhaps the most significant contribution to the identification of this later occupation comes from the Lonetree site, located on a terrace overlooking the Santa Cruz River, south of Point of the Mountain. Based on evidence from this site, Bernard-Shaw (1990:122, 209) has proposed the Tortolita phase (A.D. 600–800) as a red ware horizon coeval with the Vahki phase in the Phoenix Basin. The most substantial Tortolita phase remains, however, were uncovered recently in one locus of the Valencia site (B. Huckell 1993; Wallace, personal communication 1998). Less substantial evidence of a similar phenomenon may be present at the Dairy site, near the northern end of the valley (Fish et al., ed. 1992) and at the Houghton Road and other sites in the eastern Tucson Basin (Deaver and Ciolek-Torrello 1993; Huckell et al. 1987).

The diagnostic of this phase is Tortolita Red, a ceramic type that, although highly variable with regard to paste, slip color, and surface finish (Heidke 1990a:87), can be distinguished easily from the highly micaceous Vahki Red. The end of the phase is indicated by the disappearance of the early red wares, as late Pioneer and early Colonial period decorated ceramics appear in Tucson Basin assemblages. Heidke (1990a:76, 94–95) has argued that Tortolita Red is clearly a Hohokam ceramic type, as indicated by paddle-and-anvil manufacture and the abundance of flare-rim bowl forms—a Hohokam hallmark—whereas the earlier plain ware horizon ceramics reflect closer affiliation with contemporary Mogollon ceramics (Whittlesey 1995, 1998b). Jar forms are rare, and the only type identified is the neckless seed jar (Heidke 1990a:81), indicating continuity with the earlier plain ware horizon.

Tortolita phase structures are similar in size and construction to the Vahki phase houses in the Phoenix Basin and contrast with the more informal Archaic period houses (Bernard-Shaw 1990:124), as well as the Snaketown phase house at Hodges Ruin (see below). The ground and flaked stone assemblages are diverse and include new forms that became abundant in later Hohokam sites (Eppley 1990:135). Botanical evidence reveals a wide spectrum of economic plant remains, including corn, beans, and squash and a variety of wild plant foods (Bernard-Shaw 1990:211). The nature of the habitations and their arrangement with extramural features, trash, and inhumations suggest the emergence of a larger village structure and a permanent and cohesive settlement (Bernard-Shaw 1990:121, 202–203, 206). The arrangement of the houses within the settlement, however, reflects a far less formal pattern than the courtyard groups that characterized later periods.

Recent evidence is accumulating in support of this Early Formative period occupation in the Tucson Basin, which was characterized by an undecorated, red-slipped and plain ware pottery tradition; small and relatively formal pit houses; informal house arrangements and large communal houses; and inhumation burial. The presence of such a tradition here and elsewhere in southern Arizona (see Cable and Doyel 1987; Sayles 1945) and western New Mexico raises questions about Hohokam origins and revives the issue of basic distinctions between the Hohokam and Mogollon cultures.

Limited information concerning the late Pioneer period comes from excavations at several sites in the northern and western portions of the basin. Kelly's excavations at Hodges Ruin yielded Hohokam ceramics dating to the Sweetwater phase around A.D. 650, but the earliest documented house at the site is a house floor that dates

to the subsequent Snaketown phase, possibly between A.D. 700 and 800 (Kelly et al. 1978:15). A small but significant late Pioneer period component was identified at the Valencia site, toward the southern end of the middle Santa Cruz valley (Doelle 1985, 1988). Although the paucity of late Pioneer period remains found makes the nature of this occupation highly problematic, the close association of late Pioneer period sites with the Santa Cruz River floodplain indicates that agriculture was the primary means of subsistence. Functional distinctions in architecture also were emerging at this time, as indicated by small and informal structures at such sites as Hawk's Nest (Czaplicki and Ravesloot 1989b) and the larger, more formal houses at the Lonetree and Valencia sites. Mortuary practices included inhumation, as well as cremation (Bernard-Shaw 1990; Fish et al., ed. 1992). Although Pioneer period decorated ceramics in the Tucson Basin traditionally have been viewed as indistinguishable from the Phoenix Basin types (Kelly et al. 1978:3), new information suggests that a local ceramic tradition was well developed in the Early Formative period and that decorated types may have been locally made (Deaver 1989a:53).

Colonial Period

The Colonial period witnessed dramatic changes involving an increase in the number of settlements, innovations in ceremonial architecture, the spread of new material culture elements and an elaborate mortuary ritual, and the development of new patterns in settlement and domestic group organization. These changes are generally associated with the spread of Hohokam culture from the Gila River area and the development of a Hohokam regional system that encompassed most of prehistoric Arizona (Doyel 1991; Wallace et al. 1995; Wilcox 1979; Wilcox and Sternberg 1983). The early portion of the period, the Cañada del Oro phase, is not as well known as the later Rillito phase, although reported sites are located throughout the Tucson Basin, except for its eastern extremity.

Until recently, Hodges Ruin was the only source of excavated Cañada del Oro phase material in the region. The presence of four house floors and one transitional Rillito phase structure provided meager evidence regarding continuity with settlement and subsistence trends of preceding periods. Recent excavations have greatly expanded our knowledge of this phase, as well as the earlier Snaketown phase, and have suggested the establishment of settlement and subsistence patterns that were to continue through several successive phases. Excavations at the Redtail site (Bernard-Shaw 1989b), located near the Lonetree site, and the Dakota Wash site (Craig 1988), located near the West Branch site south of Sentinel Peak, revealed significant early Colonial period remains. These and other sites indicate that increasing numbers of sedentary farming settlements were established along the Santa Cruz River by this time. Large, formal pit houses were constructed and cremation became the standard mortuary treatment. A local decorated ceramic tradition also emerged at the end of the Snaketown phase, although the Phoenix Basin appears to have remained the predominant trading partner with sites of the Santa Cruz valley throughout the Colonial and Sedentary periods, as evidenced by the common presence of imported buff ware ceramics. Exactly what was exchanged for the buff ware is unknown, as Tucson Basin ceramics were not common in Phoenix Basin sites at that time. Layhe (ed. 1986:290) suggested that perishables, such as cotton, may have been traded to the north. Not all sites in the Tucson Basin appeared to be equally involved in this trading system, however. Hodges Ruin and other sites located north of the Rillito–Santa Cruz confluence have considerably higher percentages of buff ware than do sites farther south, along the Santa Cruz River and in the southern Avra Valley (Layhe, ed. 1986:289; Wallace 1988:316).

The number of recorded and excavated Rillito phase sites and features increases dramatically over those of the preceding phase (Doelle 1988; Mayberry 1983). Recent, large-scale excavations have been completed at several Colonial period sites located along the length of the Santa Cruz River within the Tucson Basin, including the Redtail site (Bernard-Shaw 1989b), components of Hodges Ruin (Kelly et al. 1978; Layhe, ed. 1986), and the Punta de Agua sites (Greenleaf 1975). These excavations have provided a more detailed picture of occupation than for any earlier period, including internal site structure, subsistence, regional exchange, and mortuary patterns. Domestic, village, and community structure reflected patterns that were to be crystallized in the ensuing period. A formal household arrangement characterized as courtyard groups (J. Howard 1985; Wilcox et al. 1981) appeared for the first time, along with a diversified settlement system consisting of large, permanent villages; smaller, permanent or seasonal farmsteads and hamlets; and temporary settlements. Several discrete communities, consisting of large villages associated with clusters of hamlets, can be distinguished by this time. Together with the emerging evidence for small-scale canal irrigation, the even spacing of these communities along the Santa Cruz River suggests the development of intervillage networks, although these never achieved the complexity of those in the Phoenix Basin (Doyel 1984). Special cremation areas appear to have been characteristic of larger villages, such as Hodges Ruin and the Punta de Agua sites. Mayberry (1983:42) and Doelle (1988) have maintained that these cemeteries were part of an important community integrative system that was focused on

ball courts; large cemeteries and ball courts declined in the following period (Doelle 1988:306).

In the Cañada del Oro phase, settlement organization appears to have involved a series of small, independent, widely dispersed settlements rather than hierarchically structured, linked communities. Increasing settlement density and village complexity characterize the Rillito phase; individual villages increased dramatically in size (Vokes 1988a, 1989). An important feature of the Rillito phase is the appearance of primary villages (Doelle 1985:76)—large settlements exhibiting greater intensity of occupation, and often associated with ball courts and an array of smaller, satellite settlements. The ball court at the Valencia site is reputed to have been originally constructed in the Cañada del Oro phase (Doelle et al. 1987:81). Ball courts, a form of public architecture in which members of the community participated in ritual activities and exchange, appear to have been a sudden introduction that spread rapidly and rather uniformly (Doelle 1988:297). Many of these large ball court villages are clustered south of Martinez Hill, including the Punta de Agua sites investigated by Greenleaf (Doelle 1988:282). Others are present at the Valencia site complex, the Dakota Wash site, Hodges Ruin, and Los Morteros at the northern end of the basin. Still other ball courts are located along the major tributary drainages and other outlying areas of the Tucson Basin. The wide distribution of ball courts supports the notion that a region-wide community network was established by the Rillito phase, and suggests that the Tucson Basin Hohokam had become fully integrated into the larger Hohokam regional system (Wilcox and Sternberg 1983). This network was made up of individual communities, each focused on a ball court.

Doelle (1988:282) has attributed the development of this large community settlement pattern and concomitant, rapid population growth to a major environmental change that occurred around the beginning of the Rillito phase. After A.D. 800, the Santa Cruz River changed from a deeply entrenched channel to a broad, sandy floodplain that was ideal for floodwater farming (Waters 1987). In this scenario, it is not clear whether improved farming conditions in the floodplain were the primary causal factor in the dramatic changes that occurred during the Rillito phase, or if the improvement was localized to the San Xavier area. The introduction of new varieties of corn undoubtedly had an important impact, as well (Doelle 1988).

Settlements were located in the floodplain and associated riverine terraces, alluvial fans, and the mountain pediment. Although the intensity of occupation appears to have varied within each zone (Doelle and Wallace 1986:75), there was a preference for the riverine zone. Rillito phase sites, including the first large villages, are

33

situated along the length of the Santa Cruz River, suggesting an increasing focus on agriculture and exploiting riverine resources (Mayberry 1983:39). Small-scale canal systems may have been developed during this phase, as well (Bernard-Shaw 1988:167; Doyel 1984; Mayberry 1983:41). These systems probably never rivaled the complex systems developed in the Phoenix Basin, and remained small-scale systems serving a single village (Doyel 1984). The first dry-farming systems also appear to have begun during the late Colonial period, suggesting the development of a variety of agricultural systems (Mayberry 1983:41).

Sedentary Period

The Sedentary period, as represented by the Rincon phase in the Tucson Basin, often has been viewed as representing the height of the Hohokam occupation in the region, the time of maximum integration of the regional system, and the time of the greatest intensity of interregional contacts (Mayberry 1983:42). Alternatively, others view this period as reflecting a gradual breakdown in the regional system, and the first stage in the development of a local Tucson Basin cultural system (Deaver and Ciolek-Torrello 1993). Perhaps the most intensively investigated period in Tucson Basin prehistory, the Sedentary period is well known from excavations at Hodges Ruin (Kelly et al. 1978; Layhe, ed. 1986), the Punta de Agua sites (Greenleaf 1975), the West Branch site (Altschul et al. 1996; Huntington 1986), the Valencia site (Doelle 1985), and the Tanque Verde Wash site (Elson 1986). Research along the southern end of the middle Santa Cruz valley—especially that conducted by Desert Archaeology—has contributed immeasurably to this understanding. A wealth of knowledge about this time period has resulted from the intensive survey of large areas, coupled with a further refinement of Greenleaf's (1975) ceramic typology (Wallace 1986c), and recent intensive excavations at the West Branch and Valencia site complexes by Desert Archaeology and SRI.

More sites are attributed to this time period than any other, and no other prehistoric period is as well documented in the archaeological record of the Tucson Basin. The Sedentary period also is characterized by occupational continuity, in that most Rincon phase sites were established in the preceding Rillito phase and continued to be occupied in the Tanque Verde phase that followed. This continuity stands in sharp contrast to the Phoenix Basin, where few Sedentary period sites survived the Sedentary-Classic period transition (Mayberry 1983:42).

It is unclear, however, whether the Tucson Basin continued to be characterized by rapid population growth, as

is suggested for the Rillito phase. For example, Doelle (1988:283–284) has argued that a major reorganization of settlement and village structure took place during the middle Rincon subphase. The beginning of the Sedentary period was marked by changes in settlement pattern and population that may have correlated with minor environmental fluctuations, such as changes in the floodplain environment along the Santa Cruz River. In the western Tucson Basin, many of the large, centralized villages of the Rillito phase were replaced with a much more dispersed pattern involving an almost continuous band of small settlements along the southern portion of the Santa Cruz River (Doelle 1988:283). Doelle has suggested that this change was caused by another major disruption of the floodplain environment involving deep downcutting of the southernmost portion of the Santa Cruz River. In the eastern part of the basin, residential expansion is indicated. Settlements increased in number, upland elevations were settled, and expansion into agriculturally marginal areas occurred (Elson 1986:446–447; Simpson and Wells 1983, 1984). There were shifts in the foci of communities, especially in those villages centered on ball courts (Craig 1988:5; Doelle 1988; Doelle and Wallace 1986:80–81). Traditionally, these changes have been seen in the context of a burgeoning local population and associated socio-economic shifts that probably affected all portions of the Tucson Basin equally. The ball court system apparently never developed in the eastern basin, however, and the communities in that area therefore did not undergo the same kinds of shifts. Functional and social differentiation among Rincon phase settlements was marked. Larger villages were characterized by households occupying multiple, functionally differentiated structures (Elson 1986; Huntington 1986). Mortuary practices remained variable, although urn cremations and secondary cremations appear to have increased in frequency (Kelly et al. 1978).

Although the Rincon phase chronology based on Wallace's (1986c) refined ceramic typology has not been tested independently, it has proven to be of great utility in studying both regional and local patterns. The dispersion of Rillito phase villages appears to have been a gradual process that, by the late Rincon subphase, also included a gradual shift from the west to the east bank of the Santa Cruz River, south of San Xavier. This shift was completed during the Classic period (Doelle 1988:286). In addition, the more refined chronology has made possible research into the internal structure of Rincon phase villages and households (Doelle et al.1987; Huntington 1986). The West Branch site represents a large, dispersed settlement, the southernmost locus of which is the Colonial period Dakota Wash site. The northern set of loci was initially occupied during the early Rincon subphase, reached its peak occupation during the middle Rincon subphase, and declined during the late Rincon subphase. By the Tanque Verde phase, settlement had shifted back to the Dakota Wash site vicinity (Craig 1988; Doelle et al. 1987:83). The ball court at the Dakota Wash site was not replaced by a Rincon phase structure when settlement shifted north, as had occurred in the nearby Valencia site when this site experienced a similar shift (Doelle et al. 1987:82).

The Dakota Wash–West Branch site complex is regarded as one large village occupied from the early Colonial period to the early Classic period. The individual loci comprising this village represent precincts, the intermediate level of social and political organization between the village and smaller corporate groups, such as individual households (Doelle et al. 1987:83). Each precinct consisted of a series of domestic structures, a common courtyard, trash mounds, borrow areas, and sometimes cemeteries that were clustered together as a discrete unit. These clusters, in turn, represent the material domain of households (see also Ciolek-Torrello 1988b; J. Howard 1985; Sires 1987; Wilcox et al. 1981). Huntington (1986; Doelle et al. 1987) defined three household types at the West Branch site, based on the number and size of component structures. He accounted for this variability in terms of the developmental cycle of domestic groups and, more importantly, the economic power of the head of the household. Well-defined households were present in the early and middle Rincon subphases, with a trend toward increasing household size. This increase was associated with a diversification of subsistence and production activities at the West Branch site. Huntington maintained that larger households with skilled leaders were better able to manage the labor requirements and scheduling conflicts created by this diversification.

Morphological and formal changes are evident in Rincon phase pottery. A localized area of decorated ceramic production has been inferred for the southwestern Tucson Basin at this time (Harry 1996; Wallace and Heidke 1986). Large quantities of decorated pottery are believed to have been exchanged with communities in the eastern Tucson Basin, which apparently produced little or none. Huntington (1986) suggested that the West Branch site was one area of specialized ceramic production.

Evidence for subsistence diversification is found at both the West Branch and Valencia sites with the development of dry-farming systems located away from the floodplain (Doelle et al. 1987:93; Huntington 1986). Several new cultigens also were introduced during the Sedentary period, including tepary beans, jack beans, grain amaranth, and tobacco (Miksicek 1988:52). Agave utilization became increasingly important at the Valencia site by the late Rincon subphase. Specialization in subsistence practices at Rincon phase settlements correlates with the diversification in settlement function observed at

this time (Huckell et al. 1987; Huntington 1988:219; Miksicek 1988:52). These economic changes may have been associated with considerable stress to riverine resources that resulted from major human alterations to the riverine landscape, as evidenced in faunal (Szuter 1986, 1988b) and pollen (Fish 1986) remains.

By the late Rincon subphase, many of the earlier sites were abandoned and the West Branch site was considerably reduced. Ball courts, long considered to have been the mechanism of intra- and intercommunity integration, also were abandoned at this time (Wilcox and Sternberg 1983). The Hohokam regional system appears to have collapsed by the end of the Sedentary period. The middle Rincon subphase had witnessed a significant reduction in the use of Hohokam Buff Ware. By the late Rincon subphase, buff ware was absent, and small numbers of Mimbres Classic Black-on-white ceramics suggest a major shift in external ties at that time (Doelle et al. 1987:94).

Classic Period

By the late Rincon subphase, the Hohokam regional system essentially had collapsed, along with its ritual accouterments and even many nodes in the network. Ball courts fell into disuse, central villages were abandoned, and locations of existing hamlets shifted. The degree to which social factors were responsible for these changes has yet to be assessed adequately, although it is probable that nonenvironmental factors played a greater role in these changes than has been believed (Altschul 1988). The Classic period was a time of marked organizational change, as new settlement systems replaced the collapsed structure that had tied desert communities together for the past few centuries.

The two phases of the Classic period, the Tanque Verde and the Tucson phases, traditionally are distinguished by ceramics. The early Classic period Tanque Verde phase is better known than the later Tucson phase. Tanque Verde Red-on-brown is the diagnostic of the Classic period, persisting throughout both phases. The Tucson phase is usually distinguished by the addition of Roosevelt Red Ware, Tucson Polychrome, and nonlocal pottery types, such as White Mountain Red Ware, although these distinctions are problematic (see Wallace and Holmlund 1984). The low frequency of these later decorated pottery types makes temporal identification of Classic period sites suspect. The absence of these rare ceramic types at a site could result from a lack of participation by site residents in the exchange system that procured them (Mayberry 1983:47), or to sampling error. The latter may be a major problem, as few late Classic period sites have been intensively investigated.

Many of the sites that have served as the major sources of information on the pre-Classic and early Classic periods in the Santa Cruz valley did not have late Classic period components. Large villages occupied during the preceding period were abandoned or experienced dramatic depopulation by the late Classic period, and villages were established in new locations. The Marana community, Los Morteros, Hodges Ruin, the West Branch and Valencia sites, and the Punta de Agua sites were abandoned before or during the early Classic period. What little we know of the late Classic period comes from early excavations at University Indian Ruin, located in the eastern Tucson Basin (Hayden 1957), as well as the smaller-scale investigation of the Martinez Hill site, in the southern part of the valley (Gabel 1931). Because these excavations focused on the obvious architectural features and only portions of the work have been reported, information about this poorly understood period remains extremely limited (Wallace and Holmlund 1984:181). Thus, SRI's recent excavations at a small Tucson phase component of the Dairy site will contribute crucial information about this time period.

The substantial shift in settlements that occurred over the course of the Classic period is clearly seen in the northern Tucson Basin community of Marana. There, multiple-function settlements arranged in a zonal pattern focused on a platform mound village, and associated walled, residential compounds were established in previously unused portions of the Tortolita Mountains bajada during the early Classic period (Fish 1989; Fish et al. 1988:227), although bajada habitations were decreasing in other areas of the valley (Mayberry 1983:48). Similar shifts took place in the eastern Tucson Basin, where large villages consisting of several compounds were built in areas of previous low population density (Deaver and Ciolek-Torrello 1993; Slaughter and Roberts 1996; Whittlesey and Harry 1990:9). The occupation of the Point of the Mountain area reached its peak at that time (Lange and Deaver 1989; Wallace 1995), and the shift of settlement from the west side of the Santa Cruz to the east was completed in the San Xavier area (Doelle 1988). A new settlement type, *trincheras*, became important, with major examples near Cerro Prieto (AZ AA:7:11 [ASM]), Los Morteros, Tumamoc Hill (AZ AA:16:6 [ASM]), Black Mountain (AZ AA:16:12 [ASM]), and Martinez Hill (Downum 1993; Mayberry 1983:48; Wallace and Holmlund 1984:180). These settlements were located on walled terraces built on the slopes of peaks flanking the Santa Cruz River, and were used for residential and agricultural purposes, although their defensive nature also is clear (Downum 1993; Fish et al. 1984).

New types of domestic architectural forms were developed during the transition between the late Sedentary and early Classic periods, including puddled adobe construction, contiguous rectangular surface rooms, and compound enclosures (Greenleaf 1975:25; Greenwald and Ciolek Torrello 1988:357; Henderson 1987). There was, however, considerable regional variability in architecture, and the closing years of the Classic period were marked by a return to pit house construction (Ciolek-Torrello and Greenwald 1988a:142–143; Ravesloot 1987; Sires 1984a). Nondomestic architecture also underwent striking changes during the Classic period, as the focus of the ceremonial system moved from ball courts to platform mounds. Construction of platform mounds evidently was begun during the early Classic period (Ciolek-Torrello 1988a:307; Fish et al. 1988:227). The platform mound at University Indian Ruin, however, appears to have been constructed during the late Classic period (Hayden 1957). It is evident that, although superficially similar, not all platform mounds were used for the same purposes (cf. Gasser and Ciolek-Torrello 1988:499). The number of villages with such public facilities appears to have declined from that of the Sedentary period, suggesting increasing ceremonial integration concomitant with population aggregation.

These changes traditionally have been associated with the arrival of the Salado culture in south and central Arizona during the Tucson phase. The Salado phenomenon has been variously identified as a group of immigrants, an interaction sphere encompassing various cultural entities, and a trading network. It is becoming increasingly clear, however, that these changes were presaged in the late Rincon subphase, and that most occurred before the presumed Salado intrusion. For example, rectangular, adobe-walled rooms, polychrome pottery, and compound walls first made their appearance during the Tanque Verde phase, and possibly as early as the late Rincon subphase (Deaver and Ciolek-Torrello 1993). Sires (1987) attributed contemporaneous developments in compound architecture in the Phoenix Basin to an indigenous evolution of the Hohokam courtyard group. Accordingly, it seems highly unlikely that any one process is responsible for these various new patterns that characterize the Classic period.

The settlement shifts and *trincheras* sites appear to have been associated with shifts in subsistence, as many of the new site locations were closer to extensive dry-farming areas in the bajada zone. A major focus of these dry-farming areas appears to have been agave cultivation, as evidenced by large areas of rock pile features and associated roasting pits (Doelle 1988:285; Fish 1989; Whittlesey et al. 1994), although excavation and survey data indicate an increasing reliance on traditional cultigens, as well (Mayberry 1983:48). Agave may have been sporadically cultivated prior to the Classic period, but the presence of enormous rock pile fields and processing areas of Classic period age indicates a significant elaboration of agave cultivation and an increased importance in agave use. Large agave fields are reported in the southwestern Tucson Basin (Doelle 1988:285), the Marana community (Fish et al. 1988:230), and along McClellan Wash, east of the Picacho Mountains (Ciolek-Torrello and Halbirt 1987). Agave cultivation may have been more or less continuous between the Tortolita and Picacho Mountains (Sires et al. 1988:22).

Despite the extensive Tanque Verde phase research, the nature of inter- and intracommunity patterns during that time remains difficult to characterize (Doelle 1988:285). Doelle has argued for continuity in household and precinct organization from the Sedentary period. The internal structure of Tanque Verde phase villages is not nearly as well documented as in early Classic period contexts in the Phoenix Basin, however, and it thus seems premature to make this argument. To the contrary, existing evidence suggests that community organization in the Tucson Basin differed from contemporary Phoenix Basin settlements at that time (Doelle 1988:286). The Marana community, for example, is the only one associated with a platform mound, which was the most common integrative feature in Classic period communities in the Phoenix Basin. Platform mounds were never as common in the Tucson Basin as in other areas of southern and central Arizona, and the only other platform mounds in the Tucson Basin did not appear until the late Classic period (Wallace and Holmlund 1984:181–183). Classic period mortuary practices are poorly understood as well, although inhumations also appear to be less common at Tucson Basin Classic period sites than at contemporary Phoenix Basin sites. Cremation burial continued to be the dominant form in the Tucson Basin, at least during the Tanque Verde phase. Tanque Verde Red-on-brown differs from earlier Tucson Basin Brown Ware in design, technology, and morphology. The low diversity observed in Tanque Verde phase designs relative to previous periods is consistent with a model of production in which a few settlements produced the bulk of the decorated pottery, which was then widely exchanged (Whittlesey 1987d, 1988). Technological homogeneity in paste and temper also may suggest such an interpretation.

The Classic period phenomenon in the Tucson Basin was apparently short-lived, as little evidence for Tucson phase occupation has been found. There appears to have been a reduction of population during the Tucson phase, but the difficulty associated with identifying Tucson phase sites makes this proposition difficult to assess. Many of the locales that had been continuously occupied from the Pioneer period were abandoned by the Tucson phase. Although there was a major Tucson phase occupation at University Indian Ruin (Hayden 1957) and Martinez Hill Ruin (Gabel 1931), other large settlements, such as Hodges Ruin (Kelly et al. 1978), Sabino Canyon

Ruin (AZ BB:9:32 [ASM]), Los Morteros, and the Marana community (Fish et al. 1988:232), seem to have been abandoned at this time. The very high density of Tucson phase material at the few remaining sites is more indicative of intense nucleation than major population reduction, however, although this process of nucleation may have been associated with some population decline. By the Tucson phase, population appears to have been concentrated in a few locations that probably were the most favorable riverine settings for agriculture (Doelle 1988:286; Wallace and Holmlund 1984:183). Tucson phase sites along the middle Santa Cruz River include the Martinez Hill and the Zanardelli sites near San Xavier, near the southern end of the valley, as well as Rabid Ruin (AZ AA:12:46 [ASM]) and two large settlements near the Santa Cruz–Rillito River confluence (Wallace and Holmlund 1984). The dry-farming fields located on the bajadas do not appear to have continued in use after the Tanque Verde phase (Doelle 1988). The larger Tucson phase villages contained platform mounds, or at least massive, walled compounds containing pueblo-like roomblocks (Wallace and Holmlund 1984:183), yet other forms of architecture also were present. A Tucson phase pit house has been excavated at Rabid Ruin, for example (Wallace and Holmlund 1984).

The overall impression of this little-studied time, however, is one of depopulation, reorganization of existing populations, and relocation to other areas. For example, population apparently expanded in the Picacho Mountain area during the late Classic period (Ciolek-Torrello 1988b; Marmaduke and Henderson 1995). Traditionally, the cultural phenomena of this period have been attributed to the Salado, who were thought to have migrated south to the Phoenix and Tucson Basins to dwell alongside the Hohokam (Haury 1945). This theory has few proponents today. The considerable reorganization that took place during the Classic period has generally been regarded, in the absence of the Saladoan intrusion, as response to environmental stresses, some of which were natural and others undoubtedly man-made (Mayberry 1983; Wallace and Holmlund 1984:189; Whittlesey et al. 1994). The disruptions, first evident in the late Rincon subphase, may have become progressively greater. Waters (1989:121) noted that flooding during this time has been documented on the Salt River (Nials et al. 1989:69–70). He observed that similar events in both the Phoenix and Tucson Basins may have contributed to the decline of the Hohokam. Graybill's unpublished revisions of his 1989 paleoflood model, using refined tree-ring chronologies, reveal an even closer correlation between the collapse of the Hohokam and Salado cultural systems in the Phoenix Basin and surrounding areas, and a sequence of flooding events and extreme droughts in the late fourteenth and early fifteenth centuries (Van West and

Altschul 1994). The reduction of regional water tables (Dean 1988) that also occurred at this time would have served only to exacerbate the problems caused by these floods and droughts. It is not surprising that irrigation-based societies, such as the Classic period Hohokam and Salado, could not survive such calamities. Although the Tucson Basin was not as dependent upon irrigation as those populations residing along the Salt River, environmental deterioration, catastrophic events, and social factors, such as violent conflict, could have been critical to the decline of Hohokam culture there.

Protohistoric to Historical Period Transition

This important period in the occupational history of the region, which spans the end of the prehistoric sequence and the beginning of the historical period, remains poorly understood due to the small sample of excavated materials, poor chronometric control, and lack of a cohesive interpretive framework (Ravesloot and Whittlesey 1987). The Jesuit priests whose mission was to spread Christianity throughout what is today southern Arizona and northern Sonora encountered a homogenous linguistic stock of Native Americans, collectively called the Upper Pimans. According to Father Eusebio Kino, the Spaniards recognized five distinct subgroups who occupied different geographical territories within Sonora. One of these groups, the Sobaipuri, occupied the valleys of the Santa Cruz and San Pedro Rivers from their headwaters to the northern end of the Tucson Mountains (Brew and Huckell 1987; Di Peso 1953; Huckell 1984c; Masse 1981, 1985; Seymour 1989), whereas another group, the Papago (Tohono O'odham), who originally dwelled in the desert region west of the Tucson Mountains, subsequently played an important role in the Native American history of the region. When Kino first arrived in the Tucson Basin, he found the Sobaipuri concentrated in a small number of settlements along the Santa Cruz River. One of the largest was the village of Bac, where the mission of San Xavier was later established. A second large settlement, San Agustín de Oyaur, was located along the Santa Cruz south of its juncture with the Rillito River. Four smaller villages, called rancherías by the Spaniards, were located between San Agustín and Bac, including San Cosme de Tucson, near Sentinel Peak. San Clemente was located at the northern terminus of the Tucson Mountains (Burrus 1965:Plate VIII; Doelle 1984:200). Manje (Burrus 1971:377–378) reported a population of 1,680 Sobaipuri living in these villages in 1697—a minimal figure, according to Doelle (1984:203).

Agriculture was the mainstay of Sobaipuri subsistence, and included canal irrigation in those portions of the valley where surface water was available, as well as floodwater farming (Burrus 1971:348, 464). Doelle (1984:207) has attributed the dense, aggregated population to intensive agriculture and associated sociopolitical developments. Population movements created by Apache raiding and warfare influenced the Sobaipuri population living in the Santa Cruz River valley. In 1762, the entire remnant San Pedro River Sobaipuri population merged with resident populations in the villages of the Santa Cruz River valley. Subsequent loss of cultural identity and extinction by disease has been amply documented (Di Peso 1953; Dobyns 1963, 1976; Masse 1981:28).

Archaeological evidence for Sobaipuri occupation of the Tucson Basin is minimal, which is extraordinary, given the historical evidence for sustained and intensive occupation of the Santa Cruz River valley during the protohistoric period. Isolated and disturbed materials that may date to the protohistoric period have been recovered in a number of Tucson Basin localities. These include a surface scatter in the Tucson Mountain foothills that produced a calibrated radiocarbon date of A.D. 1650 through 1720 (Doelle 1984:199; Huckell and Huckell 1981; Ravesloot and Whittlesey 1987:Table 7.4); the Pima Canyon site (AZ BB:9:53 [ASM]) (Spoerl 1987; Whittlesey 1987a); and an isolated inhumation inferred to be protohistoric Sobaipuri (Brew and Huckell 1987). A number of features at the San Xavier Bridge Site (AZ BB:13:14 [ASM]) (Ravesloot 1987) may postdate the Tanque Verde phase occupation, given their stratigraphic position, and may be protohistoric in age (Ravesloot and Whittlesey 1987:91).

Although the collapse of Hohokam culture at the end of the Classic period is generally accepted, the fate of the Hohokam is unknown. The ancestors of the Native Americans presently populating southern Arizona variously have been suggested to be the Hohokam (Haury 1976), the O'otam (Di Peso 1956), the Amargosans (Hayden 1970), and Sonoran Indians (Masse 1980:312). A Hohokam-Piman continuum has not been demonstrated conclusively. Regardless of which prehistoric–historical-period social continuum is accepted, it remains to be determined by what processes one group "became" the other (Altschul 1988:15). Thus, it is critical to identify and study closely the Sobaipuri occupation of the Tucson Basin, for it speaks directly to questions concerning the Hohokam-Piman continuum, the decline of the Hohokam culture, and related issues.

Historical Period

The Tucson Basin has been subjected to a number of far-reaching changes in its three hundred years of recorded history. The small number of Sobaipuri rancherías came under increasing Spanish influence in the early

1700s, until a royal presidio was finally established in 1776. The modern city of Tucson developed out of this presidio settlement, whose original function was to protect the northern frontier of New Spain and communication routes to Alta California against both foreign (European) and domestic (Apache) enemies (Barnes 1983, 1984). During the middle years of the 1800s, Tucson went through a lengthy transitional period when Spanish rule was replaced first by Mexican and finally by U.S. administration. Tucson society changed as it became rapidly incorporated into the burgeoning and expansionistic U.S. economy. The Hispanic-Indian ties that had formed the backbone of presidial Tucson for a century were progressively weakened, and eventually overwhelmed by the influx of Euroamerican settlers. In the early years of the Territorial period, Tucson was essentially an amiably bifurcated city, with Hispanics and Euroamericans sharing rough parity. As the number of Euroamericans increased and as Tucson underwent a series of technological transformations around 1880, the town gradually became a predominantly Euroamerican city with Hispanic enclaves. It has continued in this vein up to the present day.

The Spanish Era, Late 1600s–1821

Spain has left an indelible mark on the Tucson area, but at the beginning of the colonial era, its presence was rather marginal. During the period when the Jesuits were in charge of the Sonoran frontier, Spanish missionaries and their military escorts maintained only the barest presence among Piman rancherías. Only during the Franciscan period was Tucson really established as a pueblo and mission, to which was finally added a royal presidio. After more than a decade of direct confrontations with the Apaches, the Tucson presidio and mission community entered into a period of florescence that lasted from about 1790 to 1820. It was during this period that Spanish rule had its greatest impact.

The first European known to have visited the area was a Jesuit missionary, Father Eusebio Francisco Kino. Credited with reorganizing and expanding New Spain's frontier northward, Kino first traveled through the Santa Cruz valley in 1694, visiting and making permanent contacts with the Piman settlements he encountered along the way. He is perhaps best known in local history for establishing the mission at San Xavier del Bac as the center of Jesuit work in the Tucson Basin. Kino died in 1711, having established a string of missions and *visitas* in the southern Arizona region.

Following Kino's death, Spain's presence in the area waned until the 1736 discovery of silver approximately 70 miles south of Tucson. This event marked the beginning of a permanent Hispanic presence in southern

Arizona, with prospectors and settlers streaming into a community that became known as "Arizonac." The influx of Hispanic settlers disturbed the Pimans and was one of many causes that led first to the plundering of the mission at San Xavier del Bac in 1744, and later to the Pima revolt of 1751. Although Spanish forces quickly restored order in the region, these troubles began a period of increased hostility between indigenous tribes and Spaniards. In an attempt to strengthen their foothold in the area, Spain established a military presence in the area in 1752 with the construction and garrisoning of the royal presidio at Tubac, 40 miles south of Tucson. By the end of the 1750s, San Ignacio de Tubac housed several hundred Hispanic settlers and soldiers paid by the Spanish crown (Officer 1987:4). Another revolt by the Pima took place in 1756, however, and the next year they forced the Jesuits from the mission at San Agustín.

The 1750s also marked the beginning of serious Apache raiding into southern Arizona. The Sobaipuri in the San Pedro Valley were exposed to the worst of these attacks and were forced to abandon the valley (Whittlesey et al. 1994). In 1762, the surviving remnants of the San Pedro valley Sobaipuri relocated to the Tucson Basin. In 1767, the Jesuit Order was expelled from southern Arizona as part of a hemisphere-wide change mandated by the Spanish crown, and members of the Franciscan Order assumed responsibility for the Sonoran frontier.

Between 1770 and 1773, Fray Francisco Garcés, a Franciscan, helped supervise the construction of a second church and fortified mission complex in the Tucson Basin. The new mission was located near the foot of Sentinel Peak and on the west side of the river, across from the Sobaipuri settlement of San Agustín. Following its completion, the complex was formally consecrated as San Agustín del Tucson (the name "Tucson" is a hispanicized version of a Papago/North Piman word meaning "at the foot of the Black Mountain" [Sentinel Peak] [Greenleaf and Wallace 1962:18]), and it became the location of a pueblo that came to rival Tubac and Bac (Dobyns 1976:33; Officer 1987:48). In an effort to reallocate Spain's military strength in northern Sonora, the Spanish commander Hugo O'Connor selected a location on the east side of the Santa Cruz River, approximately three-quarters of a mile northeast of mission San Agustín, as the site of a new presidio (Ciolek-Torrello and Swanson 1997:32–33). Construction began in 1777 and was almost complete when a major force of Apaches attacked the presidio and the older settlement across the river.

The new presidio, together with the deployment of a policy to subsidize the Apaches, quelled raiding activities along the frontier and initiated a period of relative peace for the Hispanic occupants of the area. By 1797 (the date of the first census), some 395 people were identified as inhabitants at the presidio, including 102 soldiers,

25 servants, and 21 civilian households (Officer 1987:71). Among Tucson's residents were about 100 Aravaipa Apaches (*Apaches mansos*) who were resettled by Spanish authorities outside of San Agustín del Tucson. An additional 236 Pinal Apaches were settled there in 1819. Perhaps the most comprehensive census conducted for the settlement was completed in 1804 by José de Zúñiga, a former commandant at San Diego and administrator for the Tucson area from 1795 through 1810 (Greenleaf and Wallace 1962:22). This census gave the total population of the Tucson presidio and pueblo, as well as San Xavier del Bac, as 1,015, composed mainly of ranchers and farmers who had spread throughout the valley during this peaceful period (Ciolek-Torrello and Swanson 1997:35). In addition to the human population, 3,500 cattle, 2,600 sheep, 1,200 horses, 120 mules, and 30 burros were accounted for in the valley.

Although Hispanics continued to populate the area throughout this period, their presence in the Santa Cruz valley remained tenuous. Tucson represented the northern frontier of Spanish expansion in what was later to become Arizona, and Hispanic and local Indian populations remained generally segregated through this period. In the first two decades of the nineteenth century, Spain's involvement in the Napoleonic wars, as well as a series of insurrections in Sonora, drained both the wealth of the frontier settlements and the resources to protect them (Barnes 1983:74–75).

The Mexican Era, 1821–1856

Mexico achieved her independence from Spain in 1821, in the wake of the Napoleonic wars, whereupon conditions deteriorated on the northern frontier. The policy of subsidizing and resettling peaceful Apaches was terminated, and Apache raiding quickly resumed (Sheridan 1986:21). By 1828, the Sonoran missions had been secularized and the Franciscans replaced with regular parish priests. Civil war in Sonora led to increasing conflicts between Mexican and other Indian groups as well, leading to the "Papago War" between 1840 and 1841. By the end of the Mexican period, Hispanic settlement within the entire area was limited essentially to the immediate surroundings of the Tucson presidio because of the threat from Apache raiders (Williams 1988:178).

The Mexican War and the first U.S. military presence in the area in 1846 only contributed to the general disorder characterizing the region during this period. The war ended in 1848 with the signing of the Treaty of Guadalupe Hidalgo, in which Mexico lost its claim to California and much of the Southwest. A new, international border was established 60 miles north of Tucson, along the Gila River, leaving Tucson a Mexican possession. The Treaty of Mesilla, signed by President Antonio Lopez de Santa Anna in 1853, formalized the Gadsden Purchase and relocated the international border to the south of Tucson. The Mexican military finally withdrew from the area in 1856, with the arrival of the U.S. First Dragoons. It was at this time that Euroamericans began moving into the Tucson area, principally to supply the military contingent (Officer 1987:283; Sheridan 1986:30).

The American Era, 1856–Present

When the United States formally assumed control of Tucson in 1856, the town's population did not exceed 500 persons (estimates range from 300 to 400 Mexicans and 50 Euroamericans). The arrival of large numbers of U.S. military personnel brought many new settlers to the area, who in turn opened mercantile shops in Tucson or established ranches or farms in the outlying areas. The result was an economic boom for Tucson, which quickly regained its former prosperity. With all trade barriers broken and the influx of Euroamerican influence and settlement, the town ceased to serve primarily as a military outpost, becoming instead the primary redistribution point for raw materials from the increasing mines and ranches in southern Arizona and for finished goods from the east and west coasts (Barnes 1983:26). Tucson quickly became the center of trade with Sonora and the Greater Southwest, a major stop on the southern route to California, and the source of goods and protection for local mining and ranching interests (Barnes 1983:104). By 1860, when the first U.S. census was taken, the population had expanded to include some 925 people, with 653 Mexicans and 168 Euroamericans (Sheridan 1986:37). In the earliest years of U.S. control, however, Tucson was a rude, frontier town that was not viewed kindly by travelers.

The American Civil War temporarily halted economic development in the area. In March of 1861, the secessionist convention was held in Mesilla, and the southern half of New Mexico Territory—which included Tucson and what was to become southern Arizona—seceded from the Union. In July, Mesilla was occupied by Texan troops, and federal troops abandoned their military outposts in southern Arizona (Ciolek-Torrello and Swanson 1997:39). Tucson was named a second judicial seat of the new Confederate state of Arizona, and at about this same time, 68 Tucson residents passed their own ordinance of secession. They requested Confederate troops for protection from the Apaches, who regarded the withdrawal of federal troops as a sign of victory and an opportunity to renew their raids with greater vigor. In February 1862, Captain Sherod Hunter led a company of mounted Texas riflemen into Tucson to establish a Confederate garrison. They were forced to abandon Tucson in May, however, as the first party of the California Volunteers entered the Santa Cruz valley. General Carleton, commander of these

Union forces, placed Tucson under military occupation. In August, Carleton left Major D. Fergusson in control of Tucson with a detachment of troops, as the California Volunteers moved east in pursuit of the Confederates. The Territory of Arizona was organized in 1863. Tucson would have been the territorial capital, but for its secessionist sympathies; because the war was still on, the first capital was established at Prescott.

Up until the Civil War, Tucson was the primary and most prosperous Euroamerican settlement in what came to be the Territory of Arizona. But the war severely disrupted life in southern Arizona, causing tremendous economic upheaval in Tucson and quickly bringing its prosperity to an end. One of the first casualties was the Butterfield stage route, which was immediately shut down. Traffic along the Santa Fe Trail also ceased, and Apache raiding increased dramatically, forcing abandonment of outlying mines and ranches. By the time Captain Hunter raised the Confederate Flag over Tucson, the only surviving settlements in southern Arizona were at Tucson, the Mowry Silver Mine in Patagonia, and Pete Kitchen's ranch on Portrero Creek. The Confederates lived off the land, using Tucson as a base to confiscate food, stock, and other property of Union loyalists. When the federal troops retook Tucson, Carleton seized the property of Confederate sympathizers, most notably Sylvester Mowry's silver mine and the Tucson property of William and Granville Oury, who were among the most prominent of the town's Euroamerican citizens (Ciolek-Torrello and Homburg 1990:124–125; Smith n.d.).

The Euroamerican population suffered disproportionately during the war. Much of that population hailed from southern states and supported the Confederate cause. Many left to serve the Confederacy and others were expelled by the Union forces. By the end of the war, the Euroamerican population had decreased by 36 percent and Euroamerican per capita wealth, as measured by the census, had decreased to about 26 percent of the 1860 figure (McGuire 1979:86). Alternatively, the Mexican population of Tucson for the same period more than doubled, as increasing unrest in Mexico during the 1860s and 1870s led to a new wave of Mexican migration into southern Arizona. Whereas the share of wealth held by the Mexican population represented only 12 percent of the town's total wealth in 1860, by 1864 it comprised almost 60 percent. The combined wealth of both ethnic groups, however, had decreased by more than 50 percent. Euroamerican settlers suffered greater loss during the war because much of their wealth, tied up in mining and commercial interests, dissipated as mining and trade were halted and goods were seized or destroyed. The destruction of the means of production and the loss of military payrolls that accompanied the original Union withdrawal also took most of the money out of circulation. By

contrast, most of the Mexicans were traditional farmers and small ranchers who were not perceived as Confederate sympathizers (McGuire 1979:89–90).

Tucson recovered slowly in the immediate postwar years, but the occupation of the town by the California Volunteers had many favorable repercussions. Notably, in August 1862, Fergusson undertook the first mapping of Tucson in an attempt to survey and record all property holdings. For this task he appointed the former Confederate sympathizer, William Oury—now apparently in favor with the Union forces—as registrar (Oury, who became the first mayor of the town in May 1864, and served as Pima County sheriff between 1873 and 1877, in 1871 organized and led the infamous Camp Grant massacre [see Ciolek-Torrello and Homburg 1990:124–125; Smith 1967, n.d.]). Under Fergusson's order, Oury conducted the first legal registration of land ownership in Tucson (Officer 1989:288–290).

An economic spurt was aided by the return of large numbers of Union troops and the 1865 establishment of Camp Lowell as a military garrison on the outskirts of the town, the relocation of the territorial capitol to Tucson in 1867, and the reestablishment of the Butterfield Stage line and other forms of communication and shipping. By 1870, Tucson's total wealth had increased by almost fourfold over its level prior to the war, and Euroamericans had reestablished their former economic control, although the Mexican community's wealth also tripled over the 1864 level. The population of both groups increased dramatically, but the Mexican population grew more rapidly with a steady flow of new settlers from Sonora, pushed northward by French intervention in Mexico and the Mexican civil war (McGuire 1979:86, 90). The Apaches again came under military control, and mines and ranches were reopened in southern Arizona, with Tucson becoming firmly established as a commercial hub. The federal payroll brought many new merchants, increasing the flow of goods and competition. As a result, the variety of goods increased and prices fell. Many of the Euroamerican immigrants brought new capital and skills that the Mexican community could not provide. Despite the increased flow of Euroamericans and their goods, however, Tucson retained its Mexican character throughout the 1870s (Bourke 1971:63–64; Hinton 1970:267–271). The town remained attached to Hispanic ways far longer than many other communities in the Southwest, Texas, and California, its isolation contributing to this state of affairs, as did the Mexican immigrant surges of the 1860s and 1870s. These surges allowed the Hispanic population to keep pace with Euroamerican immigration, which was rather limited compared to California, or even Texas (Sheridan 1986:88). The Mexican community was more stable in Tucson than in many other areas, having its own middle class that could not be displaced easily by financially adventurous Americans (Sheridan 1986:93).

In the early days of U.S. control, Euroamericans often mixed with Hispanics, with many of the Euroamerican pioneers marrying Hispanic women (McGuire 1979). This became less the rule as the influx of Euroamericans allowed them to create their own community. During the 1860s and 1870s, Tucson became a bifurcated town, Hispanic and Euroamerican—held together by mutual respect and the absolute need to preserve order in the face of the Apache threat and a harsh environment, but culturally divided. As Euroamerican merchants moved into the old presidial district, Hispanic residents tended to move into the area immediately south (Sheridan 1986:6).

McGuire (1979:91) attributed early Tucson's character to the inability to bring in Euroamerican goods in sufficient quantities or at low enough cost to make them available to most members of the community. Its character was due in part to the poverty that lingered despite the economic boom. A major aspect of Tucson's new wealth, and another cause of its retaining its Mexican character, was the continuation of strong ties with Mexico, particularly Sonora. Mexicans continued to dominate the non-Indian population, their numbers augmented by immigrants from Sonora. Tucson also monopolized the Sonoran trade, obtaining substantial quantities of food from Hermosillo and other parts of Sonora by exchanging Euroamerican dry goods for large quantities of flour, mescal, corn, beans, chile, and dried fruit (Bourke 1971:59–63; Hinton 1970:267). Apparently, southern Arizona was unable to provide sufficient food to feed itself, probably because Apache raiding continued to restrict the location of farms (McGuire 1979:83).

As Euroamericans moved into Tucson in numbers, it became clear that they would make their own changes to the community, which they hoped to refashion along more Euroamerican lines. The critical comments about Hispanic Tucson made by the first Euroamericans suggested the gulf that would some day arise between the two communities. The city remained "made of mud" until the turn of the century. George Hand's map of Tucson (Schneider 1941), compiled over a 10-year period in the 1870s, indicated that Tucson houses were made almost exclusively of adobe, with 8-inch- to 2-foot-thick, dirt roofs supported by small poles laid over rafters, the ceilings often cloth-lined to provide some protection from falling dirt. Since initial Mexican occupation, wood was very scarce and relatively expensive, and fired brick was unknown (Greenleaf and Wallace 1962:24–25; Thiel et al. 1995:55). Tucson during this period had no paving, no sidewalks, no lawns, few trees, and buildings constructed right on the edge of the street (Wagoner 1970:72)—features that made the town unpleasant to Euroamericans.

Despite the cultural conservatism of Tucson during this time, Euroamerican norms became more common as the city grew. By the early 1870s, Tucson had an estimated population of around 3,500, only 500 of whom were Euroamerican (Greenleaf and Wallace 1962:25), but it was the Euroamerican population that was in the forefront of the movement to make Tucson an incorporated community. Although William Oury had compiled the first property records in 1862, under Major Fergusson's orders, conflicts over land ownership developed between the Mexican descendants of the presidio and the Euroamerican newcomers. Tucson's civic leaders realized that a resolution to these conflicting land claims was necessary. Surveyed in 1872 by S. W. Foreman (Thiel et al. 1995:42), the town became incorporated the same year when it paid the federal government $1,600 for the patent to two sections of land for a "village site" (Barter 1881). The incorporated area was bounded by what is now Speedway Boulevard to the north, 22nd Street to the south, First Avenue to the east, and an area between the old presidio and Interstate 10 to the west (Sheridan 1986:238, Figure 4.3). Sunset Mesa lay far outside of the new townsite.

By 1880, the population of Tucson had increased to more than 7,000 (Sheridan 1986:56–57). The entry of the Southern Pacific Railroad into Tucson that same year provided the catalyst for a number of sweeping changes that would forever separate Tucson from its growing reputation as a "ramshackle" Mexican town. The railroad brought a flood of new Euroamerican immigrants, along with European and U.S. products and building materials that were to reshape Tucson into a Euroamerican town. Brick houses with peaked roofs gradually replaced the older, flat-roofed adobe houses. Within two years of the railroad's arrival, contracts were let for the construction and maintenance of gas works and gas lighting for the city, as well as for the construction and operation of the city's first street railway. During this two-year period, the first street numbers were assigned to houses within the city limits, and telephone service was inaugurated. The city's first water works was completed by December of 1881. In 1885, an act passed by the territorial legislature established the University of Arizona on a 40-acre parcel, located on what were then the northeastern outskirts of town. Several of the main campus buildings were constructed between 1887 and 1891.

The 1880s also saw the beginning of the collapse of traditional irrigation practices on the Santa Cruz River. Population growth led to mill dams and more fields, stretching available water to the limit even before the introduction of alfalfa, which needed more water than traditional crops. The introduction of Chinese truck farms only aggravated the situation. All of these demands on the water table led to the degradation of the Santa

Cruz floodplain, making traditional agriculture impossible (Sheridan 1986:63–67). The situation was similar on the ranches around Tucson, which increasingly shifted from Hispanic to Euroamerican ownership. Not familiar with the law or Euroamerican methods of land recording, many Hispanic ranchers were squeezed off the land, joining the influx of farmers in the movement to Tucson. A common expression described this situation: *"del rancho al barrio* (from the ranch to the barrio)" (Sheridan 1986:55–92).

Its economy closely related to the mining and cattle industries, Tucson experienced a series of boom-and-bust cycles at the end of the nineteenth century, but by the early twentieth century, with an increasing influx of immigrants, its economy diversified. Population continued to increase until the Great Depression, when Tucson experienced a tremendous population loss (Bufkin 1980). Much of its population was regained during World War II, when defense-related industries moved into the area. In the 1950s and 1960s, the population of Tucson exploded, increasing almost twentyfold (Barnes 1983:115), a process that has continued unabated into the 1990s.

Historical-period settlement outside of Tucson began in the 1850s, with a few settlers living along the Agua Caliente and Tanque Verde Washes as early as 1858, shortly after the area was incorporated into the U.S. (Gregonis and Huckell 1980:15). In 1873, Camp Lowell was moved from the townsite of Tucson to a location near the confluence of Tanque Verde and Pantano Washes, and was renamed Fort Lowell. Ranches and farms existed along the Rillito River and the Tanque Verde, Agua Caliente, and Cañada del Oro Washes before the fort was moved, despite the problems with Apache attacks, but with the establishment of this and other military posts throughout Arizona, the Apache problem was resolved and rural settlement increased throughout the region. The Rillito River area was one of the first to benefit from the economic prosperity associated with the establishment of

peace in Arizona Territory, and by the 1880s, many farmers began to irrigate the bottomlands along the stream.

The earliest settler along the Rillito River was a man from Arkansas named Robert Rolette, who cultivated the bottomland just above the future location of Fort Lowell, beginning in 1858 (Smith 1910:98; Turner 1982:6). He sold out to the Robertson brothers in 1862. At least nine civilians had established farms or ranches near the fort by the time it was founded, and three canals also had been built at this early time (Turner 1982). By 1886, there were enough people living on the Rillito to warrant the formation of an irrigation company. Between 1886 and 1888, the Santa Catalina Ditch and Irrigating Company attempted to build an irrigation system capable of watering 1,200–1,600 ha of land on the north side of the river. The only parts of this system to be completed were a small segment of a canal, an inverted siphon, and a 0.4 km-long concrete infiltration gallery. The gallery emptied into a canal that ran along the south side of the river to a point west of present-day Dodge Boulevard, and then ran into a siphon under the bed of the river in order to carry the water to the north side. The siphon, a pipe built of redwood planks, was destroyed by heavy flooding in 1887, putting an end to the entire project. The first functional irrigation system along the Rillito was not developed until after 1910, when Mormon settlers built a system to supply water for their fields in the Binghampton area.

By 1909, 920 ha of land were under cultivation along the Rillito River (Gregonis and Huckell 1980:61), most of it watered by several small irrigation systems. With dropping water tables and the gradual loss of surface water along the river, these systems were abandoned and replaced by individual wells. Farming and stock raising continued to be the major use of the Rillito River area until after World War II, when the area was gradually absorbed by the expansion of Tucson. Large tracts along the river, however, retained their rural character into the 1990s.

CHAPTER 4

Field Methods

Robert B. Neily, Edgar K. Huber, and Richard Ciolek-Torrello

Data recovery at Sunset Mesa Ruin involved mechanical trenching and stripping, complete hand excavation of all pit houses and the historical-period homestead identified during the testing and data recovery phases, and the sample excavation of extramural features. These procedures were designed to obtain the necessary data to address the research themes outlined in Chapter 1. As surface artifact sampling had been undertaken during the testing phase (Harry and Ciolek-Torrello 1992:50), only limited, judgmental surface samples were obtained during the data recovery phase. Backhoe trenching and mechanical stripping were used throughout to locate, identify, and expose various features that were subsequently subjected to complete or sample excavation. A total of 48 prehistoric and historical-period features was located by these various procedures. These included houses, food-processing areas, a canal segment, and numerous pit features. All of the houses were completely excavated and about half of the other features were sample excavated. The remaining features, which consisted of extramural pits, were recorded but not sampled. Two cremations, Features 4 and 10, had been excavated during the testing phase (Harry and Ciolek-Torrello 1992:35, 40). No additional human remains were encountered during data recovery. The fieldwork extended from August 8 to September 27, 1994. A total of 172 person-days of effort was expended during the data recovery phase.

Backhoe Trenching

During the testing phase, backhoe trenching was undertaken across the entire site area within the APE, to assess the extent of subsurface cultural deposits. At that time, nine 20-m-long trenches were laid out about 20 m apart, generally in two parallel rows with approximately 20 m between them (see Figure 4). Two additional trenches were placed perpendicular to these alignments and just outside the APE, to test further an area of dense surface and subsurface cultural deposits. Although extensive cultural deposits were observed in the westernmost portion of the APE, relatively few features could be identified. These consisted primarily of small pit features, although one possible house, two cremations, and a historical-period adobe house foundation also were identified. Because of the paucity of features in the presence of dense artifact deposits, it was decided to excavate many more trenches during the data recovery phase. Seventeen additional trenches, totaling approximately 425 m in length, were excavated at this time (Figure 8). Combined with the 220 m of backhoe trenching in the testing phase, almost 650 m of trenches were excavated within the APE and its immediate vicinity. Placed near the concentration of deposits found during testing, most of the new trenches were 18 m in length and less than 1 m in width; these were arranged in a systematic pattern at approximately 10-m intervals. Three trenches were extended across the southern boundary of the APE, along with two of the 18-m trenches. Most of the trenches excavated during data recovery were aligned north-south and perpendicular to those excavated during the testing phase. To augment the standard backhoe trenches investigated during data recovery; seven broadside trenches, 5–18 m in length and 2 m in width, were excavated in selected areas along the western edge of the Qt2 terrace.

The trenching carried out during the data recovery phase was designed primarily to evaluate more intensively the portion of the APE where subsurface features were suspected as a result of previous investigation. This portion was centered on the area between Trench 1 and Trench 9 on the west, and Trench 11 on the east (see Figure 8). Based on the results of the surface and subsurface investigations carried out during the testing phase at

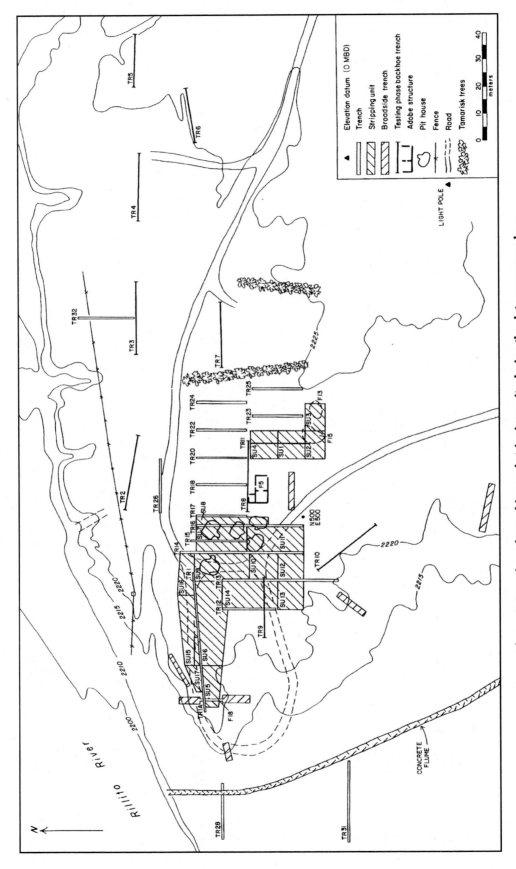

Figure 8. Location of trenching and stripping units during the data recovery phase.

Sunset Mesa Ruin, the densest concentration of artifacts and most of the identified and likely buried features were projected to be located primarily along the western margins of the Qt2 terraces, both within and just south of the APE (Ciolek-Torrello and Homburg 1990; Harry and Ciolek-Torrello 1992). Furthermore, previously identified features, including two cremations along Trench 8 and a possible pit house along Trench 1, indicated that this area might represent a habitation area containing pit houses and associated features. The historical-period, turn-of-the-century homestead component also was centered in this area.

The first step toward the intensive investigation of this area involved excavating a series of systematic, staggered, north-south-oriented trenches in untested areas surrounding the identified testing phase features. These trenches were excavated at 10-m intervals and generally were 18 m long, although four trenches (Trenches 13–16) were extended as much as 27 m longer, based on the deposits and features encountered during the initial trenching. Trench 26 was excavated to verify the northern boundary of the possible habitation area, whereas Trench 32 was excavated north of testing phase Trench 3 to evaluate a possible feature that had been identified there. Only one of the original testing phase trenches (Trench 1) was reexcavated during data recovery. This trench, which contained a possible pit house and other features, was also lengthened to 51 m to investigate the full length of a narrow terrace ridge in the extreme northwest portion of the site.

Two other testing phase trenches that contained features, Trenches 8 and 11, were not reopened because their precise locations could not be found. To avoid further damage to the segment of the historical-period adobe structure (Feature 5) identified along Trench 8 and the possible pit house in Trench 11, it was decided to strip the areas in their vicinity rather than place more trenches. The outlines of Feature 5 were located by hand-excavation. The remainder of the area around Trench 8 was left unexcavated, as the cremations in this trench had been removed during the testing phase and no features or cultural deposits were located in Trenches 17, 18, 20, and 22, which were laid out perpendicular and to the north of Trench 8. The area around Trench 11 was stripped mechanically to locate the possible pit house and associated features. In addition, Trenches 23 and 25 were excavated to the east of Trench 11 and south of the APE. Unfortunately, the pit house could not be located, although a food-processing area was identified in this area subsequently.

No additional excavations were planned in the vicinity of the historical-period adobe structure west of Trench 11 and south of Trench 8 until after the structure and any associated features were excavated. Subsequently, a 14-by-2-m, broadside trench was excavated in this untested area south of Feature 5.

Two of four planned trenches (Trenches 28 and 31) were excavated perpendicular to the historical-period, concrete flume on the lower T1 terrace, west of the previously defined site boundary. Based on the presence of the historical-period canal, it was anticipated that prehistoric or other buried historical-period canals might be present along the base of the Qt2 terrace. Archaic period features also were anticipated on this lower terrace, as they had been found recently in a similar geomorphic setting a short distance to the south (see Mabry et al. 1997). To locate such features, Trenches 28 and 31 were excavated between approximately 2 and 4 m in depth; no prehistoric or historical-period features were found, however.

After the identification of a prehistoric canal segment (Feature 18) in Trench 1, along the edge of the terrace in the extreme northwest portion of the site, five more broadside trenches were excavated along the western and northwestern edges of the terrace to track the canal alignment. A vertical cut also was made along the terrace edge north and east of the canal alignment to obtain a profile of the canal and to examine the geomorphic structure of the surrounding terrace sediments. Because of the eroded condition of the terrace edge, there were few possible locations at or near the canal's elevation where other intact segments might have been preserved. These areas included the north-facing terrace edge along the Rillito River, east of the canal segment, and two locations to the south and outside of the APE. The canal, however, could be located only in the one broadside trench placed perpendicular to Trench 1A and in the vertical cut in the terrace edge. The canal was completely excavated within this segment. No segments of the canal were identified in the other broadside trenches.

Mechanical Stripping

Approximately 2,200 m^2 of the site area overlying known and suspected features also was subject to mechanical stripping. To assess subsurface artifact density and distribution, 10-by-10-m (100-m^2) stripping units were planned. The size and dimensions of some of these stripping units differed, however, because of their location on the terrace, the presence of modern disturbance, and other uncontrolled factors. All artifacts recovered from each stripping unit were provenienced separately.

Feature Excavation

The prehistoric component of the site included five pit houses (Features 21–23, 25, and 27), a ramada (Feature 13) and an associated food-processing/storage area (Feature 15), a canal segment (Feature 18), and 25 extramural features (Figure 9). The latter consisted of small pits, trash areas, and two isolated vessels. All five houses were completely excavated, whereas the ramada, work area, and canal, and 12 extramural features were tested or sampled. The historical-period component consisted of an adobe building foundation (Feature 5) and 12 historical-period to recent pit features. Feature 5 was excavated, and seven of these pit features were tested or sampled. The locations, associations, and presumed function of the remaining 18 prehistoric and historical-period pit features were recorded.

Excavation methods for each of the five pit houses were identical, and each structure was completely excavated. The historical-period foundation also was excavated in its entirety. Each of the extramural features was sampled, although several unique features—including Features 13 and 15, the ramada and associated work areas, and Feature 18, the canal segment—were sampled more extensively.

Pit Houses

Each of the five pit houses was exposed in the backhoe trenches, although only small portions of Features 22 and 27 were identified in profiles along Trenches 14 and 15. The overlying natural and cultural deposits were then mechanically removed to expose and define the feature outlines. The excavation proceeded by initially quartering the approximate outline of each structure along its longitudinal and transverse axes, if possible; otherwise, it was divided into four approximately equal sections. It was expected that the transverse axis would bisect the entry. Each quarter of the fill was excavated separately, and at least one quarter was screened with $\frac{1}{4}$-inch mesh. Undifferentiated house fill was excavated in 20-cm arbitrary levels, unless finer vertical control was needed during feature excavation.

The burned roof fall/wall fall stratum, if present, was excavated separately, as was floor fill, which consisted of an arbitrary 5–10-cm level immediately above the floor. Any artifacts in contact with the floor were mapped, point-provenienced, and collected separately. Pollen and macrobotanical flotation samples were taken from a number of fill contexts. Some arbitrary pollen samples were taken from upper fill strata, and systematic pinch samples

were obtained from floor-contact proveniences across each of the quarters. Additional pollen samples were obtained where possible from good covered or sealed contexts, such as under floor-contact ground stone artifacts or ceramic vessels. Four-liter flotation samples were taken from roof fall contexts exhibiting abundant carbonized material, or where specific economic plant remains were detected. Systematic floor fill samples also were taken from each of the excavated quarters of the structure. Additional samples were obtained from good floor fill contexts where carbonized material was observed.

Interior floor features, such as hearths, other thermal features, and floor pits, were excavated in their entirety. In some cases, the entire fill of the feature was removed as a sample; in others, a portion was sampled and the remainder was screened. Larger pits were halved, with at least one half screened. Fill from postholes and floor grooves generally was not screened. At least one 4-liter flotation sample was obtained from the fill of floor pits, although multiple 4-liter-sized samples often were taken from the larger pits. Pollen samples were obtained from hearths, floor pits, intrusive pits (if present), and some postholes.

Historical-Period Structure

A 1.85-m portion of the adobe foundation of Feature 5 was originally identified along the west end of Trench 8 during the testing phase. Subsequent hand excavation exposed a 6.5-m-long wall segment extending to the south, defining the west wall and southwest corner of Room 3 and a portion of the west wall of Room 1 (Harry and Ciolek-Torrello 1992:38–39).

During data recovery, these wall segments were re-exposed and additional hand stripping revealed the remainder of Feature 5. Disturbance was noted in the northeast corner of Room 3 (along Trench 8), most of the east wall of Room 1, and the southeast corner of Room 2. Each of the defined rooms was approximately quartered and excavated separately. Only the northwest quarter of Room 1 was screened with $\frac{1}{4}$-inch mesh. Because of the lack of historical-period material in the fill, no additional screening in this or the other two rooms was conducted. The scant number of artifacts on the floor were mapped, point-provenienced, and collected, where possible. No pollen or flotation samples were obtained.

Ramada and Food-Preparation Area

The ramada and food-preparation area consisted of two adjacent and functionally interrelated features, Features 13

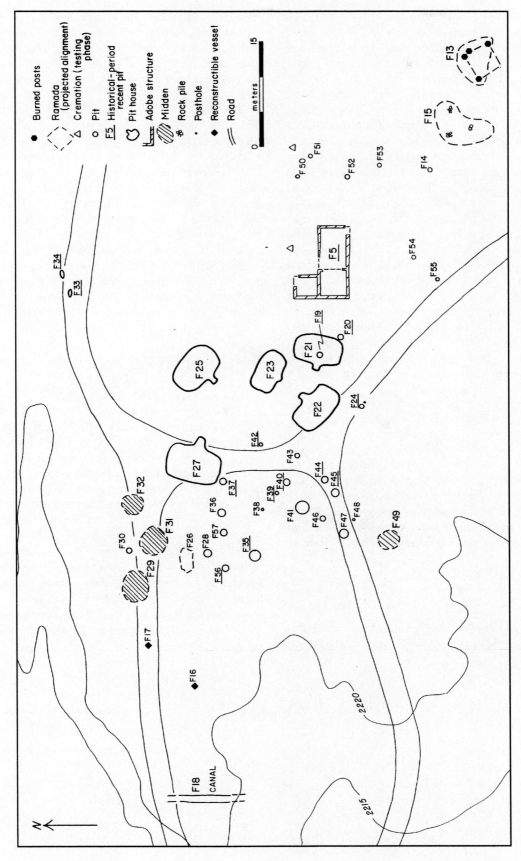

Figure 9. Location of features investigated at Sunset Mesa Ruin during the data recovery phase.

and 15. The ramada, Feature 13, was initially identified in Stripping Unit 3. Shovel scraping was used to define further the extent of the scatter. Exposed artifacts were mapped, and specific artifacts and artifact clusters were point-provenienced and collected.

Because a distinct feature boundary could not be determined, two screened test pits—a 1-by-2-m unit and an adjacent 2-by-2-m unit—were excavated in the densest part of the concentration to assess whether an activity surface was present. No surface was found in these units. Additional shovel scraping around these excavation units, however, yielded a configuration of four burned posts, a small remnant of a use-compacted surface, additional ceramic clusters, and clusters of charred seeds. Macrobotanical and pollen samples were obtained from around and under the artifact clusters.

The food-storage and cooking area, Feature 15, was initially located during the testing phase and identified as a possible pit house, Feature 9, at the south end of Trench 11. In an attempt to relocate this feature, the south end of Trench 11 was mechanically stripped during data recovery (Stripping Units 1 and 2), but to no avail. Identified instead was Feature 15, which consisted of a dense scatter of artifacts with several clusters and three spatially distinct piles of fire-cracked rock.

Shovel scraping was used to define the general extent of the scatter. Exposed artifacts were mapped, and specific artifact clusters were point-provenienced and collected. Because a distinct feature boundary could not be determined after initial shovel scraping, a 1-by-2-m test pit was excavated in an area of high artifact density to assess the depth of the cultural deposits and the presence of an activity surface, although none was found. Pollen and flotation samples were taken from both of the fire-cracked rock clusters, as well as several artifact clusters.

Canal

Feature 18 was initially identified in both the north and south profiles at the western end of Trench 1A. The terrace remnant, across which the canal extended, was less than 8 m wide, approximately 1.4 m to the north and 5.4 m to the south of the trench. The northern edge of the terrace had been truncated by the Rillito River, whereas the southern portion was dissected by several erosional channels.

The longer portion of the canal segment, to the south of the trench, was shovel scraped to the distinct, silty clay fill of the canal. This segment of the canal was longitudinally bisected and the west half was completely excavated and screened. A 50-cm section of the canal just south of the trench also was completely excavated to assess the cross-sectional morphology of the canal. The shorter portion of the canal north of the trench was completely excavated, as well.

Sediment samples were systematically taken from the canal, along with a series of matched pollen and ostracode samples. Radiocarbon samples were obtained from canal sediments and from sheet trash deposits that underlay a portion of the canal north of the trench.

Extramural Pit Features

Thirty-seven extramural pit and trash features were documented during data recovery, of which 12 were historical-period or recent features and 25 were prehistoric. Twelve features also had been identified during the testing phase, including two cremations (Features 4 and 10) that were completely documented at that time; of the other 10 features, only Feature 5, the historical-period adobe house foundation, was investigated during data recovery. All of the extramural features found during data recovery—with the exception of Features 33 and 34, which were identified in Trench 26—were found in the course of mechanical stripping. Ten of the prehistoric features and six of the historical-period features were tested or sampled. Of these, two isolated ceramic vessels were completely excavated, whereas the other features were bisected and then sampled for macrobotanical and pollen remains.

CHAPTER 5

Feature Descriptions

Robert B. Neily and Edgar K. Huber

This chapter describes the features encountered in the northwestern portion of Sunset Mesa Ruin, along the Rillito River terrace edge. This roughly 100-by-40-m area corresponds with the western end of the APE, where previous testing suggested a high potential for subsurface cultural deposits and the presence of habitations dating to the prehistoric and historical periods. Excavations were extended slightly south of the APE boundary during testing and data recovery to expand the sample and to obtain closure on the habitation areas found in the APE. Despite this extension, only a small portion of this site was excavated and is described in this report. Extensive surface midden deposits similar to those found in the investigated area are distributed for another 150 m south along the western terrace edge and as much as 100 m to the east. It is highly likely that this portion of the site contains subsurface deposits similar to those found in the western end of the APE. Thus, the concentration of habitations and associated features in the APE probably represented roughly no more than 20 percent of the inhabited portion of the site.

Five prehistoric pit houses (Features 21, 22, 23, 25, and 27) were identified in a 25-by-25-m (625-m^2) area of the APE (see Figure 9). At least three of these houses (Features 21, 25, and 27) probably were contemporaneous and represented a courtyard group (see Wilcox et al. 1981). The other two houses may have represented older structures employed by the residents of this house group. In addition, 25 other prehistoric extramural features were arrayed to the west of this courtyard group and probably were associated with this habitation area. These included 5 trash deposits (Features 28, 29, 31, 32, and 49) located to the northwest and southwest, 18 pits distributed primarily to the west and southeast, and 2 isolated vessels (Features 16 and 17) located to the northwest. Two cremations related to this courtyard group were located to the east of the structures during the testing phase (Harry

and Ciolek-Torrello 1992). A discrete food-preparation area was situated a short distance to the southeast of the courtyard group. This area contained two closely spaced, dense artifact clusters (Features 13 and 15), one of which was associated with a ramada. These features appear to have represented a kitchen area involving storage, cooking, and food-preparation activities. The distinct location of these two features makes it unclear as to whether they also were associated with this courtyard group, or were related to another courtyard group located in unexplored areas to the south and southwest.

A prehistoric canal segment (Feature 18) also was identified along the northwest edge of the terrace on which the site was located. This north-south-oriented segment, which was fed with water flowing from the Rillito River, represents one of only a few known prehistoric canals within the Tucson Basin. The presence of a canal clearly associates the occupation of Sunset Mesa with irrigation agriculture and possibly an irrigation community that may have linked several settlements.

A historical-period, turn-of-the-century component was present within the APE, as well, located directly east of the prehistoric courtyard group. This component was represented by a three-room adobe house (Feature 5) that was probably associated with the Cuevas homestead (Roskruge 1893), 12 thermal and other pits, and a general surface scatter of trash related to the occupation of the adobe house, the Sunset Dairy after 1915, and modern dumping activities.

The following description first presents a brief overview of the features recorded during the testing phase. This is followed by descriptions of the prehistoric pit houses, the ramada and kitchen area complex, the various prehistoric extramural features, and finally, the irrigation canal. The discussion is concluded with a description of the adobe structure and other historical-period features.

Testing Phase Features

During the initial testing phase, a total of 271 m of trenches was excavated in the vicinity of the APE, which encompassed approximately 25 percent of the total site area. In the western portion of the tested area, 12 features were identified (Harry and Ciolek-Torrello 1992). Of these, 2 features (Features 2 and 3) were relocated along Trench 1 during data recovery, 2 (Features 9 and 12) were investigated along Trench 11, and 1 feature (Feature 5) was relocated along Trench 8 (see Figure 9).

Feature 2 was originally described as a probable pit house visible in both the north and south backhoe trench walls. After Trench 1 was reopened and the adjacent Stripping Units 6 and 15 were exposed, however, a distinct pit boundary or floor was not identifiable. Rather, the feature appeared to represent a trash deposit, and was similar to nearby deposits containing abundant artifactual trash—Features 29, 30, and 32—all located north of Trench 1. Given the proximity of these trash features and the generally high artifact density in Stripping Units 6 and 15, it is likely that the combined area represented a trash mound that had been leveled and disturbed through subsequent historical-period and modern use.

Feature 11, described as a circular pit, was originally recorded along Trench 1, adjacent to Feature 2. The feature was not relocated.

Feature 3, a hearth that exhibited an oxidized, basin-shaped base, was relocated along the north face of Trench 1, within 15 cm of the present-day ground surface. No artifacts were identified in association with the pit. Although the feature was not deeply buried, the recovery near the surface of two nearby in situ jars, Features 16 and 17, suggests that this feature might have been prehistoric in origin. No further work was conducted, however.

Although Trench 11 was not reopened, the area to either side of it was mechanically stripped (Stripping Units 1 and 4, and part of Stripping Unit 2) to expose two previously identified features, Features 9 and 12, for planned excavation. Whereas Feature 9 was described as a probable pit house, Feature 12 was described as a probable storage pit, although it was suspected that Trench 11 had cut through a corner of a pit house. Mechanical stripping revealed only a vague outline of Feature 12, and given the general lack of distinct fill or abundant artifactual material, further work was not undertaken. In the area where Feature 9 had been identified, mechanical stripping exposed a dense area of artifacts and clusters of fire-cracked rock. No pit house was discernible, but this feature was recorded and subsequently tested as Feature 15 (see below).

Feature 5 was originally identified along Trench 8. Although the trench was not reopened during data recovery, the originally exposed adobe wall segments of Feature 5 were relocated. Feature 5 was completely defined and excavated.

Seven other features were recorded during testing. These included a probable roasting pit situated outside of the APE to the south, two cremations, a small roasting pit containing fire-cracked rock, and a ephemeral hearth. None of these features were relocated or subject to further investigation during data recovery. Feature 1, a probable roasting pit, was identified on the surface, south of the APE. Because fire-cracked rock is prevalent in eroded areas of the site's southwest portion, where Feature 1 was located, it is likely that other cooking features and roasting pits are present in this area. Another roasting pit, Feature 8, was identified along the south wall of Trench 9, along the northwest periphery of the site. Similarly, this portion of the terrace margin might also have been used for cooking functions.

Features 4 and 10 both represented secondary cremations located in Trench 8 (Harry and Ciolek-Torrello 1992), which was not reopened during data recovery. The location of these cremations east of the habitation structures indicates that the area may have been an associated cemetery. Feature 4, a "mixed burial," consisted of a pit containing calcined bone and large plain ware and red ware sherds along the north wall of Trench 8. Feature 10, an urn cremation, consisted of a small plain ware bowl containing calcined bone, covered with a large sherd. This cremation, also situated along the north wall of Trench 8, was recovered during the testing phase (Harry and Ciolek-Torrello 1992:40–46).

Feature 7, located along the north wall of Trench 8 between Features 4 and 10, represented a small cooking pit containing fire-cracked rock. Feature 6 consisted of an ephemeral hearth along the north wall of Trench 3. Because the location of this feature was far removed from other identified features at the site, its functional association is not clear. The trench was not reopened.

Prehistoric Features

Pit Houses

Feature 21

Feature 21 was a pit house with a lateral entryway oriented to the northwest (Figures 10 and 11). Although the house pit was indistinct, the structure appears to have been

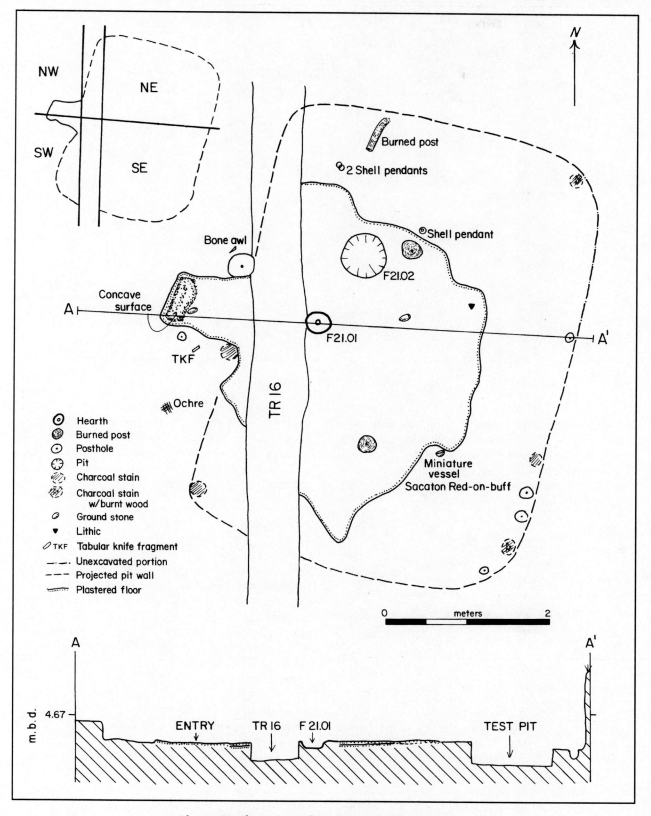

Figure 10. Plan map and cross section of Feature 21.

Figure 11. Feature 21, west view.

roughly subrectangular in shape. Two floor features, a hearth (Feature 21.01) and a large pit (Feature 21.02), were recorded. Two partial, plastered and superimposed floors were noted, both centered around the hearth and the entry. Floor artifacts were sparse, but included three shell pendants and a miniature ceramic vessel.

Type: pit house
Function: habitation
Temporal assignment: Rincon phase
Dimensions: approximately 6 m long by 4.05 m wide
Floor area: 24.3 m^2 (excluding entryway)
Entry orientation: 280°
Shape: subrectangular
House pit depth: approximately 20 cm

Excavation Methods

The structure was initially identified in profile on both sides of Trench 16. Approximately 60 cm of overburden on each side of the trench was mechanically removed to expose the rough outline of the structure. Although the hearth (Feature 21.01) was identified along the east side of the trench, the orientation and location of the entry and the long axis of the structure could not be determined at first. Structure fill, therefore, was excavated in quarters using the north-south trench and an arbitrary grid line

south of the hearth. Excavation of the fill was undertaken in 20-cm arbitrary levels. The fill in the southwest quadrant was completely screened, whereas only floor fill (Level 3) was screened across the remainder of the structure.

Stratigraphy

Level 1
This 20-cm-thick level (4.55–4.75 m below datum [mbd]) contained the upper fill of the house. It consisted of a compact, light brown sandy to silty loam with some scattered fire-cracked rock. Refuse was sparse, consisting primarily of sherds. A historical-period pit (Feature 19) intruded into the upper portion of this level.

Level 2
This 20-cm-thick level (4.75–4.95 mbd) contained the remainder of the fill and the burned remains of the roof. It was a lightly compacted, light brown to dark gray silty clay loam containing charcoal and ash with some scattered fire-cracked rock. Artifact content again was low, consisting primarily of sherds.

Level 3
This 5-cm-thick level (4.95–5.00 mbd) consisted of the fill directly over the floor. It was a dark gray silty clay

loam to sandy clay loam in the southeast quadrant, with numerous charcoal chunks, some daub, and abundant sherds. Macrobotanical samples recovered from this level contained only the remains of wild plant species, such as hedgehog and mallow seeds, and monocotyledon tissue with calcium oxalate crystals that possibly represents agave (see Chapter 9).

Level 4

This 3-cm-thick level (5.00–5.03 mbd) corresponds with Floor A. This surface was plastered only in the central portion of the house and in the entry ramp. Coarse sand to silty clay loam sediments were encountered elsewhere at a level equivalent to the floor. The floor surface and floor level contained numerous small sherds. In addition, a miniature ceramic vessel was probably associated with these sherds.

Level 5

This level corresponds with the fill between Floor A and an earlier plastered floor segment, Floor B, that was present at 5.03 mbd around the hearth (Feature 21.01) and between 5.00 and 5.04 mbd in the inner portion of the entryway. This fill consisted of a compact, gray silty clay loam containing sherds. Pollen and macrobotanical remains included wild plants, such as chia, cholla, and cheno-am, as well as corn and squash. Level 5 extended to a depth of 30 cm (5.03–5.33) in the two eastern quadrants and consisted of a silty clay loam to coarse sand that contained artifacts, charcoal chunks, and some burned daub. Artifact density decreased substantially below 5.13 mbd.

Artifact Summary

Artifacts were sparse in the house fill above the roof fall, consisting primarily of sherds, but including a few pieces of flaked stone debitage, two mano fragments, and several burned and unburned bone fragments. The roof fall stratum, however, yielded abundant artifacts—again, mostly sherds—as did the floor fill in the central portion and northeast quadrant of the structure. Lower densities were present in the southeast quadrant of the floor fill. Resting on the surface for Floor A, and adjacent to the entryway, were a shell pendant fragment; a pair of complete, zoomorphic shell pendants; a complete, miniature Sacaton Red-on-buff cauldron; a bone awl fragment; two mano fragments; a flake; a tabular knife fragment; and a chunk of red ochre. Artifacts from Floor B and the fill between the two floors consisted of scattered small sherds, some of which were encased in floor plaster.

Construction Details

Wall and Roof Construction

Two main support postholes, containing burned post remnants, were centrally located along the long axis of the structure. Both measured 18 cm in diameter, extended 33–45 cm deep, and were reinforced with rocks that partially lined the posthole. Six postholes, three burned posts without defined postholes, and several circular charcoal stains were arranged around the periphery of the house and etntryway, and probably represented the remains of the house walls. The postholes averaged 13 cm in diameter and 18 cm deep. One large posthole, which flanked the entry ramp, contained one rock at the bottom, measured 24 cm in diameter, and extended 20 cm deep.

Floor Construction

Only the entry ramp and the central portion of Floor A were plastered. The remainder of the floor was represented by loosely compacted, silty to coarse sands containing cultural material. An underlying plastered floor (Floor B), identified only around the hearth (Feature 21.01) and the inner portion of the entry, was overlain by 3 cm of mixed cultural fill.

Floor Features

Feature 21.01 was a basin-shaped, circular, plastered hearth, measuring 30 cm in diameter by 11 cm deep. The hearth, whose rim was flush with Floor A, was centered in front of the entry. Feature 21.02 was a circular, roughly vertical-walled pit with a level base, measuring 57 cm in diameter by 21 cm deep. Its fill consisted of silty clay loam containing some charcoal, ash, and sherds. The pit was constructed into silty clay loam deposits underlying the floor down to coarse sand deposits at the base. The pit rim, which was flush with Floor A, was plastered and partially oxidized.

Entryway

The lateral entry ramp measured 1.15 m long by 0.80 m wide, and was completely plastered. Although the ramp exhibited a slight concave surface at the extreme west end, it was essentially level with the house floor, sloping up only 4 cm. A portion of the lower Floor B, which was exposed along the backhoe trench, extended into the entry for an undetermined distance.

Dating

Ceramic: Rincon phase
Archaeomagnetic: *Feature 21.01(hearth), Sample 5ua:* A.D. 1005 (1150) 1170 (Table B.3)

Remarks

No distinct pit walls were distinguished even after stripping the upper Level 1 fill to within 25 cm of the floor. The absence of distinct pit walls made it impossible to determine precisely the dimensions of the structure. The limited placement of floor plaster around the center of the house and in the entryway, and the generally unprepared nature of the remainder of the floor, is consistent with a construction pattern that employed raised wooden floor platforms supported by numerous interior posts (Ciolek-Torrello 1994; Deaver 1998 ; Haury 1932), yet no interior postholes that might have contained floor supports were noted. Alternatively, benches or shelves may have surrounded the periphery of the floor area (see Motsinger 1994), but these interior features also would have been supported on posts. This house was burned and apparently was cleared of refuse prior to abandonment. The paucity of refuse in the fill suggests that it was one of the last houses occupied in the area.

Feature 22

Feature 22 was a subrectangular pit house with a lateral step entry oriented to the northeast (Figures 12 and 13). Floor features consisted of a hearth (Feature 22.01), and four possibly intrusive pits along the margins of the structure (Features 22.02–22.05). Few artifacts were identified on the floor, although a large quantity of artifacts, including reconstructible vessels, was derived from one of the intrusive pits (Feature 22.04).

Type: house
Function: habitation
Temporal assignment: Rincon phase
Dimensions: 6.6 m long by 4 m wide
Floor area: 26.4 m^2 (excluding entryway)
Entry orientation: 38°
Shape: subrectangular
House pit depth: 29 cm

Excavation Methods

The southwest corner of Feature 22 was initially identified along Trench 14. Mechanical stripping over the feature removed the overburden and revealed the outline of the structure, although the location of its entry was not identified initially. The structure outline was quartered perpendicular to its long and short axes and each quadrant was excavated separately. The southeast quadrant of fill was completely screened to the floor, whereas only the floor fill in the other three quadrants was screened.

Stratigraphy

Level 1

This 10-cm-thick level (4.67–4.77 mbd) contained the structure fill. It consisted of loosely compact, ashy gray sandy silt loam with a moderate density of artifacts—mostly sherds—and a mano fragment.

Level 2

Representing the roof fall, this 10-cm-thick level (4.77–4.87 mbd) consisted of loosely compact, ashy gray sandy silt loam with burned adobe, wood, and grasses. Artifact density was low to moderate, consisting mainly of sherds, but also including some flaked stone debitage, shell, bone, a mano, a metate fragment, and an axe fragment.

Level 3

This 9-cm-thick level (4.87–4.96 mbd) consisted of roof fall and the fill directly over the floor. The fill composition was similar to Level 2. Artifact density was low except in the northwest quadrant, where there was a substantial quantity of sherds, including reconstructible vessels associated with an intrusive pit (Feature 22.04).

Level 4

This level corresponds with the floor (4.96 mbd), which was plastered. Artifacts on the floor included two complete manos.

Artifact Summary

Artifacts in upper fill, roof fall and floor fill consisted primarily of sherds, along with some flaked stone debris, ground stone fragments, faunal bone, and worked shell. A high density of sherds was concentrated in a portion of the house's northwest quadrant, where at least one pit, Feature 22.04, intruded through the fill and into the floor. The two floor-contact manos were situated in the west half of the structure. The abundance of maize pollen derived from beneath the mano near the center of the pit house suggests that food processing of that domesticate probably took place in this structure.

Construction Details

Wall and Roof Construction

Two main support postholes, measuring 28 cm in diameter and 23–38 cm deep, were identified along the long axis of the structure. Twenty-one additional postholes, averaging 13 cm in diameter and extending 5–20 cm deep, were identified around the periphery of the floor. A 5-cm-wide-by-4–5-cm-deep floor groove, with several of the peripheral postholes in direct association, was identified along

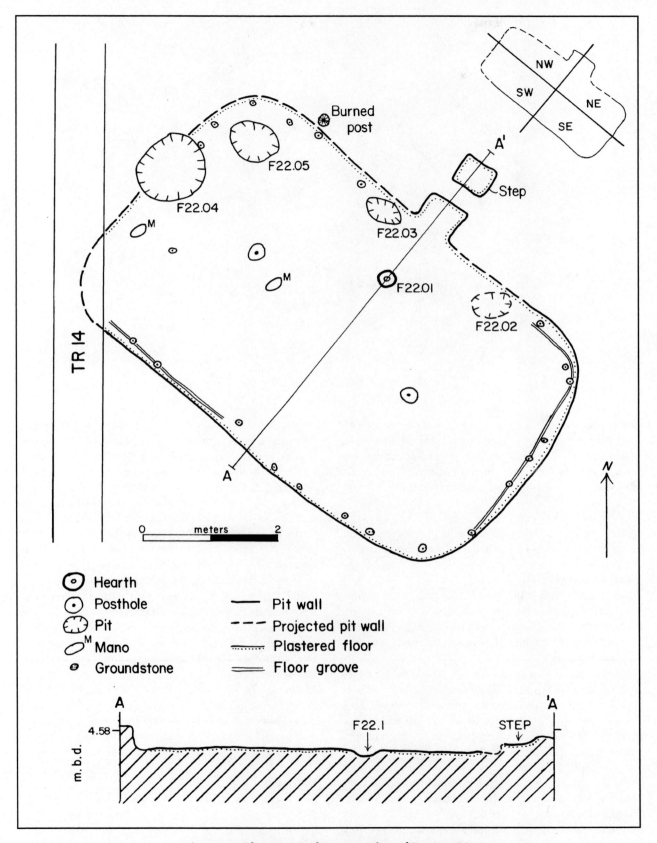

Figure 12. Plan map and cross section of Feature 22.

Figure 13. Feature 22, south view.

two portions of the floor edge. One small, interior post-hole was located in the southwest quadrant. A burned post, measuring 10 cm in diameter, was located adjacent to the pit wall outside the house, near the northwest corner. Its association with the house is undetermined.

Floor Construction
The floor consisted of a plastered silty clay loam surface. The surface exhibited burning across its entire extent.

Floor Features
Feature 22.01 was a circular, basin-shaped hearth that measured 28 cm in diameter by 8 cm deep. The ashy fill contained no artifacts. Macrobotanical remains included wild plant foods, including cheno-am and mallow seeds, and grass grains.

Feature 22.02 was an indistinct, oval pit measuring 48 by 35 cm, by 18 cm deep. The fill consisted of probable roof fall material, with charcoal chunks but no artifacts. Because the feature intruded into the wall posthole alignment and also exhibited rodent disturbance, this pit might have resulted from disturbance.

Feature 22.03, another indistinct, oval pit, measured 58 by 36 cm, by 15 cm deep. The fill consisted of ashy, possible roof fall material that contained several sherds. This feature was situated along the north edge of the floor and intersected the wall posthole alignment, suggesting that it also might be a product of disturbance.

Feature 22.04 was a large, circular pit measuring 95 cm in diameter by at least 64 cm deep. This slightly bell-shaped pit intruded into the floor and the west pit wall of the house. A high density of ceramics was initially recovered from Level 1 fill of the structure at approximately 29 cm above the floor. The outline of a pit or the presence of distinct fill was not noted, however. Because the ceramic artifact density in this portion of the pit house continued down through the fill and roof fall of the structure, it is likely that the pit originated within Level 1, suggesting that the total depth of the feature was closer to 93 cm. The sandy silt fill of the pit below the Feature 22 floor contained daub and charcoal chunks, and the high sherd density continued. Some flaked stone debitage, a biface, a scraper, and worked shell also were recovered. The base of the pit was constructed down to coarse alluvial sand deposits.

Feature 22.05 was a roughly circular pit, 72 by 62 cm, by 46 cm deep. The fill consisted of a moderately compact, sandy silt with some charcoal flecks and a small quantity of artifacts. The basin-shaped base was constructed down to coarse alluvial sand deposits.

Entryway
The lateral stepped entry ramp measured 1.2 by 0.6 m. The lower portion of the entry extended 40 cm out from the structure and was at the same level as the structure floor. A roughly rectangular, plastered surface that was

approximately 45 cm long, the step portion was 12 cm higher than the lower portion. Natural silty clay loam deposits separated the two segments of the entry. No postholes bordering the entryway were identified.

Dating

Ceramic: Rincon phase
Archaeomagnetic: *Feature 22.01 (hearth), Sample 9ua:* A.D. 950–1100 (see Table B.3)

Remarks

This is a typical Hohokam house-in-a-pit with walls, represented by the floor groove and peripheral posts, constructed within the excavated house pit (see Haury 1976). Because of the very close placement and inward orientation of Feature 22 to two other structures, Features 21 and 23, it is unlikely that any of the three structures were contemporaneous. Although the floor level of Feature 23 is 15 cm higher than that of Feature 22, archaeomagnetic results suggest that the occupation of Feature 23 preceded that of Feature 22 (see Appendix B). The house was burned and its floor apparently was cleared of household implements prior to abandonment. It was subsequently filled with trash, although the presence of roof fall material within the intrusive pits suggests that the house was still standing after it was abandoned and used as a trash repository. Feature 22.04, an intrusive trash-filled pit constructed through the burned structure fill and into the Feature 22 floor, was probably used in conjunction with the continued occupation of nearby courtyard structures, Features 25 and 27, after Feature 22 was abandoned.

Feature 23

Feature 23 was a subrectangular pit house with an ill-defined lateral entry oriented to the southwest (Figures 14 and 15). Floor features consisted of a hearth (Feature 23.01) and an irregular, oval, ash-filled pit (Feature 23.02). Floor artifacts consisted of two possible reconstructible vessels, a complete metate, one mano, and one ground stone artifact.

Type: pit house
Function: habitation
Temporal assignment: Rincon phase
Dimensions: 5.6 m long by 3.3 m wide
Floor area: 18.48 m^2 (excluding entryway)
Entry orientation: 204°
Shape: subrectangular
House pit depth: 17 cm

Excavation Methods

Initially identified in the east and west faces of Trench 16, the structure profile was manifested by a roughly level surface overlain by gray, ash- and charcoal-stained fill. The 60 cm of overburden was then mechanically stripped to expose the outline of the structure. An entryway was not distinguished at this time. To maintain horizontal control in the excavation of the structure fill, the structure outline was quartered along the long and short axes. The roof fall stratum was excavated in one 10-cm level, and floor fill was excavated in one 4–7-cm level to floor contact.

Stratigraphy

Level 1

This 10-cm-thick level (4.72–4.82 mbd) represented roof fall. The west half consisted of loosely compacted, ashy gray sandy silt containing some charcoal, with the densest ash concentration in the northwest quadrant. The artifact density was high in this half, consisting primarily of sherds, with some flaked stone and faunal bone. Compact, silty clay fill with possible unburned daub and a few artifacts characterized the east half.

Level 2

This 7-cm-thick level (4.82–4.89 mbd) consisted of roof fall and the fill directly over the floor, and was characterized by loosely compacted, ashy gray sandy silt containing charcoal. The artifact density was high, with a large number of sherds and probable reconstructible vessels, in addition to a bone awl and worked shell.

Level 3

At 4.89 mbd, this level corresponds with the floor, which was plastered only around the hearth and at the entry. The remainder of the floor was a disturbed, hard-packed surface.

Artifact Summary

Artifacts in the roof fall and floor fill included a large quantity of sherds representing several reconstructible vessels, some flaked stone, a polishing stone, a bone awl, faunal bone, and worked shell fragments. Artifacts on the floor consisted of one inverted, complete metate; one mano fragment; a fragment of a ground stone artifact; and two partially reconstructible vessels—a Gila Plain flare-rimmed bowl near the hearth (Feature 23.01), and a Rincon Red subhemispherical bowl near a large, irregular, ash pit (Feature 23.02).

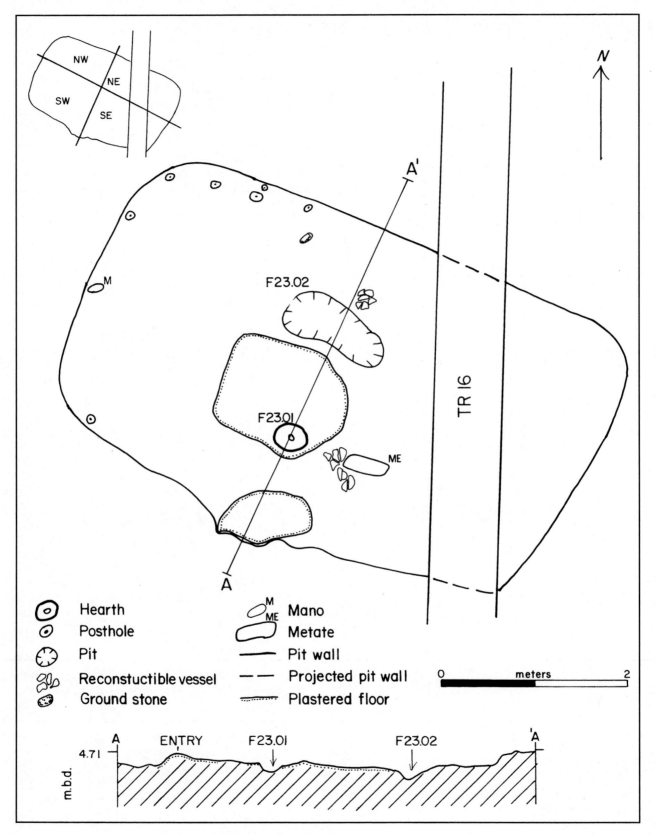

Figure 14. Plan map and cross section of Feature 23.

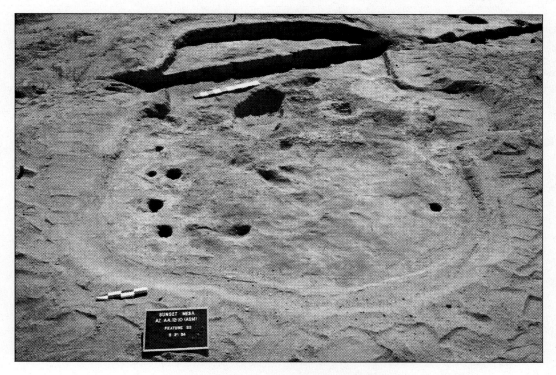

Figure 15. Feature 23, east-southeast view.

Construction Details

Wall and Roof Construction
Because of the disturbed nature of the hard-packed floor, and in part due to the placement of Trench 16, no main support postholes were identified. Seven peripheral wall postholes, averaging 12 cm in diameter and 17 cm deep, were located mainly in the northwest quadrant.

Floor Construction
The floor consisted of a hard-packed, silty clay loam surface. Burned plastered floor areas were confined to two locations, one around the hearth (Feature 23.01) and the other in front of the entryway.

Floor Features
Feature 23.01 was a plastered, basin-shaped hearth measuring 27 by 26.5 cm, by 14 cm deep. Feature 23.02 was an irregular, ash-filled, oval pit measuring 1.1 by 45 cm, by 17 cm deep. Macrobotanical remains from these features included wild plant foods, such as grass grains from the hearth, and chia, cheno-am, and saguaro seeds from the ash-filled pit. Monocotyledon tissue with calcium oxalate crystals (possibly agave), as well as maize and cholla pollen, also were identified in samples from Feature 23.02.

Entryway
The entryway consisted of a short, plastered section of floor that barely extended beyond the southwest wall. The approximate entryway measured 30 cm long by 72 cm wide. Excavations extending around the plastered entryway segment failed to identify any postholes or an entryway step.

Dating

Ceramic: Rincon phase
Archaeomagnetic: *Feature 23.01 (hearth), Sample 6ua:* A.D. 930 (1025) 1045, A.D. 1230 (1275) 1370 (see Table B.3)

Remarks

Although the floor was extensively disturbed, only the central hearth and entryway area appear to have been plastered. The lack of evidence for plastering over the remainder of the structure suggests that Feature 23 might have had a raised floor overlying the unplastered areas. No interior floor support postholes were identified, however. Prickly pear pollen, identified from composite samples taken from floor contact, represents the only evidence of this taxon in a pit house context at the site. Cholla pollen also was represented in these floor samples. Although charcoal and ash were found in the fill, this house contained less evidence for postabandonment burning than the other houses. The floor was cleared of household implements prior to abandonment, and the house was subsequently filled with refuse.

Feature 25

Feature 25 was a subrectangular pit house with a lateral step entry ramp oriented to the southwest (Figures 16 and 17). Floor features included two central main support postholes, 29 entryway and wall postholes, a floor groove that extended around most of the floor periphery, and a plastered hearth (Feature 25.01). Floor artifacts were sparse and consisted of sherds, flaked stone debitage, and some faunal bone.

Type: pit house
Function: habitation
Temporal assignment: Rincon phase
Dimensions: 6.6 m long by 4.2 m wide
Floor area: 27.7 m^2 (excluding entryway)
Entry orientation: 217°
Shape: subrectangular
House pit depth: 20 cm

Excavation Methods

Feature 25 was initially identified along both sides of Trench 16. Mechanical stripping removed the overburden and exposed the rough outline of the structure. To maintain horizontal control in the excavation of the structure fill, the structure outline was quartered, but because the exact feature orientation could not be determined at this time, the feature was divided east-west along an arbitrary grid line and north-south by Trench 16. The southwest quadrant was initially excavated in one level (Level 1) to the floor. In the other three quadrants, roof fall was excavated in a 17-cm natural level (Level 1), and floor fill (Level 2) was excavated in a 9-cm arbitrary level. The fill from all four quadrants was completely screened.

Stratigraphy

Level 1

This 17-cm-thick level (4.76–4.93 mbd) contained the burned remains of the roof. It was characterized by ashy silty loam with charcoal, burned daub, burned roofing material, charred and fused *Zea mays* kernels, a light to moderate density of artifacts, and some faunal bone.

Level 2

This 9-cm-thick level (4.93–5.02 mbd) contained the fill directly over the floor, and consisted of sandy silty loam with burned wood, a light density of artifacts, and some faunal bone. *Zea mays* kernels were recovered in the northwest quadrant.

Level 3

At 5.02 mbd, this level corresponds with the structure's floor, which was plastered in its entirety. Floor artifacts consisted of some scattered artifactual debris.

Artifact Summary

Both roof fall and floor fill contained a light to moderately light quantity of sherds and flaked stone debris, two scrapers, a projectile point tip, faunal bone, and worked shell fragments. Floor-contact artifacts were sparse, consisting of scattered sherds, flaked stone debitage, and faunal bone fragments.

Construction Details

Wall and Roof Construction

Two main support postholes were identified along the structure's central main axis. The northwest posthole measured 50 cm in diameter and extended 40 cm deep. Post support stones in the posthole included a 17-by-20-cm flat rock situated on the bottom and six small rocks on the west side. The dimensions of the southeast posthole, which was partially cut by Trench 16 and also extensively disturbed by a likely pot hole, could not be determined. Four rocks, including two possible hammer stones and probably representing supports for the posts, were found in the posthole. Arranged around the periphery of the house pit and entryway were 29 postholes and a continuous floor groove. Only two small interior postholes were present.

Floor Construction

A plastered clay surface was present across the entire floor.

Floor Features

Feature 25.01 was a plastered hearth, measuring 30 cm in diameter by 10 cm deep. Its fill consisted of ashy, silty loam with several burned bone fragments and charred grass grains, mallow seeds, and corn kernel fragments.

Entryway

The lateral stepped ramp measured a total of 1.8 m long and 0.8–1.1 m wide. The lower, bulbous portion of the entryway was plastered, extended approximately 90 cm, and was inclined only slightly above the level of the house

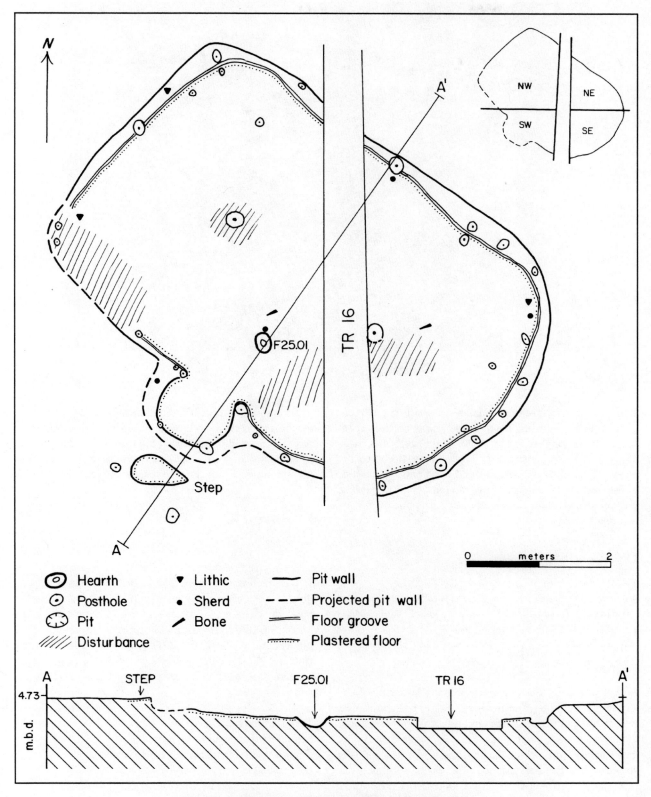

Figure 16. Plan map and cross section of Feature 25.

Figure 17. Feature 25, east view.

floor. A separate, irregular plastered step, situated 30 cm beyond and 15 cm higher than the lower portion, measured 50 cm long by 70 cm wide. Eight postholes, averaging 15 cm in diameter and 18 cm deep, bordered the entry. This house was burned and apparently cleared of household implements prior to abandonment. Little refuse was present in the fill, indicating this was one of the last occupied houses.

Dating

Ceramic: Rincon phase
Archaeomagnetic: *Feature 25.01 (hearth), Sample 3ua:* A.D. 1005 (1100) 1195; *sample floor plaster, Sample 4ua:* A.D. 930 (950–975) 1020 (see Table B.3)

Remarks

A portion of the floor in the southeast quadrant of the structure, including one of the main support postholes, was disturbed by probable pot hunting activity. Additional disturbance was noted along the southwest corner. The general lack of floor-contact artifacts suggests that the structure had been abandoned prior to its burning. Feature 25 (27.7 m²) is the second largest structure, after Feature 27 (30.83 m²), in overall floor area. Again, the paucity of trash in the fill suggests that this was one of the last houses to be occupied.

The identification of charred and fused *Zea mays* kernels in a burned roof fall context indicates that corn might have been dried or stored on the roof. A low percentage of maize pollen was identified in a composite floor sample, but no other subsistence resources were identified.

Feature 27

Feature 27 was a subrectangular pit house with a lateral step entry ramp oriented to the southeast (Figures 18 and 19). Floor features included 2 central main support postholes, 30 entryway and wall postholes, 1 probable interior posthole (Feature 27.04), 2 sections of floor groove along portions of the southeast and northeast perimeter, 2 floor pits (Features 27.02 and 27.03), and a plastered hearth (Feature 27.01). Floor artifacts were sparse, consisting of scattered sherds, flaked stone debitage, and some ground stone.

Type: pit house
Function: habitation
Temporal assignment: Rincon phase
Dimensions: 6.85 m long by 4.5 m wide
Floor area: 30.83 m² (excluding entryway)
Entry orientation: 107°
Shape: subrectangular
House pit depth: 25+ cm

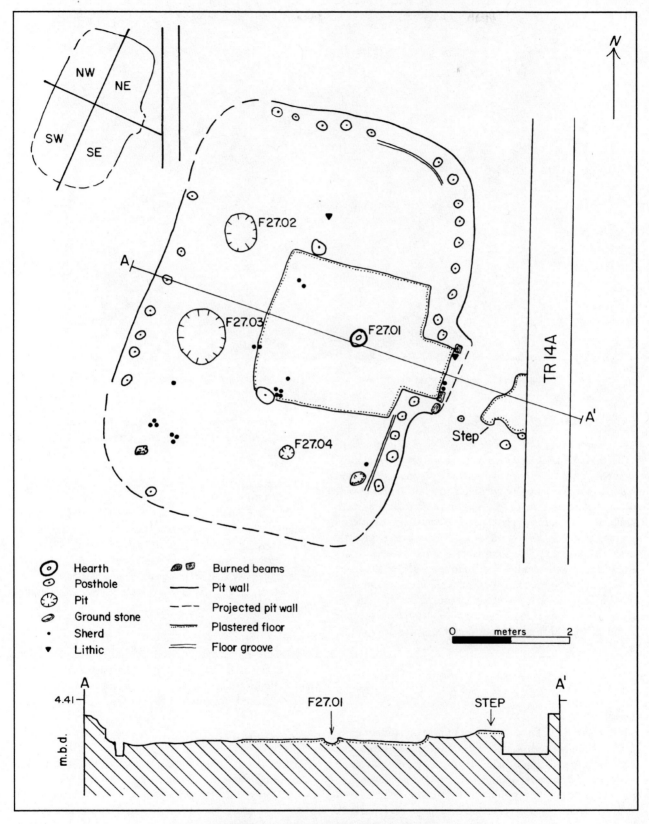

Figure 18. Plan map and cross section of Feature 27.

Figure 19. Square, plastered floor and entryway of Feature 27, northwest view.

Excavation Methods

The plastered entry step of Feature 27 was initially identified along the west side of Trench 14A. Mechanical stripping of the overburden exposed a distinct outline and a dense concentration of oxidized daub in the north half of the structure, but only a vague outline in the south half. For excavation purposes, the structure was quartered perpendicular to its long axis and short axis extending through the entry. The southwest quadrant was initially excavated in one level (Level 1) to the floor. In the other three quadrants, roof fall was excavated in a 24-cm arbitrary level (Level 1). Additional roof fall and floor fill (Level 2) were excavated in a 6-cm arbitrary level to floor contact. The fill from all four quadrants was completely screened.

Stratigraphy

Level 1

This 24-cm-thick level (4.69–4.93 mbd) contained upper fill and unburned roof fall in the southeast and southwest quadrants, consisting of hard, silty clay loam with small quantities of charcoal and artifacts. In the northwest and northeast quadrants, the entire level contained burned roof fall, which consisted of compact, gray silty clay loam with abundant chunks of burned daub and charcoal. Artifacts

were sparse throughout, including sherds, flaked stone debris, a mano fragment, two metate fragments, and burned bone.

Level 2

This 6-cm-thick level (4.93–4.99 mbd) of floor fill and roof fall consisted of loose, dark gray silty clay loam with abundant charcoal and some burned daub chunks. Artifacts were sparse in the north half of the structure, primarily sherds and flaked stone debris. A slightly higher artifact density, mainly of larger sherds, was present in the south half. Cheno-am and grass seeds were identified in the northeast quadrant.

Level 3

This 4-cm-thick level (4.99–5.03 mbd) corresponds with the floor, which was plastered only around the hearth and entry. Floor-contact artifacts were sparse and consisted of sherds, flaked stone debitage, and ground stone.

Artifact Summary

Artifact density through roof fall and floor fill was light, consisting primarily of sherds and flaked stone artifacts, with some ground stone fragments, faunal bone, and shell. Very few artifacts were associated with the extensive burned daub material in the north half. Artifacts on the floor also were sparse, consisting of scattered sherds, some flaked stone debitage, a grinding slab, and a metate fragment.

Construction Details

Wall and Roof Construction

Two ill-defined main support postholes were identified along the central main axis of the structure. The postholes measured, respectively, 22 and 30 cm in diameter by 22 and 30 cm deep and contained only a small quantity of charcoal flecks in their sandy silt loam fill. Twenty-one burned wall post remnants—some extending as much as 10 cm above the floor—and six additional postholes containing only charcoal-stained fill were defined around the floor periphery. Three additional burned posts bordered the south side of the entry ramp. The peripheral wall posts averaged 8 cm in diameter and the postholes averaged 13.5 cm deep.

A 1-m-long, collapsed segment of carbonized wattle-and-daub wall was identified along the northeast corner of the structure (Figure 20) inside the alignment of peripheral posts. This wall segment consisted of sections of burned daub; closely spaced, horizontally aligned twigs extending between the burned wall post remnants; and clumps of common reed (*Phragmites australis*) stems that were oriented perpendicular to—and therefore were probably originally interwoven with—the twigs.

Floor Construction

The well-prepared, plastered floor consisted of a discrete, 2.6-by-2.5-m rectangular area that encompassed the hearth (Feature 27.01) and extended between the two main support postholes. A short segment of the plastered floor, measuring 60 cm long by 1 m wide, extended into the lower portion of the entry, curving up 20 cm at the entry step. The remainder of the floor consisted of an unprepared, somewhat disturbed, and loosely compacted to hard-packed, silty to sandy loam that was very indistinct along the southern edge and portions of the western periphery. The plastered surface and portions of the unprepared floor exhibited evidence of burning.

Floor Features

Feature 27.01 was a plastered hearth measuring 28 cm in diameter by 9 cm deep. Flush with the floor, the hearth was basin shaped. Its fill consisted of a loosely compact, ashy and charcoal-flecked silt. Macrobotanical remains included cheno-am and mallow seeds.

Feature 27.02 was an irregular, oval pit measuring 62 by 56 cm, by 20 cm deep. The pit exhibited oxidation on its walls, and its fill consisted of ashy loam with some burned faunal bone.

Figure 20. Remains of wall posts and wattle in northeast corner of Feature 27, north view.

Feature 27.03 was a large, oval pit, measuring 99 by 86 cm, by 70 cm deep, that exhibited some oxidation along its rim. The insloping to vertical-sided, unplastered pit wall was mostly indistinct, due to its construction in subfloor sandy loam deposits. Its fill consisted of silty loam throughout, with some charcoal, burned daub, and fire-cracked rock in the upper fill. The pit contained a moderate density of artifacts, including decorated and plain ware sherds, flaked stone debitage, one scraper and an abrader, some bone, and two "Apache Tear" obsidian nodules. Corn and grass pollen derived from the base of the feature suggest possible storage of these resources.

Feature 27.04 was a pit that measured 27 by 21 cm, by 23 cm deep. Its fill consisted of sandy loam with some charcoal flecks. The location of this feature suggests that it might have functioned as a posthole for a raised floor support post.

Entryway

The lateral, stepped entry ramp measured 2.25 m long by 1 m wide, its outer edge attenuated by Trench 14A. The ramp consisted of three sections: the lower, plastered extension of the house floor; an intermediate, unplastered step; and an outer, plastered segment. The lower, 1-m-wide portion of the entry extended 60 cm from the rectangular, plastered floor centered around the hearth, its outer edge raised 20 cm from floor level to form the lip leading up to the step. Burned beam or post segments were laid partially across this lip, suggesting the presence of a wooden riser. The middle portion of the entry consisted of a 90-cm-long, unplastered, gently sloping ramp consisting of undisturbed silty loam sediments. The level outer portion of the entry consisted of an irregularly shaped, plastered segment that measured roughly 75 cm long by 1 m wide. Two burned posts, averaging 10 cm in diameter, framed each side of the lower plastered portion of the entry. Only three other posts, all on the south side, lined the remainder of the entry.

Dating

Ceramic: Rincon phase
Archaeomagnetic: *Feature 27.01(hearth), Sample 10ua:* A.D. 1005 (1100) 1170 (see Table B.3)

Remarks

The configuration of the floor, consisting of a rectangular-shaped, central, plastered surface and an unprepared surface elsewhere, suggests that the living surface surrounding the plastered floor might have been elevated on a wooden platform. Only one possible interior posthole (Feature 27.04) that might have served as a support post for a raised floor was identified, however. The general lack of floor-contact artifacts suggests that the structure was probably abandoned prior to burning. Little trash was subsequently deposited in this house, suggesting that it was abandoned late in the occupational sequence.

Irrigation Canal (Feature 18)

Feature 18 represented a 7.4-m, north-south-oriented segment of a prehistoric canal located along the western edge of the Qt2 terrace, at the extreme northwest corner of the Sunset Mesa site (see Figures 8 and 9). The canal is approximately 3.45 m (11.32 feet) above the modern Qt1 terrace that borders the Santa Cruz River to the west (Figure 21) and the Rillito River to the north. A smaller ditch, measuring roughly 45 cm wide and 30 cm deep, appears to have been set in the upper, eastern portion of the original canal sediments subsequent to the abandonment of the main canal. Backhoe testing within the site boundary along the edge of the Qt2 terrace to the south and to the east failed to expose any additional segments of the canal.

Figure 21. Overview of canal alignment, viewed southwest toward Qt1 terrace and Santa Cruz River.

Given its physiographic location, Feature 18 appears to have been used to irrigate fields located along the roughly 300-m-wide Qt1 terrace southeast of the Santa Cruz–Rillito River confluence. At the present time, however, the Qt1 terrace is more than 3 m lower than the canal, suggesting that erosion has substantially lowered the level of the terrace since the canal was in use.

During the 1930s, a concrete flume was constructed along the lower edge of the Qt2 terrace, in conjunction with the operations of the Sunset Dairy, to irrigate alfalfa fields located on the Qt1 terrace. The previous owner of the property indicated that this canal, which was fed by water pumped from wells, was in operation through the early 1950s (Ellen Wheller, personal communication 1994). Other than erosion along the banks of the Qt1 terrace facing both the Santa Cruz and the Rillito Rivers, the level of the Qt1 terrace has not degraded appreciably since the construction and use of this historical-period canal.

The tops of house pits at Sunset Mesa Ruin were found between 4.4 and 4.7 mbd, only 30–60 cm above the rim of the prehistoric canal. The prehistoric inhabitants of the site were probably living on the Qt2 terrace and farming its lower edges, which likely extended north into the existing, channelized Rillito River and west beyond the eroded edges of the modern Qt1 terrace.

Based on an evaluation of canal sediments (see Appendix A), Feature 18 tapped the Rillito River rather than the Santa Cruz River. It is likely, then, that the canal headed upstream on the Rillito River and extended downstream to the west, along the since-eroded, northern edge of the Qt2 terrace, before turning south in the vicinity of the segment identified as Feature 18. Although the resulting flow would have been upstream with regard to the Santa Cruz River, the elevation of the canal on the Qt2 terrace probably provided a sufficient gradient for the canal to irrigate the portion of the Qt1 terrace that lies along the Santa Cruz River, south of its confluence with the Rillito. Today, it covers only about 35 acres, but this lower terrace area could have been much larger in prehistoric times, as it has undergone several episodes of erosion by the Santa Cruz River in this century alone (Bruce Knapp, personal communication 1990).

Dimensions: 7.4 m long by 1.24 m wide by 73 cm deep
Elevation: *Rim:* 4.98 mbd, 677 m (2,222 feet) AMSL; *base:* 5 .7 mbd
Orientation: 2°

Excavation Method

Feature 18 was initially identified in both the north and south profiles at the western end of Trench 1A, a 25-m-long extension of Trench 1, which was excavated during the testing phase (Figure 22). The terrace remnant, across which the canal extended, was less than 8 m wide as a result of extensive erosion of the terrace to the north and south. The Qt2 terrace was terminated approximately 1.4 m to the north by the Rillito River, and 5.4 m to south of Trench 1A by a gully eroding its western edge.

The longer portion of the canal segment to the south of the trench was shovel scraped to remove the upper 5–8 cm of loose, loamy fine sand containing both prehistoric and historical-period material, and to expose the distinct, silty clay fill of the canal. This segment of the canal was then longitudinally bisected and the west half was completely excavated in natural levels down to the manganese- and iron oxide-stained and indurated sediments at the base of the canal (Figure 23). All of the excavated fill was screened. Archaeomagnetic samples from the upper portion of the oxide-stained zone at the base of the canal did not yield a reliable date (see Table B.3).

A 50-cm section of the canal just south of Trench 1A was completely excavated in one natural unit to assess the cross-sectional morphology of the canal (see Figure 23).

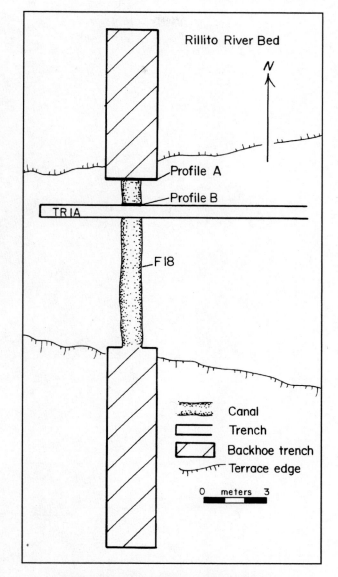

Figure 22. Plan map of canal, Feature 18.

The shorter portion of the canal north of Trench 1A also was completely excavated in natural levels. In this latter section, a possible later but smaller ditch was identified in the upper, eastern portion of the fill (Figures 24 and 25). This upper fill was excavated as a separate stratum (Figure 26).

Sediment samples were taken systematically from the north-facing Profile A, located 1.4 m north of Trench 1A and along the south bank of the Rillito River. A series of matched pollen and ostracode samples also were taken from the south-facing canal Profile B, which was located along Trench 1A (see Figure 24). Radiocarbon samples were obtained from canal sediments and from sheet trash deposits that underlay the canal, but were not submitted for analysis.

Figure 23. Canal segment (Feature 18) excavated south of Trench 1A, southeast view.

Figure 24. Profile of canal, Feature 18, in north wall of Trench 1A.

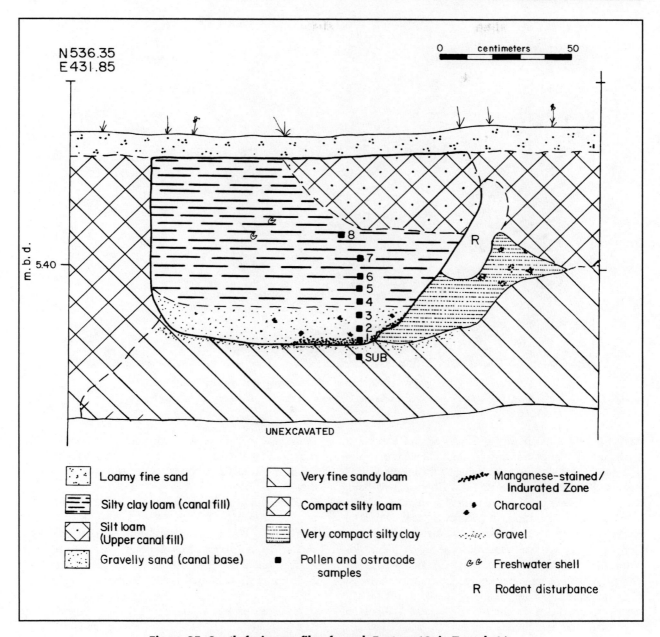

Figure 25. South-facing profile of canal, Feature 18, in Trench 1A.

Stratigraphic Context

Seven strata were identified in the north-facing, 2.4-m, vertical exposure of Profile A (Figure 27). The lower sediments, Strata IV–VII, represented alternating compact, silty loam, alluvial floodwater deposits (Strata IV and VI) and blocky, silty clay slack water deposits (Strata V and VII) of the Qt2 terrace. The uniform and level nature of the deposits indicates a long period of active aggrading, after which Stratum IV deposits were subject to erosion, as suggested by the irregular boundary between Stratum IV and the overlying Stratum III.

Stratum III, situated within 6 cm of the canal's base, consisted of an irregular 15–52-cm-thick, brown (10 YR 5/3) sandy loam, colluvial deposit containing sherds, worked marine shell, unburned bone, and charcoal flecks. This stratum was identified only in Profile A, indicating that the trash deposit over which the canal was constructed was limited in areal extent, perhaps along a portion of the Qt2 terrace edge. The irregular boundary between Stratum III and Stratum II indicates that the trash deposits were subject to sheetwash erosion.

Based on the presence of diagnostic artifacts (see Chapter 6), Stratum III appears to have been roughly

Figure 26. Canal segment (Feature 18) excavated north of Trench 1A, showing upper and main channels, viewed north, toward the Rillito River.

coeval with the occupation of Sunset Mesa Ruin. Given this stratigraphic relationship, it is possible that irrigation agriculture was not undertaken during the initial occupation of the site, when the Stratum III trash was being deposited, or that canals were built elsewhere.

The overlying Stratum II sediments, into which the canal was constructed, represented colluvial deposits consisting of gravelly sandy loam to fine sandy loam sediments that contain some charcoal flecks, but no artifacts. This stratum appears to have been of primarily anthropogenic origin, added as fill along the edge of the Qt2 terrace to provide a foundation for the canal alignment over the underlying, eroded Stratum III trash deposits.

The 10–12 cm of overburden above the canal (Stratum I) consisted of loamy fine sand subject to root, rodent, and modern mechanical disturbance. The abundant artifacts in this stratum consisted of mixed prehistoric, historical-period, and modern material.

Canal Stratigraphy

Stratum I fill contained a later ditch set within the Stratum II fill of the canal. Stratum I consisted of a compact, very fine sandy loam to silty clay loam. Macrobotanical material recovered from this stratum yielded a mixture of fuelwoods, reed-grass stems, *Zea mays* kernels, and a

Phaseolus sp. cotyledon. Dark slack water deposits, expressing some manganese–iron oxide staining, were present at the base of the ditch, along the contact between Strata I and II.

The fill within the main canal consisted of 65 cm of grayish brown blocky silty clay (dry: 10YR 6/2; moist: 10YR 4/3). Inclusions consisted of several freshwater shells, flecks of charcoal, and a low density of small sherds and some flaked stone debitage. The lower 5–25 cm of fill exhibited a considerable amount of manganese–iron oxide staining. Small areas of stained deposits also were present adjacent to the canal on the east side, and probably represented clean-out sediment from the canal.

Dating

Ceramic: Rincon phase
Archaeomagnetic: *Feature 18, Sample 7ua:* no date, poor sample (see Table B.3).

Remarks

The pollen spectra represented in the Stratum II fill support the probability that the canal's headgate was situated

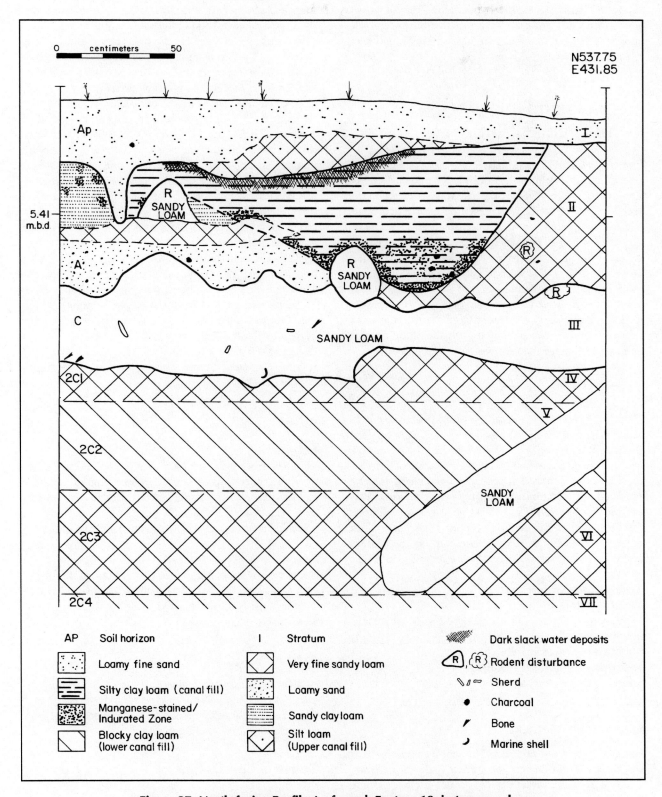

Figure 27. North-facing Profile A of canal, Feature 18, in terrace edge.

along the Rillito River rather than along the Santa Cruz River (see Chapter 10). In addition, the presence of sediments derived from the Catalina Mountains suggests origins along the Rillito River.

Ramada and Food-Preparation Area

Two adjacent and functionally interrelated, dense artifact concentrations, Features 13 and 15, were identified in an area approximately 50 m southeast of the courtyard group (see Figure 9). Feature 13 represented a ramada, probably used in conjunction with food-storage and -processing activities, whereas Feature 15 represented a related kitchen area used for storage and cooking-related activities. Both features, which were identified during mechanical stripping (Stripping Units 2 and 3), exhibited gray, charcoal- and ash-stained sandy loam deposits with abundant artifacts, particularly clusters of large sherds representing broken vessels. Because they lay outside of the APE, the full extent of these features was not determined.

Feature 13

Feature 13 was characterized by several ceramic clusters representing broken jars, along with manos, a complete palette, and a configuration of burned posts partially encompassing a remnant of a use-compacted activity surface. Food resources that probably were being stored or prepared were represented by masses of charred tansy mustard (*Descurainia* sp.) "seed meal", other wild plant material, and some kernels of corn (*Zea mays*). Fire-cracked rocks also were distributed among the artifacts, although specific cooking features were not identified.

Type: ramada/artifact cluster
Function: storage/food processing
Dimensions: about 4.7 m long by 3.6 m wide (ramada interior)
Floor area: approximately 16.92 m^2
Entry orientation: not identified
Shape: incompletely defined

Excavation Methods

Feature 13 was initially identified approximately 70 cm below the present-day ground surface in Stripping Unit 3. The feature was characterized by a dense cluster of artifacts at the same level as Feature 15 (4.77–4.84 mbd), but situated 3 m to the east. Shovel scraping was used to define the extent of the scatter. Exposed artifacts were mapped, and specific artifacts and artifact clusters were point provenienced and collected (Figures 28 and 29).

Because no distinct feature boundary could be determined, a 1-by-2-m test unit was excavated in the densest part of the concentration to assess whether an activity surface was present. The unit was excavated in six 10-cm screened levels to 5.34 mbd, but no activity surface could be identified. Artifacts were recovered from each level, although artifact density diminished 25 cm below the initially defined artifact cluster. To assess further the feature, an adjacent 2-by-2-m test unit also was excavated. This unit was excavated in seven 10-cm screened levels to 5.48 mbd. As with the adjacent unit, artifacts were identified in each level, substantially diminishing below Level 3. Despite these efforts, no activity surface could be identified.

Subsequent to the excavation of these two adjacent test units, seasonal rains substantially increased soil moisture and somewhat eroded the corners of the test pits, exposing a burned post. Additional shovel scraping around these excavation units yielded a configuration of four burned posts, a small remnant of a use-compacted surface, additional ceramic clusters, and "seed meal" cakes primarily made of charred tansy mustard seeds and some corn kernels.

Stratigraphy

Level 1
This 10-cm-thick level (4.77–4.87 mbd) contained fill overlying the ramada surface, consisting of charcoal-stained, dark loamy sand with abundant flat-lying artifacts and burned seeds (4.75–4.84 mbd). A remnant of a use-compacted surface was identified at 4.77 mbd.

Level 2–7
These 10-cm levels comprised 61 cm (5.04–5.48 mbd) of dark loamy sand to tan coarse sand and compact silty sand. Artifact density diminished in Levels 2 and 3, and artifacts were sparse in Levels 4–7).

Artifact Summary

Artifact density was greatest in Level 1, consisting primarily of broken ceramic jars, nine manos, two metate fragments, an abrading stone, one complete palette, and some flaked stone, shell, and faunal bone.

Construction Details

Wall and Roof Construction
An alignment of 3–4 burned posts delineated the eastern boundary of the feature, and another burned post defined

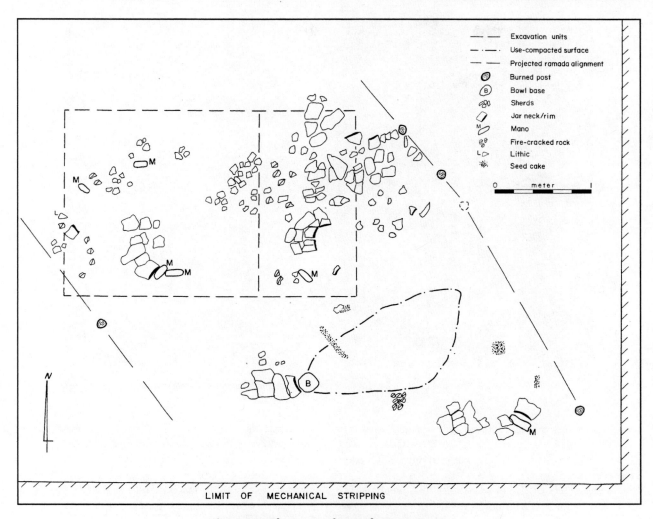

Figure 28. Plan map of ramada, Feature 13.

the southwest corner. No other wall or roof construction material was identified. The overall configuration of the burned posts suggests a rectangular ramada superstructure with its long axis oriented northwest-southeast.

Floor Construction
A 0.9-by-1.8-m, roughly oval area, consisting of thinly compacted silty loam, represented a likely use-compacted surface. No other remnants of this unprepared surface were identified.

Floor Features
No floor pits were identified.

Dating
Ceramic: Rincon phase

Remarks

The presence of grinding tools, storage vessels, and tansy mustard seed cakes, along with other economic plant products, suggests that the facility was probably used for food preparation and storage. In the absence of thermal features (although scattered fire-cracked rocks and one small rock cluster were present), it is possible that only limited cooking activities, such as seed parching, were undertaken in this area.

Feature 15

Feature 15 also contained several clusters of large sherds, possibly representing storage vessels, and a cake of mostly tansy mustard seeds, similar to ones recovered from Feature 13. Other economic plants stored or prepared in this area included corn and cholla, as indicated by the

Figure 29. Ramada area, Feature 13, and associated artifacts, north view.

recovery of aggregates of these plants under a reconstructible vessel fragment. Although ground stone was present at Feature 15, no complete grinding implements were recovered.

Three clusters of fire-cracked rock also were associated with Feature 15. Pollen derived from one of these rock clusters yielded cholla and prickly pear, suggesting the accumulation of these resources. The overall assemblage represented at Feature 15 suggests that a predominance of cooking-related activities were probably undertaken in this area. Only three small and shallow cooking pits were identified, however, and no formal hornos or hearths were found within the tested area of the feature.

Type: kitchen area
Function: food preparation/cooking
Temporal assignment: Rincon phase
Approximate areal extent: 7.5 by 7 m

Excavation Methods

Feature 15 was initially identified during the testing phase (as Feature 9) at the south end of Trench 11. At that time, the feature was described as a possible pit house, based on the presence of burned daub, abundant artifacts, and numerous flat-lying sherds in contact with what was

described as a deteriorated plastered surface situated about 75 cm below the present-day ground surface.

During data recovery, despite mechanical stripping at the south end of Trench 11 (Stripping Units 1 and 2), no pit house outline was discernible. Rather, an irregular area of charcoal-stained sediments containing some burned daub and charcoal chunks, abundant artifacts, and three spatially distinct clusters of fire-cracked rock (Features 15.01–15.03) was identified (Figure 30). The feature was exposed primarily in the northeast corner of Stripping Unit 2, but cultural material also extended into the adjacent Stripping Unit 1, into the northeast corner of Stripping Unit 3 to the east, and continued into an unstripped area to the northeast. Although the main concentration of artifacts was found at the same general elevation (4.80–4.85 mbd) as Feature 13 to the east, some artifacts and fire-cracked rock were identified 24 cm higher (4.56 mbd), in association with Feature 15.03.

Shovel scraping was subsequently used to define the general extent of the scatter, although no distinct feature boundary was identified. Exposed artifacts were mapped, and specific artifact clusters were point provenienced and collected. Unfortunately, during the initial phase of excavation, the feature was vandalized and some of the large, partially exposed sherds at the north end, including several seed jar sherds, were removed before they could be mapped and collected.

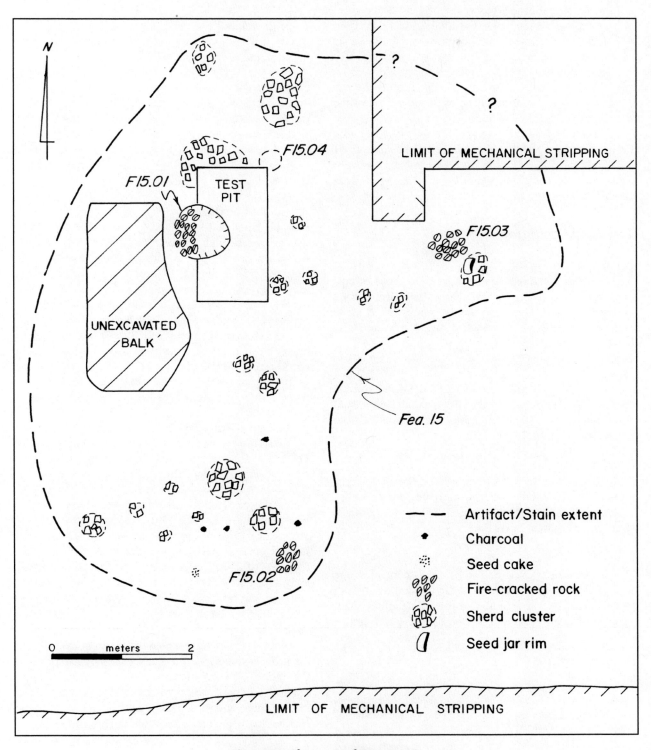

N

F15.04

F15.01

TEST
PIT

UNEXCAVATED
BALK

LIMIT OF MECHANICAL STRIPPING

?

?

F15.03

Fea. 15

F15.02

Artifact/Stain extent

Charcoal

Seed cake

Fire-cracked rock

Sherd cluster

Seed jar rim

0   meters   2

LIMIT OF MECHANICAL STRIPPING

Figure 30. Plan map of Feature 15.

Because a distinct feature boundary could not be determined after initial shovel scraping, a 1-by-2-m control unit was excavated in an area of high artifact density to assess the depth of the cultural deposits and the presence of an activity surface. The unit was excavated in five 10-cm screened levels to 5.30 mbd. Artifacts were recovered from each level, although as with Feature 13, the density of artifacts diminished some 25–30 cm below the initially defined artifact cluster.

As a result of the excavation of the 1-by-2-m test unit, Features 15.01 and 15.04 were identified and Feature 15.01 was subsequently excavated. No use-compacted surface or deteriorated floor, as Feature 9 in Trench 11 was described during the testing phase, was identified.

Test Unit Stratigraphy

Level 1–2
These levels contained 19 cm (4.81–5.00 mbd) of cultural fill, consisting of dark charcoal-and ash-stained loamy sand with abundant sherds, some flaked stone and burned shell, and fire-cracked rock (associated with Feature 15.01).

Level 3
This 10-cm-thick level (5.00–5.10 mbd) of cultural fill consisted of dark charcoal-and ash-stained loamy sand and compact silty sand. Artifacts were numerous, but fewer than in Level 2.

Level 4
This 10-cm-thick level (5.10–5.20 mbd) contained cultural fill and culturally sterile alluvium consisting of compact silty sand overlying coarse sand. Fewer artifacts were present than in Level 3.

Level 5
This 10-cm-thick level (5.20–5.30 mbd) contained one artifact in what was otherwise culturally sterile alluvium characterized by coarse sand. The artifact, a shotgun shell, was probably introduced through rodent disturbance.

Artifact Summary

The greatest artifact density, consisting mainly of large sherds, was present in Levels 1 and 2. Flaked stone, marine shell fragments, and faunal bone also were recovered in small quantities. Artifact density diminished through Levels 3 and 4. Although artifacts were recovered throughout Level 5, their association with the essentially culturally sterile, light-colored, coarse sandy alluvium near the bottom of that level appears to be the result of animal burrow disturbance.

Construction Details

Roof Construction
There were no indications that the activity area was covered.

Floor Construction
A use-compacted surface was not identified, although a deteriorated floor surface had been tentatively identified during the testing phase. The level at which Feature 15.01 was constructed was indistinct, but appeared to have been constructed in dark loamy sand cultural deposits at 4.92 mbd.

Associated Features
One pit filled with fire-cracked rock (Feature 15.01) was associated with Feature 15, as were two clusters of fire-cracked rock that possibly represented other pits (Features 15.02 and 15.03), and one possible pit (Feature 15.04). An informal cooking pit, Feature 15.01 (Figure 31) was irregular, basin shaped, and unlined, measuring 90 cm in diameter and 16 cm deep. The pit walls, set into cultural fill, exhibited little oxidation. The fill consisted of dark ashy loamy sand with abundant fire-cracked rock fragments, numerous sherds, three metate fragments, flaked stone debris, and a tabular knife fragment. Pollen recovered from the fill included cholla and prickly pear.

Although neither was tested, Features 15.02 and 15.03 probably represented features similar to Feature 15.01. Feature 15.02 consisted of a 50-cm-diameter cluster of fire-cracked rock; one fire-cracked, plano-convex mano fragment, numerous sherds, several stone flakes, and a hammer stone. Two clusters of large sherds were situated near the feature. Feature 15.03 consisted of a 40-by-60-cm area of fire-cracked rock. Sherds and several stone flakes were in association, and several sherds from a large fragment of a plain ware seed jar were situated immediately adjacent to this cluster. Because only limited shovel scraping was undertaken in the general area around Feature 15.03, it is expected that additional adjacent ceramic clusters were present.

Feature 15.04 represented an unexcavated, 25-cm-diameter basin-shaped pit that was exposed in profile in the northeast corner of the test unit. The fill within the feature was similar to the surrounding sediments of Feature 15, but somewhat darker. Sherds and some burned marine shell were recovered from the profile.

Dating

Ceramic: Rincon phase

Figure 31. Fire-cracked rock cluster, Feature 15.01, before excavation, west view (feature number on line board is missing a digit).

Remarks

Because several clusters of large sherds representing primarily necked and seed jars were identified at Feature 15, as well as Feature 13, it is likely that one of the primary functions carried out in both areas was food storage of such resources as tansy mustard (which was found in the form of "seed meal cakes"), other wild plants, and some corn. The lack of intact manos or other grinding tools, such as those recovered in association with ramada Feature 13, suggests that meal grinding probably was not undertaken at Feature 15. Rather, the presence of pits filled with fire-cracked rocks suggests that cooking activities—seed parching, for example—were important. No formal hearths or hornos were identified in the excavated portion of the feature, however.

Prehistoric Extramural Features

In addition to the ramada and cooking areas, 37 extramural pit, trash, and other, undefined features were identified, of which 25 were prehistoric (Table 3). Ten of these prehistoric features were sampled for macrobotanical and pollen remains. The other features were simply located and their fill and artifact associations described. Most of the prehistoric, as well as the historical-period, features were situated immediately west of

the structures. This area, unfortunately, has been subjected to periodic mechanical disturbance from bulldozers, and the dumping of construction materials and modern trash to reinforce the terrace edge. Such activities undoubtedly have affected the integrity of these features and their deposits.

Four of the 10 tested prehistoric features (Features 20, 41, 46, and 47), containing charcoal, ash, and artifacts, probably functioned as cooking pits. Pollen derived from 3 of them (Features 41, 46, and 47) was characterized primarily by cholla and prickly pear cacti, suggesting resources that might have been processed. The only other economic plants in evidence were cheno-ams, represented by a few seeds recovered from Feature 46, and *Zea mays,* represented by one cupule recovered with wood charcoal from Feature 47, although this probably is a product of fuel use rather than food.

Two of the features were reconstructible jars. Feature 16, a Sacaton Red-on-buff shouldered jar (Figure 32), and Feature 17, a large, plain ware globular jar (Figure 33), were exposed during mechanical stripping. No identifiable context, such as a pit, occupation surface, or ramada, could be determined for either of these vessels, due to the disturbance of the overlying sediments. Each vessel, although badly cracked and missing its rim, was resting largely intact in an upright position on culturally sterile deposits, suggesting that the two had been buried in prehistoric times to perhaps serve as lined storage pits.

Table 3. Prehistoric Extramural Features

Feature Number	Function	Dimensions	Fill	Comments
14	unknown pit	50 cm diameter	indistinct	
16	storage vessel	see Chapter 6	natural sediments	Sacaton Red-on-buff jar, excavated
17	storage vessel	see Chapter 6	natural sediments	plain ware jar, excavated
20	cooking pit	70 cm diameter	ash, charcoal	not oxidized, sampled
26	unknown	indeterminate	sandstone, artifacts	excavated
28	trash-filled pit	90 × 65 cm	burned rock, charcoal, bone, artifacts	trash-filled pit, sampled
29	midden	4 m diameter	ashy sediments, artifacts	
30	unknown pit	75 cm diameter	indistinct	
31	midden	4 m diameter	ashy sediments, artifacts	
32	midden	3 m diameter	ashy sediments, artifacts	
36	unknown pit	1 m diameter	burned rock, charcoal, daub	
38	unknown	40 × 40 cm	charcoal, burned sediments	pit?
41	cooking pit	1.89 × 1.86 m	ash	oxidized, sampled
43	unknown pit	60 × 30 cm	burned rock, artifacts	
46	cooking pit	58 × 61 cm	ashy sediment	oxidized, sampled
47	cooking pit	indeterminate	ash, charcoal, bone, artifacts	sampled
48	posthole	12 × 10 cm	ash, charcoal	oxidized, sampled
49	midden	3 m diameter	burned rock, ash, charcoal, artifacts	may be disturbed, sampled
50	unknown pit	indeterminate	burned rock	
51	unknown	25 cm diameter	burned rock, daub	disturbed
52	unknown	50 cm diameter	burned rock, artifacts	ill-defined
53	unknown	indeterminate	indistinct	
54	unknown pit	50 cm diameter	burned rock	
55	unknown pit	40 cm diameter	burned rock	
57	unknown pit	70 × 85 cm	burned rock, charcoal, artifacts	

If they had been left on the surface, they undoubtedly would have washed away or been crushed by subsequent activities, before they could be buried. The absence of a definable pit outline indicates only that they were excavated into a homogenous matrix.

Four of the 25 prehistoric features were classified as trash or midden deposits, based on the abundance of recovered artifacts and the lack of distinct pit boundaries. Three adjacent, high artifact density areas, Features 29, 31, and 32, were identified during mechanical stripping northwest of pit house Feature 27. These artifact concentrations, together encompassing an area of approximately 8 by 15 m, probably represented the remnants of one larger midden associated with the courtyard group, but because the area has been disturbed by modern bulldozing activities, only the lower portion of the deposits remained intact.

Another possible trash area, Feature 49, identified during mechanical stripping to the southwest of pit house Feature 22, is characterized as a high artifact density area measuring approximately 3 m in diameter. Only one potentially economic plant part, a charred mallow seed, was recovered in a flotation sample from the fill.

Historical-Period Features

Feature 5

Feature 5 consisted of a three-room building with an adobe foundation that was probably constructed by Basillio Cuevo some time after A.D. 1880 (Figures 34 and 35). The preserved portion of the foundation, which was not

Figure 32. Isolated Sacaton Red-on-buff jar in pit, Feature 16, east view.

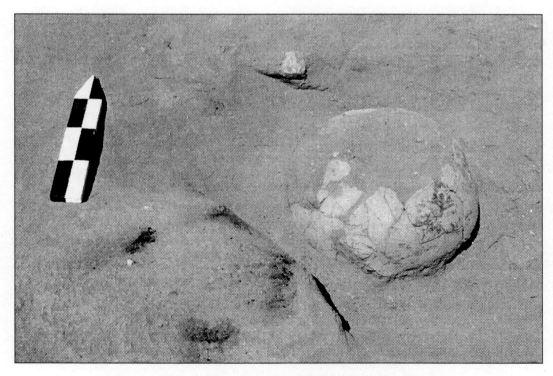

Figure 33. Isolated plain ware jar in pit, Feature 17, north view.

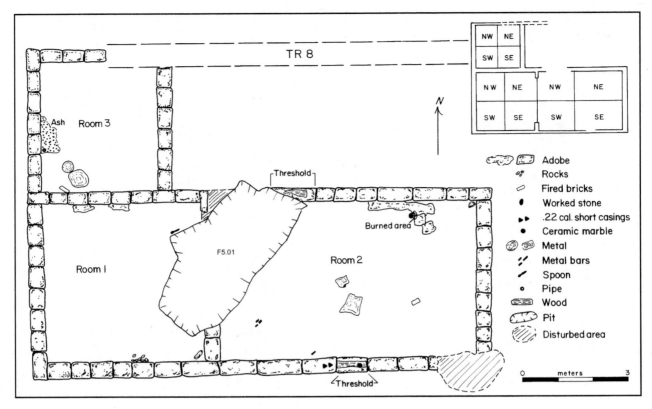

Figure 34. Plan map of historical-period adobe structure, Feature 5.

Figure 35. Historical-period adobe foundation, Feature 5, southeast view.

exposed on the surface, stood no more than two courses high. Only one possible interior feature, a rough alignment of adobes along the north wall of Room 2, was identified. The L-shaped house contained one large, east-west-oriented room (Room 2) with two doorway thresholds oriented to the north and the south, and two small rooms (Rooms 1 and 3) with no notable entries. A large intrusive pit (Feature 5.01) disturbed most of the east wall of Room 1 and part of the north wall of Room 2. Floor artifacts were sparse, and metal artifacts were mostly eroded and fragmented.

Type: adobe house
Function: homestead
Temporal assignment: ca. 1880–1910
Dimensions: *Room 1:* 12.14 feet (3.7 m) long by 11.81 feet (3.6 m) wide; *Room 2:* 19.06 feet (5.81 m) long by 11.65 feet (3.55 m) wide; *Room 3:* 10 feet (3.05 m) long by 8.96 feet (2.73 m) wide
Floor area: *Room 1:* 143.4 feet^2 (13.32 m^2); *Room 2:* 222 feet^2 (20.63 m^2); *Room 3:* 89.6 feet^2 (8.33 m^2)

Excavation Methods

The structure was initially identified along Trench 8 during the testing phase, although the east portion of the north wall of Room 3 was disturbed as a result. Subsequent hand trenching exposed the west wall of Room 3 and a portion of the west wall of Room 1. During the data recovery phase, the previously exposed wall segments were redefined, and the remaining walls were traced by removing the 10 cm of sediments that covered the wall remnants. To assure that the structure was completely defined, shovel scraping was carried out around the outside of the structure. Disturbance from a large pit (Feature 5.01) had destroyed most of the east wall of Room 1, as well as the west end of the north wall of Room 2, including a portion of the doorway sill. The wall in the southeast corner of Room 2 also was disturbed.

Each of the rooms was quartered to maintain horizontal control in the excavation of the fill. In the northwest quadrant of Room 1, the 18 cm of fill was screened in two arbitrary levels to floor contact. Based on the limited historical-period material derived from this fill, the remaining three quadrants of Room 1 were excavated in one unscreened level. The fill of Rooms 2 and 3 were similarly excavated in one unscreened level.

Stratigraphy

Room 1

Level 1. This 10-cm-thick level (3.99–4.09 mbd) contained a compact, tan silty sand fill that included a light

density of historical-period artifacts mixed with prehistoric sherds, some flaked stone debitage, and faunal bone.

Level 2. This 8-cm-thick level (4.09–4.17 mbd) contained a compact, silty sand fill. A few historical-period and prehistoric artifacts were present.

Level 3. At 4.17 mbd, a compact, silty clay surface represented the floor of the structure. A concentration of ash covered the central portion of the floor.

Room 2

Level 1. This 31-cm-thick level (3.89–4.20 mbd) contained a moderately compact, tan silty sand fill that included a light density of glass and metal artifacts mixed with prehistoric sherds and some flaked stone debitage.

Level 2. At 4.20 mbd, the floor consisted of compact, silty clay, except where it had been disturbed by an intrusive pit (Feature 5.01).

Room 3

Level 1. This 19-cm-thick level (4.02–4.21 mbd) contained a compact, silty clay loam fill (adobe wall melt). Included was a light density of metal and glass fragments mixed with prehistoric sherds, flaked stone debitage, and ground stone.

Level 2. At 4.21 mbd, the floor consisted of a moderately compact, silty loam. A concentration of ash covered the floor along a portion of the west wall.

Artifact Summary

The fill in each room of Feature 5 contained a small quantity of prehistoric sherds, flaked stone debris, and ground stone mixed with fragments of historical-period metal, glass, brick, and pottery. Several marbles and cartridge shell casings also were recovered. Artifacts on the floor consisted of a metal spoon fragment in Room 1; a marble, a brick fragment, a shell casing, unidentified metal pieces, and a metal door hinge adjacent to the south entry in Room 2; and a brick fragment, a segment of metal pipe, and two possible metal basins (25 cm in diameter by 7 cm deep, and 40 cm in diameter by 11 cm deep) in Room 3.

Construction Details

Wall and Roof Construction
No roof support material or roofing material was recovered. Douglas fir board fragments were recovered from

the upper fill of the intrusive pit (Feature 5.01). This wood, similar to that used in the thresholds of the doorways, may have been used in the construction of the walls, as well as the door and window frames.

The foundation of the structure was constructed mostly with uniformly sized, adobe bricks measuring 19 by 13 by 5 inches (48 by 33 by 13 cm). A section of the wall dividing Room 1 from Room 3 stood two courses, or approximately 10 inches (25 cm), high.

Floor Construction

A hard-packed, silty clay loam plastered surface was present in Rooms 1 and 2. The floor surface in Room 3, however, consisted only of a moderately compact, silty loam surface.

Floor Features

An intrusive pit intrusive pit (Feature 5.01), measuring 3.9 by 1.76 m, by 0.69 m deep, disturbed the adobe wall foundation dividing Rooms 1 and 2 , as well as the west end of Room 2's north wall. The loosely compacted, silty loam fill contained fragments of redwood board in the upper portion, and several prehistoric artifacts, along with some glass and metal fragments. A curving, irregular mass of adobe was identified in Room 2, adjacent to the north wall. This adobe material exhibited a small area of burning from an unidentified source. No interior features were identified in Room 3.

Entryways

Two doorways or thresholds were indicated by redwood planks covering adobe bricks along the north and south walls of Room 2. The entry in the north wall was offset to the west, whereas the south entry was centered along the wall. An entry was not identified for Room 3. It is possible that the intrusive pit (Feature 5.01) removed a likely doorway connecting Rooms 1 and 2.

The south doorway threshold of Room 2 was represented by a 12-by-70-cm, Douglas fir board set flush into the center of an adobe brick. The north doorway threshold of Room 2 was similarly constructed, although its west half had been disturbed by Feature 5.01. The remnant portion of the north doorway extended about 20 inches (50 cm) across. A metal hinge fragment and a fragment of wood with screw or nail holes, found on the floor near the south entry threshold, probably were part of the south door.

Dating

Diagnostic Artifacts: Diagnostic artifacts were scarce in the fill and on the floor of the building. Based on those

diagnostic artifacts recovered during the testing phase (Harry and Ciolek-Torrello 1992:55–56) and data recovery, however, the building appears to date between 1880 and the early 1900s, prior to the founding of the Sunset Dairy in 1915. Specific diagnostic artifacts in and around the building include sun-colored amethyst (SCA) and aqua soft drink and condiment bottle glass, shell casings, square cut nails, and metal cans.

Remarks

Room 2 probably functioned as the primary living space in the house, based on its large size and two exterior doorways. The burned adobe area along its north wall suggests that a stove might have been located in this part of the room. Although Room 1 might have functioned as a bedroom, given its intermediate size and lack of exterior doorways, the presence of a spoon and an ash deposit on the floor suggest that the room might have been used as a kitchen. Room 3, based on its small size, lack of exterior doors, unprepared floor, and the presence of several metal containers, might have functioned as a utility room, storeroom, or bathroom. The room also might have been equipped with some type of plumbing, as evidenced by a small metal pipe set vertically 16 cm into the floor. The concentration of ash along the west wall of the room suggests that a stove might have been present.

The construction of the house itself remains unknown. At the end of the nineteenth century, most houses in Tucson—especially those associated with Hispanic households—continued to be made primarily of local materials, such as adobe. Despite the availability of fired brick and milled lumber following the railroad's arrival in 1880, only wealthy households could make use of these relatively expensive imported materials (Ciolek-Torrello and Swanson 1997; Mabry et al. 1994). The presence of redwood planks in Feature 5 suggests, however, that the Cuevas family employed imported materials to some extent. Whether milled wood was included in wall construction or was used just for doors and window frames remains unknown. It is possible that adobe was used to construct the walls and that only the buried foundation remained preserved. Except for the small fragment of adobe in Room 2, there was no evidence of adobe melt, but given the extensive evidence for modern bulldozing activities in this vicinity of the site, it is possible that the walls were demolished and scraped away. However, the fact that Bruce Knapp had no recollection of a house in this area, although he had resided on the property since at least the 1920s, suggests it was removed long ago.

Table 4. Historical-Period Extramural Features

Feature Number	Function	Dimensions	Fill	Comments
19	unknown	70 cm diameter	ash, charcoal, sandstone, historical-period artifacts	sloping pit sidewalls, flat bottom, tested
24	unknown	56 × 37 cm	ash, artifact	shallow pit
33	unknown	70 × 50 cm	ash, charcoal, sandstone, bone, metal	oxidized pit, tested
34	unknown	77 × 50 × 35 cm		tested
35	unknown	indeterminate	burned rock	
37	unknown	1 m diameter	burned rock, historical-period artifacts	
39	burned pit	55 × 50 × 20 cm	burned rock, cobbles, charcoal	circular basin, tested
40	unknown	80 × 70 × 10 cm	burned rock, sandstone, cobbles, charcoal	burned sediments in fill, tested
42	unknown	50 × 40 cm	bone, historical-period shoe	
44	basin pit	60 × 53 × 26 cm	burned rock, cobbles, ash, charcoal, bone	rock in upper levels, tested
45	unknown	100 × 30 cm	cobbles, ash, charcoal	
56	hearth ?	1 m diameter	charcoal, artifact	oxidized rim

Extramural Historical-Period Features

Twelve pit and trash features were identified that related to either the turn-of-the-century Cuevas homestead, the twentieth-century Sunset Dairy, or more recent times (Table 4). Ten features were recorded as a result of mechanical stripping west of Feature 5, and 2 others (Features 33 and 34) were identified along Trench 26, to the north of Feature 5. At least 4 of the 10 features were associated with the Cuevas homestead, as indicated by the artifacts recovered from them.

Seven features were sampled to evaluate their temporal affinity and to assess their function. Four of these features (Features 19, 33, 34, and 44) yielded historical-period to more recent artifacts. Two other features (Features 37 and 42) also had historical-period artifacts in association, although the features themselves were not tested. One of the tested features (Feature 34) contained burned cow bone. Cow bone was also recovered from the surface of an untested feature (Feature 42). Two of the tested features (Features 33 and 39) and one untested feature (Feature 56) exhibited burning or oxidized pit walls. Finally, three of the tested features (Features 39, 40, and 44) contained burned and unburned cobbles, fire-cracked rock, and charcoal and ash.

CHAPTER 6

Ceramics

Robert A. Heckman and Stephanie M. Whittlesey

This chapter reports on the analysis of a sample of 5,504 prehistoric sherds, 30 prehistoric reconstructible vessels, and 5 historical-period and possible historical-period Native American sherds from data recovery investigations at Sunset Mesa Ruin. The collection we recovered indicates that the site was occupied primarily during the middle portion of the Rincon phase, which is the Sedentary period equivalent to the Sacaton phase in the Phoenix area. Although a few sherds found during previous investigations indicated a possible transitional pre-Classic–Classic period or later occupation at Sunset Mesa Ruin, no ceramic evidence of such an occupation was found during data recovery. The historical-period occupation is only minimally represented in the recovered ceramics.

Research issues for data recovery (Harry and Ciolek-Torrello 1992; Neily 1994) focused on household organization, subsistence and settlement, ceramic production and exchange, mortuary practices, the pre-Classic–Classic period transition, and irrigation systems, along with several historical-period research themes (see Chapter 1). Ceramics can contribute to most of these issues, in addition to chronology, site occupation, and abandonment. It became evident as analysis progressed that no pottery dating to the pre-Classic–Classic period transition or later occupation was recovered; thus, it was not possible to address this research theme as it was originally defined. We did not recover sufficient quantities of relatively complete, reconstructible vessels from de facto refuse contexts, such as floors, to permit a formal-functional analysis of the ceramic assemblage, which hampered our ability to address settlement and subsistence from a ceramic perspective. Lastly, there was no ceramic information to assist in answering historical-period research themes.

Our most important research focus among those defined therefore became ceramic production and exchange.

In the Tucson Basin, archaeologists have made a considerable research investment in defining local areas of production and determining the distribution of ceramics made in these areas. These studies have focused on the pre-Classic period, particularly the Rincon phase. There also has been an interest in examining the relative proportions of nonlocal pottery, particularly Hohokam Buff Ware, and attempting to explain unusual patterns in the distribution of this pottery. Sunset Mesa Ruin could certainly contribute to the body of research concerning these issues.

The presence of a variety of decorative styles in the painted pottery from Sunset Mesa Ruin made it possible to address the collection from a stylistic perspective. The description of decorative styles, correlation of these styles with technological and morphological characteristics, and investigating temporal change in styles became a second important research focus.

This chapter presents the methods used to study the ceramic collection and the results of our research. Following this introduction, we set forth the methods and sampling strategy used for plain ware, red ware, and painted pottery. We then present the results, discussing first the recovery context and how the ceramic collection can inform on abandonment processes and depositional events. Results are summarized by general ware (e.g., plain ware), and information on vessel form, temper, and other characteristics of the collection is provided for each category. The Tucson Basin painted pottery is discussed by decorative style (Rincon Red-on-brown Style A, Style B, and indeterminate style). We then summarize the ceramic study according to broad research themes: ceramic dating, decorative styles in painted pottery, and ceramic production and distribution. Supporting information is presented in Appendix E, including details of attributes recorded and examples of recording forms, along with specific data for reconstructible vessels.

Methods

Sampling

Excavations at Sunset Mesa Ruin produced 12,320 sherds and 30 reconstructible vessels. The sherd collection consisted of three general ware categories: painted (n = 1,953), plain ware (n = 10,213), and red ware (n = 154) pottery. The first analytic step involved sampling the sherd collection. Painted, red ware, and plain ware ceramics yield different kinds of information, and different attributes are recorded for each of these categories. Because painted and red ware ceramics typically provide important information to assist in placing features and sites in time, we decided to analyze all sherds in these categories. Plain ware pottery is less likely to yield temporal information, but as the all-purpose utility pottery, it provides excellent functional data. Plain ware is also the most common pottery in archaeological contexts, however, and to avoid collecting redundant information, it was necessary to sample the plain ware sherds.

Because research questions centered on issues of settlement function, household organization, subsistence, and ceramic production and distribution, we believed that the prehistoric pit house contexts would provide the best information. The structures, which were thoroughly excavated and dated archaeomagnetically, represent the strongest contexts. Therefore, we analyzed the plain ware pottery from all excavated contexts in the five pit houses (Features 21, 22, 23, 25, and 27). We recorded only the painted and red ware pottery from other contexts, including extramural features, stripping units, and trench backdirt. The unpainted pottery from Feature 5, the historical-period Basillio Cuevas homestead, was scanned for historical-period Native American pottery. Data were recorded for all reconstructible vessels.

Recording

Once the plain ware sample had been selected, the collection was divided into the appropriate general wares, and each category was analyzed. The attributes we recorded and the forms we used are presented in Appendix E. The coding form used for sherds is reproduced in Figure E.1, and that used for reconstructible vessels is shown in Figure E.2. Figure E.3 is the coding index used for all analyses. Figures E.4–E.8 depict morphological attributes used for reconstructible vessels and rim sherds.

Ceramics were classified using a combination of standard southwestern classificatory systems and additional design and technological attributes, as necessary. For example, Rincon Red-on-brown pottery was classified using Deaver's (1984) subdivision of the type into several design styles. Plain ware and red ware pottery that could be assigned to traditionally defined types was identified conservatively. Thus, the plain ware and red ware assigned to Gila Plain or Rincon Red, for example, exhibit a limited degree of variation. The remaining categories used for classifying plain and red ware pottery are based on qualitative observations.

Painted Ceramics

All painted ceramics were analyzed, regardless of provenience. To facilitate identification of crossmatching (conjoining) sherds, the painted sherds from a feature were laid out on a table by stratigraphic provenience. If intrusive features were present, ceramics from those contexts were laid out at the same time. Each sherd was recorded individually, except in cases of conjoining sherds, where they were recorded collectively. Conjoining sherds from different proveniences, such as different levels or features, were recorded as originating in the provenience from which they were collected, and a note of the crossmatch was made in the database.

Vessel form was recorded for each painted sherd, whenever possible. Criteria developed by Shepard (1968) were used to identify vessel form. A bowl is defined as a vessel that exhibits no corners or inflection points that create a restriction less than the maximum body diameter at any point in the profile contour. The end point (at the lip) of a bowl is either vertical, or inclined outward. By contrast, a jar is defined as a vessel that does exhibit such a restriction point. In the case of a "seed" or neckless jar, the restriction is at the orifice, whereas on a jar with a flaring rim, the restriction is at the aperture. It should be noted that the location of paint makes vessel form easier to recognize in painted pottery, even among body sherds. Metric data (other than sherd thickness) were recorded only for rim sherds (see Figure E.3). Vessel forms are depicted in Figure E.6, and rim forms and lip finishes in Figures E.7 and E.8. Only vessel form and temper were recorded for sherds smaller than a 25-cent coin, except rims and conjoining sherds. Sherd weight was not recorded.

The Tucson Basin red-on-brown ceramics were classified using previously defined technological and design attributes (Deaver 1984; Greenleaf 1975; Kelly et al. 1978; Wallace 1986b, 1986c; Whittlesey 1986a). Painted pottery in the Tucson Basin dating to the Sedentary period exhibits a florescence of technological and design variation that distinguishes it from earlier painted ceramics. There are several paint and slip combinations, and variety in painted designs. Ceramicists have approached the classification of this variability in different ways. Deaver (1984) was one of the first to deal with the technological variability of Rincon phase painted pottery in his analysis of ceramics from the Rosemont project. He defined four technological varieties of Rincon Red-on-brown: (1) micaceous; (2) white-slipped; (3) smudged; and (4) the unslipped, nonmicaceous, unsmudged "typical" variety (Deaver 1984:320). We follow Deaver in recognizing white-slipped painted pottery separately, although we do not name this as a variety. We did not, however, identify smudged varieties of Rincon Red-on-brown. Deaver (1984:322) also defined black-painted Rincon pottery as a separate type, Rincon Black-on-brown. As with red-painted Rincon pottery, the black paint can be present on either the unslipped brown background, or on a white slip applied to the underlying brown paste. According to Deaver (1984:324), "Stylistically and technologically Rincon Black-on-brown is indistinguishable from its red-on-brown counterpart, supporting the inference that this type is produced in the Tucson Basin. The only distinguishing attribute is the use of a blackish pigment." By contrast, offering the justification that proliferation of "minor technological distinctions such as paint color" would be "counterproductive to our perception of ceramic variability," Wallace (1986c:21) has recognized both black-painted and white-slipped Rincon Red-on-brown as "varieties." We follow Deaver's usage in this study, recognizing Rincon Black-on-brown as a separate type.

Rincon Red-on-brown also has been subdivided in various ways using technological, morphological, and design attributes. Each subdivision of Rincon Red-on-brown is designed to elicit different kinds of information, and serves different purposes. Deaver (1984:243) developed what he calls a stylistic approach to painted decoration, "defining a model of decorative changes which focuses on identifying a sequence of decorative styles rather than a sequence of pottery types." Each style is a "particular decorative configuration in design structure, decorative units, and execution, that can be recognized independently of archaeological context or association." He defined three styles of Rincon painted pottery, Rincon Style A, B, and C (Deaver 1984:Table 4.1). Wallace (1986b, 1986c), by contrast, has used a standard typological approach explicitly to achieve chronological control. He has defined three subtypes of Rincon Red-on-brown—Early, Middle, and Late—each coterminous with a Rincon subphase. Each approach to Rincon phase painted pottery has its advantages and limitations. This study uses Deaver's (1984:242–265) scheme, with its three styles of Rincon phase painted pottery (Rincon Styles A, B, and C). Only Styles A and B are present in the Sunset Mesa Ruin collection. Style was recorded for all Rincon painted pottery, regardless of technological

variation. The styles and their implications are discussed in greater detail in a subsequent section.

Painted brown ware sherds exhibiting attributes consistent with Rincon phase ceramics in the Tucson Basin, but too small to identify by specific style, were classified as Rincon Red-on-brown or Rincon Black-on-brown, indeterminate style. Some of the specific attributes used to identify sherds as Rincon phase pottery were the presence of a painted rim lip and wavy lines in the design.

Indeterminate red-on-brown pottery was recognized by technological criteria. These sherds have the brown ware paste characteristic of Tucson Basin painted pottery—dense paste with few or no voids, considerable variability in color, and variable temper—which is consistent with Tucson Basin painted pottery identifiable by type. For consistency with typed categories, sherds with a white slip were identified separately. Unlike Hohokam Buff Ware, which can be easily recognized in sherd form even if it lacks paint, Tucson Basin painted ceramics can be difficult to distinguish from plain ware pottery, because they share similar paste and temper. There is, therefore, no category of sherds without paint equivalent to indeterminate Hohokam Buff Ware without paint (see below).

Hohokam Buff Ware pottery was assigned to types within the traditional Hohokam ceramic sequence based on attributes described by Haury (1965, 1976). Assignment was conservative; if sherds exhibited insufficient criteria to justify classification by type, they were recorded as indeterminate red-on-buff (painted) or indeterminate buff (no paint). The lack of paint on many sherds is typical of buff ware, which has a soft, easily eroded paste and often has poorly bonded paint.

An indeterminate buff or brown category was recognized by technological criteria. The distinction between buff and brown ware is primarily one of paste color and texture. The indeterminate buff or brown ware category consists of ceramics that exhibit characteristics of both wares. These sherds typically have the pinkish rose color of buff ware paste, but the dense, nonporous paste without voids or vugs that typifies brown ware. The temper in indeterminate buff or brown ware is schist. The same procedures were followed as for Hohokam Buff Ware, separating the indeterminate sherds into those with and those without paint.

Unpainted Ceramics

The unpainted category includes plain and red ware ceramics. As discussed previously, the plain ware was sampled; only the plain ware sherds from pit houses (all levels) were analyzed. A large proportion of these sherds proved to be too small for analysis; these are listed as "indeterminate unpainted" in the tables. Although it is possible that some of these sherds are red ware, the likelihood is small because the red ware is so readily identified.

In order to make our results comparable with previous research in the Tucson Basin (see Deaver 1984; Heidke 1986; Whittlesey 1986a), we did not apply type and variety labels that have been used elsewhere for Hohokam plain ware pottery. Instead, we recorded a number of technological attributes, such as temper and surface treatment. The only traditional plain ware type we used was Gila Plain.

All of the red ware we recovered was analyzed. Standard typological descriptions were used to identify the red ware pottery. In particular, we used Kelly et al.'s (1978:67) and Wallace's (1986c:69–78) descriptions of Rincon Red to identify most of the red ware sherds as this type. Red ware sherds that did not conform to the description of Rincon Red were placed in qualitative categories, including possible intrusive red ware and indeterminate red ware. Possible intrusive red ware exhibited technological attributes, such as surface treatment and temper, that distinguish it from Rincon Red. It cannot be definitively demonstrated that these ceramics represent intrusive vessels, however. We used such categories to subdivide the collection into potentially meaningful groups in order to facilitate subsequent analyses. Indeterminate red ware is different from the possible intrusive red ware category in attributes of surface treatment, but we did not feel comfortable with assigning it to traditionally defined types. The unidentified red ware categories are described below. We did not need to use a category of indeterminate plain or red ware, as is common in analysis of desert ceramic collections, because the attributes characterizing Rincon Red pottery are so distinctive and readily distinguished, even in sherd form. All of the red ware has a well-defined slip that may be as much as 1 mm thick, and that contrasts sharply with the paste in cross section. No ambiguous cases were observed, such as red surface and paste color combined with a high polish or float.

The attributes recorded for plain ware and red ware are listed in Figures E.1 and E.3. Red ware attributes are the same as for plain ware and painted pottery, with the exception of surface treatment. Surface treatment was recorded for all red ware sherds, regardless of vessel part.

Different attributes were recorded for plain ware rim and body sherds. Vessel form and metric data were recorded only for rim sherds, whereas observations of surface treatment were limited to body sherds. Vessel forms and rim morphology are illustrated in Figures E.6–E.8.

Vessel forms were identified based on Shepard's (1968) criteria, discussed above.

Temper was identified macroscopically with the aid of a hand lens, as necessary. Temper categories found in the unpainted ceramics include sand (undifferentiated), sand and muscovite mica, schist, phyllite, indeterminate phyllite or schist, and sand (volcanic) (see Figure E.3). Schist, as used here, is distinguished from sand and muscovite mica temper by the presence of rock fragments within the schistose matrix and tiny flecks of mica. The category sand with muscovite mica was used for those sherds exhibiting relatively large booklets or individual platelets of muscovite mica, as well as rounded, sand-size mineral inclusions (predominantly quartz). Subsequent examination of the sherds coded as containing phyllite or indeterminate phyllite or schist suggests that the tempering agent could be described more accurately as gneissic rock fragments. Furthermore, the subtle, and somewhat subjective, distinction between schist and gneiss is one that could justify collapsing these two categories, as well. The important behavioral aspect reflected by the addition of a foliated metamorphic rock to the pottery is that it may represent a technological trait that corresponds to the Hohokam ceramic tradition emanating from the Gila-Salt River basin.

Sand and schist is a combination temper that was identified based on the presence of subangular to subrounded particles characteristic of stream sand, in conjunction with foliated metamorphic material. Often, the mineralogy or lithology of the stream sand was inconsistent with the presence of the metamorphic material. This circumstance can occur naturally in stream sand; however, based on a qualitative appraisal of the material, in this study it was inferred to represent the addition of metamorphic temper to a clay body containing sand-sized inclusions, or a mixture of clay, sand, and metamorphic rock. In either case, the metamorphic temper material is inferred to have been added deliberately.

Gila Plain was distinguished from schist-tempered plain ware pottery and from plain ware tempered with sand and muscovite mica by qualitative criteria. Gila Plain contains abundant, finely divided mica particles, whereas schist-tempered plain ware does not; its mica particles are larger and less abundant. Also, Gila Plain typically exhibits patterned polish striations, whereas schist-tempered plain ware does not. Pottery with sand and muscovite has abundant surface mica, but it usually represents large, single mica platelets. Most such pottery also lacks patterned polishing.

Criteria developed by Fontana et al. (1962) and Whittlesey (1986b, 1994, 1997) were used to identify historical-period Native American pottery from Feature 5.

Reconstructible Vessels

Some reconstructible vessels (RVs, defined as greater than 50 percent complete) and partial vessels (PVs, defined as between 15 and 50 percent complete) were identified in the field, and others were discovered during analysis. As is typical, some sherd clusters recorded in the field as reconstructible vessels proved upon analysis to represent only groups of individual sherds, or nonconjoining sherds from a single vessel, insufficient to reconstruct. All reconstructible vessels were separated from the sherd collection for reconstruction and subsequent analysis. The recorded attributes (see Figure E.2) were designed primarily to obtain morphological and metric data (see Figures E.4–E.6 for morphological categories and standardized measurements).

Sourcing Study

Archaeologists seeking to determine where pottery was made by identifying the provenance of its paste constituents have several choices in methods, ranging from instrumental neutron activation analysis to inductively coupled plasma spectroscopy. Sourcing studies carried out on prehistoric Tucson Basin pottery have to date relied almost exclusively on petrography (see review in Whittlesey 1987c). The petrographic technique focused on identifying sand composition sources called petrofacies, first developed by Lombard (1985, 1986a, 1986b, 1987a), has become the choice of researchers at Desert Archaeology, Inc. (DAI). A petrofacies is a mineralogically distinct sand composition zone. Petrofacies are typically identified in regions where the bedrock geology is sufficiently diverse to permit wash sands to be mineralogically varied. General procedures for sand-sample collecting, petrofacies identification, thin sectioning and point counting, and statistical analysis as carried out by DAI are detailed in Miksa and Heidke (1995).

For the Sunset Mesa Ruin study, we chose to submit a relatively large collection of prehistoric ceramics (261 samples, representing sherds and reconstructible vessels) to DAI for qualitative petrographic characterization. The sample represents about 4 percent of the plain ware, 15 percent of the red ware, and 5 percent of the painted pottery sherds recovered from Sunset Mesa Ruin. Samples were chosen from the strongest contexts, and had to be sufficiently large to permit macroscopic inspection of temper materials. We did not include Hohokam Buff Ware in the sample for temper characterization because most of it is tempered with schist. Although more recently

DAI has attempted to identify the source of metamorphic rocks, such as schist and phyllite, this work had not begun when the Sunset Mesa Ruin study was initiated.

James M. Heidke of DAI conducted the temper characterization. None of the samples were thin sectioned and point counted. Heidke provided three observations: temper type, which presents the general category of material, such as sand or mixed sand and mica; generic temper source, which notes whether the temper represents igneous, metamorphic, sedimentary, or mixed materials; and specific temper source, which attempts to pinpoint temper provenance to a specific petrofacies or subset of petrofacies. Heidke's report containing methods and results is available in Appendix D.

Results

Recovery Context and Abandonment Processes

The analyzed ceramic collection is summarized in Table 5, which presents the sherd and reconstructible vessel data for the analyzed proveniences. Because of archaeological recovery procedures and the sampling strategy employed for ceramic analysis, most of the analyzed prehistoric sherds at Sunset Mesa Ruin derive from the five excavated pit houses (82.3 percent) (Table 6). Extramural contexts yielded 12.9 percent (Table 7), stripping units and trenches provided 4.1 percent (Table 8), and Feature 5 yielded 0.7 percent (painted and red ware prehistoric sherds only) (Table 9). Few vessels were found in de facto refuse contexts, and most of these were incomplete. This suggests that much of the material found in the houses accumulated through natural rather than behavioral processes of deposition. The lack of whole vessels also precluded a detailed study of vessel formal-functional classes toward understanding house function.

Pit Houses

The pit houses labeled Features 21, 22, and 23 form a tight cluster with facing entryways around a common courtyard, but evidently not all were occupied at the same time. Feature 21 produced the largest collection of sherds (1,407) among the pit houses, and three reconstructible vessels (Table 10). This feature alone yielded half of all Rincon Red sherds found in the analyzed Sunset Mesa

Table 5. Analyzed Prehistoric Ceramic Collection

Ceramic Ware and Type	Number of Sherds	Number of RVs	Sherds Category[a] (%)	Total (%)
Painted ceramics				
Tucson Basin Brown Ware				
Indeterminate Rillito or Rincon R/Br	1	—	< 0.1	< 0.1
Rincon R/Br, Style A	54	3	2.8	1.0
Rincon R/Br, Style A (white-slipped)	9	1	0.5	0.2
Rincon R/Br, Style B	130	4	6.7	2.4
Rincon R/Br, Style B (white-slipped)	24	2	1.2	0.4
Rincon Bl/Br, Style B	1	—	< 0.1	< 0.1
Rincon Bl/Br, Style B (white-slipped)	18	—	0.9	0.3
Rincon R/Br, indeterminate style	406	1	20.8	7.4
Rincon R/Br, indeterminate style (white-slipped)	74	—	3.8	1.3
Rincon Bl/Br, indeterminate style	6	—	0.3	0.1
Rincon Bl/Br, indeterminate style (white-slipped)	11	—	0.6	0.2
Rincon polychrome	1	2	< 0.1	< 0.1
Other Polychrome	—	1	0.0	< 0.1
Indeterminate R/Br	969	—	49.6	17.6
Indeterminate R/Br (white-slipped)	5	—	0.3	< 0.1
Hohokam Buff Ware				
Sacaton R/B	125	2	6.4	2.3
Indeterminate R/B	98	—	5.0	1.8
Indeterminate buff (no paint)	13	—	0.7	0.2
Indeterminate buff or brown ware				
Painted	4	—	0.2	< 0.1
No paint	4	—	0.2	< 0.1
Subtotal painted ceramics	1,953	16	100.0	35.5
Unpainted ceramics				
Plain ware	2,481	11	69.9	45.1
Gila Plain	20	1	0.6	0.4
Subtotal plain ware	2,501	12	70.5	45.5
Red ware				
Rincon Red	133	2	3.7	2.4
Possible intrusive red ware	6	—	0.2	0.1
Indeterminate (unidentified) red ware	15	—	0.4	0.3
Subtotal red ware	154	2	4.3	2.8
Unidentified indeterminate unpainted[b]	896	—	25.2	16.3
Subtotal unpainted ceramics	3,551	14	100.0	64.5
Total	5,504	30	100.0	100.0

Key: Bl/Br = Black-on-brown; R/B = Red-on-buff; R/Br = Red-on-brown
[a] Painted, unpainted
[b] Too small to analyze

Ceramic Type	F25.02				F27				F27.03			
	3	L4	—	Subtotal for F25	L1	L2	L3	—	L1	L2	Subtotal for F27	Total
	S-R	Fill	Fill		OB	RFL	FLR Fill	FLR	Fill	FLR Fill		
Painted ceramics												
Tucson Basin Brown Ware												
Rincon R/Br, Style A	—	—	—	0	—	—	—	—	—	—	0	24
Rincon R/Br, Style A (white-slipped)	—	—	—	0	—	—	—	—	—	—	0	9
Rincon R/Br, Style B	—	—	—	4	—	—	—	—	21	—	21	46
Rincon R/Br, Style B (white-slipped)	1	—	—	1	4	—	—	—	—	—	4	5
Rincon Bl/Br, Style B	—	—	—	0	—	—	—	—	—	—	0	1
Rincon Bl/Br, Style B (white-slipped)	1	—	—	7	—	—	—	—	6	—	6	14
Rincon R/Br, indeterminate style	—	—	—	30	—	5	5	—	2	—	12	168
Rincon R/Br, indeterminate style (white-slipped)	—	—	—	8	—	6	5	—	3	—	14	54
Rincon Bl/Br, indeterminate style	—	—	—	0	—	1	—	—	—	—	1	3
Rincon Bl/Br, indeterminate style (white-slipped)	—	—	—	0	—	3	4	—	—	—	7	8
Indeterminate R/Br	—	1	—	64	—	11	16	1	17	2	47	563
Indeterminate R/Br (white-slipped)	—	—	—	0	—	—	—	—	—	—	0	1
Hohokam Buff Ware												
Sacaton R/B	—	—	—	0	—	—	4	—	—	—	4	26
Indeterminate R/B	—	—	—	3	—	—	3	—	—	—	3	56
Indeterminate buff (no paint)	—	—	—	0	—	—	—	—	—	—	0	9
Indeterminate buff or brown ware												
Indeterminate R/B or R/Br (painted)	—	—	—	0	—	—	—	—	—	—	0	1
Indeterminate buff or brown (no paint)	—	—	—	1	—	—	—	—	—	—	0	4
Subtotal painted ceramics	2	1	0	118	4	26	37	1	49	2	119	992
Unpainted ceramics												
Plain ware	2	—	—	292	—	26	134	7	160	—	327	2,481
Gila Plain	—	—	—	0	—	—	—	—	—	—	0	20
Red ware												
Rincon Red	1	—	—	20	—	3	1	—	7	—	11	122
Possible intrusive red ware	—	—	—	0	—	1	3	—	—	—	4	6
Indeterminate red ware	—	—	—	2	—	—	—	—	—	—	0	15
Indeterminate unpainted	—	—	2	218	—	10	63	—	67	—	140	896
Subtotal unpainted ceramics	3	0	2	532	0	40	201	7	234	0	482	3,540
Total	5	1	2	650	4	66	238	8	283	2	601	4,532

Key: BD = backdirt; Bl/Br = Black-on-brown; F = feature; Fl

Subtotal for F15	F17	F18					Subtotal for F18	F20	F26	F31	F32	F40	F47	F49	Total
	L1	—	—	L1	L2	L3		L1	L1	—	—	L1	L1	L1	
	Fill	Fill/SFLR	OB	OB	Fill	FLR		Fill	Fill	BD	BD	Fill	Fill	Fill	
0	—	—	—	—	—	—	0	—	—	—	—	—	—	—	1
25	—	—	—	—	—	—	0	—	—	5	—	—	—	—	30
28	1	—	3	—	—	—	3	—	—	24	6	—	1	—	68
15	—	—	—	—	—	—	0	—	—	1	1	—	—	—	18
2	—	—	2	—	—	—	2	—	—	—	—	—	—	—	4
40	2	1	13	12	2	1	29	—	12	15	9	1	15	2	152
6	—	—	2	1	—	—	3	—	—	2	—	—	—	—	15
0	—	—	—	1	—	—	1	—	—	—	—	—	—	—	2
86	4	—	16	20	5	1	42	1	38	24	18	2	10	4	284
0	—	—	—	—	—	—	0	—	1	—	—	1	—	—	4
86	—	—	—	—	—	—	0	—	1	—	—	—	3	—	90
13	2	—	—	—	—	—	0	—	1	—	4	—	—	—	25
2	—	—	—	1	—	—	1	—	—	—	—	—	—	—	3
0	—	—	—	—	—	—	0	—	—	—	—	—	1	—	3
303	9	1	36	35	7	2	81	1	53	71	38	4	30	6	699
6	—	—	—	—	—	—	0	—	—	—	—	—	—	—	10
6	0	0	0	0	0	0	0	0	0	0	0	0	0	0	10
309	9	1	36	35	7	2	81	1	53	71	38	4	30	6	709

Table 8. Painted and Red Ware Sherds from Stripping Units and Trench Backdirt Contexts

Ceramic Type	Backdirt						Overburden											Total
	SU10	TR12	TR13	TR14	TR15	TR16	SU1	SU2	SU4	SU6	SU11	SU12	SU13	SU14	SU15	SU16	SU17	
Painted ceramics																		
Tucson Basin Brown Ware																		
Rincon R/Br, Style B	1	—	1	—	—	—	2	5	2	2	2	—	—	—	1	—	—	16
Rincon R/Br, Style B (white-slipped)	—	—	—	—	—	—	—	—	—	1	—	—	—	—	—	—	—	1
Rincon Polychrome	—	—	—	—	—	—	—	—	—	1	—	—	—	—	—	—	—	1
Rincon R/Br, indeterminate style	1	1	—	—	6	2	13	5	—	24	6	—	2	4	4	5	3	76
Rincon R/Br, indeterminate style (white-slipped)	—	—	—	—	—	—	1	2	—	1	—	—	—	—	1	—	—	5
Rincon Bl/Br, indeterminate style	—	—	—	—	—	—	—	—	—	—	—	—	—	—	—	3	—	3
Rincon Bl/Br, indeterminate style (white-slipped)	—	—	—	—	—	—	—	—	—	—	—	—	—	—	1	—	—	1
Indeterminate R/Br	1	—	1	4	3	2	13	13	—	39	6	1	2	2	4	3	2	96
Hohokam Buff Ware																		
Sacaton R/B	—	—	—	—	—	—	—	—	—	7	—	—	—	—	1	—	1	9
Indeterminate R/B	—	—	—	—	—	—	3	2	1	8	1	—	—	—	—	1	—	16
Subtotal painted ceramics	3	1	2	4	9	4	32	27	3	83	15	1	4	6	12	12	6	224
Unpainted ceramics																		
Red ware																		
Rincon Red	—	—	—	—	—	—	1	—	—	—	—	—	—	—	—	—	—	1
Subtotal unpainted ceramics	0	0	0	0	0	0	1	0	0	0	0	0	0	0	0	0	0	1
Total	3	1	2	4	9	4	33	27	3	83	15	1	4	6	12	12	6	225

Key: Bl/Br = Black-on-Brown; R/B = Red-on-Buff; R/Br = Red-on-Brown; SU = stripping unit; TR = trench

Table 9. Prehistoric Painted Sherds from Feature 5 (Basillio Cuevas Homestead)

Ceramic Type	OB	L1 Fill	L2 Fill	L3 Fill	Fill/SFLR	Total
Painted ceramics						
Tucson Basin Brown Ware						
Indeterminate Rillito or Rincon R/Br	—	—	—	—	—	0
Rincon R/Br, Style A	—	—	—	—	—	0
Rincon R/Br, Style B	—	—	—	—	—	0
Rincon R/Br, Style B (white-slipped)	—	—	—	—	—	0
Rincon Bl/Br, Style B (white-slipped)	—	—	—	—	—	0
Rincon R/Br, indeterminate style	—	5	4	1	—	10
Rincon R/Br, indeterminate style (white slipped)	—	—	—	—	—	0
Rincon Bl/Br, indeterminate style (white-slipped)	—	—	—	—	—	0
Indeterminate R/Br	1	16	7	1	1	26
Indeterminate R/Br (white-slipped)	—	—	—	—	—	0
Hohokam Buff Ware						
Sacaton R/B	—	—	—	—	—	0
Indeterminate R/B	—	1	—	—	—	1
Indeterminate buff (no paint)	—	1	—	—	—	1
Indeterminate R/B or R/Br	—	—	—	—	—	0
Total	1	23	11	2	1	38

Key: Bl/Br = Black-on-brown; L = level; OB = overburden; R/B = Red-on-buff; R/Br = Red-on-brown; SFLR = subfloor

Ruin collection. Sherds were particularly abundant in Level 3, floor fill, and Level 5, subfloor fill between the structure floor (Floor A) and an earlier, plastered floor segment (Floor B). The general lack of floor artifacts (see feature description, Chapter 5), the abundance of sherds in floor fill and subfloor contexts, and the lack of an areally extensive, plastered floor are consistent with the presence of a raised house floor in this structure, and suggest that the ceramics represent primary or secondary refuse, or both. It should be noted, however, that only the southwest quarter of the house was completely screened; floor fill only was screened across the remainder of the structure (see feature description). About 28 percent of the unpainted sherds were too small to be analyzed, which also indicates the house was probably filled by natural erosional processes. The archaeomagnetic sequence (Deaver and Murphy, Appendix B) places Feature 21 as essentially contemporaneous with Features 25 and 27, a pair of pit houses located to the north of the cluster containing Features 21–23.

The vessels were recovered from several contexts in Feature 21. Floor fill (Level 3) yielded PV 30, a partial, polychrome effigy vessel. Sherds from PV 8, a Rincon Red-on-brown, Style A flare-rimmed bowl, were found in roof fall (Level 2), floor fill, and a fill layer (Level 5)

between Floor A and the earlier Floor B. Level 5 also produced RV 7, a miniature Sacaton Red-on-buff cauldron (see Table 10).

The adjacent Feature 23 yielded the second-largest collection of sherds (1,175) and several vessels from floor fill and other contexts. Ceramics were most abundant in roof fall/floor fill (Level 2), with fill (Level 1) providing the next-highest quantity. The high yield of sherds from floor fill is not inconsistent with the notion of a raised house floor (see feature description, Chapter 5). One-fourth of the ceramics from Feature 23 came from the fill deposits, contrasted with only about 8 percent in Feature 21. This may suggest different abandonment sequences for these features. No excavation methods are noted that may be responsible for the differences in fill sherd density between Features 21 and 23 (see feature description). The archaeomagnetic sequence (Deaver and Murphy, Appendix B) places Feature 23 as the first structure in the pit house cluster to be abandoned, and Feature 22 as the last, with Feature 21 intermediate. The high density of sherds in the fill of Feature 23 is consistent with this abandonment sequence. The low proportion of small, unpainted sherds in the structure (about 11 percent) is more consistent with primary or secondary refuse deposition than deposition by natural processes, such as

Table 10. Attribute Data for Whole, Reconstructible, and Partial Vessels

	RV1	RV2	RV3	RV4	PV5	PV6	RV7	PV8	PV9	RV10
Feature	23	23	23	22	22.04	22.04	21	21	27.03	27
Bag number	363	461	480	603	704	704	409	516	676	672
Context	fill	floor fill and floor	floor fill	floor	intrusive pit fill	intrusive pit fill	fill between floors	roof fall, floor fill, fill between floors	fill of floor pit	floor
Type	Rincon Red-on-brown, Style B	Rincon Red-on-brown, Style A	Rincon Red-on-brown, Style A (white-slipped)	Rincon Red-on-brown, Style A	Rincon Polychrome	Rincon Red-on-brown, Style B (white-slipped)	Sacaton Red-on-buff	Rincon Red-on-brown, Style A	Rincon Polychrome	Rincon Red-on-brown, Style B (white-slipped)
Completeness (%)	50	50	55	99	30	20	100	30	25	50
Vessel form	shouldered jar	flare-rimmed bowl	shouldered jar	hemispherical bowl	shouldered jar or cauldron	indeterminate jar	miniature cauldron	flare-rimmed bowl	subhemispherical bowl	subhemispherical bowl
Temper	sand	schist	sand	sand	sand	sand	schist	schist	sand	sand
Petrofacies	Beehive Peak (J1)	Beehive Peak (J1)	Twin Hills (J2)	Beehive Peak (J1)	Beehive Peak (J1)	Beehive Peak (J1)	not analyzed	Beehive Peak (J1)	Beehive Peak (J1)	Beehive Peak (J1)
Rim diameter (cm)	24	21	indeterminate	17	indeterminate	21	6	25	27	23
Orifice diameter (cm)	23.3	20	indeterminate	16.4	indeterminate	20	5.7	24.4	26.3	22.5
Aperture diameter (cm)	21	16.5	indeterminate	16.4	indeterminate	19	4.7	22	26.3	22.5
Throat diameter (cm)	21.7	n/a	indeterminate	n/a	indeterminate	20	4.7	22	n/a	n/a
Max. body diameter (cm)	41	21	40	17	47	indeterminate	5	25	27	23
Shoulder height (cm)	indeterminate	n/a	n/a	n/a	indeterminate	indeterminate	n/a	n/a	n/a	n/a
Rim height (cm)	1.4	1	indeterminate	n/a	indeterminate	1.3	1	3	n/a	n/a
Neck height (cm)	2.7	n/a	indeterminate	n/a	indeterminate	2	n/a	n/a	n/a	n/a
Total height (cm)	indeterminate	indeterminate	indeterminate	6.8	indeterminate	indeterminate	4.3	14	12	14
Thickness (cm)	0.7	0.5	0.5	0.6	0.7	0.5	0.3	0.6	0.7	0.5
Volume (ml)	indeterminate	indeterminate	indeterminate	750	indeterminate	indeterminate	75	indeterminate	indeterminate	indeterminate
Rim form	slight flare	moderate flare	indeterminate	direct	indeterminate	slight flare	slight flare	moderate flare	direct	direct
Rim finish	rounded	tapered	indeterminate	rounded	indeterminate	exterior bulge or overhang	interior bevel	rounded	interior bevel	rounded
Shoulder	Gila	n/a	Gila	indeterminate	Gila	indeterminate	n/a	n/a	n/a	n/a
Base shape	indeterminate	indeterminate	rounded	rounded	rounded	indeterminate	rounded	flat	indeterminate	rounded
Interior surface finish	SP, blackened	UP, blackened	HS, blackened	UP, fire clouded	slip, SP	UP, blackened	HS	UP, blackened	slip, SP	UP
Exterior surface finish	UP, fire clouded	UP	UP, fire clouded	UP, fire clouded	slip, UP	UP	HS	SP, fire clouded	UP, fire clouded	UP, fire clouded
Modifications	none	none	none	none	none	none	none	none	none	none
Use wear	none-indeterminate	none-indeterminate	none-indeterminate	none	none-indeterminate	none-indeterminate	exterior basal abrasion	exterior basal abrasion	interior basal abrasion	exterior basal abrasion
Comments	lower portion of pot missing	lower portion of pot missing	rim and base missing		no rim; base missing	base missing			interior red slip with exterior decoration (black-on-brown)	

Key: HS = hand smoothed; mbd = meters below datum; SP = striated polish; UP = uniform polish

Table 10 (continued).

	RV11	PV12	RV13	PV14	RV15	RV16	RV17	RV18	PV19	RV20
Feature	18	48	13	13	16	22	22	22	22	23
Bag number	90	758	793	795	146	704	576	576	622	35
Context	backdirt	fill	on use-compacted surface	on use-compacted surface	isolated vessel	fill, floor fill, pit fill	fill	fill	fill	floor fill
Type	Rincon Red-on-brown, Style B	Rincon Red-on-brown, Style B	Rincon Red-on-brown, Style B	Rincon Red-on-brown (indeterminate style)	Sacaton Red-on-buff	plain ware	plain ware	plain ware	plain ware	Gila Plain
Completeness (%)	70	40	80	30	80	70	100 (reworked)	100 (reworked)	30	60
Vessel form	subhemispherical bowl	cauldron	hemispherical bowl	indeterminate bowl	shouldered jar	indeterminate jar	informal plate	informal plate	indeterminate jar	jar ("bean pot")
Temper	schist	sand	sand	sand	sand	sand and muscovite mica	sand	sand	sand	schist
Petrofacies	Beehive Peak (J1)	Beehive Peak (J1)	indeterminate	indeterminate	not analyzed	indeterminate	Twin Hills (J2)	indeterminate	indeterminate	indeterminate
Rim diameter (cm)	31	38	26	indeterminate	indeterminate	29	24	34	25	20
Orifice diameter (cm)	30	37	25	indeterminate	indeterminate	28.2	24	34	24	19.7
Aperture diameter (cm)	30	35	24.6	indeterminate	19	27	24	34	22	17.5
Throat diameter (cm)	n/a	35	n/a	indeterminate	19	27	n/a	n/a	22	17.5
Max. body diameter (cm)	31	43	26	indeterminate	46	indeterminate	24	34	indeterminate	20
Shoulder height (cm)	n/a	n/a	n/a	n/a	13.6	indeterminate	n/a	n/a	indeterminate	n/a
Rim height (cm)	n/a	1.2	0.8	indeterminate	indeterminate	1.8	n/a	n/a	1	1.5
Neck height (cm)	n/a	1.4	n/a	n/a	indeterminate	1.5	n/a	n/a	1	0.5
Total height (cm)	n/a	indeterminate	indeterminate	indeterminate	indeterminate	indeterminate	1.8	2.1	indeterminate	12
Thickness (cm)	0.4	0.7	0.4	0.6	0.65	0.6	0.6	0.7	0.7	0.3
Volume (ml)	indeterminate	indeterminate	indeterminate	indeterminate	indeterminate	indeterminate	n/a	n/a	indeterminate	indeterminate
Rim form	direct	slight flare	slightly everted	indeterminate	indeterminate	slightly everted	n/a	n/a	slight flare	slightly everted
Rim finish	flat	rounded	rounded	indeterminate	indeterminate	rounded	n/a	n/a	rounded	tapered
Shoulder	n/a	n/a	n/a	n/a	Gila	rounded	n/a	n/a	rounded?	n/a
Base shape	rounded	indeterminate	indeterminate	rounded	rounded	rounded	rounded	rounded	rounded	rounded
Interior surface finish	UP, blackened	SP, blackened	HS, blackened	UP	HS	HS	UP, blackened	indeterminate	SP	SP, blackened
Exterior surface finish	SP, fire clouded	UP, fire clouded	UP, fire clouded	UP	HS	SP, fire clouded	UP, fire clouded	UP	SP, fire clouded	SP, fire clouded
Modifications	none	repair hole	none	reworked rim	none	none	reworked into an informal plate	reworked into an informal plate	none	none
Use wear	none	none	none-indeterminate	none	base	none-indeterminate	none	exterior basal abrasion	none-indeterminate	none
Comments			exterior decoration	decoration is interior, exterior trailing lines; the rim has been reworked (ground to make it smooth after it had broken)		surface treatment identical to Gila Plain	reworked from jar base; dimensions are those of the reworked plate	reworked from jar base; dimensions are those of the reworked plate	base and portions of the body are missing	

Key: HS = hand smoothed; mbd = meters below datum; SP = striated polish; UP = uniform polish

Table 10 (continued).

	RV21	PV22	PV23	RV24	RV25	PV27	RV28	RV29	PV30	RV31
Feature	23	23	23	13	13	15	15	15	21	17
Bag number	405	400	403	795	792	894	898	894	374	141
Context	floor fill	floor fill	floor fill	on use-compacted surface	on use-compacted surface	fill	fill	fill	floor fill	isolated vessel
Type	Rincon Red	plain ware	plain ware	plain ware	plain ware	plain ware	Rincon Red	plain ware	polychrome effigy	plain ware
Completeness (%)	50	20	40	80	60	30	100 (reworked)	100 (reworked)	15	60
Vessel form	subhemispherical bowl	subhemispherical bowl	globular jar	indeterminate jar	neckless jar	shouldered jar	informal plate	informal plate	anthropomorphic?	globular jar
Temper	sand	sand	sand	sand and muscovite mica	sand	sand and muscovite mica	sand	sand	sand	sand
Petrofacies	Beehive Peak (J1)	not analyzed	Twin Hills (J2)	indeterminate	indeterminate	indeterminate	Beehive Peak (J1)	Beehive Peak (J1)	not analyzed	unanalyzed
Rim diameter (cm)	20	27	20	26	25	23	25	32	n/a	indeterminate
Orifice diameter (cm)	19.5	26.4	19	24	25	21	25	32	n/a	indeterminate
Aperture diameter (cm)	19.5	26.4	19	23	25	20	25	32	n/a	indeterminate
Throat diameter (cm)	n/a	na	19	23	n/a	indeterminate	n/a	n/a	n/a	indeterminate
Max. body diameter (cm)	20	27	indeterminate	45	indeterminate	indeterminate	25	32	(5.6 × 5.2)	47
Shoulder height (cm)	n/a	n/a	n/a	indeterminate	indeterminate	indeterminate	n/a	n/a	n/a	indeterminate
Rim height (cm)	n/a	n/a	1	1.5	indeterminate	1	n/a	n/a	n/a	indeterminate
Neck height (cm)	n/a	n/a	1	2	indeterminate	1.4	n/a	n/a	n/a	indeterminate
Total height (cm)	7	9	indeterminate	indeterminate	indeterminate	indeterminate	2.6	3.4	indeterminate	indeterminate
Thickness (cm)	0.5	0.6	0.7	0.5	1	0.4	0.5	1	0.5	0.5
Volume (ml)	indeterminate	indeterminate	indeterminate	indeterminate	indeterminate	indeterminate	indeterminate	indeterminate	indeterminate	indeterminate
Rim form	direct	direct	slight flare	slight flare	direct	slight flare	n/a	n/a	n/a	indeterminate
Rim finish	rounded	flat	rounded	rounded	rounded	tapered	n/a	n/a	n/a	indeterminate
Shoulder	n/a	n/a	rounded	rounded	rounded	Gila	n/a	n/a	n/a	rounded
Base shape	rounded	rounded	rounded	rounded	rounded	rounded	rounded	rounded	n/a	rounded
Interior surface finish	slip, SP	UP, fire clouded	HS, blackened	HS, blackened	HS, blackened	HS	SP, fire clouded	UP, blackened	unfinished, blackened	unfinished
Exterior surface finish	slip, SP	UP	UP, fire clouded	SP, fire clouded	UP, fire clouded	SP	SP, fire clouded	UP, fire clouded	UP	UP, fire clouded
Modifications	none	none	none	none	none	none	reworked rim	reworked into an informal plate	none	none
Use wear	exterior basal abrasion	exterior basal abrasion	indeterminate	none	none	none	none	none	none	exterior basal abrasion
Comments		lower portion of pot missing		surface treatment identical to Gila Plain			reworked from a bowl sherd; dimensions are those of the reworked plate	reworked from a jar sherd; dimensions are those of the reworked plate	red and white paint; all measurements taken from the single sherd that represents the vessel	J1 petrofacies assigned as temper by ceramic analyst; not part of the vessel petrographic sample

Key: HS = hand smoothed; mbd = meters below datum; SP = striated polish; UP = uniform polish sheetwash. Feature 23 yielded only six Rincon Red sherds.

A Rincon Red-on-brown, Style A flare-rimmed bowl (RV 2) was found on the floor (Level 3), with some sherds in floor fill contexts. RV 20, a Gila Plain "bean pot," and PV 23, a plain ware globular jar, derived from floor fill. Three additional vessels also were found in the floor fill (Level 2): RV 3, a white-slipped, Rincon Red-on-brown, Style A shouldered jar; RV 21, a subhemispherical Rincon Red bowl; and PV 22, a subhemispherical plain ware bowl. Fill deposits (Level 1) yielded a Rincon Red-on-brown, Style B shouldered jar (RV 1) (see Table 10).

The remaining pit houses (Features 22, 25, 27) produced fewer sherds, between 600 and 700 sherds each (see Table 6). Feature 22 is part of the cluster formed by Features 21–23. Level 3, roof fall/floor fill, produced the highest frequency of sherds in Feature 22, followed by roof fall (Level 2). Only one quadrant of the house was completely screened; floor fill only was screened in the remaining quadrants. The general layout of the house cluster suggests that Feature 22 could have been contemporaneous with Feature 21 or Feature 23, or both houses. The orientation of Feature 22, with its entry less than 2 m from the pit wall of Feature 21, makes contemporaneity of these two houses less likely. The archaeomagnetic data (Deaver and Murphy, Appendix B) suggest that Feature 22 was abandoned after Feature 21, which groups temporally with Features 25 and 27. Deaver and Murphy state that, although Feature 22 is later than Feature 25, it is not detectably later than Features 21 and 27. No calendrical date was provided for Feature 22; Deaver and Murphy suggest the low-latitude position of the sample may indicate a date around A.D. 1100.

Approximately 22 percent of the Feature 22 sherds were recovered from fill, a quantity similar to that recovered from fill in the early-abandoned Feature 23. About 26 percent of the unpainted sherds in the feature were too small to be analyzed, which is similar to the proportion in Feature 21. Feature 22 yielded 18 Rincon Red sherds.

A large, intrusive trash-filled pit (Feature 22.04) postdates the occupation of the structure. Although the feature description notes a high density of sherds in this pit, only 38 were recovered, 29 of which originated in the upper level of pit fill. Some of the sherds noted in the field also derived from two reconstructible vessels found in Feature 22.04: PV 5, a Rincon Polychrome shouldered jar or cauldron, and PV 6, a white-slipped Rincon Red-on-brown, Style B indeterminate jar.

Five additional vessels from Feature 22 were found in several contexts (see Table 10). RV 4, a Rincon Red-on-brown, Style A hemispherical bowl, was found on the floor. Three vessels derived from fill: RVs 17 and 18, informal plain ware plates reworked from jar bases, and

PV 19, an indeterminate plain ware jar, were found in Level 2. Pieces of RV 16, an indeterminate plain ware jar, were found in several different contexts, including fill, Level 3 floor fill, and pit fill. The recovery of conjoining sherds in different contexts indicates that the damage to the structure created by the intrusive pit Feature 22.04 was substantial. The number of reconstructible vessels in the upper levels of fill is consistent with the notion that these deposits represent secondary refuse.

The archaeomagnetic data (Deaver and Murphy, Appendix B) place Feature 22 as the last of the Sunset Mesa Ruin dated structures to be abandoned. There is no ceramic evidence that indicates this late an occupation, however. The quantity of sherds in the fill is more consistent with the earlier-abandoned houses. Clearly, there was occupation at Sunset Mesa Ruin postdating the use of Feature 22, as indicated by the intrusive pit that cuts through the structure, and the later use of the area may be responsible for the relatively high density of sherds in the fill. We must also assess the intrusive pit as a factor potentially disturbing the structure deposits.

Features 25 and 27 form a pair of houses located northwest of the Feature 21–23 cluster. Feature 25 yielded the second-smallest quantity of sherds (see Table 6). It differs from other structures in that the roof fall level (Level 1) yielded many more sherds than floor fill, representing two-thirds of recovered ceramics from that feature. Excavation methods do not seem responsible, as the fill from every unit was screened completely (see feature description). No reconstructible vessels were found in this house. Two archaeomagnetic dates were obtained from Feature 25, and they are temporally discrete, with the floor date earlier than the hearth date. The archaeomagnetic data place the Feature 25 floor context as the first to be abandoned at Sunset Mesa Ruin. The floor and later hearth dates bracket Feature 23. Deaver and Murphy (Appendix B) place Features 21, 25, and 27 as essentially contemporaneous, an assessment that is not contradicted by the ceramic data. Orientation indicates that Features 25 and 27 may have been paired, forming a courtyard group that included Feature 21. Feature 25 yielded 41 percent unpainted sherds that were too small to be analyzed, which is the highest proportion of small sherds among the houses. This suggests that natural erosional processes, rather than human activities, were responsible for filling the structure.

Feature 27 yielded the smallest quantity of sherds (see Table 6), including 11 Rincon Red sherds (1.8 percent). This structure was consistent with most other houses, in that most sherds from the structure derived from the floor fill/roof fall level, and few were found in other levels. Level 1 yielded 11 percent of the recovered sherds, whereas Level 2, floor fill, produced almost 40 percent. Feature 27 yielded a quantity of small unpainted sherds

(29 percent), similar to Features 21 and 22. A large, oval floor pit (Feature 27.03) produced almost as many sherds as the entire floor fill/roof fall level.

Two vessels were found in Feature 27 (see Table 10). One, a white-slipped Rincon Red-on-brown, Style B sub-hemispherical bowl (RV 10), was found on the floor. The second, PV 9, a Rincon Polychrome subhemispherical bowl, was found in the fill of the pit Feature 27.03. The relative scarcity of sherds in the house and the presence of vessels on the floor are consistent with the notion that the house was one of the later ones at Sunset Mesa Ruin to be abandoned, and that the sherds represent refuse deposited through natural processes.

Extramural Features

Extramural features yielded considerable quantities of ceramics, although only painted and red ware pottery was analyzed (see Table 7). Pottery was particularly abundant in Features 13 and 15, a ramada and food-preparation area located southeast of the pit houses. These features represented dense concentrations of artifacts. Burned posts in Feature 13 partially encompassed a use-compacted activity surface and evidently represented an outdoor food-storage and food-preparation area, as indicated by charred tansy mustard and maize remains, grinding stones, and other artifacts. Four reconstructible vessels were recovered from the activity surface of Feature 13: RV 13, a Rincon Red-on-brown, Style B hemispherical bowl; PV 14, an indeterminate-style Rincon Red-on-brown bowl; RV 24, a plain ware jar; and RV 25, a neckless plain ware jar (see Table 10).

Feature 15 lacked a definitive use-compacted activity surface, but represented a similarly dense artifact concentration along with considerable fire-cracked rock. No postholes were found. Cooking is a likely activity to have taken place in this feature; no grinding tools were noted, such as those found in Feature 13. Three vessels were found in Feature 15: PV 27, a shouldered plain ware jar; RV 28, an informal plate made from a Rincon Red bowl; and RV 29, also an informal plate, reworked from a plain ware jar (see Table 10).

There are no ceramic indicators that these features represent substantially earlier or later activities than the excavated pit houses. The quantity of sherds and reconstructible vessels, along with the other artifacts and activity indicators, such as pits, suggest primary refuse deposition in both features. We lack unpainted-sherd-size data to help confirm this interpretation. Rincon Red sherds were found in both features.

Small quantities of painted and red ware pottery were recovered from other extramural features, including Feature 18, the prehistoric irrigation canal; two pits (Features 20 and 47); midden areas (Features 31, 32, and 49);

an unidentified feature (Feature 26) containing sandstone and artifacts; and an unidentified, historical-period feature (Feature 40) containing sandstone, cobbles, charcoal, and burned rock (see Table 7). Reconstructible vessels were recovered from several features (see Table 10). The canal yielded RV 11, a Rincon Red-on-brown, Style B sub-hemispherical bowl. PV 12, a cauldron also identified as Rincon Red-on-brown, Style B, was found in the pit Feature 48. RV 15 was an isolated Sacaton Red-on-buff shouldered jar found during mechanical stripping and labeled Feature 16. Feature 17 also was an isolated vessel (RV 31), a globular, plain ware jar. This feature produced, in addition, nine painted sherds, including indeterminate buff ware and Rincon Red-on-brown, Style B sherds.

Basillio Cuevas Homestead (Feature 5)

Feature 5 was the historical-period structure representing the Basillio Cuevas homestead (see feature description, Chapter 5). We analyzed 38 prehistoric painted sherds, primarily Rincon Red-on-brown and indeterminate painted brown ware, from the excavation units in this structure (see Table 9). No Rincon Red or other red ware was recovered, and there were no reconstructible vessels in Feature 5. One indeterminate Papago Plain or Red sherd and four sherds representing possible Tohono O'odham pottery also were found in Feature 5, which was the only context at Sunset Mesa Ruin to yield historical-period Native American pottery. The number of prehistoric sherds and the mixture of these ceramics with the historical-context deposits clearly indicate a great deal of historical-period and modern disturbance to Sunset Mesa Ruin.

Painted Ceramics

Rincon phase painted pottery signifies a point of punctuation within the continuous painted pottery tradition of the Tucson Basin. Sometime during the Rincon phase, the local potters developed several technological innovations and began to employ diverse design templates. The product of these innovations was a ceramic fabric of unprecedented technological and stylistic diversity, one which has no parallels in the Hohokam pottery of the Phoenix area. Potters began to experiment with black pigments to render their bichromatic designs, and combined black, red, and white pigments and slips with the unslipped brown background in innovative ways to create diverse bichromatic and polychromatic schemes. This technological diversity was matched by stylistic diversity within the type originally defined as Rincon Red-on-brown. Rincon Red-on-brown pottery has been characterized as stylistically diverse since its initial description by Kelly et al. (1978:47–48), who stated,

> Our Rincon phase ceramics may contain still another ingredient, and one which is more difficult to isolate. Again in association with perfectly normal Rincon Red-on-brown, if such a varied style can be so described, are several vessels which show a divergence in an over-simplification of the design (not illustrated). Counterparts can be found within the very considerable range embraced by Gila Basin Sacaton Red-on-buff (see especially Gladwin and others 1937: Fig. 69c–e; Plates CXXXIV and CXXXVII) [Kelly et al. 1978:47].

This statement appears to allude to the co-occurrence in the same contexts of vessels with simple designs (which would be characterized today as Rincon Style A), and more-intricate, subdivided designs—or in the words of Kelly et al., "normal" designs—(Rincon Style B), which are the hallmark of the painted Rincon phase ceramics. Kelly et al.'s (1978:47) conclusion that there is little point in distinguishing these stylistically distinct designs from Rincon Red-on-brown is justifiable. The fact that diversity in design can be identified within the inclusive category of Rincon Red-on-brown pottery is important, however.

The diversity of design among Rincon phase painted ceramics, particularly when coupled with its extraordinary technological diversity, has created opportunities and problems for ceramicists working with this pottery. Ceramicists may choose among three approaches, which may also be combined in various ways. One approach is typological or classificatory, and attempts to use a type-variety system to encompass the range of stylistic and technological variability in painted pottery. Types, subtypes, and varieties can be defined based on such attributes as slip and paint color, and design characteristics. A second approach uses decorative styles within single types to describe the range of design variability. A third approach is to conduct an attribute seriation, using independent stratigraphic or chronometric evidence to define a sequence of change through time in painted pottery and technological variability. Each of these approaches has been used in some fashion to describe Rincon phase painted pottery.

The typological approach is the traditional one taken by Kelly et al. (1978) in describing the painted pottery of the Tucson Basin. Deaver (1984) also used aspects of the typological approach in his classifications, designating technological varieties and new types of Rincon phase painted pottery, and Wallace (1986b, 1986c) employed

typology to create temporally based subtypes of Rincon ceramics.

The design style approach was formalized by Deaver (1984), who defined seven styles of painted pottery, three of which applied to Rincon phase ceramics. His styles were based on "design structure, style of linework, and draftsmanship within the principal fields of decoration (the interior of bowls and jar exteriors) with the intent to identify horizon markers within the decorative development." Although the term "style" has been used broadly since Deaver's description of three Rincon phase painted styles, and is so used in this study, it should be noted that Deaver's concept differs somewhat from the way style is applied elsewhere in southwestern ceramic research. His styles apply to a single pottery type only. As Colton and Hargrave (1937:15) pointed out long ago, styles are not necessarily coterminous with types; a single style may be evident on different wares, and more than one style may be present on a single type. Years later, Carlson (1970) further restricted the definition of ceramic style, applying the term to a decorative design that crosscuts different wares (e.g., Pinedale Style; see discussion in Whittlesey 1989). We have yet to determine if Rincon styles also apply to Hohokam Buff Ware, or demonstrate potential relationships with other pottery wares.

At the same time that Deaver was developing his stylistic model, Henry Wallace was developing a similar approach. Ceramics from the Valencia site (AZ BB:13:15 [ASM]) were analyzed

> to develop a seriation of Rincon Red-on-brown based on controlled excavations and independent dating. . . . Tightly controlled samples from several of the pits and floor assemblages permitted a tentative seriation which compared favorably with Greenleaf's proposed "early," "middle," and "late" varieties [Wallace 1986c:19].

Additional projects permitted Wallace to refine the model, and it was presented in full in the 1986 report focusing on the West Branch site (AZ AA:16:3 [ASM]) (Wallace 1986b). Wallace's approach is a traditional typological one with the explicit purpose of temporal control. He defined three subtypes that were correlative with subdivisions of the Rincon phase. "At the present time," Wallace (1986c:21) wrote,

> it is most appropriate to work within the existing chronology, simply subdividing the Rincon phase according to the ceramic divisions that can be developed. The term "subtype" refers to a rung on the hierarchical ladder immediately below "type" and that comprises the range of variation of the "type" within one chronologically controlled segment of its history.

A design-based approach to categorizing variability in Rincon Red-on-brown pottery has several advantages. One is avoiding the inherent circularity of embedding temporal control in subtypes that are temporally defined. The stylistic classifications are free from the inherent temporal limitations defined by the subtypes, which have a one-to-one correlation with subphases. Decorative styles should be viewed as potentially overlapping, rather than mutually exclusive; we must hold open the possibility that different styles can be present in the same proveniences without the implication of temporal mixing (see, for example, Wallace's [1986a:153–154] discussion of the floor assemblage from Feature 19 at Tanque Verde Wash site [AZ BB:13:68 (ASM)]).

Second, a design-based approach permits ceramics to be evaluated by independent means. Reid's (1982:6) statement that "style should be a formal ceramic property unencumbered in its definition and measurement by behavioral denotations" signifies the importance of independent evaluation of stylistic definitions. Vessel form can impinge upon stylistic expression, and for this reason cannot be ignored. Vessel morphology need not be an integrated component of stylistic definitions, however (see Whittlesey 1987d). This allows for the inevitable presence of designs presumed to be early on vessel forms thought to be later. For example, the Gladwin et al. (1937) plates referenced by Kelly et al. (1978) in their discussion of design variability in Rincon Red-on-brown illustrate Sacaton Red-on-buff vessels that employ simplified, presumably "early" designs, yet have Gila shoulders and the short, everted rims we associate with Sedentary period pottery. Defining styles independently of other technological attributes, such as vessel form and temper, permits the independent evaluation of design style with technological and morphological attributes that may have greater temporal resolution than elements of design.

Contrary to Wallace's (1995:446) contention that chronological control must be achieved prior to an examination of style, style can be studied without controlling for time. A third advantage of a design-based approach is that, far from excluding the chronological evaluation of style, such evaluation is facilitated. If ceramics in particular deposits or floor assemblages are classified using Deaver's (1984) stylistic approach (or indeed, any other design-based approach), they can in turn be subjected to any number of independent evaluations, including application of independent chronometric data. This is not to suggest that the styles are not temporally sensitive. Throughout the Southwest, there are horizon styles that are geographically widespread and temporally distinct. Maintaining the independence of style and chronological control strengthens each.

A final advantage of a design-based model is that it can be applied to individual sherds and vessels. As Wallace

(1986b, 1986c) makes clear in his discussion of the West Branch ceramic seriation, the criteria used to define deposits representing subphases are based on *all* of the ceramics from that deposit (see discussion in Wallace 1986b:144–147). The deposit is "dated"—assigned to a subphase on the basis of temporally sensitive criteria—and then the individual sherds or vessels in that deposit can be assigned to subtypes. In addition to its inherent circularity, this usage precludes researchers from defining independent means of assigning individual sherds and vessels to styles or chronologically sensitive "subtypes."

The following discussion treats the two Rincon Red-on-brown styles present at Sunset Mesa Ruin, Style A and Style B, separately, and also addresses the indeterminate-style Rincon Red-on-brown pottery that could not be identified according to style.

Rincon Red-on-brown, Style A

Deaver (1984:259–262) defined Rincon Red-on-brown, Style A in terms of a preference for "banded" layouts (the decorative elements are arranged in linear rows with or without framing lines), and the repetition of only one or two elements over the decorative field. These characteristics suggest that Style A was derived from the Colonial period style (Deaver 1984:259). Style A is similar to the simplified variant of Rincon Red-on-brown alluded to by Kelly et al. (1978:39) and to Greenleaf's (1975:50) presumed early Rincon style, which was formally defined by Wallace (1986c:22–36; see also Heidke 1995:297–311). The salient characteristics that distinguish Rincon Style A from its Colonial period predecessor (Rillito Red-on-brown) are the simplification of the design layout and, less important, the poor or sloppy execution of the design coupled with heavier line work (Deaver 1984:259). Style A also uses layouts characterized by elements arranged in simple horizontal (Figure 36f), oblique (see Figure 36c), and zigzag (see Figure 36a, b) rows. The more complex, horizontal-oblique rows found on Colonial period ceramics (Deaver 1984:Figure 4.5a, e) are simplified and occur less often in Rincon Style A (Figure 36e).

The offset-quartered layout continued throughout the Colonial and Sedentary period sequence. On pottery dating to the Colonial period, the quadrants of such layouts lack additional, well-delineated subdivisions (Figure 37a, b). During the Sedentary period, there appears to have been a growing preference for subdividing the design field in various ways. In Rincon Style A, we begin to see the use of bounded or bordered units, typically called panels (Deaver 1984), within the quadrants. Multiple bordered subdivisions or panels within the quadrants are rare, however; the bordered units fill the quadrants horizontally or vertically (see Figure 37c, d; Figure 38).

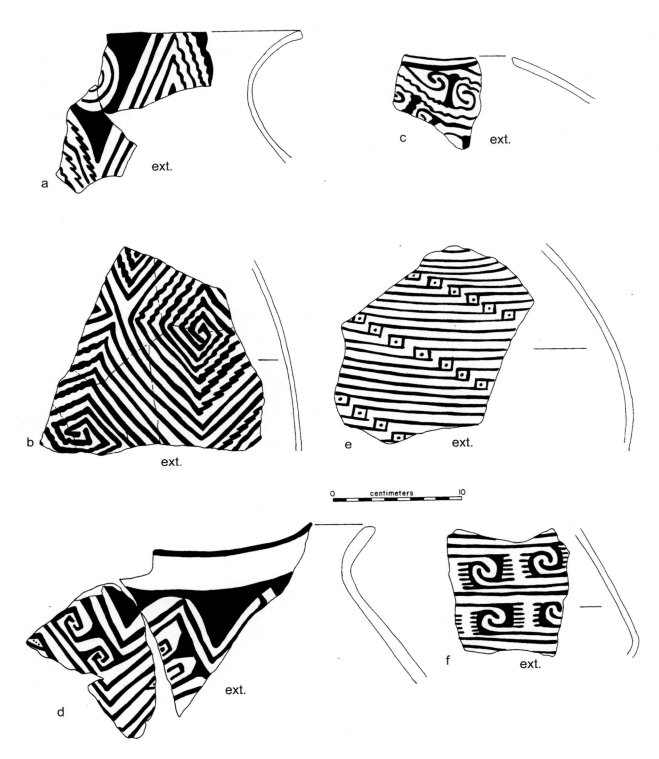

Figure 36. Rincon Red-on-brown, Style A sherds from Sunset Mesa Ruin: (a, c, e, f) unslipped; (b, d) white-slipped.

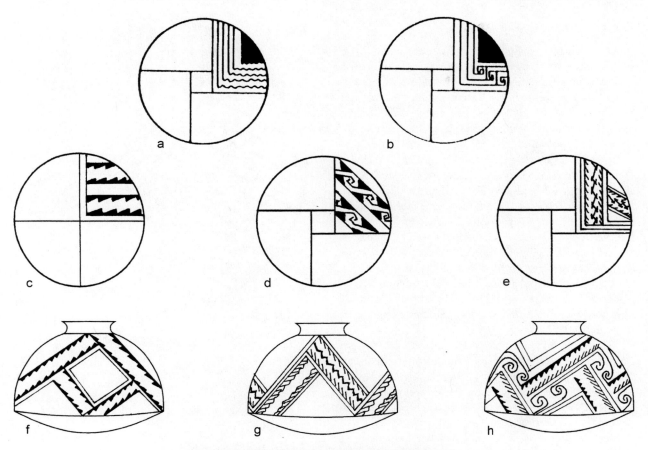

Figure 37. Examples of bowl and jar design layouts:
(a–b) unpaneled; (c–e) paneled interior bowl layouts; (f–h) paneled exterior jar layouts.

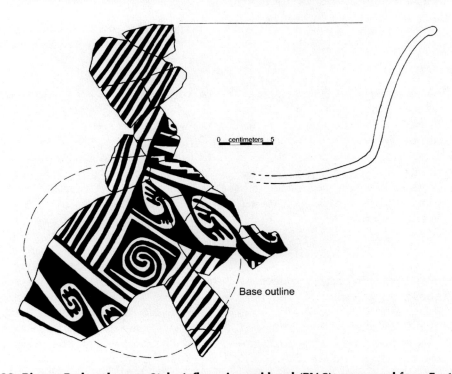

0 centimeters 5

Base outline

Figure 38. Rincon Red-on-brown, Style A flare-rimmed bowl (PV 8), recovered from Feature 21.

Distribution

Rincon Red-on-brown, Style A is represented by 63 sherds and 4 reconstructible vessels (see Table 5). The style was thus relatively rare at Sunset Mesa Ruin, representing 8.6 percent of all Rincon painted sherds, and 26.7 percent of all Rincon painted pottery that could be identified by style. Among the pit houses, no Style A pottery was recovered from Feature 25 or Feature 27.

Style A was most frequent in Feature 21 (9 of the 10 sherds identifiable by style). All 9 of these Style A sherds are white slipped, and were found in the roof fall of this feature (see Table 6). In addition, one Style A vessel (PV 8) (see Figure 38) was found in the deposits between the two floors of Feature 21, and in the roof fall and upper floor fill levels. Eight of 21 identifiable-style sherds from Feature 22 (38.1 percent) are Rincon Style A; all were in the Level 1 fill deposit (see Table 6). A second Style A vessel (RV 4) was recovered from the floor of Feature 22. This bowl (see Table 10) exhibits a trisected design layout (Figure 39).

Sixteen of 25 identifiable sherds in Feature 23 (64 percent) are Style A, and were recovered from floor fill and floor contexts (see Table 6). The remaining two Style A reconstructible vessels were recovered from Feature 23; one (RV 2) was found on the floor (Figure 40), and the second (RV 3) derived from floor fill (Figure 41).

Rincon Style A was present in limited quantities in extramural contexts (see Table 7). It was found in Feature 15, the extramural kitchen, representing 25 of the feature's 70 Rincon painted sherds that were identifiable by style (35.7 percent). It also was present in Feature 31, a midden area (5 of 30 identifiable sherds, or 16.7 percent).

Technological Variability

Technological variation among Rincon Red-on-brown, Style A ceramics is limited compared to Rincon Red-on-brown, Style B. Nine of the 63 sherds (14.3 percent) and one of the reconstructible vessels (25 percent) classified as Rincon Style A exhibit a white slip applied to the decorative field (see Table 5). None of the Style A sherds represent Rincon Black-on-brown, however; the use of black pigment is restricted to Rincon Style B and indeterminate-style Rincon phase painted pottery.

Vessel Form

Previous research in the Tucson Basin has suggested that vessel form has a strong temporal signal (Deaver 1984; Greenleaf 1975; Heidke 1995; Kelly et al. 1978; Wallace 1985, 1986b, 1986c; Whittlesey 1986a). Kelly et al. (1978:41) described a dramatic drop in the production of flare-rimmed bowls at Hodges Ruin (AZ AA:12:18

0   centimeters   5

Figure 39. Rincon Red-on-brown, Style A bowl (RV 4), recovered from Feature 22.

[ASM]) between the late Colonial period and the Rincon phase. Although Deaver (1984:307) and Wallace (1986c:37) documented the presence of the flare-rimmed bowl in contexts postdating the Colonial period, it is limited almost exclusively to the early portion of the Sedentary period. The subhemispherical (or outcurved) bowl form is thought to have replaced the flare-rimmed bowl by the middle portion of that period. At Sunset Mesa Ruin, the frequency of the flare-rimmed bowl form (see Figures 38 and 40) is greater among Style A ceramics (47 percent of sherds and 66.7 percent of reconstructible vessels) than among Style B pottery (1.3 percent of sherds and none of the reconstructible vessels) (Table 11).

Jar shapes also changed during the Sedentary period. The rounded shoulders and tall, gently curving necks found on Colonial period jars were replaced by the squat, sharp Gila shoulder and short, abrupt neck forms (Deaver 1984; Kelly et al. 1978; Wallace 1986c; Whittlesey

interior

0   centimeters   5

exterior

Figure 40. Rincon Red-on-brown, Style A flare-rimmed bowl (RV 2), recovered from Feature 23.

0   cm   3

Figure 41. Rincon Red-on-brown, Style A (white-slipped variant) shouldered jar (RV 3), recovered from Feature 23.

Table 11. Vessel Form among Rincon Red-on-brown and Rincon Black-on-brown Ceramics

Vessel Form	Style A			Style B			Indeterminate Style		
	Sherds		RVs	Sherds		RVs	Sherds		RVs
	n	%	n	n	%	n	n	%	n
Bowls									
Indeterminate	—	—	—	18	22.8	—	174	66.7	1
Flare-rimmed	8	47.0	2	1	1.3	—	21	8.0	—
Subhemispherical	9	53.0	1	57	72.1	2	61	23.4	—
Hemispherical	—	—	—	3	3.8	1	5	1.9	—
Subtotal bowls	17	100.0	3	79	100.0	3	261	100.0	1
Jars									
Indeterminate	17	42.5	—	80	85.1	1	207	88.5	—
Globular	21	52.5	—	6	6.4	—	8	3.4	—
Neckless	2	5.0	—	—	—	—	2	0.8	—
Gila-shouldered	—	—	1	8	8.5	1	17	7.3	—
Subtotal jars	40	100.0	1	94	100.0	2	234	100.0	0
Other									
Cauldron	6	100.0	—	—	—	1	—	—	—
Scoop	—	—	—	—	—	—	2	100.0	—
Subtotal other	6	100.0	0	0	0.0	1	2	100.0	0
Total	63	100.0	4	173	100.0	6	497	100.0	1

1986a). The vessel forms evidenced by the Style A rim sherds are consistent with the short neck characteristic of Sedentary period jars, yet globular or round-shouldered jars are the dominant jar form among the Style A sherds (see Table 11). None of the jar sherds exhibit the sharp or Gila shoulder, although there is one reconstructible jar with a Gila shoulder (RV 3; see Figure 41).

Temper

The use of foliated metamorphic rocks as one temper constituent is, like vessel form, thought to have temporal meaning (Deaver 1984:318; Wallace 1986a:89–90, 1986c:22). Deaver (1984:318) and Wallace (1986c:22) have argued that the use of schist or gneiss as a tempering agent was most frequent during the Colonial period and the early portion of the Rincon phase. The dominant temper in the Rincon Red-on-brown, Style A sherds from Sunset Mesa Ruin is undifferentiated sand (n = 49, or 77.8 percent). The remaining 14 Style A sherds (22.2 percent) were tempered with metamorphic material (schist or gneiss).

Rincon Red-on-brown and Rincon Black-on-brown, Style B

Six reconstructible vessels and 173 sherds from the Sunset Mesa Ruin collection were classified as Rincon Style B (see Table 5). Deaver (1984:262) defined Style B as "a recrystallization of the pottery craft . . . a movement away from the banded designs toward geometric, grid-like patterns in plaited and paneled designs for both bowls and jars." The bordered subdivisions or panels can occur on bowls and jars. Multiple, bordered subdivisions of the design field, which often overlap in the complicated pattern resembling woven textiles that Deaver labels plaiting, are the hallmark of the Style B design repertoire (see Figure 37c–h). The triangles and diamonds created by these layouts can in turn be subdivided (Figure 42; see Deaver 1984:Figure 4.8b) or filled with a single element (Figure 43; see Deaver 1984:Figure 4.10d; Wallace 1985:Figure 7.8a). A common motif is multiple subdivision of the design field in conjunction with interlocking and single scrolls (Figure 44a, c, e, f). Another

Figure 42. Rincon Red-on-brown, Style B shouldered jar (RV 1), recovered from Feature 23.

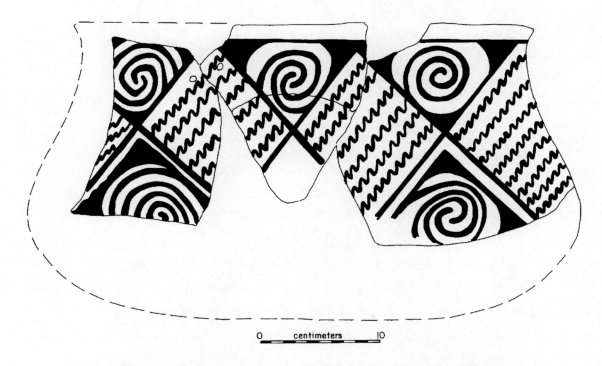

Figure 43. Rincon Red-on-brown, Style B cauldron (RV 12), recovered from Feature 48.

Figure 44. Rincon Red-on-brown and Rincon Black-on-brown, Style B pottery from Sunset Mesa Ruin: (a, e, f) Rincon Red-on-brown; (b–c) Rincon Red-on-brown, white-slipped variant; (d) Rincon Black-on-brown, white-slipped variant.

distinguishing characteristic that separates Style B from Style A and Colonial period pottery is the use of several different design units or motifs, rather than the repetition of only one or two (Deaver 1984:262) (Figure 45; compare a, b with c, d).

Distribution

Because it is more abundant relative to Style A, Rincon Style B ceramics were more widely distributed. Style B was found among all the pit houses and most of the extramural features, representing 23.6 percent of all Rincon phase painted pottery and 73.3 percent of sherds that

were identifiable to style (see Tables 6 and 7). Pit house Feature 21, which had the highest proportion of Style A sherds, correspondingly had the lowest percentage of Style B sherds (1 of 10 identifiable-style Rincon painted sherds). Thirteen of 21 identifiable-style sherds from Feature 22 (61.9 percent) are Style B, as are 9 of 25 identifiable sherds from Feature 23 (36 percent) and all of the identifiable sherds from Features 25 and 27. Extramural contexts with a high proportion of (or all) Style B sherds include Features 13, 18, 31, and 32 (see Table 7).

One Rincon Style B vessel (PV 6; Figure 46) was found in the late-abandoned Feature 22, in the fill of the intrusive pit Feature 22.04. A Style B jar (RV 1; see Figure 42)

Figure 45. Rincon Red-on-brown, Style A and Style B vessels (not to scale): (a) Style A, from Los Morteros (Heidke 1995:Figure 5.39); (b) Style A, from Hodges Ruin (Kelly et al. 1978:Figure 4.25c); (c) Style B, from the Tanque Verde Wash site (Wallace 1986b:Figure 6.6d); (d) Style B, from AZ DD:8:122 (ASM) (Doyel 1977a:Figure 14a; see also Deaver 1984:Figure 4.9a).

Figure 46. Rincon Red-on-brown, Style B (white-slipped variant) jar (PV 6), recovered from Feature 22.04.

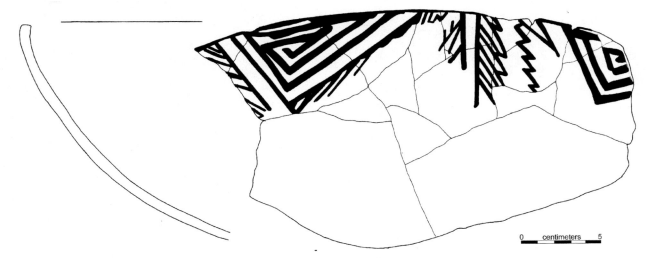

Figure 47. Rincon Red-on-brown, Style B (white-slipped variant) subhemispherical bowl (RV 10), recovered from Feature 27.

was found in the early-abandoned Feature 23, in the upper levels of fill. The floor of Feature 27 yielded RV 10, a bowl (Figure 47). Feature 27 is considered by Deaver and Murphy (Appendix B) to be one of the later-abandoned houses at the site, and is thought to be essentially contemporaneous with Features 21 and 25. Three reconstructible, Style B vessels were found in extramural contexts. RV 13 (Figure 48) was found on the use-compacted activity surface of Feature 13, and Feature 18 (the canal)

yielded RV 11 (Figure 49). Feature 48 also contained a Style B vessel, PV 12 (see Figure 43).

Technological Variability

The appearance of black pigment in the Rincon phase has been documented by several researchers (Deaver 1984:322, 1989b:71–73; Doyel 1977a:36, 80; Ervin 1983:25; Wallace 1986c:37). Deaver (1984:322, 1989b:71–73) and

Figure 48. Rincon Red-on-brown, Style B bowl (RV 13), recovered from Feature 13.

0   centimeters   10

Figure 49. Rincon Red-on-brown, Style B bowl (RV 11), recovered from Feature 18.

Wallace (1986c:37) have argued that the appearance of black pigment can be dated to the middle portion of the Rincon phase. Rincon Black-on-brown (Deaver 1984:322–326) is represented by 19 sherds at Sunset Mesa Ruin; all of these are Style B (11 percent of Style B sherds) (see Table 5). The remaining 154 sherds (89 percent) and the 6 reconstructible vessels have red-painted designs (see Table 5). The frequency of white-slipped Rincon Red-on-brown and Rincon Black-on-brown pottery is thought to have increased over the span of the phase (Deaver 1984:Table 4.3; Heidke 1995:306; Wallace 1986a:146, 1986c:37; Whittlesey 1986a:92). Forty-two Style B sherds (24.3 percent) exhibit a white slip. There is evidently a correlation between the use of black pigment and white slip applied to the decorated field (Deaver 1984:322, 1989b:71–73; Wallace 1986c:37). At Sunset Mesa Ruin, only 1 Style B sherd with black pigment did not also have a white slip.

Vessel Form

Previous research has suggested that the Colonial–Sedentary period transition marked a dramatic decrease in the use of the flare-rimmed bowl form (Deaver 1984; Heidke 1995; Wallace 1986c). Similarly, the appearance of the

Gila shoulder on jars has been associated with the middle portion of the Rincon phase (Deaver 1984; Wallace 1986c). At Sunset Mesa Ruin, Rincon Style B and Style A ceramics show a marked difference in vessel forms (see Table 11). The number of Style B flare-rimmed bowls decreases relative to Style A; there is only one flare-rimmed bowl sherd (1.3 percent), and none of the reconstructible vessels represent this form. The dominant Rincon Style B bowl form is subhemispherical (57 sherds, or 72.1 percent, and 2 of 3 reconstructible bowls). Among jar forms, the acute, or Gila, shoulder is present primarily on vessels classified as Rincon Style B. It represents 8.5 percent of Style B sherds compared to none of the Style A sherds, and one of two reconstructible jars, RV 1 (see Figure 42); the second is of indeterminate form (see Table 11).

Temper

Style A and Style B ceramics differ little in temper. The dominant temper among Style B sherds, as among Style A, is sand. The relative percentage of sherds with schist temper (13.9 percent, n = 24) is only slightly lower than that recorded for the Style A sherds (22.2 percent, n = 14).

Rincon Red-on-brown and Rincon Black-on-brown, Indeterminate Style

This category consists of 497 sherds and one reconstructible vessel (see Table 5) that exhibit characteristics of the type Rincon Red-on-brown or Rincon Black-on-brown (i.e., a rim with a painted lip), but are not large enough, or do not have sufficient diagnostic characteristics, to permit a finer classification by style. These sherds constitute most of the Rincon phase painted sherd collection (67.7 percent). They also are the most widely distributed of all Rincon painted sherds, having been found in almost all proveniences at Sunset Mesa Ruin (see Tables 6–9).

Technological Variability

White-slipped sherds represent 17.1 percent, and black-painted sherds 3.4 percent, of the indeterminate-style sherds (see Table 5). These percentages contrast with 24.3 percent white-slipped and 11 percent black-painted sherds among Style B, and 14.3 percent white-slipped and no black-painted Style A sherds. This implies, but does not confirm, that many of the black-painted sherds represent vessels that would be classified as having Style B designs if they were larger or more clearly painted.

Vessel Form

As Table 11 indicates, the vessel forms represented among the indeterminate-style Rincon sherds (rims and bodies) differ from those found on both Style A and Style B sherds. Flare-rimmed bowls, which predominate among Style A sherds, represent 8 percent of indeterminate-style sherds. Subhemispherical bowls, which are 72.1 percent of Style B sherds, represent 23.4 percent of the indeterminate sherd collection (see Table 11). It is possible that the much larger collection of indeterminate-style sherds is more representative of vessel forms in Rincon phase painted pottery than the smaller Style A and Style B collections. Inferences about vessel form and design style presented above should therefore be accepted with caution.

Temper

Most of the indeterminate-style sherds are tempered with sand (n = 455, or 91.5 percent). Forty-one sherds exhibit a sand and schist mixture, and only one sherd that contains volcanic sand was identified. The latter contains dark red or maroon (possibly rhyolitic), well-rounded inclusions in large quantities. This material was also observed in sherds identified as tempered with undifferentiated sand, but in much smaller quantities.

Rincon Phase Polychromes

Sometime during the Rincon phase, polychrome pottery began to be produced in the Tucson Basin. This pottery, representing one of the earliest polychrome traditions in the Southwest, exhibits considerable technological and design variation. Although previously recognized by Isabel Kelly (as cited in Greenleaf 1975:67), Rincon Polychrome was first formally defined by Greenleaf (1975:67–73). His description was based on 67 sherds and 3 vessels, recovered primarily from the Tucson area (Greenleaf 1975:113–114). He summarized Rincon Polychrome as follows:

> Rincon Polychrome was created by applying black and white designs on a slipped and polished redware. In general, the pottery utilized was constructed of the same materials and was finished in the same manner as Rincon Redware. The paste, temper, color of slip, and surface finish were identical. All shapes common to Rincon Red, as well as the low-shouldered, incurved jar form, were utilized. Fine mica particles, however, were notably absent from the polychrome vessels [Greenleaf 1975:67].

In his original description of Rincon Polychrome, Greenleaf (1975:67) characterized the black pigment as

carbon. Deaver (1984:326) subsequently conducted refiring experiments, and concluded that the pigment used is mineral (see also Wallace 1986c:84).

Greenleaf's (1975:68–73) discussion of design draws distinctions within Rincon Red-on-brown, and only hints at the possibility of design variability. He observed that "the overall concept gave the effect of bold use of open, widely spaced, simple major design elements" (Greenleaf 1975:70). "[E]ven from a relatively small collection," he wrote, "there was a considerable range in the decorative treatment on Rincon Polychrome" (Greenleaf 1975:73), and he noted that Isabel Kelly had thought two types might be present in polychrome ceramics. Because similar elements were used among different vessels and combined in consistent ways, Greenleaf (1975:73) concluded that "Rincon Polychrome would best be understood as the end result of local decorative experiments upon the local redware," with elements borrowed from Hohokam Buff Ware and White Mountain Red Ware.

Subsequent research has confirmed the extraordinary design variation that exists within Rincon phase polychrome pottery. It may not be too extreme to state that no two vessels are the same, in contrast to later Tanque Verde Red-on-brown, which exhibits equally extraordinary design homogeneity (Whittlesey 1987d, 1988). The variability in design structure, layout, and color scheme in Rincon Polychrome appears to preclude an all-inclusive, workable type description. Attempts to cope with this variability have created a situation that can be described as highly confused, at best. Some researchers have employed a typological strategy to define new polychrome types. Deaver (1984:328–229), for example, defined Sahuarita Polychrome on the basis of five sherds recovered from the Rosemont area. The type was described as combining the exterior decoration of Rio Rico Polychrome (Doyel 1977a) with a red-slipped interior. Exterior decoration might be black-on-brown, red-on-brown, or polychrome red, black, and brown (Deaver 1984:328). The few sherds were too small to discuss design in a meaningful fashion.

Another solution has been to define multiple variants of the type Rincon Polychrome (Table 12). The placement of the three colors on the vessel and the ways in which colors are combined appear to govern definition of these variants. Further confusing the situation, Heidke (1995:336) has defined a bichrome variant of Rincon Polychrome, and argues that some of the previously defined variants of Rincon Polychrome are really bichromes, "as only one color of paint was used in the decorated portion of the vessel." The white-on-red vessel from Los Morteros (AZ AA:12:57 [ASM]) described by Heidke (1995:336-342) as Rincon Polychrome, bichrome variant, cannot be considered polychrome, as by definition a polychrome must exhibit more than two colors (Carlson

Table 12. Rincon Polychrome Color Combinations

Color Combination	Reference
Red-and-black-on-brown exterior, red interior[a]	Ervin (1983:41)
Black-on-brown exterior, red interior[a]	Wallace (1986a:Figure 3.5j)
Black-on-white exterior, red interior	Wallace (1986a:Figure 3.4e)
Black-on-red interior, red exterior	Wallace (1986a:Figure 3.6b)
Black-and-white-on-red interior, red exterior	Wallace (1986a:Figure 3.5d)
White-on-red	Heidke (1995:Figure 5.10c–d)

[a] Could be classified as Sahuarita Polychrome (Deaver 1984:328–329)

1982:201). Further, there is no stipulation concerning the placement of color combinations on the vessel to define a pottery type as polychrome. For example, if we were to use Heidke's (1995:336) reasoning, we would not describe Gila Polychrome as a polychrome, because it has only one color of paint in the decorated portion of the vessel.

This taxonomically confused situation illustrates extremely well both the technological variation within Rincon phase painted pottery, and the inherent limitations of using a typological framework to describe variation. Moreover, expanding typological categories to encompass variation obscures the intriguing and behaviorally significant implications of extreme design and technological variability. A cursory review of the literature (e.g., Bubemyre 1996; Greenleaf 1975; Wallace 1986c) reveals that almost every Rincon Polychrome vessel is unique in the structure of the design layout, elements of painted decoration, and use of the black, white and red color scheme—as if these ceramics were the product of either a few extraordinarily inventive potters, or a large group of potters employing different conventions. Research effort should be invested in attempting to discover the behaviors responsible for this intriguing diversity, its implications for the organization of ceramic production and distribution, and other ramifications, rather than masking variability through taxonomic devices. Toward this end, we offer descriptive information for the three polychrome vessels recovered from Sunset Mesa Ruin.

Partial Vessel 5

This vessel (Figure 50) is a restricted-orifice vessel with a Gila shoulder (see Table 10), recovered from an intrusive pit (Feature 22.04) cut into the fill of the pit house Feature 22. Interior and exterior surfaces of the entire vessel are coated with the red slip characteristic of Rincon Red pottery. The decorative fields were delimited by the application of a white slip over the red, which defines unconnected, floating design units or medallions of varied shapes. These floating design units recall those used on the polychrome vessels illustrated by Greenleaf (1975:Figure 3.22a, c). The painted designs within the floating units were executed with black pigment. The largest white-slipped areas are triangular with rounded corners. The central unit, which provides the most completely preserved painted designs, is subdivided by bounded subunits or panels that are slightly oblique to the rim line. These smaller units are filled with scrolls and wavy-capped fringe motifs that are characteristic of Rincon Red-on-brown, Style B (see Figure 44a, c, d, f).

Partial Vessel 9

A subhemispherical bowl, PV 9 (Figure 51) has a red-slipped interior and a black-on-brown design on the exterior (see Table 10). The exterior placement of the design is rare on subhemispherical bowls, which provide a shallow exterior decorative field. Typically, exterior decoration is reserved for jars and cauldron forms. In color placement and combination, this vessel meets Deaver's (1984:328–329) criteria for the type Sahuarita Polychrome. Its design layout and treatment are consistent with Rincon phase red-on-brown and black-on-brown painted pottery. In light of the small sample of Sahuarita Polychrome ceramics, and the status of this type as a "hybrid" of two other, relatively rare and poorly defined types (Rincon Polychrome and Rio Rico Polychrome), we have chosen not to categorize the vessel as Sahuarita Polychrome.

The design shows a striking similarity to a partial vessel from the Tanque Verde Wash site (Wallace 1986a:Figure 6.5a). The bordered units (panels) in this design create the woven or plaited effect. The panels are filled with opposing, straight-line fringes, with a zigzag central element typical of Rincon Red-on-brown, Style B. The rim is painted black, and in some areas covers the interior red slip, suggesting that the red slip was applied first. Abrasion on the exterior portion of the rim may indicate that the vessel was used as a scoop.

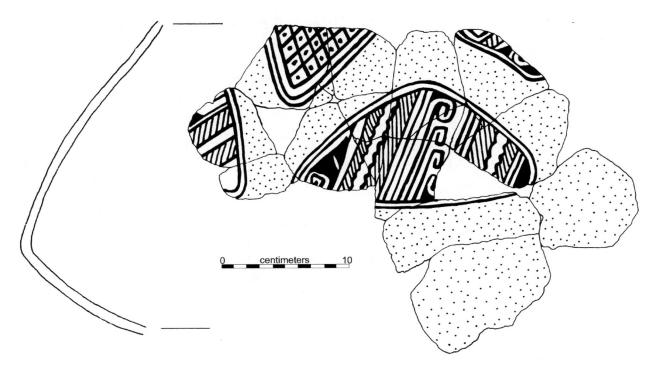

Figure 50. Rincon Polychrome shouldered jar or cauldron (PV 5), recovered from Feature 22.04.

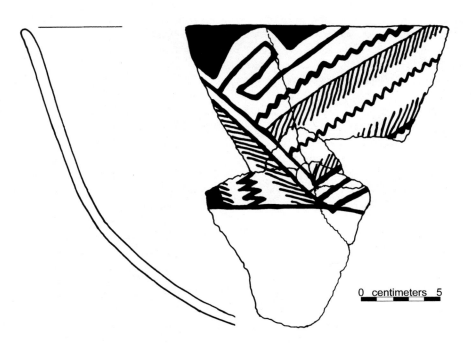

Figure 51. Rincon Polychrome bowl (PV 9), recovered from Feature 27.03.

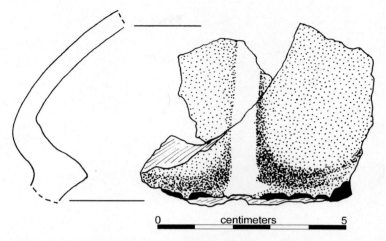

Figure 52. Polychrome anthropomorphic (?) effigy vessel (PV 30), recovered from Feature 21.

Partial Vessel 30

This unusual vessel (Figure 52) was recovered from floor fill context in Feature 21 (see Table 10). It could represent a portion of a human effigy vessel, although other possibilities certainly exist in light of its fragmentary condition. A sharp "shoulder" represents the juncture between parts of the possible body, along which the vessel broke. The brown paste is typical of Tucson Basin painted pottery; it is sandy, with some muscovite mica and possibly small schist or gneiss fragments. The interior is blackened and the exterior unslipped and lightly polished. White slip or paint separates the two protuberances that may represent anatomical parts. The juncture exhibits tiny areas of reddish brown paint typical of Rincon Red-on-brown; it is impossible to determine the original design, although it could represent wavy lines.

The vessel may represent a censer or effigy container. The existing portion is hollow, clearly suggesting a container rather than figurine. Depending on orientation, the vessel could be perceived as the ventral side of a human upper torso (chest or breasts), or the dorsal side of the lower torso (buttocks). Haury (1976:Figure 12.15s) illustrated an effigy vessel that could be similar to the former.

Intrusive Ceramics: Hohokam Buff Ware

Painted intrusive pottery in the Sunset Mesa Ruin collection is exclusively from the Phoenix Basin. Hohokam Buff Ware pottery constitutes 12.1 percent (n = 236) of the painted sherds, and 5.2 percent of the total sherd collection recovered from pit houses (see Table 5). Two Sacaton Red-on-buff vessels make up 6.7 percent of the reconstructible vessel collection and 12.5 percent of the painted vessels (see Table 10). Sacaton Red-on-buff (n = 125) is the only type represented among the sherds that could be identified by type. The remainder are indeterminate red-on-buff (98 sherds) or indeterminate buff ware (13 sherds). One Gila-shouldered jar (RV 15) (see Figure 32), which was an isolated vessel in Feature 16, and one miniature cauldron (RV 7) (Figure 53), found in Feature 21, also were classified as Sacaton Red-on-buff.

Some Sacaton Red-on-buff sherds from Sunset Mesa Ruin exhibit a sectioned or subdivided design creating a plaited effect, with a fringe motif characteristic of the type. The design layout on RV 15 consists of interlocking, rectilinear scrolls arranged in oblique rows. This

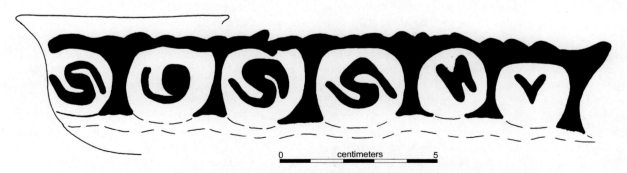

Figure 53. Miniature Sacaton Red-on-buff cauldron (RV 7), recovered from Feature 21.

Table 13. Hohokam Buff Ware Vessel Forms

Vessel Form	Sacaton Red-on-buff			Indeterminate Red-on-buff		
	Sherds (Rims and Bodies)		RVs	Sherds (Rims and Bodies)		RVs
	n	%	n	n	%	n
Bowls						
Flare-rimmed	10	33.3	—	1	2.4	—
Indeterminate	20	66.7	—	41	97.6	—
Subtotal bowls	30	100.0	0	42	100.0	0
Jars						
Gila-shouldered	11	11.6	1	15	33.3	—
Indeterminate	84	88.4	—	30	66.7	—
Subtotal jars	95	100.0	1	45	100.0	0
Other						
Miniature cauldron	—	—	1	0	—	—
Scoop	—	—	—	1	25.0	—
Plate	—	—	—	3	75.0	—
Subtotal other	0	0.0	1	4	100.0	0
Indeterminate form	—	—	0	7	100.0	—
Total	125	100.0	2	98	100.0	0

layout is characteristic of the Colonial period (Gladwin et al. 1937:Plate CLVIIe, f, h, i), and may be analogous to Rincon Red-on-brown, Style A designs as defined by Deaver (1984).

Sacaton Red-on-buff was most abundant in extramural Feature 15, which alone yielded 68.8 percent of all Sacaton Red-on-buff sherds. Sherds were found in most other proveniences; none were found in the canal (Feature 18). In pit house contexts, Sacaton Red-on-buff was most abundant in Feature 21, which yielded 16 sherds, or 12.8 percent of recovered Sacaton Red-on-buff (see Tables 6–9).

Vessel forms differ between red-on-brown and red-on-buff ceramics. We identified 357 Rincon painted sherds as bowls and 368 as jars, for a bowl-to-jar ratio of almost 1:1 (see Table 11). Among Sacaton Red-on-buff sherds, roughly 25 percent are bowls, for a ratio of about 3 jars to 1 bowl (Table 13). The flare-rimmed bowl is the only identifiable bowl form in the Sunset Mesa Ruin collection. There are no identifiable globular jar sherds; all have acute, Gila shoulders. These patterns also differ from Rincon painted pottery, which exhibits greater variability in vessel forms. Twenty-five of 64 jar sherds having determinable forms (39.6 percent) are Gila-shouldered jars, and neckless jar forms also are present (compare Tables 11 and 13). Among bowls, there are subhemispherical, hemispherical, and flare-rimmed forms.

Unpainted Ceramics

Plain Ware

We analyzed 2,481 plain ware sherds, exclusive of indeterminate unpainted sherds, of which there are 2,368 body sherds and 113 rim sherds. Eleven plain ware reconstructible vessels were recovered and examined.

Vessel Form

Plain ware represents the utilitarian pottery that presumably was made within the Tucson Basin. This category can potentially inform, therefore, on domestic activities related to food preparation, consumption, and storage. We assume that utilitarian pottery was constructed and designed for, but not limited to, a specific functional purpose. Several studies using ethnographic cross-cultural comparisons extrapolated to archaeological data have attempted to arrive at original vessel function using morphological characteristics (Braun 1980; Crown 1984; Lindauer 1988; Whittlesey 1994). Each of these studies used similar, but not identical, morphological characteristics to arrive at formal-functional classes. The limited number and small size of rim sherds recovered from the sampled Sunset Mesa Ruin deposits preclude a detailed

Table 14. Plain Ware and Red Ware Vessel Forms

Vessel Form	Plain Ware			Rincon Red		
	Sherds (Rims Only)		RVs	Sherds (Rims and Bodies)		RVs
	n	%	n	n	%	n
Bowls						
Hemispherical	1	2.8	—	2	1.6	—
Subhemispherical	27	75.0	1	6	4.7	1
Incurved	—	—	—	1	0.8	—
Indeterminate	8	22.2	—	118	92.9	—
Subtotal bowls	36	100.0	1	127	100.0	1
Jars						
Neckless	4	6.1	1	—	—	—
Globular	—	—	2	—	—	—
Gila-shouldered	—	—	1	—	—	—
Indeterminate	62	93.9	3	—	—	—
Subtotal jars	66	100.0	7	0	0.0	0
Other						
Scoop	2	100.0	0	—	—	—
Informal plates	—	—	3	—	—	1
Subtotal other	2	100.0	3	0	0.0	1
Indeterminate form	9	100.0	0	6	0.0	0
Total	113	100.0	11	133	100.0	2

analysis of function relating to morphological characteristics. Some observations can be made, however, based on orifice diameters among the rim sherds, augmented by the more complete metric and morphological data the reconstructible vessels provide.

Ethnographic data suggest that vessels with unrestricted openings are usually used in food preparation, serving, and eating (e.g., Fontana et al. 1962:47–48). The size and volume of such vessels are related to the size of the consuming group. Bowls used to prepare large meals or facilitate serving a large group have a greater volume than bowls used by individuals. Among rim sherds, bowls represent 34.6 percent of sherds identifiable as to form; only 1 of 11 plain ware reconstructible vessels is a bowl (Table 14).

None of the rim sherds represent shallow bowls, which are unrestricted vessels with a sidewall angle of less than approximately 30°. Shallow bowls can be loosely correlated with Braun's (1980:182) orifice and shape classification "plain bowls," which he subdivided into four categories based on orifice size: narrow (7–12 cm), medium (13–25 cm), wide (26–31 cm), and very wide (32–38 cm). In the Sunset Mesa Ruin collection, the most-common size group is the medium-orifice bowl (Figure 54), which Braun (1980:183) associated with small-scale food preparation, small-group serving, and extremely short-term storage.

Three reconstructible vessels categorized as informal plates could have served functions similar to those of bowls. Two plates were reworked from the bases of jars whose original form is indeterminate, and the third from the base of a bowl of indeterminate form. Use-wear abrasion is visible on the exterior base of one plate (RV 18). The one bowl, PV 22, is subhemispherical. Its height-to-maximum-diameter ratio of 1:2.88 fits comfortably within the middle of the range Lindauer defined (1988:Table 13) as characterizing bowls used for serving and food preparation (see also Whittlesey 1994:420). There also are two scoops among the rim sherds (1.9 percent); scoops are presumed to have been used for the transfer of foods or other materials from storage vessels, for serving, and perhaps for other activities, as well (see Crown 1984).

Bowls, when inverted over or placed upright within the orifice of a jar, also make perfect lids. The Pinaleno cotton cache, a group of vessels and baskets containing cotton and other materials found in the Pinaleno

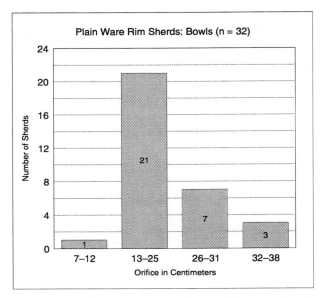

Figure 54. Orifice diameters among plain ware bowl rim sherds from Sunset Mesa Ruin, grouped according to Braun's (1980) orifice diameter classes.

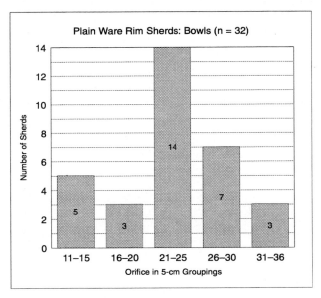

Figure 55. Orifice diameters among plain ware bowl rim sherds from Sunset Mesa Ruin, grouped by 5-cm increments.

Mountains near Safford, Arizona, illustrates the prehistoric use of bowls as lids (Haury and Huckell 1993:Figure 2). To explore the feasibility of bowls being used as lids, a simple comparison of Sunset Mesa Ruin rim sherds was carried out. In order for an inverted bowl to be used as a lid, the orifice must be slightly greater than that of the jar. Comparing orifice diameters (in 5-cm increments) of bowls (Figure 55) and jars (Figure 56) reveals concordance among the size groups. There is a range among bowl size groups sufficient to have permitted them to have served as lids for the range of sizes among the jars. For example, the 21–25-cm group of bowls (n = 14) could have served perfectly as lids for the 16–20-cm group of jars (n = 23). These are the two largest size groups of rim sherds. Although this distribution certainly does not confirm that bowls were used as lids, neither does it refute the possibility.

Jars make up 63.5 percent of determinable rim sherds in the Sunset Mesa Ruin collection, and represent variable forms (see Table 14). The proportions of jar forms among rim sherds cannot be considered representative of the entire collection or the prehistoric assemblage. Neckless or "seed" jars can be identified only among rim sherds, and shoulder form only among body sherds representing the shoulder portion of the vessel. We note, however, that four rim sherds are neckless jars, and one of seven reconstructible jars also is neckless. Two globular jars and one shouldered jar are present among the Sunset Mesa Ruin plain ware vessels.

The relative proportions of a jar are indicative of function. For example, jars exhibiting only a slight re-

striction (a small ratio of orifice to maximum diameter) are ideal for cooking. The Tohono O'odham vessels classified as bean pots by Fontana et al. (1962:Figures 29–31, 32) are examples of such vessels. Jars that have a larger ratio of maximum diameter to orifice have generally been associated with storage of dry and liquid materials and with liquid transport (Braun 1980; Lindauer 1988; Whittlesey 1994). Most jars in the Sunset Mesa Ruin sample represent examples of the latter. The plain ware jars represent what Braun (1980:182) would classify as "intermediate and recurved-restricted vessels" with medium (13–25 cm) and wide (25–31 cm) orifices (Figure 57), and the Sunset Mesa Ruin jars have short, everted rims with short or no necks. These vessels would fit into what Whittlesey (1994:419–420) has classified as dry-storage vessels. The rim sherds are similar, in that short, everted rims dominate the collection and reflect a similar inferred function.

Temper

The predominant tempering material in plain ware ceramics is sand, representing 71.7 percent of plain ware sherds (Table 15). We did not attempt to formally subdivide sand temper further based on constituent lithology and mineralogy, but did observe that sand temper, in most cases, represents a mixture of volcanic and igneous plutonic material—which is not surprising, given Sunset Mesa Ruin's location at the confluence of the Rillito and Santa Cruz Rivers. The Rillito conveys the runoff from the southern aspect of the Santa Catalina Mountains and the

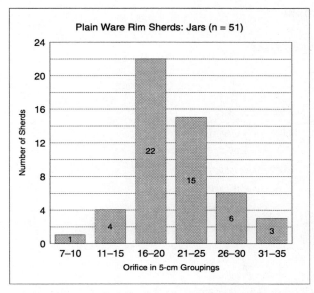

Figure 56. Orifice diameters among plain ware jar rim sherds from Sunset Mesa Ruin, grouped by 5-cm increments.

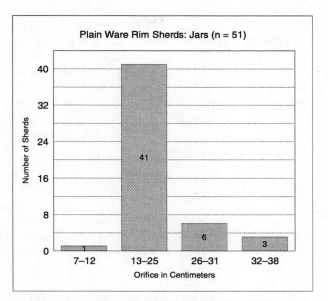

Figure 57. Orifice diameters among plain ware jar rim sherds from Sunset Mesa Ruin, grouped according to Braun's (1980) orifice diameter classes.

western and southern aspects of the Rincon Mountains, both of which are igneous plutonic units. The Tucson Mountains watershed is largely volcanic, and the Santa Cruz River, as a trunk stream, also should have a mixed lithology. The second most abundant tempering material is sand and muscovite mica, a temper category that, except for two Tucson Basin painted sherds, is exclusive to plain ware. Sand and muscovite mica temper is present only in plain ware jars, at least in the rim sherd collection. We do not know if this is also the case for the body sherds, as vessel form was not recorded. The three reconstructible vessels that exhibit sand and muscovite mica temper are plain ware jars (see Table 10). Although suggestive of a functional distinction between plain ware jars and bowls, the data are limited. The use of sand and mica temper produces a strong visual impact. The large, individual platelets of muscovite mica create a micaceous surface

sheen that is similar to, yet qualitatively different from, that seen among Gila Plain pottery. The latter has abundant, extremely finely divided mica deriving from fine schistose particles (Haury 1965), whereas the pottery tempered with sand and muscovite mica has relatively large (1–1.5 mm), individual mica platelets. Two of the reconstructible vessels with sand and muscovite mica temper also exhibit zonal polishing striations identical to Gila Plain (e.g., Haury 1976:Figure 12.57).

Intrusive Plain Ware: Gila Plain

Intrusive plain ware was limited to Gila Plain. One reconstructible vessel (RV 20) and 20 sherds were identified (see Table 5), representing less than 1 percent of the plain ware sherds in pit house contexts, and 8.3 percent of plain

Table 15. Sherds from Selected Categories Showing Tempering Material

Temper	Tucson Basin Painted		Plain Ware		Red Ware	
	n	%	n	%	n	%
Sand	1,554	90.9	1,778	71.7	146	94.8
Sand and muscovite mica	2	0.1	643	25.9	—	—
Sand and schist	34	2.0	—	—	8	5.2
Schist	120	7.0	58	2.3	—	—
Phyllite	—	—	2	0.1	—	—
Total	1,710	100.0	2,481	100.0	154	100.0

ware reconstructible vessels. Sixteen of the sherds (80 percent) were found in Feature 23, and the remainder in Feature 21. RV 20 can be classified as a jar because of the slight restriction created by the corner point defining the rim-body juncture. This vessel, which is approximately half complete, is morphologically similar to the historical-period Tohono O'odham bean pot illustrated by Fontana et al. (1962:Figure 31), and its shape and size are consistent with a small cooking vessel.

Red Ware

Most of the red ware sherds (86.4 percent, n = 133) and two reconstructible vessels (all of the red-slipped vessels) were classified as Rincon Red (see Table 5). The remaining 21 sherds were placed in either indeterminate red ware or possible intrusive red ware, based on slip and paste characteristics that varied from those described for Rincon Red pottery (Deaver 1984; Greenleaf 1975; Kelly et al. 1978; Wallace 1986c).

Rincon Red

The Rincon Red recovered from Sunset Mesa Ruin fits well with Kelly et al.'s (1978:67) original description of this pottery:

> Rincon Red is of coarse, granular paste, usually sand in color and generally non-micaceous. The surface finish is good to excellent; exterior, interior, or both may be highly polished. What, with further data, might prove to be a separate redware type tends to be less highly polished and more micaceous. The red of Rincon is clear and deep, but sometimes through weathering it becomes powdery and fugitive; the surface tends to pit and flake with weathering.

Wallace (1986c:69–78) provided a description of the type that emphasizes its characteristic and consistent slip and horizontal polishing striations.

Distribution

Half of the Rincon Red sherds were found in pit house Feature 21. Features 22 and 25 also had considerable percentages of this pottery, but it was scarce in pit house Feature 23 (six sherds). Oddly, Rincon Red was found in extramural contexts only in the outdoor activity area Features 13 and 15 (see Table 7).

Surface Finish

Rincon Red pottery from Sunset Mesa Ruin exhibits random polishing striations on both surfaces (Table 16), and some sherds have partially exfoliated slips from

Table 16. Surface Finish on Red Ware Sherds

Red Ware	Surface Finish	Interior
Rincon Red		
Uniform polish	—	19
Striated polish	—	10
Slipped, hand smoothed	1	—
Slipped, uniform polish	47	—
Slipped, striated polish	85	—
Slipped, uniform polish, fire clouds	—	51
Slipped, striated polish, fire clouds	—	53
Subtotal Rincon Red		133
Intrusive red ware		
Uniform polish	—	4
Uniform polish, fire clouds	—	1
Slipped, uniform polish	3	1
Slipped, striated polish	3	—
Subtotal intrusive red ware		6
Indeterminate red ware		
Uniform polish	—	3
Uniform polish, blackened	—	1
Slipped, hand smoothed	1	—
Slipped, uniform polish	13	5
Slipped, striated polish	—	4
Slipped, uniform polish, fire clouds	1	2
Subtotal indeterminate red ware		15

weathering. All of the sherds typed as Rincon Red had an interior slip. Most (78.2 percent) were also slipped on the exterior (see Table 16). The presence of fire clouding was noted on 78.2 percent of the exterior surfaces. Fire clouding produces a distinctive, mottled light brown and red color on the slipped surface. Wallace (1986c:72) has noted that this characteristic is a useful diagnostic in recognizing the presence of a slip.

Vessel Form

Bowls dominate over jars among Rincon Red pottery throughout the Tucson Basin (Ervin 1983; Greenleaf 1975; Heckman 1994; Heidke 1995; Kelly et al. 1978; Wallace 1986b, 1986c; Whittlesey 1986a, 1987b). This is also true at Sunset Mesa Ruin. All of the sherds of determinable form and both of the reconstructible vessels are or were bowls (see Table 14; see also Table 10). This contrasts strikingly with the plain ware, which is dominated by jars (63.5 percent). Clearly, red ware and plain ware vessels served different purposes.

Six of nine rim sherds are from hemispherical (or outcurved) bowls, and one of two reconstructible vessels is a subhemispherical bowl (RV 21). These vessel forms dominate in other collections. Wallace (1986c:73) reported hemispherical and "deep outcurved" forms as forming more than half of the West Branch site collection, with the latter form predominating. Wallace also reported flare-rimmed bowls from the West Branch site. The other vessel (RV 28) represents an informal plate that was reworked from an original bowl sherd of indeterminate form. RV 21 falls into Braun's (1980) medium-size class (orifice diameter is 19.5 cm).

Temper

All of the Rincon Red sherds and both of the reconstructible vessels are tempered with sand. The dominant lithology within the sand temper is volcanic.

Intrusive and Indeterminate Red Ware

Possible intrusive red ware (n = 6) and indeterminate red ware (n = 15) represent sherds that did not conform to published type descriptions of Rincon Red pottery. The two non-Rincon Red categories were separated on the basis of slip color, paste, and temper characteristics.

All of the indeterminate red ware sherds have a purple-red slip that is relatively thin compared to the slip on Rincon Red sherds. All are bowl sherds. Most (13 sherds) have a uniformly polished interior surface, whereas exterior surface treatment varies (see Table 16). There is more variability in temper among indeterminate red ware than among either Rincon Red or possible intrusive red ware pottery. Eight of the 15 sherds have sand temper consistent with the volcanic material found in the Rincon Red sherds. The remaining 7 sherds were tempered with a mixture of sand from a volcanic source and schist, suggesting that the metamorphic material was added as a deliberate tempering agent.

The six sherds classified as possible intrusive red ware exhibit a deep, crimson-colored slip. Five sherds have an extremely hard paste, and they appear to represent well-fired vessels. These sherds are qualitatively consistent with published descriptions of San Francisco Red variants found in southern (Whittlesey 1998a) and southeastern (Sayles 1945) Arizona. The sherds are primarily uniformly polished (see Table 16). The identification of these sherds as a variant of San Francisco Red may have temporal implications. San Francisco Red is one of the earliest red wares in the Southwest, if not the earliest, first appearing in Early Formative contexts dating to the Mogollon I period (Wheat 1955). In southern Arizona,

pottery closely resembling San Francisco Red was found at the Houghton Road site (AZ BB:13:398 [ASM]), where it may date as early as A.D. 400 (Whittlesey 1998a). Among ceramics from Alder Wash Ruin (AZ BB:6:9 [ASM]), a multicomponent site located along the lower San Pedro River, Masse (1985) identified a variant of San Francisco Red that he called Peppersauce Red. He argued that it dates to the Sacaton phase and early Classic period, but this dating is problematic (see discussion in Whittlesey 1998:152). San Francisco Red was the most abundant intrusive pottery at Snaketown (AZ U:13:1 [ASM]), recovered from contexts dating to all phases (Haury 1965:217). It may be that locally made variants of San Francisco Red had a longer lifespan in desert contexts than the original type in its mountain heartland. For example, red wares identical to San Francisco Red are found with Sedentary period Hohokam pottery in southern Arizona contexts (Sayles 1945; Tuthill 1947).

The remaining possible intrusive red ware sherd is consistent with Haury's (1976) description of Sacaton Red. This sherd is slipped on the interior with powdery, poorly bonded hematite. Its exterior is fire clouded and, although not tool polished, has a uniform finish. The temper is a sand and schist mixture, with the sand exhibiting an extremely diverse lithology and mineralogy, possibly consistent with sedimentary or volcanic material (or both), as well as igneous parent material.

Unidentified red ware is relatively common in Sedentary period contexts. Wallace (1986c:69) reported that 16 percent of the red ware at the West Branch site was not identified as Rincon Red, although he failed to provide a description of the indeterminate red ware. This proportion of Rincon Red to other red wares is virtually identical to that observed at Sunset Mesa Ruin. At the Tanque Verde Wash site, 5.7 percent of the Sedentary period red ware was categorized as "indeterminate" (Wallace 1986a:167). Approximately 23 percent of the Sedentary period red ware from Los Morteros was categorized as either (1) unidentified, not Rincon Red, or (2) unidentified, possibly Rincon Red (Heidke 1995:Table 5.2). Wallace (1985:Table 7.6) recorded 28.8 percent of the red ware at the Valencia site as indeterminate.

Evidently, there is considerable variability in Tucson Basin red ware that should be explored further. The red ware ceramics that do not fit comfortably within the type description for Rincon Red probably represent locally manufactured variants of Rincon Red. The possibility that all of these indeterminate or unidentified red wares represent intrusive pottery is unlikely, given the limited presence of intrusive ceramics in the Tucson Basin among Sedentary period contexts. A reevaluation of the type Rincon Red also may be warranted.

Historical-Period Native American Pottery

We recovered a small quantity of historical-period and possible Tohono O'odham sherds, all from Rooms 1 and 2 of Feature 5 (not included in tables). These include one indeterminate Papago Plain or Red sherd and four possible Papago Plain sherds. All are body sherds, and none could be identified as to vessel form. The definitely identified sherd is manure tempered and carbon cored, with the porous, black paste and linear voids representing carbonized hay or grass pieces that typify this pottery. One surface is red, but exhibits no definite slip. Because the slip is poorly bonded to the paste surface, Papago Red sherds often exhibit this eroded but oxidized surface (Whittlesey 1987a). This sherd is thick (about 1 cm), which is consistent with Papago Plain pottery.

The possible Tohono O'odham sherds have a dark core (dark gray to black), but do not have the characteristic carbonized core of manure-tempered pottery. They are thick (7–8 mm) and have abundant sand temper, creating a coarse, crumbly paste. None exhibit the characteristic voids of manure-tempered pottery.

Tohono O'odham pottery tempered with materials other than manure is extremely difficult to distinguish from prehistoric Classic period plain ware (see discussion in Whittlesey 1997). For this reason, and particularly in light of the tiny collection, we can say only that these may be historical-period Tohono O'odham, an inference strengthened by the presence of ceramics that are definitely Tohono O'odham in origin.

Additional pottery was found previously during testing at Sunset Mesa. Harry et al. (1992:49) reported two manure-tempered Papago Red sherds, and one was observed in the Midvale collection at ASM (Ciolek-Torrello and Homburg 1990). Fontana et al. (1962:104–105) placed Papago Red pottery in their Period 1 ceramic complex, dating from 1700 to 1860. The use of manure temper began as early as the late 1700s. Pottery recovered from the Spanish presidio of Santa Cruz de Terrenate (AZ EE:4:11 [ASM]), along the San Pedro River in southeastern Arizona, is tempered with both manure and sand, but the sand-tempered reconstructible vessels (classified by Di Peso [1953] as Whetstone Plain) were restricted to the site's earlier component. This suggests that manure temper came into use during the four-year occupation of the presidio between 1776 and 1780 (Whittlesey 1997:461–462). Most turn-of-the-century Tohono O'odham pottery in the Tucson area is manure tempered (e.g., Whittlesey 1997). It seems probable that the widespread use of manure temper postdates 1800, and that it was more common in heavily acculturated, urban areas, where horses were common.

Harry et al. (1992:51) also reported pottery from testing that resembled Whetstone Plain. The sherds had a sand temper and rough, wiped surface. This type has been identified as protohistoric Sobaipuri (Masse 1981, 1985). No similar pottery was identified during data recovery. It is unlikely that these sherds represent a protohistoric period occupation; rather, they probably are simply variants of prehistoric plain ware.

According to Sterner (this volume), the Basillio Cuevas homestead was established in 1890. In 1915, the property was purchased by William A. Knapp, who established the Sunset Dairy. Use of the property after this time remains poorly known, although the area clearly has been extensively disturbed and used as a trash dump in modern times. This is certainly indicated by the quantity of prehistoric pottery recovered from Feature 5.

The Tohono O'odham pottery found at Sunset Mesa Ruin is consistent with the dating of the Cuevas homestead reported by Sterner. It is not unusual to find Tohono O'odham pottery in turn-of-the-century, urban contexts occupied by Euroamericans (Ayres 1990; Rogge et al. 1992; Whittlesey 1997). Tohono O'odham pottery was prized for its ability to keep water cool and fresh in the days before refrigeration. Making and selling *ollas* to Tucsonans was an important industry for Tohono O'odham women, who used the proceeds (cash or barter) to supplement family income. Nearly every turn-of-the-century home had a Tohono O'odham water jar in the courtyard.

Research Issues Revisited

Ceramic Dating

The painted and red ware pottery recovered from Sunset Mesa Ruin is consistent with a relatively short-term occupation during the Rincon phase. Most of the painted pottery is Rincon Red-on-brown; all variants represent 81 percent of the typable painted sherds and 68.7 percent of painted reconstructible vessels. Although only one Rincon Polychrome sherd was recovered, there are two partial vessels, and a third polychrome vessel lacking red slip, and some of the black-painted and white-slipped sherds may represent portions of polychrome vessels. Rincon Red represents 2.4 percent of the sherd collection, and we found two vessels of this type. The Hohokam Buff Ware identifiable to type also represents the Sedentary period. Sacaton Red-on-buff constitutes 14.5 percent of the typable painted sherds and 12.5 percent of the painted reconstructible vessels.

Only one possibly earlier sherd, classified as indeterminate Rillito or Rincon Red-on-brown, was found. It was recovered from an extramural context (Feature 13, the ramada/food-preparation area). No later ceramics, such as Late Rincon Red-on-brown (Rincon Style C), Tanque Verde Red-on-brown, or Roosevelt Red Ware pottery, were identified. A few sherds of Late Rincon Red-on-brown, transitional Rincon–Tanque Verde Red-on-brown, and Tanque Verde Red-on-brown were found during the testing phase of the project and among previous collections house at ASM (Harry et al. 1992:49). We know from stratigraphic evidence that there is a later occupation postdating the Rincon phase structures at Sunset Mesa Ruin, but we found no ceramic evidence for such occupation during data recovery. The later pottery identified among previously collected material may represent Rincon Red-on-brown, Style B that was classified as transitional Rincon or Tanque Verde Red-on-brown, or indeed may represent a later occupation at a portion of the site that we did not excavate.

The only nonlocally made pottery found at Sunset Mesa Ruin is Hohokam Buff Ware that evidently originated in the Gila River valley. The complete absence of crossdated intrusive pottery, such as white ware, hampers our ability to make temporal inferences but is not atypical of the Tucson Basin during the Sedentary period. Much larger sites typically fail to yield non-Hohokam intrusive pottery. Neither Kelly et al. (1978:Table 4.1) nor Whittlesey (1986a:Table 6.15) found any during excavations at Hodges Ruin, for example. One of the exceptions is the Tanque Verde Wash site, which produced nine Cibola White Ware sherds (Wallace 1986a:177). Mimbres Black-on-white also has been reported in some late Rincon phase contexts (e.g., Doelle and Wallace 1986:41; Wallace 1985:132–133).

The lack of intrusive, well-dated pottery types, the confusing signal sent by an examination of formation processes as revealed by ceramic information, and the apparent lack of temporal significance in design styles of painted pottery, discussed below, suggest that a prudent approach to site and intrasite chronology among Rincon phase sites is to rely as heavily as possible upon chronometric data, supplementing these data with ceramic information.

Design and Technological Variability in Rincon Painted Pottery

As discussed previously, two models of design variability in Rincon painted pottery have been developed. Both Wallace's (1986c) seriational, subtype model and Deaver's (1984) stylistic model recognize an implicit sequence of change through time in painted decoration. Although Deaver's design-style model holds open the possibility that different styles may be contemporaneous—there is no a priori embedding of chronological information in the concept of style—temporal information is nevertheless built into the model. In a typological approach, the sequence of development is represented in pottery types; in Deaver's model, it is a sequence of decorative styles (Deaver 1984:243). A continuous sequence of design development through time is implicitly acknowledged by ceramicists working with the model. In practice, styles are viewed as coterminous with temporal units. According to Deaver (1984:252–253),

This model has been defined to identify those pottery styles that are indicative of time. Controlling for time, not only for the purpose of dating the sites, but for documenting the technological and formal traditions of the pottery was a major concern. This model is purely seriational, based upon observations of whole and restorable vessels in published accounts and those housed at the Arizona State Museum. Because the model is not based upon chronometric, associational, or stratigraphic information, its validity must await confirmation from such detailed studies.

Despite the acknowledged lack of verification, Deaver's model was used to provide chronological control for unpainted pottery that Deaver (1984) analyzed from the Rosemont sites, and for the Rosemont project in general.

Wallace's approach is designed specifically to achieve chronological control; it has no other purpose. He has written, for example, that

One could realistically define two or three types from the range of variability encompassed in Rincon Red-on-brown (based on decorative styles), but the types would be seen to overlap in time and they would be more difficult to deal with for chronological control [Wallace 1986b:21].

The explicit use of typology to create chronological subdivisions is an appropriate use of the typological approach—classification must, by definition, have one or more purposes—but Wallace's exclusive focus on temporal issues differs from the typological approach used by most southwestern ceramicists, who seldom build an exclusively research objective into their type definitions and descriptions. Huckell (1987:134) succinctly stated the distinction between Wallace's and Deaver's approaches: "Deaver's is the study of ceramic art through time, and Wallace's is the study of time through ceramic art."

Each Rincon Red-on-brown subtype represents a set of ceramic attributes that correlate with a particular segment of time. The Early Rincon Red-on-brown subtype, for example,

> comprises the range of stylistic variability in the earliest chronological segment of Rincon Red-on-brown. Subphases in this system are directly related to subtypes, just as phases are to types. They are intended to represent portions of the sequence of cultural change embodied within phases [Wallace 1986c:21].

This unique application of a phase may represent a misunderstanding of the purpose of such culture-history units. Phases refer not simply to units of time, but to *culture* as it was manifest within particular units of time. In the case of the early to late Rincon subphases, units of time are coterminous with a single material culture trait, in this case, variations of one pottery type. Although in Hohokam archaeology, phase has come to be synonymous with units of time, this application differs from traditional usage.

The relatively short, apparently single-component prehistoric occupation of Sunset Mesa Ruin provides an opportunity to examine the presumed temporal sequence of decorative styles in Rincon phase painted pottery. The distribution of Rincon Style A and Style B pottery at Sunset Mesa Ruin indicates that the styles co-existed. Both styles were found in all but two of the excavated pit houses, Features 25 and 27, in which only Style B was found. Extramural deposits produced fewer examples of co-existence; only Features 15 and 31 yielded both styles. The possibility that the deposits yielding both styles are temporally "mixed" cannot be completely ruled out. That possibility is difficult to evaluate independently, however, given the apparent brief occupation of the site and lack of superpositioning among features. As the discussion of abandonment and depositional processes reveals, there are no clear ceramic indicators that would distinguish early-abandoned and late-abandoned houses and, except for the disturbance created by intrusive features in Feature 22, no indicators of prehistoric postdepositional disturbance. The lack of de facto floor assemblages, the partial state of most of the recovered vessels, and characteristics of fill deposits indicate an archaeological context created by the cleaning of house floors prior to abandonment, and the filling of the houses by predominantly natural erosional processes. There were no catastrophic abandonment events.

There are few examples of de facto refuse that would assist in dating the styles. Two of the Style A vessels were recovered from Feature 23; one (RV 2) was found on the floor, and the second (RV 3) derived from floor fill. Feature 23 was one of the earliest structures to be abandoned

at Sunset Mesa Ruin, and is the earliest if the confusing archaeomagnetic date from the structure floor is discounted (see Deaver and Murphy, Appendix B). Another Style A vessel (PV 8) was found in the roof fall, floor fill, and intrafloor fill deposits of Feature 21, which was one of the late-abandoned pit houses at the site (Deaver and Murphy, Appendix B). A second Style A vessel (RV 4) was recovered from the floor of Feature 22, which was the latest archaeomagnetically dated feature to be abandoned at Sunset Mesa Ruin (Deaver and Murphy, Appendix B). Thus, Style A vessels were present in floor or floor fill contexts in both the earliest- and latest-abandoned houses at Sunset Mesa Ruin. This would indicate a temporal range between A.D. 930 and 1100 for Style A, if the estimate for the latest-abandoned Feature 22 is accepted.

The six Rincon Style B reconstructible vessels were found in pit house and extramural contexts. Only one, however, was in floor context. RV 10 was found on the floor of Feature 27, which is considered by Deaver and Murphy (Appendix B) to be one of the later-abandoned houses at the site, and is thought to be essentially contemporaneous with Features 21 and 25. The remaining Style B reconstructible vessels were found in extramural contexts or in the upper levels of fill in pit houses. One was in the fill of the intrusive pit (Feature 22.04) into Feature 22. Vessels representing Rincon Styles A and B were not present on the same house floors. No particular weight should be given to this fact, however, in light of the limited number of *any* painted vessels in floor context and the overall numerical superiority of Style B pottery.

Limited information in support of a temporal sequence between Styles A and B can be found in a few instances. A Style B jar was found in the upper levels of fill of the early-abandoned Feature 23, which contained Style A vessels in floor context. All but one of the Style B sherds in this house also came from upper fill levels, and all of the Style A sherds were from lower levels. The intrusive pit Feature 22.04 contained a Style B jar, and a Style A bowl was found on the floor of Feature 22. The small sample, however, coupled with the lack of ceramic evidence for stratified deposits, makes any temporal inferences from these contexts extremely tenuous.

Other examples of the co-ocurrence of stylistically "early" (Style A, Early Rincon) designs with "later" (Styles B and C, Middle and Late Rincon) designs have been documented in the Tucson Basin. Huckell (1987:129–130), for example, noted that Style B was found in association with Style A ceramics consistently at two sites (AZ EE:1:157 and AZ EE:1:158 [ASM]) excavated during the Corona de Tucson project. He echoed Deaver's (1984:309–310) assertion that decorative treatments representing Rincon Style A were long lived, spanning much of the Sedentary period. One of the best examples of co-occurrence of Rincon Style A and Style B is found in an assemblage of vessels from de facto refuse context on the floor of Feature 19 at the Tanque Verde Wash site, described by Wallace (1986a:153). The two vessels Wallace (1986a:153) referred to as "discordant notes in the assemblage," Tanque Verde Wash vessels RV 2 and RV 8, can clearly be classified as Rincon Style A (see Wallace 1986a:Figures 6.6b [RV 2] and 6.9a [RV 8]). The remaining vessels from the floor assemblage could comfortably be classified as Rincon Style B (Wallace 1986a:Figures 6.6–6.9).

To summarize, the data suggest that Rincon Styles A and B were used together at Sunset Mesa Ruin within a relatively brief occupation span dating between A.D. 930 and 1100. This supports the inference that Style A endured throughout much of the Sedentary period. Style A would, therefore, appear to be a design variation with a behavioral signal other than time alone. Future research should determine the spatial and temporal distribution of Style A in more detail, and attempt to discover its behavioral implications. Does it represent the product of a particular social group or pottery-making group, for example? The correlation of particular vessel forms and technological variations with design styles may imply that the makers of Style A pottery were more influenced by the Hohokam tradition, whereas Style B producers may have been influenced more heavily by other ceramic traditions.

We cannot conclude on the basis of our limited sample that there is *no* temporal progression in painted decoration during the Sedentary period. As we have discussed, most researchers familiar with Tucson Basin ceramics have implicitly recognized the temporal signal of design diversity and have applied the progression from "early" Style A to "late" Style C as a relative dating tool (e.g., Greenleaf 1975). The evidence suggests, however, that variables other than time may influence the distribution of these styles, and this possibility should be examined.

There is no easy way to address this issue. Wallace's approach appears to be extremely circular. It is impossible to independently evaluate the temporal assignment of types that are temporally defined. Attribute data that Wallace (1986c:21–27) presents in support of the Early, Middle, and Late Rincon Red-on-brown subtype descriptions are revealing. One set of data uses sherd lots, selecting "the groups of units assigned to each *subphase* as the units for typological analysis. This approach assumes that all sherds in each of the groups represent the ceramic subtype associated with the particular subphase" (Wallace 1986c:21; emphasis in original). Wallace used the first data set to segregate all the sherds attributed to each subtype. Because the subphase assignments were based on typological distinctions, there is no independent means of verifying the selection of attributes used to define the subtypes.

Moreover, Wallace's (1986b, 1986c) Early-Middle-Late Rincon temporal typology cannot be evaluated with chronometric data. The units of time encompassed by the subtypes and subphases are beyond the resolution of contemporary chronometric dating techniques. There is no ready means of confirming the typology. The Style A–C sequence avoids this difficulty, but given the typically broad range of archaeomagnetic dates, requires additional steps to confirm the dating of styles. Statistical clustering of archaeomagnetic data to provide a relative occupation sequence within or among sites (e.g., Deaver and Altschul 1996) may provide the necessary framework to assess contemporaneity of styles. As we have seen with Sunset Mesa Ruin, assessment of intramural and site stratigraphy and formation processes may provide little useful supporting information.

The Sunset Mesa Ruin data also suggest that technological variability in Rincon painted pottery—the use of black paints and white slips in combinations—began to flourish during the middle portion of the phase. Moreover, both Rincon Red and polychrome pottery appear in the later contexts at the site. The sole Rincon Red vessel found in a pit house was recovered from floor fill context in the early-abandoned Feature 23, and Rincon Red sherds were most abundant in Feature 21, one of the later-abandoned houses. The two Rincon Polychrome vessels were found in later-abandoned houses. One (PV 5) was found in the fill of the intrusive pit in Feature 22, and the second (PV 9) was found in a floor pit in Feature 27. The polychrome effigy (PV 30) was recovered from floor fill in Feature 21. Feature 22 is the latest-abandoned house at Sunset Mesa Ruin, and Features 27 and 21 appear to have been essentially contemporaneous and abandoned toward the end of the sequence. This would place the appearance of polychrome pottery around or slightly before A.D. 1100. Polychrome pottery is also relatively rare at Sunset Mesa Ruin (one sherd and three vessels).

Ceramic Production and Distribution

Ceramic sourcing studies attempt to define the provenance of paste materials (plastic materials, or clay, and aplastic inclusions, commonly called temper) as a proxy measure of the locale of ceramic production. The assumption is made that local materials—those found at the site or near it—represent those used by the inhabitants to produce pots recovered in the archaeological context. Materials found at some distance, within catchment areas defined by crosscultural ethnographic studies, are assumed to indicate pottery made elsewhere. The sourcing study reported here relies on this assumption, as it is employed by researchers at DAI. Only qualitative petrographic analysis was carried out, so we can report only on the aplastic inclusions or temper in the Sunset Mesa Ruin pottery. This provides an incomplete, and possibly nonrepresentative, view of ceramic paste composition.

Sourcing studies in the Tucson Basin have relied almost exclusively on petrography, with a particular focus on the definition of sand composition zones or petrofacies and the matching of sand temper in prehistoric pottery to particular petrofacies. The petrofacies concept was pioneered by geologist James Lombard in the 1980s, and has since been expanded and refined by archaeologists at DAI. DAI's work has concentrated on the western portion of the Tucson Basin, where a distinctive set of adjacent petrofacies and their subsets has been identified with a presumed ceramic-production area at the West Branch settlement. Originally identified as the Cat Mountain petrofacies by Lombard (1987a; see also Lombard 1986a, 1986b) and now subdivided, the Beehive Peak petrofacies (Petrofacies J1) (see Figure D.1) in the southern portion of Lombard's original sand composition zone is distinguished by a biotite-bearing rhyolite grain. As defined by Lombard (1987a), the Cat Mountain petrofacies encompasses the narrow, eastern bajada of the Tucson Mountains. The southern and eastern boundaries of the petrofacies are the West Branch of the Santa Cruz River to its confluence with the main branch, at which point the Santa Cruz River becomes the eastern boundary of the petrofacies. The northern boundary is near the intersection of Silverbell Road and Sunset Road. Lombard (1987a:351) first suggested that biotite-bearing rhyolite was distinctive of the southern portion of the Tucson Mountains. DAI tested this hypothesis by collecting additional sand samples (none were point counted, however). The new samples confirmed Lombard's notion; only those in the southern Tucson Mountains contained abundant biotite-bearing rhyolite (Heidke 1996). This newly distinguished Beehive Peak petrofacies encompasses the West Branch site, which has been proposed as a specialized ceramic-production settlement (Harry 1996; Wallace and Heidke 1986). The distinctive character of the biotite-bearing rhyolite grain in Beehive Peak sand permits it to be readily identified by binocular microscope inspection.

North of Beehive Peak is the Twin Hills petrofacies (Petrofacies J2) (see Figure D.1). Sand samples collected by DAI demonstrated abundant hypabyssal volcanic grains and siltstone grains in a sand sample adjacent to St. Mary's Ruin (AZ AA:16:26 [ASM]). This became the basis for distinguishing the Twin Hills petrofacies (Heidke 1996). The Wasson petrofacies (Petrofacies J3) (see Figure D.1) is the northernmost petrofacies in the eastern slopes of the Tucson Mountain. Also volcanic,

this petrofacies is perhaps best described as lacking the distinctive grains that identify Twin Hills and Beehive Peak.

Many other petrofacies in the Tucson Basin and adjacent areas have been identified since Lombard (1987a) presented his initial petrofacies map for the area. The Avra Valley area has been sampled and several petrofacies defined on the eastern slopes of the Roskruge and Silverbell Mountains and the western slopes of the Tucson Mountains. The eastern Tucson Basin is encompassed by the Rincon petrofacies, and the northern basin by the Catalina petrofacies (see Figure D.1).

We use DAI's petrographic identifications and our own macroscopic observations of temper materials in the Sunset Mesa Ruin sample to discuss possible patterns in ceramic production and distribution. This discussion makes two a priori assumptions about the temper identifications. We assume that DAI's temper identifications are correct (although previous experiments have demonstrated a high percentage of incorrect identifications [Harry 1997]). We also assume that temper provenance indicates production locale, despite the fact that this extremely critical assumption has yet to be demonstrated (see discussion in Whittlesey 1987c).

The most unusual pattern we see among the Sunset Mesa Ruin ceramics is the complete lack of evidence for local manufacture. Although located within the area encompassed by the Wasson petrofacies (see Figure D.1), according to Heidke (Appendix D) the site is assigned to the Santa Cruz River petrofacies because it is situated on the Qt2 terrace of this trunk stream. Archaeologists at DAI use two definitions of "local" temper materials. The "geologically compatible" temper resource corresponds to the petrofacies in which the site is located (Heidke, Kamilli, and Miksa 1996:43)—in the case of Sunset Mesa Ruin, the Santa Cruz River petrofacies. The "behaviorally local" resource is defined by Arnold's (1985) ethnographic data indicating that potters using sand temper typically travel less than one kilometer to collected materials, and few travel as far as a maximum of three kilometers. Therefore, "any sand-tempered pottery containing a composition similar to that available in washes located within 3 km of the archaeological site from which the vessel was recovered should, in a behavioral sense, be considered the product of 'local' manufacture" (Heidke, Kamilli, and Miksa 1996:43; see also Miksa and Heidke 1995:133–134). For Sunset Mesa Ruin, the "behaviorally local" petrofacies is the Wasson petrofacies.

Using these assumptions, we can state that *none* of the ceramics recovered at Sunset Mesa Ruin were locally made. No Santa Cruz River petrofacies sand (the "geologically compatible" temper resource) was observed among the identified petrofacies (Table 17). It is certainly possible that such sand is represented among the many

Table 17. Specific Temper Source by Ware or Type

| Specific Temper Source | Rincon Red | | Plain Ware | | Rincon Red-on-brown | | | | | | Rincon Polychrome | | Total | |
| | | | | | Style A[a] | | Style B[a] | | Indeterminate Style[a] | | | | | |
	n	%	n	%	n	%	n	%	n	%	n	%	n	%
Beehive Peak (J1) petrofacies	18	94.7	60	46.5	9	90.0	29	87.9	35	71.4	2	100.0	153	63.2
Twin Hills (J2) petrofacies	—	—	17	13.2	1	10.0	1	3.0	12	24.5	—	—	31	12.8
Tortolita (E) petrofacies	—	—	2	1.5	—	—	—	—	—	—	—	—	2	0.9
Indeterminate	1	5.3	50	38.8	—	—	3	9.1	2	4.1	—	—	56	23.1
Total	19	100.0	129	100.0	10	100.0	33	100.0	49	100.0	2	100.0	242	100.0

Note: Based on DAI identifications (see Appendix D). Excludes intrusive plain and red ware and indeterminate red-on-brown.
[a] Includes black-on-brown and white-slipped variants.

Table 18. Generic Temper Source among Plain Ware with Unidentified Specific Temper Source

Generic Temper Source	Frequency	Percentage
Metamorphic core	1	2.0
Igneous plutonic	6	12.0
Igneous plutonic (Tortolita or Sutherland)	3	6.0
Igneous plutonic or metamorphic core	5	10.0
Igneous volcanic	8	16.0
Igneous volcanic (Twin Hills or Wasson)	2	4.0
Igneous volcanic or igneous plutonic and mixed lithic	3	6.0
Indeterminate	22	44.0
Total	50	100.0

Note: Based on DAI identifications (see Appendix D).

unidentified samples, however (about one-fourth of the samples were characterized as having an indeterminate specific temper source). Because of geomorphic and hydrologic conditions, sands from trunk streams exhibit mixed mineralogy and lithologies. These characteristics are also expected to change considerably over time, unlike the conditions affecting smaller drainages.

To explore the possibility that some of the samples were tempered with Santa Cruz River sand, we looked at the plain ware pottery—as the utility ware, probably the most likely of the Sunset Mesa Ruin ceramics to have been locally made—that Heidke (see Table D.1) identified as having indeterminate temper (a summary of Heidke's possible generic temper source identifications is provided in Table 18). It is intriguing that eight of the indeterminate samples (16 percent) have mixed lithologies that might indicate a trunk stream. These are indeterminate igneous plutonic or metamorphic core complex, and indeterminate igneous volcanic or igneous plutonic and mixed lithic materials.

It seems unlikely that potters residing at Sunset Mesa Ruin would have restricted themselves to using sand from the Santa Cruz riverbed, however. We therefore looked for evidence of sand temper originating in the Wasson petrofacies, which is the nearest petrofacies other than the Santa Cruz River petrofacies (see Figure D.1) and thus "behaviorally local." Apparently, people living at Sunset Mesa Ruin did not travel even short distances to obtain sands to use in locally made pottery. No Wasson petrofacies sands were identified among the Sunset Mesa Ruin ceramics (see Tables 17 and D.1).

None of the identified petrofacies among the analyzed sample are "behaviorally local," and most are from the southern end of the Tucson Mountains. Sand from the Beehive Peak petrofacies predominates (63.2 percent of the analyzed "local" samples) (see Table 17). Beehive Peak petrofacies sand is present in all local wares that were analyzed. Twin Hills petrofacies sand, the second

most common temper (12.8 percent), is most prevalent among the indeterminate-style Rincon Red-on-brown samples, although it is also found in all wares except Rincon Red and Rincon Polychrome. The only other petrofacies represented is Tortolita (Petrofacies E), located northeast of Sunset Mesa; this petrofacies drains the bajada west of the Cañada del Oro Wash (see Figure D.1). Several important sites are located in the Tortolita petrofacies, including Badger Hole Ranch (AZ AA:12:40 [ASM]) (Doolittle and Ezzo 1995; Whittlesey et al. 1998) and large sites reported during the Rancho Vistoso survey (Craig and Wallace 1987). Two analyzed sherds in the Sunset Mesa Ruin sample (less than 1 percent), both plain ware, were identified as containing Tortolita petrofacies sand.

A second intriguing pattern hints at possible variable sources for ceramic wares. Plain ware, red ware, and painted ceramics were made with different temper materials, which implies that they were made in different places. The plain ware pottery in our sample represents the most varied ware; it contains materials originating in different locations and representing kinds of materials, such as phyllite, not found in the painted and red ware pottery. Most striking is the emphasis on micaceous sand containing muscovite, resulting in a vessel with a surface sheen and sparkle. By contrast, most of the Rincon Red, Rincon Red-on-brown, and Rincon Polychrome pottery in the sample was tempered with nonmicaceous, volcanic sand (see Table 15). Looking at the specific temper source, we find that plain ware pottery originated in several locales, and less than half contained Beehive Peak sand (see Table 17). By contrast, Beehive Peak predominates among the Rincon Red and painted ceramics. The selection of varied temper materials may have been functional (different materials were used in different vessel forms, possibly because of their performance characteristics), ideological (for the symbolic value of the materials or their appearance), or cultural (potters represented differing traditions of pottery making that were culturally defined and learned).

No specific provenance can be assigned to the material we identified as sand and muscovite mica. Fifteen of the sherds submitted for macroscopic temper characterization display this material. Of these, none were identified by Heidke (Appendix D) to a specific temper source. The generic temper source for most (10 sherds) was characterized as either an igneous plutonic or metamorphic core. According to Heidke (Appendix D),

> These sherds are either tempered with a metamorphic core complex sand or a granitic sand. Although foliated sand grains, a clear indicator of a metamorphic core complex source, were not observed in these sherds, the observance of polycrystalline quartz and feldspar grains in some of these sherds indicates that some of these pots may be tempered with metamorphic core complex sand.

Sand sources in the Tucson Basin identified as metamorphic core complex are the Rillito Creek, Pantano Wash, Tanque Verde Creek, Rincon, Catalina, and Owl Head petrofacies (Appendix D). All of these are either in the eastern Tucson Basin, or are secondary streams draining the slopes of the Catalina and Rincon Mountains (see Figure D.1). The metamorphic materials (granitic gneiss and schist) in this area are a probable source of the muscovite observed in this temper category. Taken at face value, this information suggests an eastern Tucson Basin production locale for one-fourth of the plain ware pottery recovered at Sunset Mesa Ruin (see Table 15).

In direct contrast to the plain ware pottery, the specific temper identifications (Appendix D) indicate that most of the painted and red ware pottery was made with sand originating in the western Tucson Basin, along the margins of the Tucson Mountains. Sand from the Beehive Peak petrofacies was the most commonly used. Previous research has identified the West Branch village, located in the Beehive Peak petrofacies, as a specialized production area for Rincon Red-on-brown, Rincon Red, and Rincon Polychrome pottery (e.g., Harry 1996; Heidke 1996; Huntington 1986; Wallace and Heidke 1986). The Sunset Mesa Ruin data do not necessarily contradict this notion. In our sample, Beehive Peak petrofacies sand is most common among Rincon painted and Rincon Red pottery (see Table 17). We remain concerned, however, about other potential explanations that have not been eliminated to date. In particular, we would like to explore the possibility that the key biotite-bearing rhyolite grain is more widely distributed among deposits likely to have been used as potting clay than DAI's petrofacies model indicates.

We also think that archaeologists need to make a theoretical distinction between processes of ceramic *distribution* from processes of ceramic *exchange*. Many behaviors other than specialized production and exchange can result in the wide distribution of pottery beyond its locale of production. In particular, the daily and seasonal movement of people across the landscape in their subsistence, economic, and social pursuits can distribute pottery widely. Ceramic production data can serve as a proxy for settlement pattern (Whittlesey 1998c:443). Although this possibility has been little explored, the Sunset Mesa Ruin ceramic production data are certainly consistent with the notion of small-scale residential mobility. The site was occupied for a relatively short time, and the abandonment and site structure data together suggest that Sunset Mesa Ruin may have been a short-term residential settlement possibly devoted to farming pursuits. Evidence is emerging that this dispersed settlement pattern may have distinguished the Rincon phase throughout the Tucson Basin. Large, year-round settlements, such as the West Branch site, may have provided the long-term social, economic, and ritual foundation for seasonal movement to small, outlying communities for farming, resource collecting, and other activities. Pottery made at the West Branch site would have accompanied the residents on these seasonal dispersions, resulting in a distribution identical to that produced by specialized production and exchange. Distinguishing between residential mobility and exchange is not easy (see Stark et al. 1995), but is critical if we are to reconstruct Rincon phase economic processes accurately.

Fourth, the multiple sources among the identified petrofacies, which imply the pottery was made in different places, are intriguingly correlated with style among Rincon Red-on-brown pottery (see Table 17). Roughly equal, and high, proportions (88–90 percent) of Rincon Style A and B pottery (including black-painted and white-slipped variants) are tempered with Beehive Peak sand. A lesser proportion of indeterminate-style Rincon Red-on-brown pottery (71.4 percent) shares this temper, whereas a significant proportion (24.5 percent) is tempered with Twin Hills petrofacies sand. In addition to indicating at least two production locales for painted ceramics, this suggests the possibility of stylistic microtraditions among Tucson Basin potters that were geographically restricted. The pottery we identified as indeterminate style (unidentifiable as Style A or Style B) may represent an alternative design tradition among potters using Twin Hills petrofacies sand. Twin Hills encompasses St. Mary's Ruin and other important sites sandwiched between the larger communities to the north, such as Los Morteros, and those in the south, such as the West Branch site. It is the second-nearest petrofacies to Sunset Mesa on the west side of the Santa Cruz River, located between Wasson and Beehive Peak. We suspect that our implicit sampling procedures may have influenced these patterns, but we do not know to what extent or how. Certainly these possibilities need to be explored with a larger and more randomly selected sample.

Nonlocally made pottery also presents some interesting distributions. The only nonlocally made pottery we identified originated in the Phoenix area. This was Gila Plain, Hohokam Buff Ware, and possible Sacaton Red. Gila Plain was found in minor quantities (less than 1 percent of all plain ware sherds), and one possible Sacaton Red sherd was found. The role played by micaceous utility pottery in Tucson Basin ceramic assemblages was apparently reserved for pottery that appears to have been made in the Tucson Basin and tempered with sand and muscovite mica. Ceramic collections in other so-called peripheral Hohokam areas, such as the Tonto Basin, often have considerable quantities of schist-tempered plain ware apparently derived from the Phoenix Basin (e.g., Stark et al. 1995). Because of the lack of petrographic analyses designed to identify the provenance of schist-tempered pottery found in the Tucson Basin, we cannot say if this pattern is common, or eliminate the local metamorphic core complexes as the source of the schist-tempered pottery. In short, there is much work to be done in sourcing schist-tempered pottery.

In contrast to the plain ware, there is a considerable amount of intrusive painted pottery at Sunset Mesa Ruin that originated in the Phoenix Basin. Hohokam Buff Ware represents 12.1 percent of the painted sherds, and 5.3 percent of the total sherd collection recovered from pit houses. Several researchers have noted that, when compared to the Colonial period, the Sedentary period witnessed a dramatic decrease in the frequency of buff ware ceramics (Doelle and Wallace 1986; Greenleaf 1975; Wallace 1985). In comparison to other Tucson Basin collections, the proportion of buff ware at Sunset Mesa Ruin is anomalous. Wallace (1986b:102) reported less that 1 percent buff ware pottery in contexts dating to the middle portion of the Rincon phase at the West Branch site. Bubemyre (1996:6–20) reported 2 percent buff ware at the SRI locus of the West Branch site. At the Tanque Verde Wash site, 11 Hohokam Buff Ware sherds were recovered among more than 29,000 sherds (less than half of 1 percent), and buff ware represented 0.2 percent of the painted collection (Wallace 1986a:176).

These relatively low percentages do not necessarily represent a simple decrease through time, for Hohokam Buff Ware is not evenly distributed across the Tucson Basin. Doelle and Wallace (1991) plotted the percentages of Santa Cruz Red-on-buff and Rillito Red-on-brown ware, and found that sites located in the southern and southwestern portions of the basin had much lower percentages of Santa Cruz Red-on-buff than sites in the northern and eastern portions of the basin. There is no simple fall-off pattern, however, as frequencies of buff ware increase, once again, south of the Tucson Basin (Doelle and Wallace 1991:287, Figure 7.9). A clear zone is defined that exhibits low percentages of Hohokam Buff Ware and correspondingly high percentages of Tucson painted pottery. Its northern border appears to be somewhere between Hodges Ruin and St. Mary's Ruin. Although they are less than 7 km apart, Hodges Ruin exhibits 54 percent buff ware compared to less than 6 percent at St. Mary's Ruin (Doelle and Wallace 1991:287). Indeed, the frequency of buff ware and other imported goods at Hodges Ruin, along with the site's strategic location, led Layhe (1986b:289) to characterize it as a point of entry into the Tucson Basin, and a central place that may have functioned in the distribution of exotic goods.

The high frequency of buff ware pottery at Sunset Mesa Ruin may be indicative of the site's location, which is well north of the boundary represented by Hodges Ruin. By virtue of this location, the inhabitants may have had greater opportunity to obtain buff ware pottery coming south from the Phoenix area. Another possibility is maintenance of greater social contacts, through kinship, marriage, membership in religious groups, or other mechanisms, with the Hohokam of the Phoenix area. The relatively small size of the settlement implies that settlement function is not a likely explanation.

Concluding Remarks

The ceramic collection from Sunset Mesa Ruin represents a Rincon phase occupation of relatively brief duration. There are no substantial ceramic indicators of earlier or later occupation at the site, with the exception of the few sherds representing the historical-period component. The Sunset Mesa Ruin ceramic collection has provided an opportunity to add to a growing body of information concerning the Tucson Basin ceramic tradition. As many researchers have recognized implicitly (e.g., Deaver 1984, 1989b; Greenleaf 1975; Heidke 1995; Huckell 1987; Wallace 1986c; Whittlesey 1986a), Hohokam pottery of the Tucson Basin was not simply a copy of Hohokam ceramics produced in the Phoenix Basin. For whatever social, ritual, economic, or cultural reasons, the traditions were distinct. In many respects—particularly the technological and design diversity among the painted pottery, the apparently contemporaneous stylistic expressions, the flourishing red ware tradition, and the development of a polychrome pottery tradition—the Tucson Basin was unique. Moreover, these innovations appear to have taken place within a relatively brief period of time during the Rincon phase. The current Tucson Basin chronology (Dean 1991; Wallace and Craig 1988) implies that introduction of black pigment, development of polychrome ceramics, and blossoming of red ware all took place within a short time span, perhaps half a century or less. Combined with the appearance of radical changes in tempering materials and in vessel form, a time of extreme and rapid change in the ceramic art is indicated—one that was unparalleled in the Phoenix Basin. Without question, the Rincon phase represents the fluorescence of the Tucson Basin ceramic tradition.

Coupled with this understanding is the striking possibility that these innovations were produced by a relatively small group of potters concentrated in the western portion of the Tucson Basin on the flanks of the Tucson Mountains. Taken at face value—which must be the case, in the absence of experimental studies—the petrographic data indicate the predominant use of Beehive Peak petrofacies sand and other western-basin petrofacies sand to temper Rincon painted pottery and Rincon Red pottery. The discovery of pottery-making equipment and materials in

houses at the West Branch site (Harry 1996; Huntington 1986) implies that ceramic production took place at this settlement located in the Beehive Peak petrofacies. The possibility exists that potters living at this relatively large settlement were responsible for the Rincon phase ceramic innovations. Discovering the reasons for these innovations is an important direction for future study.

As suggested previously, another critical direction for future research is distinguishing among alternative possibilities for ceramic production and distribution. Was the West Branch settlement a locale for specialized production and wide exchange of pottery during the Rincon phase? Or were Rincon phase people employing a dispersed residential and economic settlement system that created many small settlements linked to a large and permanent village? Such research directions are likely to yield a better understanding of Tucson Basin Hohokam than continued efforts to demonstrate the existence of vast ceramic production and distribution networks (e.g., Wallace and Heidke 1986), or village-based craft specialization (e.g., Harry 1996).

CHAPTER 7

Flaked and Ground Stone Analyses

Anthony Della Croce

A total of 867 flaked and ground stone artifacts was recovered from Sunset Mesa Ruin. Although neither assemblage is temporally diagnostic, the general characteristics of both resemble other lithic collections from Rincon phase sites in the Tucson Basin. A relatively high ratio of unmodified flakes (56 percent) to formally produced flaked tools (less than 1 percent) (Table 19) is indicative of what has been termed an "expedient" flake technology (Rozen 1984), interpreted as the result of both increased sedentism and a growing reliance on agriculture (Parry and Kelly 1987).

Table 19. Artifact Types and Frequencies in the Sunset Mesa Ruin Lithic Assemblage

Artifact Type	n	%
Debitage	487	56
Flaked stone tools	6	< 1
Shatter	173	20
Cores	68	8
Hammer stones	6	< 1
Manos	40	5
Metates	19	2
Polishing stones	8	1
Abrading stones	3	< 1
Tabular knives	2	< 1
Axes	2	< 1
Mortar	1	< 1
Pestle	1	< 1
Other	7	< 1
Ground stone fragments	44	5
Total	867	

Research Questions

Four research questions are discussed based on the analysis of the Sunset Mesa Ruin lithic assemblage. As defined in the data recovery plan, these are (1) type of production of lithic implements (i.e., technology); (2) activities represented by tool types; (3) site function; and (4) evidence for trade and exchange. The results for the flaked and ground stone artifacts are described separately. A related analysis is the sourcing of three pieces of obsidian, which is not indigenous to the Tucson Basin (see Appendix C).

Flaked Stone Analysis

Methods

The flaked stone assemblage was separated into four classes, including cores, shatter, unmodified flakes (debitage), and tools. Raw materials were recorded for both flaked and ground stone assemblages. Weight, directionality, and degree of reduction were recorded for cores. Recorded attributes for tools include tool type (based on morphology) and metric data (weight, length, width, and thickness). Only six tools were recovered, all of which lacked diagnostic qualities for addressing such issues as chronology, use, and formal tool production at Sunset Mesa Ruin. Consequently, a combined analysis of flaked and ground stone was employed for maximum interpretive efficiency (Table 20).

The largest component of the Sunset Mesa Ruin collection—debitage—warranted a more intensive analysis than that of other recovered flaked artifact classes. The examination of unmodified flakes has played a prominent

Table 20. Provenience Designations for Flaked Stone Tools and Ground Stone Artifacts

Provenience, by Artifact Type	Context	n	Provenience, by Artifact Type	Context	n
Flaked stone tools			F 15.01, L 1	feature fill	3
Projectile point (1)			F 22, L 2	roof fall	1
F 25, L 1	feature fill	1	F 23, L ?	floor	1
Biface (1)			F 27, L 1	roof fall	2
F 22.04, L 2	feature fill	1	F 27, L 3	floor	1
Scrapers (4)			Pestle (1)		
F 22.04, L 2	feature fill	1	F 26, L 1	feature fill	1
F 25, L 1	feature fill	1	Mortar (1)		
F 25, L 2	feature fill	1	SU 1	overburden	1
F 27.03, L 1	feature fill	1	Abrading stones (3)		
			F 13, L 1	feature fill	1
Ground stone			F 21, subfloor	feature fill	1
Utilitarian			F 27.03, L 1	feature fill	1
Manos (40)			Axes (2)		
Trench 13	backdirt	1	SU 17	overburden	1
SU 1	overburden	2	F 22, L 2	roof fall	1
SU 4	overburden	3	Polishing stones (8)		
SU 5	overburden	2	SU 1	overburden	2
SU 6	overburden	1	SU 2	overburden	1
SU 16	overburden	2	SU 4	overburden	1
F 5, Room 1, L 1	feature fill	4	SU 5	overburden	1
F 5, Room 1, L 2	feature fill	1	F 21, L 2	feature fill	1
F 13, L 1	feature fill	9	F 21, subfloor	feature fill	1
F 21, L 2	feature fill	2	F 23, L 1	feature fill	1
F 21, L 4	floor	1	Tabular knives (2)		
F 22, L 2	roof fall	1	SU 9	overburden	1
F 22, L ?	feature fill	1	F 15.01, L 1	feature fill	1
F 22, L 4	floor	2	Other (2)		
F 23, L ?	floor	1	F 22, L 1	fill	1
F 26, L 1	feature fill	1	F 27, L 3	floor	1
F 27, L 1	roof fall	1	Nonutilitarian		
F 31	backdirt	3	Ornament (1)		
F 48, L 1	feature fill	1	F 13, L 4	feature fill	1
Metates (19)			Cruciform (1)		
Trench 16	backdirt	5	F 26, L 1	feature fill	1
SU 5	overburden	1	Palettes (2)		
SU 17	overburden	1	F 13, L 1	feature fill	1
F 5, Room 2, L 1	feature fill	1	F 22.04, L ?	feature fill	1
F 5, Room 3, L 1	feature fill	1	Incised bowl (1)		
F 13, L 1	feature fill	2	SU 1	overburden	1

Key: F = Feature; L = Level; SU = Stripping Unit

role in Hohokam lithic analysis as a result of their frequently dominating presence in collections. Rozen (1984; see also Sullivan and Rozen 1985) has shown that flaked-based assemblages, contrary to commonly held assumptions, do have interpretive value. The present study uses applications from such prior research, in addition to what has been termed a "minimum flake attribute set" (Schott 1994:79–81).

Recorded attributes for debitage (here used in the strict sense as unmodified flakes) include raw material, technology (reduction stage), size, platform type, flake status (completeness), and visible edge wear. the reduction stage (that is, tertiary, secondary, primary, and bifacial thinning) of flakes was recorded based on morphology and percentage of exterior cortical coverage. Size was measured using a 10-cm concentric scale marked at 1-cm intervals. Five platform types were recorded, including plain, trimmed, cortical, faceted, and indeterminate, the last class including removed platforms. Flaked status comprised complete, split, proximal and fragmented categories. Finally, the presence or absence of visible (to the naked eye) edge damage was recorded as a binary attribute.

Results

Following is a discussion of the results from the flaked stone analysis. The discussion is organized by a consideration of raw material procurement, followed by three artifact classes: flakes, cores, and tools.

Raw Material Procurement

An analysis of raw materials by flaked artifact class (Table 21) indicates that chert was the preferred material (30 percent) at Sunset Mesa Ruin. It is likely that this material was traded or quarried from AZ AA:16:187 (ASM), a chert quarry located south of the junction of the Santa Cruz River and its West Branch arroyo, approximately 8 km from Sunset Mesa. The chert that comes from AA:16:187 is a milky brown color with few phenocrysts, similar to much of the chert found at Sunset Mesa Ruin. The next most commonly used material was rhyolite (23 percent), which was probably procured from nearby Safford peak, a popular source of prehistoric rhyolite in the Tucson Basin.

A. igneous and P. igneous represent aphanitic (microcrystalline) and phaneritic (macrocrystalline) igneous rocks, respectively. Generalized terms such these are employed to avoid the inconsistency with which igneous rocks, recovered from stream proveniences, are identified. Most of the other materials in the flaked stone assemblage, excluding obsidian and argillite, were probably procured from local washes. Three pieces of obsidian were sourced using x-ray fluorescence analysis. Two pieces could not be identified, but the third was sourced

Table 21. Raw Material by Flaked Stone Artifact Class

Raw Material	Flake		Shatter		Cores		Tools		Total
	n	%	n	%	n	%	n	%	n
Chert	167	34	39	23	11	17	1	17	218
A. igneous	97	20	86	50	13	19	1	17	197
P. igneous	45	9	20	12	7	10	—	—	72
Quartzite	26	5	—	—	9	13	—	—	35
Mineral quartz	3	1	1	< 1	—	—	1	17	5
Chalcedony	3	1	4	2	—	—	1	17	8
Greenstone	4	1	1	< 1	3	4	—	—	8
Rhyolite	128	26	17	10	24	36	1	17	170
Obsidian	2	< 1	1	< 1	—	—	—	—	3
Sandstone	4	1	—	—	—	—	—	—	4
Vesicular basalt	5	1	1	< 1	—	—	—	—	6
Argillite	—	—	—	—	—	—	1	17	1
Redstone	3	1	3	2	—	—	—	—	6
Limestone	—	—	—	—	1	1	—	—	1
Total	487		173		68		6		734

Table 22. Debitage Raw Material by Flake Status

Raw Material	Complete		Split		Proximal		Fragmented		Total
	n	%	n	%	n	%	n	%	n
Chert	125	35	13	48	4	44	25	27	167
A. igneous	78	22	3	11	1	11	15	16	97
P. igneous	34	9	—	—	—	—	11	12	45
Quartzite	11	3	5	19	1	11	9	10	26
Mineral quartz	1	< 1	—	—	—	—	2	2	3
Chalcedony	1	< 1	—	—	—	—	2	2	3
Greenstone	4	1	—	—	—	—	—	—	4
Rhyolite	98	27	5	19	3	33	22	24	128
Obsidian	2	< 1	—	—	—	—	—	—	2
Sandstone	1	< 1	—	—	—	—	3	3	4
Vesicular basalt	1	< 1	—	—	—	—	4	4	5
Redstone	2	< 1	1	4	—	—	—	—	3
Total	358		27		9		93		487
Percentage of total flakes		73		6		2		19	100

Flakes

As indicated by Table 22, most flakes recovered from the site were complete (n = 358; 73 percent). According to Sullivan and Rozen (1985), a high ratio of whole to broken flakes may indicate a preference for core reduction over tool manufacture, as the latter often produces a higher percentage of flake fragmentation during manufacture. Although this has been challenged by subsequent studies (Baumler and Downum 1989; Tomka 1989), a preference for the production of flakes over formal tools seems to be the emerging pattern of Tucson Basin Hohokam flaked stone assemblages. This preference is evidenced by high percentages of complete flakes in all raw materials except mineral quartz, chalcedony, and vesicular basalt, which by their very nature produce higher proportions of fragmentation during primary flaking.

Table 23 shows that most complete flakes are 4–5 cm in maximum dimensions. Flakes in this size range may have resulted purely from preference, as flakes this large are easily held in the hand. Or, a standard reduction method and platform angle may have been chosen, creating flakes of similar metric attributes. Experiments by Dibble and Whittaker (1981) have shown that consistency of the platform angle and position of the core at the moment of flake initiation can produce flakes similar in size.

As indicated in Table 24, high proportions of plain and cortical platforms, combined with a high ratio of complete core reduction flakes (primary, secondary and tertiary) to prepared bifacial thinning flakes, indicate little reliance on formal tool reduction and a preference for sharp, freshly struck flakes at Sunset Mesa Ruin. In general, high proportions of plain platforms accompany technologies that place a lesser emphasis on the controlled production of flakes. In order to better control a flake's metric qualities, such as size, the preparation of platforms (only 7 percent at Sunset Mesa Ruin) is often necessary. The high ratio of flakes without visible edge damage to that of flakes exhibiting signs of use may be misleading (see Table 24). Cutting activities involving meat and other soft materials may not leave noticeable edge damage, in contrast to using flakes on such harder materials as wood and bone (Keely 1980). In addition, the identification of such use wear is often unreliable (Young and Bamforth 1990).

Cores

A total of 68 cores was recovered from Sunset Mesa Ruin (Table 25). Raw materials present in the core assemblage (see Table 21) are similar to those in the debitage assemblage, with one important exception. Chert is present in a much smaller proportion in the core assemblage than among the debitage. This may indicate that chert was used

Table 23. Debitage Raw Material by Size Class for Unmodified Complete Flakes

Raw Material	1 cm	2 cm	3 cm	4 cm	5 cm	6 cm	7 cm	8 cm	9 cm	10 cm	Total Flakes
Chert	—	14	25	30	38	6	5	5	—	2	125
A. igneous	1	7	13	19	25	4	5	2	2	—	78
P. igneous	—	—	3	16	10	2	1	1	1	—	34
Quartzite	—	1	3	3	2	1	—	—	1	—	11
Mineral quartz	—	1	—	—	—	—	—	—	—	—	1
Chalcedony	—	—	1	—	—	—	—	—	—	—	1
Greenstone	—	—	—	2	2	—	—	—	—	—	4
Rhyolite	—	9	19	24	20	19	4	1	1	1	98
Obsidian	—	2	—	—	—	—	—	—	—	—	2
Sandstone	—	—	—	—	1	—	—	—	—	—	1
Vesicular basalt	—	—	—	1	—	—	—	—	—	—	1
Redstone	—	—	—	1	1	—	—	—	—	—	2
Total	1	34	64	96	99	32	15	9	5	3	358

Table 24. Flake Attribute Frequencies

Flake Attribute	n	%
Reduction stage		
Primary	43	9
Secondary	115	24
Tertiary	327	67
Bifacial thinning	2	< 1
Total reduction stage	487	
Platform type		
Plain	212	44
Prepared	36	7
Cortical	125	26
Indeterminate	93	19
Faceted	21	4
Total platform type	487	
Edge wear		
Yes	40	8
No	447	92
Total edge wear	487	

Table 25. Core Attribute Frequencies

Core Attribute	n	%
Core size (g)		
0–100	36	53
100–200	12	18
200–300	11	16
300–400	6	9
400–500	1	1
500–1000	2	3
Total core size	68	
Core type (direction)		
Unidirectional	44	65
Bidirectional	5	7
Multidirectional	19	28
Total core type	68	
Core completeness (percentage remaining)		
Exhausted	30	44
10	14	21
25	6	9
50	7	10
75	5	7
90	4	6
95	2	3
Total core completeness	68	

more efficiently because of its better knapping qualities and the increased energy needed for its procurement. Of the 30 cores classified as exhausted, 11 (37 percent) were chert. Ten of these were reduced using a multidirectional flake removal technique, suggesting that chert was a highly desired material at the site. The other materials generally were reduced unifacially and often incompletely, indicating that efficiency in flake removal was not a priority when making use of the abundant local materials.

Flaked Stone Tools

Six flaked stone tools were recovered from Sunset Mesa Ruin, two bifaces and four scrapers (see Table 20). The two bifaces include one broken projectile point tip made from chert, and a crude biface or preform made from rhyolite (Figure 58). Neither artifact is temporally diagnostic. The point tip was broken during manufacture, as shown by the presence of a lateral pressure fracture. The four scrapers are all backed. Two of these are made from finer materials, chalcedony (see Figure 58) and argillite. The remaining two were made from local river pebbles and flaked unifacially, an attribute common among many Hohokam scraper tools in the Tucson Basin.

Ground Stone Analysis

Methods and Results

The ground stone from Sunset Mesa Ruin was divided into two different typological groups—utilitarian and nonutilitarian—that do not reflect the actual function of described artifacts (Tagg 1984). Utilitarian ground stone is defined as those items with established functions, such as manos, metates, tabular knives, polishing stones, pestles, mortars, abrading stones, and axes. The functions of nonutilitarian items, in contrast, are not readily apparent or cannot be ascertained with any degree of certainty. Such items include censers, palettes, and ornaments. Table 26 lists both utilitarian and nonutilitarian items recovered from the site, whereas provenience designations for both classes of ground stone are provided in Table 20.

Utilitarian Ground Stone

Each class of utilitarian artifacts was analyzed using a variety of attributes: raw material, completeness, indication of thermal alteration, interior (where possible) and exterior texture, overall shape (mostly for manos and

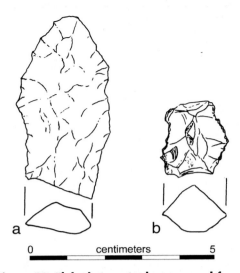

Figure 58. Flaked stone tools recovered from Sunset Mesa Ruin: (a) biface from Feature 22.04; (b) chalcedony scraper from Feature 27.03.

Table 26. Ground Stone Artifact Types and Frequencies

Tool Type	n	%
Utilitarian		
Manos[a]	40	31
Metates[a]	19	15
Pestle	1	< 1
Mortar	1	< 1
Abrading stones	3	2
Axes	2	2
Polishing stones	8	6
Tabular knives	2	2
Other	2	2
Subtotal utilitarian	78	61
Nonutilitarian		
Ornaments	1	< 1
Cruciform	1	< 1
Palettes[a]	2	2
Incised bowl	1	< 1
Subtotal utilitarian	5	4
Indeterminate fragments	44	35
Total	127	

[a] Count includes fragments

140

Table 27. Utilitarian Ground Stone Raw Materials by Artifact Type

Raw Material	Manos	Metates	Pestles	Mortars	Abrading Stones	Axes	Polishing Stones	Tabular Knives	Other	Total n	%
Vesicular basalt	18	14	—	1	—	—	—	—	—	33	42
Quartzite	12	—	—	—	2	1	—	—	—	15	19
A. igneous	3	2	—	—	1	1	2	—	—	9	11
P. igneous	2	—	—	—	—	—	—	—	—	2	3
Granite	2	2	—	—	—	—	—	—	—	4	5
Sandstone	1	—	1	—	—	—	—	—	—	2	3
Schist	2	—	—	—	—	—	—	—	—	2	3
Basalt	—	1	—	—	—	—	—	—	2	3	4
Slate	—	—	—	—	—	—	—	2	—	2	3
Indeterminate	—	—	—	—	—	—	6	—	—	6	8
Total	40	19	1	1	3	2	8	2	2	78	

metates), and extent of shaping. Most of these attributes suggest an intensity of use prior to discard or breakage. Manos, if complete or nearly so, were classified as one-hand or two-hand, based on overall length.

The types of raw materials exploited for utilitarian ground stone tools (Table 27) exhibit a pattern common among sites in the Tucson Basin. Vesicular basalt, quartzite, and various igneous rocks make up most of the materials used in the production of ground stone tools. Vesicular basalt probably was obtained from a source on Tumamoc Hill, where a large supply is present today. The remaining materials also are probably from local sources, with the exception of schist, which is found in the Santa Catalina Mountains, to the north.

The variety of utilitarian ground stone recovered from Sunset Mesa Ruin (see Table 20) indicates that food-processing tasks were carried out at the site. A high proportion (n = 31; 78 percent) of both one- and two-hand manos are completely shaped. In addition, two of the three complete metates were ground into deep, trough-shaped basins, such as the large granite metate (Figure 59) recovered from the floor of Feature 23. This extensive shaping of the ground stone assemblage suggests either a continuously extended or repeated seasonal occupation at the site.

Additional artifacts include one axe and one maul (Figure 60). Because both are broken, the extent of grooving could not be ascertained. The maul was used as a hammer stone and flaked following breakage. The recovery of two tabular knives (Figure 61) suggests the processing of plant materials, possibly agave, although no residue analysis was done on the artifacts. One is pierced near a corner, possibly for hanging from a rope or belt. The other is a crescent-shaped knife that was refit from three separate fragments. Also recovered were a possible pestle and a mortar (Figure 62); the two artifacts were not in direct association (see Table 20). Whereas the mortar is made from vesicular basalt, the pestle is sandstone, and shows signs of having been worn down and discarded.

Two basalt rocks were placed in the utilitarian "other" category because of the unclear nature of their use. One, recovered from the floor of Feature 27, is roughly rectangular and blocky, measuring 25.6 by 21.2 cm and 7.8 cm thick. It displays some pecking on its upper, flattish surface; the pecking could be the product of excavation, however. This rock may have served as an anvil or perhaps was simply a manuport, brought in for use as a flat, raised surface. The second rock, from the fill of Feature 22, has been shaped to a wedge form with rounded edges created by pecking; it exhibits a smooth polish on its two wide surfaces, possibly from use with a soft material, such as hide or fiber. Measuring 21.5 by 21 cm and 6.3 cm thick, this rock may have served as a lap stone.

Nonutilitarian Ground Stone

Five ground stone artifacts classified as nonutilitarian were recovered (see Table 20). The four classes of artifacts (ornamental stone, palettes, a cruciform and an incised bowl) are not commonly found at sites in the Tucson Basin. At the present time, it is not known whether this is due to a lack of production on the part of the Tucson Basin Hohokam, or the results are perhaps skewed because of pot hunting, which targets such items.

The cruciform and the ornamental stone (Figure 63) are interesting for different reasons. The argillite cruciform

Figure 59. Trough-shaped basin metate recovered from the floor of Feature 23 at Sunset Mesa Ruin.

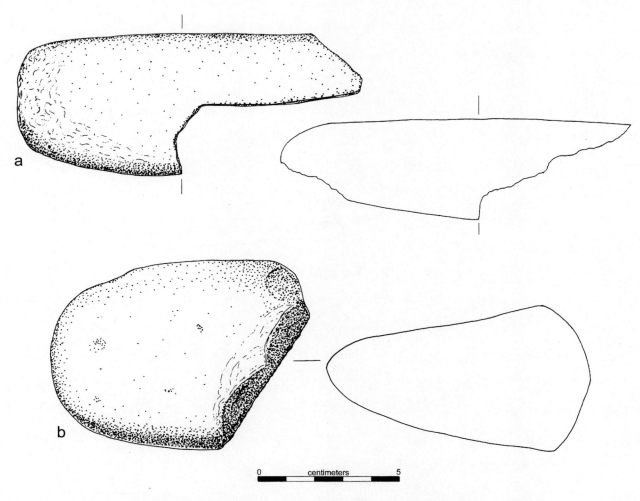

Figure 60. Utilitarian ground stone artifacts recovered from Sunset Mesa Ruin:
(a) axe fragment from Stripping Unit 17; (b) maul fragment from Feature 22.

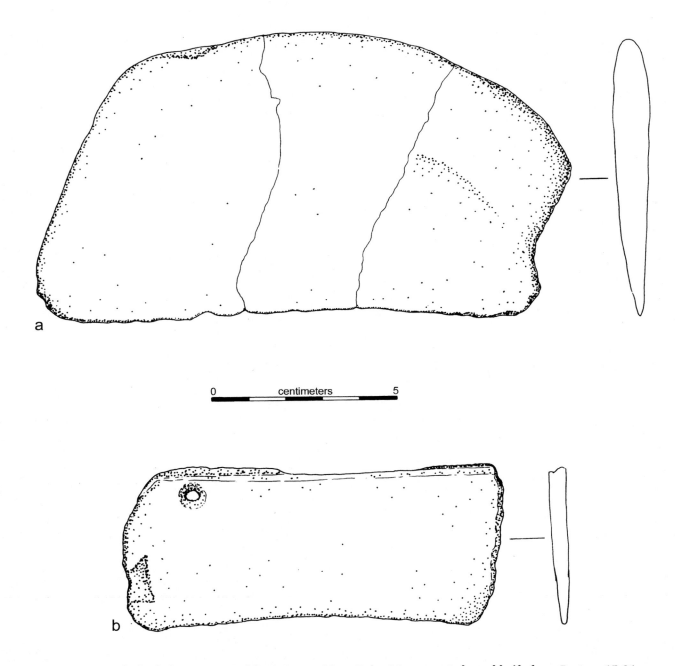

0   centimeters   5

Figure 61. Tabular knives recovered from Sunset Mesa Ruin: (a) crescent-shaped knife from Feature 15.01; (b) pierced knife from Stripping Unit 9.

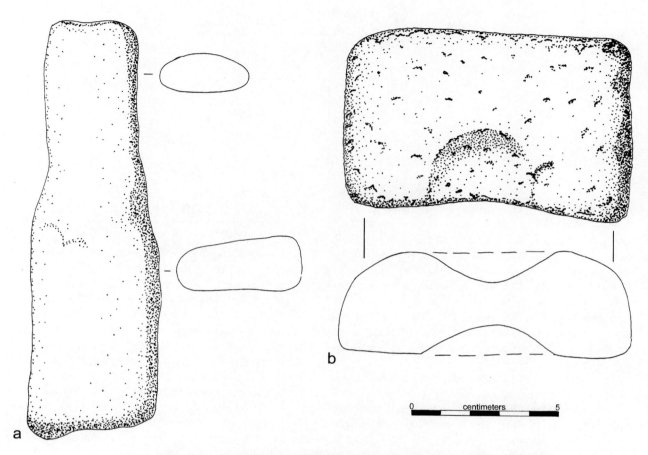

**Figure 62. Utilitarian ground stone artifacts recovered from Sunset Mesa Ruin:
(a) pestle from Feature 26; (b) mortar fragment from Stripping Unit 1.**

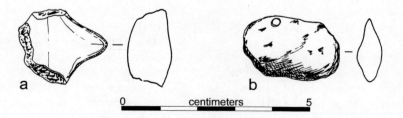

**Figure 63. Nonutilitarian ground stone artifacts recovered from Sunset Mesa Ruin:
(a) argillite cruciform fragment from Feature 26; (b) jasper pendant from Feature 13.**

Table 28. Nonutilitarian Ground Stone Raw Materials by Artifact Type

Raw Material	Ornamental Stone	Cruciform	Palette	Incised Bowl	Total	
					n	%
Jasper	1	—	—	—	1	20
Argillite	—	1	—	—	1	20
Schist	—	—	1	—	1	20
Slate	—	—	1	—	1	20
Tuff	—	—	—	1	1	20
Total	1	1	2	1	5	

(Table 28) is fragmentary, and may have been an "heirloom" piece procured from an earlier site or context. This inference is based on an artifact found at the Archaic period Santa Cruz Bend site (AZ AA:12:746 [ASM]) (Mabry et al. 1997), south of Sunset Mesa, that is very similar in form and size. The ornamental stone is perforated and made of jasper. The perforation, which is very well executed, is quite small and shows no signs of having been drilled; rather, it is more like a puncture of the material. Most probably the artifact was a pendant used as jewelry.

Palettes and incised bowls have been recorded from a variety of Sedentary period sites (Ferg 1984; Haury 1937b, 1976; Sayles 1937). Of the two palettes recovered from Sunset Mesa Ruin, one is complete. Made from schist, it has a criss-cross-style, incised border that is flush with its interior (Figure 64), a trait thought to belong to the Sedentary period (Haury 1937b, 1976). As pointed out by Ferg (1984), however, technological limitations imposed by the thin nature of the schist played an important role in the overall form of the palette. This complete specimen, which was found in the fill of the ramada area (Feature 13), is not burned and was not associated with a cremation, as is often the case with palettes. The other specimen, a small corner fragment made of slate and burned, was found in an intrusive pit (Feature 22.04) in pit house Feature 22.

The incised bowl, made of tuff, is cylindrical in shape and nearly complete. Its sides are incised in a cross-hatched style, creating a diamond-shaped pattern. This artifact type has been referred to as a censer (Haury 1976; Sayles 1937), and may have functioned as such. This particular example, however, does not exhibit signs of anything having burned in it. Unfortunately, the stylistic attributes of the incising are not temporally diagnostic, as they appear throughout much of the Hohokam sequence.

Conclusions

The Sunset Mesa Ruin lithic assemblage shares common attributes with other Rincon phase sites in the Tucson Basin, such as the West Branch site (AZ AA:16:3 [ASM]) (Eppley 1986) and the Valencia site (AZ BB:13:15 [ASM]) (Graff 1985). A high proportion of core reduction flakes to formal tools, coupled with the lack of evidence for the production of formal tools, is typical of these sites and supports the notion of an expedient, flake-based industry (Parry and Kelly 1987). The high proportion of whole flakes and plain platforms, and the low incidence of visible use wear also support this conclusion. In addition, the low number of temporally diagnostic tools recovered suggests only that the assemblage reflects a Formative period occupation.

Activities involving the lithic assemblage probably were dominated by the processing of food materials and small animals. Steep-sided scrapers, similar to those recovered (n = 4) have been shown to be very effective in the butchering of small rodents and lagomorphs (Jobson 1986). The lithic assemblage does not seem to have been concentrated in any one area (Table 29). This is true for individual classes of artifacts, as well as for the entire assemblage. Although 24 lithic items were recovered from floor contexts, the integrity of these proveniences is somewhat in doubt. During the course of analysis approximately 12 pieces of railroad slag were recorded from subfloor contexts in the same features that produced floor-contact assemblages. Evidently, the intrusion of small objects from the surface was an active taphonomic process at Sunset Mesa Ruin. However, the uncovering of such artifacts as complete metates (Feature 23, floor) certainly suggests that the processing of plant materials with ground stone implements did take place in some of the features.

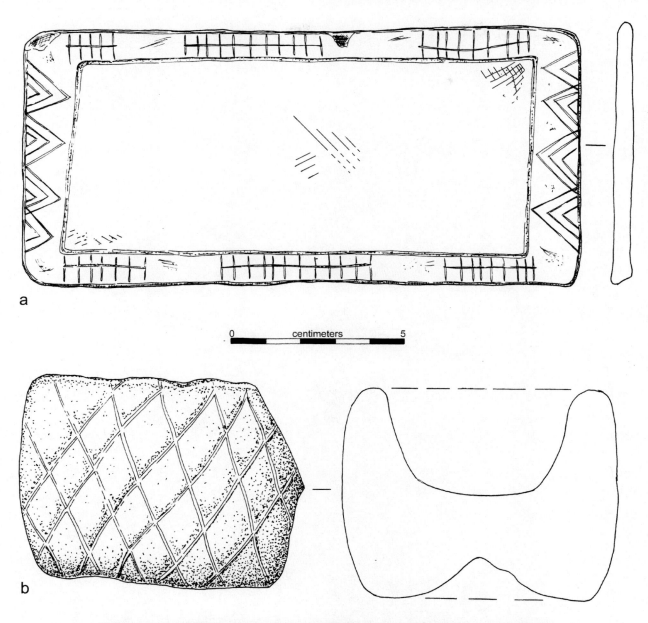

0   centimeters   5

Figure 64. Nonutilitarian ground stone artifacts recovered from Sunset Mesa Ruin: (a) decorated palette from Feature 13; (b) incised bowl from Stripping Unit 1.

Other activities represented at the site, as indicated by the lithic assemblage, possibly include the production of pottery. Eight polishing and three abrading stones were recovered from various contexts (see Table 20). Few formal lithic tools were used by the site's inhabitants, an observation that is not surprising, given the declining importance of formal tools often associated with increased sedentism. Although there is evidence in the form of obsidian for a minor amount of trade, the vast majority of the lithic assemblage at Sunset Mesa Ruin seems to have involved the local procurement of raw materials and their subsequent reduction for use as simple flake tools.

Table 29. Lithic Collection, by Feature

Feature No.	Feature Type	Age	Debitage	Shatter	Cores	Tools	Hammer Stones	Utilitarian Ground Stone[a]	Nonutilitarian Ground Stone[a]	Total n	Total %
5	adobe structure	historical period	21	7	2	—	—	8	3	41	5
5.01	intrusive pit	historical period	12	7	2	—	—	1	—	22	3
13	ramada	Rincon phase	45	15	7	—	1	17	3	88	10
15	kitchen area	Rincon phase	17	5	2	—	—	—	—	23	3
15.01–15.03	fire-cracked rock	Rincon phase	17	—	6	—	2	8	2	35	4
17	reconstructible vessel	Rincon phase	3	1	—	—	—	—	—	4	<1
18	irrigation canal	Rincon phase	35	7	2	—	—	—	—	44	5
20	pit	Rincon phase	1	—	—	—	—	—	—	1	<1
21	pit house	Rincon phase	85	23	8	—	—	6	4	126	15
22	pit house	Rincon phase	41	8	9	—	1	13	—	72	8
22.01	hearth	Rincon phase	2	4	1	—	—	1	—	7	<1
22.02–22.05	intrusive pits	Rincon phase	—	4	—	2	—	1	1	8	<1
23	pit house	Rincon phase	29	13	5	—	1	5	1	54	6
23.02	intrusive pit	Rincon phase	2	1	—	—	—	—	—	3	<1
24	pit	historical period	1	—	—	—	—	—	—	1	<1
25	pit house	Rincon phase	68	51	5	3	—	2	—	130	15
25.02	unknown	Rincon phase	2	—	3	—	—	2	—	7	<1
26	scatter	unknown	16	3	1	—	—	2	2	24	3
27	pit house	Rincon phase	47	7	1	—	—	7	—	62	7
27.03	intrusive pit	Rincon phase	4	—	—	1	—	1	—	6	<1
31	trash area	Rincon phase	2	—	—	—	—	2	—	4	<1
41	pit	Rincon phase	2	—	1	—	—	—	—	3	<1
47	pit	Rincon phase	8	4	—	—	—	—	—	12	1
48	posthole	Rincon phase	2	—	—	—	—	—	—	2	<1
SU1–SU17	stripping units	unknown	20	11	11	—	1	22	6	71	8
TR13 & 16	trenches	unknown	1	—	1	—	—	8	—	10	1
Surface & backdirt	surface and backdirt	unknown	4	2	1	—	—	—	—	7	<1
Total			487	173	68	6	6	103	24	867	

[a] Indeterminate ground stone fragments included in count.

CHAPTER 8

Shell Analysis

Arthur W. Vokes

The excavations undertaken by SRI at Sunset Mesa Ruin produced a shell assemblage of more than 61 pieces of marine, freshwater, and terrestrial shell that is estimated to represent approximately 57 specimens. The sample includes finished artifacts, material in the process of production, unworked fragments and whole valves. This chapter provides a descriptive summary of the different artifact forms present, and a comparison and interpretation of these results within the framework of the Tucson Basin during the Sedentary period.

Methods

The assemblage was subjected to a detailed analysis that involved the creation of a descriptive record, including a scale drawing, along with a set of linear measurements obtained by using a digital vernier caliper. Notes on condition, shape, decorative motifs, and technological aspects were recorded. For purposes of analysis, fragments that could be refitted were considered to be a single specimen, with the number of pieces recorded in the notes. Similarly, in instances where the fragments could not be refitted but evidence indicated that the pieces are from a single specimen, the number of pieces was recorded in the notes and counted as one in the analysis.

The artifact classification structure employed during this analysis is based largely upon that developed by Haury (1937a, 1945, 1976) for the material from Snaketown and Los Muertos. Generally, additions or modifications of the system are noted in the text. The nomenclature and biological determinations were made in accordance with Keen's (1971) *Sea Shells of Tropical West America*. An additional source employed for identification is Abbott's (1974) *American Seashells*, which provided information regarding species endemic to the California coast. I have previously provided figures illustrating the major components of both univalves and bivalves (see Vokes 1984, 1986a).

Genera and Species

Two general sources for marine shell that were available to the prehistoric inhabitants of the region are the Gulf of California and the west coast of North America, off the present state of California. Archaeologists working in the U.S. Southwest benefit from a natural division of oceanic environments that exists off the western coast of the Baja Peninsula. To the south of this area is the warm tropical current of the Panamic province, whereas the Californian province to the north is characterized by colder waters derived from the Arctic circle. The two currents converge and turn out to sea in the area of Magdalena Bay. Because of the differences in these environments, many species of mollusca are confined to one of the two zones exclusively, or have a limited distribution and frequency in the one zone relative to the other. Although both biotic communities contributed to some degree to the shell material available to the prehistoric inhabitants of the Southwest, the principle source appears to have been the Gulf of California.

The shell genera and species identified in the Sunset Mesa Ruin assemblage are summarized in Table 30. Of the seven marine genera identified, *Glycymeris* and *Laevicardium* are the most commonly represented, accounting for approximately 85 percent of the marine shell in the sample. The popularity of *Glycymeris* is related largely to its use as the principal medium for shell bracelets and rings. Although there are species of *Glycymeris*

149

Table 30. Shell Genera and Species Present in the Sunset Mesa Ruin Assemblage

Genus/Species	Frequency	MNI	Province
Marine shell			
Pelecypods			
Glycymeris			
Glycymeris sp.	13	13	Panamic
Glycymeris gigantea	3	3	Panamic
Glycymeris maculata	1	1	Panamic
Laevicardium			
Laevicardium elatum	30	25	both
Pecten			
Pecten vogdesi	1	1	Panamic
Spondylus sp.	1	1	Panamic
Spondylus or *Chama*	2	2	Panamic
Gastropods			
Olivella sp.	1	1	Panamic (probably)
Turritella			
Turritella leucostoma	1	1	Panamic
Haliotis sp.	1	1	Californian
Freshwater and terrestrial shell			
Gastropods			
Helisoma sp.	5	5	
Succinea sp.	2	2	
Unidentified snail[a]	?	1	
Total	61	57	

[a]Condition too fragmentary to permit a count.

present in the Californian province, they are quite small and would not have been suitable for bracelet production; large, unworked *Glycymeris* valves were probably obtained from the Gulf of California. Valves from the northern zone might have been suitable for producing rings, but it seems likely that the smaller valves also were obtained from the gulf, where they are quite common as beach drift today.

Laevicardium elatum is one of the few species present in both biotic communities. Its northern range extends into the area near San Pedro, California (Abbott 1974:486), but it does not appear to be as abundant in the colder waters off the California coast as it is in the gulf (Keen 1971:160). In addition, there is little evidence for its extensive use by the prehistoric aboriginal populations of southern California (Gifford 1947). It therefore appears more likely that most, if not all, of the *Laevicardium* recovered from sites in the southern portion of the Southwest originated in the Gulf of California.

Both *Pecten vogdesi* and *Turritella leucostoma* are species restricted to the warmer waters of the gulf. There is a closely related species of *Pecten—P. diegensis*—recovered along the lower portion of the Californina province, but the shape of its rib's cross section is diagnostic.

All Pacific species of the genus *Spondylus* are endemic only to the warmer waters of the Gulf of California and south, to Panama. The purple coloration often found in *Spondylus calcifer* valves has been used as a diagnostic trait by archaeologists in the past. However, specimens of the genus *Chama* also can exhibit this purple coloration, and possess a comparatively thick shell wall. For this reason, the two lizard effigy pendants recovered from Feature 21 at Sunset Mesa can be attributed to either *Spondylus* or *Chama*.

Olivella is a genus represented in both provinces, although the species are exclusive of each other. Certain features, such as the shape of the callus along the inner lip, can be employed to distinguish between most of the

Table 31. Sunset Mesa Ruin Shell Assemblage Summarized by Artifact Form and Genus

Artifact Forms	Pelecypods					Gastropods			Total
	Glycymeris	Laevicardium	Pecten	Spondylus	Spondylus or Chama	Olivella	Turritella	Haliotis	
Finished artifacts									
Beads									
Whole shell	—	—	—	—	—	1	—	—	1
Claw-shaped	—	—	—	1	—	—	—	—	1
Pendants									
Whole shell	—	—	1	—	—	—	—	—	1
Cut shell	—	—	—	—	2	—	—	1	3
Bracelets									
Plain	8	—	—	—	—	—	—	—	8
Decorated	1	—	—	—	—	—	—	—	1
Perforated shell	—	1	—	—	—	—	—	—	1
Ring	3	—	—	—	—	—	—	—	3
Earspool?	1	—	—	—	—	—	—	—	1
Etched shell	—	1	—	—	—	—	—	—	1
Manufacturing evidence									
Artifacts in process	3	—	—	—	—	—	—	—	3
Debris	—	1	—	—	—	—	—	—	1
Whole valves	1	—	—	—	—	—	—	—	1
Fragmentary material									
Worked, unknown form	—	1	—	—	—	—	—	—	1
Unworked	—	21	—	—	—	—	1	—	22
Total	17	25	1	1	2	1	1	1	49

species in the two regions (Silsbee 1958). The callus area on the one specimen in the current sample indicates it is a species endemic to the Gulf of California. The general shape of the valve is consistent with *Olivella dama*, but without the diagnostic color patterning of the body whorl, this designation must remain tentative.

The only genus in the current sample—represented by one specimen—to be exclusively endemic to the colder waters of the Californian province is *Haliotis*. This genus was used extensively by the cultural groups of the Pacific coast, and was widely traded throughout the Southwest. Studies of Hohokam shell assemblages indicate that *Haliotis* was consistently available in low quantities throughout the occupational sequence (Vokes 1984:470–472).

The presence of freshwater and terrestrial gastropods is probably fortuitous, in that neither genera identified has ever been found in contexts suggesting they held any value for the local inhabitants. Most of the *Helisoma* valves were recovered from canal deposits (Feature 18) and were probably in their natural habitat. One of the most widely distributed aquatic gastropods, *Helisoma* appears to prefer slow-moving bodies of water (Bequaert and Miller 1973:108–109) and, historically, is often re-

covered with stream-associated debris. It is a relatively large, but very fragile, mollusk. The presence of *Succinea* also is probably fortuitous. Although it is a terrestrial snail, this genus favors moist, well-vegetated areas along the edges of marshes and streams. It may have been introduced into the archaeological record when the site's inhabitants were collecting vegetation, mud, or driftwood from the river's edge. In both cases, the current specimens do not appear to have been deliberately used by the site's inhabitants, and will not be included in the following discussion of artifact materials.

Artifact Assemblage

Discounting the freshwater and terrestrial snails, the assemblage comprises 49 complete and fragmentary specimens (Table 31). These include finished artifact forms, specimens in the process of manufacture or being reworked, and whole shell representing raw material, along with worked and unworked fragments.

Finished Artifacts

Seven different forms of artifacts are represented by finished examples in the assemblage (see Table 31). Finished artifacts are specimens for which the manufacturing process appears to have been concluded, and are sufficiently complete to permit identification of the resulting artifact form. In the Sunset Mesa Ruin assemblage, the finished artifacts include bracelets, several types of pendants, beads, and other, less common artifact forms.

Beads

Two beads representing very different forms are present in the assemblage. One whole shell bead made from an *Olivella* valve was recovered from Feature 13 (Figure 65a), an activity area southeast of the main habitation zone as defined by the structures. The bead was produced by grinding away the apex of the valve's spire. This is a very common form of bead and is known from assemblages throughout the Southwest and virtually its entire occupational history, beginning with the Late Archaic period.

The second bead is a nearly complete, claw-shaped bead that appears to have been carved from the dorsal margin of a *Spondylus* valve. The bead has a biconical perforation near one end that has been partially broken out. From this perforation, it curves down to a rounded, bulbous end. The specimen is similar to some examples illustrated by Haury (1976:Figure 15.15a), which he referred to as "bead-pendants." Although less common than other types of cut shell beads (e.g., disk beads), examples of this type of bead have been reported from contexts at other sites in the Tucson Basin that date to the Colonial and Sedentary periods (Officer 1978:114 [triangular prism beads]; Vokes 1986a:233).

Pendants

Four pendants representing whole shell and cut shell forms were recovered during the course of the project (see Figure 65b–e). An incomplete pendant made from the flattened left-hand valve of a *Pecten vogdesi* shell was recovered from Floor A in Feature 21 (see Figure 65c). The specimen has been reworked from a larger pendant that had previously broken across one corner, resulting in the loss of nearly one-third of the valve. The break, which passed through the original perforation, has been ground smooth and the valve reperforated. The natural side margin also has been ground to form a relatively straight edge. *P. vogdesi* pendants have been reported in considerable quantities from the Grewe site (Woodward 1931:19) and from a cremation area and neighboring features at Snake-

town (Nelson 1991:47). This association with rich crematory areas and other artifact forms of perceived status has led Nelson (1991:49) to suggest that *P. vogdesi* pendants may have served as markers of status or rank during the Sedentary period.

Three cut shell pendants, all representing zoomorphic images, were recovered. Two of these constituted a matching pair of complete, abstract, lizard forms recovered from Floor A in Feature 21 (see Figure 65d–e). The shell employed is a mottled purple and white, with a heavy white callus layer on the inner surface, suggesting it is either *Spondylus* or *Chama*. The "head" of each lizard is roughly trapezoidal in form, with biconical perforations passing through the body near the juncture of the head with the forelimbs. Both the front and hind legs are shown as subtriangular extensions projecting to the sides with no effort to show detail or to depict the body's trunk as a separate feature. The tail extends down from the hind legs as a roughly rectangular block.

The third zoomorphic pendant, which is incomplete, is a small fragment of *Haliotis* carved to represent the leg and foot of a quadruped. Because that portion of the specimen that would have been perforated is missing, the designation as a pendant is supposition. All quadruped examples of which I am aware are pendants, however, and it therefore seems probable that this specimen also is one. Shown is a foot with toes or claws, represented by a series of shallow notches cut into the nacreous face. Quadruped pendants are found mainly at sites dating to the Colonial and Sedentary periods, and became increasingly abstract with time (Jernigan 1978:59–60, Vokes 1984:482).

Bracelets

Nine bracelet segments were recovered from Sunset Mesa Ruin, making the bracelet the most common artifact form in the assemblage (see Figure 65f–g, j–k). Eight of these are portions of plain bands, whereas the ninth is a carved and incised band segment.

One specimen represents roughly three-quarters of a plain bracelet (see Figure 65f). The missing portion is essentially one complete side. The remaining plain bands are fragments representing less than 30 percent of the bracelets. All are portions of the side and ventral margins. The more complete band is the only specimen to retain any portion of the dorsal margin, including the umbo, or beak area, of the valve. This band is uniformly quite thin around its entire perimeter—width average is around 2.3 mm—but has a well-defined, low, triangular hump centered on the back of the taxodontic plate with one corner extended to intercept a drilled perforation, which passes thought the umbo. The beak has been ground, tapering to a broad point.

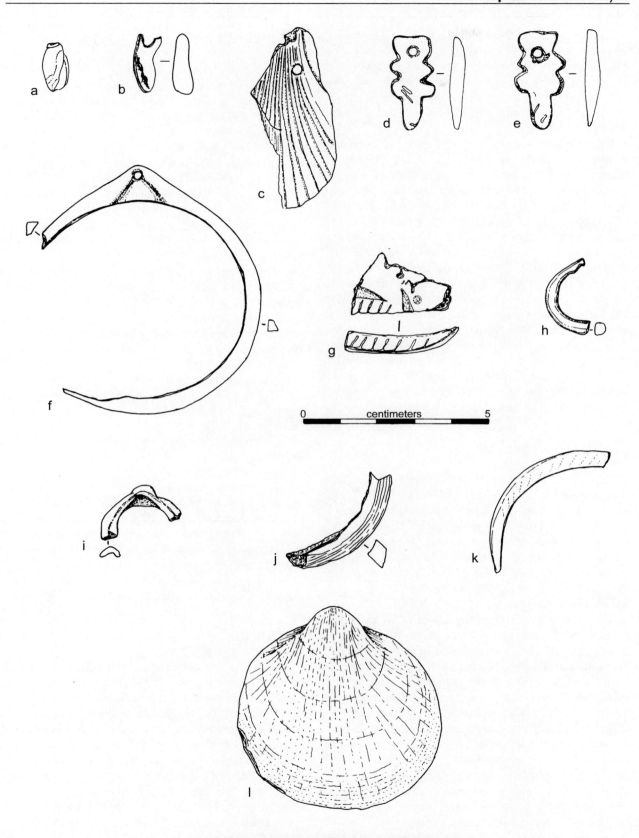

Figure 65. Shell artifacts from Sunset Mesa Ruin.

In three-quarters of the plain bands (n = 6), exterior surfaces are ground to form an steep angle to the face. The exterior surfaces of the two additional plain bands also are ground, but they retain the natural slope of the valve wall. The width of the band segments ranges from 2.3 mm to a maximum of 6.43 mm. Most (n = 6) are between 4 and 6 mm.

The one decorated band is from the dorsal portion of a wide band bracelet/armlet (see Figure 65g). This band has been carved, incised, and drilled in an effort to create a complex design that appears to represent the intertwined body or bodies of (a) snake(s). Part of a rattle is visible tucked against the lower portion of the snakes's undulated body, indicating a body completely wrapped around the band (or possibly depicting two snakes). The snake motif lends itself to the shape of the bracelet/armlet and has been reported from other sites both within (Officer 1978:118–119) and outside (Haury 1937a:142–144; 1976:314–315) the basin. Often the wider band versions, as represented by the current specimen, are combined with a bird motif, with the umbo carved to depict the bird clasping the snake in its talons or beak (Jernigan 1978:67). Because the umbo portion of the dorsal margin is missing, however, this association cannot be demonstrated with the current specimen.

Perforated Shell

The use of the "perforated shell" taxonomic classification was first employed by Haury (1937a:Plate CXVII) to refer to a series of shell bands that seem to possess a discrete set of morphological characteristics. Principal among these features is a large perforation, either centered on the back or shifted toward the ventral margin. The larger specimens, generally made from the large valves of *Laevicardium elatum*, appear to have functioned as armlets (DiPeso et al. 1974:494).

One fragment of a large version of perforated shell was identified in the current assemblage. The specimen, from Feature 23, was manufactured from a large *Laevicardium elatum* valve. The fragment is from the lower back, where a portion of the central perforation forms one side of the fragment. The edge of this perforation was ground to a smoothed, even arc with a pronounced inward bevel, which presumably was intended to conform to the side of the arm. The arc of the perforation extends for nearly 50 mm, and it is estimated that the interior diameter of the perforation may have approached 75 mm. Two shallow grooves, closely spaced, have been cut across part of the interior face, originating from the beveled edge. It is possible that these represent an effort to rework the fragment after the perforated shell had broken.

Ring-Pendants

Three plain ring-pendants were recovered, one each from the floor fill of Features 21, 23, and 25 (see Figure 65h). All are fragmentary specimens manufactured from *Glycymeris* valves. Treatment of the umbo is observable in only one of the cases. It is not perforated, but has been ground down to a small, dome-like projection. In all of the specimens, the band was ground in a manner to create a steep, nearly vertical exterior face. One of the bands has been ground in such a manner that the exterior has a faceted appearance when viewed from above.

Band width ranges between 3.14 and 5.68 mm; the widest specimen is a segment from the dorsal margin. Band thickness ranges from 2.23 to 2.5 mm. The interior diameter of only one ring can be directly measured; it is 14.22 mm across. The other two bands are estimated to be between 16 and 18 mm in interior diameter.

There has been some question as to the role of this artifact form. Fewkes (1896:362) reported finding some ring-pendants in situ on the fingers of inhumations. More recently, while analyzing shell material from Grasshopper pueblo and from the Tonto Basin, I also have encountered instances where *Glycymeris* bands have been found encircling fingers in burials. An alternative use was identified by DiPeso (1956:92), who reported several inhumations with multiple specimens in the area of the neck, suggesting they may have been worn as pendants. Pailes (1963:174) and Urban (1981:317) have argued that the gracile nature of some bands would have made them unsuitable for use as finger rings, and have pointed out that some were too small to fit onto most adult fingers. In the Sunset Mesa Ruin sample, the specimens appear to be robust enough to have been employed in either role, although the diameters of several do appear small for use as finger rings by adults. That would not preclude their use by adolescents or children, however.

Earspool?

A fragment of a somewhat unusual, flared, ring-like artifact was recovered from the fill of the canal Feature 18, along the northwest portion of the site area. Approximately one-third of the artifact was recovered (see Figure 65i). Manufactured from a relatively thick-walled *Glycymeris* valve, the fragment retains the dorsal margin and portions of both side margins. It is probable that the back was reduced using a process similar to that employed in the manufacturing of rings and bracelets. The internal edge is well finished, and the exterior surface has been ground down in a manner that left a cylindrical collar forming the inner margin, from which a relatively thin sheet of shell flares out like a funnel.

Haury (1950:370) was the first to identify this form and suggested it may have been part of a composite earspool assemblage. Eleven fragments of this artifact type were recovered during the 1982–1984 excavations at Las Colinas (Vokes 1988b:357–360). In addition, five sites in the Tucson Basin have produced examples. A complete specimen was recovered from Hodges Ruin (ASM Catalog No. A-7306), and three fragments were identified in the Tanque Verde Wash site assemblage (Vokes 1986b:319). One fragment was recovered from Rincon phase deposits at the Los Morteros site (Vokes 1995). A specimen was recovered from a small Rincon phase farmstead near Sabino Springs (Vokes 1994), and another was reported from excavations at the Rincon phase site of West Branch (Vokes 1996b). In all cases where the specimens were in a datable context, they were associated with the Sedentary period and may have been restricted to the middle or late portion of the period (Vokes 1986b:319, 1988b:359, 1994, 1996b).

Etched Shell

A fragment of a relatively large *Laevicardium elatum* valve was recovered from the floor fill of Feature 25. This specimen, which is a segment from along the ventral margin, has been etched on its interior face. The etching was designed in such a way that the margin's inner surface forms an even, raised border, roughly 7 mm wide, that extends along the entire length of the fragment. The etched surface is clearly recessed back from the natural face.

The technique of etching shell through the use of an acidic bath apparently was pioneered by the Hohokam, and was not developed in other parts of the world until the sixteenth century (Haury 1937a:148). Among the Hohokam, etching appears to have been restricted to the early and middle Sedentary period, with one possible example in a late Colonial period deposit at La Ciudad (Howard 1987:103); the date of that specimen is suspect, however. One of the more spectacular examples of etching technology is a complete, painted *Laevicardium* valve recovered near the town of Rillito, along the Santa Cruz River, to the north of Sunset Mesa Ruin (Pomeroy 1959). Other specimens from nearby sites include several pieces recovered at Hodges Ruin (Officer 1978:120; Pomeroy 1959) and the Los Morteros site (Vokes 1995:589–590).

Manufacturing Evidence

Evidence for local production of shell artifacts was recovered in three forms: unfinished artifacts, along with a fragmentary specimen being remodeled; waste material;

and a whole, unmodified valve. Although all of these lines of evidence are present, none are in any great number.

Unfinished Artifacts and Reworked Artifacts

Two plain bracelet segments, still in the late stages of production, were recovered. One was found on the modern surface in the vicinity of Feature 13, whereas the other was in the fill between the two floors of Feature 21. In both instances, the pieces are from the side-ventral margin portions of the bands, and they clearly represent two, discrete bracelets. The interior margins of both bands have been roughly flaked to shape with no attempt made to finish this face by grinding it smooth. In one case, the marginal edge of the band's exterior face has been ground smooth, giving the band a faceted profile. The other band's exterior face is unmodified (see Figure 65j).

A third specimen still in the manufacturing process is a nearly finished needle, or needle-pendant, recovered from the floor fill of Feature 21 (see Figure 65k). It was made from a side-ventral fragment of a *Glycymeris* plain bracelet. In general, the band is relatively narrow, with a width of 3.67 mm. One end has been ground to a blunt point, whereas the other is beveled to form a thin, wedge-shaped end. This thinning is often found on needle-pendants, where it provides a platform through which the artifact could be perforated. The artifact in question lacks this final step.

Waste Material

A relatively small fragment of *Laevicardium,* with two contiguous worked edges, was recovered from a trash deposit (Feature 2). One side has been carefully ground to a straight, smooth edge. The other is formed by a cut that partly penetrated the valve's exterior wall; the piece was then broken along the groove, leaving an edge with a rough lip that was not modified further. The fact that the finished edge does not wrap around the corner, or round off the rough corner, suggests the groove-and-snap process was done after the first edge was ground. That the groove-and-snap edge was left raw suggests the fragment was discarded as waste.

Unmodified Valve

A complete, medium-size *Glycymeris maculata* valve was recovered from a posthole in the floor of Feature 25 (see Figure 65l). There are a few small chips missing from the ventral margin, but these are not patterned and appear to be natural. The valve is roughly 55 mm in diameter, which would have been sufficient to make a small bracelet or a whole shell pendant.

Worked and Unworked Fragments

In assemblages of any size, it is not uncommon to recover shell fragments that either are worked but too incomplete to be classified, or appear to be unworked. These fragments may derive from three possible sources: fragmentation of finished artifacts, manufacturing activities, or the breakage of whole valves.

Worked Fragments

Two fragments of *Laevicardium* that appear to represent one artifact were recovered from the northwest quadrant of Feature 22. This is an area where a large pit intruded into the structure, and their association is therefore unclear. All of the edges of these fragments are rough breaks, but the exterior surface of the pieces has been abraded. The striations vary from shallow to deep, but are consistent in direction.

Unworked Fragments

Twenty-six unworked shell fragments were recovered from throughout the excavated portion of the site. These are estimated to represent approximately 22 different specimens. All but one of these fragments are *Laevicardium*.

The *Laevicardium* fragments are mostly from the middle and lower back regions of the various valves, although there are a few pieces from the umbo. The valves represented range from large, robust specimens to medium-size valves. These fragments were recovered from nearly every major feature investigated, the exception being Feature 25, which contained the *Turritella* fragment. This specimen was probably a whole shell pendant, or was intended to be such a pendant, as it is the only artifact form that employs *Turritella*.

Discussion

The shell assemblage recovered during the excavations in many ways reflects the nature and temporal association of the site's occupation. The placement of the settlement at the confluence of the Rillito and Santa Cruz Rivers made it an ideal location for accessing trade material entering the basin from the north. Although the current assemblage is not especially large, it is quite diverse. As is typical of virtually all Hohokam shell assemblages, the collection is dominated by bracelets, which represent roughly 43 percent of the finished artifacts. There are, however, several artifacts present—principally the perforated shell of *Laevicardium*, the possible earspool fragment, and the fragment of etched shell—that had restricted tenure and are generally associated with occupations at larger hamlets or villages (Vokes 1984:544, 1988b:382–383, 1996b).

The assemblage's diversity appears to extend to local manufacturing activities, as well. Although it is not uncommon for assemblages to contain limited evidence of localized shell carving to produce pendants and beads (Officer 1978:111; Vokes 1986a, 1986c, 1995, 1996b), the Sunset Mesa Ruin assemblage contains two specimens of bracelets in the manufacturing process. There are other assemblages in the basin that have produced evidence of local bracelet production (Table 32), but these are generally associated with relatively large samples. With the exception of AZ BB:9:54 (ASM), a relatively small, late Rincon phase site associated with the Hardy site complex (Huntington 1982), all of these sites were large habitation sites located along the Santa Cruz River. In general, the level of production in the Tucson Basin during the Sedentary period was quite limited in comparison with settlements to the north, along the periphery of the Papaguería (A. Howard 1993; Vokes 1993a), and appears to be restricted mainly to the larger communities on the western side of the basin, which would have been near the probable trade route by which shell entered the region.

A comparison with other assemblages in the basin that date to the Sedentary period (see Table 32) illustrates the general concordance between this assemblage and other collections. The relative frequency of bracelets is somewhat lower than what has been found at some other sites, but it is comparable. Bracelets always played an important role in the Hohokam culture. In some early assemblages, bracelets represent more than 80 percent of the finished artifacts. Over time, their relative importance appears to have suffered somewhat as new artifact forms appeared, but they were always prominent.

Within the site, the shell material is somewhat concentrated in the area of the house cluster. Features 21, 23, and 25 all appear to have had a relatively high number of shell artifacts associated with them (Table 33), although most of this material was incorporated within the roof fall and floor fill levels of the house pits, and probably represents secondary trash. Feature 21 was, in part, an exception. Two complete, carved lizard shell pendants and a nearly complete, *Pecten* whole shell pendant were recovered from the floor area of this structure. These, along with the

Table 32. Sites within the Tucson Basin with Comparable Sedentary Period Assemblages

Site	Whole Beads (Cylindrical)		Cut Beads		Finished Artifacts								Manufacturing Evidence			Total[b]
	Frequency	Occurrence	Frequency	Occurrence	Whole Shell Pendant	Tinkler	Cut Pendant Forms	Pendant (Other/Unknown Forms)	Bracelet	Perforated Shell	Rings	Other Artifacts	Bracelet/Ring	Carved/Other[a]	Whole Valve	
Sunset Mesa Ruin	1	1	1	1	1	—	3	—	9	1	3	2	2	2	1	26
West Branch site[c]	15	15	6	5	1	—	24	4	193	9	18	16	4	15	4	309
Tanque Verde Wash site[d]	1	1	1	1	—	1	6	4	40	2	6	4	—	—	—	65
Julian Wash[e]	4	3	6	3	—	—	—	—	4	—	—	—	—	—	—	14
Los Morteros[f]	13	12	4	4	8	—	21	7	142	19	14	8	4	24	6	270
AZ BB:9:54 (ASM)[g]	1	1	—	—	—	—	2	—	5	—	2	—	7	2	—	19
Valencia site[h]	2	2	—	—	—	—	5	2	35	2	1	—	1	7	—	55
Vactor Ranch site[i]	11	2	1	1	—	—	—	—	4	—	—	—	—	—	—	16

[a]Includes carved waste by-product.
[b]Total number of specimens using bead frequency figures.
[c]Vokes (1986a, 1996b, 1996d); [d]Vokes (1986b); [e]Vokes (1996a); [f]Vokes (1995); [g]Vokes and Huntington (1982); [h]Mayro (1985); [i]Vokes (1996c).

Table 33. Sunset Mesa Shell Assemblage Summarized to Provenience

Artifact Form, by Unit Description and Quadrant/Level	Genus	Count	MNI	Artifact Form, by Unit Description and Quadrant/Level	Genus	Count	MNI
Nonfeature contexts				Floor contact			
N490, E520				Pendant-lizard	*Spondylus* or *Chama*	2	2
SU 2							
Unworked fragment	*Laevicardium*	3	2	Whole shell pendant	*Pecten*	1	1
Trench backdirt				Between Floors A and B, NE			
TR 14				Claw-shaped bead	*Spondylus*	1	1
Plain bracelet	*Glycymeris*	1	1	Bracelet in process	*Glycymeris*	1	1
Features				Unworked fragment	*Laevicardium*	2	2
Feature 2: trash deposit				1 × 2			
SU 6				Unworked fragment	*Laevicardium*	1	1
Carved shell debris	*Laevicardium*	1	1	Feature 22: pit house			
Unworked fragment	*Laevicardium*	2	1	Roof fall, SE			
SU 15				Plain bracelet	*Glycymeris*	1	1
Plain bracelet	*Glycymeris*	1	1	Floor fill, NW			
Feature 13: activity area/ ramada				Worked fragment— unknown	*Laevicardium*	2	1
SU 3				Unworked fragment	*Laevicardium*	1	1
Plain bracelet	*Glycymeris*	1	1	Subfloor test			
Bracelet in process	*Glycymeris*	1	1	Whole valve	*Succinea*	1	1
Unworked fragment	*Laevicardium*	1	1	Feature 23: pit house			
Level 3				Floor fill			
Whole shell bead	*Olivella*	1	1	SW			
Feature 15: activity area/ kitchen area				Plain bracelet	*Glycymeris*		
Surface				SE			
Unworked fragment	*Laevicardium*	1	1	Plain bracelet	*Glycymeris*	1	1
Level 1				Plain ring	*Glycymeris*	1	1
Unworked fragment	*Laevicardium*	2	1	Unworked fragment	*Laevicardium*	2	2
Level 2				Whole valve	*Helisoma*	1	1
Unworked fragment	*Laevicardium*	1	1	Backdirt			
Level 3				Perforated shell	*Laevicardium*	1	1
Unworked fragment	*Laevicardium*	2	2	Plain bracelet	*Glycymeris*	1	1
Feature 18: canal				Feature 25: pit house			
Level 1				Roof fall			
Unworked fragment	*Laevicardium*	1	1	NW			
Whole valve	*Helisoma*	1	1	Carved bracelet	*Glycymeris*	1	1
Level 2				Plain bracelet	*Glycymeris*	1	1
Earspool?	*Glycymeris*	1	1	SW			
Whole valve	*Helisoma*	1	1	Unworked fragment	*Turritella*	1	1
Level 3				Floor fill			
Whole valve	*Helisoma*	2	2	NW			
Unworked fragment	unidentifiable freshwater/ terrestrial snail	—	1	Etched shell fragment	*Laevicardium*	1	1
				NE			
				Plain ring	*Glycymeris*	1	1
Feature 21: pit house				SE			
Roof fall, NW				Whole valve	*Succinea*	1	1
Unworked fragment	*Laevicardium*	2	1	Subfloor-posthole			
Floor fill				Whole valve	*Glycymeris*	1	1
NE				Feature 26: unknown			
Plain ring	*Glycymeris*	1	1	Fill, Level 1			
Needle-pendant in process	*Glycymeris*	1	1	Unworked fragment	*Laevicardium*	1	1
Unworked fragment	*Laevicardium*	1	1	Feature 27: pit house			
SE				Floor fill, NW			
Unworked fragment	*Laevicardium*	2	2	Pendant (quadruped)	*Haliotis*	1	1
				Total		**61**	**57**

Key: MNI = minimum number of individuals; SU = Stripping Unit; TR = Trench presence of a miniature vessel on the floor, suggest the structure may have been abandoned with an intact floor assemblage. Feature 21 was also found to have two super-imposed floors. The fill between these produced some shell material, as well, although its fragmentary condition suggests it was more in the nature of discarded trash.

One other deposit that may reflect purposeful placement is the complete *Glycymeris* valve in a posthole in Feature 25. It is possible this may represent some form of offering put there prior to the installation of the post during construction of the house.

There does not appear to be any clear spatial trend with regard to the evidence for manufacturing. The carved waste and the unfinished artifacts are widely dispersed across the site area. The same is generally true for un-worked fragments that might reflect manufacturing activities, although there is some concentration in the afore-mentioned structures and in the area incorporated by Feature 15, a kitchen area to the southeast of the structures. However, the sample of material related to manufacturing is too small to present a clear picture.

The Sunset Mesa Ruin assemblage is quite representative of Sedentary period assemblages with respect to the relative frequency of the various shell genera and artifacts present. The popularity of *Glycymeris* is a reflection of its use as the principal medium in bracelet production. That it was also employed for other artifact forms, such as the earspool, only served to strengthen its position. The relative frequency of *Laevicardium elatum* (50 percent of the marine shell) also corresponds to that seen in other collections. In assemblages that date prior to the Colonial period, this species was relatively scarce (A. Howard 1985:173; Vokes 1984:533, 1993b:372). Its percentage in assemblages rapidly increased after the middle of the Colonial period, although there is a ten-dency for many specimens to be unworked fragments. This is likely a reflection of the shell's relatively gracile nature, which results in a tendency for it to fragment into numerous, relatively small pieces, but is also an indica-tion of the shell's increasing popularity as a medium for carving pendants and other forms of ornaments.

The presence of other, less numerous forms, such as perforated shells, rings, and earspools, also reflects the temporal placement of the occupation. The large version of the perforated shell form made from *Laevicardium* valves has proven to be largely, although not exclusively, limited to the Sedentary period; it appears to have at-tained its greatest popularity during the early and middle portions of this period. These bands, which appear to have been armlets, possibly were later replaced by the heavy, wide "bracelets." DiPeso (1956:97) noted that in the Classic period component at Paloparado, bracelets with

band widths greater than 10 mm, when found in situ, were worn about the upper arm.

Ring-pendants also became increasingly popular dur-ing the Sedentary period. Few have been found in con-texts that can be dated prior to the later half of the Colonial period. It is at that time that the form appears to have gained acceptance. During the Sedentary period, ring-pendants continued to increase in popularity. In con-trast to the perforated shells, this form continued on into the Classic period, when it was relatively common. Its continued popularity may be a reflection of the multiple ways in which it was worn.

One other artifact form that warrants review is the possible earspool. Whereas artifacts of this form appear in low frequency, they are consistently associated with Sedentary period occupations and may be restricted to the middle and late portions of that era. Whether or not these bands were elements of composite earspools cannot be determined at this time. Regardless, they appear to have been made over a relatively limited interval, and may prove to be an index of the middle and late Sedentary period.

Trade

With the exception of the one *Haliotis* fragment, the marine shell recovered from the excavations was probably derived from the Gulf of California. Access to this source of raw material is likely to have been through an exchange system, although direct procurement cannot be ruled out. There are two general routes by which shell was possibly obtained through exchange. The first lies across the cen-tral Papaguería, whereas the other would have followed the river systems of northern Sonora. The southern, or riverine, route does not appear to have been very active with respect to the Hohokam of the Tucson Basin during the Sedentary period (Craig 1982). In contrast, the route crossing the Papaguería is known to have been quite active (Ferg 1980; Hayden 1972; Teague 1981; Vokes 1992, 1993a), and it seems likely that this would have been the source for most of the shell entering the Tucson Basin during that time.

Conclusion

Sunset Mesa Ruin's shell assemblage corresponds well to other collections from large habitation sites that have been attributed to the Sedentary period. Relatively diverse in composition, it is composed primarily of finished artifacts, with bracelets the dominant form. There is some evidence for on-site production; however, these efforts appear to have been relatively limited in scope and would not have satisfied local demand, much less regional needs. For the most part, the inhabitants of the Sunset Mesa community were consumers of finished shell products, probably imported from the more northern communities along the Gila River and the periphery of the Papaguería.

CHAPTER 9

Archaeobotanical Remains

Karen R. Adams

A total of 21 macrofossil samples and 20 4-liter flotation samples was analyzed from houses and extramural features. The results of these analyses are reported below. At least 27 charred plant taxa have been identified from this site (Table 34). Complete data sets are available in Appendix F (flotation data, macrofossil data, and criteria of plant part identification).

Feature Discussions

Feature 5

A historical-period, adobe homestead, occupied in the period of 1880–1910, preserved four partially charred pieces of douglas fir (*Pseudotsuga*) wood, one of which is 8 cm or more in diameter. Identification was verified by the Laboratory of Tree-Ring Research at the University of Arizona. One piece has what appears to be a nail hole, confirming its use during the historical-period occupation. Milled lumber used in turn-of-the-century house construction can represent a variety of species, some clearly not local.

Feature 13

Feature 13 likely represented a covered work area or ramada, used primarily for food preparation (especially grinding) and storage during the Rincon phase. Two macrobotanical samples from fill contexts yielded a total of 900 ml (263 g) of charred tansy mustard (*Descurainia*) "seed meal," in addition to hundreds of loose tansy

mustard seeds. The "seed meal" has broken into pieces, and some of the pieces are nearly flat and/or smooth in contour; the largest piece measures 7 by 6 by 1 cm. The meal is composed almost entirely of thousands of tansy mustard seeds, many of which appear mature (Figure 66a), but some of which are sunken in and small, suggesting they were immature when harvested (see Figure 66b). A few additional items (for example, an *Atriplex* fruit, a Paniceae grain [caryopsis], and a *Sphaeralcea*-type seed) were embedded in the meal. The presence of many broken tansy mustard pieces suggests some of the seeds were actually ground into meal, perhaps to help hold the seed cake together. Fifteen flint kernels of *Zea mays* accompanied the seed meal. A sherd associated with the meal may be from the storage container that held it. The smoothness of the "meal" pieces may have more than one explanation: (a) the seeds were pressed into smooth cakes by hand; (b) the meal rested against smooth storage pot interiors; or (c) the meal has eroded over time to have smooth contours.

Feature 15

Feature 15, a nearby kitchen area, also contained stored food; one of its primary functions may have been small-scale, household cooking. Similar to Feature 13, a macrofossil sample preserved charred *Descurainia* "seed meal" (100 ml, or 39 g)—primarily as one, large piece measuring 8 by 6.5 by 3.5 cm—and a small amount of loose tansy mustard seeds. Embedded in the meal were single, charred specimens of globemallow (*Sphaeralcea*) seed, a *Zea mays* embryo, and a Gramineae grain. A flotation sample recovered a saguaro (*Carnegiea*) seed and a Malvaceae-type seed, as well as charcoal of mesquite (*Prosopis*), which apparently was used for fuelwood.

Table 34. Charred Plant Taxa and Parts Identified from Macrobotanical and Flotation Samples (Organized Alphabetically by Taxon) from Sunset Mesa Ruin

Taxon	Common Name	Part(s)
Acacia type	acacia	charcoal
Ambrosia type	ragweed	charcoal, twig
Ambrosia/Pluchea type	ragweed/arrowweed	charcoal
Atriplex type	saltbush	charcoal, fruit, twig
Carnegiea type	saguaro	charcoal, seed
Celtis reticulata type	hackberry	twig
Cercidium type	palo verde	charcoal
Cheno-am[a]	cheno-am	seed
Descurainia type	tansy mustard	seed meal, seed
Echinocereus type	hedgehog	seed
Eragrostis type	lovegrass	caryopsis (grain)
Gramineae type	grass	caryopsis (grain), stem
Hymenoclea type	burro-brush	twig
Helianthus type	sunflower	charcoal
Larrea type	creosote bush	charcoal, twig
Leguminosae type	legume	seed
Malvaceae type	mallow	seed
Monocotyledon	monocot/agave	tissue
Morus microphylla type	elderberry	charcoal
Olneya type	ironwood	charcoal
Paniceae	grass	caryopsis (grain)
Phaseolus (domestic)	bean	cotyledon (seed half)
Phragmites australis	reedgrass	stem
Populus type	cottonwood	charcoal, twig
Populus/Salix type	cottonwood/willow	charcoal
Prosopis velutina	mesquite	charcoal
Pseudotsuga type	douglas fir	charcoal, wood
Salvia type	chia	seed
Sphaeralcea type	globemallow	seed
Zea mays	maize	cupule, embryo, kernel

[a] Cheno-am represents a combination of goosefoot (*Chenopodium*) and pigweed (*Amaranthus*), assigned to ancient seeds that could represent either genus.

Feature 18

Feature 18, a canal segment identified along the northwest edge of the terrace on which the site is located, is one of only a few known prehistoric canal segments within the Tucson Basin. The charred plant remains recovered in a macrofossil sample from this canal segment include: *Prosopis, Larrea, Atriplex,* and *Ambrosia* charcoal fragments, at least 50 *Zea mays* kernels (both flint and flour endosperm), a *Phaseolus* cotyledon that would be either a large tepary (*P. acutifolius*) or a small common bean (*P. vulgaris*), and some reedgrass (*Phragmites australis*) stem segments and fragments. Because of the mixture of foods and likely fuelwoods, these materials may represent midden deposits that filled the canal. However, burned plant materials within canal segments in the Queen Creek area have been interpreted as representing the burning of canal-clogging plant debris and adjacent fields for planting (Bohrer 1992).

Figure 66. *Descurainia* "seed meal," recovered from Feature 13 (Bag 796):
(a) plump, mature seeds; (b) sunken, immature seeds. Both views at 20×.

Feature 21

Feature 21 was a Rincon phase pit house with two floor features (hearth Feature 21.01 and large pit Feature 21.02), and two plastered floor surfaces (Floor A and Floor B) that were both centered around the hearth and entryway. Three separate support post macrofossil samples were identified as multiple fragments of *Prosopis velutina* charcoal, revealing use of this wood as a construction element. One piece is at least 20 cm in diameter. One of the three support post samples also contained some *Populus*-type charcoal, perhaps a second construction timber choice.

A flotation sample from the hearth fill contained saltbush- (*Atriplex-*) and *Carnegiea*-type charcoal and two charred chia- (*Salvia-*) type seeds. Floor A preserved hedgehog (*Echinocereus*) seeds; lovegrass (*Eragrostis*) grains (caryopses); Malvaceae seeds; monocotyledon tissue with calcium oxalate crystals (possibly agave); Gramineae stem segments; and charcoal of cottonwood/willow (*Populus/Salix*), mesquite (*Prosopis*), and an unknown wood. The reproductive parts may have once been foods prepared at the hearth, using the wood as fuel. Lower Floor B retained cheno-am, Leguminosae, and *Salvia* seeds; *Eragrostis* grains; and charcoal of creosote bush (*Larrea*) and *Prosopis*. As with Floor A, Floor B seems to have been a locus of food preparation near the hearth.

Feature 22

Two samples were analyzed from a second Rincon phase pit house, Feature 22. The ashy fill of a circular basin hearth (Feature 22.01) preserved a variety of charred reproductive parts likely representing food preparation, including a cheno-am seed, a Malvaceae seed, and at least 20 Gramineae grains. The rest of the materials (*Carnegiea*, *Morus microphylla*, and *Prosopis* charcoal, and a *Zea mays* cupule) probably reflect fuel uses. The *Morus* (elderberry) recovery is interesting, as the taxon grows at higher elevations, and perhaps came down a major drainage as driftwood, or was used for some material culture use. *Prosopis velutina* was sought as a main support post. Floor fill retained charred stems of *Carnegiea*, sunflower (*Helianthus*), *Phragmites,* and smaller grasses. Possibly these materials were related to smaller layers of roofing construction.

Feature 23

Feature 23 was another Rincon phase pit house. Flotation samples from two floor features, a hearth (Feature 23.01)

and an irregular, oval ash-filled pit (Feature 23.02), preserved remains suggestive of foods. These include Gramineae grains from the hearth, and *Carnegiea*, cheno-am, and *Salvia* seeds from the ash-filled pit. Monocotyledon tissue from the pit, having calcium oxalate crystals, possibly indicates past use of agave in this location. *Prosopis* charcoal was preserved in both floor features and in floor fill, suggesting reliance on mesquite for heating and cooking.

Feature 25

Two samples were analyzed from Feature 25, yet another Rincon phase pit house. A plastered hearth (Feature 25.01) preserved charred remains of foods, including Gramineae grains, Malvaceae seeds, and *Zea mays* kernel fragments. On the floor, excavators recovered 100 ml (28.5 g) of charred and fused *Z. mays* flour kernels, possibly the remains of a food product in storage. Other preserved charred plant remains on the floor, such as charcoal of *Ambrosia/Pluchea*, *Larrea*, *Phragmites,* and *Prosopis*, could signal either roofing needs or fuelwood needs. Both *Ambrosia/Pluchea* and *Prosopis* charcoal preserved in the hearth. Excavators recovered *Larrea* twig fragments from roof fall, and a *Prosopis velutina* support post. One lot of uncharred rodent pellets suggest post-abandonment disturbance.

Feature 27

The final Rincon phase pit house to be discussed is Feature 27. Flotation samples from floor fill and a plastered hearth (Feature 27.01), along with a variety of macrofossils representing roof fall, floor fill, and support posts, reveal past plant choices in this house.

Two support posts of *Prosopis velutina* and an entry beam of *Cercidium* reveal selection of materials as major construction elements. Smaller twigs (ranging from 0.3 to 1.2 cm in diameter) that preserved in both roof fall and floor fill layers reveal the range of plant taxa considered useful in roof construction. These include *Ambrosia*, *Atriplex*, *Celtis reticulata*, *Larrea*, *Populus* and *Hymenoclea* twigs, *Carnegiea* and *Phragmites* stems, and *Prosopis* wood. The presence of small Gramineae stems (1–2 mm diameter), some with bases still attached, may signal a type of roof-closing layer. Some reproductive parts present in floor fill (cheno-am seeds and Gramineae grains) correspond to those found in hearth fill and, along with a Malvaceae seed, may represent past food preparation in the house. *Prosopis* charcoal in the hearth signals fuel use.

Pit Fill and Midden

Flotation samples from three separate extramural pits (Features 41, 46, and 47) and a midden area (Feature 49) contain primarily a rather diverse charcoal record. This includes *Prosopis* from all four features, *Cercidium* type from Features 46 and 47, *Atriplex* type from Features 47 and 49, and a variety of other woody types from one feature each. *Olneya, Pseudotsuga,* and an unknown type were found in Feature 46, and *Acacia* and *Celtis reticulata* were found in Feature 49. *Zea mays* cupules were present in Feature 47. Only two seed types (cheno-am and Malvaceae) hint at food-preparation activities in Features 47 and 49.

Vessel Fill

Charcoal of *Prosopis* was recovered from the fill of both isolated vessels, Features 16 and 17, and the latter vessel also held charcoal of *Pseudotsuga* in its fill. In addition, the fill from both vessels yielded charred seeds (cheno-ams and an unknown type), which may reflect either items in storage, or midden debris that came in afterward with the charcoal.

General Patterns of Plant Use at Sunset Mesa Ruin

An overview of the archaeobotanical record at Sunset Mesa Ruin reveals patterns in plant use during the Rincon phase. House support posts (n = 6) were primarily of *Prosopis velutina*, though one was of *Populus*. *Cercidium* provided the material for at least one entry beam. Smaller roofing layers were constructed of twigs or stems (0.4–1.2 cm in diameter) of a variety of taxa, including *Ambrosia, Atriplex, Carnegiea, Celtis reticulata, Larrea, Phragmites,* and *Populus*. Even small layers of grass stems were chosen.

Hearths within five separate habitation structures (Features 21, 22, 23, 25, and 27) and an interior pit filled with ashy debris (Feature 23.02) were used to prepare cheno-am seeds, grass grains, Malvaceae seeds, and on occasion, *Zea* kernels, and *Carnegiea* and *Salvia* seeds. *Prosopis* fuelwood preserved in these thermal features most often, along with leftover *Zea* cobs, *Carnegiea* stems, and a few other woody resources. Four extramural pits preserved a record of primarily charcoal, including *Prosopis, Atriplex, Cercidium,* and other types of charred

wood. Limited evidence of seeds (cheno-ams and Malvaceae) and monocotyledon tissue (possibly agave) preserved in two of these pits.

Other possible foods at Sunset Mesa Ruin were preserved in floor fill, either as items spilled during preparation, or as midden debris that entered postabandonment. These include *Echinocereus* seeds, *Eragrostis* grains, and a Leguminosae seed. A possible storage cache of *Zea mays* flour kernels preserved on the floor of one habitation, Feature 25.

The record of foods suggests that both domesticates (*Z. mays* and *Phaseolus*) and wild plant products were relied upon. The actual amount of maize and bean remains is rather low, suggesting either a low dependence on agricultural crops, or that the plant record reflects a season of the year (for example, late winter, spring, early summer) in which agricultural crops and their secondary by-products were not readily available.

The archaeobotanical record suggests spring (*Descurainia* seeds), summer (*Carnegiea* fruit), and fall (*Eragrostis* grains) use of the area. A spring and summer residency also is implied by the presence of the agricultural products; perhaps people were in residence even earlier, to attend to canal maintenance.

The record of plant use at Sunset Mesa Ruin agrees in most details with archaeobotanical reports from other Rincon phase sites in the Tucson Basin, especially smaller agricultural and nonvillage sites (Miksicek 1988). The domesticates maize and beans, weedy cheno-ams, tansy mustard, chia and globemallow, saguaro and hedgehog cacti, grains of various grasses, and potential evidence of agave use recognized at Sunset Mesa Ruin have all been commonly reported elsewhere for this phase. Sunset Mesa Ruin is similar to smaller sites that yielded primarily crops, weeds, and encouraged plants, and that contained minimal evidence for a reliance upon wild perennials, such as mesquite pods and saguaro fruit.

Notable Plant Taxa at Sunset Mesa Ruin

Three plant taxa recovered from Sunset Mesa Ruin are of special note. The recovery of more than 1,000 ml of charred tansy mustard (*Descurainia*) "seed meal" at the site is an important addition to the developing record of past tansy mustard importance in the Tucson Basin. Tansy mustard seeds have been recovered in as many as 67 percent of examined flotation samples from some Tucson Basin archaeological sites, particularly those dating to the pre-Classic period (Miksicek 1988:51). Although the seeds usually are not abundant in any given sample, two Rincon phase Punta de Agua sites, south of Tucson, yielded significant quantities. One olla from a habitation at AZ BB:13:41 (ASM) held at least 400 ml of tansy mustard seeds, and a second olla in an extramural hearth at nearby AZ BB:13:50 (ASM) contained more than 890 ml of the same small seeds (Bohrer, Cutler, and Sauer 1969:2–3) The Sunset Mesa Ruin find offers the additional insight that, at times, some of the tansy mustard seeds were harvested while still immature. *Descurainia* is one of the spring-ripening mustards.

The ethnographic record of tansy mustard use is extensive (Adams 1988). The leaves and young plants have provided both edible greens and pottery paint. Because the seeds ripen during the spring, their value as a "cool season" resource would be high. Numerous southwestern groups once gathered them (Adams 1988), including Navajo, who ground the seeds and made the resulting meal into cakes (Vestal 1952:28). Among the Tohono O'odham (Papago), they were once noted as the "most common of seed crops" (Castetter and Underhill 1935:24). It is possible that some form of human management, such as scattering the seeds in a favored place, may have occurred in the past.

Two woody taxa were probably not in the immediate vicinity at the time that Sunset Mesa Ruin was occupied. The limited amount of elderberry (*M. microphylla*) charcoal recovered from the fill of hearth Feature 22.01 probably represents either driftwood from the Rillito or Santa Cruz Rivers, or the leftover debris of a wood sought for some specific material culture need. Likewise, the presence of douglas fir (*Pseudotsuga*) charcoal in the fill of a cooking pit (Feature 46) and within vessel fill (Feature 17) also probably represents driftwood use. The partly charred *Pseudotsuga* beam with a possible nail hole from the historical-period structure (Feature 5) attests to the greater ease with which high-elevation woods were acquired in historical times.

CHAPTER 10

Sunset Mesa Ruin Pollen Analysis

Susan Smith and Jim Hasbargen

This report presents the results of the analysis of 25 pollen samples from Sunset Mesa Ruin, a Rincon phase (A.D. 1000–1150), Hohokam settlement. The sample set includes 1 surface control sample, 1 sample from a historical-period context, and 23 samples from prehistoric features. Five of the samples were composites, combined from 2 to 4 discrete samples. The pollen samples were processed and analyzed at the Laboratory of Paleoecology, Northern Arizona University, Flagstaff.

Limitations of Pollen Data

Pollen assemblages from archaeological contexts are the product of natural processes and cultural activities. The natural component is determined by different plant species' pollination ecology (pollen production and dispersal) and the physical environment (vegetation, geomorphology, and climate). Pollen dispersal of most plant species is divided into two categories, wind- or insect-pollinated. Most trees, shrub, and grass species are wind pollinated, and produce abundant, aerodynamic pollen that can travel hundreds of kilometers. Insect-pollinated taxa, which include cacti and most herb species, produce small amounts of ornamented, heavy pollen, deposited generally within meters of the parent plant. Of course, the biological realm never strictly follows generalizations. Corn (maize), a member of the wind-pollinated grass family, does not disperse pollen far from the parent plant (Raynor et al. 1972), and its presence in archaeological assemblages signifies a local source.

The soil/sediment context of archaeological samples present special problems for pollen analysis (Pearsall 1989). Bioturbation from insects, rodents and humans; the effects of water movement through soil; chemical and physical gradients in sediment profiles; and variations in the morphology of different pollen types can affect the composition of pollen assemblages. The strength of a cultural signal in archaeological samples is a function of the sampled context's integrity and the type and intensity of use. Pit houses, pits, vessels, and other roofed or covered contexts are assumed to have been "protected" from natural, ambient pollen, preserving pollen evidence of cultural activities. Open, extramural contexts are often characterized by a mix of atmospheric pollen rain and pollen associated with cultural activities.

Methods

Analytical Methods

The criteria used to discern ethnobotanical resources in this analysis are the presence of cultigen pollen, and an abundance of any taxon that would indicate representation in excess of what could be expected from natural processes. The search for prehistoric, natural pollen analogs to characterize "what could be expected from natural processes" is a difficult proposition, however. Modern surface pollen samples are generally not appropriate, because historical-period land uses have significantly altered vegetation communities. In this analysis, two samples from a prehistoric canal and a surface sample are used to derive some measure of a prehistoric, natural pollen analog.

The absolute abundance of pollen in each sample was estimated by relating the sample pollen count to a count of exotic spores (tracers) added to each sample prior to processing. Sample pollen concentrations were calculated by the following formula:

$$Concentration = \frac{\frac{Pollen\ Counted}{Tracers\ Counted} \times Tracer\ Concentration}{Sample\ Volume}$$

Pollen concentration is expressed as the number of pollen grains per cubic centimeter of sample sediment, abbreviated as gr/cc.

Pollen concentrations are an index to the abundance of plant material that may have been associated with cultural activities. Concentrations provide the first level of comparison, followed by comparison of pollen percentages, which relate the taxon counts to the pollen sum ([taxon counted/pollen sum] × 100). Pollen percentages express the relative importance of each taxon in a given sample.

Laboratory Methods

Most of the samples were collected in the field in September and December 1994; two samples (Samples 241 and 783) were collected in August 1994. In the laboratory, sample bag contents were thoroughly mixed and 20 cc subsamples extracted. A known concentration (27,000 grains) of exotic spores (*Lycopodium*) was added to each sample to estimate pollen concentration. Samples then were treated with 10 percent hydrochloric acid (to remove carbonates), screened (0.18-mm mesh), and treated for approximately 20 hours with hydrofluoric acid (to dissolve silicates). After the hydrofluoric step, samples were floated in zinc bromide (specific gravity 2.0), followed by acetolysis (to reduce organics).

Pollen assemblages were identified by counting slide transects at 400-power magnification to a 200-grain pollen sum, if possible, then scanning the entire slide at 100-power magnification to record additional taxa. Aggregates (clumps of the same taxon) were counted as one grain per occurrence, and the taxon and size were recorded separately. The distinction between hi-spine and low-spine Compositae was based on the height of spines, using 2 micrometers as a cutoff (Hevly et al. 1965). Maize pollen was discriminated from grass pollen by pore morphology and size, using 60 micrometers as the minimum size for maize (Faegri and Iversen 1989; Martin and Schoenwetter 1960).

Sample Set Overview and Pollen Types Identified

Table 35 documents the provenience of all 25 samples, and also shows for each sample the pollen sum and

concentration, the number of taxa identified, and the percentage of degraded grains. Individual sample counts are documented in Appendix G. Only one sample produced a count of less than 200 grains; the sample from Feature 27.03, a floor pit associated with a pit house, was counted to a 100-grain sum. Pollen concentrations were high, with an average concentration for all 25 samples of 34,909 gr/cc (maximum 270,000 gr/cc; minimum 1,971 gr/cc). The number of pollen taxa identified in each sample ranged from 3 to 14, with an average of 8. The percentage of grains too degraded to identify averaged 15 percent, with a range of 4 to 37 percent.

A total of 21 different pollen types was identified among the 25 samples. Table 36 lists the pollen types identified, with common names, and indicates the pollination mode (wind or insect), the flowering season, and possible cultural uses for each taxon. Pollen types are discussed by common names throughout the report, except for cheno-am and Compositae. Cheno-am and Compositae were the dominant pollen types in the Sunset Mesa Ruin samples, and are also characteristic of modern Sonoran Desert pollen assemblages from floodplain and alluvial terrace sediments (Hevly et al. 1965; Solomon et al. 1982). The cheno-am category encompasses several genera from the Chenopodiaceae and Amaranthaceae families, which were important prehistoric subsistence resources, and both categories include several taxa that colonize disturbed ground. Other identified weed types that have been used as disturbed ground indicators (Gish 1991:244) include globemallow, spiderling type, and summer poppy. The Sunset Mesa Ruin samples were characterized by low percentages of spiderling type.

Low percentages of pine, Mormon tea, and sagebrush pollen were calculated for some of the pollen samples. These are attributed to long-distance atmospheric transport from highlands near Tucson or river transport from the Santa Cruz and Rillito Rivers. Because the site is located on an alluvial terrace adjacent to two rivers, the terrace deposits undoubtedly contain some component of river-deposited pollen that could come from anywhere in the drainage basins.

Maize and squash are the obvious economic pollen types identified, and cholla also is evaluated as an important, potentially economic resource. Cholla was identified in 14 of the 23 prehistoric samples from Sunset Mesa Ruin, primarily pit house floors and extramural features. There are extensive ethnographic accounts of consumption of cholla buds—roasted, boiled, or dried for storage. Gasser and Kwiatkowski (1991) have proposed that cholla was a Hohokam trade commodity, and Fish (1984) and Bohrer (1991) have suggested that cholla was deliberately cultivated, or at least encouraged, at Hohokam sites in the Salt and Gila River valleys. Cacti and prickly

Table 35. Sunset Mesa Pollen Samples

Feature	Sample Number[a]	Context	Pollen Sum	Pollen Concentration (gr/cc)	Number of Taxa	% Degraded
Surface	902	control	200	33,750.0	10	4.0
35	807	historical-period pit fill	200	22,500.0	5	6.5
21	composite (2)	pit house Floor A (entry)	200	135,000.0	14	12.5
21	546	pit house Floor B (hearth)	200	6,585.4	12	15.5
21.02	473	intramural posthole fill	209	4,340.8	8	7.2
22	644	pit house floor (beneath mano)	204	22,950.0	10	6.9
22	composite (4)	pit house floor	200	270,000.0	10	12.0
23	composite (2)	pit house floor	200	22,500.0	7	11.5
23	composite (4)	pit house floor	200	45,000.0	10	12.0
23.02	852	intramural floor pit	200	9,310.3	7	23.5
25	391	pit house floor	200	30,000.0	7	11.0
25	composite (4)	fill	200	30,000.0	5	29.5
27	composite (4)	pit house floor	200	54,000.0	5	26.5
27.01	659	intramural hearth	200	8,709.7	6	26.5
27.03	675	intramural pit	100	4,655.2	6	37.0
13	797	kitchen area (ramada)	200	19,285.7	9	17.0
15	897	kitchen area	221	7,851.3	8	7.2
15.01	241	fire-cracked-rock pit fill	200	13,500.0	10	10.0
41	800	extramural pit fill	200	11,739.1	7	4.0
46	767	extramural thermal pit fill	200	45,000.0	6	14.0
47	805	extramural pit fill	200	33,750.0	13	9.0
49	788	burned-rock midden	205	14,565.8	11	5.4
18	826	canal fill, sample 5 (see Figure 24)	200	22,500.0	12	13.0
18	783	canal base	200	1,970.8	3	19.5
18	836	below canal	200	3,253.0	6	25.5

[a] Composites show number of samples combined in parentheses.
Key: gr/cc = pollen grains per cubic centimeter of sample sediment.

pear, both evident in the Sunset Mesa Ruin pollen data, also are evaluated as subsistence resources. The cacti designation refers to a pollen type that is identifiable to the Cactaceae family, but is not cholla, prickly pear, or saguaro. The cacti type may reflect hedgehog (*Echinocereus*) cactus.

Results and Interpretations

Figure 67 displays bar graphs of the pollen percentage data for all 25 samples and also shows sample pollen concentration and number of pollen types identified. The following details the results by feature.

Historical-Period Feature 35

A fill sample from an ash-filled pit, Feature 35, was submitted for analysis. The pollen assemblage from this sample contributed little information as to use of the pit or plant resources that may have been associated with the feature. The pollen assemblage was dominated by cheno-am and cheno-am aggregates (84 percent and 6 percent of the pollen sum, respectively), which suggests the pit may have been a favorable site for cheno-am weeds.

Table 36. Pollen Types Identified with Ecological and Ethnobotanical Significance

Pollen Taxa	Common Name	Pollination Mode	Flowering Season	Ethnobotanical Uses					
				Food	Medicinal	Ceremonial	Fuel	Building	Other
Abies	fir	wind	summer			x	x	x	x
Pinus	pine	wind	summer	x	x	x	x	x	x
Pinus pinyon type	pinyon	wind	summer	x	x	x	x	x	x
Ephedra	Mormon tea	wind	spring		x	x	x		
Artemisia	sagebrush	wind	summer	x	x	x	x		x
Prosopis	mesquite	insect	spring	x			x	x	x
Cactaceae	cactus family	insect	spring	x					
Cylindropuntia	cholla	insect	early summer	x		x			
Platyopuntia	prickly pear	insect	spring	x					
Cucurbita	squash	insect	summer	x		x			x
Zea	maize	wind	summer	x		x	x		x
Cheno-am	includes saltbush, goosefoot, pigweed and others	wind/insect	spring–fall	x	x	x	x		x
Hi-spine Compositae	includes sunflower, aster, seepwillow and others	insect	spring–fall	x	x	x	x		x
Low-spine Compositae	bursage, ragweed	wind	summer–fall	x			x		
Gramineae	grass family	wind	spring–fall	x		x			x
Sphaeralcea	globemallow	insect	summer–fall	x	x	x			
Boerhaavia type	spiderling, four o'clock	insect	summer–fall	x	x				x
Kallstroemia	summer poppy	insect	summer	x					
Cruciferae	mustard family	insect	spring	x	x				
Eriogonum	buckwheat	insect	spring–summer	x	x	x			
Onagraceae	evening primrose family	insect	spring–summer	x	x	x			

Notes: Pollination mode and flowering period referenced primarily from Kearney and Peebles (1960). Information on ethnobotanical uses based on prehistoric data from Bohrer (1991), Gasser and Kwiatkowski (1991), and Huckell (1993), and on ethnographic information primarily from Stevenson (1915), Whiting (1939), Castetter and Bell (1942), and Curtin (1984).

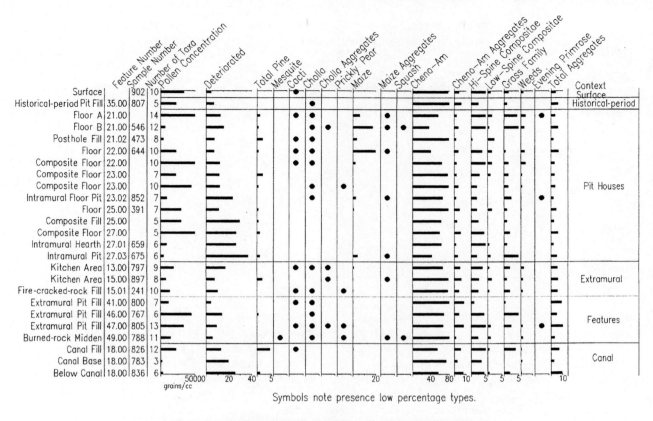

Figure 67. Pollen percentage diagram, Sunset Mesa Ruin.

Canal Feature 18

Three samples were analyzed from the canal feature: a sample from below the canal (Sample 836), one from the base of the canal (Sample 783), and one from canal sediments (Sample 826). The greatest contrast among pollen concentrations in all the samples was evident in the precanal and canal base samples (3,253–1,971 gr/cc) as compared to the canal sample (22,500 gr/cc). High pollen concentrations are typical of fine-grained, fluvial sediments (Fall 1987; Solomon et al. 1982). The results from the three canal samples indicate that the samples represent water-laid sediments. The dominant pollen types in all three samples were cheno-am and Compositae, but differences in the percentages suggest the precanal and canal base samples reflect Santa Cruz River floodplain sediments, whereas the canal sample was more similar to pollen spectra from the Rillito River.

Solomon et al. (1982) analyzed pollen from fresh clay samples deposited by six flood events between July and November 1974 in the Santa Cruz and Rillito Rivers, near Sunset Mesa Ruin. Table 37 shows pollen percentage data for selected taxa from the three canal samples, and average percentages from the Santa Cruz and Rillito

River flood samples (calculated from Appendix A, Solomon et al. 1982:68–69).

The most significant contrast in the river samples was the average percentages of cheno-am and Compositae pollen. The Santa Cruz River flood samples were characterized by higher percentages of cheno-am (average 64 percent) and lower percentages of Compositae (hi-spine, 7 percent; low-spine, 5 percent), compared to average percentages from the Rillito River (cheno-am, 38 percent; hi-spine, 12 percent; and low-spine, 13 percent). Another difference between the two rivers was the slightly higher average percentage of pine pollen from the Rillito River (3 percent) than from the Santa Cruz River (2 percent). These differences are attributed to the larger Santa Cruz catchment, which includes a greater area of floodplain and desert vegetation communities than does the Rillito River.

The canal sample pollen percentages were more similar to the Rillito River flood samples, and the pre-canal and canal base samples were comparable to the Santa Cruz River samples. The canal sample was characterized by higher percentages of hi-spine Compositae and pine pollen, as compared to the precanal and canal base samples. The percentages of cheno-am pollen from the canal

171

Table 37. Pollen Percentages for Selected Taxa from Canal Feature 18 and
Average Percentages from River Flood Samples (Solomon et al. 1982)

Pollen Taxa	Canal Feature 18			Rillito River Average % 13 Flood Samples	Santa Cruz River Average % 5 Flood Samples
	Pre-Canal	Canal Base	Canal		
Cheno-am	56.5	73.5	54.9	38.4	63.8
Hi-spine Compositae	4.5	3.5	14.5	12.3	7.2
Low-spine Compositae	0.5	—	0.5	12.8	5.1
Grass	2.0	—	4.0	18.9	13.3
Riparian trees and shrubs	—	—	—	0.5	0.8
Oak	—	—	—	1.9	1.0
Total pine	1.0	—	4.5	2.9	1.5
Juniper	—	—	—	1.5	0.4
Mesquite	—	—	—	1.1	0.4

and precanal samples were comparable, but a significantly greater percentage of cheno-am pollen was calculated from the canal base sample. The comparison of the flood samples and the three canal samples (see Table 37) suggests that the canal Feature 18 was supplied by Rillito River water, and that the precanal and canal base samples were composed of alluvial sediments deposited by the Santa Cruz River.

Prehistoric Pollen Analog: Canal and Surface Samples

The pollen data from the precanal and canal base samples are interpreted to provide a measure of the natural, prehistoric pollen composition in sediments near the site, probably a mixture of atmospheric pollen rain, river-deposited pollen, and prehistoric cultural activities. The pollen results from the surface sample provide some support for the use of the precanal and canal base samples as prehistoric analogs. The surface sample was characterized by a high percentage of cheno-am pollen (78 percent), moderate Compositae (hi-spine, 8 percent; low-spine, 1 percent), and grass (2 percent) pollen, and no pine or other weed types, except for buckwheat pollen (2 percent). The surface sample results are somewhat surprising, as higher representation from weed and grass pollen was expected, given the modern use of the terrace by a dairy. Considered together, the surface, precanal, and canal base samples indicate that natural background percentages of the dominant pollen types fall within the following ranges: cheno-am, 57–78 percent; hi-spine Compositae, 4–8 percent; low-spine Compositae, 1 percent; grass, 2 percent; and all weed types combined (globemallow, spiderling type, summer poppy, mustard, and buckwheat), less than 2 percent .

Comparison of these numbers to percentages from the archaeological pollen samples does not identify any context in which cheno-am was significantly high enough to interpret cultural use. Cheno-am taxa were probably harvested for greens and seeds at the site, because cheno-am taxa undoubtedly were accessible in the natural plant community, and cheno-ams were important ethnobotanical resources. But there is no pollen evidence that any particular feature was associated with cheno-ams. In fact, cheno-am percentages calculated for most of the features were generally less than 70 percent, which indicates that the pervasive, natural cheno-am pollen rain was restricted by roofs and coverings over pit houses and pits. The same pattern was observed in the weed pollen types, with most contexts yielding a combined weed percentage of less than 2 percent. Samples from pit house Features 21 and 22 were the only ones to yield higher weed percentages (3–4 percent). A few of the archaeological samples were characterized by higher percentages of Compositae and grass pollen, and these are discussed in the next section.

Pit House Feature 21

Three pollen samples from Feature 21 were analyzed, including a fill sample from a primary posthole pit (Feature 21.02) and two floor samples—one from Floor A, from the plastered area in the structure entry, and the other from Floor B, from the plastered area around the hearth. The fill sample yielded a relatively low pollen concentration (4,341 gr/cc) compared to Floor A (135,000 gr/cc), but was comparable to Floor B (6,585 gr/cc). The pollen assemblage from the fill contrasted with both floor samples, with higher percentages of cheno-am and low-spine Compositae pollen, and lower percentages of hi-spine

Compositae and grass. Maize and cholla pollen were identified in all three samples, but the percentages of maize and cholla were higher from the floor samples, and aggregates of maize and cholla were identified only from the floor samples. Cacti pollen was identified from Floor A and the fill sample, but a higher percentage was calculated for the fill sample (3 percent) than for Floor A (1 percent).

The Floor B sample from around the hearth was characterized by a high percentage (18 percent) of maize pollen and the presence of cholla, squash, and pollen aggregates of maize and cholla. Squash pollen was rare in this analysis, and was identified in only one other sample (Feature 49, a burned-rock midden). Floor B was also distinguished by the maximum hi-spine Compositae percentage (13 percent) in the sample set. The Floor A sample from the structure's entry was characterized by a lower percentage of maize (6 percent) compared to Floor B. Cholla and cacti pollen and aggregates of maize pollen also were identified from Floor A. The percentage of grass pollen in both floor samples was notable (5–6 percent), compared to a total absence of grass pollen in the fill sample. The percentages of both grass and hi-spine Compositae pollen were also higher than the defined analog. The contrasts among the floor and fill samples, and between the entry and hearth areas of the floor, indicate that hi-spine Compositae and grass may have been ethnobotanical resources used in the structure, in addition to maize, cholla, and squash. The high pollen concentration from Floor A, in the structure entry, suggests this area captured more pollen from foot traffic, and perhaps sweepings from the structure's interior.

Pit House Feature 22

Two samples from the surface of a plastered floor in Feature 22 were analyzed, a composite of four samples and a sample from beneath a mano. The composite sample was distinguished by the maximum pollen concentration of the sample set, at 270,000 gr/cc. A concentration of 22,950 gr/cc was calculated for the sample from beneath the mano, which is high for such a protected context. The percentages of the dominant pollen types (cheno-am and Compositae) were similar between both samples. A higher percentage of hi-spine Compositae (10 percent) was calculated for the composite floor sample, compared to 4 percent hi-spine from the sample beneath the mano. Maize pollen was identified from both samples, but the floor sample from beneath the mano was characterized by the maximum percentage of maize (35 percent) and highest number of maize aggregates (five) out of all 25 samples. Cholla pollen was identified during scans of both floor samples, and low percentages

of cacti pollen (less than 2 percent) were calculated for both. Maize was obviously associated with the floor mano in Feature 22, and the abundance of maize pollen under the mano suggests maize processing. Cholla, hi-spine Compositae, and possibly cacti also may have been used in Feature 22.

Pit House Feature 23

Three samples analyzed from Feature 23 include a sample from a floor pit, Feature 23.02, and two composite floor samples. One composite was combined from four samples from roof fall and fill material just above the pit house floor, and the other composite combined two samples that included one from beneath a floor metate. Pollen concentrations from the two floor samples were high (22,500 and 45,000 gr/cc) compared to the intramural pit sample (9,310 gr/cc). A moderate percentage of degraded pollen (24 percent) was calculated from the pit sample, compared to lower percentages from the two floor samples (12 percent). The percentages of hi- and low-spine Compositae pollen were comparable among the three samples, but a slightly higher percentage of grass pollen was calculated from the pit sample (3 percent) than from the floors (2 percent grass). Cholla and maize pollen and aggregates of maize were identified in the pit sample. Cholla and prickly pear pollen were identified from one of the composite floor samples (four sample composite), which was the only identification of prickly pear pollen from all the pit house samples. The pollen data indicate that maize, cholla, and prickly pear were used in this structure. The slightly higher representation of grass pollen from the pit feature may reflect some use of grass as a subsistence resource, textile material, or pit lining.

Pit House Feature 25

A floor and a composite fill sample (combined from four samples) were analyzed from pit house Feature 25. Both samples yielded sample concentrations of 30,000 gr/cc, but the fill sample was characterized by a higher percentage of degraded grains (30 percent) compared to the floor sample (11 percent). The percentages of cheno-am, Compositae, and grass pollen were comparable between both samples. The only cultigen pollen identified was a low percentage (less than 1 percent) of maize from the pit house floor sample. No cacti, cholla, or prickly pear were identified from either sample. The low representation of maize pollen from the floor sample is the only indication of subsistence resources in this structure.

Pit House Feature 27

Three samples were analyzed from Feature 27: a composite of four samples from the floor, a hearth sample (Feature 27.01), and a floor pit sample (Feature 27.03). A high sample pollen concentration was calculated for the composite floor sample (54,000 gr/cc), and relatively low concentrations were calculated for the hearth (8,710 gr/cc) and the intramural pit (4,655 gr/cc). All three samples were characterized by a high percentage of degraded pollen (27–37 percent), but the pit yielded the highest amount (37 percent). Hi-spine Compositae percentages from the floor and hearth (5–7 percent) were higher than from the pit, but the percentage of grass pollen was significantly higher from the pit (7 percent) than from the floor and hearth (less than 2 percent). The intramural pit sample was the only context with maize pollen (4 percent). No cacti, cholla, or prickly pear were identified from any of the three samples. The pollen data from Feature 27 suggest that maize was stored or used in the intramural pit, and that grass may have been stored or used in some way in the pit context. There may have been some use of taxa from the hi-spine Compositae category within the pit house.

Kitchen Area: Features 13 and 15

One fill sample was analyzed from Feature 13, a food-preparation area associated with a ramada. The sample was characterized by a high concentration (19,286 gr/cc), and an assemblage that included cacti, cholla, an aggregate of cholla, and a low percentage of maize pollen (less than 1 percent). Two samples were analyzed from the food preparation area Feature 15, a fill sample and a sample from a concentration of fire-cracked rock. A higher sample pollen concentration was calculated for the fire-cracked-rock sample (13,500 gr/cc) than for the fill sample (7,851 gr/cc). Pollen aggregates of maize and cholla were identified in the fill sample, and the fire-cracked-rock sample included cacti, cholla, and prickly pear pollen. The pollen from these two kitchen areas indicate that cacti, cholla, prickly pear, and maize were processed or consumed near Features 13 and 15.

Extramural Features 41, 46, 47, and 49

Four fill samples were analyzed from each of four extramural features, which included one burned-rock midden area, Feature 49. The latter may represent an actual cooking area, or the clean-out of a nearby cooking pit. Pollen concentrations were similar among the four pit samples, ranging from 11,739 to 45,000 gr/cc. The pollen assemblages also were remarkably similar among all four features, and were characterized primarily by cacti pollen. Cholla pollen was present in all four fill samples, and prickly pear was identified from Features 47 and 49. Other cacti pollen was present in Features 41 and 47. Maize and squash pollen were identified only from Feature 49, which was the only context out of all 25 samples to include mesquite pollen. A high percentage (4 percent) of mesquite pollen and several mesquite aggregates characterized the fill sample from Feature 49. Feature 46 was not significantly different from any of the other samples, with the exception of a slightly higher percentage of grass pollen (7 percent) There were no significant percentages of cheno-am or Compositae pollen in any of the pit fill samples.

The pollen results from the extramural features indicate that they were used to process and/or store cacti, especially cholla. The results from Feature 49 suggest that maize, squash, cholla, prickly pear, and mesquite were either disposed in the feature or directly associated with the burned rock in the midden. The presence of mesquite pollen and aggregates in Feature 49 suggests that mesquite flowers—or a branch with flowers—were incorporated in the midden fill, and does not necessarily indicate that mesquite beans were processed or stored nearby. Mesquite pollen is rarely recovered from archaeological samples, because it is an insect-pollinated type that produces small amounts of poorly dispersed pollen. The presence of mesquite pollen in Feature 49 could reflect cultural use of mesquite, natural deposition from the local vegetation community, or use of river water that contained mesquite flowers. Regardless of the origin of the mesquite pollen, its presence indicates a spring deposition in the context.

Summary and Conclusions

The analysis of the canal samples provides tentative evidence that canal Feature 18 may have been supplied by the Rillito River. Table 38 summarizes the interpretations of significant pollen types for the prehistoric pit house and extramural features. The ubiquity of maize pollen across all of the feature samples indicates that maize agriculture was a main activity at the site. The presence of squash pollen in two samples indicates that squash also was grown at Sunset Mesa Ruin. The glimpse of mesquite pollen in one pit sample suggests that mesquite was a local

Table 38. Summary of Ethnobotanical Pollen Types by Feature

Feature	Maize	Squash	Cholla	Prickly Pear	Other Cacti	Hi-Spine Compositae	Grass
Pit houses							
21	x	x	x			x	x
22	x		x		x	x	
23	x		x	x			x
25	x						
27	x					x	x
Trash areas							
13	x		x	x	x		
15	x		x	x	x		
Extramural pits							
41			x		x		
46			x				
47			x	x	x		
49	x	x	x	x		(mesquite)	

resource probably harvested for both fuel and construction wood, as well as mesquite beans. The consistent presence of cholla pollen in most of the features indicates that cholla flower bud harvesting and processing constituted another important activity at the site. Prickly pear and other cacti also appear to have been subsistence resources.

The cholla pollen signature from this site raises the question of whether cholla was gathered from natural communities near the site, or was deliberately cultivated or encouraged at or near the site. The question of cholla cultivation cannot be resolved from the pollen data, but there is increasing evidence in the archaeological pollen record that cholla was cultivated at Hohokam sites (Bohrer 1991; Fish 1984).

The distribution of pollen types shown on Table 38 shows that pit house Features 21, 22, and 23 contained more pollen evidence of cultural activity than pit house Features 25 and 27. Although maize was associated with all of the pit houses, it was more abundant in Features 21–23, which suggests a more intensive focus on maize within these three houses. The consistent presence of cholla pollen in most of the features, with the exceptions of Features 25 and 27, implies a seasonal difference in occupation. Cholla flowers from April to May, and

the absence of cholla pollen (and other spring-flowering cacti) in Features 25 and 27 suggests these houses were not in use during the spring. The scarcity of ethnobotanical pollen data from Features 25 and 27 could reflect that these two structures represent a different occupation that was focused on summer maize agriculture. Both Features 25 and 27 were characterized by a higher percentage of degraded pollen than Features 21–23, which suggests that Features 25 and 27 are older. Alternatively, Features 25 and 27 may not have been used for habitation or plant processing for some cultural reason.

One of the more interesting patterns in the pollen results summarized in Table 38 is the ubiquity of cacti (cholla, prickly pear, and other cacti) pollen and the rare presence of maize pollen in all of the extramural features. If maize agriculture was a main focus of the site, where was surplus maize stored? Was maize grown, processed, and stored as a meal? Or was maize grown at Sunset Mesa and traded as a commodity to other Hohokam communities? The macrobotanical results may contribute to this question, as mature cobs of maize stored in extramural pits (or pit houses) may not register in the pollen record. The correspondence between cacti pollen and extramural pit features definitely shows that prickly pear, other cacti, and especially cholla, were processed and used at the site.

CHAPTER 11

Faunal Analysis

Kellie M. Cairns and Edgar K. Huber

A total of 508 faunal bone fragments was recovered from Sunset Mesa Ruin. The assemblage, which includes worked bone artifacts and unworked bone, represents the site's prehistoric and historical-period components.

Analytical Methods

All 508 of the faunal bone fragments recovered were analyzed, including the worked bone specimens. Identifications were made with the consultation of a variety of resources, including published literature (Gilbert 1973; Gilbert et al. 1985; S. J. Olsen 1968, 1973, 1979) and the comparative collection located in the zooarchaeology laboratory of the Arizona State Museum (under the direction of Professor Stanley J. Olsen).

For each specimen, information was recorded on provenience, species, element, portion of the bone, symmetry, burning, observable modifications, historical-period butchering marks, and count. A 16× hand lens facilitated small vertebrate identifications and determinations of butchering marks, striations, and polishing. Identifications were made to the most explicit taxonomical level possible. Tentative assignments are indicated by "cf." (compares favorably with), followed by genus or species designations. Bone fragments not identified to at least a family level were assigned to small, medium, and large size classes for birds and mammals. These classifications were judged on relative body size and the thickness of the bone wall. The indeterminate class category was used for severely splintered bones that could not be placed in one of these categories.

Species identification was determined by diagnostic features on identifiable bone. The qualities that render a bone unidentifiable are mainly incompleteness and

formlessness, but analysts may disagree on what constitutes the latter. Few analysts would regard an epiphysis as nonidentifiable, for example, but they may strongly disagree on a fragmentary one. In many cases, the availability of a complete comparative collection and the skill of the analyst may determine whether or not a fragment can be identified. If possible, all fragments were identified to a particular element, such as humerus or ulna. When this was not possible, identifications were left at a more general level. For instance, fragments of an unidentifiable leg bone were identified as long-bone fragments. Although the unidentified remains do not belong to a true taxonomic category, these size categories may still reflect the general nature of animal use at the site.

Various problems arise when identifying and distinguishing among various species of lagomorphs and artiodactyls. At least two species of cottontail rabbit reside in the project area, *Sylvilagus audubonii* (desert cottontail) and *S. floridanus* (eastern cottontail). These two species are virtually indistinguishable on the basis of postcranial elements alone. Only when complete skulls are present can the distinction be made. For this report, the category of *Sylvilagus* sp. was used for all cottontail remains. Similar problems arise in distinguishing between black-tailed jackrabbits (*Lepus californicus*) and the antelope jackrabbit (*L. alleni*). Both inhabit the project area today and also can be difficult to distinguish based on postcranial elements. However, the mature antelope jackrabbits are substantially larger than their adult, black-tailed jackrabbit counterparts. Antelope jackrabbits have longer leg-bone shafts in relation to the epiphyses and the shafts are heavier (Strand 1996). Only one specimen was positively identified as *L. alleni*; all other specimens were left at the genus level. One faces the same identification problems when distinguishing between white-tailed and mule deer, or bison and domestic cow. Extreme caution was used in identifying these species and more often than not, identifications were left at the genus level.

After the identifications were made, the NISP (number of identified specimens per taxon [Grayson 1984; Lyman 1982]) measure of taxonomic abundance was recorded to show the total number of bones in the collection. Some analysts take a very literal view of NISP, including only those bones that can be identified to a certain taxonomic level—usually to at least family—or to a specific element (for example, the femur). For this report, I have used a very liberal interpretation of NISP as being all fragments of bone from any particular level of taxonomic identification. Thus, the total sum of all NISP equals the number of all bone fragments for the collection. One advantage of this approach is that it permits a comparison of the NISP for a more specific taxon to a less specific one, and the use of such a comparison to make inferences concerning the degree of fragmentation for the collection. For example, we could compare the NISP for artiodactyls to the NISP for the more generic, ungulate-size class to determine the ratio of bone fragments that are too small or broken to be identified to a specific taxon, or to determine the ratio that can be identified. This may provide a crude measure of the degree to which bone is being broken during food processing or by later, taphonomic processes. The problem with NISP as a measure of taxonomic abundance lies in its extreme sensitivity to the degree of fragmentation, and to differences in the total number of bones in the skeletons of various taxa (Grayson 1984; Ringrose 1993).

The Modern Living Community

The living community of animals that resided in the area of Sunset Mesa Ruin 850–1,050 years ago was probably very similar to that which exists today. This suite of animals probably has changed little over this time, with the exception of a few introduced species. However, the relative proportions of native species in the modern living community have drastically changed from their prehistoric proportions. Changes in habitat caused by human use, and competition with introduced species—particularly domesticated animals—has altered the proportions of these native species to various degrees.

One of the most important aspects of Sunset Mesa Ruin is its location near two major rivers. The riparian communities along these streams would have supported high biotic diversity and attracted a wide array of species, ranging from fish and amphibians to mammals and birds. Native animal life in the area today consists of black-tailed and antelope jackrabbits, desert and eastern cottontails, mule deer, javelina, coyote, kit fox, badger, bobcat, spotted and striped skunk, and various rodents. Birds include the mockingbird, cactus wren, Gambel's quail, dove, roadrunner, turkey vulture, red-tailed hawk, and sparrow hawk. Various reptiles also inhabit the area, ranging from toads and lizards to rattlesnakes (Rozen 1979).

Assemblage Composition

The following discussion is based on the analysis of 508 specimens of unworked bone and worked bone artifacts from 14 features and 1 nonfeature. Of the features represented, 10 have been identified as prehistoric and 4 (Features 5, 34, 42, and 44) appear to date to the historical period. Table 39 presents the various species represented and their relative frequencies per taxon. Table 40 divides the species list by feature. In all, 17 fragments are presumed to represent historical-period fauna, whereas the remaining 491 specimens relate to the prehistoric occupation and intrusive species.

Most of the collection (71 percent) could not be identified beyond the level of class. Of the identifiable remains, however, at least 8 or 9 species were represented. The identified collection consists mostly of mammals (92 percent, n = 135), followed by birds (8 percent, n = 11). One of the most interesting aspects of the Sunset Mesa Ruin assemblage is the high frequency of artiodactyl specimens, which account for approximately 34 percent of the identifiable remains. Hohokam faunal assemblages are usually characterized by high frequencies of lagomorphs and artiodactyls, but, as will be discussed later, most of the artiodactyl remains were recovered from a unique context.

Taxonomic Composition

Mammals

Represented among the identifiable remains are lagomorphs, rodents, perissodactyls, artiodactyls, and Aves. A breakdown of these various orders, their context and relative frequencies is presented below. No fish, reptile, or amphibian remains were found; however, the absence of these taxa may be due in part to data recovery methods that relied on $\frac{1}{4}$-inch-mesh screens, which are too large to recover the small bones usually associated with these animals.

Table 39. Vertebrate Species Recovered from Sunset Mesa Ruin

Scientific Name, by Class and Order	Common Name	NISP
Mammalia		
Lagomorpha		
Lepus alleni	antelope jackrabbit	1
cf. *Lepus alleni*	antelope jackrabbit	3
Lepus sp.	jackrabbit	42
Sylvilagus sp.	cottontail	12
Indeterminate Leporidae	indeterminate rabbit	6
Subtotal		64
Rodentia		
Neotoma sp.	woodrats	1
Perognathus sp.	pocket mice	1
Indeterminate Rodentia	indeterminate rodents	19
Subtotal		21
Perissodactyla		
cf. *Equus caballus*	domestic horse	2
Subtotal		2
Artiodactyla		
Bison bison/Bos taurus	bison/domestic cow	14
cf. *Bison bison/Bos taurus*	bison/domestic cow	1
Odocoileus sp.	deer	27
cf. *Ovis* sp.	bighorn/domestic sheep	2
Indeterminate Artiodactyla	indeterminate artiodactyl	4
Subtotal		48
Unidentified		
Rodent-sized	small mammal	66
Rabbit/rodent-sized	small mammal	9
Rabbit-sized	small mammal	109
Skunk-sized	small-medium mammal	1
Carnivore-sized	medium mammal	16
Ungulate-sized	large mammal	117
Subtotal		318
Aves		
Zenaida macroura	mourning dove	5
Indeterminate small Aves	indeterminate small birds	1
Indeterminate medium Aves	indeterminate medium birds	2
Indeterminate Aves	indeterminate birds	3
Subtotal		11
Indeterminate class	indeterminate	44
Indeterminate	indeterminate	44
Total		508

Table 40. List of Animal Species Recovered from Sunset Mesa Ruin, by Feature (in NISP)

Scientific Name	Prehistoric												
	13	15	17	21				22				23	
	Fill	Fill	Fill	Fill	Roof Fall	Floor Fill	Fill (Subfloor)	Fill	Roof Fall	Floor Fill	Floor	Fill	Floor Fill
Lagomorpha													
Lepus alleni	—	—	—	—	—	—	—	—	—	—	—	—	—
cf. Lepus alleni	1	—	—	—	—	—	—	—	—	—	—	—	—
Lepus sp.	6	—	—	—	2	3	3	2	1	—	—	2	3
Sylvilagus sp.	—	—	—	—	2	—	—	—	—	—	—	—	1
Indeterminate Leporidae	—	—	—	—	—	—	—	—	—	—	—	1	—
Rodentia													
Neotoma sp.	—	—	1	—	—	—	—	—	—	—	—	—	—
Perognathus sp.	—	—	—	—	—	—	—	—	—	—	—	—	—
Indeterminate Rodentia	—	—	7	—	4	—	1	—	—	—	—	2	5
Perrissodactyla													
cf. Equus caballus	—	—	—	—	—	—	—	—	—	—	—	—	—
Artiodactyla													
Bison bison/Bos taurus	—	—	—	—	—	—	—	—	—	—	—	—	—
cf. Bison bison/Bos taurus	—	—	—	—	—	—	—	—	—	—	—	—	—
Odocoileus sp.	—	—	—	—	—	—	—	—	1	—	—	—	—
cf. Ovis sp.	—	—	—	—	—	—	—	—	—	—	—	—	—
Indeterminate Artiodactyla	—	—	—	—	—	—	—	—	—	—	—	—	1
Subtotal	7	0	8	0	8	3	4	2	2	0	0	5	10
Aves													
Zenaida macroura	—	—	—	—	—	—	—	—	—	—	—	—	—
Indeterminate small Aves	1	—	—	—	—	—	—	—	—	—	—	—	—
Indeterminate medium Aves	—	—	—	—	—	—	—	—	—	—	—	—	—
Indeterminate Aves	2	—	—	—	—	—	—	—	—	—	—	—	—
Subtotal	3	0	0	0	0	0	0	0	0	0	0	0	0
Unidentified Mammalia													
Rodent-sized	8	—	—	1	—	1	3	—	—	—	—	1	1
Rabbit/rodent-sized	5	—	1	—	—	—	2	—	—	—	—	—	—
Rabbit-sized	7	—	—	3	1	—	1	1	2	1	—	—	1
Skunk-sized	—	—	—	—	—	—	—	—	—	—	—	—	—
Carnivore-sized	1	—	—	—	—	—	—	—	—	—	—	—	—
Ungulate-sized	3	—	—	—	—	—	—	—	—	—	1	—	1
Subtotal	24	0	1	4	1	1	6	1	2	1	1	1	3
Indeterminate class	—	1	—	—	—	—	—	—	—	—	—	1	1
Total	34	1	9	4	9	4	10	3	4	1	1	7	14

Table 40 (continued).

Scientific Name	Prehistoric (continued)							5		Historical-Period					Total
	25			26	27		28			34	42	44	Backdirt	Overburden	
	Fill	Roof Fall Floor Fill	Floor	Fill	Fill	Roof Fall Floor Fill	Fill	Overburden	Fill	Fill	Surface	Fill			
Lagomorpha															
Lepus alleni	—	1	—	—	—	—	—	—	—	—	—	—	—	—	1
cf. *Lepus alleni*	1	2	—	—	—	—	—	—	—	—	—	—	—	—	3
Lepus sp.	1	9	—	—	—	—	—	—	—	—	—	—	—	—	42
Sylvilagus sp.	—	3	1	—	—	—	—	—	3	—	—	—	—	—	12
Indeterminate Leporidae	—	5	—	—	—	—	—	—	—	—	—	—	—	—	6
Rodentia															
Neotoma sp.	—	—	—	—	—	—	—	—	—	—	—	—	—	—	1
Perognathus sp.	—	—	—	—	—	—	—	—	1	—	—	—	—	—	1
Indeterminate Rodentia	—	—	—	—	—	—	—	—	—	—	—	—	—	—	19
Perissodactyla															
cf. *Equus caballus*	2	—	—	—	—	—	—	—	1	—	—	—	—	1	2
Artiodactyla															
Bison bison/Bos taurus	1	1	—	—	—	—	—	—	8	—	4	—	—	1	14
cf. *Bison bison/Bos taurus*	—	1	—	—	—	—	—	—	—	1	—	—	—	—	1
Odocoileus sp.	3	3	20	—	—	—	—	—	1	—	—	—	—	—	27
cf. *Ovis* sp.	—	—	1	—	—	—	—	—	1	—	—	—	—	—	2
Indeterminate Artiodactyla	—	—	3	—	—	—	—	—	—	1	—	—	—	—	4
Subtotal	3	24	25	0	2	0	0	0	14	1	4	0	0	2	135
Aves															
Zenaida macroura	—	—	—	—	—	—	—	2	3	—	—	—	—	—	5
Indeterminate small Aves	—	—	—	—	—	—	—	—	1	—	—	—	—	—	1
Indeterminate medium Aves	—	—	—	—	—	—	—	—	—	—	—	—	—	2	2
Indeterminate Aves	—	—	—	—	—	—	—	1	1	—	—	—	—	—	3
Subtotal	0	0	0	0	0	0	0	3	3	0	0	0	0	2	11
Unidentified Mammalia															
Rodent-sized	—	14	—	2	2	2	34	—	—	—	—	—	—	—	66
Rabbit/rodent-sized	—	1	—	—	—	—	—	—	—	—	—	—	—	—	9
Rabbit-sized	8	46	—	—	4	6	—	—	5	—	—	—	15	1	109
Skunk-sized	—	—	—	—	—	—	—	—	—	—	—	—	1	—	1
Carnivore-sized	1	1	3	—	—	3	—	—	—	—	—	—	—	—	16
Ungulate-sized	1	21	53	—	1	—	12	1	12	—	—	1	—	1	117
Subtotal	1	58	56	0	8	11	54	1	17	0	0	1	16	2	318
Indeterminate class	—	9	—	5	—	—	13	—	1	1	—	—	—	—	44
Total	4	77	82	81	5	10	11	67	4	35	1	4	1	16	5	508

Lagomorphs

Lagomorphs are the most abundant taxa in the assemblage, constituting 44 percent of the identifiable remains. Table 41 presents the lagomorph remains by feature. Most of the elements (n = 46) examined were identified as jackrabbits. Although both cottontails and jackrabbits can be found within the project area, they have very different behavioral patterns. For instance, cottontails generally prefer environments with more vegetative cover. This dense cover allows them to hide when pursued, but they have also been known to retreat to the nearest burrow when threatened. Jackrabbits, on the other hand, tend to flee rather than hide. Environments with less vegetative cover allow them to reach high speeds while attempting to elude their predators. Because of these behavioral differences, the methods of hunting these two genera may be different. As Szuter (1991:204) has pointed out, communal drives tend to catch much higher frequencies of jackrabbits, compared to cottontails. Cottontails are more easily captured by solitary hunters who stalk them individually or with traps (Szuter 1991:204).

Based on the assumption that cottontails prefer more brushy areas, whereas jackrabbits prefer more open ones, archaeofaunal analysts (Szuter 1991; Szuter and Bayham 1989) have developed an equation to measure various aspects of faunal diversity. The lagomorph index is a taxonomic ratio based on the NISP of antelope jackrabbit (*Lepus alleni*), black-tailed jackrabbit (*L. californicus*), and cottontails (*Sylvilagus*), as well as the faunal remains identified simply to order or family; it compares the relative proportion of cottontails (*Sylvilagus*) to jackrabbits (*Lepus*). This measure is determined by dividing the total NISP of *Sylvilagus* by the total NISP of all leporid specimens (S/L, where S = *Sylvilagus* and L = Lagomorphs).

Citing work by Gillespie (1989) suggesting that the lagomorph index tends to decline in areas of long-term, human habitation, Szuter (1991:206–209) has argued that this decline is in response to the increasing impacts of sedentary populations on both wild resources and habitat. In the case of Sunset Mesa Ruin, the lagomorph ratio of 0.187 is consistent with the lower indexes cited by Szuter (1991:208, Table 6.5) for the later occupations of the Tanque Verde Wash (AZ BB:13:68 [ASM]), Valencia (AZ BB:13:15 [ASM]), and West Branch (AZ AA:16:3 [ASM]) sites in the Tucson Basin, indicating a higher percentage of jackrabbit remains compared to cottontails. Rather than providing a true reflection of the inhabitants' preference for jackrabbits, or environmental degradation, however, this index may result from a combination of factors. For instance, use of ¼-inch mesh may underrepresent smaller taxa, especially fish and cottontails. James (1995) has concluded that, when compared to the use of ⅛-inch mesh, the use of ¼-inch mesh creates a bias against cottontails and other small fauna in favor of the larger species, such as jackrabbits. Thus, recovery methods have a potentially significant effect on the lagomorph and artiodactyl indexes, and could alter our interpretations of the use of faunal resources and degree of exploitation of certain habitats. Considering this problem, the lagomorph index should be used with extreme caution.

The high frequencies of both cottontails and jackrabbits clearly represent the economic importance of these animals during the occupation of Sunset Mesa Ruin. When compared to most other small mammals, cottontails and jackrabbits are a great source of meat protein because of their relatively large size and fecundity. The latter is such that human hunters rarely eradicate their populations, but can at most only temporarily depress their numbers (Shelley and Cairns 1998). This results in a fairly constant and reasonable supply of meat protein, regardless of hunting pressure. Moreover, lagomorphs not only provided a source of meat, but also fur that was used for blankets and a variety of other purposes. The bones also have been used as raw materials for manufacturing tools and ornaments (Shelley 1993).

The skeletal representation among lagomorph body parts appears to be relatively uniform. Cranial elements, forelimbs, hind limbs, scapulae, pelves, and vertebral specimens are represented for each genera. This suggests that both cottontails and jackrabbits were brought back to the site in their entirety and then butchered.

Rodents

Rodents constitute approximately 14 percent (n = 21) of the identifiable faunal collection. Within this count, pocket mice, wood rats and indeterminate rodents were recorded. Their bones show no cultural modifications and their use as an economically important species is not certain.

Before an adequate discussion of the importance of these animals can begin, a basic methodological problem needs to be addressed: Are the rodent remains recovered from Hohokam sites the result of human subsistence activities, or are they the result of intrusions into cultural deposits by burrowing animals? Nor is it possible to distinguish rodents that intruded into cultural deposits while a site was actively occupied from those that entered the deposits after the site was abandoned. This problem is of concern in addressing subsistence issues, as well as understanding the local environment during the site's occupation.

Szuter (1982) called for a thorough examination of the ethnographic, taphonomic, and archaeological evidence to differentiate the possible causes for the presence of rodent bones at an archaeological site. Ethnographic records indicate that rodents can provide a readily available supply of meat, the acquisition of which does not

Table 41. Frequencies of Lagomorph Elements by Feature (in NISP)

Element, by Scientific Name	Prehistoric												Historical-Period		Total
	13	21			22		23			25			27.03	5	
	Fill	Roof Fall	Floor Fill	Fill (Subfloor)	Fill	Roof Fall	Fill	Floor Fill	Fill	Roof Fall	Floor Fill	Floor	Fill	Fill	
Lepus alleni															
Mandible	—	—	—	—	—	—	—	—	—	1	—	—	—	—	1
cf. *Lepus alleni*															
Humerus	1	—	—	—	—	—	—	—	—	—	—	—	—	—	1
Radius	—	—	—	—	—	—	—	—	—	1	—	—	—	—	1
Tibia	—	—	—	—	—	—	—	—	—	1	—	—	—	—	1
Lepus sp.															
Blade	—	—	—	1	—	—	—	—	—	—	—	—	—	—	1
Calcaneus	—	—	—	—	—	—	—	—	—	—	—	—	1	—	1
Femur	—	—	—	—	—	—	1	—	—	—	1	—	—	—	2
Humerus	—	—	—	1	—	—	—	—	—	—	—	—	1	—	2
Indeterminate metacarpal	3	—	—	—	—	1	—	1	—	1	—	—	—	—	6
Indeterminate metatarsal	—	—	1	—	—	—	—	1	—	1	—	—	—	—	3
Ischium	1	—	—	—	—	—	—	—	—	1	—	—	—	—	2
Mandible	—	—	—	—	—	—	—	—	—	1	—	—	—	—	1
Phalanx	1	—	2	—	2	—	—	—	—	—	3	—	—	—	8
Radius	—	—	—	1	—	—	—	2	—	2	2	—	—	—	7
Rib	1	—	—	—	—	—	—	—	—	—	—	—	—	—	1
Tibia	—	—	—	—	—	—	—	—	—	3	—	—	—	—	3
Ulna	—	2	—	—	—	—	—	—	—	—	2	—	—	—	4
Vertebra	—	—	—	—	—	—	1	—	—	—	—	—	—	—	1
Sylvilagus sp.															
Femur	—	—	—	—	—	—	—	—	—	—	1	—	—	—	1
Humerus	—	1	—	—	—	—	—	—	—	—	—	—	—	1	2
Indeterminate metacarpal	—	1	—	—	—	—	—	—	—	—	—	—	—	—	1
Indeterminate metatarsal	—	—	—	—	—	—	—	—	—	1	—	—	—	—	1
Innominate	—	—	—	—	—	—	—	—	1	—	—	—	—	—	1
Ischium	—	—	—	—	—	—	—	—	—	1	—	—	—	—	1
Mandible	—	—	—	—	—	—	—	—	—	—	—	1	—	—	1
Phalanx	—	—	—	—	—	—	—	—	—	—	1	—	—	—	1
Radius	—	—	—	—	—	—	—	—	—	—	—	—	—	1	1
Tibia	—	—	—	—	—	—	—	—	—	1	—	—	—	—	1
Ulna	—	—	—	—	—	—	—	—	—	—	—	—	—	1	1
Indeterminate Leporidae															
Incisor	—	—	—	—	—	—	1	—	—	—	—	—	—	—	1
Vertebra	—	—	—	—	—	—	—	—	—	5	—	—	—	—	5
Total	7	4	3	3	2	1	3	4	1	20	10	1	2	3	64

interfere with the scheduling of agricultural activities, as does the hunting of large game mammals. Agricultural fields, food stores, and middens actually attract rodents, and by setting small traps within their fields, a site's inhabitants would not only help to rid those fields of the pesky creatures, but at the same time would obtain a reliable source of meat protein without having to expend much energy. In addition, the condition of a rodent bone found at a site may reflect its mode of deposition. Rodent remains deposited at the same time should exhibit the same degree of weathering. Other indicative attributes would include burning or butchering marks, but these are rarely evident on rodent bones in the Southwest.

No modifications were found on any identifiable rodent remains recovered from Sunset Mesa Ruin. However, 40 specimens identified as rodent-sized mammals were burned and calcined, indicating some economic importance. Most of these specimens were recovered from the fill of features, which suggests that they were burned prior to their final deposition. They may have been deposited in the features as a result of hearth-cleaning activities.

Perissodactyls

Two elements were not positively identified, but most closely resemble the domestic horse (*Equus caballus*). These elements were identified as a phalanx recovered from overburden, and a rib fragment from the fill of Feature 5 (Room 3), a turn-of-the-century adobe house. The rib element displays butchering marks characteristic of the historical period. Both elements most likely relate to the occupancy of the historical-period structure.

Artiodactyls

The artiodactyls may be one of the most interesting aspects of the Sunset Mesa Ruin assemblage. A total of 48 elements was identified to this order, including both prehistoric and historical-period specimens. Table 42 presents the frequencies of artiodactyl elements by feature.

Fourteen fragments have been identified as bison or domestic cow (*Bison bison/Bos taurus*), and an additional fragment was not positively identified, but most closely resembles *Bison bison/Bos taurus*. Differentiating between the two species is not possible with most postcranial elements; however, the recovery of 13 specimens from historical-period features and evidence of historical-period butchering marks on 5 specimens indicate that most of the remains probably belong to domestic cattle rather than bison. One specimen recovered from the roof fall of prehistoric pit house Feature 25 shows no evidence of burning or historical-period butchering marks and may represent bison, but more likely is intrusive to the feature.

Of particular interest is the distribution of deer (*Odocoileus* sp.) and possible bighorn or domestic sheep (cf. *Ovis* sp.) remains. A total of 27 fragments of deer (n = 26) and possible sheep (n = 1) was recovered from the fill, roof fall, floor fill, and floor of Feature 25, a prehistoric pit house. Astonishingly, of the 27 elements, 25 represent innominate fragments. The remaining 2 elements are a left proximal humerus and an incisor of *Odocoileus* sp. With the exception of one possible bighorn or domestic sheep (cf. *Ovis* sp.) pubis, all of the innominate elements belong to deer (*Odocoileus* sp.). All of the innominate elements are burned, but none appear to have been worked. They are heavily fragmented, but no butchering marks were observed. At least eight individuals of *Odocoileus* sp. have been recorded from this context, as evidenced by eight right acetabulums, and one individual of cf. *Ovis* sp. is represented by one pubis. Also recovered from this provenience were 53 smaller fragments, classified as ungulate-sized mammals, that most likely can be refitted to the identified elements.

Such a high frequency of meat-bearing elements (innominates) is unusual at sites in the Tucson Basin. The frequency of innominates was also unusually high in Szuter's (1991) sample, due largely to the contribution of one site, Muchas Casas, near Marana (James 1987). At Muchas Casas, 9 *Ovis* sp. and 36 *Odocoileus* sp. innominates were found from one context (Pit House 496), where large numbers of minimal elements (MNEs)—primarily horn cores, antlers, and skulls—also were recovered (James 1987:Table 8.7). This might represent some special utilization of these animals, perhaps related to dry season predation as the animals sought water, occupation of the house by a skilled hunter, or ceremonial feasting activities associated with the household.

Szuter (1991) compiled data from a large number of Hohokam sites and determined that artiodactyls compose roughly 14.5 percent of the identifiable remains. Artiodactyls account for approximately 26 percent of the identifiable, presumed prehistoric specimens from Sunset Mesa Ruin. An artiodactyl index developed by Bayham (1982) compares changes in the relative proportions of artiodactyls to lagomorphs through time. This index (Szuter and Bayham 1989) is determined by dividing the NISP of artiodactyl remains by the sum of the artiodactyl and leporid specimens (A/A+L, where A = artiodactyls and L = leporids). Unlike the lagomorph index, the artiodactyl index is not used solely as an environmental indicator, but as an indicator of the intensity of use of lagomorphs versus deer at Hohokam sites.

Szuter and Brown (1986) reported that artiodactyl indexes for sites in the Tucson Basin rarely exceed 0.20 (see also Szuter 1991:247, Figure 7.1), and indicated that leporids usually contribute most of the identifiable remains. Based on these data, they inferred a preference for

Table 42. Frequencies of Artiodactyl Elements by Feature (in NISP)

Element, by Species Name	Prehistoric						Historical-Period			Overburden	Total
	22	23		25			5	34	42		
	Roof Fall	Floor Fill	Fill	Roof Fall	Floor Fill	Floor	Fill	Fill	Surface		
Bison bison/Bos taurus											
Accessory	—	—	—	1	—	—	—	—	—	—	1
Glenoid	—	—	—	—	—	—	—	—	1	—	1
Third phalanx (terminal)	—	—	—	—	—	—	1	—	—	—	1
Radius	—	—	—	—	—	—	1	—	—	—	1
Rib	—	—	—	—	—	—	1	—	—	—	1
Vertebra	—	—	—	—	—	—	5	—	—	1	6
[Not recorded]	—	—	—	—	—	—	—	—	3	—	3
cf. *Bison bison/Bos taurus*											
Rib	—	—	—	—	—	—	—	1	—	—	1
cf. *Ovis* sp.											
Phalanx	—	—	—	—	—	—	1	—	—	—	1
Pubis	—	—	—	—	—	1	—	—	—	—	1
Indeterminate Artiodactyla											
Innominate	—	—	—	—	—	3	—	—	—	—	3
Metapodial	—	1	—	—	—	—	—	—	—	—	1
Odocoileus sp.											
Acetabulum	—	—	1	1	—	13	—	—	—	—	15
Glenoid	1	—	—	—	—	—	—	—	—	—	1
Humerus	—	—	—	—	1	—	—	—	—	—	1
Ilium	—	—	1	—	—	—	—	—	—	—	1
Incisor	—	—	—	1	—	—	—	—	—	—	1
Ischium	—	—	—	1	—	7	—	—	—	—	8
Total	1	1	2	4	1	24	9	1	4	1	48

leporids over deer. At 0.34, the artiodactyl index for Sunset Mesa Ruin is relatively high, but this does not necessarily indicate a greater preference for deer on the part of the site's residents. Similar to the lagomorph index, the artiodactyl index may not be a true indicator of the animal preference. Artiodactyl bones are often highly fragmented—possibly the result of intentionally breaking apart the bone to extract grease or to manufacture bone tools—which may critically affect the index value.

Although cottontails and jackrabbits provided most of the bone, artiodactyls were probably not less economically important. Artiodactyls provide more meat protein and marrow per individual than rabbits, making wider sharing of meat and marrow a possibility. Artiodactyl bones also are more frequently shaped into tools or ornaments than either bird or rabbit bones (Szuter 1991).

The collection of deer and sheep elements from Feature 25 is a rare find among Hohokam faunal assemblages. All of the bone recovered is burned and represents high meat-bearing elements. Similar finds have been recorded from the Classic period settlements of Gibbon Springs (Strand 1996), at the base of the Santa Catalina Mountains, and Muchas Casas (James 1987), at the base of the Tortolita Mountains.

Strand (1996:389, Table 10.8) recorded 58 identified artiodactyl specimens recovered from the floor fill of one feature (Feature 106) at Gibbon Springs. A total of 57 pelves fragments was identified to deer (n = 14), white-tailed deer (n = 5), bighorn sheep (n = 4), and indeterminate artiodactyl (n = 34). The pelves were not worked and the amount of burned bone is unknown. Strand concluded that the pelves in Feature 106 may represent access to the better cuts of meat.

James (1987:Tables 8.5, 8.7) recorded a very similar situation at Muchas Casas. Feature 496 contained a total of 551 fragments of *Odocoileus/Ovis* (n = 10), *Odocoileus/Antilocapra/Ovis* (n = 17), cf. *Odocoileus* sp. (n = 132), *Odocoileus* sp. (n = 23), *Odocoileus hemionus* (n = 1), and *Ovis canadensis* (n = 368). From these counts, nine pelves were identified as bighorn sheep, and 36 pelves were identified as deer. Other elements recovered with less frequency were skull fragments, femurs, and metapodials. According to James (1987:187), this pattern suggests a "gourmet butchering strategy" for Locus H. Pelves and proximal femurs are high meat-bearing elements and may indicate a differential access to the better cuts of meat for that locus.

Aves

The Aves remains account for only 2 percent of the total assemblage. Most of the Aves remains could not be identified beyond the level of indeterminate small or medium Aves. The only species identified is the mourning dove (*Zenaida macroura*), which is represented by five elements recovered from the overburden and fill of Feature 5. It is very likely that these elements were intrusive because the condition of the bone is excellent. The elements identified—primarily wing fragments that most likely were articulated at one time—include two left coracoids, one left humerus, one left carpometacarpus, and one sternum. Doves are relatively common in most Hohokam sites.

The paucity of avian elements recovered from Sunset Mesa Ruin is curious. Szuter (1991) observed that in terms of richness, birds are by far the most diverse class of animals recovered from Hohokam sites, with an abundance similar to that of reptiles. Many of the birds are dependent on open water or associated with irrigated fields. The location of Sunset Mesa Ruin would have provided an attractive habitat for many species of birds. Once again, excavation methods (that is, 1/4-inch screens) may have biased the record against small remains, leading to an underrepresentation of avian species.

Unidentified

The unidentified remains constitute 71 percent (n = 362) of the total faunal assemblage. Most of these fragments were not identifiable beyond the size classes of small, small-medium, medium, and large mammals; the remaining fragments were indeterminate as to class. Generally, most Hohokam assemblages contain as much as 60 percent unidentifiable remains (Bayham and Hatch 1985). The high number of unidentifiable remains from Sunset Mesa Ruin evidences a highly fragmented assemblage. Large-sized mammals make up the bulk of the collection (n = 117), followed closely by rabbit-sized mammals (n = 109). High frequencies of unidentifiable remains may be the result of butchering and pounding of the bones to extract the marrow.

Most (n = 181) of the unidentifiable remains were recovered from Feature 25. Feature 28, a prehistoric trash-filled pit, contained the second highest amount of unidentifiable bone (n = 67). Following close behind were Feature 13 (n = 24), a prehistoric kitchen area/ramada, and Feature 27 (n = 23).

Modified Bone

Burned and Calcined Bone

Overall, 55 percent of the faunal collection from Sunset Mesa Ruin is burned and calcined. Various genera are represented and were recovered from numerous features and strata (Table 43). Of the identifiable remains, *Odocoileus* sp. constitutes the bulk of the burned collection, with a total of 24 fragments. These pelves were recovered from Feature 25, most of them (n = 20) from the floor. Also recovered from the floor of this feature was one burned pubis of cf. *Ovis* sp. Other genera present with decreasing frequency within the burned collection are jackrabbits (n = 9), cottontails (n = 3), indeterminate artiodactyl (n = 1), and cf. *Bison bison/Bos taurus* (n = 1). When examining the burned collection as a whole, the unidentifiable remains dominate the collection. Most of these are classified as ungulate-sized mammals making up approximately 31 percent of the entire burned collection. It is possible that many of these fragments refit to the identified pelves of deer and bighorn, as these specimens were recovered from the same proveniences as the identified elements.

The burned collection emphasizes the economic importance of deer, lagomorphs, and small-sized mammals. Although deer account for most of the identified remains, this measure is not the sole indicator of the relative importance of large game for the site's prehistoric inhabitants. The data reveal a reliance on small game, as well. Both rabbits and rodents, readily available and hunted with little advance preparation, would have provided a reliable source of meat protein. Large game requires more planning, and possibly traveling some distance, thus taking away from equally important tasks, such as farming and foraging.

Most of the burned bone (52 percent, n = 146) was recovered from the fill, roof fall, floor fill, and floor of Feature 25. Feature 28 contained the second highest amount of burned bone, with all of its 67 fragments recovered from fill.

Butchered Bone

Historical-period faunal remains, as evidenced by distinct striae of saw marks, also were recovered from Sunset Mesa Ruin. Table 44 presents the species and elements displaying historical-period butchering marks. Figure 68 illustrates a specimen identified as a glenoid from a bison or domestic cow that displays common butchering techniques identified in the collection (the blade has been removed and saw marks are visible). Other animals represented in the butchered bone collection include ungulate-sized mammal (n = 8) and possibly domestic horse (n = 1). These historical-period remains most likely relate to the Basillio Cuevas homestead dating from 1890 to 1915, although modern trash also was found scattered across the site.

The butchering patterns of the bison/domestic cow remains are characteristic of Euroamerican butchering methods. Based on the elements recovered, which include foot elements, vertebrae, a radius, a glenoid, and rib fragments (see Table 42), it is possible to assume that some of them represent discarded refuse, along with choice cuts of meat. Cranial and foot bones of cows are commonly discarded in the butchering process because of their low food value, whereas portions proximal to the wrist and ankle have high food value, as do the vertebrae and ribs (Lyman 1987). The scapula and humerus area produces chuck steaks and roasts. Both the butchered scapula and the humerus elements in the collection were sawn transversely on parallel planes across the long axis. The rib fragments are represented by midsections and also were sawn transversely. This rib midsection commonly becomes "short ribs" and produces rib steaks and roasts, according to Clonts (1983), who also has observed that Mexican butchering patterns generally do not employ the same techniques because the consumption of meat in Mexico does not follow the same patterns.

Bone Tools

Three bone tools are included in the Sunset Mesa Ruin faunal assemblage (Table 45). One tool has been classified as an awl, and the other two as awls or hairpins. Two of these tools include both tips and shafts, whereas the third includes only the tip. Awls and hairpins are by far the most common worked bone artifacts from Hohokam sites. Distinguishing between them is difficult, however—but possible, depending on the completeness of the artifact.

S. L. Olsen (1979, 1981) identified the ratio of tip width to thickness as a distinguishing characteristic between awls and hairpins. She suggested that awls generally have a symmetrical, cross section of the shaft about 5 mm above the working tip, whereas hairpins have an asymmetrical cross section at the same position, with width about twice the thickness. In addition, hairpins exhibit polish on the tip and up most of the shaft. Awls, on the other hand, appear to have polish only on the tip, which may be a result of incidental use of the tool.

The shafts of the tools recovered from Sunset Mesa Ruin are in poor condition from weathering or burning, or covered in caliche-like material, making it difficult to observe any polish. The tips of the three awl/hairpins are basically round in cross section, making determination of the tip-width-to-tip-thickness ratio problematic. The identification of the awl was made on the basis of its length in conjunction with the width of its shaft. Awls appear to be shorter and wider, whereas hairpins are longer and more slender. This shape of the awl gives it support to withstand the torque needed to penetrate heavy material. Hairpins do not need to have as much girth, and are preferred thinner, to allow them to slide through a knot of hair—somewhat like a pencil.

Table 43. Burned and Calcined Bone from Sunset Mesa Ruin by Feature (in NISP)

Element, by Scientific Name	Prehistoric										
	13	21				22	23	25			
	Fill	Fill	Roof Fall	Floor	Fill (Subfloor)	Roof Fall	Floor Fill	Fill	Roof Fall	Floor	Floor Fill
Lepus alleni											
Mandible	—	—	—	—	—	—	—	—	1	—	—
cf. *Lepus alleni*											
Humerus	1	—	—	—	—	—	—	—	—	—	—
Radius	—	—	—	—	—	—	—	—	1	—	—
Lepus sp.											
Blade	—	—	—	—	1	—	—	—	—	—	—
Indeterminate metatarsal	—	—	—	—	—	—	1	—	—	—	—
Radius	—	—	—	—	—	—	1	—	2	—	1
Sylvilagus sp.											
Innominate	—	—	—	—	—	—	—	—	—	—	1
Mandible	—	—	—	—	—	—	—	—	—	1	—
Phalanx	—	—	—	—	—	—	1	—	—	—	—
Indeterminate Artiodactyla											
Metapodial	—	—	—	—	—	—	1	—	—	—	—
cf. *Bison bison/Bos taurus*											
Rib	—	—	—	—	—	—	—	—	—	—	—
Odocoileus sp.											
Acetabulum	—	—	—	—	—	—	—	1	1	13	—
Ilium	—	—	—	—	—	—	—	1	—	—	—
Ischium	—	—	—	—	—	—	—	—	1	7	—
cf. *Ovis* sp.											
Pubis	—	—	—	—	—	—	—	—	—	1	—
Rodent-sized											
Long bone, complete or undetermined	1	—	—	—	1	—	—	—	—	—	—
Radius	—	1	—	—	—	—	—	—	—	—	—
Splinters, probable long bone	1	—	—	—	—	—	—	—	—	—	—
Rabbit/Rodent-sized											
Long bone, complete or undetermined	1	—	—	—	—	—	—	—	—	—	—
Radius	—	—	—	—	—	—	—	—	—	—	1
Rabbit-sized											
Long bone, complete or undetermined	2	—	1	—	—	—	2	—	5	—	5
Splinters, probable long bone	—	—	—	—	—	1	—	—	—	—	2
Undetermined element	—	1	—	—	—	—	—	—	—	—	10
Carnivore-sized											
Rib	—	—	—	—	—	—	—	—	—	1	—
Splinters, probable long bone	—	—	—	—	—	—	—	—	—	—	—
Undetermined element	—	—	—	—	—	—	—	—	—	—	—
Ungulate-sized											
Acetabulum	—	—	—	—	—	—	—	—	—	1	—
Long bone, complete or undetermined	—	—	1	—	—	—	—	—	—	—	—
Rib	—	—	—	—	—	—	—	1	1	—	1
Splinters, probable long bone	1	—	—	—	—	—	—	—	—	—	—
Undetermined element	1	—	—	—	—	—	—	—	7	50	10
Indeterminate class											
Undetermined element	—	—	—	—	—	—	1	—	9	—	10
Total	8	2	1	1	2	1	7	3	28	74	41

Table 43 (continued).

Element, by Scientific Name	Prehistoric (continued) 26 Fill	27 Fill	27 Roof Fall	27 Floor Fill	28 Fill	Historical-Period 5.01 Fill	34 Fill	Backdirt	Total
Lepus alleni									
Mandible	—	—	—	—	—	—	—	—	1
cf. *Lepus alleni*									
Humerus	—	—	—	—	—	—	—	—	1
Radius	—	—	—	—	—	—	—	—	1
Lepus sp.									
Blade	—	—	—	—	—	—	—	—	1
Indeterminate metatarsal	—	—	—	—	—	—	—	—	1
Radius	—	—	—	—	—	—	—	—	4
Sylvilagus sp.									
Innominate	—	—	—	—	—	—	—	—	1
Mandible	—	—	—	—	—	—	—	—	1
Phalanx	—	—	—	—	—	—	—	—	1
Indeterminate Artiodactyla									
Metapodial	—	—	—	—	—	—	—	—	1
cf. *Bison bison/Bos taurus*									
Rib	—	—	—	—	—	—	1	—	1
Odocoileus sp.									
Acetabulum	—	—	—	—	—	—	—	—	15
Ilium	—	—	—	—	—	—	—	—	1
Ischium	—	—	—	—	—	—	—	—	8
cf. *Ovis* sp.									
Pubis	—	—	—	—	—	—	—	—	1
Rodent-sized									
Long bone, complete or undetermined	—	1	—	1	—	—	—	—	4
Radius	—	—	—	—	—	—	—	—	1
Splinters, probable long bone	—	—	—	—	34	—	—	—	35
Rabbit/Rodent-sized									
Long bone, complete or undetermined	—	—	—	—	—	—	—	—	1
Radius	—	—	—	—	—	—	—	—	1
Rabbit-sized									
Long bone, complete or undetermined	—	—	3	1	—	5	—	—	24
Splinters, probable long bone	—	—	—	4	—	—	—	—	7
Undetermined element	—	5	—	1	—	—	—	15	32
Carnivore-sized									
Rib	—	—	—	—	—	—	—	—	1
Splinters, probable long bone	—	—	—	—	8	—	—	—	8
Undetermined element	—	—	—	2	—	—	—	—	2
Ungulate-sized									
Acetabulum	—	—	—	—	—	—	—	—	1
Long bone, complete or undetermined	—	—	—	—	—	—	—	—	1
Rib	—	—	—	—	—	—	—	—	3
Splinters, probable long bone	—	—	—	—	6	—	—	—	7
Undetermined element	—	—	—	—	6	—	—	—	74
Indeterminate class									
Undetermined element	5	—	—	—	13	—	—	—	38
Total	5	6	3	9	67	5	1	15	279

Table 44. Historical-Period Butchered Bone from Sunset Mesa Ruin by Feature (in NISP)

Element, by Scientific Name	Butchering Marks	5			34	42	44	Overburden	Total
		Fill	Room 2 Fill	Room 3 Fill	Fill	Surface	Fill		
Bison bison/Bos taurus									
Glenoid	butchered, visible saw marks	—	—	—	—	1	—	—	1
Radius	transverse cut	—	—	1	—	—	—	—	1
Rib	transverse cut	1	—	—	—	—	—	—	1
Vertebra	butchered	—	—	—	—	—	—	1	1
cf. *Bison bison/Bos taurus*									
Rib	2 transverse cuts	—	—	—	1	—	—	—	1
cf. *Equus caballus*									
Rib	butchered	—	—	1	—	—	—	—	1
Ungulate-sized mammal									
Humerus	transverse cut	1	—	—	—	—	—	—	1
Rib	butchered	—	—	—	—	—	1	—	1
Rib	transverse cut	—	—	2	—	—	—	—	2
Undetermined element	butchered	—	4	—	—	—	—	—	4
Total		2	4	4	1	1	1	1	14

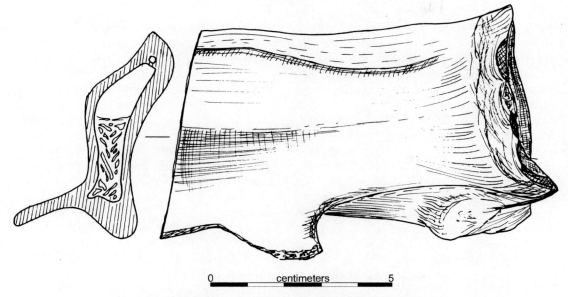

0   centimeters   5

**Figure 68. Butchered glenoid of bison or domestic cow
recovered from the surface of Feature 42 at Sunset Mesa Ruin.**

Table 45. Bone Artifacts from Sunset Mesa Ruin

Feature No.	Context	Scientific Name	Elements	Burned/ Calcined	Tool Type	Tip (cm)	Length (cm)	NISP
21	floor	ungulate-sized mammal	long bone, complete or undetermined	burned	awl/hairpin	5 × 5	7.7	1
23	floor fill	indeterminate Artiodactyla	metapodial	burned	awl	5 × 4	6.9	1
23.02	fill	indeterminate class	undetermined element	—	awl/hairpin tip	5 × 6	1.4	1

The one awl identified (recovered from the floor fill of Feature 23) (Figure 69) was manufactured from a metapodial of an indeterminate artiodactyl. Szuter (1988a) has noted that the metapodial is the preferred element because the straightness of its shaft and its vascular groove make it an ideal body part for fashioning awls and hairpins. This is not the case for sheep, as no such groove exists in the sheep metatarsal. The longitudinal split technique appears to have been used in manufacturing this awl, a technique that involves the splitting of the metapodial between the distal condyles along the vascular groove, then working and grinding the split elements down to the desired shape.

Summary and Conclusions

Overall, the faunal data from the Sunset Mesa Ruin contribute to several important research issues concerning

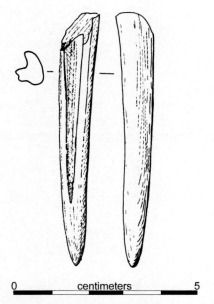

0   centimeters   5

**Figure 69. Bone awl recovered from
floor fill of Feature 23 at Sunset Mesa Ruin.**

191

Rincon phase settlement and subsistence in the Tucson Basin. In most respects, the collection is typical of similar-sized and contemporary Hohokam settlements. The faunal mix leans heavily toward exploitation of lagomorphs, along with some other species. The lagomorph ratio calculated for this collection indicates a higher recovery of jackrabbits compared to cottontails, a pattern interpreted in previous studies of similar desert settings as indicating environmental degradation resulting from long-term human habitation in large agricultural settlements (see Bayham and Hatch 1985; Szuter 1991). The size of the settlement at Sunset Mesa is consistent with this conclusion, but the brevity of occupation in the area is not. It has been noted previously that the lagomorph ratio is affected by data recovery methods, hunting patterns, and other factors, in addition to environmental conditions (Cairns and Ciolek-Torrello 1998; Shelley and Cairns 1998), and these factors should be considered in interpreting the Sunset Mesa results.

Despite the location of the site near the confluence of two major drainages, there is no evidence for the exploitation of riparian faunal species. With a few notable exceptions (see James 1991, 1995), this pattern is typical of Hohokam subsistence practices. The absence of fish and amphibian remains at Sunset Mesa Ruin and many other Hohokam sites, however, may be due in part to the size of screen mesh used during data recovery (see James 1995).

The most unusual aspect of the faunal collection from Sunset Mesa Ruin was the high proportion of large game remains, especially the pelves of deer and bighorn sheep, which are considered major meat-bearing elements. Similar cases have been found in only a few Hohokam sites. The large populations of the Formative period apparently had eradicated most of the large game animals from the environs of most valley settlements, pushing large game into peripheral upland locations; hunting large game during this time probably required long-distance travel and elaborate logistical arrangements to avoid conflicts with agricultural activities (Szuter 1991). Because it was difficult to carry back most of the kill to the home village, it appears that much of the meat was butchered and consumed at the kill site. As a result, artiodactyl remains are relatively rare in Hohokam settlements and are usually restricted to cranial and distal elements that were apparently selected for tool manufacture, and perhaps ceremonial activities (Weaver 1988). Thus, the presence of numerous large meat-bearing elements at Sunset Mesa Ruin is especially unusual.

Most of the artiodactyl remains were contained within one house, Feature 25, which also contained most of the faunal remains recovered from the excavations at Sunset Mesa Ruin. The identified fauna represented within this one feature include lagomorphs (n = 32) and artiodactyls (n = 30), whereas unidentified fauna include rabbit-sized (n = 54) and ungulate-sized (n = 86) mammals that probably represent many more lagomorphs and artiodactyls. The bulk of the faunal remains from this house were recovered from the floor and floor fill, and nearly all of the bone was burned or calcined. Most of the artiodactyl remains represent choice cuts of meat, whereas the lagomorphs are represented by the entire skeleton. None of the other houses exhibited any evidence of such intense faunal exploitation, especially of large game.

Based on the faunal evidence from the courtyard group, it appears that most of the inhabitants were relying more on small-sized game, using an opportunistic hunting strategy. The inhabitants of Sunset Mesa Ruin were able to supply themselves with a steady supply of meat protein while ridding their fields of pesky rodents and lagomorphs. Large-game hunting was practiced in at least one household. As such an activity probably required a greater expenditure of time and more elaborate logistical arrangements than those involved in the more typical opportunistic hunting strategy, the residents of this household may have been hunting specialists, or collected and processed game animals for ceremonial feasting.

The historical-period faunal assemblage indicates that settlement and subsistence practices of the Cuevas household and later users of the Sunset Mesa site are consistent with those observed at other early Euroamerican homesteads in the northwestern Tucson Basin. That is, subsistence was aimed primarily at use of domestic cattle and perhaps, to a lesser extent, the horse.

CHAPTER 12

Historical-Period Resources at Sunset Mesa Ruin

Matthew A. Sterner

Sunset Mesa Ruin has been recognized as a moderate-sized prehistoric hamlet since Midvale initially discovered it in the late 1930s (Ciolek-Torrello and Homburg 1990:46). During a survey conducted by SRI in 1989 (Ciolek-Torrello and Homburg 1990), a large quantity of historical-period artifacts were identified at the site, although much of the artifact accumulation reflected recent activity. It was not until SRI conducted further archival research and field testing in 1990 (Harry and Ciolek-Torrello 1992) that a significant historical-period component was identified at the site, principally in the form of a section of adobe building foundation.

Testing of the site in 1990 provided the structure for much of the subsequent investigation conducted during SRI's data recovery efforts in 1994, at which time 12 historical-period features were identified (see Table 4). The adobe foundation remnant identified during the 1990 testing phase, Feature 5, was exposed in its entirety during this data recovery effort. Most of the features appeared to represent later twentieth-century trash-dumping episodes, although some late-nineteenth–early-twentieth-century materials were identified. A detailed discussion of each of the features will be presented below.

Preliminary archival research conducted during the course of the data recovery project identified Sunset Mesa Ruin as the location of a historical-period homestead established in 1890, belonging to a nationalized Mexican citizen by the name of Basillio Cuevas. Roskruge's 1893 map of Pima County shows the Cuevas residence at the confluence of the Rillito and Santa Cruz Rivers, in the approximate location of the adobe foundation identified as Feature 5. The Pima County Range and Township Book (on file at the Arizona Historical Society), a land ownership document dating to the early decades of the twentieth century, indicates that Basillio Cuevas retained free and clear ownership of his homesteaded property as of 1907.

The adobe homestead remnant identified at Sunset Mesa Ruin presents us with an excellent opportunity to address several issues pertinent to historical-period homesteading in the northern Tucson Basin. Unfortunately, little in the way of informant interviews was available to augment the history of the Basillio Cuevas family. However, the identification of the adobe structure and documents pertaining to the homesteading of the property serve to further our understanding of the challenges faced by early homesteaders in Tucson. In an effort to understand the context into which the Cuevas homestead fits, a brief overview of several historical-period trends will be addressed.

The Foundations of Homesteading

In 1862, the United States government passed the Homestead Act into law. The purpose of the act was to entice farmers, ranchers, and settlers to settle large tracts of uninhabited government lands in an effort to extend the population base across the country. When discussing the concept of homesteading, we use the word "homestead" in its narrower sense, as related only to the settling of lands under the provisions of a set of federal legislation enacted in the nineteenth and twentieth centuries. This "set" of federal legislation actually refers to several laws passed by the United States government between the years of 1862 and 1916: the Homestead Act of 1862, the Desert

Land Act of 1877, the Forest Homestead Act of 1906, the Enlarged Homestead Act of 1909, and the Stock Raising Homestead Act of 1916. All of these laws shared a common underlying principle rooted in Jeffersonian law, namely that every citizen had a right to a share of the soil, and public lands should be granted to people in small tracts (Stein 1990:2). From 1862 until the repeal of the legislation in 1976, homesteading would provide the vehicle for transferring more than 270 million acres of land from public stewardship to private ownership (Stein 1990:2).

All federal land was potentially available to interested homesteaders, with just a few exceptions. The available land (1) could not abut saline bodies of water; (2) could not possess significant mineral resources; (3) could not have been previously withdrawn or reserved; (4) could not be occupied for trade or business undertakings; and (5) did not lie within an incorporated city or town.

The initial act enabling the homesteading of federal lands entitled heads of households or persons at least 21 years of age to file for 160-acre parcels (contiguous lands) otherwise sold by the government for $1.25 per acre, or 80-acre parcels (contiguous lands) that would otherwise be sold by the government for $2.50 per acre. The higher-priced lands were generally those that lay within the limits of railroad grants—in most states, grants extended 20 miles on either side of the railroad track right-of-way, although in Arizona Territory, the grants extended 40 miles on either side of the track right-of-way (Stein 1990:3). The limitation that potential homesteaders could enter only 80 acres within railroad grants was eventually removed by the Act of March 3, 1879 (Stein 1990:3).

Each individual homesteader could petition for one claim only and, to fulfill the requirements to eventually own the parcel, had to reside on the claimed homestead continuously for a period of five years. Residency requirements also dictated that improvements be made to the property, generally in the form of cultivating the land during the final four years of occupation. The homesteader (generally called the "entryman"—the man or woman who filed the claim) had to establish residency within six months or risk losing his or her claim to a later applicant (Stein 1990:3). These residency requirements were amended in 1872, when Congress allowed military veterans to substitute as much as four years of the residency requirement with time served in military duty (the fifth year of the residency requirement had to be served on the claimed homestead). At the end of the five year residency, the entryman was required to "prove up," an act that finalized the title transfer in the eyes of the government. For a nominal filing fee, the land was transferred to the entryman free and clear.

The history of the evolution and implementation of the various homestead acts is extensive and complex. Among

several scholars who have tackled this subject over the years, Stein (1988, 1990) and Gates (1968) have been the most successful in unraveling this convoluted maze of federal legislation. According to Stein (1990), "in view of all of the laws, amendments, and regulations . . . it may come as no surprise that the early days of homesteading were not its heyday." The greatest boom in the application for homestead claims came, in fact, after the passage of the Enlarged Homestead Act of 1909, with more than a quarter of the total acreage transferred to private ownership in the 10-year period during and after World War I (Stein 1990:7).

Allen (1987:136) attributes the 1910s boom in homesteading to the timing of the 1909 law, coupled with the economic panic of 1907. Widespread fear that public lands were vanishing triggered an enormous response, "somewhat akin to last-minute shopping on Christmas Eve":

> Anything would do. People who had never considered homesteading along with those who had tried it more than once before, became land-seekers, even though the lands opened under the Enlarged Homestead Act were, in the words of one bitter commentator, "the parings and scraps and crumbs of the Old West" [Allen 1987:136].

It is important to grasp the significance of the homestead legislation during the nineteenth and twentieth centuries. As illustrated in the discussion of the Basillio Cuevas homestead, embarking upon the homesteading process was not an easy undertaking. But hard work, perseverance, and patience all paid off for the unlanded entryman who wanted little more than a piece of land to call his or her own. The process was at times cumbersome and convoluted, but the rewards for some amounted to the proverbial pot of gold at the end of the rainbow.

Homesteading in Arizona

No comprehensive study of homesteading in Arizona has been compiled to date. Stein (1990), however, has culled from a variety of sources several very interesting statistics that provide some general trends in Arizona homesteading.

+ Arizona was one of only 31 states or territories to have homesteading. No homestead claims were ever filed in New England and generally very few were ever filed east, or immediately west, of the Mississippi (BLM 1962:1, in Stein 1990:7).

- No successful claims were entered in Arizona Territory until 1878. Prior to that time, scores of homesteads had been filed for in Arizona (most along the Salt River valley), but all had been canceled or relinquished (Stein 1990:7).

- More homesteads failed than succeeded in Arizona. Documents on file at the State Office of the Bureau of Land Management indicate that failures outnumbered successes throughout the history of the homestead movement (Stein 1990:8).

- Despite the failure rate, between 21,000 and 22,000 entries were successfully fulfilled in Arizona, resulting in the conveyance of title patents (BLM 1962:2–28, in Stein 1990:8).

- More than 4,748,000 acres of Arizona land passed from public to private ownership through the various homesteading acts. Of these lands, more than 1 million acres were eventually repurchased by the government through the Bankhead-Jones Act, but more than 3 million acres acquired through the various homestead acts remain in private ownership today (Stein 1990:8).

- The railroads courted homesteaders tenaciously. Because increased settlement led to increased business along transportation corridors, such companies as the Atchison, Topeka, and Santa Fe (ATSF) formed "Colonization Departments" to promote the homestead process. These departments provided literature with sufficient technical information to assist the prospective homesteader, in addition to glorifying and romanticizing a return to the land. Such enticement and propaganda stood in marked contrast to the more wary approach urged by most government officials (Allen 1987:133, in Stein 1990:8).

In the Tucson Basin, no comprehensive work has been completed to date regarding the extent or success of homesteading. The only substantive work was conducted by Pat Stein (1983), in the early 1980s, for an area along the Santa Cruz River and the Cañada del Oro Wash. This area, located little more than one mile to the northwest of Sunset Mesa Ruin, first witnessed homestead activity in the 1880s and 1890s. A total of ten claims was filed during this period, most as desert land entries (Stein 1983:46). Nine of these claims were canceled by the government, whereas one was relinquished by the claimant. According to Stein (1983:46), no evidence of any irrigation devices or water management infrastructure relating to these claims was identified during that survey.

By the 1890s, homesteading was gaining more of a foothold throughout the area. Apart from the Cuevas claim at the confluence of the Rillito and the Santa Cruz Rivers, seven more claims were filed on lands around the Cañada del Oro Wash and the Santa Cruz River. During Stein's investigation of this area, she identified four claims for which title patents were issued in the late 1890s and early 1900s. Although she identified three claims that never resulted in the issuance of a patent (Stein 1983:46), it is clear that homesteaders were beginning to make more effective use of the Tucson Basin landscape. Table 46 lists those homestead claims identified by Stein (1983) within her survey area for which claim information was available.

The Basillio Cuevas Homestead

The discussion on homesteading in Arizona is particularly appropriate in the case of Sunset Mesa Ruin. Documents

Table 46. Homestead Claims Identified by Stein (1983)

Homestead	Location[a]	Size (acres)	Site Number
Esteban and Guadalupe Flores homestead	Lot 4 and the southwest quarter of the northwest quarter of Section 5, and Lot 1 and the southeast quarter of the northeast quarter of Section 6	159.98	AZ AA:12:257
Antonio Alvarez homestead	southwest quarter of Section 15	160	AZ AA:12:370
Sotero Ruelas homestead	south half of the southeast quarter of Section 8 and north half of the northeast quarter of Section 17	160	(destroyed)
J. Landis homestead	northwest quarter of Section 6	160?	(destroyed)
Antonio Canas homestead	southeast quarter of Section 35	160?	AZ AA:12:313?
Alejandro Molina homestead	west half of the southeast quarter and east half of the southwest quarter of Section 22	160	(destroyed)

[a] All locations listed fall in Township 12 South, Range 12 East.

Table 47. Documents Associated with the Basillio Cuevas Homestead Claim, 1890–1891

Date	Document Description
September 4, 1890	certificate of citizenship
September 20, 1890	nonmineral affidavit
September 20, 1890	affidavit for homestead application (declaring age, intent of citizenship, etc.)
September 20, 1890	homestead application
September 30, 1890	receipt for $15.77, for homestead claim (processing fees)
September 30, 1890	receipt for $15.77, for homestead claim (processing fees), amended
September 30, 1890	registration of land with Registrar of the Land Office
September 30, 1890	cover of homestead application[a]
October 16, 1890	legal document citing change in legal description of property
October 16, 1890	witness accounts for change in legal description of homestead claim
September 10, 1891	receipt for $.23, for 6.2 acres[b]
September 10, 1891	affidavit by Cuevas verifying he had not applied for any more lands under the homestead provision[c]

[a] September 30 probably indicates the date of approval, whereas September 20 was the date of application.
[b] This corrects the processing fee for a homestead claim on 160 acres (bringing it to a total of $16.00).
[c] Cuevas apparently signed one of these in 1890, but for some reason (probably something to do with the amendment in acreage) he was required to sign a second one.

photocopied from materials held at the National Archives, Washington, D.C., provide a good picture of the homestead process undertaken by Basillio Cuevas in 1890. Like many homesteaders of the time in southeastern Arizona, Basillio Cuevas was a Mexican immigrant from the state of Sonora who applied for and was granted United States citizenship in 1890. Records do not exist to identify the reasons that brought Basillio and his family to Tucson, but records of the application and disposition of his homestead claim provide many answers to the fate of the Cuevas family after they reached the Tucson Basin.

Basillio Cuevas first applied for land provisioned under the 1862 Homestead Act on September 20, 1890, in homestead application number 1429 (Table 47). The application was initially for 153.8 acres of land along the Rillito River in Section 7 of Township 13 South, Range 13 East, although the application was later amended to include an additional 6.2 acres, to bring the total application allotment to 160 acres of land. As a fee to process the initial application for land, Cuevas had to pay the sum of $15.77. A footnote in the margin of the initial application document indicates that the land claim was amended on March 3, 1891, to include the extra acreage that brought the total claim up to 160 acres. Associated documents indicate that Cuevas did not pay the processing fee for this additional property ($.23 for the additional 6.2 acres) until September 10, 1891 (see Table 47).

What we know about Cuevas and his family is sketchy at best, derived from snippets of information contained on documents submitted in 1897 to "prove up" the claim. Cuevas was 37 years old when he first claimed the parcels indicated as the southeast one-quarter of the northwest one-quarter, and the northeast one-quarter of the southwest one-quarter, and the north one-half of the southeast one-quarter of Section 7, Township 13 South, Range 13 East. He first settled the land on September 30, 1890, with his wife and one child. During the course of his occupation of the property, he constructed a 12-by-18-foot adobe house, a well, a corral, and a chicken house, and constructed a post-and-brush fence around approximately 40 cleared acres. Cuevas actively cultivated 5 acres of the 160, and had been raising crops on this portion since 1891. The testimony of witness statements dated 1897, submitted by Loreto Yguera (age 59) and Francisco Manzo (age 77), indicate that the land claimed by Basillio Cuevas was "level prairie land suitable for farming and grazing." No mention is made, however, regarding the ownership of any stock animals or the use of the lands for the purposes of grazing livestock.

Basillio Cuevas applied for patent to the land he had been homesteading on April 26, 1897. Receiving final patent for a homestead claim was in some ways even more difficult and exhaustive than the initial filing. First, a letter of intent to make final proof on the claim had to be completed at least 30 days prior to the intended date of

Table 48. Documents Associated with the Basillio Cuevas Homestead Patent Application, 1897

Date	Document Description
n.d.	agreement from Herbert Brown (Arizona Citizen) not to charge the government for costs related to publishing the homestead claim
March 9, 1897	Cuevas's letter of intention to make final proof on claim on April 26, 1897; witnesses listed include Francisco Manzo, Jesus Cocio, Loreto Yguera, and Ysabel Garcia[a]
March 9, 1897	notice of application publication in newspaper, stating the Arizona Citizen to be the paper closest to holding
April 26, 1897	nonmineral affidavit
April 26, 1897	copy of proof of citizenship certificate
April 26, 1897	homestead proof, Testimony of Witness Loreto Yguera[a]
April 26, 1897	homestead proof, Testimony of Witness Francisco Manzo[a]
April 26, 1897	homestead proof, Testimony of Claimant Basillio Cuevas
April 26, 1897	final affidavit, with signatures of Cuevas and Pima County Registrar Eugene J. Trippel
April 26, 1897	notarized copy of letter from the Arizona Citizen indicating that the property was properly listed in the newspaper for the requisite amount of time
April 26, 1897	affidavit that Cuevas had not applied for any other homestead lands
April 27, 1897	Registrar and Receiver's Report (affirming validity of all documents)
April 27, 1897	receipt for $6.00, for final dispensation of the claim (160 acres)
April 27, 1897	certificate for payment in full on Cuevas land, acting as a patent for the claim
April 27, 1897	certificate that the homestead claim had been posted at the Land Claims office (posted since March 11, 1897)
November 5, 1897	final Land Office approval and patent for Cuevas claim (approved June 30, patented Nov. 5)

[a] Although Cuevas had to list several witnesses, only two actually had to be present.

patent application, and certificates verifying the posting of the claim in the local newspaper had to be requested and obtained at that time. Both of these tasks were completed in the case of Basillio Cuevas on March 9, 1897. In his letter of intent, Cuevas indicated that he would "prove up" on April 26. A list of all documents associated with his final patent is presented in Table 48.

When the date of final petition arrived, the entryman had to complete a statement of testimony verifying his or her statements regarding occupation on and improvements made to the claim for which he or she was seeking patent. At least two witnesses had to accompany the entryman to the General Land Office to corroborate the statements of the petitioner. In the case of homestead application 1429, Basillio Cuevas had to sign a second nonmineral affidavit (the first having been signed during the initial claim process), attesting to the fact that no mineral resources were located on the homestead. Cuevas also had to produce his certificate of citizenship for a second time. In addition, he signed another document verifying that he had not applied for any other claims

under the 1862 Homestead Act. Only after the generation of all of these documents could Basillio Cuevas sign the final affidavit required of homestead claimants, indicating his compliance to all of the rules and regulations governing the dispensation of homestead lands. The ordeal certainly must have been intimidating, especially for someone like Basillio Cuevas, a naturalized citizen who could not write his own name—all of his signatures consisted simply of an "X."

But his work was not yet over. On the following day, April 27, 1897, Cuevas had to return to the offices of the governing powers for several additional responsibilities. It was at this time that he paid the final installment of $6.00 for final deed to his homestead claim. Following his payment, Cuevas received a certificate for payment in full, a document that also served as his patent for claim to his lands.

Little is known of the ultimate disposition of Basillio Cuevas and his family. Local historical accounts, both written and oral, indicate that William A. Knapp bought the land encompassing Sunset Mesa Ruin in 1915. Soon after assuming ownership, Knapp founded the Sunset Dairy on land adjacent to the Cuevas homestead. William Knapp's son, Bruce, who was born on the property, had no knowledge of the Cuevas homestead (Harry and Ciolek-Torrello 1992:55). Although the property remains in the hands of the Sunset Dairy, it is unclear for what purpose the area is used today.

Archaeological Investigation of Historical-Period Features at Sunset Mesa Ruin

A total of twelve archaeological features dating to the historical period was identified during data recovery efforts at Sunset Mesa Ruin. A background discussion of Feature 5, the Basillio Cuevas homestead, provides an excellent beginning in determining the historical context of the site. As in any discussion of historical-period archaeological features, archival research has served to complement the physical evidence identified during the field investigation. A discussion of the Cuevas homestead and all of the associated historical-period features identified during the data recovery effort is presented below.

Feature 5, the Basillio Cuevas Adobe

Certainly, the most prominent feature identified at Sunset Mesa Ruin was the remnants of the adobe structure attributed to Basillio Cuevas (see Figures 9 and 34). Overall, the archaeological context of Feature 5 was generally poor. In addition, the area of the site surrounding Feature 5 had been used as a trash dump over the past 50 years, and a great deal of recent trash and building materials obscured the visibility of older artifacts associated with the Cuevas adobe. No systematic surface collection was attempted. Diagnostic "early" historical-period artifacts were collected when observed, both from the surface and from the mechanical stripping of overburden conducted in search of prehistoric features. Only the foundation bricks remained from the Feature 5 adobe, and it is likely that the structure had been scavenged for building materials at some time in the past. The amount of overburden that remained during stripping suggests that most of the adobe

brick had been removed prior to the structure's dilapidation, and did not melt in place.

A large subsurface pit (Feature 5.01) had been dug into the floor of Feature 5 at some time after its abandonment and presumably after the removal of its building materials. The purpose of this pit is not known, but it may represent a pot hunter's hole. The prehistoric portion of Sunset Mesa Ruin has been extensively pot hunted, and the slightly mounded area of the historical-period adobe may have been mistaken for a prehistoric feature.

Feature 5 was excavated in 3 levels: overburden, general fill, and room fill. The few artifacts identified within the feature were point provenienced as floor artifacts. The following discussion will present a brief summary of artifact recovery by provenience. The large intrusive pit (Feature 5.01) was excavated as one unit and the few artifacts it contained were point provenienced separately from those in the house.

Artifacts from Surface and Overburden

Metal

Metal artifacts include three cartridge casings. One was a .45-70 Government, internally primed case without a head stamp that was manufactured by the United States military between 1873 and 1877 (Herskovitz 1978:50). Also present was a caliber .40-60 Winchester Center Fire cartridge casing that was head-stamped "W.R.A. Co. .40-60 W.C.F." This casing was manufactured by the Winchester Repeating Arms Company between 1876 and 1934 to fit the Model 1876 Winchester lever action rifle. Manufactured between 1876 and 1894, the Model 1876 Winchester is the only firearm to use this cartridge (Barnes 1989:118). The third was a .38 Smith and Wesson cartridge casing that was head-stamped "REM-UMC 38 S&W" and manufactured by the Remington Arms Company after 1911 (Barnes 1989:69). This cartridge fit pistols made by a wide variety of companies in the general period of 1877 to the 1930s. It was one of the most common American pistol cartridges until superseded by more powerful cartridges in the 1930s (Barnes 1989:163).

Other metal artifacts included a hole-in-top, crimp seam, soldered-top, No. 1 square meat tin from approximately 1880–1910 (Fontana and Greenleaf 1962:72), a 12-by-0.625-inch piece of metal strapping with two hand-hammered rivets, a 6.5-by-1.5-inches piece of metal strapping with a square hole for a carriage bolt, a possible bracket, and a 1-by-1.5-inches metal buckle. The two pieces of strapping may represent wagon parts, whereas the bracket is an unidentified metal object designed to be attached to wood or metal to support a square rod.

Ceramics

Ceramic artifacts recovered include one Mexican glazed earthenware sherd with a brick-red paste, light yellow green lead glaze, brown underglaze, and hand-painted decoration on the exterior. The sherd is similar to ceramics found at Rancho Punta de Agua (AZ BB:13:18 [ASM]) (McGuire 1979:27), a historical-period ranch site with an 1880 terminal date.

Also recovered was one body sherd from an English or American cup. The sherd is of nonvitreous, white-bodied earthenware with exterior overglaze, with a green, gray, pink, and yellow floral decal decoration, that dates to about the 1930s or later (Majewski and O'Brien 1987). The pattern matches a sherd from a different vessel that was located inside Room 3 (see below).

Two refitting base sherds of undecorated, semivitreous, white-bodied earthenware vessel (probably English) also were found. A portion of a black, underglaze transfer-printed, coat-of-arms maker's mark is visible on the exterior, with an undecipherable impressed mark over part of the quartered-shield portion of the transfer-printed mark.

Glass

One bottle neck with a double-bead finish from a half-pint- or pint-size medicine or flask bottle was recovered. The bottle neck is a sun-colored amethyst, indicating a date prior to 1918 (Toulouse 1969:534). Another bottle neck, also from a half-pint-or pint-size medicine or flask bottle, displays a hand-applied, single-bead finish.

Artifacts from General Fill

Metal

Two 12-gauge shotgun shells, manufactured by the Winchester Repeating Arms Company, were recovered from the fill of Feature 5. One shell is head-stamped "1901 Repeater No 10," and the second is head-stamped "Winchester Repeater No 12." Both of these shotgun shells date to the twentieth century, but Winchester shotgun shells have not proven suitable for finer temporal subdivision.

Other metal artifacts recovered include: four wire nails (machine made—two large and two small) and one nail that was too corroded to identify; half of an exterior shutter hinge designed to hold a 1-inch-thick wooden shutter; one metal rod—4.75 inches long and made of 0.625-inch diameter steel, with a flared fitting 1 inch in diameter present on one end—that may be the hinge-pin for a large hinge; and 143 g of unidentified ferrous metal objects consisting of rusted sheet metal, wire, and/or nail fragments.

Ceramics

Six sherds of English or American, nonvitreous or semivitreous, white-bodied earthenware were recovered. All are undecorated, except for a plate body sherd with relief molding on the interior, near what would have been the rim. Of the remaining sherds, two represent cup rims, one represents a plate base, and two are indeterminate body sherds.

Glass

Included among the glass artifacts is one milk glass fragment, a vessel leg in the Geneva pattern manufactured by Northwood and Associates between 1896 and 1922. These dates indicate the entire production range of two Northwood and Associates factories. Based on the pattern's appearance in a 1900 Montgomery Wards Catalog, however, this pattern likely was made only at the earlier of the two factories and dates between 1896 and 1904.

A bottle neck fragment with a crown cap finish also was recovered. The crown cap was patented in 1892, becoming universal for carbonated beverage bottles by 1912 (Berge 1980). The fragment is aqua colored and appears to represent a soda or beer bottle.

Other glass artifacts recovered include one large (1.5 inches in diameter) marble made of swirled green and white glass; one clear glass stopper, probably from a half-pint- or pint-size medicine bottle; three blue glass fragments from a ribbed condiment bottle; two dark green glass fragments, probably from a wine, brandy, or whiskey bottle; and seven glass bottle fragments that are indeterminate as to shape.

Artifacts from Room 1

Metal

Metal artifacts recovered include one can lid of the removable, pry-out-top kind, 3 inches in diameter; a U-shaped object that appears to represent a stirrup (presumably this metal portion would have been covered with wood and leather); one fragmentary, very rusted teaspoon found on floor; one very corroded sheet metal object found on the floor—possibly a can or lard pail—weighing 199 g, with small sections of crimped seam and wire visible; five wire nails (machine made)—three medium size, and two small nails too corroded to identify the pennyweight; and one piece of galvanized wire.

Ceramics

One English or American, nonvitreous, white-bodied, earthenware sherd—possibly from the base of a plate—

was recovered. Undecorated, the sherd has two concentric lines on its base, perhaps from the jiggering process. In addition, a red common-brick fragment was found on floor.

Glass

Glass artifacts recovered include three dark green glass fragments—probably from a wine, brandy, or whiskey bottle—and two clear glass fragments that are indeterminate as to shape.

Artifacts from Room 2

Metal

Among the metal artifacts recovered from Room 2 are two .22 short cartridge casings with no head stamp present, and one .22 long rifle cartridge casing head-stamped "Super X," indicating it was manufactured by the Winchester-Western Arms Company and dates between 1934 and the present (Barnes 1989:61). Also recovered was one white metal ornament displaying a decorative star pattern within a circle; the function of the ornament is unknown. Other metal artifacts include one key-opened, round can lid, 2.5 inches in diameter; one metal strap, possibly the fragment of a wagon spring, that measures 17 by 2.5 inches; another metal strap that measures 11 by 1 inches; a very corroded sheet metal object that weighs 126 g; and one wire nail (machine made).

Ceramics

The sole ceramic artifact recovered from Room 2 is a rim sherd from a hard paste porcelain saucer. The sherd is undecorated, except for an overglaze gilded band around the interior lip, of which only traces remain.

Glass

One dark green glass bottle fragment was recovered.

Artifacts from Room 3

Metal

Several metal artifacts were recovered from Room 3, among them 2 very corroded sheet metal containers found in situ on the floor (see Figure 35). One of these containers measures 12 inches in diameter by 3 inches tall and weighs 1,015 g, whereas the other is larger, measuring 18 inches in diameter by 4.5 inches tall and weighing 1,647 g. In addition, a 7-by-1 inch pipe was found embedded in the floor, and two shotgun shells were recovered:

a 16-gauge shell with partial head stamp visible that reads "Western 16," and a 12-gauge shell head-stamped "Winchester Repeater No 12."

Other artifacts recovered include one wagon part (a whiffletree coupling [Herskovitz 1978:90]); one wire hood (portion of a cork-capped bottle closure); one carriage bolt fragment, 0.25 inches in diameter; one 2-inch, No. 12 wood screw; one 2.5-inch, heavy gauge fence staple; one machine made, 8d farriers nail, and five wire nails (machine made). Of the latter, one nail is 10d, three nails are smaller but too corroded to size, and one nail is fragmentary.

Also recovered was a total of 88 g of unidentified ferrous metal objects, consisting of rusted sheet metal, and wire or nail fragments.

Ceramics

One body sherd of an English or American, nonvitreous, white-bodied, earthenware saucer or plate was recovered. The exterior displays an overglaze green, gray, pink, and yellow floral decal decoration that dates the sherd to the 1930s or later (Majewski and O'Brien 1987). This pattern belongs to the same set as a cup sherd recovered from the surface and overburden surrounding Feature 5.

Three brick fragments also were recovered. Two are unmarked, red common brick, and one is fire brick with a partial maker's mark ("& CO") stamped into it.

Glass

One bottle neck fragment with a crown cap finish was recovered. This finish indicates a date after 1892 (Berge 1980). The fragment is clear glass and probably represents a soda or beer bottle. Other glass artifacts from Room 3 include two clear-glass, kerosene lampshade fragments; one aqua glass marble, 0.75 inches in diameter; one fragment of flat, clear window glass; one dark green glass fragment, probably from a wine, brandy, or whiskey bottle; and two glass bottle fragments, one clear and one of sun-colored amethyst glass.

Artifacts from Feature 5.01 (Intrusive Pit)

Metal

Metal artifacts recovered from this pit include two .357 caliber, lead, soft-nose pistol bullets (both have been fired); one 2-inch, No. 12 wood screw; and five wire nails. Of the latter, one nail is 20d, one is 8d, one is 6d, and two are too corroded to size. Also recovered were 95 g of unidentified ferrous metal fragments, consisting of rusted sheet metal, and wire or nail fragments.

Ceramics

The sole ceramic artifact recovered consists of one body sherd of an English or American, undecorated, nonvitreous, white-bodied, earthenware cup.

Glass

Glass artifacts recovered include five fragments of clear glass from one bottle, two fragments of clear window glass, and five small fragments of clear and aqua bottle glass.

Other Historical-Period Features

Apart from the Basillio Cuevas house, several historical-period features were identified at Sunset Mesa Ruin (see Table 4). Most of these features represent trash pits, surface dumps or other accumulation. Remarkably few historical-period features were found in proximity to the Cuevas homestead (Feature 5), and no other features directly related to the Cuevas occupation were identified during the current project. Generally, most of the historical-period features were clustered along two-track roads that criss-crossed the site (see Figure 9).

Feature 19

Feature 19 was a circular, shallow pit located approximately 6 m west of Feature 5. The pit measured approximately 2 feet, 4 inches (70 cm) in diameter and extended to a depth of no more than 4.74 mbd, making the pit approximately 6–7-inches deep. The feature fill was generally characterized as an ashy silt, with gravels, charcoal, ash, and some historical-period artifacts distributed throughout. Some evidence of rodent and root disturbance was identified in the feature fill. Although the interior edges of the feature exhibited some level of burning, the feature did not appear to have been used as a firepit or hearth. Several artifacts were recovered from the feature, and are described below.

Metal

A total of 275 g of extremely corroded sheet metal fragments from a large canister and a portion of a bail-type handle was recovered from Feature 19. The handle indicates that these fragments may represent a lard pail. Other metal artifacts include one 3-lb, single-bit axe head; four wire nails (one 8d, one 6d, and two 4d); and 245 g of unidentified ferrous metal objects, consisting of rusted sheet metal, strapping, wire, and nail fragments.

Ceramics

Two marble fragments were recovered, portions of two different earthenware. Apart from the fact that they are made of earthenware, these marbles are similar to what Carskadden and Gartley (1990:57) would probably identify as German-made (stoneware) marbles of the type called "Benningtons" and "crockers" by Americans, based on the similarity of their glaze to that of the popular Rockingham pottery made in Bennington, Vermont. Carskadden and Gartley (1990:61) date this type of marble from 1875 until 1920, with a peak of popularity between 1890 and 1915.

Glass

One broken but complete condiment bottle was recovered. With "H. J. HEINZ CO. No. 79 PATD JUNE 9TH 1891" stamped on the bottom, the mustard bottle retains part of its paper neck label containing the words "Heinz Prepared Mustard."

Feature 33

Feature 33 was a pit identified in the south wall of Trench 23, in the northern portion of the site. The feature appeared to be relatively deeply buried, approximately 31.5 inches (80 cm) below the present-day ground surface. Exposure of the feature area identified an oval pit shape measuring 27.5 by 19.75 inches (70 by 50 cm), with an overall depth of 13.5 inches (34 cm). The base of the feature was bowl or basin shaped.

The feature was filled with lightly compacted silts with high ash and charcoal inclusion. The walls of the pit exhibited only very slight thermal alteration, suggesting limited use of this feature, or low-temperature burning associated with the secondary deposition of hearth material. In addition, an amount of horse (or other large mammal) manure was observed in the feature fill. Artifact recovery was low, limited to several metal fragments.

Metal

Six fragments of wire or a large nail are the only artifacts recovered from Feature 33.

Feature 34

Feature 34, also a pit, was identified in Trench 26, less than 3 m east of Feature 33. Similarly, this feature was filled principally with ash, charcoal, rocks, and a few historical-period artifacts. Identified approximately 19.75 inches (50 cm) below the present-day ground surface, almost 11.75 inches higher than the adjacent Feature 33, Feature 34 was capped by a thin gravel lens that measured approximately 3.5 inches in thickness.

The feature was slightly ovoid in shape, measuring 30.25 by 19.75 inches (77 by 50 cm). Total depth of the feature was 13.75 inches. No evidence of burning or other thermal activity was identified in the feature fill or adjacent profile. Artifacts recovered from the feature are limited.

Metal

Metal artifacts recovered include one 5-lb dumbbell-shaped object with a strap handle—possibly a weight for a balance scale—and one copper sheet (3.25 by 0.5 inches) with a small nail (?) hole in the center.

Ceramic

The sole ceramic artifact recovered is the handle of an English or American, undecorated, nonvitreous, white-bodied, earthenware cup.

Feature 42

Feature 42 was a pit identified approximately 82 feet (25 m) northwest of Feature 5. The feature was first exposed as the general area, characterized by a generally darkened fill, was scraped. During the scraping, a portion of a leather shoe and several bone fragments were exposed, defining the temporal designation of the feature.

Feature 42 measured approximately 19.75 by 15.75 inches (50 by 40 cm). Its depth is unknown. This feature was not tested, primarily because of time constraints and its small nature.

Leather

One shoe sole was recovered, the width of which indicates it is from a woman's shoe.

Features 39, 40, and 44

Features 39, 40, and 44 were tentatively assigned a historical-period temporal affiliation. Although these features produced no artifacts, the temporal designation was based on general elevation, adjacent artifact recovery, and the presence of large quantities of charcoal in the fill matrix. These features varied in size from the relatively small Feature 39 (21.75 by 19.75 inches [55 by 50 cm]) to the larger Feature 40 (31.5 by 27.5 inches [80 by 70 cm]). All three features may represent the remnants of firepits or hearths used during the historical period or more recent times.

Features 24, 37, 45, and 56

Features 24, 37, 45, and 56 were identified during surface stripping in the western portion of the site, but were not tested during the field investigation. These features generally are either circular or oval stains that appeared at an elevation significantly higher than the prehistoric occupation horizon. No artifacts were recovered from any of the four features.

CHAPTER 13

Summary and Conclusions

Richard Ciolek-Torrello, Joseph A. Ezzo, and Jeffrey H. Altschul

Data recovery at Sunset Mesa Ruin (AZ AA:12:10 [ASM]) has made a valuable contribution to the sample of Rincon phase habitation sites in the Tucson Basin, as well as providing a rare glimpse of turn-of-the-century Hispanic homesteading in the basin. Based on testing results, we oriented the data recovery research design around seven themes. Of those, five can now be addressed: chronology, household organization and site structure, settlement pattern and subsistence, ceramic production and exchange, and mortuary practices. The lack of a Classic period component within the data recovery area of the site precludes addressing the pre-Classic–Classic period transition. The final research theme, irrigation systems, is integrated here in the discussion of settlement patterns and subsistence. The treatment of these issues will be considered in a broader, regional picture of Rincon phase occupation of the Tucson Basin, particularly the area of the northern Tucson Basin near the confluence of the Santa Cruz and Rillito Rivers.

The focus of excavation at Sunset Mesa Ruin centered on a house group composed of five pit houses (Features 21, 22, 23, 25, and 27), and associated trash mounds and extramural pit features, as well as a nearby food-preparation and storage area (Features 13 and 15). Extramural features investigated included cooking pits and buried storage jars. A fairly extensive midden (originally defined as a series of trash pits) lay just to the northwest of the habitations, and a prehistoric irrigation canal (Feature 18), coming off the Rillito River near the western boundary of the data recovery area, was defined and excavated. As noted in Chapter 1, the data recovery concentrated on only a very small portion of the site that contained subsurface features and was located within and immediately adjacent to the APE. In addition, the foundation of the adobe-walled Cuevas homestead, located adjacent to the prehistoric house group, was completely excavated during data recovery.

Recent testing and data recovery excavations by Desert Archaeology for an unrelated project (Lindeman 1999; Swartz and Adams 1998) has resulted in a much more complete investigation of the site and the discovery of other segments of this prehistoric settlement. A group of more than a dozen houses (Locus A) was encountered about 65 m southeast of the SRI locus, in the area of high surface artifact concentrations encompassed by Collection Units 2 and 4 (Figure 70; see Figure 4). Two similarly sized house groups (Loci B and C) were found more than 250 m east of Locus A and the SRI locus, in the vicinity of the recently abandoned cattle pens. Only a scatter of houses was found in the large central area between these various loci. Desert Archaeology investigators also found a cemetery immediately east of the houses in the SRI locus, in the vicinity of the two cremations identified during the testing phase (see Harry and Ciolek-Torrello 1992), as well as another cemetery in Locus B.

Chronology

Archaeomagnetic dates were obtained from floors and hearths of the five pit houses (see Appendix B). Five samples from four of the pit houses (Features 21, 23, 24, and 27) date between A.D. 950 and 1200, which places the site comfortably in the Rincon phase of the Sedentary period. Multiple determinations for two samples suggest later thirteenth- and fourteenth-century occupations, but no independent evidence is available to support such temporal interpretations. A sixth sample from Feature 22 produced good results but was not datable, as the sample's location was off of the established dating curve. Refinements in the analysis of individual dates, as discussed in

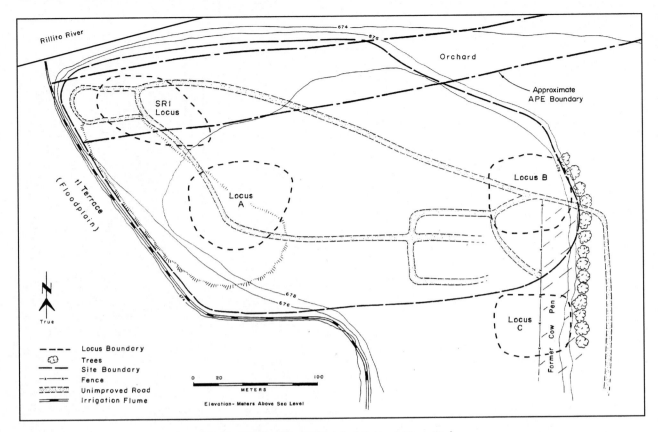

Figure 70. Residential loci at Sunset Mesa Ruin.

Appendix B, have permitted the tentative chronology of construction and occupation of all five houses in the house group (see below). The temporally diagnostic ceramics from floor fill and floor contexts of the pit houses confirm an early to middle Rincon subphase occupation. It should be noted that only one of the houses exhibited evidence of remodeling. Feature 21, which contained two superimposed floors with a layer of trash between them, appears to have been reoccupied after an abandonment. The lack of remodeling among the other four houses suggests that only one episode of occupation occurred for each. It is interesting that ceramics that bridge the pre-Classic–Classic period transition were reported on the surface of the site during our initial assessment, causing us to suspect a late Rincon subphase or Tanque Verde phase occupation at the site (Harry and Ciolek-Torrello 1992). No features associated with these ceramics were encountered during data recovery, suggesting that the entire area was occupied for a relatively brief period during the early and middle Rincon subphases, and that the few Tanque Verde sherds relate to later incidental use of the site area. Alternatively, it is possible that the other loci at Sunset Mesa Ruin were the source of the late Rincon subphase and Tanque Verde phase ceramics. Again, however, no late Rincon subphase or Tanque Verde phase features were identified in the

recent investigations by Desert Archaeology. Their results also suggest a primarily middle Rincon subphase occupation, with only ephemeral use of the site during later periods (Lindeman 1999; Swartz and Adams 1998).

Although chronometric data from Hohokam sites are rarely of sufficient precision for fine-scale temporal distinctions, a combination of archaeomagnetic, architectural, and ceramic data, together with spatial relationships, make possible a finer temporal resolution than the 100–200-year-long Rincon phase. For example, statistical analysis of the original archaeomagnetic data provides a relative sequence of features occupied within this phase by assessing their contemporaneity (see Appendix B). Features 21, 22, 25, and 27 appear to represent a cluster of houses that were occupied and abandoned at about the same time. The temporal placement of Feature 25 is based on the hearth date, as the floor date is anomalous and may be unreliable. A sequence of abandonment is suggested within this temporal cluster; the dates for Features 22 and 25 are significantly different, indicating that Feature 25, the earlier of the two, may have been abandoned first in this cluster, whereas Feature 22 may have been abandoned last. Feature 23 is an outlier to this temporal cluster, and appears to have been the first house to be abandoned.

The ceramic evidence tentatively supports this sequence. Heckman and Whittlesey (Chapter 6) maintain that Rincon Red-on-brown, Style A ceramics are not temporally sensitive, as they were present throughout the occupational sequence. This style was clearly more common in the earlier dated contexts, however, whereas Style B ceramics were restricted to later-dated contexts. For example, a Rincon Red-on-brown, Style A vessel was found on the floor of Feature 23, presumably the earliest abandoned house. Another was found on the floor of Feature 22, which is inferred to be the last abandoned house. Still another Style A vessel was found above the earlier floor of Feature 21; a relatively late date was obtained from the hearth that was associated with the later floor. By contrast, Style B vessels were found only in later contexts: on the floor of Feature 27, one of the later houses; in the upper fill of Feature 23; and in an intrusive pit in Feature 22. All the Style B sherds in Feature 23 were found in the upper fill, whereas Style A sherds were restricted to the floor. In addition, Feature 23 contained the highest quantities of sherds in the upper fill and floor fill, suggesting trash deposition, whereas Features 22 and 27 contained the lowest frequencies, indicating that relatively little refuse was deposited in these houses after abandonment.

Although no stratigraphic superpositioning of houses was identified, the placement of houses in relation to one another can provide another clue to their relative contemporaneity. For example, the entryways of Features 22 and 23 directly faced each other, separated by a distance of about 3 m, which would have left an extremely small courtyard between them. Furthermore, the entryway of Feature 21 faced into the northwest corner of Feature 22 and was separated from it by an even shorter distance. These arrangements suggest that Feature 22 was not occupied at the same time as the other two houses.

Taken together, these various lines of evidence suggest the following sequence of construction and abandonment within this house group. Feature 23, which contained the most refuse, the oldest style Rincon Red-on-brown ceramics, and the earliest date, may have been the founding house, followed by Features 21 and 25. The presence of Rincon Red-on-brown, Style A vessels on the floor of Feature 23 and the earlier floor in Feature 21 suggests that these two surfaces were contemporaneous. The hearth associated with the later floor in Feature 21, however, clearly postdates Feature 23. Feature 23 was probably abandoned prior to the construction of Feature 25, as the latter is located slightly behind it. Feature 21 also may have been abandoned about that time, as refuse was deposited between the two floor surfaces. The archaeomagnetic data suggest that Feature 25 was contemporaneous with the later floor of Feature 21. Feature 21 apparently was remodeled and reoccupied when

Feature 25 was built. The various lines of evidence are consistent in indicating that Features 22 and 27 were probably the last houses built in this group, most likely after the other three houses were abandoned. The archaeomagnetic data suggest that Feature 25 was abandoned before Feature 22. The Rincon Red-on-brown, Style A vessel present on the floor of this house may represent a curated item. Although the archaeomagnetic data also indicate that Features 21 and 22 were abandoned at the same time, the physical placement of Feature 21 suggests that it was not contemporary with Feature 22. It is possible, however, that the occupations of all three houses overlapped.

None of the extramural features were dated by independent analysis, nor was the canal. Reliable archaeomagnetic dates could not be obtained from the canal sediments, the two pit features sampled, or from the historical-period samples. Ceramics recovered from the fill of the prehistoric features showed uniformity in type with the assemblage derived from the pit houses, suggesting but not confirming contemporaneity. Thus, the temporal relationship of the associated extramural features and the nearby kitchen area (Features 13 and 15) cannot be determined with any degree of precision, other than to note that they were generally contemporary with the overall occupation of the house group. At least some of the pit features, however, postdated the occupation, as Feature 22 was intruded by several pits, and several broken vessels were deposited in the fill. The association of these intrusive pits is unknown; it is possible that additional undiscovered houses were present in the vicinity of this house group (see below) or that these pits were associated with houses in one of the other residential loci. The absence of Tanque Verde phase ceramics in the excavated portion of the canal suggests it was active for only a short time. This finding may imply short-term shifts in the hydrology and/or water tables that allowed for canals this high on the terrace. This idea is explored further below (see "Subsistence"). Artifacts recovered from the historical-period features support the turn-of-the-century occupation of the adobe house, as well as indicating use of the site during the period of the Sunset Dairy and in more recent times.

In summary, at least four discrete occupational episodes can be distinguished in the 100–150 year span of the early and middle Rincon subphases in the portion of the site investigated by SRI. The first episode is represented by the occupation of one to two houses, Features 23 and 21; the second is represented by the occupation of two to three houses, Features 21, 25, and possibly 22; and the third by Features 22 and 27. A fourth episode is indicated by pits that intruded into Feature 22. This complex pattern of construction and abandonment within such a small area is not surprising within this short span of time. Similar occupational sequences have been found regularly in contemporary sites in the Tucson Basin (Altschul et al. 1996; Elson 1986; Huntington 1986; Wallace 1995). Wallace (1995:455) has argued that a much finer temporal resolution for the occupational sequences at these sites can be obtained from a determination of the number of occupational episodes and the use life of individual houses. The use life of houses built of wood and thatch is estimated to have been relatively short, and they frequently were abandoned because of accidental fires, termite infestations, wood rot, and other factors. Ahlstrom (1985:638) and Schlanger (1985, 1986) have estimated from better-dated contexts on the Colorado Plateau of northern Arizona that prehistoric pit houses lasted no more than 15–20 years, and only slightly longer if they were remodeled. Wallace (1995:455) derives roughly similar use life estimates of 14–30 years from an assessment of house construction and abandonment patterns during the Rincon phase occupation at Los Morteros. Using similar reasoning, it can be concluded that each of the four occupational episodes in the SRI locus lasted no more than 20 years, and the entire occupation represented by all five houses and associated features lasted no more than 80 of the 150 years of the early and middle Rincon subphases. If the area was first inhabited during the early Rincon subphase, as might be argued from the presence of Rincon Red-on-brown, Style A pottery, then it was probably abandoned by the middle of the middle Rincon subphase, unless there was an occupational hiatus between the abandonment of the older houses and the construction of new ones.

Household Organization and Site Structure

Over the last two decades, work in the Phoenix and Tucson Basins, as well as in other areas of southern Arizona, has revealed regular patterns in the spatial configuration of Hohokam settlements. Beginning at least as early as the late Colonial period (Rillito phase), Hohokam settlements were structured into a set of hierarchically arranged components, the elemental component of which was the individual pit house. Although there was much uniformity in the construction and function of Hohokam houses, considerable variability in size, construction, and internal features is recognized by some archaeologists as reflecting different house functions and household arrangements (Ciolek-Torrello and Greenwald 1988a, 1988b). Huntington (1986) and his colleagues

(Doelle et al. 1987:85–88), for example, recognized four house sizes and distinct storage houses arranged in various combinations to create three types of households at the West Branch site (AZ AA:16:3 [ASM]). The smallest households consisted of a single, moderately large habitation representing the dwelling of a founding nuclear household. The most common type of household contained a second, smaller house, reflecting the growth of the founding household, whereas the largest households consisted of three habitations, including an extremely large house and a large storage structure. Wallace (1995:790–793) recognized a similar variety of household arrangements and sequence of growth that started with a single large house at Los Morteros (AZ AA:12:57 [ASM]). Henderson (1987:121) also suggested that courtyard groups in the Phoenix Basin settlement of La Ciudad (AZ T:12:1 [ASM]) may have been founded by a household occupying a single large habitation, although she attributed the rapid growth of courtyard groups in this settlement to immigration.

House Types

Hohokam habitations were relatively large (10–20-m^2), formally constructed houses built in shallow pits with well-prepared floors, well-defined walls, a centrally located, plastered hearth, and a lateral entry ramp centered along one wall (see Ciolek-Torrello and Greenwald 1988a). Smaller, informally constructed houses with unlined, often off-centered firepits and poorly defined or off-centered entryways represent field houses and other special-function structures (see also Crown 1985). Storage structures also can be distinguished by an absence of the central, plastered hearth, and the presence of numerous vessels on the floor, or interior storage pits or shallow vessel rests (Ciolek-Torrello and Greenwald 1988a; Wallace 1995:97). In Rincon phase hamlets and villages, however, almost all houses were moderate to large in size and contained the formal arrangement of features associated with residential structures. Although interior partitions, benches, and storage pits are often observed in these residential houses, few attempts have been made to integrate such functional patterning into household reconstructions (see Ciolek-Torrello and Greenwald 1988a; Motsinger 1994).

Courtyard Groups

Individual houses were arranged into courtyard groups, a pattern that is the hallmark of the Sedentary period, and certainly the Rincon phase. Courtyards are thought to have begun with a single large house, representing a founding household. Additional pit houses, likely the result of new households budding off of the founding household, are arranged to form the courtyard group. Courtyard groups are defined as the space occupied by two or more contemporaneous houses whose doorways open into a common use area or courtyard and share cooking and probably storage facilities (Wilcox et al. 1981:155). Often associated with the houses in a courtyard group are refuse middens, extramural cooking and food-processing areas, and cemeteries. In most cases, such courtyard groups consist of only two or three houses (Huntington 1986; Wallace 1995; Wilcox et al. 1981), although in some cases larger groupings are recognized (J. Howard 1985, 1990). In most cases where larger house groups are found around a common courtyard area, however, only two or three were actually occupied at the same time (Wilcox et al. 1981:155). The other houses in such a grouping reflect the continuity of the same social group within the area, and often reveal slight shifts in the location of the courtyard over time, although establishing which houses were contemporary is often difficult in Hohokam contexts, where temporal precision is not great (see Wallace 1995:765 for a discussion). There also appears to have been regularities in the area encompassed by courtyard groups (about 100–200 m^2), with a pattern of increasing density as the number of houses increases (Ciolek-Torrello et al. 1998; Henderson 1987; Klucas et al. 1998; Mitchell 1988).

Conventional wisdom holds that courtyard groups consisted of related households or extended families (Ciolek-Torrello 1988b; Dean 1987; Doelle 1988; Doelle et al. 1987; Elson 1986; Huntington 1986; Whittlesey et al. 1994). Although in their original formulation of the courtyard group, Wilcox et al. (1981:154) equated households with the domestic domain, and facilities and implements associated with sets of residential, food-processing, cooking, and storage activities (see also Ciolek-Torrello 1985, 1988b; Ciolek-Torrello and Reid 1974), in practice, most Hohokam archaeologists equate households with the presence of one or more habitation structures.

Precincts and Village Segments

As many as two other residential groupings have been recognized between the level of the individual courtyard group and the entire settlement or village. The residential precinct is a commonly recognized structural component of Hohokam settlements that consists of clusters of courtyard groups associated with a common cemetery and, in many cases, hornos or formal earth ovens (Doelle et al. 1987; Henderson 1987; Rice 1987a; Sires (1984b); Wallace 1995). The component courtyard groups in these precincts may surround a large common use area sometimes referred to as a plaza (Doyel 1991; Wilcox et al. 1981). These residential clusters also are of a regular size, with diameters of 50–100 m and areas of more than 2,400 m^2 (Sires 1984b:523–524; Wallace 1995:766). Howard (1990), however, restricted the plaza to a much larger residential aggregate, which he termed the village segment. These larger aggregates are composed of clusters of residential precincts and massive trash disposal areas arranged around a communal use area containing hornos, which together encompass areas with diameters of 200–300 m (Howard 1990:Figure 30). Wallace (1995:770) has argued that the existence of these larger groupings has not been adequately demonstrated and that most investigators equate the village segment with the smaller village precincts.

Villages and Communities

As a form of public architecture, ball courts were integral parts of Hohokam villages during the Colonial period, but do not appear to have functioned beyond the early Sedentary period (early Rincon subphase). All the ball courts with reliable dates were built during the Cañada del Oro or Rillito phases of the Colonial period (Wallace 1995:772). Colonial period settlements with ball courts consisted of several village precincts or segments clustered around a central plaza and ball court complex. In some cases, a large cemetery has been found in the plaza area (Wallace 1995:773). The internal structure of village precincts during the Colonial period is not well known. Courtyard groups, if present, were small and probably did not exceed two structures (Czaplicki and Ravesloot 1988, 1989a). Less formal arrangements composed of a variety of house types also may have been common at this time in place of courtyard groups (Ciolek-Torrello 1988b; Ciolek-Torrello and Greenwald 1988b). Nevertheless, houses in the larger settlements were arranged in well-defined precincts. Colonial period and early Rincon subphase villages appear to have been relatively compact and tightly integrated settlements that were focused around the central plaza–ball court complex (Wallace 1995:804). Although the plaza–ball court complexes may still have been in use by the middle Rincon subphase, these features were no longer the focus of settlements. Instead, middle Rincon subphase villages were more dispersed settlements that spread out in linear arrangements, presumably along fields and water sources. Huntington (1986:346–347) argued for a shift from the centralized precinct or village cemeteries to household cemeteries associated

Figure 71. Artist's reconstruction of pit house with plastered entry and floor platform (adapted from Vanderpot et al. 1994:Figure 6.52).

with individual courtyard groups during the Rincon phase. By contrast, Wallace (1995:794) sees a continued strong association between cemeteries and precincts at Los Morteros. Wallace (1995:773, 804) also has suggested that some middle Rincon subphase settlements no longer fit the criteria of primary villages (see Doelle et al. 1987) because of their lack of identifiable public architecture and more dispersed arrangement. A more structured arrangement did not develop until the Tanque Verde phase, with the advent of platform mounds as new forms of public architecture.

Despite their relative lack of structure, Rincon phase villages did represent discrete population aggregations that were distinct from other such settlements. Los Morteros, for example, consisted of 20–26 contemporaneous precincts, each of which contained 2–4 contemporaneous courtyard groups with 2–3 contemporaneous houses (Wallace 1995:804–805; see also Elson 1986). The courtyards within each precinct shared a cemetery and one or more communal hornos. Each courtyard also had its own refuse disposal areas.

At a still larger scale, Hohokam communities in the Tucson Basin consisted of such primary villages, as well as hamlets, farmsteads, and temporary resource-extraction or -processing areas. Hamlets are discrete settlements comparable in size to village precincts but lacking any evidence of plazas or public architecture, whereas farmsteads are still smaller residential settlements comparable in size and composition to individual courtyard groups (Ciolek-Torrello 1988b; Doelle et al. 1987; Wallace 1995:773).

Site Structure at Sunset Mesa Ruin

The pit houses in the SRI locus at Sunset Mesa Ruin appear to have been part of one courtyard group that was occupied for an extended period of time. Probably no more than two or perhaps three of these houses were occupied at the same time. The houses were quite uniform and likely functioned in a similar manner as the primary dwellings for individual nuclear households. All were subrectangular in shape, with a central, plastered interior hearth, a lateral stepped entry, and few other interior features. All fit in the largest size class for habitations (see Ciolek-Torrello and Greenwald 1988a; Doelle et al. 1987), except for Feature 23, which was a moderately large habitation. All were typical Hohokam houses-in-pits rather than true pit houses. The distinction involves the construction of house walls along the edge of the floor at the base of the pit instead of incorporating the wall of the pit into the construction of the house wall (see Haury 1976; Wheat 1955). Haury (1976) considered the former to be the architectural idiom of the Hohokam, although true pit houses are found in Hohokam sites, especially in those that date prior to the Sedentary period. True pit houses, however, usually make up a very small minority of the Rincon phase houses (Bernard-Shaw 1990; Kelly 1978; Layhe, ed. 1986; Wallace 1995).

The floors of Features 21, 23, and 27 exhibited an unusual pattern in which only the central area around the hearths and entryways were plastered and the remainder of the pit floors were unsurfaced. This plastering pattern is typical of that found in houses with raised wooden platforms that served as the house floor (Figure 71), and is distinct from the raised collar or apron found around hearths and entryways on plastered floors (compare Wallace 1995:Figures A.23 and A.68). The regularity of the floor plaster, especially in the case of Features 23 and 27 (see Figures 14 and 18), indicates that the pattern is not the product of disturbance or differential preservation of the floor surface. In houses with wooden platforms, only the portion of the house pit surrounding the hearth and entryway is plastered and used as a floor, whereas the rest of the house pit is covered by the platform. The presence of raised wooden floor surfaces in these three houses could not be confirmed by evidence of either stone or wooden floor supports, or the interior postholes found in examples of this type of architecture (see Deaver 1998; Haury 1932; Vanderpot et al. 1994), although wooden posts may have rested directly on the pit floor without the benefit of postholes. Ciolek-Torrello (1994) has argued that pit houses with raised wooden platforms are an unusual but widespread form of Hohokam architecture that reflects stylistic preferences rather than functional considerations.

Artifacts in floor fill and floor contexts do not particularly distinguish activities in the various structures, except for the large collection of artiodactyl remains found in Feature 25, suggesting that the house was a locus for the storage or preparation of meat. The unusually large quantity of meat-bearing elements on this floor, which has been observed in only a few other contexts in the Tucson Basin, exceeds what is usually associated with subsistence needs of individual households and suggests that the inhabitants of this household directed or were involved in communal feasting activities. Although Feature 25 was a relatively large house, it was not the largest in the courtyard group (it was exceeded in size by Feature 27), did not appear to have a raised floor, and was otherwise undistinguished.

The temporal-spatial arrangements between these five houses reflect many, but not all of the patterns that other investigators have observed among Hohokam courtyard groups. The group apparently was founded with the construction of Feature 23 (Figure 72a), which, contrary to the norm, was the smallest of the five houses. At some point during the occupation of Feature 23, the courtyard group was expanded to include Feature 21, located only about 2 m southeast of Feature 23. The entryways of both houses were placed at right angles to one another in the pattern most diagnostic of a courtyard pair, creating a courtyard that opened to the southwest (see Figure 72b). Although the two houses in this pair were of different size classes, as Huntington (1986) predicted for the most

common type of courtyard group, the pattern differed from the typical arrangement in that the new house was larger than the older house. This discrepancy suggests an alternative temporal reconstruction for these houses. It is possible that Feature 21 was the founding household and that Feature 23 was added later. Feature 23 was abandoned early, however, and Feature 21 was remodeled and incorporated into a new courtyard with the construction of Feature 25 (see Figure 72c). This reconstruction is consistent with the temporal data, which indicate that Feature 23 was the first house to be abandoned and that Feature 21 was remodeled before being abandoned. At the same time, this alternative conforms with the general pattern of house growth observed at other sites. The doorways of Features 21 and 25 were oriented in the same manner as the previous pair, but the new courtyard group encompassed an area almost three times as large. The entryways of Features 21 and 23 were less than 5 m apart, and the courtyard area they encompassed was about 15 m in diameter (about 180 m^2). By contrast, the entryways of Features 21 and 25 were almost 15 m apart and the courtyard was about 25 m in diameter (490 m^2). The new group also represented a total increase in interior floor area from about 43 m^2 to 52 m^2, reflecting the growth of the resident household. The final courtyard arrangement is represented by Features 22 and 27, whose entryways also are arranged at right angles to one another (see Figure 72d). This group represents a slight, additional increase in interior floor area (57 m^2) and a shift in orientation of the courtyard to the northeast (see Figure 12). The spacing between the two houses and the area encompassed by the courtyard is about the same, however. It is possible that Feature 25 also was a part of this group, although archaeomagnetic and ceramic evidence indicate that it was abandoned prior to these other two houses.

These various courtyard groups represent the residence of what was probably one social group, comparable to an extended family, that inhabited the area over a period of several generations. A nuclear family probably established residence in the area occupying a single large habitation structure, either Feature 23 or Feature 21. The family quickly expanded and added a second house. These two houses were replaced by a pair of similar houses on two different occasions. With the first replacement, the size of the courtyard area used by the household increased dramatically, whereas the interior floor area increased only slightly. In its final configuration, the size of the courtyard area remained stable and interior floor area again increased slightly. This type of residential continuity has often been interpreted as evidence for the development of land rights or ownership (Ciolek-Torrello et al. 1998; Elson 1986:408; Wilcox et al. 1981). Old

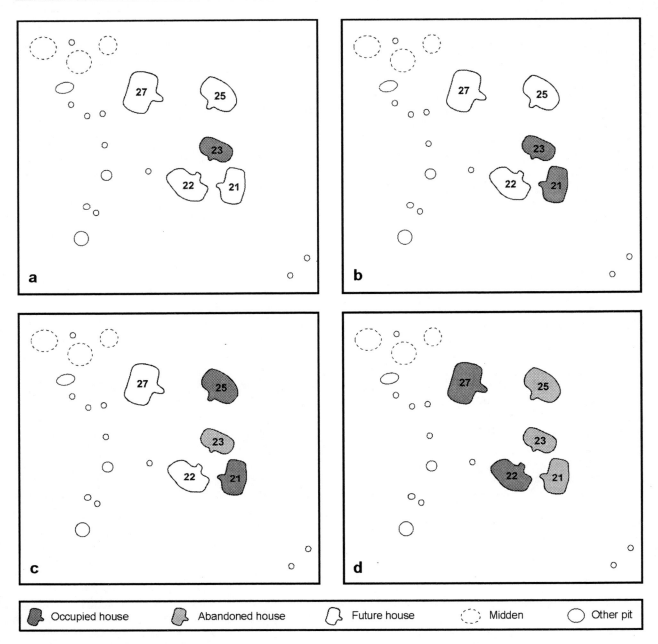

Figure 72. Chronological reconstruction of houses and courtyard groups at SRI locus of Sunset Mesa Ruin.

houses were abandoned or remodeled as the size of the family grew and their needs for dwelling space changed over a span of no more than 60 years. Although the same general area was inhabited during this time, the actual courtyard area shifted slightly, along with the change in houses. Food-processing pits were placed to the west of the group and trash was deposited in one or more large pits to the northwest. A short distance to the southeast was the kitchen area, represented by Features 13 and 15, and a number of additional pit features. This kitchen area contained a ramada that functioned as a food-storage and

-processing area (Feature 13)—possibly comparable to the storage rooms found by Huntington (1986) and Wallace (1995)—and roasting pits (Feature 15) functionally comparable to hornos. It is likely that these also were a part of this house group, as the houses found in Desert Archaeology's more recent excavations (Lindeman 1999; Swartz and Adams 1998) are at a greater distance. These recent excavations also confirmed the presence of a cemetery at the eastern edge of the courtyard group. Such associations support Huntington's (1986) hypothesis that cemeteries, and perhaps even hornos, were associated with individual courtyard groups rather than precincts during the Rincon phase.

Although the courtyard group grew over time, its internal composition remained the same after its initial expansion. The group never achieved the size of the large, four-house courtyard groups identified by Huntington (1986) and his colleagues (Doelle et al. 1987) at contemporary sites. It cannot be determined when the ramada area was integrated into this courtyard, or if it was shared with other nearby courtyards (see below). This feature appears to have functioned in a manner analogous to the storage houses associated with Huntington's large households, and suggests the possibility that the courtyard at the SRI locus did achieve some level of complexity at some point of time in its history. However, the distance between the storage area and the houses indicates a lower level of integration of storage into the household domain than in the case where the storeroom is in the courtyard group.

It is possible that additional houses and at least one other courtyard group was present in this area. The two buried vessels, Features 16 and 17, may represent the locations of additional houses in the heavily eroded area west of the house group. Isolated storage vessels buried in pits are unusual features in Hohokam settlements, although they are found in Sedentary period house floors (Ciolek-Torrello and Greenwald 1988a:149). Wallace (1995:97) observed large storage vessels that were deeply seated in house floors at Los Morteros. He also identified six isolated vessels in pits, at least five of which he suspected were contained within house floors that may have been removed by stripping operations (Wallace 1995:253). At Sunset Mesa, extensive erosion and earlier bulldozer activity at the western edge of the terrace may have destroyed the houses associated with these vessels, leaving only their subfloor contexts, which were then exposed by our stripping activities. This interpretation is consistent with the leveling of the midden area and the three remnant trash deposits (Features 29, 31, and 32) found there. If true, then this house group, with at least seven houses in two courtyard groups, would be comparable in size to the other loci at Sunset Mesa investigated by Desert Archaeology, and would conform better with other Rincon phase residential precincts. It would include two courtyard groups and a communal midden, a cemetery, and a roasting area. Together, these features encompass an area of about 100 by 45 m, which compares favorably with Sires's (1984b) and Wallace's (1995) estimates of precinct size.

At least three other similarly sized residential precincts were investigated by Desert Archaeology at Loci A, B, and C, located on the eastern and western flanks of the formation known as Sunset Mesa (Lindeman 1999; Swartz and Adams 1998). The two better preserved loci,

Loci A and B, contained between 8 and 14 houses dating to the middle Rincon subphase, along with associated extramural pit features, cemeteries, and refuse areas (Lindeman 1999). It remains to be demonstrated, however, whether the structural patterns identified at the SRI locus are replicated in these areas. It also remains unclear whether these various loci fit the more focused and integrated pattern reflected in Colonial period villages or the more dispersed Sedentary period pattern. The isolated pit houses found in the large central area between these loci (Swartz and Adams 1988:Figure 1.2) tentatively suggest a dispersed residential pattern rather than the central plaza–ball court complex of the Colonial period.

Subsistence

Macrobotanical and palynological data (Chapters 9 and 10) indicate a clear use of locally available botanical resources for food, fuel, and construction materials. Mesquite and palo verde were the most frequently used materials for construction posts in the pit houses, with such species as creosote bush used as thatch. Mesquite was the preferred fuel, although saltbush and paloverde charcoal were likewise found in hearths. Seeds or grains of a variety of grasses, weeds, and cacti, all of which were locally available, were recovered from hearths or pits within the pit houses (see Table 34). The prevalence of saguaro is somewhat unusual at a regional comparative level, as is the rather remarkable number of seeds, both mature and immature, of tansy mustard. Tansy mustard is ubiquitous and abundant in Rincon phase contexts (Bohrer et al. 1969:2–3; Miksicek 1986a, 1986b; Wallace 1995:809) and was used more extensively in the Tucson Basin than in other Hohokam regions (Gasser and Kwiatkowski 1991:449). At Hodges Ruin, Huckell (1986:259) also identified large numbers of tansy mustard seeds, many recovered as cakes or fused aggregates similar to those identified at Sunset Mesa Ruin. Tansy mustard is a weedy plant that is often associated with cultivated fields. The presence of tansy mustard, saguaro, and grains of lovegrass attest to use of the site at least from early spring until autumn. One can presume that if foods—particularly maize—were stored for the winter, then Sunset Mesa Ruin was occupied year-round.

Agave apparently also was used by the residents of Sunset Mesa, although only limited evidence in the form of oxalate crystals was identified. Agave was an important staple throughout the occupational sequence in the Tucson Basin (Gasser and Kwiatkowski 1991:426), and there is strong evidence that by the Classic period, agave was cultivated on a large-scale basis in the bajada areas surrounding the basin (Fish et al. 1985; Wallace 1995). Agave is also common in Rincon phase contexts (Huckell 1986:Table 12.4). Miksicek (1986a:308, 1986b:392) included agave among the cultivated plants in Rincon phase contexts at the West Branch and Tanque Verde Wash sites, and it is possible that it was cultivated on a widespread basis during this time, as well.

Maize, not surprisingly, is prominent in the botanical assemblage, and was almost certainly the dietary staple, probably grown in an irrigated field on the Qt1 terrace just below the site. Common and tepary beans also were recovered. A wide variety of beans has been recovered from Tucson Basin contexts, and the area is noted as a regional center for raising beans in the desert Southwest (Gasser and Kwiatkowski 1991:430–431). Squash, the third of the so-called Mexican triumvirate, and cotton, another important cultigen, were not in evidence. Squash is rarely preserved in open sites, but presumably was grown along with maize and beans. Cotton, by contrast, has an uneven distribution, and evidence for its cultivation is most common along the Salt and Gila Rivers, where large-scale irrigation was practiced (Gasser and Kwiatkowski 1991:427). Evidence for cotton was recovered at the West Branch and Tanque Verde Wash sites, and it was prominent in the collection from Hodges Ruin (Huckell:260, Table 12.4). Thus, its absence at Sunset Mesa Ruin may be significant. In this respect, it will be important to determine if cotton is present in the other loci being investigated at Sunset Mesa by Desert Archaeology. Sunflower also may have been grown, although the only part of this taxon recovered was charcoal. Such weeds as ragweed and the cheno-ams, which grow well in disturbed areas, likely sprang up in the cultivated fields and were used accordingly. It is not possible to evaluate how much domesticates contributed to the diet, but the ubiquity of maize at Rincon phase sites in the Tucson Basin (as well as at earlier and later sites) attests to its importance in maintaining a certain level of stability in the food base.

In terms of faunal resource exploitation, the record at Sunset Mesa Ruin (see Chapter 11) is very typical of Rincon phase occupations of the Tucson Basin, with one exception. In general, the faunal record appears to indicate a preference for small, local game, particularly jackrabbits. The lagomorph index of 0.187 is lower than the minimum estimated for hamlets and farmsteads, and comparable to larger Hohokam settlements (Szuter 1991:199). This low ratio suggests extensive land clearing associated with large-scale agricultural activities and wood collecting. The short occupation span of the site, however, is inconsistent with the extensive land modification usually associated with such low lagomorph indices. Many small settlements have been documented in the

confluence area (Ciolek-Torrello and Homburg 1990), some with evidence of Colonial period occupation that indicates greater time depth for occupation in the immediate area of Sunset Mesa. It is also possible that other factors, such as a preference for the larger jackrabbits or erosion in the confluence area, affected the selection of lagomorphs. Deer and bighorn sheep also are well represented in the assemblage, but are found almost exclusively on the floor of one house, Feature 25. Nearly all the identified elements in this house are innominates, a high meat-bearing element. The abundance of deer bone, especially high meat-bearing elements, is quite unusual in desert agricultural sites and suggests that the residents of this house were hunting specialists or gathered meat for ceremonial meals. Similar concentrations of deer have been found in early Classic period contexts in Marana (Rice 1987), and at the Gibbon Springs site (AZ BB:9:50 [ASM]) in the eastern Tucson Basin (Slaughter and Roberts 1996), but not in Rincon phase contexts.

Situated at the confluence of the Santa Cruz and Rillito Rivers, the two largest drainages in the Tucson Basin, and near several large expanses of some of the finest arable land in the Tucson Basin (see Figures 5 and 6), Sunset Mesa Ruin occupies an optimal location for farming. As discussed in Chapter 2, the site is located on the Qt2 terrace, an extensive alluvial formation that abuts much of the Santa Cruz River and is where most sites present along the river are located. At the present time, this terrace is approximately 6 m above the active channel of the Santa Cruz River, and 3.5 m above a large expanse of the Qt1 terrace and Comorro sandy loam soils, which, subject to periodic flooding, would have provided the best arable land in the area. The canal Feature 18 had its headgate in the Rillito River, and diverted water from there to the Qt1 terrace adjacent to the Santa Cruz River. The ostracode analysis (see Appendix A) suggests that the canal segment investigated by SRI was located near its outtake from the Rillito River, and initially the canal was subjected to a rapid input of water in a high energy environment. Subsequently, the flow energy decreased considerably, but a steady flow of water was maintained throughout the short life of the canal.

A reconstruction of the paleohydraulics of this canal (Appendix H) suggests that it could have had a maximum discharge of between about 11 and 19 cubic feet per second (cfs) depending on the actual gradient. Several arbitrary gradient values are used, as it is impossible to determine the gradient from a single segment of the canal. All of these values, however, are below the maximum value established by the natural gradient of the Rillito River channel (see Howard 1993:279 for a discussion). If it is assumed that the average discharge of this canal was about 25 percent of the maximum (see Ackerly 1989) and about 10 percent of the water was lost to evaporation and

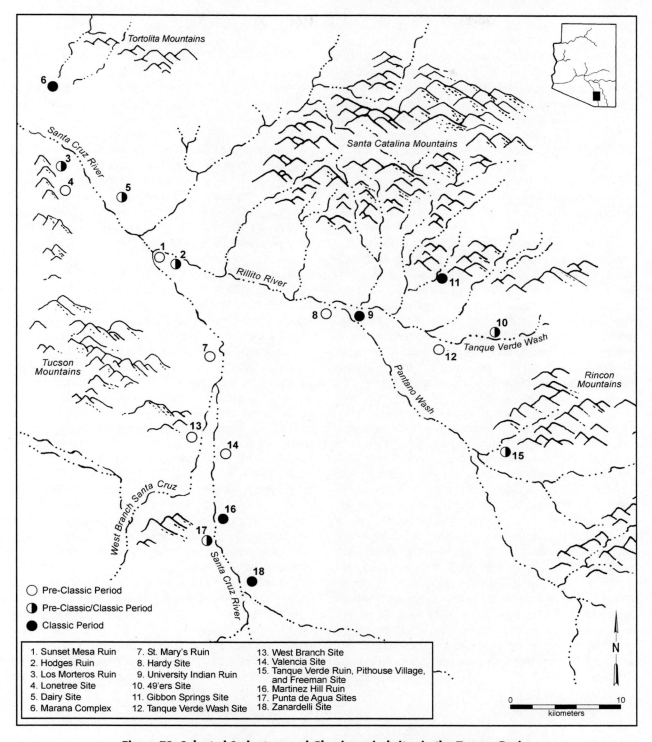

Figure 73. Selected Sedentary and Classic period sites in the Tucson Basin.

○ Pre-Classic Period
◐ Pre-Classic/Classic Period
● Classic Period

1. Sunset Mesa Ruin
2. Hodges Ruin
3. Los Morteros Ruin
4. Lonetree Site
5. Dairy Site
6. Marana Complex
7. St. Mary's Ruin
8. Hardy Site
9. University Indian Ruin
10. 49'ers Site
11. Gibbon Springs Site
12. Tanque Verde Wash Site
13. West Branch Site
14. Valencia Site
15. Tanque Verde Ruin, Pithouse Village, and Freeman Site
16. Martinez Hill Ruin
17. Punta de Agua Sites
18. Zanardelli Site

seepage (see Howard 1991, 1993), it could have irrigated an area of between 99 and 171 acres (see Table H.1), depending on the gradient. The current remnant of the Qt1 terrace west of Sunset Mesa is only about 35 acres. It is possible that this terrace segment was larger in prehis-

toric times, having been reduced by erosion, especially lateral migration of the Rillito and Santa Cruz channels (Pearthree and Baker 1987). The terrace probably extended a short distance northward into the current channel of the Rillito River and farther west into the existing

213

channel of the Santa Cruz River. The canal, which appears to turn east at its northern limit, is truncated at this point, suggesting that the northern end of the terrace has indeed been eroded since the Rincon phase. The terrace could also have extended farther south along the east bank of the Santa Cruz River. Even if the terrace was twice its current size, however, it would have been considerably smaller than the 99 acres that the canal could have irrigated based on the lowest estimated gradient.

The smaller channel inset into the fill of the canal had a much lower discharge of only 1.7–3 cfs and could have irrigated only between about 16 and 27 acres, again depending on the gradient. These acreage estimates conform much more closely with the observable amount of arable land in the vicinity of the canal. Initially, it is possible that the canal was too large and its capacity was much larger than that required for the amount of arable land. It may have been filled or allowed to fill naturally with sediment until a much smaller canal could be constructed in its channel. At an average capacity of 50 percent (as opposed to the 25 percent capacities calculated for most canals [see Ackerly 1989]) and a moderate gradient, this small canal could have supplied sufficient water to irrigate the entire Qt1 terrace area west of Sunset Mesa.

These estimates of discharge and irrigable land derived from the hydraulic reconstruction of the canal can be used to estimate maize yields and the size of the human population that could be supported by this resource (Appendix H). Potential maize production estimates that range between 29,784 and 46910 kg and population estimates of 26–40 individuals are derived for the early canal (see Table H.2). These numbers can be doubled if we assume that at least an equal area of arable land was available on the east side of Sunset Mesa. If the estimates are based on the smaller, later canal or the actual amount of farmland that was available on the Qt1 terrace (about 40 acres, or 15 hectares), we derive a maximum potential maize yield of 11,169 kg of maize and a total of less than 10 people for the western half of the settlement, or 20 people for the entire settlement, if we again assume that another canal may have irrigated an equal area on the east side of Sunset Mesa.

Settlement Patterns

The location of Sunset Mesa Ruin at this confluence is one of the most strategic in the Tucson Basin, a location to which Layhe (1986b:289) attributed the importance of Hodges Ruin. Given its closer association to this strategic setting, it is reasonable to ask why Sunset Mesa Ruin did not become the primary village, and why it was occupied so briefly. Why were sites located upstream along the Rillito River, such as Hodges Ruin, not smaller outliers of Sunset Mesa Ruin? The answers to these questions are anything but clear. For whatever reason, Hodges Ruin was established earlier, at the end of the Pioneer period, and was occupied much longer, into the early Classic period. By the time Sunset Mesa Ruin was founded, Hodges Ruin was already a sizeable village with a ball court (Kelly et al. 1978:5), perhaps the largest village in the Tucson Basin during the pre-Classic period (Layhe 1986b:289). Sunset Mesa Ruin appears to have been a briefly occupied outlier or satellite of Hodges Ruin, the nearest primary village (Figure 73). Economic, social, and political factors may have precluded the possibility of two villages emerging so close to one another.

As noted in Chapter 1, the sites are barely 3 km apart, well within the catchment area for a settlement and its agricultural fields (Doyel 1985; Gregory 1995:164). Chisholm (1979:127) has argued that a distance greater than 4 km between a settlement and its associated fields usually necessitates the establishment of a new permanent settlement closer to the fields. The construction of the canal at the confluence would have opened up irrigated fields along the eastern bank of the Santa Cruz River. Sunset Mesa Ruin may have been founded by residents of Hodges Ruin to exploit these fields. Thus, Sunset Mesa Ruin may have functioned as an agricultural hamlet that supplemented the food base of Hodges Ruin. Alternatively, Sunset Mesa Ruin and Hodges Ruin may have been equivalent settlements during the Sedentary period. Hodges Ruin was a prototypical example of a primary village during the Colonial period. The construction and use of the ball court is attributed to this time, although limited evidence suggests it may have continued in use during the Rincon phase (Kelly et al. 1978:5). Furthermore, most of the pre-Classic period houses date to the Colonial period, and Rincon phase houses are in the minority (Kelly et al. 1978:10; Layhe 1986a:49). It is possible that, as in the case of Los Morteros and many other Sedentary period settlements in the Tucson Basin (see Doelle et al. 1987; Wallace 1995:804), Hodges Ruin became a much more dispersed settlement during the Rincon phase. From this perspective, the founding of Sunset Mesa Ruin can be seen as part of a general pattern of population dispersal from the formerly nucleated settlement at Hodges Ruin.

As in the case of Los Morteros (Wallace 1995), this population dispersion was related to the opening of new field areas along a newly constructed canal. The occupation of the SRI locus and Locus A at Sunset Mesa Ruin fit this scenario well, but it does not account for the occupation of Loci B and C unless another, as yet undiscovered canal segment was built to exploit fields at the eastern foot of Sunset Mesa. This is not an unreasonable possibility. Sunset Mesa is a higher landform that projects northward to the edge of the Rillito River, dividing a large expanse of Comorro sandy loam soils into two roughly equivalent areas of arable land (see Figures 5 and 6). At least 5 acres of arable land lies on the west side of Sunset Mesa, below the SRI locus and Locus A. The canal that supplied water to this area could easily have been taken out of the Rillito River at the constriction in the floodplain created by the tip of Sunset Mesa. A similar area of arable land lies on the east side of the mesa at the foot of Loci B and C. No constriction in the floodplain is present upstream of this possible field area to facilitate an outtake canal. However, the Rillito River makes a prominent horseshoe bend to the southeast on the east edge of this possible field area (see Figure 5). It might have been relatively easy to take out a canal at the upstream end of this bend to irrigate fields in this area. The area where such a canal may have originated, however, has been subjected to extensive lateral stream erosion in historical times, as the Rillito River has repeatedly tried to cut a straight channel across the bend (Pearthree and Baker 1987), and it would be difficult to find evidence of a prehistoric canal.

The Sedentary period was a time of settlement expansion and dispersion throughout the desert regions of southern and central Arizona. In the southern Tucson Basin, for example, Colonial period settlement had been concentrated along the west bank of the southern portion of the Santa Cruz River in four, evenly spaced, primary villages and several hamlets, with a fifth large village on the east bank (Doelle 1988:Figure 19.2). By the middle Sedentary period, however, all but one of these large villages were abandoned, replaced by many more, smaller hamlets distributed in an almost continuous belt of habitation along the west bank and in several clusters on the east bank. Field houses also were established on the higher terraces above the river. Doelle (1988:283–285) has suggested that these rapid and radical changes in settlement were due to a major disruption of the floodplain environment involving deep downcutting of the southernmost portion of the river, reducing the agricultural potential of this area and creating improved conditions for floodwater farming downstream.

A similar situation may have occurred farther downstream along the Santa Cruz River, in the northern Tucson Basin. Such downcutting, in fact, more recently forced abandonment of the farmland on the west side of Sunset Mesa during the 1930s (Knapp, personal communication 1990). Supplying this land with water from the Rillito River may have been a Sedentary period response to this same type of problem. Sunset Mesa Ruin may have been established by residents of Hodges Ruin to build and maintain a canal for this purpose.

Alternatively, the occupants of Sunset Mesa Ruin may have had little or no interaction with the residents of Hodges Ruin. One of the peculiar characteristics of the Rincon phase is the establishment of scores of small residential sites throughout the Tucson Basin. Many of these sites were small farmsteads, consisting of a few pit houses and associated extramural features, some of which were located away from the floodplain, in areas that today could not support dry farming agriculture. Yet, the assemblages from these sites suggest not only that corn and other crops were grown there, but also that the sites were occupied year-round. Cairns and Altschul (1994) excavated one such farmstead in the eastern Tucson Basin. They pointed out that the petrocalcic horizon at many of these sites is only 40–50 cm below surface. Water from rains and run-off from nearby alluvial fans that seeps into the ground will naturally move along the surface of the calcic horizon. Water, therefore, will be perched below the surface, and soil moisture will be conserved. The fine silts commonly found in the Tucson Basin bajada contain sufficient nutrients to support domesticates, if adequate soil moisture is available (Karen Adams, personal communication 1997). For crops to grow in these areas in the absence of irrigation presupposes that environmental conditions were more mesic than they are today. Wallace (1995:805) has attributed the dispersion of Colonial period settlements to particularly favorable riverine and rainfall conditions that improved irrigation agriculture and *ak chin* farming during the middle Rincon subphase, although he also believes that the collapse of the Hohokam regional system was an important factor in the breakup of Colonial period villages.

There are precious few data from which to reconstruct precipitation patterns for the Sonoran Desert during the Sedentary period. Utilizing paleoclimatic reconstructions derived from tree-ring data, Van West and Altschul (1994, 1998) have modeled agricultural productivity in the Transition Zone of central Arizona. Although their reconstructions are not directly applicable to the Tucson Basin, the climate of the Tucson Basin probably shared many of the general features of that of central Arizona. According to Van West and Altschul (1994:399),

[T]he most striking feature of the Sedentary period is its relatively salubrious nature. It possesses a uniquely long period between A.D. 1042 and 1083 (42 years) when, with the notable exception of A.D. 1067, there was almost no drought years of any magnitude. These were the longest, continuously productive years in the entire 631-year (A.D. 740–1370) sequence.

Contributing to this extended period of high productivity was the absence of flooding. By contrast, the preceding Colonial period was characterized by cycles of catastrophic floods and devastating droughts that would have hampered a variety of agricultural pursuits (Van West and Altschul 1994). For example, under these conditions, canals could have been damaged periodically by flooding and left dry during droughts. A recent extension of the paleoclimatic reconstruction to the modern period does not alter this picture of the salubrious Sedentary period (Van West and Altschul 1998). In short, the most favorable period for agricultural pursuits within the last 1,500 years corresponds with that portion of the Sedentary period identified as the middle Rincon subphase.

It may be due in part to such favorable climatic conditions that canal construction appeared to expand in the Tucson Basin during the Rincon phase. Not only was the canal built at Sunset Mesa, but a much larger canal was constructed along the Santa Cruz River in the northern Tucson Basin, forming the foundation for radical changes in settlement in the Los Morteros and Marana site complexes (Wallace 1995). Whether these favorable climatic conditions also coincided with greater precipitation and elevated water tables, and whether these forces combined also would have allowed dry-farming techniques to be successful in the Tucson Basin, are questions that cannot be answered at the present time. It is worth noting that the Rincon phase settlement, which is unlike the pattern for any other period in the Hohokam sequence of the Tucson Basin, is consistent with a dispersed dry-farming regime.

One plausible model to explain the origin of Sunset Mesa Ruin is that favorable environmental conditions led to the breakup of ball court villages into their constituent elements. Large, nucleated settlements with populations of several hundred individuals, such as those of the Colonial period, were probably particularly important when farming was restricted to areas of the floodplains of major drainages that were protected from flooding and erosion. During these periods, access to these limited amounts of arable land was paramount, and villages provided a unit with sufficient sociopolitical strength to define and defend territories. Ball courts may have operated within the context of regional networks that maintained communication between communities and helped to move people and resources around to even out resource differences during periods of climatic fluctuations (Ciolek-Torrello 1998; Van West and Altschul 1998). When climatic and hydrological conditions permitted the successful pursuit of a variety of farming methods in an equally diverse set of environmental contexts, the inherent social centrifugal forces that plague small-scale tribal entities led to the fission of these villages into smaller units and the abandonment of the ball courts. The largest of these units were hamlets corresponding in size to the precincts that formerly comprised nucleated villages. Although much smaller than villages, hamlets were still many times larger than farmsteads. Their size probably

gave them an advantage in claiming the best lands in the basin. Thus, during the Rincon phase we find most hamlets on terraces overlooking major drainages, whereas farmsteads tend to be found on more marginal lands.

Sunset Mesa Ruin was a settlement that compares in size with a large hamlet or small village. It consisted of four precincts, each of which probably contained no more than two to four contemporaneous households. Utilizing Wallace's (1995:805) estimates of 5–8 persons per household, a range that conforms with Cook and Heizer's (1968) household size estimates for houses of the size found at Sunset Mesa Ruin, we obtain population estimates of 40–128 persons. This population is considerably smaller than what has been estimated for villages (Doelle et al. 1987; Wallace 1995) and is consistent with that usually associated with a hamlet.

These estimates can be compared with those derived independently from the paleohydraulic reconstruction and the currently existing amount of available arable land (see above). For example, the range in population size estimated for the minimum household size (5 individuals) and 2–4 contemporary houses in the two western precincts (20–40 people) corresponds well with the estimates derived independently from the amount of land that could have been irrigated by Feature 18 (26–40 people). As noted above, however, this canal could have supplied much more water than there was land to irrigate in this area. The discharge from the later canal conforms better with the amount of arable land, but the estimates derived from the later canal (7 people) or the area of Qt1 terrace (9 people) are too small for the size of the settlement found at Sunset Mesa. If we assume that a similar irrigation system operated on the eastern side of Sunset Mesa to serve the two eastern precincts, only 14–18 people could have been supported by the combined systems. Even at the minimum household size and the minimum number of contemporary houses (2) per precinct, the minimum momentary population of the settlement would have been 40 people.

These estimates are quite likely inaccurate, as they are each based on a number of assumptions, which are, in turn, affected by many variables that we cannot control adequately as yet. Nevertheless, comparison of the variously derived estimates is informative. If accurate, the inconsistencies between these estimates suggest that some of the underlying assumptions should be modified. Crop production on the limited amount of arable land available to the residents of Sunset Mesa could have been increased dramatically if fallowing was eliminated. Van West and Altschul (1998) present this as the most likely strategy in their reconstruction of irrigation systems in the lower Verde River valley. The paleohydraulic reconstruction (Appendix H) suggests that the prehistoric farmers at Sunset Mesa were able to obtain more than enough water for their fields, but arable land was the limiting factor. Eliminating fallow and cultivating the maximum amount of arable land would have been likely under these circumstances. Alternatively, a larger population could also have been supported if per capita demand were decreased by reducing storage capacity. The common occurrence, for the first time, of specialized storage structures in Rincon phase settlements, however, and the presence of the ramada used for food storage at the SRI locus of Sunset Mesa indicate that food storage capacity may actually have increased during this period. The presence of such structures suggests that Rincon phase households had begun to accumulate food surpluses, perhaps in the form of the two-year supply that has been documented ethnographically. Thus, reduction of the fallow cycle is a more likely possibility and may provide a clue as to why the settlement was occupied for such a brief period. It is possible that a reduced fallow cycle was not practical under the less favorable climatic conditions that characterized the late Rincon subphase, or that soil fertility was reduced or depleted over an extended period of intensive cultivation. Although it has great appeal as an explanation for the short occupation of the settlement, this conclusion presupposes that the residents of Sunset Mesa confined their agricultural activities to the southern bank of the Rillito River. A much larger expanse of Qt1 terrace and Comorro soils, however, exists on the north bank opposite Sunset Mesa (see Figures 5 and 6). Whether this area was cultivated by the residents of Sunset Mesa or another settlement remains unknown. Midvale reported the possible remains of another large settlement in this area (AZ AA:12:9 [ASM]), but the area has been destroyed by gravel pit operations and freeway construction, and no evidence of this settlement remains (Ciolek-Torrello and Homburg 1990).

The diversity of material culture at the Sunset Mesa Ruin is similar to that found in other large habitation sites in the Tucson Basin, and compares favorably with that recovered from excavations at Hodges Ruin. The ceramic assemblage includes a great variety of decorated pottery from a number of different sources (see below). The shell collection, although small, conforms closely in terms of species and artifact diversity with those from other large Rincon phase settlements, and limited evidence for on-site bracelet manufacture was observed. Although it may have been founded by people from Hodges Ruin, Sunset Mesa Ruin does not appear to have been subsidiary to this older settlement and, in fact, may have been equivalent to it in size and function during the Rincon phase.

Even though it was a relatively small settlement, Sunset Mesa Ruin may actually have been one of the more important settlements in this part of the Tucson Basin. As discussed earlier, the canal at the site appears to date exclusively to the middle Rincon subphase, which corresponds closely with the occupation of the site. The ability to divert water from the Rillito onto the Santa Cruz floodplain may have required the unique juxtaposition of high water tables coinciding with a lack of droughts and floods. If this is the case, it suggests that ditch irrigation technology was readily available to Rincon phase farmers, and they took advantage of this technology when conditions allowed. Such an inference is quite reasonable, given that canals have been found throughout the prehistoric sequence in the Tucson Basin, beginning with the introduction of domestics in the Late Archaic period (Ezzo and Deaver 1998). It also may imply that people moved purposely to Sunset Mesa when these conditions arose, and stayed there until conditions changed. Their movement to the confluence of the Rillito and Santa Cruz Rivers, and their abandonment of the settlement shortly thereafter, may imply that the strategic location was coveted, but unuseable without the aid of peculiar environmental conditions.

The favorable climatic conditions that characterized the salubrious Sedentary period came to an abrupt end in the early decades of the eleventh century with a series of severe and extended droughts (Van West and Altschul 1994, 1998). It may be purely coincidental, but the end of these salubrious conditions corresponds with dramatic changes to the entire fabric of Hohokam society in the Tucson Basin and elsewhere. Another major restructuring of settlement systems occurred within the short span of 50 years represented by the late Rincon subphase, when there were wholesale abandonments of entire settlements and large segments of settlements. By the early Classic period, these settlements were replaced by larger aggregations, often in areas that had only seen minimal settlement in previous times. These new sites were composed of courtyard groups contained within walled compounds distributed around a central plaza area in which is often found a central structure. At the nearby Badger Hole Ranch Ruin, the plaza area contained a large adobe structure and a relatively large cemetery. Cemeteries have been found elsewhere on the site, as well, but are smaller and may reflect familial plots, as opposed to communal areas. In the Marana complex and at University Indian Ruin (AZ BB:9:33 [ASM]), Martinez Hill Ruin (AZ BB:13:3 [ASM]), and several other settlements, large platform mounds form the focal points of Classic period settlements. Regardless, the nucleated and focused structure of Classic period settlements is highly reminiscent of the Colonial period ball court villages, but with platform mounds and other structures replacing the ball court. A host of changes in architectural forms, burial practices, ceramics, ceremonial paraphernalia, and subsistence and economic pursuits accompanied these changes in settlement pattern and site structure.

Ceramic Production and Exchange

The first point to be made with regard to this issue is that the ceramic assemblage from Sunset Ruin Mesa is typical of the Rincon phase, except for the relatively high frequency of ceramics imported from the Phoenix Basin. Partial and reconstructible vessels exhibit a trend toward squat, Gila-shouldered jars, a manifestation seen throughout the Tucson Basin during this time. Rim sherds likewise lend evidence to this trend. Of the nearly 2,000 decorated sherds recovered, 87.5 percent fall into the Tucson Basin Brown Ware series, being various styles of Rincon Red-on-brown or Rincon Black-on-brown. The remaining decorated ceramics were from the Hohokam Buff Ware series, consisting largely of Sacaton Red-on-buff. Plain ware ceramics dominated the unpainted ceramic assemblage (69.9 percent), and Rincon Red sherds accounted for 3.7 percent (see Table 5).

In terms of nonlocal ceramics, one Gila Plain jar and the Hohokam Buff Ware sherds represent intrusive ceramics from the Phoenix Basin. As discussed in Chapter 6, the percentage of Hohokam Buff Ware (12.5 percent of the decorated ceramic assemblage) is unusual for the Rincon phase. During the Sedentary period in the Tucson Basin, there was a general tendency toward a decrease in Hohokam Buff Ware (about 1–2 percent of the decorated ceramic assemblage seems to be the norm). Although unusual, the high frequency of Sedentary period buff ware is not unique to Sunset Mesa Ruin. High frequencies of Sacaton Red-on-buff also were present at Los Morteros, and outnumbered Colonial period buff ware by a factor of almost 10 to 1 (Heidke 1995:Table 5.2). Red-on-buff ceramics were also common in early excavations at Hodges Ruin, where they made up as much as 40 percent of the decorated ceramics in some excavation units, and 49 vessels were recovered from cremations (Kelly et al. 1978:77). Among the latter, 20 vessels were Sacaton Red-on-buff. In the more recent excavations at Hodges Ruin, buff ware constitutes 28.7 percent of the decorated collection and 3.5 percent of the entire ceramic assemblage (Whittlesey 1986a). Santa Cruz Red-on-buff, however, is the overwhelmingly dominant type, and Sacaton Red-on-buff constitutes a relatively small part of the collection.

These data suggest a continued link between the settlements of the northern Tucson Basin and the Hohokam of the Phoenix Basin during the Sedentary period. It is most likely that the high frequency of Sacaton Red-on-buff at Sunset Mesa Ruin is the result of its location, given that the Santa Cruz River was a likely route of ceramic distribution between the two regions, or perhaps the inhabitants of these northern settlements continued to have access to Phoenix Basin ceramics through some sort of alliance or exchange network. The similarities between Sunset Mesa Ruin and Hodges Ruin in the relatively high percentages of intrusive buff ware supports the notion that the two settlements were closely related and participated equally in the same exchange networks.

According to the petrographic data (see Appendix D), 75 percent of the analyzed sherds that could be identified to a Tucson Basin petrofacies bore the distinct characteristics of the J1 (Beehive) petrofacies, which is located just north of the west branch of the Santa Cruz River in the southern Tucson Basin (see Figure D.1). This is also the location of the West Branch site, a large village that had a substantial Rincon phase occupation (Altschul et al. 1996; Huntington 1986). It is tempting to postulate that the West Branch site was a production locus for ceramics at this time, trading to neighboring sites up and down the Santa Cruz River and its principal tributaries (see Harry 1996; Heidke 1996a; Wallace 1986b). This is far too simplistic an interpretation, however, as a number of different mechanisms could account for the same patterning. Was it the pottery or the people that were moving throughout the basin? Heckman and Whittlesey (Chapter 6) argue that the relatively dispersed settlement system of the Rincon phase may have produced this ceramic distribution as pottery was circulated throughout the basin by a mobile population. The petrographic data require several independent lines of evidence about ceramic production and exchange before such inferences can be made with any degree of confidence. Whereas there is little question that ceramic manufacture took place at the West Branch site, the nature of any sort of exchange network, or the idea that ceramics made at the site were being traded throughout the basin, remains very poorly understood at the present time. Mechanisms for the exchange are inadequately explained, not to mention the ways in which such exchange networks may have been integrated into the social systems. Therefore, the petrographic data must be considered with considerable caution, and cannot be used alone to infer ceramic production loci and trade networks.

Wallace (1986b) has pointed to the abundance of clays, pigments, and polishing stones at the West Branch site as additional evidence for ceramic production, a finding that has been reinforced by more recent excavations at the site (Altschul et al. 1996). Similar evidence for ceramic vessel manufacture was not found at Sunset Mesa Ruin, suggesting that pottery was imported in some manner. Thus, the notion of the West Branch site as a center for the production of decorated ceramics during the Rincon phase cannot be rejected out of hand, either. There is evidence to suggest that the residents of Sunset Mesa Ruin may have participated in this exchange network, by whatever mechanisms it may have functioned.

It would not be a great stretch of the imagination to infer that the Sunset Mesa Ruin inhabitants were well aware of the inhabitants of the West Branch site, located several miles to the south on the western banks of the Santa Cruz River, as well as the inhabitants of other sites in that area. Similarities in material culture and general adaptation suggest strong cultural affinity, which likely meant a common language and common solutions to adaptive problems. Whereas territoriality played a role in relationships, and encroachment may have resulted in conflict, the mobile heritage of these people suggests certain levels of interaction that may have been expressed in trade, marriages between families from different sites, periodic relocation of families or households from one site to another, and an additional range of interactions. All of these factors may have been involved in the movement of pottery in the basin.

Unlike some other Rincon phase settlements, however, which may have obtained all their ceramics from the West Branch area (see Elson 1986), the residents of Sunset Mesa Ruin also obtained a small but significant number of vessels manufactured with tempering materials obtained from nearby petrofacies. They may have obtained these tempering materials directly or in the form of finished vessels from neighboring settlements. The large number of Phoenix Basin ceramics also attests to the fact that the residents of Sunset Mesa maintained an unusually diverse and wide network for obtaining their decorated pottery.

Mortuary Practices

Two cremations were identified during the testing phase outside of the APE, and one was recovered at that time (Harry and Ciolek-Torrello 1992:40–46). They were located to the east of the house group (see Figure 9). The second cremation was not relocated, and no additional cremations were identified, during data recovery. Recent excavations by Desert Archaeology have revealed a number of additional cremations in this area, suggesting the presence of a formal cemetery (Lindeman 1999). The absence of other houses to the east of this cemetery suggests that it was associated with the houses found in the SRI locus. Desert Archaeology also found evidence for another cemetery in association with Locus B, suggesting that each precinct maintained its own cemetery area.

At the outset of data recovery, we also had hoped to address issues related to mortuary behavior and to explore

the possibilities of different kinds of mortuary treatments and their social correlates. In this endeavor, we have been stymied by the lack of data. Although disappointing, this result is not surprising. Rincon phase mortuary practices are perhaps the most poorly understood of the Tucson Basin Hohokam sequence. Unlike the preceding Colonial period and the following Classic period, cemeteries are generally lacking. Rincon phase burials are often found distributed as isolated features both within structures and in extramural areas, which suggested to Huntington (1986) that Rincon phase burials were associated with individual households. The discovery of more centralized cemeteries at Sunset Mesa Ruin indicates that mortuary patterns were more complex at this time. This is an important research avenue that we must leave to Desert Archaeology to pursue.

Historical-Period Homesteading

As discussed in Chapter 1, and examined in Chapter 12, a late-nineteenth–early-twentieth-century homestead was located at the edge of the APE at Sunset Mesa Ruin. The homestead patent was applied for by Basillio Cuevas in April, 1890; he began farming this land in 1891, and final Land Office approval and patent were completed in November 1897. Twelve archaeological features were identified in association with the Cuevas homestead. Features included remains of the Cuevas house (Feature 5), one intrusive pit in the house, and several pits of various shapes that contained historical-period trash.

Four research questions relating to historical-period homesteading were framed in Chapter 1. The first, regarding the number of occupants and association with Cuevas, was answered in part by documentary evidence. Whereas we know this was the Cuevas homestead, and that the three-room adobe house constructed on the site (Feature 5) was occupied by Cuevas and his family, we do not know the makeup of the family or how many people actually resided within the house.

The second question concerns the range of activities in evidence. This is somewhat problematic, given that the site has been used as a dump for some time, and much of the material in the fill is recent trash. The types of glass, metal, and ceramic artifacts recovered from the rooms suggest domestic and basic farming activities. Archival evidence indicates that Cuevas cleared 40 acres but actively cultivated only 5 acres. A corral, chicken house, and fence were constructed, in addition to the house. The archival documents make no mention of canals or ditches that Cuevas may have used to irrigate his small cultivated plot. Which crops were cultivated and what stock, other than chickens, were raised by the Cuevas family remains unanswered, as do the reasons for which the property was subsequently sold to Knapp.

The third question relates to the length of occupation. This is not known, but we do know that by 1915 the land was purchased by William A. Knapp, who soon after founded the Sunset Dairy on land adjacent to the former Cuevas homestead. Therefore, the Cuevas family lived in the adobe house no more than 25 years. This occupational span is tentatively supported by the temporal range of the associated cultural material recovered from the excavations.

The final question deals with the socioeconomic status of the Cuevas family. This cannot be deduced from archaeological or documentary records, but given that Cuevas was a naturalized citizen who could not sign his name (see Chapter 12), one can surmise that his socioeconomic status, and that of his family, was relatively low. The small size of the house and the utilitarian nature of most of the associated artifacts do not contradict this conclusion. Several clues, however, suggest that the status of the Cuevas household was not marginal. The house was a well-built, multiroom structure that featured what were probably expensive redwood door frames. Although the sample is small, the butchered bone suggests the consumption of relatively high-valued meat cuts that were probably purchased from a butcher shop, as well as the preparation of menudo from the waste bone, a common practice of Mexican families (Jones 1997). No evidence for the consumption of chickens was found, despite the mention in archival documents of a chicken house on the property. The paucity of ceramics of Tohono O'odham manufacture is also disconcerting, as these were usually abundant in turn-of-the-century contexts in the Tucson Basin, especially in Hispanic contexts (see Whittlesey 1997). In most other respects, the limited archaeological and archival data are in general agreement.

Conclusions

We have only begun to scratch the surface of understanding the human dynamics that characterized the prehistoric and historical-period occupation of Sunset Mesa Ruin. The relatively small percentage of the site that was investigated opens a narrow window to many of the most important issues that archaeologists working in the

Tucson Basin have been grappling with for the past two decades. Despite the small scale of our investigations, we are able to address these issues precisely because of the fact that so many of the basic aspects of Rincon phase culture are known, and because of the extensive comparative context that is available to us. We can be confident that the portion of the site investigated represents a typical Rincon phase occupation of an agricultural hamlet, a common pattern of settlement during the Sedentary period in the Tucson Basin, when population aggregations were dispersed along major drainages and agricultural fields. One of the most important contributions derived from this investigation has been our ability to map the structure of a residential courtyard and its change through time. Also important has been the documentation of the subsistence system and the unique suite of cultigens and wild plants that formed the basis of the Sedentary period socioeconomic system in the Tucson Basin. Like other contemporary settlements in the region, the residents of Sunset Mesa Ruin focused on maize, beans, agave, tansy mustard, and other weedy annuals that grew in field areas. The discovery of a canal also adds to our understanding of the role that irrigation technology played in the developments that characterized the subsistence and settlement systems of the middle Rincon subphase. Some characteristics of the site, such as the importation of Hohokam Buff Ware from the Phoenix Basin, the use of several ceramic production sources, and the presence of centralized cemeteries, further enhance our understanding of variability during this period, and again compel us to respect the remarkable complexity inherent in human systems.

What the excavations at Sunset Mesa Ruin can contribute to is the growing database of Sedentary period occupation in the Tucson Basin. The Sedentary period was a time of considerable change for the region's inhabitants, when the region was experiencing major growth and expansion of settlement. It was also at this time that much of the basis of the Hohokam socioeconomic system was undergoing significant change and adaptation, which would find expression in a series of cultural and behavioral innovations that became the hallmarks of the Classic period. The task of better understanding such critical transitions remains at the core of Hohokam research, and likely will be an issue of significance for years to come.

Investigations of the historical-period Cuevas homestead were even more limited in scope, and we were able to address few of the related research issues. Nevertheless, this study also contributes to the little known subject of turn-of-the century rural homesteading in the Tucson Basin, particularly that relating to Mexican immigrants.

APPENDIX A

Ostracode Analysis

Manuel R. Palacios-Fest

This report presents the results of the analyses of nine canal samples from the Sunset Mesa site, north of Tucson, Arizona. Samples are identified by their bag numbers preceded by the suffix SR (Statistical Research). All samples analyzed derive from the following provenience: Site AZ AA:12:10 (ASM); Feature 18; Grid N 536.35 and E 431.85.

Sample SR-821 (Level 8): Grayish brown blocky clay consisting of 3 percent sand and 97 percent silt and clay. Sand fraction consists of medium to fine grains of quartz, feldspars, biotite, muscovite, gypsum, calcite, charcoal, rock fragments, and shell fragments. Particles are well sorted and subangular to subrounded. Massive. Contains fossils of ostracodes, gastropods, and plant debris. Ostracode fauna consists of *Ilyocypris bradyi* (73 individuals), *Limnocythere* sp. (2), *Potamocypris* sp. (3), *Cypridopsis vidua* (8), and *Herpetocypris reptans* (1).

Sample SR-823 (Level 7): Grayish brown blocky clay consisting of 8 percent sand and 92 percent silt and clay. Sand fraction consists of medium to fine grains of quartz, feldspars, biotite, muscovite, calcite, gypsum, charcoal, rock fragments, and shell fragments. Particles are well sorted and subangular to subrounded. Massive. Contains some fossil ostracodes, gastropods, and plant debris. Ostracode fauna consists of *Ilyocypris bradyi* (6) and *Cypridopsis vidua* (5).

Sample SR-285 (Level 6): Yellowish brown blocky clay consisting of 24 percent sand and 77 percent silt and clay. Sand fraction consists of medium-sized grains of quartz, feldspars, biotite, muscovite, calcite, gypsum, and, rock fragments. Particles are moderately well sorted and subangular to subrounded. Massive. Contains no fossils.

Sample SR-827 (Level 5): Grayish brown blocky clay consisting of 11 percent sand and 89 percent silt and sand.

Sand fraction consists of medium-size grains of quartz, feldspars, biotite, muscovite, calcite, gypsum, rock fragments, and shell fragments. Particles are moderately well sorted and subangular to subrounded. Massive. Contains few fossils of gastropods and ostracodes (1 specimen of *Ilyocypris bradyi*).

Sample SR-829 (Level 4): Grayish brown blocky clay consisting of 15 percent sand and 85 percent silt and clay. Sand fraction consists of medium-size grains of quartz, feldspars, biotite, muscovite, calcite, gypsum, and rock fragments. Particles are moderately sorted and subangular to subrounded. Massive. Contains no fossils.

Sample SR-831 (Level 3): Reddish brown gravelly sand consisting of 7 percent gravel, 11 percent sand, and 82 percent silt and clay. Coarse fraction consists of quartz, feldspars, calcite, biotite, muscovite, gypsum, and rock fragments. Particles are poorly sorted and angular to subangular. Massive. Contains no fossils.

Sample SR-833 (Level 2): Reddish brown gravelly sand consisting of 75 percent with a minor silt and clay component (25 percent). Coarse fraction consists of quartz, feldspars, biotite, muscovite, gypsum, and rock fragments. Particles are poorly sorted and angular to subangular. Massive. Contains no fossils.

Sample SR-835 (Level 1): Reddish brown gravelly sand (89 percent) with a minor silt and clay component (11 percent). Coarse fraction consists of quartz, feldspars, biotite, muscovite, calcite, gypsum, and rock fragments. Particles are poorly sorted and angular to subangular. Massive. Contains no fossils.

Sample SR-837 (Level sub): Yellowish brown compact silty clay (71 percent) with minor gravelly sand component (29 percent). Coarse fraction consists of quartz, feldspars, biotite, muscovite, calcite, gypsum, and rock fragments. Particles are poorly sorted and angular to subangular. Massive. Contains no fossils.

Interpretation

Table A.1 shows the fossil ostracode content of the Sunset Mesa canal sediments. The microstratigraphic sequence indicates that the canal was subject to rapid water input in Level 1. High energy characterized this event; no ostracodes were able to survive under these conditions. Subsequent canal flooding suggests decreasing flow energy from Level 2 to Level 4. However, no ostracodes are present because energy was still too great to preserve the ostracode valves. In Level 5, a rare occurrence of *Ilyocypris bradyi* indicates that running waters were still entering the canal. From Level 6 to Level 8, an evident increase in ostracodes suggests that flow energy decreased considerably during this interval. The dominant occurrence of *I. bradyi* is indicative of flowing waters. The occurrence of *Cypridopsis vidua*, *Herpetocypris reptans*, and *Potamocypris* sp. also suggests running or discharge waters. The faunal assemblage from Level 8 suggests that the deposition site was near the canal headgate. It also suggests that input waters were fresh to slightly saline, as indicated by the rare occurrence of *Limnocythere* sp.

Grain-size ratios derived from bulk-to-residual-weight analysis also supports the interpretation of a high energy environment. Energy gradually decreased from Level 1 to Level 8. Other fossils (gastropods and plant debris) are in good agreement with this interpretation, as well.

Table A.1. Ostracode Record from the Sunset Mesa Site (AZ AA:12:10 [ASM]) Canal

Sample No.	Bulk Wt. (g)	Residual Wt. (g)	Level	Depth (mdb)	Ostracodes/g	I. bradyi	Limnocythere sp.	C. vidua	Potamocypris sp.	H. reptans	Fragmentation	Encrustation	Abrasion	Other	Other	Fossils
							Species (%)					**Taphonomic Features (%)**				
SR-821	26.57	0.85	8	5.28	87	84	2	9	3	1	40	30	—	—	mollusks	plant debris
SR-823	29.08	2.36	7	5.36	11	55	—	45	—	—	60	—	—	—	mollusks	plant debris
SR-825	29.69	7.04	6	5.43	—	—	—	—	—	—	—	—	—	—	mollusks	
SR-827	31.90	3.64	5	5.48	1	100	—	—	—	—	—	—	—	—		
SR-829	30.92	4.65	4	5.53	—	—	—	—	—	—	—	—	—	—		
SR-831	34.46	6.35	3	5.58	—	—	—	—	—	—	—	—	—	—		
SR-833	43.99	32.84	2	5.63	—	—	—	—	—	—	—	—	—	—		
SR-835	37.04	32.88	1	5.68	—	—	—	—	—	—	—	—	—	—		
SR-837	27.33	8.05	sub	5.75	—	—	—	—	—	—	—	—	—	—		

Archaeomagnetic Sampling, Analysis, and Dating at Sunset Mesa Ruin

William L. Deaver and Barbara A. Murphy

We obtained 12 archaeomagnetic dating samples from prehistoric and historical-period archaeological features discovered during excavations at Sunset Mesa Ruin (AZ AA:12:10 [ASM]), by SRI (Table B.1). The site is located in Tucson, Arizona, at a latitude of 32.31° north and a longitude of 248.95° east. The local magnetic declination is 11.86° east. Five of the seven prehistoric dating samples were collected from clay-lined firepits in pit houses. One sample was collected from a section of the floor in a pit house that had burned. The remaining prehistoric dating sample was obtained from the basal oxides and manganese deposits associated with a canal. The available independent chronological information indicates that the structures and canal were used and abandoned during the early to middle Rincon phase (ca. A.D. 950–1100). The historical-period dating samples were collected from a historical-period building and four associated trash-burning pits. Several fired adobe bricks in an adobe building may have been the remains of a fireplace. Based on historical maps, documents, and local informants, the building is estimated to have been occupied in the late nineteenth through early twentieth century (ca. A.D. 1890–1915).

The prehistoric samples were collected to estimate when the pit houses were used and to determine an internal site chronology. The samples from the historical-period features were acquired for methodological reasons. We could not reasonably expect to archaeomagnetically

Table B.1. Archaeological Contexts for Archaeomagnetic Samples from Sunset Mesa Ruin

Sample Number[a]	Sample Context	Archaeological Phase or Period	Estimated Calendrical Age (A.D.)
-1ua	Feature 19, pit	historical period	1890–1915
-2ua	Feature 24, pit	historical period	1890–1915
-3ua	Feature 25.01, pit house hearth	Rincon	950–1100
-4ua	Feature 25, pit house floor	Rincon	950–1100
-5ua	Feature 21.01, pit house hearth	Rincon	950–1100
-6ua	Feature 23.01, pit house hearth	Rincon	950–1100
-7ua	Feature 18, canal basal oxides	Rincon	950–1100
-8ua	Feature 5, structure fireplace (?)	historical period	1890–1915
-9ua	Feature 22.01, pit house hearth	Rincon	950–1100
-10ua	Feature 27.01, pit house hearth	Rincon	950–1100
-11ua	Feature 33, pit	historical period	1890–1915
-12ua	Feature 34, pit	historical period	1890–1915

[a]All sample numbers prefixed with the site number AZ AA:12:10(ASM).

date the historical-period building any more precisely than is already possible with historical documents. The age of the firing is reasonably well known, and the results from these samples will provide additional information for tracing the behavior of the regional magnetic field in the late historical period.

Basis of Archaeomagnetic Dating

Two fundamental principles underlie archaeomagnetic dating. The first principle is that many desert sediments contain ferromagnetic minerals that, under certain conditions, will acquire a magnetic remanence parallel to the prevailing magnetic field. The most common situation is when sediments and soils at archaeological sites were heated to relatively high temperatures such as occurred with the use of hearths and cooking pits, or such as occurred during the destruction of a structure by fire (for more information on this and other processes see Aitken 1974; Butler 1992; Eighmy and Howard 1991; Eighmy and Sternberg 1990; Irving 1964; McElhinny 1973; Sternberg 1982, 1990; Tarling 1983). The magnetic remanence is acquired upon cooling, and once established, this magnetization is stable and enduring. The second principle is that the direction and strength of the prevailing magnetic field is constantly changing, a phenomenon referred to as *secular variation*. Although the direction and strength of the magnetic field change, archaeomagnetic studies in the southwestern United States have concentrated on documenting directional secular variation. Changes in the magnetic field direction are typically monitored by shifts in the apparent location of the magnetic north pole. Change in the apparent location of the magnetic north pole is commonly referred to as *polar drift* or *polar wander*. Because of polar wander, each archaeomagnetic remanence is an observation of the apparent location of the magnetic north pole at a specific point in time.

We refer to the moment that the remanence is acquired as the *archaeomagnetic event*. To have meaning in archaeological analyses, we must associate the archaeomagnetic event with a specific archaeological event.[1] In the case of hearths and cooking pits that were probably reused, we assume that each heating and cooling cycle successfully erased any previously acquired magnetization and a new remanence was acquired. Following this logic, the recorded remanence represents the last heating and cooling cycle associated with that feature. When these firepits are associated with structures, we assume that the last use and abandonment of the hearth corresponds to the

abandonment of the structure. In the case of samples collected from walls and floors heated during the burning of structures, the archaeomagnetic event is clearly equivalent to the destruction event. In most situations, the archaeomagnetic event probably corresponds to an archaeological abandonment event, but at the most unresolved level, the archaeomagnetic event represents some archaeological event that occurred some time within the use life of the archaeological feature.

Experimental Methods

An archaeomagnetic sample consists of a set of individually oriented and measured specimens obtained from the baked archaeological sediments. We follow standard sampling procedures as described by Eighmy (1990) and apply laboratory procedures well established at the Paleomagnetic Laboratory, Department of Geosciences, University of Arizona.

We have adopted a sample designation protocol similar to that used by the Archaeometric Laboratory at Colorado State University. Most archaeological sites from which we have obtained archaeomagnetic samples have been assigned unique designations in inventories maintained by private, local, state, or federal agencies. The archaeomagnetic sample number is prefaced with this site inventory designation. Within each archaeological site, samples are numbered sequentially. In Arizona, sites often have been assigned designations in several inventory systems. When this occurs, we use the site designation that will be used in the archaeological report in which the archaeomagnetic data will appear. On occasion, we obtain samples from a site that was previously studied by Colorado State University. In these situations we attempt to assign a series of numbers that do not duplicate the previous sample numbers. To avoid potential duplication, we suffix our sample number with the initials "ua" to indicate that the sample was measured at the Archaeomagnetic Program, University of Arizona.

The 12 specimens were collected from baked sediments or soil representing the same archaeomagnetic event. Each specimen was carefully isolated from the remaining matrix and was surrounded by an aluminum mold. The mold was leveled and filled with plaster encasing each specimen. This procedure preserved the integrity of the specimens and allowed us to control for the orientations of the molds. The azimuth of the mold surrounding each specimen was always measured relative to magnetic north using a Brunton compass. The axis along which the azimuth was measured, the sample number, and the specimen designation were etched into the plaster on top of the specimen. Weather permitting, the azimuth also was measured using a sun compass. When corrected for the geographic location, time of year, and time of day, the sun azimuth provides the orientation of the specimen relative to true north. The difference between the magnetic and sun azimuths is the *local magnetic declination* at the time of sampling. We averaged the individual differences between the sun and magnetic azimuths to obtain an *average magnetic declination* for the sampling sites. We have opted for this procedure because we do not always obtain a sun azimuth for each specimen. The local magnetic declination is determined by taking the average difference between the sun and magnetic azimuths for all samples from the archaeological site.

After collection, the samples were returned to the laboratory and stored in a magnetically shielded room with an average field intensity < 200 nT. During analysis, all specimens were stored in a Mu metal shield for additional protection. All measurements were made with a cryogenic magnetometer. Initially, we measured the natural remanent magnetization (NRM) of each specimen and then computed preliminary sample averages to evaluate the cohesiveness of the NRM. Our experience has been that samples characterized by large variance rarely improve during further analysis and probably represent materials that have a weak and unreliable remanence (Sternberg 1982). Even if we recover a measurable archaeomagnetic remanence, the poor precision makes archaeomagnetic dating useless. Sample means with very large confidence intervals (for example $\alpha 95 \geq 9°$) at NRM are not analyzed beyond the NRM stage.

The magnetic profiles of archaeomagnetic samples from the Southwest are fairly consistent. Experimental evidence indicates that magnetite or titanomagnetite is the primary carrier of the remanence (Sternberg 1982:34–37). The archaeomagnetic signal that we are interested in is often overlain by a weaker secondary component acquired during the several hundred years of burial. Alternating field (AF) demagnetization is a useful and appropriate means of removing the secondary magnetization (Sternberg 1990:20). All specimens are demagnetized at peak AF strengths of 2.5, 5.0, 7.5, 10, 15, 20, 30, 40, 50, 60, 70, and 80 mT. This series of measurements provides a broad spectrum of data for evaluating the magnetic profile of each specimen. The results of AF demagnetization are analyzed by principal component analysis (Kirschvink 1980) to obtain the declination and inclination of the remanence for each specimen. No fewer than four demagnetization steps are used, and only specimens with minimum angular deviations less than 5.0° are considered reliable and are used for computing the sample means.

Sample means were obtained by averaging the individual specimen directions using statistical methods based on the Fisherian distribution of points on a sphere. Use of these methods is long established in paleomagnetic studies (Fisher 1953; Irving 1964; McElhinny

1973). Specimens that exhibited irregular demagnetization behavior or that deviate excessively from the other specimens were considered as potential outliers. Each was evaluated individually for physical or experimental evidence to explain the deviation. If there was corroborating evidence that a specimen was different from the others, it was deleted from computation of the final mean. If there was no physical or experimental evidence, the specimen was evaluated as a potential statistical outlier. Specimens that deviated from the mean by more than 3 standard deviations were considered outliers and deleted from computation of the mean. By convention, a virtual geomagnetic pole (VGP) is computed for each sample mean direction (Shuey et al. 1970). The resulting VGP is a standardized measure that facilitates comparison of data from across a relatively large region.

Archaeomagnetic Dating

Because of polar wander, each archaeomagnetically determined VGP has a temporal moment that we refer to as T. It is the value of T that we try to ascertain through archaeomagnetic dating. We make a distinction between two types of archaeomagnetic dating: *calendrical dating* and *relative dating*. The primary difference between calendrical and relative dating is not in the analytical methods, but in the referents. The objective in calendrical dating is to determine when events occurred according to the modern Christian calendar by reference to a master polar wander curve that has been independently calibrated. The objective in relative dating is to determine when archaeological events occurred relative to other archaeomagnetically documented archaeological events. These two forms of dating are similar, but each addresses different kinds of chronological questions, and each is capable of achieving different levels of chronological resolution. Relative dating is the most straightforward and is the more refined temporal method. If a researcher's goal is to associate the age of an archaeomagnetic event to a cultural chronology, or to differentiate between contemporaneous and noncontemporaneous events, or to order archaeological events, relative dating is the most appropriate choice. If a researcher's goal is to determine when an archaeological event occurred in years A.D./B.C., the calendrical approach is more appropriate.

Calendrical Dating

Calendrical dating is a pattern-matching technique similar to dendrochronological dating and is not a radiometric technique, such as radiocarbon dating (Sternberg 1990).

Therefore, determining the age of an archaeomagnetic event of unknown age requires first having a master reconstruction of the pattern of ancient polar wander that is calibrated in years A.D./B.C. The polar wander path, or "master dating curve" as it is often called, is constructed from archaeological contexts where the age of the archaeomagnetic events can be estimated by independently derived dates. In the Southwest, these independent dates are produced by dendrochronology, radiocarbon assays, or cross-dated ceramic associations.[2]

We used the SWCV590 dating curve developed by the Archaeometric Laboratory at Colorado State University (Eighmy 1991) to date these samples. This curve is constructed using Sternberg's (1982:59–64; see also Sternberg and McGuire 1990) moving-window method with 40-year windows advanced by 25-year intervals. Although this is not the only dating curve that has been developed, it is the curve most widely used. Consequently, we maintain its use to foster comparability with the archaeomagnetic dates presented by Colorado State University.

We have adopted a format for the presentation of the calendrical dates that is similar to that for modern radiocarbon calibrations: A.D. 950 (1000) 1050. This date consists of a 95 percent confidence interval surrounding a *best-fit* date.[3] We apply the mathematical dating procedure established by Sternberg (1982:104–105; also Sternberg and McGuire 1990) to obtain the 95 percent confidence interval. This procedure applies the statistical methods of McFadden and Lowes (1981) for the comparison of paleomagnetic directions.[4] The statistics are all interpreted at 0.05 significance, and the dates associated with the master VGPs are applied to the VGP of unknown age following the guidelines suggested by Sternberg.

The best-fit date is intended as a measure of the central tendency of the 95 percent confidence date. Because the ancient pattern of polar wander appears as a squiggly line on the surface of the earth, sample VGPs rarely intercept the polar wander curve, but instead tend to cluster around this curve. Although the best fit date is not the interception of the measured value with the polar wander curve, it does represent the point along the polar wander curve to which the sample VGP is most similar. Our objective in presenting the best-fit date is to present information about the inherent structure of the 95 percent confidence date range.

We obtain the best-fit date by calculating the angular distance between the sample VGP and the master VGPs composing the dating curve; we refer to this statistic as *angle*. The best-fit date is that segment of the master dating curve for which angle takes on the minimum value. Typically, in evaluating the values for angle, we encounter one of two situations. The first is what we refer to as

the "unimodal situation." Within each 95 percent confidence date, there is one minimum value with all other values becoming progressively larger on either side of this minimum. These are straightforward to interpret; the value of the best-fit date is the midpoint of the age window associated with the master VGP at this minimum value. The second type is what we refer to as the "bimodal situation." The plot of the angles exhibits two major troughs of differing magnitudes. These troughs result because the curve loops back on itself. When archaeomagnetic dates span these loops, we often encounter the bimodal situation. One minimum value represents the best fit on the early side of the loop, and the other represents the best fit on the late side of the loop. As an example, given a 95 percent date range of A.D. 930–1350, the best-fit dates may be A.D. 1025 and 1300. These are the smallest values obtained on either side of A.D. 1150, which represents the apex of the A.D. 1000–1200 loop (see Eighmy 1991). Occasionally there are other minor troughs, as well, but we are interested only in the minimum values on either side of the loops. The best-fit date represents the central tendency of the 95 percent confidence date, and we include it to illustrate that the 95 percent confidence dates are not necessarily symmetrical.[5]

Calendrical dating, as it is currently implemented, has three limitations for resolving the age of archaeomagnetic events. The first and most common limitation is that multiple, mutually exclusive, date options may be assigned to a one archaeomagnetic VGP. We cannot distinguish archaeomagnetically which date option is most correct. It is the responsibility of the archaeologists to evaluate these date options against other lines of evidence to determine the most probable date. The second limitation is that the resolution of archaeomagnetic dates is not directly proportional to the uncertainty of the sample VGP. Rather, the resolution is dependent upon the period of time to which the unknown sample dates, the precision of the dating curve, and the distance of the sample VGP from the curve (Sternberg et al. 1990). Increasing the number of specimens to provide for a more accurate and precise estimation of the VGP for a critical context will not result in a more precise archaeomagnetic date using this mathematical dating method. A third limitation is that often, seemingly strong and reliable archaeomagnetic determinations do not date. In recent years we have observed that this phenomenon tends to occur with samples expected to date to the periods ca. A.D. 800 and ca. A.D. 1100. Although the moving-window method used to generate the polar wander curve has the desirable effect of reducing errors associated with independently dating archaeomagnetic events, it also has the undesirable effect of smoothing some of the real variation in the polar wander path. In the case of the A.D. 800 and A.D. 1100 loops, the effect is to reduce the magnitude of these loops. Precisely measured samples that fall along these loops may not date because the polar wander curve underestimates the course of polar wander.

Relative Dating

In relative dating, we apply many of the same methods and procedures used in calendrical dating, but the referents are different. The location of each VGP_i is taken as a proxy for the age, T_i, of the associated archaeological event. For a set of VGPs (VGP_1, VGP_2, . . . VGP_n), there is an equivalent set of temporal moments (T_1, T_2, . . . T_n). Thus, the spatial relationships among the VGPs are equivalent to the temporal relationships among the associated archaeological events. We can then evaluate an hypothesis such as $T_1 = T_2$ by evaluating the equivalent hypothesis that $VGP_1 = VGP_2$. Similarly, based on the assumption that polar wander will tend to be linear over short periods of time, we can identify the linear trajectory inherent in a distribution of VGPs and arrange them into an objective relative sequence based on the position of the VGPs relative to the linear trajectory.

Assessing Contemporaneity of Archaeomagnetic Events

The goal of this analysis is to evaluate the hypothesis if $T_i = T_j$ and thus identify contemporaneous events. An apparently simple solution would be to evaluate the calendrical dates obtained above to determine if the date ranges for any set of samples overlap. If the estimated calendrical dates overlapped, there would seem to be some probability that the archaeomagnetic events were contemporary. However, many archaeomagnetic events with overlapping calendrical dates can be shown empirically to be temporally discrete (see Deaver 1988:114).[6] This seemingly contradictory situation arises because we can measure the location of the ancient VGP more precisely than we can estimate when the VGP was in a particular location. The most direct way of assessing whether or not any two archaeomagnetic events could have occurred at the same time is to statistically compare the calculated VGPs.

To do this, we apply the statistical methods of McFadden and Lowes (1981). These are the same methods used to compare a VGP of unknown age with the archaeomagnetic dating curve. In this situation, however, we use these methods to evaluate the similarity or dissimilarity between any two archaeomagnetically determined VGPs. We perform a series of pairwise comparisons between

VGPs in preselected data sets. The null hypothesis is that the two archaeomagnetic VGPs being compared are the same ($VGP_1 = VGP_2$). If the computed probability for the F-statistic is greater than 0.95, we reject the null hypothesis and conclude that $VGP_1 \neq VGP_2$. It follows then that $T_1 \neq T_2$. Alternatively, if the computed probability for the F-statistic is equal to or less than 0.95, we must accept the null hypothesis and conclude that the difference between the VGPs is due to chance alone, and thus $T_1 \approx T_2$. The ages of the two events are not necessarily equal, but they cannot be differentiated at the desired level of significance.

Whenever the temporal span represented by VGP_1 . . . VGP_n is large enough that the pattern of polar wander loops back on itself, we will derive spurious comparisons, because archaeomagnetic events of dissimilar age will have similar VGPs. Consequently, it is helpful to create separate data sets for this analysis. Subsets should be selected on the basis of the expected or measured age of the archaeological event and the general character of polar wander as depicted in the SWCV590 curve. Generally, these comparisons can be performed for three periods: A.D. 600–800, 800–1100, and 1100–1800. Within these periods, the overall direction of polar wander appears to be unidirectional.

Determining a Relative Sequence of Events

The goal of this analysis is to provide an independent temporal ordering of archaeological contexts based on the relative position of the archaeomagnetic VGPs, so that diachronic trends in the archaeological record may be perceived. This analysis uses the same data subsets defined for the contemporaneity evaluations for similar reasons. We must have some degree of confidence that over the period of time represented by the subset of T_1 . . . T_n, the polar wander was unidirectional. This assumption appears to be generally true when the data subsets are restricted to the three calendrical periods delimited above. Even if we cannot exactly segregate the archaeological contexts to these three periods, as would occur with archaeological contexts expected to date near the boundaries, we can still derive important sequential information with the loss of some resolution near the beginning or ends of the periods.

The VGPs were analyzed by adapting Engebretson and Beck's (1978) procedures for measuring the shape of directional data to the archaeological situation at hand. As in the other archaeomagnetic dating procedures, the spatial locations of the VGPs are taken as proxies for the ages of the archaeomagnetic events relative to the one another. This analysis is accomplished in two steps. First, it is necessary to ascertain whether time is a major determinant of the VGP locations. Second, in those cases where time is found to be a determinant, a series of mathematical transformations are performed to assign values to the VGPs reflecting the relative ages of the archaeomagnetic events.

Whether or not time is a major determinant of this distribution is ascertained by evaluating the shape of the VGP distribution. We assume that the distribution of VGPs will be elliptical when time is a significant determinant to the VGP locations. Conversely, when the distribution of VGPs is circular, we assume that time is not a major factor, and that the dispersion of VGPs is determined primarily by random sampling errors. It is not time per se that creates the ellipticity of the VGP distribution. Rather, it is the effects of polar wander that occur over time that creates the ellipticity. The ellipticity of the data set is measured by an eccentricity statistic, e. The value of e varies from 0 for a circular distribution to 1 for a linear distribution. Data sets with values of e near 1 are judged to be elliptical.[7]

For elliptical distributions, we estimate the major semi-axis, l_f, for the distribution. This is the axis along which the VGPs are elongated. Accepting that the elongation is due to polar wander, l_f is then the general course of polar wander through these VGPs. It is not the polar wander path, but a general approximation of the overall trend of polar wander path. Consequently, l_f also represents the general time line through the events represented by the VGPs. The ages of the VGPs are determined according to their position relative to l_f. Variation perpendicular to l_f is caused by random sampling error and the nonlinearity of the true polar wander path. Although this method orders the VGPs, it cannot independently determine the direction in which time is progressing. Information on the direction of time is obtained from the cumulative knowledge we have amassed, first, on how past secular variation correlates with the archaeological periods and phases, and second, how this correlates with known archaeological cultural sequences (Deaver 1989c; Eighmy and McGuire 1988).

Determining the relative sequence for a data set involves six sequential steps: (1) A composite VGP is calculated for each data subset. (2) The VGPs are rotated so that the composite VGP is coincident with the Earth's rotation axis. (3) The three directional cosines, XYZ,[8] are calculated for each VGP. (4) After these coordinates are calculated, the data points are projected orthogonally onto the XY plane by setting $z = 0$. The composite mean of the distribution is now the origin on the XY plane. Because the data points are all located relatively near the Earth's rotation axis, any distortion resulting from "flattening" the distribution of VGPs from the surface of the sphere onto the XY plane is inconsequential. (5) The

e-statistic and the slope of l_f are calculated. (6) The data set is once again rotated around the composite mean so that l_f is coincident with the X axis. The relative age of each data point can now be determined by the value X_r, which is the X coordinate of each VGP after this last rotation. The value of X_r can vary between -1 and 1, but because the VGPs are located near the Earth's rotation axis, the actual values for sample VGPs typically vary over a range much smaller than this.

For the periods before A.D. 800 and after A.D. 1150, the direction of polar wander was easterly; thus, the values for X_r will have a positive correlation with the progression of time. For these periods, the value of X_r for each VGP is taken as the measure of the relative date.[9] For the period A.D. 800–1150, the direction of polar wander was westerly; thus, there will be a negative correlation between the value of X_r and the progression of time. It is important to note that the rate of polar wander was not constant, and a given distance therefore does not correspond to an exact number of calendar years. Furthermore, because of the looping character of polar wander, the relative archaeomagnetic dates assigned are specific to a given data set; the values cannot be compared from one data set to another.

Results

The final archaeomagnetic data are presented in Table B.2. Reliable archaeomagnetic measurements were obtained from all of the prehistoric samples from the pit houses, but not from the basal oxides of the canal. We conclude that the mineralization processes at the base of the canal were not sufficient to allow for the acquisition of a strong and reliable archaeomagnetic signal. As a whole, the historical-period samples were not as well magnetized as the prehistoric samples. The samples from Features 19 and 34 were very imprecise, and we conclude that they also are unreliable. The precision of the samples from two other historical-period pits and from the adobe building could be classified generally as fair to poor quality based on the precision of the measurements. Only the reliably magnetized samples from the prehistoric houses were dated (Table B.3). Because the objective of collecting and analyzing the historical-period contexts was to obtain archaeomagnetic determinations of known age, these samples were not dated even though they are listed in Table B.3.

Most of the samples represent independent archaeomagnetic events. The only exceptions are the two samples from Feature 25. One dating sample was taken from the hearth and the other from the floor. These two samples

Table B.2. Final Archaeomagnetic Data for Sunset Mesa Ruin

Sample Number[a]	N_2/N_1[b]	Paleodirection					Virtual Geomagnetic Pole			
		Inclination	Declination	J_r[c]	$\alpha95$	k	Latitude	Longitude	dm[d]	dp[d]
-1ua	12/12	75.37	288.23	1.23E-05	13.8	10.9	75.37	288.23	21.32	16.50
-2ua	12/12	79.05	309.15	3.89E-05	4.4	97.53	79.05	309.15	6.40	4.63
-3ua	12/12	77.43	192.99	3.65E-04	1.8	610.96	77.43	192.99	2.59	1.91
-4ua	12/12	86.05	238.62	2.90E-05	2.6	288.21	86.05	238.62	3.66	2.62
-5ua	12/12	75.60	195.77	3.79E-04	1.0	2,049.82	75.60	195.77	1.44	1.08
-6ua	18/18	80.99	212.66	4.67E-04	1.7	417.74	80.99	212.66	2.52	1.87
-7ua	8/12	86.77	359.80	1.67E-05	9.6	34.09	86.77	359.80	12.92	8.67
-8ua	9/13	82.88	264.83	4.72E-05	5.3	93.75	82.88	264.83	7.92	5.87
-9ua	11/12	73.87	200.22	5.42E-04	2.1	493.42	73.87	200.22	3.15	2.41
-10ua	11/12	75.60	194.82	1.03E-03	1.6	791.26	75.60	194.82	2.43	1.81
-11ua	7/12	84.98	260.65	2.97E-05	7.9	60.05	84.98	260.65	11.37	8.24
-12ua	6/12	73.11	298.71	1.68E-05	10.0	45.56	73.11	298.71	15.37	11.77

[a] All sample numbers prefixed with the site number AZ AA:12:10(ASM).
[b] N_2 = number of specimens used in computation of mean; N_1 = number of specimens collected.
[c] Intensity of magnetic moment in Gauss.
[d] dm and dp are the errors associated with the virtual geomagnetic pole location.

Table B.3. Archaeomagnetic Calendrical Dates for Sunset Mesa Ruin

Sample Number[a]	Context	Archaeomagnetic Dates at 95% Confidence (A.D.)
-1ua	Feature 19	no date, poor sample
-2ua	Feature 24	no date, historical-period context
-3ua	Feature 25.01	1005 (1100) 1195
-4ua	Feature 25	930 (950, 975) 1020 1330 (1450) 1645
-5ua	Feature 21.01	1005 (1025) 1045 1080 (1150) 1170
-6ua	Feature 23.01	930 (1025) 1045 1230 (1275) 1370
-7ua	Feature 18	no date, poor sample
-8ua	Feature 5	no date, historical-period context
-9ua	Feature 22.01	no date, off curve
-10ua	Feature 27.01	1005 (1150) 1170
-11ua	Feature 33	no date, historical-period context
-12ua	Feature 34	no date, poor sample

[a]All sample numbers prefixed with the site number AZ AA:12:10(ASM).

should be effectively representing the same archaeological event, the abandonment of the house. The virtual geomagnetic pole locations from these two samples are statistically distinct. We cannot reconcile this discrepancy. It seems unlikely that the two samples are representing discrete events, although it is possible. The field notes indicate that the floor area sampled was resting on soft sand and was difficult to sample. The precision of the measured magnetization (see Table B.2), however, suggests that sampling error was minimal. In view of the inconsistencies, both samples are maintained in the dating interpretations below. These samples provide two different scenarios for the temporal relationship of Feature 25 with the other structures.

Archaeomagnetic Chronology of the Rincon Phase Component

The results of the calendrical dating of the Rincon phase component are presented in Table B.3. Generally, these dates confirm the hypothesized age based on the archaeological information previously available. Two of the samples, -4ua and -6ua, have two potential dates because of the A.D. 1000–1200 loop in the dating curve. The early date option in both cases is consistent with the archaeological information. The later date options have values greater than A.D. 1200. A third sample, -5ua, also has two date options, one with a value between A.D. 1005 and 1025 and the other with a value between A.D. 1080 and 1170. In this case, the early option is not due to a loop in the curve, but to the fact that the A.D. 1005–1025 segment of the SWCV590 curve is the least precisely defined segment. The later date option is the more probable estimate of the age. Sample -9ua did not produce a calendrical date. The magnetization of this sample defines a relatively low VGP position (73.87° north latitude) that is significantly lower than the dating curve at the nearest point, ca. A.D. 1100. We do not believe, however, that the sample determination is in error. As noted above, we have consistently observed similar low latitude positions for samples that should date around A.D. 1100 from the Hohokam, Anasazi, and other culture areas. Our conclusion is that the ancient path of secular variation probably reached a lower latitude position than is currently modeled by the dating curve. We cannot provide a calendrical date for sample -9ua, but we can suggest that its VGP location is indicative of a low latitude magnetic pole ca. A.D. 1100.

The VGPs determined for the samples from the Rincon phase houses show patterns in their spatial distribution that may indicate the relative ages of the represented

Table B.4. Results of Pairwise Statistical Comparison of Rincon Phase Archaeomagnetic Poles

Sample Number[a]	Context	-9ua	-10ua	-5ua	-3ua	-6ua	-4ua
-9ua	Feature 22.01	0.0000[b]					
-10ua	Feature 27.01	0.7554	0.0000				
-5ua	Feature 21.01	0.7979	0.0321	0.0000			
-3ua	Feature 25.01	0.9823	0.7158	0.8519	0.0000		
-6ua	Feature 23.01	1.0000	1.0000	1.0000	0.9993	0.000	
-4ua	Feature 25	1.0000	1.0000	1.0000	1.0000	0.9992	0.0000

[a]All sample numbers prefixed with the site number AZ AA:12:10(ASM). Order of presentation is predicted sequence.
[b]Computed probability of F-statistic.

houses (Table B.4). The distribution of VGPs is extremely elongated, with an eccentricity value in excess of 0.98. This value suggests that the VGPs are not randomly scattered, but reflect the course of geomagnetic secular variation that occurred during the period these houses were occupied. Relative to the elongation axis, and assuming that these houses do in fact date before A.D. 1150, the predicted sequence of structures is as follows: Feature 25 (floor), Feature 23, Feature 25 (hearth), Feature 21, Feature 27, and Feature 22. When this sequence is evaluated with regard to the results of the contemporaneity evaluations (see Table B.4), it is evident that Feature 25 (hearth), Feature 21, Feature 27, and Feature 22 are more similar to one another than to Feature 23 or Feature 25 (floor). Features 25 (hearth), 21, 27, and 22 may represent a relatively brief occupational span during which the use and abandonments of Features 25 (hearth), 21, and 27 were essentially contemporaneous. The VGPs associated with Features 22 (-9ua) and 25 (hearth) (-3ua) are significantly different. This suggests that the abandonment of Feature 22 occurred at a time detectably later than the abandonment of Feature 25. The abandonment of Feature 22, however, is not detectably later than the abandonment of Features 21 and 27. The abandonment event of Feature 22 is the terminal event among the structures represented.

The VGPs determined from the magnetization in the sample from Feature 23 (-6ua) and from the floor of Feature 25 (-4ua) are significantly different from all other VGPs. As the data stand, these archaeomagnetic events are discrete unto themselves. The fact that the fired floor of Feature 25 (sample -4ua) appears to be earlier than the hearth (sample -3ua) leads to further suspicion that, although sample -4ua was measured precisely, the location of the VGP may be unreliable.

End Notes

1. In his seminal discussion of archaeological dating theory, Dean (1978) defines four events of importance in archaeological dating. These are: the target event (E_t), the dated event (E_d), the reference event (E_r), and the bridging event (E_b). E_t is the archaeological event that we wish to date, E_d is the event we are dating, E_r is the potentially datable event most closely related to E_t, and E_b is the event or events that link E_d with E_t. In archaeomagnetic analysis E_d is the archaeomagnetic event, and in most situations E_r is an archaeological abandonment event.

2. The ages are not perfectly known and are a source of potentially significant error. While at the University of Arizona, Robert S. Sternberg developed a moving-window method for smoothing archaeomagnetic data that explicitly accounts for the age uncertainties in the independent dating of the archaeomagnetic events. This method is now commonly used by us and the Archaeometric Laboratory of Colorado State University to generate master dating curves from a collection of archaeomagnetic events of known age.

3. The 95 percent confidence date range is equivalent with the *Residual Date Range* presented by the Archaeometric Laboratory at Colorado State University. The Archaeometric Laboratory does not provide a date comparable to our *best-fit* date.

4. The equations of McFadden and Lowes (1981) are also applied to obtain relative dates.

5. In some analyses, researchers have combined and averaged archaeomagnetic dates from independent events to obtain a more finely resolved estimate for the dates of archaeological

phases and periods (see Dean 1991; Eighmy and McGuire 1988). These analyses have turned to the statistical analysis of radiocarbon dates as a model. The researchers assumed that the 95 percent confidence date range was quasi-normal and took the midpoint as the estimate of the mean. However, this is not always the case. Furthermore, the tendency for the best-fit date to be near one end or the other of the 95 percent confidence range is not random, but patterned. The midpoint of the 95 percent confidence range consistently overestimates the best-fit date in some cases, consistently underestimates the best-fit date in other cases, or it indicates a single mean date when in fact there are two competing best-fit dates.

6. In the example cited, two samples from the site of Las Colinas were obtained from hearths in two pit structures that were dated to the Sacaton phase on the basis of associated ceramics. The interpreted archaeomagnetic date for one sample was A.D. 900–1070 and for the other sample was A.D. 860–1030. Based on the archaeological age and the overlap of the archaeomagnetic dates, it seemed that these two structures were possibly contemporary. However, the results of the pairwise comparison of the mean VGPs indicated that the VGPs were different ($p > 0.999$), and thus the archaeomagnetic events were not contemporaneous. This example illustrates the typical situation in archaeological and archaeomagnetic dating, where at each level of inference the resolution of the dating information becomes more refined.

7. Although the procedures of Engebretson and Beck (1978) provide for calculating a value of e for a set of directional data, they do not provide a method of assigning a probability to a calculated value of e. We cannot determine for a data set what value of e would be significant at a desired level of significance, and the decision on whether or not a data set is sufficiently elongated for this analysis is based on our judgement that values of e greater than 0.5 indicate strongly elliptical data sets. In most of our applications the value of e is usually much greater.

8. $x = \text{cosine(longitude)} \times \text{cosine(latitude)}$; $y = \text{sine(longitude)} \times \text{cosine(latitude)}$; $z = \text{sine(latitude)}$

9. The location of the sample VGPs are not perfectly known, and there is error associated with assigning relative dates to the VGPs. Furthermore, the errors in locating the sample VGPs are not constant from one sample to the next. Because of these issues, the sequence of the VGPs should not be taken as an exact ordering, but emphasis instead should be placed on the trend in the data set. We suggest that before the relative order of two sample VGPs is accepted as presented, the researcher should evaluate the results of the contemporaneity evaluation of these two VGPs. If the VGPs are not contemporary, then the relative order of the two VGPs is probably valid. We also offer the following bootstrap method for estimating the error in the relative placement of each sample. The estimated 95 percent confidence interval for the calculated relative age is approximately $\text{sine(dm} \times \text{dp)}^{-\frac{1}{2}}$, where dm and dp are the errors given for the VGP location.

APPENDIX C

Obsidian-Source Analysis

M. Steven Shackley

The report for this analysis is necessarily brief because of the small sample size. A discussion of the analytical methods can be found in Shackley (1992, 1994, 1995a), and source standard data is discussed in Shackley (1995a). The presence of artifacts produced from Mule Creek glass is not uncommon in sites in this region, although obsidian from pre-Classic period contexts is uncommon relative to Classic period sites (Mitchell and Shackley 1995; Table C.1). The character of chemical variability in the Mule Creek Caldera area is discussed in detail in Shackley (1995b). "Unknown A" appears commonly in sites in southern Arizona in all contexts and is probably located somewhere west of Organ Pipe National Monument and south of the Sauced Mountains (Shackley 1995a). Whereas its peralkaline character is more commonly associated with the Sierra Madre Volcanic Province (Chihuahua/Sonora), it does not appear to be from a locality that far south. It probably can be considered a relatively "local" source.

Table C.1. EDXRF Concentrations for Archaeological Samples from Sunset Mesa Ruin (AZ AA:12:10 [ASM])

Sample	Ti	Mn	Fe	Rb	Sr	Y	Zr	Mb	Source
776	919.22	184.30	12,040.45	217.12	12.80	53.17	168.19	13.83	Mule Cr (Mule Mts)
811	1,548.03	516.61	27,871.44	151.43	9.55	85.67	755.63	54.70	Unknown A
878	1,578.03	427.80	24,999.83	134.77	11.75	64.06	647.01	36.66	Unknown A

Note: All measurements in parts per million (PPM).

Petrographic Analysis

Qualitative Analysis of Sedentary Period Potsherds from Tucson, Arizona, with Emphasis on Sunset Mesa Ruin

James M. Heidke

Native American pottery produced in the Southwest often contains abundant temper, such as sand, disaggregated rock, or crushed sherd. Both sand and disaggregated rock tempers can be used as indicators of the provenance of archaeological ceramics when their geological sources are identified (Arnold 1985; Miksa 1995; Miksa and Heidke 1995; Schaller 1994; Shepard 1936, 1942).

The temper composition of 428 sherds from eight sites selected by SRI was examined in order to infer the likely production source of the sherds. [*Editor's note:* In actuality 556, sherds were analyzed from nine sites. The additional sherds were selected from the Badger Hole Ranch site (AZ AA:12:40 [ASM]), which dates to the late Rincon and Tanque Verde phases. The results from this site were excluded from this report because they do not appear to be relevant to this discussion. Only a small percentage of these later sherds could be assigned to a petrofacies, and those that could reflect a distinctive and more diverse temper-use strategy (see Heidke 1996) that is not germane to the current discussion, which focuses on early and middle Rincon phase ceramic production. The Badger Hole Ranch site is currently being investigated by SRI, and the results of the petrographic analysis will be presented in reports that are being prepared for the site. In this manner, we will have the opportunity to assess these results with reference to other contemporary materials.] The eight sites, which all are assigned to the Rincon phase, are: Sunset Mesa Ruin (AZ AA:12:10 [ASM]), the Hodges site (AZ AA:12:18 [ASM]), the Hardy site (AZ BB:9:14 [ASM]), the Observatory site (AZ BB:9:101 [ASM]), AZ BB:13:45 (ASM), Punta de Agua (BB:13:50

[ASM]), the Toland site (AZ BB:13:321 [ASM]), and Seneca Terrace II (AZ BB:13:444 [ASM]). Temper data recorded from four Middle Rincon Red-on-brown vessels and one Rincon Polychrome vessel recently recovered from the Hodges site (Swartz 1996) were added to the data set to supplement that site's sample. With the addition of these vessels, the sample examined totaled 433 specimens.

Materials Procurement Attributes

Three attributes were used to characterize temper composition: temper type, temper source generic, and temper source specific.

Temper Type

The temper type variable was used to characterize whether or not the prehistoric potter added a tempering material, such as crushed gneiss or schist, to a sand temper or even substituted crushed rock for sand altogether. An example of the former is the addition of small amounts of gneiss, a metamorphic rock, to the volcanic sand temper of the Beehive petrofacies. An example of the latter is the use of crushed gneiss as the sole tempering material.

Temper Source: Generic

Sands derived from similar source rocks under similar conditions will have similar compositions. When we study sands within a well-defined region and determine that those sands can be broken into subsets on the basis of similar compositions, we have defined generic compositions. Generic compositions are also visible in sand-tempered pottery, where they are characterized as generic temper sources. Further study of the sands within a well-defined region may determine that the generic sand compositions can be broken into subsets on the basis of additional compositional data and spatial contiguity. When that is accomplished, we have defined petrofacies, or sand composition zones. Petrofacies compositions may also be visible in sand-tempered pottery, where they are characterized as specific temper sources. These specific temper source zones are also referred to as petrofacies.

Currently, 36 petrofacies are defined for the greater Tucson Basin (Figure D.1), based on the analysis of 291 point-counted sand samples. The petrofacies represent six generic compositions. Listed below are the six generic compositions, the petrofacies included in each of them, and the symbol used to indicate each petrofacies location in Figure D.1.

Granitic sand sources: Cañada del Oro (3), Tortolita (E), Sierrita (O), Amole (Q), and Sutherland (S) petrofacies.

Granitic and mixed lithic (volcanic, metamorphic, and sedimentary) sand sources: Santa Cruz River (1), Brawley Wash (2), McClellan Wash (6), Durham (F), Santa Rita (G), University (H), Black Mountain (K), Hughes (P), and Sahuarita (Z) petrofacies.

Metamorphic core complex sand sources: Rillito Creek (4), Pantano Wash (5), Tanque Verde Creek (8), Rincon (A), Catalina (B), and Owl Head (N) petrofacies.

Mixed volcanic and granitic sand sources: West Branch of the Santa Cruz River (7), Samaniego (C), Rillito (M), Rillito West (MW), and Cocoraque (U) petrofacies.

Volcanic sand sources: Avra (D), Empire (I), Beehive (J1), Twin Hills (J2), Wasson (J3), Golden Gate (L), Batamote (R), Recortado (T), Waterman (W), and Roskruge (Y) petrofacies.

Other metamorphic sand source: Dos Titos (V) petrofacies.

The six generic compositions are based on differences in the relative percentage of sand-sized quartz, feldspar, volcanic rock fragments, metamorphic rock fragments, and sedimentary rock fragments documented during petrographic point counting of thin-sectioned wash sand samples (see Heidke, Miksa, and Wiley [1996] for a discussion of sand sample preparation and point-counting method).

Temper Source: Specific

In the analysis of prehistoric pottery, the difference between the "generic" and "specific" temper source attributes lies in the finer level of spatial resolution implied by the petrofacies. In practice, the information represented by the generic attribute is redundant with the information represented by the specific attribute when the sand temper observed in a given sherd permits its assignment to a petrofacies. However, petrofacies assignments made with the aid of a low-power, reflected light microscope should be confirmed through petrographic analysis of thin sections made from a sample of the sherds.

Methods

The coding index used in this study is reproduced at the end of this report. Sherd edges were examined at 10× to 15× magnification, using a Unitron ZSM binocular microscope fitted with a Stocker and Yale Lite Mite Series 9 circular illuminator, in order to determine temper type, generic source, and specific source whenever possible. Data were entered directly into a database file.

Results

The results of the study are reported in Table D.1. The temper type, generic source, and specific source characterizations reported here could be tested by point counting sherds included in the analysis. The last column of Table D.1 reports whether or not each sherd included in the current analysis is large enough to produce a thin section for point counting.

In order to interpret the temper characterization data, one needs to know in which petrofacies each site is located. Two of the sites are located within the T2 terrace of a trunk stream and are, therefore, assigned to that stream's petrofacies: Sunset Mesa Ruin is assigned to the Santa Cruz River Petrofacies and the Hodges site to the Rillito Creek Petrofacies. Three of the sites—Observatory, Seneca Terrace II, and Toland—are located in the

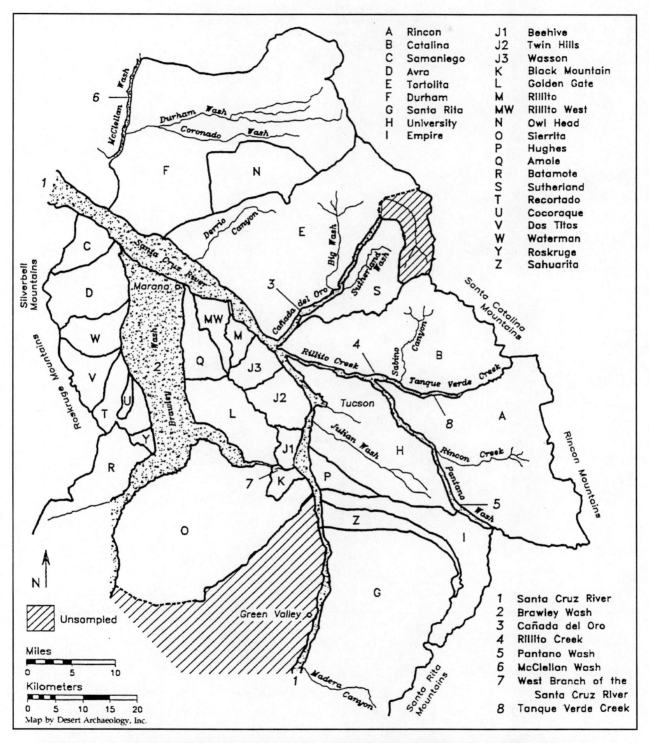

Figure D.1. Current petrofacies map of the Tucson Basin, showing their names and letter designations.

A Rincon
B Catalina
C Samaniego
D Avra
E Tortolita
F Durham
G Santa Rita
H University
I Empire

J1 Beehive
J2 Twin Hills
J3 Wasson
K Black Mountain
L Golden Gate
M Rillito
MW Rillito West
N Owl Head
O Sierrita
P Hughes
Q Amole
R Batamote
S Sutherland
T Recortado
U Cocoraque
V Dos Titos
W Waterman
Y Roskruge
Z Sahuarita

1 Santa Cruz River
2 Brawley Wash
3 Cañada del Oro
4 Rillito Creek
5 Pantano Wash
6 McClellan Wash
7 West Branch of the Santa Cruz River
8 Tanque Verde Creek

Unsampled

Miles
0   5   10

Kilometers
0 5 10 15 20

Map by Desert Archaeology, Inc.

Table D.1. Summary of Temper-Characterization Data

Sample Number, by ASM Site Number	Bag or PD Number	Temper Type	Temper Source Generic	Temper Source Specific	Comments	Section?[a]
AA:12:10						
1	363	3	1	J1		no
2	461	3	1	J1		no
3	410	4	1	J2		yes
4	603	4	1	J1		no
5	699	4	1	J1		no
6	699	4	1	J1		no
7	676	4	1	J1		yes
8	374	2	1	J1		yes
9	671	4	1	J1		no
10	90	3	1	J1		yes
11	758	3	1	J1		yes
12	70	6	-9	-9		yes
13	795	4	-9	-9		no
14	704	5	-9	-9	TSG = 2 or 3	yes
15	576	4	1	J2		yes
16	576	4	2	-9	TSS = E or S?	yes
17	622	4	1	-9		yes
18	408	7	-9	-9		no
19	504	3	1	J1		yes
20	360	3	1	J2		yes
21	42	5	-9	-9	TSG = 2 or 3	yes
22	42	4	-9	-9	TSG = 2 or 3	yes
23	894	4	2	-9	TSS = E or S?	yes
24	28	4	1	J1		yes
25	29	4	1	J1		yes
26	374	3	1	J1		no
27	516	3	1	J1		no
28	453	3	1	J1		yes
29	563	3	1	J1		no
30	564	4	1	J1		no
31	269	4	2	-9	TSS = E or S?	no
32	269	3	1	J2		yes
33	269	3	1	J2		no
34	374	4	1	J1		yes
35	374	3	1	J2		yes
36	374	3	1	J1		yes
37	374	7	-9	-9		yes
38	374	4	1	J1		yes
39	516	4	1	J2		no

Sample Number, by ASM Site Number	Bag or PD Number	Temper Type	Temper Source Generic	Temper Source Specific	Comments	Section?[a]
40	516	1	-9	-9		yes
41	516	6	3	-9		yes
42	516	3	1	J1		yes
43	516	7	-9	-9		yes
44	449	4	1	-9	TSS = J2 or J3?	no
45	449	3	1	J1		yes
46	449	5	-9	-9	TSG = 2 or 3	no
47	298	3	1	J1		no
48	298	3	1	J2		yes
49	298	3	1	J1		yes
50	298	4	1	J1		yes
51	298	4	1	J2		yes
52	298	3	1	J2		yes
53	374	4	1	J1		no
54	273	3	1	J1		yes
55	298	2	1	J1		yes
56	451	3	1	J1		no
57	451	4	1	J2		no
58	451	4	1	J2		yes
59	514	4	1	J2		no
60	514	2	1	J1		yes
61	514	4	1	J1		yes
62	514	3	1	J1		no
63	379	4	1	J2		no
64	379	4	1	J1		yes
65	516	4	1	J1		no
66	516	3	1	J2		no
67	516	4	1	J1		yes
68	516	4	1	J1		no
69	516	3	1	J1		no
70	516	4	1	J1		no
71	269	4	1	J1		no
72	269	2	1	J1		yes
73	370	3	1	J1		no
74	374	4	1	J1		yes
75	374	4	1	J2		yes
76	374	4	1	J2		yes
77	374	3	1	J2		yes
78	374	3	1	J1		no
79	374	4	1	J1		no
80	699	4	1	J1		no

Sample Number, by ASM Site Number	Bag or PD Number	Temper Type	Temper Source Generic	Temper Source Specific	Comments	Section?[a]
81	622	4	1	J1		yes
82	568	4	1	J1		no
83	344	4	1	J1		no
84	585	4	1	J1		no
85	619	4	-9	-9	TSG = 2 or 30	no
86	575	4	1	-9		yes
87	575	7	-9	-9	TSG = 2 or 3	yes
88	575	4	1	-9	TSS = J2 or J3?	yes
89	575	4	-9	-9	TSG = 1 or 30?	yes
90	575	4	-9	-9	TSG = 1/TSS = J2 or TSG = 30/TSS = 1?	yes
91	559	3	1	J1		no
92	559	4	1	J1		no
93	559	4	1	J1		no
94	559	4	2	-9		yes
95	568	4	1	J1		no
96	568	10	-9	-9	grades into schist	no
97	568	7	-9	-9	TSG = 2 or 3	no
98	532	3	1	J1		no
99	532	10	-9	-9		no
100	532	8	2	-9	TSS = E or S?	no
101	532	2	1	J1		no
102	532	10	-9	-9	grades into schist	yes
103	532	4	1	-9		yes
104	532	4	1	-9	TSS = J1 or J3?	yes
105	704	4	1	-9	TSS = J2?	yes
106	704	4	2	-9		no
107	704	5	-9	-9	TSG = 2 or 3	no
108	614	4	1	J2		yes
109	614	4	1	J1		yes
110	614	3	1	J1		no
111	614	4	1	-9	TSS = J2 or J3?	yes
112	614	4	2	-9		yes
113	577	3	1	J2		no
114	532	4	1	J1		no
115	522	4	1	J2		yes
116	581	4	1	J1		yes
117	699	4	1	J1		yes
118	699	4	1	J1		yes
119	344	3	1	J1		yes
120	585	4	1	J1		yes

Sample Number, by ASM Site Number	Bag or PD Number	Temper Type	Temper Source Generic	Temper Source Specific	Comments	Section?[a]
121	581	3	1	J2		no
122	581	4	1	J1		no
123	614	4	1	J1		no
124	614	3	1	J1		yes
125	619	3	1	J2		yes
126	577	4	1	J1		yes
127	577	4	1	J2		yes
128	577	4	1	J2		yes
129	532	4	1	J1		yes
130	476	3	1	J1		yes
131	480	4	1	J1		yes
132	422	6	1	J1		yes
133	339	4	1	J1		yes
134	476	3	1	J1		no
135	476	3	1	J1		yes
136	476	4	1	J1		yes
137	476	4	1	J2		yes
138	476	2	1	J1		yes
139	476	3	1	J1		yes
140	461	7	-9	-9		yes
141	461	4	1	J1		yes
142	461	7	-9	-9		yes
143	480	4	1	J1		yes
144	480	3	1	J2		no
145	480	4	1	J1		yes
146	422	4	1	J1		yes
147	422	4	1	J1		yes
148	422	3	1	J1		yes
149	422	3	1	J1		yes
150	422	3	1	J1		yes
151	422	4	1	J1		yes
152	410	3	1	J1		yes
153	410	4	1	J1		no
154	408	3	1	J1		no
155	408	4	1	J1		yes
156	408	4	1	J1		yes
157	363	4	1	J1		yes
158	363	3	1	J1		yes
159	400	4	1	J1		yes
160	400	4	1	J1		yes
161	405	3	1	J1		yes

Sample Number, by ASM Site Number	Bag or PD Number	Temper Type	Temper Source Generic	Temper Source Specific	Comments	Section?[a]
162	363	4	1	J1		no
163	461	4	1	J2		yes
164	480	4	1	J1		yes
165	480	4	1	J1		no
166	752	3	1	J1		yes
167	752	4	1	J1		no
168	476	4	1	J1		no
169	476	3	1	J1		yes
170	422	4	1	J1		no
171	422	3	1	J1		no
172	408	3	1	J1		yes
173	410	4	1	J1		yes
174	410	3	1	J2	not St. Mary's Ruin	yes
175	405	3	1	J1		no
176	362	3	1	J2		yes
177	362	4	1	J1		no
178	360	3	1	J1		yes
179	358	3	1	J2		no
180	362	3	1	J1		yes
181	362	4	1	J1		yes
182	461	3	1	J1		yes
183	422	4	1	J1		yes
184	410	3	1	J1		yes
185	363	4	1	J1		yes
186	405	3	1	J1		yes
187	309	4	30	-9		yes
188	369	4	1	J1		yes
189	316	4	1	J1		yes
190	334	4	1	J1		no
191	334	5	-9	-9	TSG = 2 or 3	yes
192	386	3	-9	-9	TSG = 1 or 30	yes
193	386	4	1	J1		yes
194	386	10	-9	-9		yes
195	386	7	1	J1		yes
196	369	4	1	J2		yes
197	369	-9	-9	-9	TT = 2 or 3; TSG = 1? TSS = J2?	no
198	369	4	2	-9		yes
199	369	4	1	J1		no
200	300	3	1	J2		yes
201	300	10	-9	-9		yes

Sample Number, by ASM Site Number	Bag or PD Number	Temper Type	Temper Source Generic	Temper Source Specific	Comments	Section?[a]
202	306	5	-9	-9	TSG = 2 or 3	yes
203	323	4	1	J1		yes
204	323	4	1	-9		yes
205	323	4	1	J1		yes
206	323	3	1	J1		yes
207	323	7	-9	-9		yes
208	323	4	1	-9		yes
209	438	4	1	J1		yes
210	386	3	1	J1		yes
211	323	4	1	J1		yes
212	300	3	-9	-9	TSG = 7?	yes
213	395	4	1	-9	TSS = J1 or J2	yes
214	626	4	30	-9		no
215	626	4	2	-9		yes
216	586	4	1	J1		yes
217	671	4	2	-9		yes
218	662	3	-9	-9	TSG = 2 or 3	yes
219	676	5	-9	-9	TSG = 2 or 3	yes
220	676	4	1	J1		yes
221	676	3	2	-9		yes
222	626	10	-9	-9	phyllite & sand	no
223	626	7	-9	-9		yes
224	626	4	1	J1		no
225	586	4	1	J2		yes
226	586	6	2	E		yes
227	586	4	2	E		yes
228	676	4	1	J1		yes
229	676	1	-9	-9		yes
230	648	4	1	J1		no
231	648	4	1	J1		no
232	648	4	1	J1		yes
233	648	4	1	J1		yes
234	648	4	1	J1		yes
235	648	10	-9	-9	phyllite & sand	no
236	648	6	-9	-9	TSG = 2 or 3	yes
237	769	4	1	J1		yes
238	625	4	1	-9	TSS = J2 or J3?	yes
239	683	4	1	J1		yes
240	683	4	1	J1		yes
241	676	4	1	J1		no
242	676	4	1	J1		yes

Sample Number, by ASM Site Number	Bag or PD Number	Temper Type	Temper Source Generic	Temper Source Specific	Comments	Section?[a]
243	676	4	1	J1		yes
244	600	4	1	J1		yes
245	598	4	1	J1		no
246	598	4	1	J2	not St. Mary's Ruin	yes
247	598	4	1	J1		no
248	686	4	1	J1		yes
249	245	3	1	J1		yes
250	202	3	1	J1		no
251	202	3	1	J2		yes
252	202	4	1	J1		yes
253	202	4	-9	-9		yes
254	688	3	1	J1		no
255	257	3	1	J1		yes
256	258	3	1	J1		yes
257	245	3	1	J1		yes
258	133	4	1	J1		yes
259	1	4	1	J1		yes
260	9	3	1	J1		yes
261	43	3	1	J1		no
AA:12:18						
380	1166	4	1	J1		yes
381	1275	4	1	-9	TSS = J2?	yes
382	1705	4	1	-9	TSS = J2?	yes
383	1706	4	1	J1		no
384	1770	4	1	-9	TSS = J2?	yes
385	448	3	1	J2		no
386	386	3	1	J1		yes
387	266	2	1	-9	TSG = 1 or 30	yes
388	240	3	1	J1		yes
557	103	4	1	J1		N/A
558	113	4	1	J1		N/A
559	113	4	1	J1		
560	102	3	1	J1		
561	121	4	1	J1		
BB:9:14						
298	1992	4	1	J2		yes
299	487	3	1	-9		yes
300	747	3	1	J1		no
301	1906	3	1	J1		no
302	989	4	-9	-9	TSG = 2 or 3	no
303	2847	4	1	-9		no

Sample Number, by ASM Site Number	Bag or PD Number	Temper Type	Temper Source Generic	Temper Source Specific	Comments	Section?[a]
304	0	4	3	B/8		yes
305	702	3	1	J1		no
306	194	4	1	-9		yes
307	707	4	3	B/8		yes
308	2499	3	1	J1		no
309	935	3	1	J1		no
310	0	1	-9	-9	T-1-25	no
311	1423	4	1	J2		yes
312	2392	3	1	J1		no
313	1817	4	1	J2		no
314	0	3	1	J1	3c-16	no
315	0	3	1	J1	F-9	yes
316	1544	4	3	B/8		yes
317	1209	3	1	J1		yes
318	1268	4	1	-9	TSS = J2 or J3	yes
319	0	4	1	-9	PH-1-35; TSS = J1 or J2?	no
320	1766	4	3	B/8		yes
321	679	4	1	-9	TSS = J2 or J3	yes
322	1669	4	1	J1		no
323	0	4	1	J1	PH-1-1	no
324	0	4	3	B/8	T-1-39	no
325	1169	4	3	B/8		no
326	1782	4	1	J1		no
327	1973	4	3	B/8		no
328	477	4	1	J2		yes
329	0	4	3	B/8	T-1-39	yes
330	476	4	3	B/8		yes
331	1386	4	1	J1		yes
332	1855	3	1	J1		yes
333	1356	2	1	J2		no
334	0	4	3	B/8		yes
BB:9:101						
424	51	4	3	B/8		yes
425	50	4	1	J1		no
426	57	4	1	J1		yes
427	57	4	1	J1		yes
428	61	4	1	J1		no
429	61	4	1	J1		no
430	61	4	1	-9	TSS = J2?	no
431	132	4	1	J1		no
432	132	4	1	-9		no

Sample Number, by ASM Site Number	Bag or PD Number	Temper Type	Temper Source Generic	Temper Source Specific	Comments	Section?[a]
433	132	4	1	J1		no
434	132	4	1	J1		no
435	132	4	1	J1		no
436	132	4	1	J1		yes
437	138	4	1	J1		no
438	138	4	3	B/8		no
439	138	4	3	B/8		yes
440	110	4	1	J1		no
441	110	4	1	J1		no
442	110	4	3	B/8		yes
443	110	3	1	J1		no
444	110	4	1	J2		yes
445	129	4	3	-9		no
446	131	4	3	B/8		no
447	122	4	1	J1		no
448	104	4	1	J1		no
449	104	4	3	B/8		no
450	104	4	1	J1		no
451	106	4	1	J1		no
452	106	4	3	B/8		yes
453	114	4	1	J1		yes
454	114	3	1	J1		yes
455	114	4	1	J2		no
456	117	4	1	J1		yes
457	122	4	1	J1		no
458	122	4	1	J1		no
459	124	4	1	J1		yes
460	124	3	1	J1		no
BB:13:45						
461	0	4	1	J1	Item 5	yes
BB:13:50						
462	0	4	1	J1	Item 5	yes
463	0	4	1	J1	Item 5	no
464	0	4	30	-9	Item 5	no
BB:13:321						
335	505	4	1	-9	TSS = J2?	yes
336	505	4	1	J1		no
337	434	4	1	J2		no
338	399	4	1	J1		yes
339	282	4	1	J1		yes
340	402	4	1	-9	TSS = J2?	yes

Sample Number, by ASM Site Number	Bag or PD Number	Temper Type	Temper Source Generic	Temper Source Specific	Comments	Section?[a]
341	447	4	1	J1		no
342	230	4	3	B/8		no
343	230	4	1	J1		no
344	321	4	1	J1		yes
345	371	4	2	-9		yes
346	381	3	1	J1		no
347	484	4	1	J1		no
348	375	3	1	J1		no
349	395	3	1	J1		no
350	373	4	3	B/8		no
351	429	4	1	J1		yes
352	285	4	1	J1		no
353	285	3	1	J1		yes
354	486	4	1	J1		yes
355	304	4	3	B/8		no
356	243	4	3	B/8		yes
357	393	4	1	J2		yes
358	212	4	-9	-9		no
359	499	3	1	J1		yes
360	499	4	1	J1		no
361	104	4	3	B/8		yes
362	13	4	1	J2		yes
363	278	4	1	J1		no
364	52	4	1	J1		no
365	353	4	3	B/8		no
366	29	4	3	B/8		yes
367	136	4	1	-9	TSS = J2?	yes
368	325	4	1	J1		yes
369	1	4	1	J1		yes
370	163	4	1	J1		no
371	267	3	1	J1		no
372	90	4	1	J2		no
373	90	4	1	J1		no
374	132	4	1	J1		no
375	75	4	1	J2		no
376	269	4	1	J1		yes
377	20	4	3	B/8		no
378	68	3	1	J1		no
379	329	4	1	J1		no
BB:13:444						
389	68	4	1	J1		yes

Sample Number, by ASM Site Number	Bag or PD Number	Temper Type	Temper Source Generic	Temper Source Specific	Comments	Section?[a]
390	71	4	1	J1		yes
391	71	4	-9	-9	TSG = 2 or 3	no
392	53	4	1	J1		no
393	48	3	1	J2		no
394	46	3	1	J1		no
395	107	4	3	B/8		no
396	95	4	1	J1		yes
397	95	3	1	J1		no
398	95	4	3	B/8		yes
399	77	4	1	J1		yes
400	98	4	3	B/8		yes
401	98	4	1	J1		yes
402	114	4	1	J1		yes
403	114	2	1	J1		no
404	90	4	1	J1		no
405	90	4	3	B/8		no
406	90	4	3	B/8		yes
407	90	4	3	B/8		yes
408	90	5	-9	-9	TSG = 2 or 3	yes
409	114	3	1	J1		yes
410	114	2	1	J1		yes
411	114	7	-9	-9		yes
412	114	4	3	-9		yes
413	114	3	1	J1		yes
414	77	3	1	J1		yes
415	77	4	1	J1		no
416	77	3	1	-9	TSS = J2?	no
417	141	6	3	-9		no
418	95	4	1	J1		yes
419	95	4	1	J2		no
420	95	4	1	J1		no
421	95	4	3	B/8		no
422	95	4	3	B/8		yes
423	95	4	1	J1		no

[a] Indicates whether or not the sherd is suitable for thin-sectioning.

Rincon Petrofacies. Punta de Agua is located in the Sierrita Petrofacies. The Hardy site is located in the University Petrofacies. Site AZ BB:13:45 (ASM) lies outside the sampled area.

Overall, approximately 79 percent of the sherds were assigned to a petrofacies. Four petrofacies were identified during the analysis. Ranked in order of frequency, they are: Beehive Petrofacies (n = 257), Twin Hills Petrofacies (n = 51), Catalina/Tanque Verde Creek Petrofacies (n = 33), Tortolita Petrofacies (n = 2). Characteristics of Beehive Petrofacies sand can be found in Heidke, Miksa, and Wiley (1996) and Heidke (1996). Lombard's (1986a:430, Table C-1) discussions of "biotite rhyolite" and biotite-bearing felsitic volcanic sand (1986b:480–482, 1987a:365, 1987c:330, 1990:229) also apply to the Beehive Petrofacies. Characteristics of Twin Hills Petrofacies sand can be found in Heidke, Miksa, and Wiley (1996) and Heidke (1996), as well. Lombard's (1986b:480–482) discussions of "group C" sherds and "CIENEGAc" and "CIENEGAd" sherds (1990:229) also apply to the Twin Hills Petrofacies sand temper, especially to the sands available in the vicinity of the St. Mary's Ruin. Characteristics of Catalina/Tanque Verde Creek Petrofacies sand temper are described in Lombard (1986b:476, 480–482; 1990:226, 230). Characteristics of Tortolita Petrofacies sands are described in Lombard (1987b).

Fifteen of the sherds that were not assigned to a petrofacies are accompanied by a comment that reads "TSG = 2 or 3." These sherds are either tempered with a metamorphic core complex sand or a granitic sand. Although foliated sand grains, a clear indicator of a metamorphic core complex source, were not observed in these sherds, the observance of polycrystalline quartz and feldspar grains in some of these sherds indicates that some of these pots may be tempered with metamorphic core complex sand.

Brief inspection of the characterization data during the entry-verification process confirms a number of trends previously outlined in Heidke (1990b, 1994, 1996), Heidke et al. (1994), and Heidke and Wiley (1995). First, a relatively high percentage of the Middle Rincon Red-on-brown pottery included in each site's sample is tempered with Beehive Petrofacies sand. Second, nearly all of the Rincon Polychrome sherds included in the study are tempered with Beehive Petrofacies sand. Third, there is a limited distribution of pottery tempered with Twin Hills Petrofacies sand in the west-central basin that is attenuated further from the source. Similarly, there is a limited distribution of pottery tempered with Catalina/Tanque Verde Creek Petrofacies sand in the northeastern basin that is attenuated in other parts of the basin.

Attribute Coding Index

Provenience Attributes

1. ASM Site Number (ASMSITE)
2. Sample Number (PET)
3. Bag or PD Number (BAG)

Temper Attributes

4. Temper Type (TT)
   -9 = Indeterminate
   1 = High LMT (> 25 percent gneiss/schist)
   2 = High LMT/low sand (7–25 percent gneiss/schist)
   3 = Low LMT/high sand (1–7 percent gneiss/schist)
   4 = High sand (< 1 percent gneiss/schist)
   5 = High muscovite mica (> 25 percent MUSC)
   6 = Mixed sand and muscovite mica (1–25 percent MUSC)
   7 = Gneiss/schist and muscovite mica (25 percent LMT+MUSC)
   8 = Mixed sand, gneiss/schist, and muscovite mica (1–25 percent LMT+MUSC)
   9 = Sand and crushed sherd
   10 = High phyllite (> 25 percent LMTP)
   11 = Sand and fiber (Papago types)
   12 = Sherd temper (no sand)

5. Temper Source Generic (TSG)
   -9 = Indeterminate
   1 = Igneous volcanic sands (TSS = D, I, J1, J2, J3, L, R, T, W, and Y)
   2 = Igneous plutonic sands (TSS = 3, E, O, Q, and S)
   3 = Metamorphic core complex sands (TSS = 4, 5, 8, A, B, and N)
   4 = Sedimentary sands
   7 = Mixed volcanic and granitic sands [recorded as volcano-plutonic in previous analyses] (TSS = 7, C, M, MW, and U)
   9 = Mixed volcanic and sedimentary sands
   10 = Mixed volcanic, granitic, and sedimentary sands
   11 = Mixed metamorphic and sedimentary sands
   30 = Igneous plutonic and mixed lithic (volcanic, metamorphic, & sedimentary) sands (TSS = 1, 2, 6, F, G, H, K, P, and Z)
   31 = Other metamorphic source (TSS = V)
   5 = Crushed rock [Gila or Wingfield Plain–like] (Temper Types = 1, 5, 7, or 10)
   21 = Santan/Gila Butte schist and sand (provisional RCD-derived designation)
   29 = Schist sand (LVP provisional code)

6 = Fine paste (low percentage of non-plastics, natural component of clay?)

8 = Sherd, or grog, temper

6. Temper Source Specific (TSS)
   -9 = Indeterminate
   1 = Santa Cruz River (previously recorded as TSS = P)
   2 = Brawley Wash (previously recorded as TSS = Sv ["volcanic"] & Sm ["metamorphic"])
   3 = Cañada del Oro
   4 = Rillito Creek
   5 = Pantano Wash
   6 = McClellan Wash
   7 = West Branch of the Santa Cruz River
   8 = Tanque Verde Creek
   A = Rincon
   B = Catalina
   C = Samaniego
   D = Avra
   E = Tortolita
   F = Durham
   G = Santa Rita
   H = University
   I = Empire
   J1 = Beehive (West Branch is a subset, previously recorded as "J")
   J2 = Twin Hills (St. Mary's is a subset, previously recorded as "Z")
   J3 = Wasson
   K = Black Mountain
   L = Golden Gate
   M = Rillito
   MW = Rillito West
   N = Owl Head
   O = Sierrita
   P = Hughes
   Q = Amole
   R = Batamote
   S = Sutherland
   T = Recortado
   U = Cocoraque
   V = Dos Titos
   W = Waterman
   Y = Roskruge
   Z = Sahuarita

7. Comments (COMMENTS)

8. Sample Large Enough to Section? (SECTION)
   Y = Yes, large enough to produce a thin section
   N = No, not large enough to thin section

Ceramic-Analysis Forms

Sunset Mesa Ceramics
AZ AA:12:10

Bag # _____ Feature # _____ Date _____ Box # _____

Type	Form	Part				Neck	Neck Dim.	Apert.	Rim		Shld	Surface		Temper	Thick	No.	Comments
		Rim	Shld	Body	Neck				Form	Finish		Int.	Ext.				

Figure E.1. Ceramic recording form for sherds.

Partial and Reconstructible Vessels

Site # _____ Bag # _____ Vessel #_____

Fea.# and Type _____ P.D.# _____

Location _____ Additional Bag #'s _____

PV/RV _____ Type _____

Completeness _____ % Form _____

Reconstucted _____

Rim Diameter_____ Temper _____

Orifice Diameter_____ Petrofacies _____

Aperture Diameter_____ Rim Form _____

Throat Diameter _____ Rim Finish_____

Max. Body Diameter_____ Shoulder _____

Shoulder Ht._____ Base Shape_____

Rim Ht. _____ Int. Surface Finish _____

Neck Ht._____ Ext. Surface Finish_____

Total Ht._____ Modifications _____

Thickness _____ Use Wear _____

Volume _____ Comments_____

_____

Thin Section_____

ICPS Sample #_____

Figure E.2. Ceramic recording form for partial and reconstructible vessels.

Figure E.3. Ceramic coding index.

RECORD NUMBER
BAG NUMBER
FEATURE NUMBER
CERAMIC TYPE
  Painted ceramics
  Hohokam Buff Ware
    Sacaton Red-on-Buff
    Indeterminate red-on-buff
    Indeterminate buff (no paint)
  Tucson Basin Brown Ware
    Indeterminate Rillito or Rincon Red-on-brown
    Rincon Red-on-brown, Style A
    Rincon Red-on-brown, Style A (white slipped)
    Rincon Red-on-brown, Style B
    Rincon Black-on-brown, Style B
    Rincon Red-on-brown, Style B (white slipped)
    Rincon Black-on-brown, Style B (white slipped)
    Rincon Polychrome
    Other polychrome
    Indeterminate Rincon Red-on-brown
    Indeterminate Rincon Red-on-brown (white slipped)
    Indeterminate Rincon Black-on-brown
    Indeterminate Rincon Black-on-brown (white slipped)
    Indeterminate red-on-brown
    Indeterminate red-on-brown (white slipped)
  Indeterminate buff or brown ware
    Paint
    No paint
  Unpainted ceramics
  Plain ware
  Gila Plain
  Red ware
  Rincon Red
  Intrusive red ware
  Indeterminate red ware
  Indeterminate unpainted
CERAMIC STYLE (painted database only)
  Style A
  Style B
  Blank = indeterminate style or n/a
VESSEL FORM
  00 = indeterminate
  01 = indeterminate bowl
  02 = hemispherical bowl
  03 = incurved bowl
  04 = subhemispherical bowl
  05 = flare-rimmed bowl
  06 = plate
  07 = indeterminate jar
  08 = shouldered jar
  09 = globular jar

  10 = neckless jar (seed jar)
  11 = pitcher
  12 = scoop
  17 = cauldron
PAINTED RIM
  1 = painted
  2 = indeterminate
NUMBER OF RIM SHERDS
NUMBER OF SHOULDER SHERDS
NUMBER OF BODY SHERDS
NUMBER OF NECK SHERDS
NECK DIAMETER (cm)
RIM APERTURE (cm)
RIM FORM
  00 = not applicable/indeterminate
  01 = direct (90 degrees)
  02 = slight flare (89–70 degrees)
  03 = moderate flare (69–40 degrees)
  04 = pronounced flare (< 40 degrees)
  05 = slightly everted (80–60 degrees)
  06 = moderately everted (59–45 degrees)
  07 = sharply everted (< 45 degrees)
  08 = slightly recurved (90–80 degrees)
  09 = moderately recurved (80–70 degrees)
  10 = sharply recurved (< 70 degrees)
  11 = incomplete upcurve (< 45 degrees)
  12 = complete upcurve (> 45 degrees)
  13 = incomplete incurve (< 45 degrees)
  14 = complete incurve (180 degrees)
  15 = angled (< 90 degrees)
RIM FINISH
  00 = not applicable/indeterminate
  01 = flat
  02 = interior bevel
  03 = exterior bevel
  04 = beveled, both sides
  05 = tapered
  06 = rounded
  07 = interior bulge or overhang
  08 = exterior bulge or overhang
  09 = bulged or overhung, both sides
  10 = very variable
SHOULDER
  00 = not applicable/indeterminate
  01 = Gila
  02 = Classic
  03 = rounded
  04 = seed
SURFACE FINISH INTERIOR
  00 = indeterminate
  01 = blackened
  02 = smudged
  03 = hand smoothed

04 = uniformly polished
05 = striated polished
06 = hand smoothed, blackened
07 = uniformly polished, blackened
08 = striated polished, blackened
09 = slipped, not polished
10 = slipped, uniformly polished
11 = slipped, striated polished
12 = slipped, not polished, blackened
13 = slipped, uniformly polished, blackened
14 = slipped, striated polished, blackened
15 = scraped or wiped
16 = scored or incised
17 = unfinished
18 = hand smoothed, fire clouded
19 = uniformly polished, fire clouded
20 = striated polished, fire clouded
SURFACE FINISH EXTERIOR
  (same as SURFACE FINISH INTERIOR)
TEMPER
  01 = sand

06 = sand/mica-muscovite
07 = sand/mica-biotite
08 = sand/mica-muscovite and biotite
09 = sand/schist
10 = crushed schist
11 = crushed phyllite
12 = crushed phyllite/schist
13 = crushed igneous/volcanics
14 = other crushed rock
15 = indeterminate crushed rock
16 = sherd
17 = sand/sherd
18 = indeterminate temper
19 = quartz/igneous/volcanic
THICKNESS (mm)
NUMBER OF SHERDS (unpainted database only)
OBSERVATION NUMBER (painted database only)
MNV (Minimum Number of Vessels) (painted database only)
TOO SMALL (painted database only)
COMMENTS (unpainted database only)

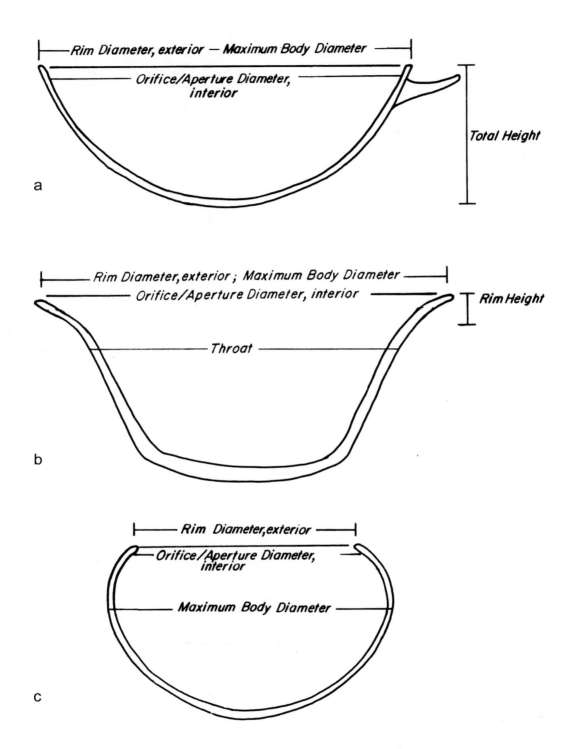

**Figure E.4. Standardized measurements for bowl dimensions:
(a) hemispherical bowl; (b) flare-rimmed bowl; (c) incurved bowl.**

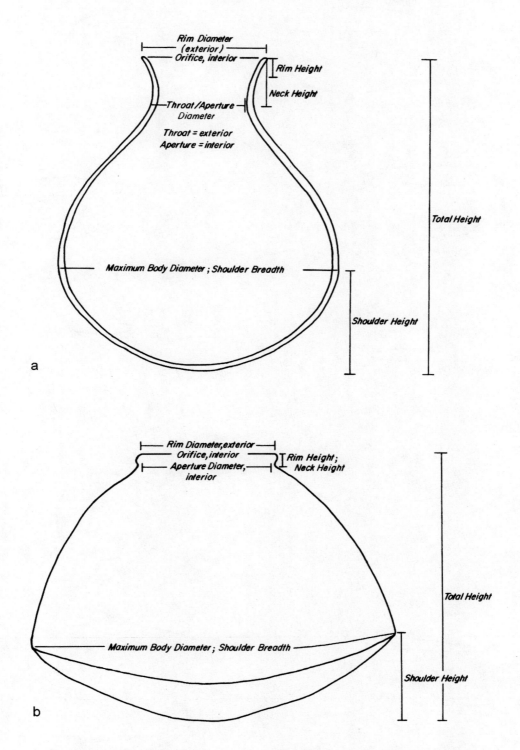

Figure E.5. Standardized measurements for jar dimensions: (a) globular jar; (b) shouldered jar.

Figure E.6. Profiles of Hohokam vessel forms: (a) hemispherical bowl; (b) incurved bowl; (c) subhemispherical bowl; (d–e) flare-rimmed bowl; (f) shouldered jar; (g) globular jar; (h) neckless or "seed" jar; (i) plate; (j) pitcher; (k) scoop; (l) cauldron (from Haury 1976:Figures 12.11, 12.15, and 12.26).

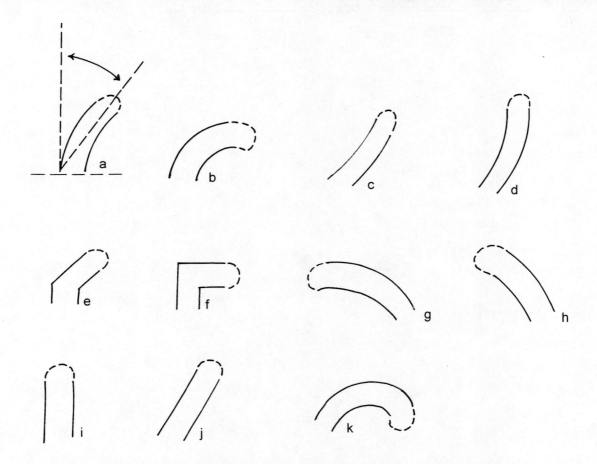

Figure E.7. Profiles of rim forms among Hohokam vessels (after Whittlesey 1991):
(a–b) flared; (c–d) upcurved; (e–f) everted; (g–h) incurved; (i) direct; (j) angled; (k) recurved.

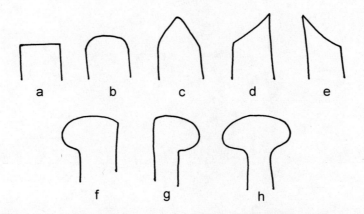

Figure E.8. Rim lip finishes used in Hohokam pottery (after Whittlesey 1991):
(a) flat; (b) rounded; (c) tapered; (d) interior bevel; (e) exterior bevel; (f) bulged/overhung interior;
(g) bulged/overhung exterior; (h) bulged/overhung both sides.

Archaeobotanical Criteria and Data Tables

Karen R. Adams

Criteria of Identification of Botanical Remains Recovered from Sunset Mesa Ruin

Acacia Type

Charcoal. Vessels present; ring porous; vessels solitary and in multiples; wavy bands of paratracheal parenchyma present in latewood; ring boundaries indistinct in mature wood; rays present, thin, numerous. *Acacia* differs from *Prosopis* by having larger vessels, more of them in pairs and multiples, and by having thinner, more discontinuous rays than *Prosopis*.

Ambrosia Type, *Ambrosia/Pluchea* Type

Charcoal. Diffuse porous, with widely scattered vessels of varying size aligned in branching radial files. Rays very thin and abundant, nearly continuous. These types often have only one to three rings, rarely as many as five. They usually are straight, even-diameter twigs not much larger than 1.5 cm across. These charcoal types are similar to another member of the Composite family, *Hymenoclea*, which also would be expected in the region (Kearney and Peebles 1960:884, 894).

Atriplex Type

Charcoal. Vessels present; rays absent or very difficult to see. Rings display a distinct ripple-like banding pattern made up of alternating arcs of vessel and nonvessel areas. This charcoal compares quite well to *Atriplex polycarpa*, known to grow in the region (Kearney and Peebles 1960:258). It does not compare well to other members of the Chenopodiaceae, such as *Sarcobatus* and *Allenrolfea*. These two charcoal types have smaller arcs and a denser background matrix of cells.

Fruit (seed enclosed in bracts). A single seed enclosed in bracts (Feature 13, Bag 796) may represent an *Atriplex*. The lenticular seed inside, measuring nearly 1 mm in diameter, appears to have an encircling embryo characteristic of many members of the Chenopodiaceae. For most of the species of *Atriplex* in Arizona, two small bracts enclose the seed (Kearney and Peebles 1960). Unfortunately, the fruit bracts are too eroded to determine whether or not they had projections, a diagnostic feature for identification of species (Benson and Darrow 1981). This specimen is probably not *Atriplex canescens*, which has four wings that protrude from a very bony fruit case.

Carnegiea Type

Charcoal. Vessels present, scattered; wood is diffuse porous. A striking feature of this wood type is its wide, relatively continuous rays. Ring boundaries are present, but barely visible. The vessels are in solitary and multiple groups, and the groups can be clustered or in radial files. A wood type with a similar appearance, *Platanus*, is distinguished by more vessels evenly distributed throughout a ring, and by the flaring of the wide rays at the ring boundaries.

Seed. Seeds are bent internally, compressed-ovoid, and with a smooth to obscurely cellular-reticulate surface and a truncate, hollow base. Seeds measure 2–4 mm in diameter.

Celtis reticulata Type

Charcoal. Vessels are present; wood is ring porous. Vessels are larger in the early wood, and smaller or in pairs or multiples in the later wood. The latewood is quite dense, and seems at times to appear as wavy bands parallel with the ring boundaries. Ring boundaries are distinct. Rays are numerous. Not a good match to *Celtis pallida*, an arid-adapted shrub.

Cercidium Type

Charcoal. Vessels are present, in a diffuse porous pattern. Rings are large and ring boundaries are indistinct. Vessels vary greatly in size and in cluster pattern; there are isolates, pairs, triplets and multiples (which are often in radial files). Because vessels and vessel clusters are widely dispersed, there is a great deal of highly light-reflective background. Rays are numerous, thin, and discontinuous, often with only one or two vessels fitting between any two of the closely spaced rays. *Acacia* and *Prosopis* are both different, in that they are noticeably ring porous, and they have banded paratracheal parenchyma.

Cheno-am

Seed. Seeds from goosefoot (*Chenopodium*) in the goosefoot family and pigweed (*Amaranthus*) in the pigweed family often look alike, especially when carbonized and degraded. The prehistoric seeds are often labeled "cheno-ams" to reflect this overlap. Specimens are compressed, circular to obovate in face view, and lenticular (lens-shaped) in cross section. Seeds vary in size, ranging from less than 1 to 1.5 mm in diameter. Broken specimens often will reveal the encircling embryo characteristic of these genera.

Descurainia Type

Seed. The Sunset Mesa Ruin tansy mustard seeds are minute, 0.8–1.0 mm long by 0.5 by 0.5 mm, oblong-oval, compressed or terete. A strongly identifying characteristic, other than the small size and oblong shape, is the finely cellular-reticulate pattern in parallel, lengthwise lines along the long axis of each seed. Some of the seeds are wrinkled, sunken in, and measure about 0.5 mm in length; it is possible these were immature when harvested. Others are larger and plump, and clearly seem to have been harvested when mature. The cellular-reticulate

surface pattern is present on all of the Sunset Mesa Ruin seeds. In modern seeds, a bent-over embryo leaves a little indentation in the proximal end, and sometimes a small projection. These features are present on some of the Sunset Mesa Ruin seeds.

Echinocereus Type

Seed. Seeds are ovoid-compressed, and have a large, hollow base or point of attachment. The seed body is characteristically rough, with a distinctly pitted surface.

Eragrostis Type

Caryopsis (grain). *Eragrostis* grains are short and sturdy; that is, the length and width measurements are similar. The grains measure 0.5–1.0 mm in length and 0.5–0.8 mm in width, are rounded in shape, and have an embryo depression approximately one-third to one-half of the grain's length.

Gramineae

Grain. A broken Gramineae grain (Feature 15, Bag 900) embedded in a matrix of *Descurainia* "meal" is identifiable only by virtue of a minute embryo depression at the base.

Stems and stem bases. One lot of charred grass stems and stem bases (Feature 27, Bag 650) is composed of narrow grass stems (~0.5 mm) and multinodal basal areas, where perhaps the grass stems were attached at the soil surface. It is possible this resource was uprooted to use.

Hymenoclea Type

Charcoal. Vessels are present; wood is diffuse porous. A distinct band of early wood vessels is present at the ring boundary. Vessel multiples occur in the latewood. Rays are wide and very numerous.

Larrea Type

Charcoal. Vessels are present, numerous, solitary, and fairly evenly distributed. Wood is diffuse porous, with a distinct band of vessels at the early wood boundary. Rays are thin, numerous, and indistinct. Wood is similar in appearance to *Cercocarpus*, which grows in upland areas of the Southwest.

Leguminosae Type

Seed. A legume is reniform (bean-shaped), with a notch along one edge and rounded ends.

Malvaceae Type

Seed. Seeds are sectoroid specimens (appearing like sections of an orange), compressed-reniform in shape, with a distinctive notch in the middle, and often measuring 1 mm in length.

Monocotyledon Type

Tissue. Tissue has scattered vascular bundles within a background matrix of cells. Some have calcium oxalate (CaO) crystals.

Morus microphylla Type

Charcoal. Vessels present; wood ring porous; larger vessels clustered at the ring boundaries are occluded and light reflective; smaller vessels in latewood; rays thin, not obvious.

Olneya Type

Charcoal. Vessels are present, in a diffuse porous pattern. However, a noticeable feature about this type of wood is the seeming lack of vessels, along with an appearance of concentric banding. The charcoal seems quite dense. Rays are obvious.

Paniceae Type

Grain. Although this specimen (Feature 13, Bag 796) lacks most of its outer coat, the remaining coat has the beaded surface texture, and the specimen has the flat ventral (palea) face and rounded dorsal (lemma) face characteristic of members of the Paniceae grass tribe. The specimen also has what appears to be an embryo

occupying more than half of its 1.4 mm length. It is 0.68 mm in width.

Phaseolus Type

Cotyledon. A single charred reniform cotyledon (Feature 18, Bag 879) is slightly broken off at both ends. The specimen measures 11 mm in length by 7 mm in width by 1.5 mm in thickness. The diagnostic embryo leaves are not available for scrutiny. This cotyledon probably represents a small common bean (*Phaseolus vulgaris*), although the measurements are also within the range of a large tepary bean (*P. acutifolius*).

Phragmites australis Type

Stem segment. A small number of charred reedgrass stem segments and fragments were recognized in Sunset Mesa Ruin deposits. They have the clearly diagnostic, cross-sectional anatomy of *Phragmites* (Adams 1990).

Populus Type, *Populus/Salix* Type

Charcoal. Vessels are present, abundant and closely spaced. The first row of earlywood vessels often makes a noticeable ring. Rays are thin and abundant. The number of vessels between any two rays ranges from one to three. Three species of *Populus* either grow in the vicinity of Sunset Mesa Ruin (*Populus fremontii*), or grow at higher elevations in the Santa Catalina Mountains (Kearney and Peebles 1960:208–209) and could be transported downstream to be picked up as driftwood (*P. angustifolia*, *P. tremuloides*). *Salix* also is present in the area.

Prosopis velutina Type

Charcoal. Vessels are present, generally as solitary isolates. Wood is clearly ring porous. Rays are of varying size, but usually quite noticeable. Banded paratracheal parenchyma is present throughout the ring. Ring boundaries are sometimes indistinct in mature wood. *Prosopis* differs from *Acacia* by having smaller vessels, more of them as solitary isolates, and by having wider, more continuous and easily seen rays than *Acacia*. However, it is easily to confuse the two types.

Pseudotsuga Type

Charcoal. *Pseudotsuga* charcoal is similar to *Pinus* type (lacking vessels; tracheids and other cell types form an even background matrix), except it has few to no resin canals, and a thick latewood band. One of the pieces (Feature 5) had a hole that could easily represent a nail hole.

Salvia Type

Seed. Seeds are oblong, compressed-triangular (with two flat facets and one rounded facet), as much as 2–5 mm in length. Similar in appearance to *Salvia columbariae* (chia).

Sphaeralcea Type

Seed. One seed from Feature 13 (Bag 796) is wedge shaped or sectoroid, rounded on the back, with a V-shaped notch opposite the rounded back. It measures 1.2 mm in diameter. Another from Feature 15 (Bag 900) is similar, measuring 1.1 mm in diameter. Both these seeds were embedded in a matrix of *Descurainia* seed "meal." Some of the Malvaceae type seeds, described above, could easily represent *Sphaeralcea*.

Unknown

Charcoal. Diffuse porous. Young growth, probably only one season. Vessels isolated, in pairs and in multiples, often in radial files. Rays very thin. One set of vessels between rays. Small amount of pith present.

Zea mays

Cupule. A cupule is a durable part of a cob, which often preserves long after other cob parts have degraded. A cupule is shaped like a cup, and holds two spikelets, each spikelet (in turn) holding one corn kernel or grain.

Embryo. *Zea* embryos have popped loose from the kernel, and are triangular in shape, with a smooth outer facet and two rough inner facets.

Kernel. The kernel is the caryopsis (fruit), also called the "grain" of corn. Criteria to distinguish flint vs. flour endosperm in charred kernels were established by Doebley and Bohrer (1983).

Table F.1. Charred Plant Materials from Sunset Mesa Ruin Flotation Samples

Taxon, by Feature, Bag Number, and Context	Part	Number	Notes
Feature 15, Bag 896, fill			
Carnegiea type	seed	4	10 ml, all examples
Malvaceae type	seed	1	10 ml, all examples
Prosopis type	charcoal	3	
Feature 15.01, Bag 240, fill			
Prosopis type	charcoal	20	40 ml, all examples
Feature 16, Bag 147, vessel fill			
Cheno-am	seed	3	10 ml, all examples
Prosopis type	charcoal	3	
Feature 17, Bag 144, vessel fill			
Prosopis type	charcoal	1	
Pseudotsuga type	charcoal	1	
Unknown	seed	1	10 ml, all examples
Unknown type	bark	5	
Feature 21			
Bag 385, pit house floor "A" fill			
Echinocereus type	seed	60	
Eragrostis type	caryopsis	14	
Gramineae	stem segment	9	30 ml, all examples
Malvaceae type	seed	6	*Sphaeralcea* type
Monocotyledon type	tissue	5	with CaO
Populus/Salix type	charcoal	1	
Prosopis type	charcoal	4	
Unknown type	charcoal	7	dense; not *Larrea*
Bag 545, pit house floor "B" fill			
Cheno-am	seed	2	25 ml, all examples
Eragrostis type	caryopsis	1	25 ml, all examples
Larrea type	charcoal	9	
Leguminosae type	seed fragment	1	likely domesticate
Prosopis type	charcoal	3	
Salvia type	seed	1	25 ml, all examples
Unknown type	bark	1	
Feature 21.01, Bag 484, hearth fill			
Atriplex type	charcoal	1	
Carnegiea type	charcoal	2	
Salvia type	seed	2	30 ml, all examples
Feature 22, Bag 558, pit house floor fill			
Carnegiea type	charcoal	16	
Gramineae	stem fragment	20+	1–2 mm diameter
Helianthus type	charcoal	8	
Phragmites type	stem fragment	11	200 ml, all examples

Taxon, by Feature, Bag Number, and Context	Part	Number	Notes
Feature 22.01, Bag 653, hearth fill			
Cheno-am	seed	1	40 ml, all examples
Carnegiea type	charcoal	1	
Prosopis type	charcoal	2	
Malvaceae type	seed	2	40 ml, all examples
Gramineae type	caryopsis	20+	40 ml, all examples
Morus microphylla type	charcoal	17	
Zea mays	cupule	1	40 ml, all examples
Feature 23, Bag 404, pit house floor fill			
Prosopis type	charcoal	16	
Feature 23.01, Bag 482, hearth fill			
Gramineae	caryopsis	2	10 ml, all examples
Prosopis type	charcoal	7	
Unknown type	bark	2	
Feature 23.02, Bag 475, pit fill			
Carnegiea type	seed	12	70 ml, all examples
Cheno-am	seed	3	70 ml, all examples
Monocotyledon type	tissue fragment	1	CaO, has vascular bundles
Prosopis type	charcoal	5	
Salvia type	seed	13	70 ml, all examples
Feature 25, Bag 392, pit house floor			
Ambrosia/Pluchea type	charcoal	10	
Larrea type	charcoal	2	
Malvaceae type	seed	1	200 ml, all examples
Phragmites australis type	stem fragment	11	200 ml, all examples
Prosopis type	charcoal	14	
Feature 25.01, Bag 442, hearth fill			
Ambrosia/Pluchea type	charcoal	2	
Gramineae	caryopsis	20+	20 ml, all examples
Malvaceae type	seed	7	20 ml, all examples
Prosopis type	charcoal	2	
Unknown type	charcoal	1	dense, vitrified?
Zea mays (flint)	kernel fragment	20+	20 ml, all examples
Feature 27, Bag 660, pit house floor fill			
Carnegiea type	charcoal	9+	
Cheno-am	seed	50+	100 ml, all examples
Gramineae	caryopsis	7	100 ml, all examples
Gramineae	stem fragment	20+	1–2 mm diameter
Phragmites australis type	stem fragment	20+	100 ml, all examples
Prosopis type	charcoal	3	

Taxon, by Feature, Bag Number, and Context	Part	Number	Notes
Feature 27.01, Bag 658, hearth fill			
Cheno-am	seed	15	
Gramineae	caryopsis	15	
Gramineae	stem fragment	10	1–2 mm diameter
Malvaceae type	seed	1	
Phragmites australis type	stem fragment	6	10 ml, all examples
Prosopis type	charcoal	6	
Feature 41, Bag 801, pit fill			
Prosopis type	charcoal	6	
Feature 46, Bag 768, pit fill			
Cercidium type	charcoal	4	
Cheno-am	seed	3	30 ml, all examples
Olneya type	charcoal	2	
Prosopis type	charcoal	1	
Pseudotsuga type	charcoal	2	
Unknown type	charcoal	2	two different types
Feature 47, Bag 806, pit fill			
Atriplex type	charcoal	1	
Cercidium type	charcoal	4	
Prosopis type	charcoal	5	
Zea mays	cupule	2	5 ml, all examples
Feature 49, Bag 790, midden fill			
Acacia type	charcoal	10	
Atriplex type	charcoal	1	
Celtis reticulata type	charcoal	1	
Malvaceae type	seed	1	10 ml, all examples
Prosopis type	charcoal	4	

Table F.2. Charred Plant Materials from Sunset Mesa Ruin Macrobotanical Samples

Taxon, by Feature, Bag Number, and Context	Part	Number	Notes
Feature 5, Bag 174, historical-period structure			
Pseudotsuga type	wood/charcoal	4	part charred, nail?
Feature 13			
Bag 740, fill			
Descurainia type	seed meal	—	700 ml
Bag 796, fill			
Atriplex type	fruit	1	embedded in meal
Descurainia type	seed meal	—	200 ml
Paniceae type	caryopsis	1	embedded in meal
Sphaeralcea type	seed	1	embedded in meal
Zea mays	kernel	15	flint endosperm
Feature 15, Bag 900, fill			
Descurainia type	seed meal	—	100 ml
Gramineae	caryopsis	1	embedded in meal
Sphaeralcea type	seed	1	embedded in meal
Zea mays	embryo	1	embedded in meal
Feature 18, Bag 879, canal			
Ambrosia type	charcoal	10	
Atriplex type	charcoal	7	
Larrea type	charcoal	20+	
Phaseolus type	cotyledon	1	
Phragmites australis type	stem segment	3	plus fragments
Prosopis velutina type	charcoal	20+	
Zea mays	kernel	50	flint and flour
Feature 21			
Bag 495, support post			
Prosopis velutina type	charcoal	1	20 cm+ diameter
Bag 498, pit house			
Prosopis velutina type	charcoal	70+	up to 6 cm diameter
Bag 502, support post			
Populus type	charcoal	20+	
Prosopis velutina type	charcoal	1	
Feature 22, Bag 714, support post			
Prosopis velutina type	charcoal	50+	main support post
Feature 25			
Bag 301, pit house			
Prosopis velutina type	charcoal	30+	
Zea mays	kernel	—	100 ml, flour endosperm
Bag 305, pit house			
Larrea type	charcoal	50+	twig fragments, roof fall
Bag 310, support post			
Prosopis velutina type	charcoal	100+	beam fragment

Taxon, by Feature, Bag Number, and Context	Part	Number	Notes
Feature 27			
Bag 649, roof fall			
Ambrosia type	twig	10+	1.0 cm diameter
Phragmites australis type	stem segments	8	0.4–0.6 cm diameter
Bag 650, roof fall			
Carnegiea type	charcoal	10+	
Gramineae type	stems, w/ bases	—	1 g, < 1 mm diameter
Prosopis velutina type	charcoal	1	
Bag 651, roof fall			
Phragmites australis type	stem segments	—	0.3–0.8 cm diameter, 33 g
Bag 652, roof fall			
Ambrosia type	twig segments	5	1.0 cm diameter
Atriplex type	twig segments	3	0.5 cm diameter
Celtis reticulata type	twig segments	10	1.2 cm diameter
Larrea type	twig fragments	10+	1.2 cm diameter
Populus type	twig segments	1	1.0 cm diameter
Bag 684, floor fill			
Phragmites australis type	stem segments	3	plus fragments
Bag 685, floor fill			
Celtis reticulata type	twig segments	3	0.5–1.0 cm diameter
Hymenoclea type	twig segments	20	0.4–0.8 cm diameter
Bag 717, entry beam			
Cercidium type	charcoal	10+	up to 10+ cm diameter
Bag 732, support post			
Prosopis velutina type	charcoal	30+	
Bag 733, support post			
Prosopis velutina type	charcoal	30+	

Sunset Mesa Pollen-Data Tables

Susan Smith and Jim Hasbargen

Table G.1. Pollen Data for Sunset Mesa (AZ AA:12:10 [ASM])

Feature Context	Surface Control	35 Historical-Period Pit Fill	21 Floor A (Entry)	21 Floor B (Hearth)	21.02 Posthole Fill	22 Floor (Mano)	22 Floor	23 Floor	23 Floor	23 Floor	23.02 Intramural Floor Pit	25 Floor	25 Fill	27 Floor
Bag number	902	807	Composite (2)	546	473	644	Composite (4)	Composite (4)	Composite (2)	Composite (4)	852	391	Composite (4)	Composite (4)
Pollen Sum	200	200	200	200	209	204	200	200	200	200	200	200	200	200
Tracers	8	12	2	41	65	12	1	6	12	6	29	9	9	5
Pollen Concentration gr/cc	33,750.0	22,500.0	135,000.0	6,585.4	4,340.8	22,950.0	270,000.0	45,000.0	22,500.0	45,000.0	9,310.3	30,000.0	30,000.0	54,000.0
Deteriorated	8	13	25	31	15	14	24	24	23	24	47	22	59	53
Unknown	1	—	1	2	—	1	1	—	—	—	1	—	2	1
Abies	—	—	—	—	—	—	—	—	—	—	—	—	x	—
Pinus	—	—	2	1	1	1	—	1	1	1	—	1	1	2
Pinus pinyon type	—	—	—	—	3	—	—	—	3	—	—	—	—	—
Ephedra	1	—	1	—	—	—	—	1	—	—	—	—	—	—
Prosopis	—	—	—	—	—	—	—	—	—	—	—	—	—	—
Cactaceae	1	—	2	—	6	3	1	—	—	—	—	—	—	—
Cylindropuntia	—	1	2	2	1	x	x	x	—	x	x	—	—	—
Platyopuntia	—	—	—	—	—	—	—	x	—	x	—	—	—	—
Zea	x	—	12	35	7	72	4	x	—	x	5	1	—	—
Cucurbita	—	—	—	x	—	—	—	—	—	—	—	—	—	—
Cheno-am	156	167	113	73	166	82	130	158	154	158	133	157	126	119
Artemisia	—	—	—	1	—	—	—	—	—	—	—	—	—	—
Hi-spine Compositae	16	5	15	25	1	8	20	4	6	4	4	4	5	9
Low-spine Compositae	2	—	3	1	5	3	3	2	2	2	—	3	—	—
Gramineae	3	2	9	11	—	1	3	3	3	3	5	2	2	4
Sphaeralcea	—	—	—	—	—	—	—	—	—	—	—	—	—	—
Boerhaavia type	x	x	5	4	—	3	4	2	2	2	1	1	—	x
Kallstroemia	x	—	x	x	—	x	—	x	—	x	—	—	—	—
Cruciferae	—	—	1	—	—	—	1	—	—	—	—	—	—	—
Eriogonum	4	—	2	2	—	4	3	—	—	—	—	—	—	—
Onagraceae	—	—	x	—	—	—	—	—	—	—	x	—	—	—
Total aggregates	8	12	7	12	4	13	6	7	6	7	4	9	5	12
Cheno-am aggregates	8 (15)	12 (7)	4 (6)	7 (100+)	3 (12)	7 (12)	4 (12)	7 (100)	4 (3)	7 (100)	3 (10)	9 (40)	5 (100)	11 (20)
Hi-spine aggregates	—	—	1 (2)	3 (30)	—	2 (10)	2 (10)	—	1 (2)	—	—	—	—	1 (20)
Low-spine aggregates	—	—	—	—	—	—	—	—	—	—	—	—	—	—
Gramineae aggregates	—	—	1 (3)	—	1 (3)	—	—	—	—	—	—	—	—	—
Boerhaavia aggregates	x (20)	—	x (3)	x (4)	1 (3)	—	—	—	1 (6)	—	—	—	—	—
Zea aggregates	—	—	x (3)	2 (2)	—	5 (3)	—	—	—	—	1 (2)	—	—	—
Cylindropuntia aggregates	—	—	—	x (2)	—	—	—	—	—	—	—	—	—	—
Cactaceae aggregates	—	1 (2)	1 (2)	—	—	1 (20+)	—	—	—	—	—	—	—	—
Prosopis aggregates	—	—	—	—	—	—	—	—	—	—	—	—	—	—

Note: x notes taxa identified during scans. Aggregate notation shows number of aggregates and size of largest aggregate in parentheses.

Table G.1 (continued).

Feature Context	27.01 Intramural Hearth	27.03 Intramural Pit	13 Kitchen Area	15 Kitchen Area	15.01 FCR Pit Fill	41 Extramural Pit Fill	46 Extramural Thermal Pit Fill	47 Extramural Pit Fill	49 Burned-Rock Midden	18 Canal Fill (Sample 5)	18 Canal Base	18 Below Canal
Bag number	659	675	797	897	241	800	767	805	788	826	783	836
Pollen Sum	200	100	200	221	200	200	200	200	205	200	200	200
Tracers	31	29	14	38	20	23	6	8	19	12	137	83
Pollen Concentration gr/cc	8,709.7	4,655.2	19,285.7	7,851.3	13,500.0	11,739.1	45,000.0	33,750.0	14,565.8	22,500.0	1,970.8	3,253.0
Deteriorated	53	37	34	16	20	8	28	18	11	26	39	51
Unknown	—	—	—	—	—	—	—	—	—	—	—	—
Abies	—	—	—	—	—	—	—	—	—	—	—	—
Pinus	x	1	—	4	x	—	1	x	x	2	—	2
Pinus pinyon type	—	—	—	—	—	—	—	—	—	7	—	—
Ephedra	—	—	—	—	—	—	—	1	—	—	—	—
Prosopis	—	—	—	—	—	—	—	—	9	—	—	—
Cactaceae	—	—	3	—	x	1	—	1	—	2	—	—
Cylindropuntia	—	—	x	—	1	x	x	1	x	—	—	—
Platyopuntia	—	—	—	—	x	—	—	1	1	—	—	—
Zea	—	4	1	x	x	x	—	x	x	x	—	—
Cucurbita	—	—	—	—	—	—	—	—	x	—	—	—
Cheno-am	127	43	133	173	155	170	138	135	167	110	147	113
Artemisia	—	—	—	—	—	—	—	—	—	—	—	—
Hi-spine Compositae	13	2	8	6	5	2	9	13	5	29	7	9
Low-spine Compositae	1	1	1	3	1	1	—	2	2	1	—	1
Gramineae	2	7	4	2	4	1	14	5	—	8	—	4
Sphaeralcea	—	—	—	—	—	—	—	—	—	x	—	—
Boerhaavia type	x	—	1	2	2	x	x	3	2	x	2	1
Kallstroemia	—	—	—	—	—	—	—	x	—	x	—	—
Cruciferae	—	—	—	—	—	—	—	—	—	—	—	—
Eriogonum	—	—	4	2	3	—	—	2	2	1	—	—
Onagraceae	—	—	—	—	—	—	—	x	—	—	—	—
Total aggregates	4	5	11	13	11	18	10	20	6	14	5	19
Cheno-am aggregates	3 (4)	3 (20)	10 (10)	13 (7)	8 (4)	17 (150)	8 (8)	16 (20)	3 (50+)	11 (4)	5 (20)	15 (30)
Hi-spine aggregates	1 (2)	—	1 (2)	—	2 (4)	—	—	3 (20)	—	2 (2)	—	3 (2)
Low-spine aggregates	—	—	—	—	—	—	—	—	—	—	—	1 (2)
Gramineae aggregates	—	1 (4)	—	x (4)	1 (2)	1 (2)	2 (2)	—	—	1 (4)	—	—
Boerhaavia aggregates	—	—	—	x (3)	—	—	—	x (2)	x (20+)	—	—	—
Zea aggregates	—	1 (5)	—	x (20+)	—	—	—	—	x (3)	—	—	—
Cylindropuntia aggregates	—	—	x (6)	—	—	—	—	1 (10)	—	—	—	—
Cactaceae aggregates	—	—	—	—	—	—	—	—	—	—	—	—
Prosopis aggregates	—	—	—	—	—	—	—	—	3 (30+)	—	—	—

Note: x notes taxa identified during scans. Aggregate notation shows number of aggregates and size of largest aggregate in parentheses.

Paleohydraulic Reconstruction of the Sunset Mesa Canal, Potential Maize Yields, and Population Estimates

Richard Ciolek-Torrello, Jeffrey A. Homburg, and Carla R. Van West

In recent years, a number of studies involving the reconstruction of the paleohydraulics of Hohokam canals have been undertaken to document canal engineering and design, and to estimate how much land they could have irrigated and the amount of production they could have supported (Ackerly 1989; Howard 1991, 1993; Howard and Huckleberry 1991; Katzer 1989b; Van West and Altschul 1998). Such reconstructions involve a series of variables and concepts that can be expressed mathematically. The most important of these is discharge, a relative measure of system capacity; that is, how much water an open channel can transport and ultimately the total area that can be irrigated (Howard 1993:277). The accuracy of estimates such as the amount of irrigable land, however, can be affected by many different variables and are often subject to high errors. Calculating the rate of discharge is dependent upon a number of factors such as the cross-sectional area of the canal and water velocity, which in turn is a function of the hydraulic radius, hydraulic gradient, and the coefficient of roughness.

According to Howard (1993:277), estimates of water velocity are necessary to calculate the rate of discharge and are critical to understanding flow regimes and their impact on canal maintenance. If the velocity is excessive, the channel will erode until its cross-sectional area increases sufficiently to reduce the velocity. If the velocity is too low, however, there is insufficient energy to transport sediments, so they build up in the canal, requiring frequent cleaning. Cross-sectional area (Table H.1) is calculated from the width at the top of the canal and its maximum depth as measured in a profile. For a parabolic profile as exhibited by Feature 18 (see Figure 25) a factor of $2/3$ of the depth-width area is applied. The profile seen in Figure 27 is not used in this calculation as it appears to represent a point in the canal alignment where it curves southwest from the Rillito River onto the Qt1 terrace and, as such, is not representative of the profile of the canal. The hydraulic radius is calculated from the cross-sectional area and the wetted perimeter, which is also derived from the canal's width and depth.

The hydraulic gradient, the slope of the water level within the canal, usually can only be estimated for Hohokam canals, because the gradient can vary substantially along the length of the canal alignment and measurements based on short segments are subject to substantial error (Ackerly et al. 1987). Howard (1993:279) argues that canal gradients should not deviate substantially from local topographic slope, as higher gradients would quickly entrench the canal to unuseable levels, and lower gradients could not continue over a great distance. Here, we use the gradient of the local Rillito River (0.0035 m/m), the source of the canal, as a maximum value. Various arbitrary gradients lower than this value are used in our calculations (see Table H.1). It should be noted that the canal runs opposite the direction of the Santa Cruz River channel and against the gradient of this river. Thus, a gradient as low as 0.001 could have been effective in this situation.

The coefficient of roughness is used to determine the effects of sidewall friction on channel velocity (Howard 1993:279). Such friction results from the irregularity of the canal sidewall, gravel on the canal bed, the sinuosity of the canal, and the amount of aquatic growth in the channel. A value of 0.030 is generally regarded as a

Table H.1. Reconstruction of Hydraulics and Amount of Irrigable Land for Feature 18

Feature	Width[a] (m)	Depth[b] (m)	Roughness Coefficient[c]	Cross-sectional Area[d] (m²)	Wetted Perimeter[e] (m)	Hydraulic Gradient[f] (m/m)	Radius[g]	Velocity[h] (m/s)	Maximum Discharge (m³/s)[i]	(cfs)[j]	Uncorrected Irrigated Acreage[k]	Corrected Irrigated Acreage[l]	Corrected Acreage with 10% Water Loss[m]	Corrected Irrigated Hectares[n]
Early canal	1.45	0.70	0.03	0.68	2.35	0.0010	0.29	0.46	0.31	10.98	439	110	99	40
	1.45	0.70	0.03	0.68	2.35	0.0015	0.29	0.56	0.38	13.45	538	134	121	49
	1.45	0.70	0.03	0.68	2.35	0.0020	0.29	0.65	0.44	15.53	621	155	140	57
	1.45	0.70	0.03	0.68	2.35	0.0025	0.29	0.73	0.49	17.36	694	174	156	63
	1.45	0.70	0.03	0.68	2.35	0.0030	0.29	0.80	0.54	19.02	761	190	171	69
Late canal	0.71	0.32	0.03	0.15	0.90	0.0010	0.17	0.32	0.05	1.73	69	17	16	6
	0.71	0.32	0.03	0.15	0.90	0.0015	0.17	0.40	0.06	2.12	85	21	19	8
	0.71	0.32	0.03	0.15	0.90	0.0020	0.17	0.46	0.07	2.45	98	24	22	9
	0.71	0.32	0.03	0.15	0.90	0.0025	0.17	0.51	0.08	2.74	109	27	25	10
	0.71	0.32	0.03	0.15	0.90	0.0030	0.17	0.56	0.08	3.00	120	30	27	11

[a] Width measurement obtained from profile drawing (Figure 25).
[b] Depth measurement obtained from profile drawing (Figure 25).
[c] Roughness coefficient of 0.03 is recommended by Howard (1993:278), Howard and Huckleberry (1991), and Katzer (1989b:224–225).
[d] Formula for a parabolic cross-sectional area is (width × depth) × 0.667.
[e] Formula for a parabolic wetted perimeter is width + ((8 × depth squared)/(3 × width)).
[f] Slope gradient is estimated at 0.0010, 0.0015, 0.0020, 0.0025, 0.0030 m/m; current gradient of the Rillito River for the segment immediately upstream is 0.0035 m/m or 0.35 percent.
[g] Formula for hydraulic radius is cross-sectional area/wetted perimeter.
[h] Velocity is estimated using the Manning formula: Velocity = ((hydraulic radius to the $^2/_3$ power) × (gradient to the $^1/_2$ power)/roughness coefficient (see Katzer 1989b:224).
[i] Formula for discharge is cross-sectional area × velocity.
[j] Formula for discharge in cubic feet per second is 35.315 × discharge in cubic meters per second.
[k] Uncorrected irrigated acreage based on 40 acres per 1 cfs (see Howard 1993:292; Haury 1976:144).
[l] Corrected irrigated acreage assumes that average discharge is 25% of maximum estimated discharge (see Ackerly 1989).
[m] Corrected irrigated acreage based on 10% water loss (see Howard 1991:4, 35, 1993).
[n] Corrected irrigated hectares based on a ratio of 2.47 acres per hectare.

good estimate for the roughness coefficient for Hohokam canals (Huckleberry 1988).

Howard (1993:289) has stressed that the discharge rates calculated in this manner represent maxima and do not accurately estimate the actual water use from a canal. Sedimentation quickly reduces channel size, and seasonal variability and use of head gates affects the amount of water introduced into the canal. Using historical data, Ackerly (1989) demonstrated that the discharge capacity as measured in the above manner significantly overestimates actual discharge used in the canal, and suggests that actual mean discharge is usually only about 25 to 30 percent of the maximum rate. Thus, the discharge rates calculated for Feature 18 are corrected accordingly, and are reduced an additional 10 percent for losses due to seepage and evaporation. Here, we calculate discharge rates for the main channel of Feature 18 as well as the smaller canal inset into its upper fill.

Estimates of maize yields and population size can be derived based on the amount of land that could be irrigated by the canal, but these estimates should be considered with caution as, like the estimates of irrigable land, they are affected by a number of other variables and can be subject to considerable error. Van West and Altschul (1994:377–378) have estimated potential agricultural productivity (PAP) under five levels of growing season conditions: poor, unfavorable, normal, favorable, and optimal. Given the advantageous conditions that characterized most of the Sedentary period and the supplementation of soil moisture with irrigation, growing season conditions at Sunset Mesa could be described as either favorable or optimal for maize production during the Rincon phase. If we are conservative and assume that conditions were on average "favorable" and that soil moisture was supplemented with irrigation, the best agricultural soils could produce up to 774.6 kg of maize per hectare (Van West and Altschul 1994:Table 14c).

Starting with such productivity estimates, Van West and Altschul (1994:382–383) derive estimates of actual maize yields and population size based on a number of assumptions about agricultural practices and annual consumption of maize per person. In an intensive agricultural economy based on maize, such as might be expected at Sunset Mesa, Van West and Altschul (1994:383), assume that only about 50 percent of the arable land is brought under cultivation at any one time, while the remainder is left uncleared or fallow. They also assume that only

75 percent of the land that is cultivated is devoted to maize production, while the remainder is devoted to other crops such as beans, squash, or cotton. Furthermore, as much as 10 percent of the crop may be lost to pests, competition, rot, or theft. Thus, only about a third of the potential productivity of the best available arable land may actually be realized in a given harvest. Van West and Altschul (1994:382) also assume that 5 percent of this total actual harvest is retained for a seed crop and, citing the ideal of storing a two-year supply of maize, that the harvest is consumed over a two-year period. An additional 10 percent of the harvest is expected to be lost to pests and rot over this period, and a further 5 percent is taken out for the second year's seed crop. Finally, they estimate an annual consumption rate of 160 kg per person of maize and 320 kg to meet the two year's per capita demand in an economy based on the intensive use of maize. Given the close association of Sunset Mesa with arable land and a canal, Van West and Altschul's (1994:383) intensive agricultural model for maize consumption is most appropriate. Using these assumptions, population is estimated according to the following formula:

$$\frac{((((PAP \times .50) \times .75) \times .90) \times .95) \times .855}{160 \text{ kg} + 160 \text{ kg}} = n$$

where PAP is the potential agricultural productivity in kg/hectare, .50 is the proportion of cultivated land, .75 is the proportion devoted to maize, .90 is the proportion of the crop that can be harvested, .95 is the proportion minus the first year's seed crop, .855 is the proportion available for consumption after a year of storage and second seed crop, and n is the estimated population size.

Estimates of maize yield and population size are derived for the initial canal as well as the later inset canal (Table H.2). For the early canal, a series of estimates are derived based on different discharge rates, which in turn are based on different possible gradients. For the much smaller inset canal, estimates are based on the maximum gradient. Similar estimates, however, can be derived from the lowest gradient by increasing mean discharge to about 50 percent of capacity. This would be a reasonable assumption for such a small canal. Estimates are also derived for comparative purposes for the amount of arable land available on the Qt1 terrace below the canal.

**Table H.2. Estimates of Maize Production in kg and Population Size
for Canal Feature 18 and Qt1 Terrace Area at Sunset Mesa**

Feature	Hectares	PAP[a] (kg)	Fallow (50%)	Maize Crop (75%)	Minus Loss (10%)	Minus Seed Crop (-5%)	Second Year Loss and Seed (15%)	First Year Demand (kg)	Second Year Demand (kg)	Population
Early canal	40	29,784	14,892	11,169	10,052	9,549	8,165	160	160	26
	49	36,485	18,243	13,682	12,314	11,698	10,002	160	160	31
	57	42,442	21,221	15,916	14,324	13,608	11,635	160	160	36
	63	46,910	23,455	17,591	15,832	15,040	12,860	160	160	40
Late canal	11[b]	8,191	4,095	3,071	2,764	2,626	2,245	160	160	7
Western Qt1 terrace	14	10,424	5,212	3,909	3,518	3,342	2,858	160	160	9

[a] Potential agricultural production: assume 744.6 kg of maize per hectare (from Van West and Altschul 1994:Table 14.6c)
[b] Assume highest gradient of 0.003 m/m or gradient of 0.001 m/m and about 50 percent average discharge

REFERENCES CITED

Abbott, R. Tucker
  1974 *American Seashells: The Marine Mollusca of*
        the Atlantic and Pacific Coasts of North Amer-
        ica. 2nd ed. Van Nostrand Reinhold, New
        York.

Ackerly, Neal W.
  1989 Paleohydrodynamic Impacts on Hohokam
        Irrigation Systems. In *Prehistoric Agricultural*
        Activities on the Lehi-Mesa Terrace: Perspec-
        tives on Hohokam Irrigation Cycles, edited by
        N. W. Ackerly and T. K. Henderson,
        pp. 46–83. Northland Research, Flagstaff.

Adams, Karen R.
  1988 *The Ethnobotany and Phenology of Plants in*
        and adjacent to Two Riparian Habitats in
        Southeastern Arizona. Unpublished Ph.D. dis-
        sertation, Department of Ecology and Evolu-
        tionary Biology, University of Arizona,
        Tucson.

  1990 Prehistoric Reedgrass (Phragmites) "Ciga-
        rettes" with Tobacco (Nicotiana) Contents: A
        Case Study from Red Bow Cliff Dwelling, Ari-
        zona. *Journal of Ethnobiology* 10(2):123–139.

Ahlstrom, Richard Van Ness
  1985 *The Interpretation of Tree-ring Dates.* Unpub-
        lished Ph.D. dissertation, Department of An-
        thropology, University of Arizona, Tucson.

Aitken, M. J.
  1974 *Physics and Archaeology.* 2nd ed. Clarendon
        Press, Oxford.

Allen, Barbara
  1987 *Homesteading the High Desert.* University of
        Utah Press, Salt Lake City.

Altschul, Jeffrey H.
  1988 *Life Away from the River: A Cultural Re-*
        sources Class II Survey of Davis-Monthan Air
        Force Base, Tucson, Arizona. Technical Series
        No. 14. Statistical Research, Tucson.

Altschul, Jeffrey H., Trixie Bubemyre, Kellie M. Cairns,
William L. Deaver, A. Della Croce, Suzanne K. Fish,
Lee Fratt, Karen G. Harry, James P. Holmlund, Gary
Huckleberry, Charles H. Miksicek, Arthur W. Vokes,
Stephanie M. Whittlesey, María Nieves Zedeño, and
L. F. Ziady
  1996 *Archaeological Investigations at the SRI Lo-*
        cus, West Branch Site (AZ AA:16:3[ASM]), a
        Rincon Phase Village in the Tucson Basin. Sta-
        tistical Research, Tucson. Draft report submit-
        ted to Pima County Department of Transporta-
        tion and Flood Control District, Tucson.

Altschul, Jeffrey H., and Jeffrey A. Homburg
  1990 The Relationship between Agricultural Sys-
        tems and Settlement Patterns in the Lukachu-
        kai Valley. Paper presented at the 55th Annual
        Meeting of the Society of American Archaeol-
        ogy, Las Vegas.

Antevs, Ernst
  1948 Climatic Changes and the Pre-white Man. *Uni-*
        versity of Utah Bulletin 38:168–191.

  1955 Geologic-Climatic Dating in the West. *Ameri-*
        can Antiquity 20:317–335.

Anyon, Roger, and Steven A. LeBlanc
  1980 The Architectural Evolution of Mogollon-
        Mimbres Communal Structures. *The Kiva*
        45:253–277.

Arnold, Dean E.
  1985 *Ceramic Theory and Cultural Process.* Cam-
        bridge University Press, Cambridge.

Ayres, James E.
1984 The Anglo Period in Archaeological and Historical Perspective. *The Kiva* 49:225–232.

1990 *Historic Archaeology at the Tucson Community Center.* Archaeological Series No. 181. Arizona State Museum, University of Arizona, Tucson.

Barnes, Frank C.
1989 *Cartridges of the World.* 6th ed. Edited by K. Warner. DBI Books, Northbrook, Illinois.

Barnes, Mark R.
1983 *Tucson: Development of a Community.* Ph.D. dissertation, Catholic University of America, Washington, D.C. University Microfilms, Ann Arbor.

1984 Hispanic Period Archaeology in the Tucson Basin: An Overview. *The Kiva* 49:213–223.

Barter, G. W. (compiler and publisher)
1881 *Directory of the City of Tucson for the Year 1881, Containing a Comprehensive List of Inhabitants with Their Occupations and Places of Residence; the Public Officers and Their Offices; with a Review of the Past, a Glance at the Present, and a Forecast of the Future of this City; Together with Other Useful Information Concerning the Same.* H. S. Crocker, San Francisco.

Baumler, M. F., and C. E. Downum
1989 Between Micro and Macro: A Study in the Interpretation of Small-Sized Lithic Debitage. In *Experiments in Lithic Technology*, edited by D. Amick and R. Maudlin, pp. 101–116. British Archaeological Reports International Series No. 528. London.

Bayham, Frank E.
1982 *A Diachronic Analysis of Prehistoric Animal Exploitation at Ventana Cave.* Unpublished Ph.D. dissertation, Department of Anthropology, Arizona State University, Tempe.

Bayham, Frank E., and Pamela Hatch
1985 Hohokam and Salado Animal Utilization in the Tonto Basin. In *Studies in the Hohokam and Salado of the Tonto Basin*, edited by G. Rice, pp. 191–210. Office of Cultural Resource Management, Department of Anthropology, Arizona State University, Tempe.

Bayham, Frank E., Donald H. Morris, and M. Steven Shackley
1986 *Prehistoric Hunter-Gatherers of South Central Arizona: The Picacho Reservoir Archaic Project.* Anthropological Field Studies No. 13. Office of Cultural Resource Management, Department of Anthropology, Arizona State University, Tempe.

Benson, Lyman, and R. A. Darrow
1981 *Trees and Shrubs of the Southwestern Deserts.* University of Arizona Press, Tucson.

Bequaert, Joseph C., and Walter B. Miller
1973 *The Mollusks of the Arid Southwest.* University of Arizona Press, Tucson.

Berge, Dale L.
1980 *Simpson Springs Station: Historical Archaeology in Western Utah.* Cultural Resource Series No. 16. Bureau of Land Management, Utah State Office.

Bernard-Shaw, Mary
1988 Hohokam Canal Systems and Late Archaic Wells: The Evidence from the Los Morteros Site. In *Recent Research on Tucson Basin Prehistory: Proceedings of the Second Tucson Basin Conference*, edited by W. H. Doelle and P. R. Fish, pp. 153–174. Anthropological Papers No. 10. Institute for American Research, Tucson.

1989a *Archaeological Investigations at Los Morteros, AZ AA:12:57 (ASM), Locus 1, in the Northern Tucson Basin.* Technical Report No. 87-8. Institute for American Research, Tucson.

1989b *Archaeological Investigations at the Redtail Site, AA:12:149 (ASM), in the Northern Tucson Basin.* Technical Report No. 89-8. Center for Desert Archaeology, Tucson.

1990 *Archaeological Investigations at the Lonetree Site, AA:12:120 (ASM), in the Northern Tucson Basin.* Technical Report No. 90-1. Center for Desert Archaeology, Tucson.

Bernard-Shaw, Mary, and William H. Doelle
1991 Tucson Basin Irrigation Systems. In *Prehistoric Irrigation in Arizona: Symposium 1988*, edited by C. D. Breternitz, pp. 25–40. Publications in Archaeology No. 17. Soil Systems, Phoenix.

Berry, Michael S.
1982 *Time, Space, and Transition in Anasazi Prehistory*. University of Utah Press, Salt Lake City.

Betancourt, Julio L.
1978 *An Archaeological Synthesis of the Tucson Basin: Focus on the Santa Cruz and Its Riverpark*. Archaeological Series No. 116. Arizona State Museum, University of Arizona, Tucson.

Betancourt, Julio L., and R. M. Turner
1988 Historic Arroyo-Cutting and Subsequent Channel Changes at the Congress Street Crossing, Santa Cruz River, Tucson. In *Arid Lands, Today and Tomorrow, Proceedings of an International Research and Development Conference, Tucson, Arizona, October 1985*, edited by E. E. Whitehead, C. F. Hutchinson, F. N. Timmerman, and R. G. Valady, pp. 1353–1371. Westview Press, Boulder.

Bohrer, Vorsila L.
1991 Recently Recognized Cultivated and Encouraged Plants among the Hohokam. *Kiva* 56:227–235.

1992 New Life from Ashes II: A Tale of Burnt Brush. *Desert Plants* 10(3):122–125.

Bohrer, Vorsila L., Hugh C. Cutler, and Jonathan D. Sauer
1969 Carbonized Plant Remains from Two Hohokam Sites, Arizona BB:13:41 and Arizona BB:13:50. *The Kiva* 35(1):1–10.

Bourke, John Gregory
1971 *On the Border with Crook*. University of Nebraska Press, Lincoln. Originally published 1891, Charles Scribner's Sons, New York.

Bradley, Bruce A.
1980 *Excavations at AZ BB:13:74, Santa Cruz Industrial Park, Tucson, Arizona*. CASA Papers No. 1. Complete Archaeological Service Associates, Oracle, Arizona.

Braun, David P.
1980 Experimental Interpretation of Ceramic Vessel Use on the Basis of Rim and Neck Formal Attributes. In *The Navajo Project: Archaeological Investigations, Page to Phoenix 500KV Southern Transmission Line*, by D. C. Fiero, R. W. Munson, M. T. McClain, S. M. Wilson, and A. H. Zier, pp. 171–221. Research Paper

No. 11. Museum of Northern Arizona, Flagstaff.

Brew, Susan A., and Bruce B. Huckell
1987 A Protohistoric Piman Burial and a Consideration of Piman Burial Practices. *The Kiva* 52:163–191.

Brown, David E., and Charles H. Lowe
1980 *Biotic Communities of the Southwest*. General Technical Report No. RM-78. USDA Forest Service, Rocky Mountain Forest and Range Experiment Station, Fort Collins, Colorado.

Bubemyre, Trixi
1996 Ceramics. In *Archaeological Investigations at the SRI Locus, West Branch Site (AZ AA:16:3 [ASM]), a Rincon Phase Village in the Tucson Basin*, by J. H. Altschul, T. Bubemyre, K. M. Cairns, W. L. Deaver, A. Della Croce, S. K. Fish, L. Fratt, K. G. Harry, J. Holmlund, G. Huckleberry, C. H. Miksicek, A. W. Vokes, S. M. Whittlesey, M. N. Zedeño, and L. F. Ziady, Chapter 6. Draft report submitted to Pima County Department of Transportation and Flood Control District, W. O. 4 BISCO. Statistical Research, Tucson.

Bufkin, Donald
1980 Tucson, Arizona Territory, c. 1880. Prepared to accompany article "The Landmarks of Historic Tucson, a Descriptive Guide to 100 Sites." *Arizoniana, The Journal of Arizona History*. Arizona Historical Society, Tucson.

Bureau of Land Management (BLM)
1962 *Homesteads*. U.S. Government Printing Office, Washington, D.C.

Burrus, Ernest J., S.J.
1965 *Kino and the Cartography of Western New Spain*. Arizona Historical Society, Tucson.

1971 *Kino and Manje: Explorers of Sonora and Arizona*. Sources and Studies for the History of the Americas, Vol. 10. Jesuit Historical Institute, St. Louis.

Butler, Robert F.
1992 *Paleomagnetism: Magnetic Domains to Geologic Terranes*. Blackwell Scientific Publications, Boston.

Cable, John S., and David E. Doyel
1987   Pioneer Period Village Structure and Settle-
        ment Pattern in the Phoenix Basin. In *The
        Hohokam Village: Site Structure and Organi-
        zation*, edited by D. E. Doyel, pp. 21–70.
        Southwestern and Rocky Mountain Division,
        American Association for the Advancement of
        Science, Glenwood Springs, Colorado.

Cairns, Kellie M., and Jeffrey H. Altschul
1994   *Testing and Data Recovery at Seneca Terrace II.*
        Technical Report 94-2. Statistical Research,
        Tucson.

Cairns, Kellie M., and Richard Ciolek-Torrello
1998   Faunal Analysis. In *Early Farmers of the Sono-
        ran Desert: Archaeological Investigations at
        the Houghton Road Site, Tucson, Arizona*,
        edited by R. Ciolek-Torrello, pp. 169–184.
        Technical Series No. 72. Statistical Research,
        Tucson.

Carlson, Roy L.
1970   *White Mountain Redware: A Pottery Tradition
        of East-Central Arizona and Western New
        Mexico.* Anthropological Papers No. 19.
        University of Arizona, Tucson.

1982   The Polychrome Complexes. In *Southwestern
        Ceramics: A Comparative Review*, edited by
        A. H. Schroeder, pp 201–234. The Arizona
        Archaeologist No. 15. Arizona Archaeological
        Society, Phoenix.

Carskadden, Jeff, and Richard Gartley
1990   A Preliminary Seriation of Nineteenth Century
        Decorated Porcelain Marbles. *Historical
        Archaeology* 24(2):55–69.

Castetter, Edward F., and Willis H. Bell
1942   *Pima and Papago Indian Agriculture.* Univer-
        sity of New Mexico Press, Albuquerque.

Castetter, Edward F., and Ruth M. Underhill
1935   *The Ethnobiology of the Papago Indians.* Eth-
        nobiological Studies in the American South-
        west No. 2, University of New Mexico Bulle-
        tin No. 275, Biological Series Vol. 4, No. 3.
        University of New Mexico, Albuquerque.

Chisholm, Michael
1979   *Rural Settlement and Land Use: An Essay on
        Location.* 3rd ed. John Wiley, New York.

Ciolek-Torrello, Richard
1985   A Typology of Room Function at Grasshopper
        Pueblo, Arizona. *Journal of Field Archaeology*
        12(1):42–63.

1987   Review of *Archaeological Investigations at
        the West Branch Site: Early and Middle Rin-
        con Occupation in the Southern Tucson Basin*,
        by Frederick W. Huntington. *The Kiva*
        53:66–73.

1988a   Conclusions. In *Hohokam Settlement along
        the Slopes of the Picacho Mountains, Tucson
        Aqueduct Project*, Vol. 6: *Synthesis and Con-
        clusions*, edited by R. Ciolek-Torrello and
        D. R. Wilcox, pp. 300–314. Research Paper
        No. 35. Museum of Northern Arizona, Flagstaff.

1988b   Domestic and Community Organization. In
        *Hohokam Settlement along the Slopes of the
        Picacho Mountains, Tucson Aqueduct Project*,
        Vol. 6: *Synthesis and Conclusions*, edited by
        R. Ciolek-Torrello and D. R. Wilcox, pp. 165–
        219. Research Paper No. 35. Museum of
        Northern Arizona, Flagstaff.

1994   Site Summary, in "Riser Site, AZ U:8:225/
        1580." In *The Roosevelt Rural Sites Study*,
        Vol. 2: *Prehistoric Rural Settlements in the
        Tonto Basin*, Part 1, edited by R. S. Ciolek-
        Torrello, S. D. Shelley, and S. Benaron,
        pp. 329–336. Technical Series No. 28.
        Statistical Research, Tucson.

1995   The Houghton Road Site, the Agua Caliente
        Phase, and the Early Formative Period in the
        Tucson Basin. *The Kiva* 60:531–574.

Ciolek-Torrello, Richard (editor)
1987   *Hohokam Settlement along the Slopes of the
        Picacho Mountains, Tucson Aqueduct Project*,
        Vol. 3: *The Picacho Area Sites.* Research Pa-
        per No. 35. Museum of Northern Arizona,
        Flagstaff.

1998   *Early Farmers of the Sonoran Desert: Archae-
        ological Investigations at the Houghton Road
        Site, Tucson, Arizona.* Technical Series No. 72.
        Statistical Research, Tucson.

Ciolek-Torrello, Richard, and David H. Greenwald
1988a   Architecture and House Function. In *Hohokam
        Settlement along the Slopes of the Picacho
        Mountains, Tucson Aqueduct Project*, Vol. 6:
        Synthesis and Conclusions, edited by R. Cio-
        lek-Torrello and D. R. Wilcox, pp. 121–164.

Research Paper No. 35. Museum of Northern Arizona, Flagstaff.

1988b Site Structure and Domestic Organization in the Picacho Mountain Area. In *Recent Research on Tucson Basin Prehistory: Proceedings of the Second Tucson Basin Conference*, edited by W. H. Doelle and P. R. Fish, pp. 109–134. Anthropological Papers No. 10. Institute for American Research, Tucson.

Ciolek-Torrello, Richard, and Carl D. Halbirt
1987 The Rock Terrace Site, NA18,017. In *Hohokam Settlement along the Slopes of the Picacho Mountains, Tucson Aqueduct Project*, Vol. 3: *The Picacho Area Sites*, edited by R. Ciolek-Torrello, pp. 217–254. Research Paper No. 35. Museum of Northern Arizona, Flagstaff.

Ciolek-Torrello, Richard, and Jeffrey A. Homburg
1990 *Cultural Resources Surveys and Overviews of the Rillito River Drainage Area, Pima County, Arizona*. Technical Series No. 20. Statistical Research, Tucson.

Ciolek-Torrello, Richard, Eric E. Klucas, and Stephanie M. Whittlesey
1998 Hohokam Households, Settlement Structure, and Economy in the Lower Verde Valley. In *The Hohokam Village Revisited,* edited by D. E. Doyel, S. K. Fish, and P. R. Fish. Southwestern and Rocky Mountain Division, American Association for the Advancement of Science, Glenwood Springs, Colorado. In press.

Ciolek-Torrello, Richard, and J. Jefferson Reid
1974 Change in Household Size at Grasshopper. *The Kiva* 40:49–47.

Ciolek-Torrello, Richard, and Mark T. Swanson
1997 Introduction. In *Pit House, Presidio, and Privy: 1,400 Years of Archaeology and History on Block 180, Tucson, Arizona*, edited by R. Ciolek-Torrello and M. T. Swanson, pp. 1–55. Technical Series No. 63. Statistical Research, Tucson.

Ciolek-Torrello, Richard, and Mark T. Swanson (editors)
1997 *Pit House, Presidio, and Privy: 1,400 Years of Archaeology and History on Block 180, Tucson, Arizona*. Technical Series No. 63. Statistical Research, Tucson.

Clonts, John B.
1983 Some Long Overdue Thoughts on Faunal Analysis. In *Forgotten Places and Things: Archaeological Perspectives on American History*, edited by A. E. Ward. Center for Anthropological Studies, Albuquerque.

Colton, Harold S., and Lyndon L. Hargrave
1937 *Handbook of Northern Arizona Pottery Wares.* Bulletin No. 11. Museum of Northern Arizona, Flagstaff.

Cook, Sherburne F., and Robert F. Heizer
1968 Relationships among Houses, Settlement Areas, and Population in Aboriginal California. In *Settlement Archaeology*, edited by K. C. Chang, pp. 79–116. National Press Books, Palo Alto.

Cooke, R. U., and R. W. Reeves
1976 *Arroyo and Environmental Change in the American Southwest*. Clarendon Press, Oxford.

Craig, Douglas B.
1982 Shell Exchange along the Middle Santa Cruz Valley during the Hohokam Pre-Classic. Paper presented at the Tucson Basin Conference, University of Arizona, Tucson. Ms. on file, Arizona State Museum Library, University of Arizona, Tucson.

1988 *Archaeological Investigations at AA:16:49 (ASM): the Dakota Wash Mitigation*. Anthropology Series Archaeological Report No. 14. Pima Community College, Tucson.

Craig, Douglas B., and Henry D. Wallace (editors)
1987 *Prehistoric Settlement in the Cañada del Oro Valley: The Rancho Vistoso Survey Project.* Anthropological Papers No. 8. Institute for American Research, Tucson.

Crown, Patricia L.
1984 Classic Period Ceramic Manufacturing: Exploring Variability in the Production and Use of Hohokam Vessels. In *Hohokam Archaeology along the Salt-Gila Aqueduct, Central Arizona Project*, Vol. 7: *Material Culture*, edited by L. S. Teague and P. L. Crown, pp. 119–197. Archaeological Series No. 150. Arizona State Museum, University of Arizona, Tucson.

1985 Morphology and Function of Hohokam Small Structures. *The Kiva* 50:75–94.

Curriden, Nancy T.
1981 *The Lewis-Weber Site, a Tucson Homestead.* Publications in Anthropology No. 14. USDI, National Park Service, Western Archeological and Conservation Center, Tucson.

Curtin, Leonora Scott Muse
1984 *By the Prophet of the Earth.* University of Arizona Press, Tucson.

Czaplicki, Jon S., and James D. Mayberry
1983 *An Archaeological Assessment of the Middle Santa Cruz River Basin, Rillito to Green Valley, Arizona, for the Proposed Tucson Aqueduct Phase B, Central Arizona Project.* Archaeological Series No. 164. Arizona State Museum, University of Arizona, Tucson.

Czaplicki, Jon S., and John C. Ravesloot (editors)
1988 *Hohokam Archaeology along Phase B of the Tucson Aqueduct Central Arizona Project,* Vol. 2: *Excavations at Fastimes (AZ AA:12:384), a Rillito Phase Site in the Avra Valley.* Archaeological Series No. 178. Arizona State Museum, University of Arizona, Tucson.

1989a *Hohokam Archaeology along Phase B of the Tucson Aqueduct Central Arizona Project,* Vol. 3: *Excavations at Water World (AZ AA:16:94), a Rillito Phase Ballcourt Village in the Avra Valley.* Archaeological Series No. 178. Arizona State Museum, University of Arizona, Tucson.

1989b *Hohokam Archaeology along Phase B of the Tucson Aqueduct Central Arizona Project,* Vol. 4: *Small Sites and Specialized Reports.* Archaeological Series No. 178. Arizona State Museum, University of Arizona, Tucson.

Dart, Allen
1986 *Archaeological Investigations at La Paloma: Archaic and Hohokam Occupations at Three Sites in the Northeastern Tucson Basin, Arizona.* Anthropological Papers No. 4. Institute for American Research, Tucson.

Dart, Allen, and James Gibb
1982 An Archaeological Investigation of AZ BB:13:146, a Small Occupation Site in the Tucson Basin, Pima County, Arizona. In *Archaeological Test Excavations in Southern Arizona,* compiled by S. A. Brew, pp. 105–144. Archaeological Series No. 152. Arizona State Museum, University of Arizona, Tucson.

Davidson, E. S.
1973 *Geohydrology and Water Resources of the Tucson Basin, Arizona.* U.S. Geological Survey Water-Supply Paper 1939-E. U.S. Government Printing Office, Washington, D.C.

Davis-Monthan Air Force Base
n.d. Climatic and Environmental Conditions, Davis-Monthan AFB, Tucson, Arizona. Ms. on file, Davis-Monthan Air Force Base, Tucson.

Dean, Jeffrey S.
1978 Independent Dating in Archaeological Analysis. In *Advances in Archaeological Method and Theory,* Vol. 1, edited by M. B. Schiffer, pp. 223–255. Academic Press, New York.

1987 Thoughts on Hohokam Settlement Behaviors: Comments on "The Hohokam Village." In *The Hohokam Village: Site Structure and Organization,* edited by D. E. Doyel, pp. 253–262. Southwestern and Rocky Mountain Division, American Association for the Advancement of Science, Glenwood Springs, Colorado.

1988 Dendrochronology and Paleoenvironmental Reconstruction on the Colorado Plateaus. In *The Anasazi in a Changing Environment,* edited by G. J. Gumerman, pp. 119–167. School of American Research and Cambridge University Press, Cambridge.

1991 Thoughts on Hohokam Chronology. In *Exploring the Hohokam: Prehistoric Desert Peoples of the American Southwest,* edited by G. J. Gumerman, pp. 61–149. Amerind Foundation New World Studies Series No.1. University of New Mexico Press, Albuquerque.

Dean, Jeffrey S., Robert C. Euler, George J. Gumerman, Fred Plog, Richard H. Hevly, and Thor N. V. Karlstrom
1985 Human Behavior, Demography, and Paleoenvironment on the Colorado Plateau. *American Antiquity* 50:537–554.

Deaver, William L.
1984 Pottery. In *Hohokam Habitation Sites in the Northern Santa Rita Mountains,* Vol. 2, by A. Ferg, K. C. Rozen, W. L. Deaver, M. D. Tagg, D. A. Phillips, Jr., and D. A. Gregory, pp. 237–419. Archaeological Series No. 147. Arizona State Museum, University of Arizona, Tucson.

1988   Identifying Contemporary Archaeological Events through Comparison of Archaeomagnetic Directions. In *The 1982–1984 Excavations at Las Colinas: The Site and Its Features,* by D. A. Gregory, W. L. Deaver, S. K. Fish, R. Gardiner, R. W. Layhe, F. L. Nials, and L. S. Teague, pp. 73–120. Archaeological Series No. 162, Vol. 2. Arizona State Museum, University of Arizona, Tucson.

1989a   Ceramics, in "Excavations at Hawk's Nest (AZ AA:12:484), a Late Pioneer–Early Colonial Period Hohokam Farmstead." In *Hohokam Archaeology along Phase B of the Tucson Aqueduct, Central Arizona Project,* Vol. 4: *Small Sites and Specialized Reports*, edited by J. S. Czaplicki and J. C. Ravesloot, pp. 51–61. Archaeological Series No. 178. Arizona State Museum, University of Arizona, Tucson.

1989b   Pottery and Other Ceramic Artifacts. In *The 1979–1983 Testing at Los Morteros (AZ AA:12:57 ASM), a Large Hohokam Village Site in the Tucson Basin,* by R. C. Lange and W. L. Deaver, pp. 27–81. Archaeological Series No. 177. Arizona State Museum, University of Arizona, Tucson.

1989c   Southwestern Archaeomagnetic Secular Variation: The Hohokam Data. In *The 1982–1984 Excavations at Las Colinas: Syntheses and Conclusions,* by L. S. Teague and W. L. Deaver, pp. 7–42. Archaeological Series No. 162, Vol. 6. Arizona State Museum, University of Arizona, Tucson.

1998   The Architecture at Scorpion Point Village: Ball Courts and Pit Houses. In *Descriptions of Habitation and Nonagricultural Sites*, edited by R. Ciolek-Torrello, pp. 21–78. Vanishing River: Landscapes and Lives of the Lower Verde Valley: The Lower Verde Archaeological Project, Vol. 2. CD-ROM. SRI Press, Tucson.

Deaver, William L., and Jeffrey H. Altschul
1996   Archaeological Timeline for the SRI Locus. In *Archaeological Investigations at the SRI Locus, West Branch Site (AZ AA:16:3 [ASM]), a Rincon Phase Village in the Tucson Basin,* by J. H. Altschul, T. Bubemyre, K. M. Cairns, W. L. Deaver, A. Della Croce, S. K. Fish, L. Fratt, K. G. Harry, J. Holmlund, G. Huckleberry, C. H. Miksicek, A. W. Vokes, S. M. Whittlesey, M. N Zedeño, and L. F. Ziady,

Chapter 3. Draft report submitted to Pima County Department of Transportation and Flood Control District, W. O. 4 BISCO. Statistical Research, Tucson.

Deaver, William L., and Richard Ciolek-Torrello
1993   *Archaeological Testing in the 100-Year Floodplain at the 49ers Country Club, Pima County, Arizona.* Technical Report No. 93-13. Statistical Research, Tucson.

1995   Early Formative Period Chronology for the Tucson Basin. *Kiva* 60:481–529.

Dibble, H. L., and J. C. Whittaker
1981   New Experimental Evidence on the Relation between Percussion Flaking and Flake Variation. *Journal of Archaeological Science* 8:283–298.

Di Peso, Charles C.
1953   *The Sobaipuri Indians of the Upper San Pedro River Valley, Southeastern Arizona.* Papers No. 6. Amerind Foundation, Dragoon, Arizona.

1956   *The Upper Pima of San Cayetano del Tumacacori: An Archaeological Reconstruction of the Ootam of the Pimeria Alta.* Papers No. 7. Amerind Foundation, Dragoon, Arizona.

DiPeso, Charles C., John B. Rinaldo, and Gloria J. Fenner
1974   *Casas Grandes, a Fallen Trading Center of the Gran Chichimeca,* Vol. 6: *Ceramics and Shell.* The Amerind Foundation Series No. 9. Amerind Foundation, Dragoon, Arizona, and Northland Press, Flagstaff.

Dobyns, Henry F.
1963   Indian Extinction in the Middle Santa Cruz River Valley, Arizona. *New Mexico Historical Review* 38:163–181.

1976   *Spanish Colonial Tucson: A Demographic History.* University of Arizona Press, Tucson.

Doebley, John F., and Vorsila L. Bohrer
1983   Maize Variability and Cultural Selection at Salmon Ruin, New Mexico. *The Kiva* 49:19–37.

Doelle, William H.
1984   The Tucson Basin during the Protohistoric Period. *The Kiva* 49:195–211.

1985   *Excavations at the Valencia Site, a Preclassic Hohokam Village in the Southern Tucson Basin.* Anthropological Papers No. 3. Institute for American Research, Tucson.

1988   Preclassic Community Patterns in the Tucson Basin. In *Recent Research on Tucson Basin Prehistory: Proceedings of the Second Tucson Basin Conference,* edited by W. H. Doelle and P. R. Fish, pp. 277–312. Anthropological Papers No. 10. Institute for American Research, Tucson.

Doelle, William H., Allen Dart, and Henry D. Wallace
1985   *The Southern Tucson Basin Survey: Intensive Survey along the Santa Cruz River.* Technical Report No. 85-3. Institute for American Research, Tucson.

Doelle, William H., Frederick W. Huntington, and Henry D. Wallace
1987   Rincon Phase Organization in the Tucson Basin. In *The Hohokam Village: Site Structure and Organization,* edited by D. E. Doyel, pp. 71–95. Southwestern and Rocky Mountain Division, American Association for the Advancement of Science, Glenwood Springs, Colorado.

Doelle, William H., and Henry D. Wallace
1986   *Hohokam Settlement Patterns in the San Xavier Project Area, Southern Tucson Basin.* Technical Report No. 84-6. Institute for American Research, Tucson.

1991   The Changing Role of the Tucson Basin in the Hohokam Regional System. In *Exploring the Hohokam: Prehistoric Desert Peoples of the American Southwest,* edited by G. J. Gumerman, pp. 279–346. Amerind Foundation New World Studies Series No. 1. University of New Mexico Press, Albuquerque.

Doolittle, Christopher J., and Joseph A. Ezzo
1995   *Data Recovery at Badger Hole Ranch (AZ AA:12:40 [ASM]), a Late Rincon/Tanque Verde Phase Site in the Northwestern Tucson Basin.* Technical Report No. 95-2. Statistical Research, Tucson.

Doolittle, William E.
1990   *Canal Irrigation in Prehistoric Mexico: The Sequence of Technological Change.* University of Texas Press, Austin.

Douglas, John E., and Douglas B. Craig
1986   *Investigations of Archaic and Hohokam Sites on the Flying V Ranch, Tucson, Arizona.* Archaeological Report No. 13. Pima Community College, Tucson.

Downum, Christian E.
1993   *Between Desert and River: Hohokam Settlement and Land Use in the Los Robles Community.* Anthropological Papers No. 57. University of Arizona Press, Tucson.

Doyel, David E.
1977a   *Excavations in the Middle Santa Cruz River Valley, Southeastern Arizona.* Contributions to Highway Salvage Archaeology in Arizona No. 44. Arizona State Museum, University of Arizona, Tucson.

1977b   Rillito and Rincon Period Settlement Systems in the Middle Santa Cruz River Valley: Alternative Models. *The Kiva* 43:93–110.

1981   *Late Hohokam Prehistory in Southern Arizona.* Contributions to Archaeology, No. 2. Gila Press, Scottsdale.

1984   From Foraging to Farming: An Overview. *The Kiva* 49:147–166.

1985   The New River–Palo Verde Community System. In *Hohokam Settlement and Economic Systems in the Central New River Drainage, Arizona,* edited by D. E. Doyel and M. D. Elson, pp. 681–699. Publications in Archaeology No. 4. Soil Systems, Phoenix.

1991   Hohokam Cultural Evolution in the Phoenix Basin. In *Exploring the Hohokam: Prehistoric Desert Peoples of the American Southwest,* edited by G. J. Gumerman, pp. 231–278. Amerind Foundation New World Studies Series, No. 1., University of New Mexico Press, Albuquerque.

Eberly, L. D., and T. B. Stanley
1978   Cenozoic Stratigraphy and Geologic History of Southwestern Arizona. *Bulletin of the Geological Society of America* 89:921–941.

Eddy, Frank W., and Maurice E. Cooley
1983   *Cultural and Environmental History of Cienega Valley, Southeastern Arizona.* Anthropological Papers No. 43. University of Arizona, Tucson.

Effland, Richard W., and Adrianne G. Rankin
1988   Adaptation within the Santa Cruz River Flood-plain near Mission San Xavier: Response to Changing Environments. In *Recent Research on Tucson Basin Prehistory: Proceedings of the Second Tucson Basin Conference*, edited by W. H. Doelle and P. R. Fish, pp. 183–205. Anthropological Papers No. 10. Institute for American Research, Tucson.

Eighmy, Jeffrey L.
1990   Archaeomagnetic Dating: Practical Problems for the Archaeologist. In *Archaeomagnetic Dating*, edited by J. L. Eighmy and R. S. Sternberg, pp. 33–64. University of Arizona Press, Tucson.

1991   Archaeomagnetism: New Data on the Southwest USA Master Virtual Geomagnetic Pole Curve. *Archaeometry* 33(2):201–214.

Eighmy, Jeffrey L., and Jerry B. Howard
1991   Direct Dating of Prehistoric Canal Sediments Using Archaeomagnetism. *American Antiquity* 56:88–102.

Eighmy, Jeffrey L., and Randall H. McGuire
1988   *Archaeomagnetic Dates and the Hohokam Phase Sequence*. Technical Series No. 3. Archaeometric Lab, Colorado State University, Fort Collins.

Eighmy, Jeffrey L., and Robert S. Sternberg
1990   *Archaeomagnetic Dating*. University of Arizona Press, Tucson.

Elson, Mark D.
1986   *Archaeological Investigations at the Tanque Verde Wash Site, a Middle Rincon Settlement in the Eastern Tucson Basin*. Anthropological Papers No. 7. Institute for American Research, Tucson.

Elson, Mark D., and William H. Doelle
1986   *The Valencia Site Testing Project: Mapping, Intensive Surface Collecting, and Limited Trenching of a Hohokam Ballcourt Village in the Southern Tucson Basin*. Technical Report No. 86-6. Institute for American Research, Tucson.

1987   *Archaeological Assessment of the Mission Road Extension: Testing at AZ BB:13:6 (ASM)*. Technical Report No. 87-6. Institute for American Research, Tucson.

Engebretson, David C., and Myrl E. Beck, Jr.
1978   On the Shape of Directional Data Sets. *Journal of Geophysical Research* 83(B12): 5979–5982.

Eppley, Lisa G.
1986   Lithics. In *Archaeological Investigations at the West Branch Site: Early and Middle Rincon Occupation in the Southern Tucson Basin*, edited by F. W. Huntington, pp. 197–228. Anthropological Papers No. 5. Institute for American Research, Tucson.

1990   Lonetree Chipped and Ground Stone Analyses. In *Archaeological Investigations at the Lonetree Site, AA:12:120 (ASM), in the Northern Tucson Basin*, by M. Bernard-Shaw, pp. 127–147. Technical Report No. 90-1. Center for Desert Archaeology, Tucson.

Ervin, Richard G.
1983   *Archaeological Monitering and Salvage Excavations at AZ BB:9:101, a Late Rincon Site in Tucson, Arizona*. Revision. Arizona State Museum, University of Arizona, Tucson. Originally published 1982.

Euler, Robert C., George G. Gumerman, Thor N. V. Karlstrom, Jeffrey S. Dean, and Richar H. Hevly
1979   The Colorado Plateaus: Cultural Dynamics and Paleoenvironment. *Science* 205:1089–1101.

Ezzo, Joseph A., and William L. Deaver
1998   *Watering the Desert: Late Archaic Farming at the Costello-King Site*. Technical Series No. 68. Statistical Research, Tucson.

Faegri, Knut, and Johs Iversen
1989   *Textbook of Pollen Analysis*. 4th ed. John Wiley, New York.

Fall, Pat
1987   Pollen Taphonomy in a Canyon Stream. *Quaternary Research* 28:393–406.

Ferg, Alan
1980   Shell from Gu Achi. In *Excavations at Gu Achi: A Reappraisal of Hohokam Settlement and Subsistence in the Arizona Papagueria*, by W. Bruce Masse, pp. 371–394. Publications in Anthropology No. 12. Western Archeological and Conservation Center, National Park Service, Tucson.

1984   Nonutilitarian Ground Stone, Crystals, and Minerals. In *Hohokam Habitation in the Northern Santa Rita Mountains*, edited by A. Ferg, K. C. Rozen, W. L. Deaver, M. D. Tagg, D. A. Phillips, Jr., and D. A. Gregory, pp. 665–686. Archaeological Series No. 147, Vol. 2, Part 2. Arizona State Museum, University of Arizona, Tucson.

Fewkes, Jesse W.
1896   Pacific Coast Shell from Prehistoric Tusayan Pueblos. *American Anthropologist* (Old Series) 9:359–367.

Fish, Paul R.
1989   The Hohokam: 1,000 Years of Prehistory in the Sonoran Desert. In *Dynamics of Southwest Prehistory*, edited by L. S. Cordell and G. J. Gumerman, pp. 19–63. Smithsonian Institution Press, Washington, D.C.

Fish, Paul R., Suzanne K. Fish, and John H. Madsen
1988   Differentiation in Bajada Portions of a Tucson Basin Classic Community. In *Recent Research on Tucson Basin Prehistory: Proceedings of the Second Tucson Basin Conference*, edited by W. H. Doelle and P. R. Fish, pp. 225–239. Anthropological Papers No. 10. Institute for American Research, Tucson.

Fish, Paul R., Suzanne K. Fish, Stephanie M. Whittlesey, Hector Neff, Michael D. Glasscock, and J. Michael Elam
1992   An Evaluation of Production and Exchange of Tanque Verde Red-on-Brown Ceramics in Southern Arizona. In *Chemical Characterization of Ceramic Pastes in Archaeology*, edited by H. Neff, pp. 233–254. Monographs in World Archaeology No. 7. Prehistory Press, Madison.

Fish, Suzanne K.
1984   Agriculture and Subsistence Implications of the Salt-Gila Aqueduct Pollen Analysis. In *Hohokam Archaeology along the Salt-Gila Aqueduct Central Arizona Project*, Vol. 7: *Environment and Subsistence*, edited by L. S. Teague and P. L. Crown, pp. 111–138. Archaeological Series No. 150. Arizona State Museum, University of Arizona, Tucson.

1986   Pollen Analysis. In *Archaeological Investigations at the West Branch Site: Early and Middle Rincon Occupation in the Southern Tucson Basin*, by F. W. Huntington, pp. 315–323.

Anthropological Papers No. 5. Institute for American Research, Tucson.

Fish, Suzanne K., Paul R. Fish, and Christian E. Downum
1984   Hohokam Terraces and Agricultural Production in the Tucson Basin. In *Prehistoric Agricultural Strategies in the Southwest*, edited by S. K. Fish and P. R. Fish, pp. 55–71. Anthropological Research Papers No. 33. Arizona State University, Tempe.

Fish, Suzanne K., Paul R. Fish, and John H. Madsen (editors)
1992   *The Marana Community in the Hohokam World*. Anthropological Papers No. 56. University of Arizona Press, Tucson.

Fish, Suzanne K., Paul R. Fish, Charles Miksicek, and John Madsen
1985   Prehistoric Agave Cultivation in Southern Arizona. *Desert Plants* 7(2):107–112, 100.

Fisher, R. A.
1953   Dispersion on a Sphere. *Proceedings of the Royal Society of London* A217: 295–305.

Flannery, Kent V.
1972   The Origins of the Village as a Settlement Type in Mesoamerica and the Near East: A Comparative Study. In *Man, Settlement and Urbanism*, edited by P. Ucko, R. Tringham, and G. W. Dimbleby, pp. 23–53. Gerald Duckworth, London.

Fontana, Bernard L., and J. Cameron Greenleaf
1962   Johnny Ward's Ranch: A Study in Historic Archaeology. *The Kiva* 28:1–115.

Fontana, Bernard L., William J. Robinson, Charles W. Cormack, and Ernest E. Levitt, Jr.
1962   *Papago Indian Pottery*. University of Washington Press, Seattle.

Fraps, Clara Lee
1935   Tanque Verde Ruins. *The Kiva* 1:1–4.

Freeman, Andrea K. L. (editor)
1997   *Archaeological Investigations at the Wetlands Site, AZ AA:12:90 (ASM)*. Technical Report No. 97-5. Center for Desert Archaeology, Tucson.

Gabel, Norman E.
1931 *Martinez Hill Ruins: An Example of Prehistoric Culture of the Middle Gila*. Unpublished Master's thesis, Department of Anthropology, University of Arizona, Tucson.

Gasser, Robert E., and Richard Ciolek-Torrello
1988 Locus S. In *Hohokam Settlement along the Slopes of the Picacho Mountains, Tucson Aqueduct Project*, Vol. 2: *The Brady Wash Sites*, edited by R. S. Ciolek-Torrello, M. M. Callahan, and D. H. Greenwald, pp. 496–579. Research Paper No. 35. Museum of Northern Arizona, Flagstaff.

Gasser, Robert E., and Scott M. Kwiatkowski
1991 Food for Thought: Recognizing Patterns in Hohokam Subsistence. In *Exploring the Hohokam: Prehistoric Desert Peoples of the American Southwest*, edited by G. J. Gumerman, pp. 417–459. Amerind Foundation New World Studies Series No. 1. University of New Mexico Press, Albuquerque.

Gates, Paul W.
1968 *History of Public Land Law Development*. U.S. Public Land Law Review Commission, Washington, D.C.

Gelderman, Frederick W.
1972 *Soil Survey of the Tucson–Avra Valley Area, Arizona*. U.S. Government Printing Office, Washington, D.C.

Gifford, Edward W.
1947 *Californian Shell Artifacts*. University of California Anthropological Records, Vol. 9, No. 1, pp. 1–132. University of California, Berkeley.

Gilbert, B. Miles
1973 *Mammalian Osteo-Archaeology: North America*. Missouri Archaeological Society, Columbia.

Gilbert, B. Miles, Larry D. Martin, and Howard D. Savage
1985 *Avian Osteology*. Missouri Archaeological Society, Columbia.

Gillespie, William B.
1989 Vertebrate Remains. In *Archaeological Investigations at the Redtail Site, AA:12:149 (ASM), in the Northern Tucson Basin*, by M. Bernard-Shaw, pp. 171–190. Technical Report No. 89-8. Center for Desert Archaeology, Tucson.

Gish, Jannifer
1991 Current Perceptions, Recent Discoveries, and Future Directions in Hohokam Palynology. *Kiva* 56:237–254.

Gladwin, Harold S., Emil W. Haury, E. B. Sayles, and Nora Gladwin
1937 *Excavations at Snaketown: Material Culture*. Medallion Papers No. 25. Gila Pueblo, Globe, Arizona.

Graff, C.
1985 Flaked Stone. In *Excavations at the Valencia Site, a Preclassic Hohokam Village in the Southern Tucson Basin*, edited by W. H. Doelle, pp. 161–184. Anthropological Papers No. 3. Institute for American Research, Tucson.

Graybill, Donald A.
1989 The Reconstruction of Prehistoric Salt River Streamflow. In *The 1982–1984 Excavations at Las Colinas: Environment and Subsistence*, by D. A. Graybill, D. A. Gregory, F. L. Nials, S. K. Fish, R. E. Gasser, C. H. Miksicek, and C. R. Szuter, pp. 25–38. Archaeological Series No. 162, Vol. 5. Arizona State Museum, University of Arizona, Tucson.

Grayson, Donald K.
1984 *Quantitative Zooarchaeology: Topics in the Analysis of Archaeological Faunas*. Academic Press, New York.

Greenleaf, J. Cameron
1975 *Excavations at Punta de Agua in the Santa Cruz River Basin, Southeastern Arizona*. Anthropological Papers No. 26. University of Arizona Press, Tucson.

Greenleaf, J. Cameron, and Andrew Wallace
1962 Tucson: Pueblo, Presidio and American City, a Synopsis of Its History. *Arizoniana, The Journal of Arizona History* 3:18–27.

Greenwald, David H., and Richard Ciolek-Torrello
1988 Locus E. In *Hohokam Settlement along the Slopes of the Picacho Mountains, Tucson Aqueduct Project*, Vol. 2: *The Brady Wash Sites*, edited by R. Ciolek-Torrello, M. M. Callahan, and D. H. Greenwald, pp. 254–365. Research Paper No. 35. Museum of Northern Arizona, Flagstaff.

Gregonis, Linda M.
1981   The Hardy Site. Ms. on file, Arizona State Museum Library, University of Arizona, Tucson.

1997   *The Hardy Site at Fort Lowell Park, Tucson, Arizona.* Archaeological Series No. 175. Arizona State Museum, University of Arizona, Tucson.

Gregonis, Linda M., and Lisa W. Huckell
1980   *The Tucson Urban Study.* Arizona State Museum, Archaeological Series No. 138. University of Arizona, Tucson.

Gregory, David A.
1995   Prehistoric Settlement Patterns in the Eastern Tonto Basin. In *New Perspectives on Tonto Basin Prehistory, the Roosevelt Community Development Study,* edited by M. D. Elson, M. T. Stark, and D. A. Gregory, pp. 127–184. Anthropological Papers No. 15. Center for Desert Archaeology, Tucson.

Gregory, David A. (editor)
1999   *The Early Agricultural Occupation at Los Pozos, AZ AA:12:91 (ASM).* Draft, in preparation. Anthropological Papers No. 21. Center for Desert Archaeology, Tucson.

Grove, G. T.
1962   *Rillito Creek Floodplain Study.* Tucson–Pima County City-County Planning Department, Tucson.

Halbirt, Carl D.
1989   Worked Stone Implements from La Cuenca del Sedimento. In *Prehistoric Agricultural Activities on the Lehi-Mesa Terrace: Excavations at La Cuenca del Sedimento,* edited by T. K. Henderson, pp. 190–204. Northland Research, Flagstaff.

Halbirt, Carl D., and James M. Copus
1993   Tator Hills (AZ AA:6:18 [ASM]), a Multicomponent Campsite. In *Archaic Occupation on the Santa Cruz Flats: The Tator Hills Archaeological Project,* edited by C. D. Halbirt and T. K. Henderson, pp. 15–53. Northland Research, Flagstaff.

Halbirt, Carl D., and T. Kathleen Henderson (editors)
1993   *Archaic Occupation on the Santa Cruz Flats: The Tator Hills Archaeological Project.* Northland Research, Flagstaff.

Hard, Robert J., and William H. Doelle
1978   *The San Agustin Mission Site, Tucson, Arizona.* Archaeological Series No. 118. Arizona State Museum, University of Arizona, Tucson.

Harry, Karen G.
1996   Craft Specialization: Context, Models, and Theory. In *Archaeological Investigations at the SRI Locus, West Branch Site (AZ AA:16:3 [ASM]), a Rincon Phase Village in the Tucson Basin,* by J. H. Altschul, T. Bubemyre, K. M. Cairns, W. L. Deaver, A. Della Croce, S. K. Fish, L. Fratt, K. G. Harry, J. Holmlund, G. Huckleberry, C. H. Miksicek, A. W. Vokes, S. M. Whittlesey, M. N Zedeño, and L. F. Ziady, Chapter 13. Statistical Research, Tucson. Draft report submitted to Pima County Department of Transportation and Flood Control District, W. O. 4 BISCO.

1997   *Ceramic Production, Distribution, and Consumption in Two Classic Period Hohokam Communities.* Unpublished Ph.D. dissertation, Department of Anthropology, University of Arizona, Tucson.

Harry, Karen G., and Richard Ciolek-Torrello
1992   *Farming the Floodplain: A Look at Prehistoric and Historic Land-Use along the Rillito.* Technical Series No. 35. Statistical Research, Tucson.

Harry, Karen G., Stephanie M. Whittlesey, Ronald H. Towner, and Linda Scott Cummings
1992   Field Methods and Results. In *Farming the Floodplain: A Look at Prehistoric and Historic Land-Use along the Rillito,* by K. G. Harry and R. S. Ciolek-Torrello, pp. 23–125. Technical Series No. 35. Statistical Research, Tucson.

Hartmann, Gayle H.
1981   *Pima County Land Exchange Survey.* Archaeological Series No. 151. Arizona State Museum, University of Arizona, Tucson.

Hastings, James R., and Raymond M. Turner
1965   *The Changing Mile: An Ecological Study of Vegetation Change with Time in the Lower Mile of an Arid and Semiarid Region.* University of Arizona Press, Tucson.

Haury, Emil W.
1928   *The Succession of House Types in the Pueblo Area.* Unpublished Master's thesis,

Department of Archaeology, University of Arizona, Tucson.

1932 *Roosevelt 9:6: A Hohokam Site of the Colonial Period.* Medallion Papers No. 4, Gila Pueblo, Globe, Arizona.

1937a Shell. In *Excavations at Snaketown: Material Culture*, edited by H. S. Gladwin, E. W. Haury, E. B. Sayles, and N. Gladwin, pp. 135–153. Medallion Papers No. 25. Gila Pueblo, Globe, Arizona.

1937b Stone Palettes and Ornaments. In *Excavations at Snaketown: Material Culture*, edited by H. S. Gladwin, E. W. Haury, E. B. Sayles, and N. Gladwin, pp. 121–134. Medallion Papers No. 25. Gila Pueblo, Globe, Arizona.

1945 *The Excavation of Los Muertos and Neighboring Ruins in the Salt River Valley, Southern Arizona.* Papers of the Peabody Museum of American Archaeology and Ethnology, Vol. 24, No. 1. Harvard University, Cambridge.

1950 *The Stratigraphy and Archeology of Ventana Cave.* University of Arizona Press, Tucson.

1953 Discovery of the Naco Mammoth and the Associated Projectile Points. *American Antiquity* 19:1–14.

1965 Pottery Types at Snaketown. In *Excavations at Snaketown: Material Culture*, by H. S. Gladwin, E. W. Haury, E. B. Sayles, and N. Gladwin, pp. 169–229. Reprinted. University of Arizona Press, Tucson. Originally published 1937. Medallion Papers No. 25, Gila Pueblo, Globe, Arizona.

1976 *The Hohokam, Desert Farmers and Craftsmen: Excavations at Snaketown, 1964–1965.* University of Arizona Press, Tucson.

Haury, Emil W., and Lisa W. Huckell
1993 A Prehistoric Cotton Cache from the Pinaleño Mountains. *Kiva* 59(2):95–145.

Haury, Emil W., E. B. Sayles, and William W. Wasley
1959 The Lehner Mammoth Site, Southeastern Arizona. *American Antiquity* 25:2–42.

Hayden, Julian D.
1957 *Excavations, 1940, at University Indian Ruin.* Technical Series Vol. 5. Southwestern Monuments Association. Gila Pueblo, Globe, Arizona.

1970 Of Hohokam Origins and Other Matters. *American Antiquity* 35:87–94.

1972 Hohokam Petroglyphs of the Sierra Pinacate, Sonora, and the Hohokam Shell Expeditions. *The Kiva* 37(2):74–83.

Haynes, C. Vance
1968 Geochronology of Late Quaternary Alluvium. In *Means of Correlation of Quaternary Successions*, edited by R. B. Morrison and E. H. Wright, pp. 591–631. Proceedings of the VII Congress of the International Association of Quaternary Research Vol. 8. University of Utah Press, Salt Lake City.

Haynes, C. Vance, and Bruce B. Huckell
1986 *Sedimentary Successions of the Prehistoric Santa Cruz River, Tucson, Arizona.* Open-file Report No. 86-15. Bureau of Geology and Mineral Technology, Tucson.

Heckman, Robert A.
1994 Ceramic Analysis. In *Testing and Data Recovery at Seneca Terrace II*, by K. M. Cairns and J. H. Altschul, pp. 35–40. Technical Report No. 94-2. Statistical Research, Tucson.

Heidke, James M.
1986 Plainware Ceramics. In *Archaeological Investigations at the Tanque Verde Wash Site, a Middle Rincon Settlement in the Eastern Tucson Basin*, by M. D. Elson, pp. 181–231. Anthropological Papers No. 7. Institute for American Research, Tucson.

1990a Ceramic Analysis. In *Archaeological Investigations at the Lonetree Site, AA:12:120 (ASM), in the Northern Tucson Basin*, by M. Bernard-Shaw, pp. 53–118. Technical Report No. 90-1. Center for Desert Archaeology, Tucson.

1990b Ceramics. In *Rincon Phase Seasonal Occupation in the Northern Tucson Basin*, by M. Bernard-Shaw and F. W. Huntington, pp. 75–129. Technical Report No. 90-2. Center for Desert Archaeology, Tucson.

1994 Qualitative Temper Characterization of Potsherds from the Gibbon Springs Site. In *Petrographic and Qualitative Analysis of Potsherds from the Gibbon Springs Site, Tucson, Arizona*, by J. M. Heidke and D. C. Kamilli, pp. 7–12. Technical Report No. 94-9. Center for Desert Archaeology, Tucson.

1995   Ceramic Analysis. In *Archaeological Investigations at Los Morteros, a Prehistoric Settlement in the Northern Tucson Basin*, edited by H. D. Wallace, pp. 263–422. Anthropological Papers No. 17. Center for Desert Archaeology, Tucson.

1996   Production and Distribution of Rincon Phase Pottery: Evidence from the Julian Wash Site. In *A Rincon Phase Occupation at the Julian Wash Site, AZ BB:13:17 (ASM)*, by J. B. Mabry, pp. 47–71. Technical Report No. 96-7. Center for Desert Archaeology, Tucson.

Heidke, James M., Christine E. Goetze, and Allen Dart
1994   Schuk Toak Project Ceramics: Chronology, Formation Processes, and Prehistory of the Avra Valley. In *Archaeological Studies of the Avra Valley, Arizona: Excavations in the Schuk Toak District, Vol. 2: Scientific Studies and Interpretations*, by A. Dart, pp. 11–76. Anthropological Papers No. 16. Center for Desert Archaeology, Tucson. Submitted to the Tohono O'odham Nation, Contract No. 8-CS-32-00380.

Heidke, James M., Diana C. Kamilli, and Elizabeth Miksa
1996   *Petrographic and Qualitative Analyses of Sands and Sherds from the Lower Verde River Area*. Technical Report No. 95-1. Center for Desert Archaeology, Tucson. Appended report in *Vanishing River: Landscapes and Lives of the Lower Verde River: The Lower Verde Archaeological Project* (CD-ROM). SRI Press, Tucson.

Heidke, James M., and W. Bruce Masse
1988   *Tucson Convention Center Monitoring—AZ BB:13:383 (ASM)*. Technical Report No. 88-3. Institute for American Research, Tucson.

Heidke, James M., Elizabeth Miksa, and Michael P. Wiley
1996   Ceramic Artifacts. In *Archaeological Investigations of Early Village Sites in the Middle Santa Cruz Valley: Analyses and Synthesis*, edited by J. B. Mabry, pp. 471–544. Anthropological Papers No. 19. Center for Desert Archaeology, Tucson.

Heidke, James M., and Michael K. Wiley
1995   Petrographic and Qualitative Analysis of Tanque Verde Red-on-Brown Sherds from the Northern Tucson Basin and Avra Valley. Ms.

on file, Center for Desert Archaeology, Tucson. Submitted to Karen G. Harry, Department of Anthropology, University of Arizona, Tucson.

Hemmings, E. T., M. D. Robinson, and R. N. Rogers
1968   Field report on the Pantano site (Arizona EE:2:50). Ms. on file, Arizona State Museum Library, University of Arizona, Tucson.

Henderson, T. Kathleen
1987   The Growth of a Hohokam Village. In *The Hohokam Village: Site Structure and Organization*, edited by D. E. Doyel, pp. 97–125. Southwestern and Rocky Mountain Division, American Association for the Advancement of Science. Glenwood Springs, Colorado.

1992   A Second Look at Ceramics: Early Ceramics, Vessel Forms, and Temporal Trends. In *Prehistoric and Historic Occupation of the Lower Verde River Valley: The State Route 87 Verde Bridge Project*, by M. R. Hackbarth, pp. 185–204. Northland Research, Flagstaff.

Henderson, T. Kathleen (editor)
1987   *Field Investigations at the Marana Community Complex*. Anthropological Field Studies No. 14. Office of Cultural Resource Management, Department of Anthropology, Arizona State University, Tempe.

Hendricks, David M.
1985   *Arizona Soils*. University of Arizona Press, Tucson.

Herskovitz, Robert M
1978   *Fort Bowie Material Culture*. University of Arizona Press, Tucson.

Hevly, Richard, Peter J. Mehringer, and Harrison G. Yocum
1965   Modern Pollen Rain in the Sonoran Desert. *Journal of the Arizona Academy of Science* 3:123–135.

Hinton, Richard J.
1970   *A Handbook to Arizona, 1877*. Rio Grande Press, Glorieta, New Mexico.

Homburg, Jeffrey A., and William C. Johnson
1991   Landscape Evolution in Relation to Basketmaker III in the Lukachukai Valley. Paper presented at the 56th Annual Meeting of the Society of American Archaeology, New Orleans.

Howard, Ann Valdo

1985   The Block 24-East Prehistoric Shell Assemblages. In *City of Phoenix, Archaeology of the Original Townsite: Block 24-East*, edited by J. S. Cable, K. S. Hoffman, D. E. Doyel, and F. Ritz, pp. 169–182. Publications in Archaeology No. 8. Soil Systems, Phoenix.

1987   The La Ciudad Shell Assemblage. In *La Ciudad: Specialized Studies in the Economy, Environment, and Culture of La Ciudad*, edited by J. E. Kisselburg, G. E. Rice, and B. L. Shears, pp. 75–174. Anthropological Field Studies No. 20. Office of Cultural Resource Management, Arizona State University, Tempe.

1993   Marine Shell Artifacts and Production Processes at Shelltown and the Hind Site. In *Shelltown and the Hind Site: A Study of Two Hohokam Craftsman Communities in Southern Arizona*, edited by W. S. Marmaduke and R. J. Martynec, pp. 321–423. Northland Research, Flagstaff.

Howard, Jerry

1985   Courtyard Groups and Domestic Cycling: A Hypothetical Model of Growth. In *Proceedings of the 1983 Hohokam Symposium*, Part 1, edited by A. E. Dittert, Jr., and D. E. Dove, pp. 311–326. Occasional Paper No. 2. Arizona Archaeological Society, Phoenix.

1990   Los Hornos: Site Structure and Community Patterning at a Large Hohokam Village. In *One Hundred Years of Archaeology at La Ciudad de los Hornos,* by D. R. Wilcox, J. B. Howard, and R. H. Nelson, pp. 73–121. Publications in Archaeology No. 6. Soil Systems, Phoenix.

1991   Regression Modeling of Canal Morphology and Paleohydraulics. In *The Operation and Evolution of an Irrigation System: The East Papago Canal Study*, edited by J. B. Howard and G. Huckleberry, pp. 4.1–4.38. Publications in Archaeology No. 18. Soil Systems, Phoenix.

1993   A Paleohydraulic Approach to Examining Agricultural Intensification in Hohokam Irrigation Systems. In *Research in Economic Anthropology*, Supplement 7, pp. 263–324. JAI Press, Greenwich, Connecticut.

Howard, Jerry B., and Gary Huckleberry (editors)

1991   *The Operation and Evolution of an Irrigation System: The East Papago Canal Study.* Publications in Archaeology No. 18. Soil Systems, Phoenix.

Huckell, Bruce B.

1984a   *The Archaic Occupation of the Rosemont Area, Northern Santa Rita Mountains, Southeastern Arizona.* Archaeological Series No. 147, Vol. 1. Arizona State Museum, University of Arizona, Tucson.

1984b   The Paleo-Indian and Archaic Occupation of the Tucson Basin: An Overview. *The Kiva* 49:133–146.

1984c   Sobaipuri Sites in the Rosemont Area. In *Miscellaneous Archaeological Studies in the ANAMAX-Rosemont Land Exchange Area*, by M. D. Tagg, R. G. Ervin, and B. B. Huckell, pp. 107–146. Archaeological Series No. 147. Arizona State Museum, University of Arizona, Tucson.

1987   Ceramics. In *The Corona de Tucson Project: Prehistoric Use of a Bajada Environment*, by B. B. Huckell, M. D. Tagg, and L. W. Huckell, pp. 123–153. Archaeological Series No. 174. Arizona State Museum, University of Arizona, Tucson.

1988   Late Archaic Archaeology of the Tucson Basin: A Status Report. In *Recent Research on Tucson Basin Prehistory: Proceedings of the Second Tucson Basin Conference*, edited by W. H. Doelle and P. R. Fish, pp. 57–80. Anthropological Papers No. 10. Institute for American Research, Tucson.

1990   *Late Preceramic Farmer-Foragers in Southeastern Arizona: A Cultural and Ecological Consideration of the Spread of Agriculture in the Arid Southwestern United States.* Unpublished Ph.D. dissertation, Arid Lands Resource Sciences, University of Arizona, Tucson.

1993   *Archaeological Testing of the Pima Community College New Campus Property: The Valencia North Project.* Technical Report No. 92-13. Center for Desert Archaeology, Tucson.

1995   *Of Marshes and Maize: Preceramic Agricultural Settlements in the Cienega Valley, Southeastern Arizona.* Anthropological Papers No. 45. University of Arizona Press, Tucson.

1998   An Analysis of the Flaked Stone Artifacts. In *Early Farmers of the Sonoran Desert: Archaeological Investigations at the Houghton Road Site, Tucson, Arizona*, edited by R. Ciolek-Torrello, pp. 89–117. Technical Series No. 72. Statistical Research, Tucson.

Huckell, Bruce B., and Lisa W. Huckell
1981 Archaeological Test Excavations at the U.S. Home Corporation's Saddlewood Ranch Proposed Development Area. Ms. on file, Arizona State Museum Library, University of Arizona, Tucson.

1984 Excavations at Milagro, a Late Archaic Site in the Eastern Tucson Basin. Ms. on file, Arizona State Museum Archives, University of Arizona, Tucson.

Huckell, Bruce B., Lisa W. Huckell, and Suzanne K. Fish
1995 *Investigations at Milagro, a Late Preceramic Site in the Eastern Tucson Basin.* Technical Report No. 94-5. Center For Desert Archaeology, Tucson.

Huckell, Bruce B., Martyn D. Tagg, and Lisa W. Huckell (editors)
1987 *The Corona de Tucson Project: Prehistoric Use of a Bajada Environment.* Archaeological Series No. 174. Arizona State Museum, University of Arizona, Tucson.

Huckell, Lisa W.
1986 Botanical Remains. In *The 1985 Excavations at the Hodges Site, Pima County, Arizona,* edited by R. W. Layhe, pp. 241–269. Archaeological Series No. 170. Arizona State Museum, University of Arizona, Tucson.

1993 Plant Remains from the Pinaleño Cotton Cache, Arizona. *Kiva* 59:147–203.

1998 Appendix B: Paleoethnobotany. In *Early Farmers of the Sonoran Desert: Archaeological Investigations at the Houghton Road Site, Tucson, Arizona,* edited by R. Ciolek-Torrello, pp. 327–344. Technical Series No. 72. Statistical Research, Tucson.

Huckleberry, Gary
1988 Relict Irrigation Canals in the East Papago Freeway Corridor. In *Arizona Department of Transportation Testing Program: Part 2, East Papago Freeway,* edited by Daniel Landis, pp. 109–167. Publications in Archaeology No. 13. Soil Systems, Phoenix.

Huntington, Frederick W.
1982 *Archaeological Data Recovery at AZ BB:9:72 (ASM), the Band Quarters Kitchen and Corral Wall at Fort Lowell, and AZ BB:9:54 (ASM), a Rincon Phase Habitation Site, Craycroft Road, Tucson, Arizona.* Archaeological Series No. 163. Arizona State Museum, University of Arizona, Tucson.

1986 *Archaeological Investigations at the West Branch Site: Early and Middle Rincon Occupation in the Southern Tucson Basin.* Anthropological Papers No. 5. Institute for American Research, Tucson.

1988 Rincon Phase Community Organization. In *Recent Research on Tucson Basin Prehistory: Proceedings of the Second Tucson Basin Conference,* edited by W. H. Doelle and P. R. Fish, pp. 207–224. Anthropological Papers No. 10. Institute for American Research, Tucson.

Irving, E.
1964 *Palaeomagnetism and Its Application of Geological and Geophysical Problems.* John Wiley, New York.

Jackson, Garrett W.
1989 *Surficial Geologic Maps of the Northeastern, Southeastern, and Southwestern Portions of the Tucson Metropolitan Area.* Open-file Report No. 89-2. Arizona Geological Survey, Tucson.

James, Steven R.
1987 Hohokam Patterns of Faunal Exploitation at Muchas Casas. In *Studies in the Hohokam Community of Marana,* edited by G. Rice, pp. 171–286. Anthropological Field Studies No. 15. Office of Cultural Resource Management, Department of Anthropology, Arizona State University, Tempe.

1991 Archaeofaunal Analysis of the Water Users Site. In *The Riverine Hohokam of the Salt and Verde River Confluence Region: The Water Users Project,* Vol. 2: *Descriptive Report,* compiled by R. B. Neily and J. E. Kisselburg, pp. 10.1–10.9. Cultural Resources Report No. 47. Archaeological Consulting Services, Tempe.

1995 Hunting and Fishing Patterns at Prehistoric Sites along the Salt River: The Archaeofaunal Analysis. In *The Roosevelt Community Development Study: Paleobotanical and Osteological Analyses,* edited by M. D. Elson and J. J. Clark, pp. 85–168. Anthropological Papers No. 14, Vol. 3. Center for Desert Archaeology, Tucson.

Jernigan, E. Wesley
1978   *Jewelry of the Prehistoric Southwest*. School of American Research, Santa Fe, and University of New Mexico Press, Albuquerque.

Jobson, R. W.
1986   Stone Tool Morphology and Rabbit Butchering. *Lithic Technology* 15(1):9–20.

Jones, Bruce A.
1997   Historical Faunal Remains. In *Pit House, Presidio, and Privy: 1,400 Years of Archaeology and History on Block 180, Tucson, Arizona*, edited by R. Ciolek-Torrello and M. T. Swanson, pp. 469–502. Technical Series No. 63. Statistical Research, Tucson.

Katzer, Keith L.
1989a   The Stratigraphy and Geomorphic History of the Los Morteros Canals (AZ AA:12:57, Locus 1). In *Archaeological Investigations at Los Morteros, AZ AA:12:57 (ASM), Locus 1, in the Northern Tucson Basin*, edited by M. Bernard-Shaw, pp. 57–72. Technical Report No. 87-8. Institute for American Research, Tucson.

1989b   The Hydrological Characteristics of the Las Acequias Canals. In *Prehistoric Agricultural Activities on the Lehi-Mesa Terrace: Perspectives on Hohokam Irrigation Cycles*, edited by N. W. Ackerly and T. K. Henderson, pp. 222–234. Northland Research, Flagstaff.

Kearney, Thomas H., and Robert H. Peebles
1960   *Arizona Flora*. University of California Press, Berkeley.

Keely, L. H.
1980   *Experimental Determination of Stone Tool Uses: A Microwear Analysis*. University of Chicago Press, Chicago.

Keen, A. Myra
1971   *Sea Shells of Tropical West America: Marine Mollusks from Baja California to Peru*. 2nd ed. Stanford University Press, Palo Alto.

Kelly, Isabel T., James Officer, and Emil W. Haury
1978   *The Hodges Ruin, a Hohokam Community in the Tucson Basin*. Anthropological Papers No. 30. University of Arizona Press, Tucson.

Kinkade, Gay M., and Gordon L. Fritz
1975   *The Tucson Sewage Project: Studies at Two Archaeological Sites in the Tucson Basin*. Archaeological Series No. 64. Arizona State Museum, University of Arizona, Tucson.

Kirschvink, J. L.
1980   The Least-Squares Line and Plane and the Analysis of Paleomagnetic Data. *Journal of the Royal Physics Society* 62:699–718.

Klucas, Eric Eugene, Richard Ciolek-Torrello, and Charles R. Riggs
1998   Site Structure and Domestic Organization. In *Overview, Synthesis, and Conclusions*, edited by S. M. Whittlesey, R. Ciolek-Torrello, and J. H. Altschul, pp. 491–530. Vanishing River: Landscapes and Lives of the Lower Verde Valley: The Lower Verde Archaeological Project. SRI Press, Tucson.

Kottlowski, R. E., M. E. Cooley, and R. V. Ruhe
1965   Quaternary Geology of the Southwest. In *The Quaternary of the United States*, edited by H. E. Wright and D. C. Frey, pp. 287–298. Princeton University Press, Princeton.

Lange, Richard C., and William L. Deaver
1989   *The 1979–1983 Testing at Los Morteros (AZ AA:12:57 [ASM]), a Large Hohokam Village Site in the Tucson Basin*. Archaeological Series No. 177. Arizona State Museum, University of Arizona, Tucson.

Layhe, Robert W.
1986a   Architectural and Extramural Features. In *The 1985 Excavations at the Hodges Site, Pima County, Arizona*, edited by R. W. Layhe, pp. 47–59. Archaeological Series No. 170. Arizona State Museum, University of Arizona, Tucson.

1986b   Summary and Conclusions. In *The 1985 Excavations at the Hodges Site, Pima County, Arizona*, edited by R. W. Layhe, pp. 285–291. Archaeological Series No. 170. Arizona State Museum, University of Arizona, Tucson.

Layhe, Robert W. (editor)
1986   *The 1985 Excavations at the Hodges Site, Pima County, Arizona*. Archaeological Series No. 170. Arizona State Museum, University of Arizona, Tucson.

LeBlanc, Steven
1982 The Advent of Pottery in the Southwest. In *Southwestern Ceramics: A Comparative Review*, edited by A. H. Schroeder, pp. 27–51. Arizona Archaeological Society, Phoenix.

Lindauer, Owen
1988 *A Study of Vessel Form and Painted Designs to Explore Regional Interaction of the Sedentary Period Hohokam.* Unpublished Ph.D. dissertation, Department of Anthropology, Arizona State University, Tempe.

Lindeman, Michael W.
1999 Untitled report on archaeological investigations at Sunset Mesa Ruin (AZ AA:12:10 [ASM]). Center for Desert Archaeology, Tucson. In preparation.

Lombard, James P.
1985 Report on Sand Temper Composition from BB:13:15 Ceramics. In *Excavations at the Valencia Site, a Preclassic Hohokam Village in the Southern Tucson Basin*, by W. H. Doelle, pp. 297–304. Anthropological Papers No. 3. Institute for American Research, Tucson.

1986a A Petrographic Analysis of West Branch Site Ceramics. In *Archaeological Investigations at the West Branch Site: Early and Middle Rincon Occupation in the Southern Tucson Basin*, by F. W. Huntington, pp. 429–444. Anthropological Papers No. 5. Institute for American Research, Tucson.

1986b Petrographic Results of Point Counts on 40 Ceramic Sherds from AZ BB:13:68. In *Archaeological Investigations at the Tanque Verde Wash Site, a Middle Rincon Settlement in the Eastern Tucson Basin*, by M. D. Elson, pp. 473–484. Anthropological Papers No. 7. Institute for American Research, Tucson.

1987a Ceramic Petrography. In *The Archaeology of the San Xavier Bridge Site (AZ BB:13:14), Tucson Basin, Southern Arizona*, edited by J. C. Ravesloot, pp. 335–368. Archaeological Series No. 171. Arizona State Museum, University of Arizona, Tucson.

1987b Composition of Ephemeral Stream Sands in the Cañada del Oro Valley. In *Prehistoric Settlement in the Cañada del Oro Valley, Arizona: The Rancho Vistoso Survey Project,* by D. B. Craig and H. D. Wallace, pp. 207–216.

Anthropological Papers No. 8. Institute for American Research, Tucson.

1987c Petrographic Study of Ceramics from the Corona de Tucson Project Sites: Appendix D. In *The Corona de Tucson Project: Prehistoric Use of a Bajada Environment*, by B. Huckell, M. Tagg, and L. Huckell, pp. 313–333. Archaeological Series No. 174. Arizona State Museum, University of Arizona, Tucson.

1990 Petrographic Report on Ceramics from the Cienega Site, AZ BB:9:143. In *Rincon Phase Seasonal Occupation in the Northeastern Tucson Basin*, by M. Bernard-Shaw, and F. W. Huntington, pp. 213–232. Technical Report No. 90-2. Center for Desert Archaeology, Tucson.

Lowe, Charles H.
1964 *Arizona's Natural Environment.* University of Arizona Press, Tucson.

Lyman, R. L.
1982 Archaeofaunas and Subsistence Studies. In *Advances in Archaeological Method and Theory*, Vol. 5, edited by M. B. Schiffer, pp. 331–393. Academic Press, New York.

1987 Archaeofaunas and Butchery Studies: A Taphonomic Perspective. In *Advances in Archaeological Method and Theory*, Vol. 10, edited by M. B. Schiffer, pp. 249–337. Academic Press, New York.

Mabry, Jonathan B.
1990 *A Late Archaic Occupation at AZ AA:12:105 (ASM).* Technical Report No. 90-6. Center for Desert Archaeology, Tucson.

1993 *Treatment Plan for Archaeological Resources within the Interstate 10 Corridor Improvement Project, Tangerine Road to the I-19 Interchange.* Technical Report No. 93-2. Center for Desert Archaeology, Tucson.

Mabry, Jonathan B., James E. Ayres, and Regina L. Chapin-Pyritz
1994 *Tucson at the Turn of the Century: The Archaeology of a City Block.* Center for Desert Archaeology, Tucson.

Mabry, Jonathan B., Deborah L. Swartz, Helga Wöcherl, Jeffery L. Clark, Gavin H. Archer, and Michael W. Lindeman
1997 *Archaeological Investigations of Early Village Sites in the Middle Santa Cruz Valley:*

Descriptions of the Santa Cruz Bend, Square Hearth, Stone Pipe, and Canal Sites. Anthropological Papers No. 18. Center for Desert Archaeology, Tucson.

Majewski, Teresita, and Michael J. O'Brien
1987   The Use and Misuse of Nineteenth-Century English and American Ceramics in Archaeological Analysis. In *Advances in Archaeological Method and Theory*, Vol. 11, edited by M. B. Schiffer, pp. 97–209. Academic Press, San Diego.

Marmaduke, William S.
1983   *The Rillito River Project: Archaeological Review and Assessment.* Northland Research, Flagstaff.

Marmaduke, William S., and T. Kathleen Henderson
1995   *Archaeology in the Distribution Division of the Central Arizona Project.* Northland Research, Flagstaff. Report submitted to the Bureau of Reclamation, Arizona Projects Office.

Martin, Paul Schultz
1963   *The Last 10,000 Years: A Fossil Pollen Record of the American Southwest.* University of Arizona Press, Tucson.

Martin, Paul Schultz, and James Schoenwetter
1960   Arizona's Oldest Cornfield. *Science* 132:33–34.

Masse, W. Bruce
1979   An Intensive Survey of Prehistoric Dry Farming Systems near Tumamoc Hill in Tucson, Arizona. *The Kiva* 45:141–186.

1980   *Excavations at Gu Achi: A Reappraisal of Hohokam Settlement and Subsistence in the Arizona Papagueria.* Publications in Anthropology No. 12. USDI, National Park Service, Western Archeological and Conservation Center, Tucson.

1981   A Reappraisal of the Protohistoric Sobaipuri Indians of Southeastern Arizona. In *The Protohistoric Period in the North American Southwest, A.D. 1450–1700*, edited by D. R. Wilcox and W. B. Masse, pp. 28–56. Anthropological Research Paper No. 24. Arizona State University, Tempe.

1985   The Peppersauce Wash Project: Excavations at Three Multicomponent Sites in the Lower San Pedro Valley, Arizona. Ms. on file, Arizona State Museum Library, University of Arizona, Tucson.

Matson, Richard G.
1991   *The Origins of Southwestern Agriculture.* University of Arizona Press, Tucson.

Mayberry, James D.
1983   The Hohokam and Protohistoric Periods. In *An Archaeological Assessment of the Middle Santa Cruz River Basin, Rillito to Green Valley, Arizona, for the Proposed Tucson Aqueduct Phase B, Central Arizona Project*, edited by J. S. Czaplicki and J. D. Mayberry, pp. 27–62. Archaeological Series No. 164. Arizona State Museum, University of Arizona, Tucson.

Mayro, Linda L.
1985   Shell Artifacts. In *Excavations at the Valencia Site, a Preclassic Hohokam Village in the Southern Tucson Basin*, by W. H. Doelle, pp. 211–224. Anthropological Papers No. 3. Institute for American Research, Tucson.

McElhinny, M. W.
1973   *Paleomagnetism and Plate Tectonics.* Cambridge University Press, Cambridge.

McFadden, P. L., and F. J. Lowes
1981   The Discrimination of Mean Directions Drawn from Fisher Distributions. *Geophysical Journal of the Royal Astronomical Society* 34:163–189.

McGuire, Randall H.
1979   *Rancho Punta de Agua: Excavations at a Historic Ranch near Tucson, Arizona.* Contribution to Highway Salvage Archaeology in Arizona No. 57. Arizona State Museum, University of Arizona, Tucson.

McKittrick, Mary Anne
1988   *Surficial Geologic Maps of the Tucson Metropolitan Area.* Open-file Report No. 88-18. Arizona Geological Survey, Tucson.

Miksa, Elizabeth J.
1995   *Petrographic Analysis of Sherds for the McDowell to Shea Boulevard Portion of the Beeline Highway Excavation Project.* Technical Report No. 94-18. Center for Desert Archaeology, Tucson.

Miksa, Elizabeth, and James M. Heidke
1995 Drawing a Line in the Sands: Models of Ceramic Temper Provenance. In *The Roosevelt Community Development Study: Ceramic Chronology, Technology, and Economics*, edited by J. M. Heidke and M. T. Stark, pp. 133–204. Anthropological Papers No. 14, Vol. 2. Center for Desert Archaeology, Tucson.

Miksicek, Charles H.
1986a Plant Remains. In *Archaeological Investigations at the West Branch Site: Early and Middle Rincon Occupation in the Southern Tucson Basin*, by F. W. Huntington, pp. 289–313. Anthropological Papers No. 5. Institute for American Research, Tucson.

1986b Plant Remains from the Tanque Verde Wash Site. In *Archaeological Investigations at the Tanque Verde Wash Site, a Middle Rincon Settlement in the Eastern Tucson Basin*, edited by M. D. Elson, pp. 371–394. Anthropological Papers No. 7. Institute for American Research, Tucson.

1988 Rethinking Hohokam Paleoethnobotanical Assemblages: A Progress Report for the Tucson Basin. In *Recent Research on Tucson Basin Prehistory: Proceedings of the Second Tucson Basin Conference*, edited by W. H. Doelle and P. R. Fish, pp. 47–56. Anthropological Papers No. 10. Institute for American Research, Tucson.

Mitchell, Douglas R.
1988 Site Structure and Chronology. In *Excavations at La Lomita Pequeña, a Santa Cruz/Sacaton Phase Hamlet in the Salt River Valley*, edited by D. R. Mitchell, pp. 351–394. Publications in Archaeology No. 10. Soil Systems, Phoenix.

Mitchell, Douglas R., and M. Steven Shackley
1995 Classic Period Hohokam Obsidian Studies in Southern Arizona. *Journal of Field Archaeology* 22(3).

Motsinger, Thomas N.
1994 An Inside View of Hohokam Architecture. *Kiva* 59:395–418.

Neily, Robert B.
1990 The Pine Creek Area in Regional Context. In *Hohokam Utilization of the Intermontane Mazatzal Mountain Region: The State Route 87 Pine Creek Project*, edited by M. Green, pp. 597–610. Cultural Resources Report No. 66. Archaeological Consulting Services, Tempe.

1994 Data Recovery Plan for the Sunset Mesa Ruin (AZ AA:12:10 [ASM]). Ms. on file, Statistical Research, Tucson.

Nelson, Richard S.
1991 *Hohokam Marine Shell Exchange and Artifacts*. Archaeological Series No. 179. Arizona State Museum, University of Arizona, Tucson.

Nials, Fred L., David A. Gregory, and Donald A. Graybill
1989 Salt River Streamflow and Hohokam Irrigation Systems. In *The 1982–1984 Excavations at Las Colinas: Environment and Subsistence*, by D. A. Graybill, D. A. Gregory, F. L. Nials, S. K. Fish, R. E. Gasser, C. H. Miksicek, and C. R. Szuter, pp. 59–76. Archaeological Series No. 162, Vol. 5. Arizona State Museum, University of Arizona, Tucson.

Officer, James E.
1978 Shell. In *The Hodges Ruin, a Hohokam Community in the Tucson Basin*, by I. T. Kelly, J. E. Officer, and E. W. Haury, pp. 110–120. Anthropological Papers of the University of Arizona No. 30. University of Arizona Press, Tucson.

1987 *Hispanic Arizona, 1536–1856*. University of Arizona Press, Tucson.

Olsen, Sandra L.
1979 A Study of Bone Artifacts from Grasshopper Pueblo, AZ P:14:1. *The Kiva* 44:341–373.

1981 Appendix B: Bone Artifacts from Las Colinas. In *The 1968 Excavations at Mound 8, Las Colinas Ruin Group, Phoenix, Arizona*, edited by L. C. Hammack and A. P. Sullivan. Archaeological Series No. 154. Arizona State Museum, University of Arizona, Tucson.

Olsen, Stanley J.
1968 *Fish, Amphibian and Reptile Remains from Archaeological Sites*. Papers of the Peabody Museum of Archaeology and Ethnology No. 56, Vol. 2. Harvard University, Cambridge.

1973 *Mammalian Remains from Archaeological Sites*, Part 1: *Southeastern and Southwestern United States*. Papers of the Peabody Museum of Archaeology and Ethnology No. 56, Vol. 1. Harvard University, Cambridge.

1979   *North American Birds*. Papers of the Peabody Museum of Archaeology and Ethnology No. 56, Vols. 4 and 5. Harvard University, Cambridge.

Oppenheimer, J. M., and J. S. Sumner
1980   *Depth-to-Bedrock Map, Basin and Range Province, Arizona*. Laboratory of Geophysics, University of Arizona, Tucson.

Pailes, Richard A.
1963   *An Analysis of the Fitch Site and Its Relation to the Hohokam Classic Period*. Unpublished Master's thesis, Department of Anthropology, Arizona State University, Tempe.

Parry, W. J., and R. L. Kelly
1987   Expedient Core Technology and Sedentism. In *The Organization of Core Technology*, edited by J. K. Johnson and C. A. Morrow, pp. 285–304. Special Studies in Archaeological Research. Westview, London and Boulder.

Pearsall, Deborah
1989   *Paleoethnobotany: A Handbook of Procedures*. Academic Press, San Diego.

Pearthree, Marie Slezak, and Victor R. Baker
1987   *Channel Change along Rillito Creek System of Southeastern Arizona 1941 through 1983*. Special Paper No. 6. Arizona Bureau of Geology and Mineral Technology, Geological Survey Branch, Tucson.

Pomeroy, J. Anthony
1959   Hohokam Etched Shell. *The Kiva* 24:12–21.

Rankin, Adrianne G., and Christian E. Downum
1986   Site Descriptions. In *A Class III Archaeological Survey of the Phase B Corridor, Tucson Aqueduct, Central Arizona Project*, by C. E. Downum, A. G. Rankin, and J. S. Czaplicki, pp. 41–180. Archaeological Series No. 168. Arizona State Museum, University of Arizona, Tucson.

Ravesloot, John C. (editor)
1987   *The Archaeology of the San Xavier Bridge Site (AZ BB:13:14), Tucson Basin, Southern Arizona*. Archaeological Series No. 171. Arizona State Museum, University of Arizona, Tucson.

1989   Chemical Compositional Analyses of Rillito Red-on-Brown and Santa Cruz Red-on-Buff Pottery. In *Hohokam Archaeology along Phase B of the Tucson Aqueduct, Central Arizona Project*, Vol. 1: *Syntheses and Interpretations*, edited by J. S. Czaplicki and J. C. Ravesloot, pp. 341–347. Archaeological Series No. 178. Arizona State Museum, University of Arizona, Tucson.

Ravesloot, John C., and Stephanie M. Whittlesey
1987   Inferring the Protohistoric Period in Southern Arizona. In *The Archaeology of the San Xavier Bridge Site (AZ BB:13:14), Tucson Basin, Southern Arizona*, edited by J. C. Ravesloot, pp. 81–98. Archaeological Series No. 171, Arizona State Museum, University of Arizona, Tucson.

Raynor, Gilbert S., Eugene C. Ogden, and Janet V. Hayes
1972   Dispersion and Deposition of Corn Pollen from Experimental Sources. *Agronomy Journal* 64:420–427.

Reid, J. Jefferson
1982   Overview of Cholla Project Ceramic Studies. In *Cholla Project Archaeology*, Vol. 5: *Ceramic Studies*, edited by J. J. Reid, pp. 1–7. Archaeological Series No. 161. Arizona State Museum, University of Arizona, Tucson.

Rice, Glenn E.
1987a   La Ciudad: A Perspective on Hohokam Community Systems. In *The Hohokam Village: Site Structure and Organization*, edited by D. E. Doyel, pp. 127–158. Southwestern and Rocky Mountain Division, American Association for the Advancement of Science, Glenwood Springs, Colorado.

1987b   *Studies in the Hohokam Community of Marana*. Office of Cultural Resource Management, Arizona State University, Tempe.

Ringrose, T. J.
1993   Bone Counts and Statistics: A Critique. *Journal of Archaeological Science* 20:121–157.

Rogers, Malcolm J.
1958   San Dieguito Implements from the Terraces of the Rincon-Pantano and Rillito Drainage System. *The Kiva* 24:1–23.

Rogge, A. Eugene, Melissa Keane, Bradford
Luckingham, James E. Ayres, Pamela Patterson, and
Todd Bostwick
    1992   *First Street and Madison: Historical Archae-
            ology of the Second Phoenix Chinatown.* Re-
            search Paper No. 9. Dames & Moore, Phoenix.

Roskruge, George James
    1893   *Official Map of Pima County, Tucson, Ari-
            zona.* Map adopted as official map of Pima
            County by resolution of Board of Supervisors,
            July 23, 1893.

Roth, Barbara J.
    1988   Recent Research on the Late Archaic Occupa-
            tion of the Northern Tucson Basin. In *Recent
            Research on Tucson Basin Prehistory: Pro-
            ceedings of the Second Tucson Basin Confer-
            ence*, edited by W. H. Doelle and P. R. Fish,
            pp. 81–85. Anthropological Papers No. 10.
            Institute for American Research, Tucson.

    1989   *Late Archaic Settlement and Subsistence in the
            Tucson Basin.* Unpublished Ph.D. dissertation,
            Department of Anthropology, University of
            Arizona, Tucson.

    1992   Sedentary Agriculturalists or Mobile Hunter-
            Gatherers? Evidence on the Late Archaic
            Occupation of the Northern Tucson Basin.
            Kiva 57:291–314.

    1993   Changing Perceptions of the Late Archaic: An
            Example from the Southern Southwest. *North
            American Archaeologist* 14(2):123–137.

Roth, Barbara J., and Bruce B. Huckell
    1992   Cortaro Points and the Archaic of Southern
            Arizona. *Kiva* 57:353–370.

Rozen, Kenneth C.
    1979   *The Archaeological Survey of the Northern
            Tucson 138kV Transmission Line System: The
            Northern Tucson Basin and Lower Santa Cruz
            River Valley.* Archaeological Series No. 132.
            Arizona State Museum, University of Arizona,
            Tucson.

    1984   Flaked Stone. In *Hohokam Habitation in the
            Northern Santa Rita Mountains*, edited by
            A. Ferg, K. C. Rozen, W. L. Deaver, M. D.
            Tagg, D. A. Phillips, Jr., and D. A. Gregory,
            pp. 421–604. Archaeological Series No. 147,
            Vol. 2, Part 1. Arizona State Museum, Univer-
            sity of Arizona, Tucson.

Sayles, E. B.
    1937   Stone Implements and Bowls. In *Excavations
            at Snaketown: Material Culture*, by H. S. Glad-
            win, E. W. Haury, E. B. Sayles, and N. Glad-
            win, pp. 101–120. Medallion Papers No. 25.
            Gila Pueblo, Globe, Arizona.

    1945   *The San Simon Branch, Excavations at Cave
            Creek and in the San Simon Valley,* Vol. 1:
            Material Culture. Medallion Papers No. 34.
            Gila Pueblo, Globe, Arizona.

Sayles, E. B., and Ernst Antevs
    1941   *The Cochise Culture.* Medallion Paper 29.
            Gila Pueblo, Globe, Arizona.

Schaller, David M.
    1994   Geographic Sources of Phoenix Basin Hoho-
            kam Plainware Based on Petrographic Analy-
            sis. In *Pueblo Grande Project,* Vol. 3: *Ceram-
            ics and the Production and Exchange of
            Pottery in the Central Phoenix Basin*, edited
            by D. R. Abbott, pp. 17–90. Publications in Ar-
            chaeology No. 20. Soil Systems, Phoenix.

Schlanger, Sarah H.
    1985   *Prehistoric Population Dynamics in the Dolo-
            res Area, Southwestern Colorado.* Ph.D. disser-
            tation, Department of Anthropology, Washing-
            ton State University, Pullman. University
            Microfilms, Ann Arbor.

    1986   Population Studies. In *Dolores Archaeological
            Program: Final Synthetic Report*, compiled by
            D. A. Breternitz, C. K. Robinson, and G. T.
            Gross, pp. 493–524. USDI, Bureau of Recla-
            mation, Denver.

Schneider, Gus
    1941   George Hand's Tucson, 1870–1880. Map on
            file, Arizona Historical Society, Tucson.

Schott, M. J.
    1994   Size and Form in the Analysis of Flake Debris:
            Review and Recent Approaches. *Journal of Ar-
            chaeological Method and Theory* 1(1):69–110.

Sellers, William, and Richard H. Hill
    1974   *Arizona Climate.* University of Arizona Press,
            Tucson.

Seymour, Deni J.
    1989   The Dynamics of Sobaipuri Settlement in the
            Eastern Pimeria Alta. *Journal of the Southwest*
            31:205–222.

Shackley, M. Steven
1992 The Upper Gila River Gravels as an Archaeological Obsidian Region: Implications for Models of Exchange and Interaction. *Geoarchaeology* 7(4):315–326.

1994 Intersource and Intrasource Geochemical Variability in Two Newly Discovered Archaeological Obsidian Sources in the Southern Great Basin: Bristol Mountains, California and Devil Peak, Nevada. *Journal of California and Great Basin Anthropology* 16(1):118–129.

1995a Sources of Archaeological Obsidian in the Greater American Southwest: An Update and Quantitative Analysis. *American Antiquity* 60:531–551.

1995b Intrasource Chemical Variability and Secondary Depositional Processes in Sources of Archaeological Obsidian: A Case Study from the American Southwest. In *Method and Theory in Archaeological Volcanic Glass Studies*, edited by M. S. Shackley. Plenum Publishing, New York.

Shelley, Steven D.
1993 *Analysis of the Faunal Remains from the Wallace Ruin, a Chacoan Outlier near Cortez, Colorado.* Unpublished Ph.D. dissertation, Department of Anthropology, Washington State University.

Shelley, Steven D., and Kellie M. Cairns
1998 Prehistoric Faunal Exploitation Patterns of the Lower Verde River Valley. In *Agricultural, Subsistence, and Environmental Studies*, edited by J. A. Homburg and R. Ciolek-Torrello, pp. 205–238. Vanishing River: Landscapes and Lives of the Lower Verde Valley: The Lower Verde Archaeological Project, Vol. 2. CD-ROM. SRI Press, Tucson.

Shepard, Anna O.
1936 Technology of Pecos Pottery. In *The Pottery of Pecos*, Vol. 2, by A. V. Kidder and A. O. Shepard, pp. 389–587. Papers of the Phillips Academy Southwestern Expedition No. 7. Phillips Exeter Academy, Andover, Massachusetts.

1942 Rio Grande Glaze Paint Ware: A Study Illustrating the Place of Ceramic Technological Analyses in Archaeological Research. *Carnegie Institution Contributions to American Anthropology and History* 7(39):12–262.

1985 *Ceramics for the Archaeologist.* Publication No. 609. Carnegie Institution, Washington, D.C.

Sheridan, Thomas E.
1986 *Los Tucsonenses: The Mexican Community in Tucson, 1854–1941.* University of Arizona Press, Tucson.

Shreve, Forest, and Ira L. Wiggins
1964 *Vegetation and Flora of the Sonoran Desert.* Stanford University Press, Palo Alto.

Shuey, R. T., E. R. Cole, and M. J. Mikulich
1970 Geographic Correction of Archaeomagnetic Data. *Journal of Geomagnetism and Geoelectricity* 22:485–489.

Silsbee, Joan M.
1958 Determining the Source of California *Olivella* Shells. In *Papers in California Archaeology*, No. 64. Reports of the University of California Survey No. 41, pp. 10–11. Department of Anthropology, University of California, Berkeley.

Simpson, Kay, and Susan J. Wells
1983 *Archaeological Survey in the Eastern Tucson Basin, Saguaro National Monument, Rincon Mountain Unit, Cactus Forest Area.* Publications in Anthropology No. 22, Vol. 1. USDI, National Park Service, Western Archeological and Conservation Center, Tucson.

1984 *Archaeological Survey in the Eastern Tucson Basin, Saguaro National Monument, Rincon Mountain Unit, Tanque Verde Ridge, Rincon Creek, Mica Mountain Areas.* Publications in Anthropology No. 22, Vol. 3. USDI, National Park Service, Western Archeological and Conservation Center, Tucson.

Sires, Earl W., Jr.
1984a Excavations at El Polvorón (AZ U:15:59). In *Hohokam Archaeology along the Salt-Gila Aqueduct, Central Arizona Project*, Vol. 4: *Prehistoric Occupation of the Queen Creek Delta*, Part 2, edited by L. S. Teague and P. L. Crown, pp. 221–354. Archaeological Series No. 150. Arizona State Museum, University of Arizona, Tucson.

1984b   Excavations at Frogtown (AZ U:15:61). In *Hohokam Archaeology along the Salt-Gila Aqueduct, Central Arizona Project*, Vol. 4: *Prehistoric Occupation of the Queen Creek Delta*, Part 3, edited by L. S. Teague and P. L. Crown, pp. 357–543. Archaeological Series No. 150. Arizona State Museum, University of Arizona, Tucson.

1987   Hohokam Architectural Variability and Site Structure during the Sedentary-Classic Transition. In *The Hohokam Village: Site Structure and Organization*, edited by D. E. Doyel, pp. 171–182. Southwestern and Rocky Mountain Division, American Association for the Advancement of Science, Glenwood Springs, Colorado.

Sires, Earl W., Jr., David H. Greenwald, and Theresa C. Miskell
1988   *The Black Sands Survey: A Cultural Resources Inventory of U.S. Bureau of Land Management Lands in South-Central Pinal County, Arizona.* SWCA Environmental Consultants, Tucson.

Slaughter, Mark C., and Heidi Roberts
1996   *Excavation of the Gibbon Springs Site, a Classic Period Village in the Northeastern Tucson Basin.* Archaeological Report No. 94-87. SWCA Environmental Consultants, Tucson.

Slawson, Laurie V., S. Miller, D. C. Hanna, and P. L. Steere
1986   *The Cortaro Site: A Late Archaic Period Occupation in the Tucson Basin.* Southwest Cultural Series No. 2. Cultural and Environmental Systems, Tucson.

Smith, Cornelius C.
1967   *William Sanders Oury: History-Maker of the Southwest.* University of Arizona Press, Tucson.

n.d.   *Tanque Verde, the Story of a Frontier Ranch, Tucson, Arizona.* Privately printed, Tucson.

Smith, G. E. P.
1910   *Groundwater Supply and Irrigation in the Rillito Valley.* Technical Bulletin No. 64. Agricultural Experiment Station, University of Arizona, Tucson.

1938   *The Physiography of Arizona Valleys and the Occurrence of Ground Water.* Technical Bulletin No. 77. Agricultural Experiment Station, University of Arizona, Tucson.

Solomon, Allen M., T. J. Blasing, and J. A. Solomon
1982   Interpretation of Floodplain Pollen in Alluvial Sediments from an Arid Region. *Quaternary Research* 18:52–71.

Spoerl, Patricia M.
1987   Islands in the Desert: Prehistory of the Coronado National Forest. Ms. on file, Arizona State Museum Library, University of Arizona, Tucson.

Stacy, V. K. Pheriba, and Julian D. Hayden
1975   *Saguaro National Monument: An Overview.* USDI, National Park Service, Western Archeological and Conservation Center, Tucson.

Stark, Miriam T., James M. Vint, and James M. Heidke
1995   Compositional Variability in Utilitarian Pottery at a Colonial Period Site. In *The Roosevelt Community Development Study: Ceramic Chronology, Technology, and Economics*, edited by J. M. Heidke and M. T. Stark, pp. 273–295. Anthropological Papers No. 14, Vol. 2. Center for Desert Archaeology, Tucson.

Stein, Pat H.
1983   Historical Resources of the Northern Tucson Basin. Ms. on file, Arizona State Museum Library, University of Arizona, Tucson.

1988   *Homesteading in the Depression: A Study of Two Short-Lived Homesteads in the Harquahala Valley, Arizona.* Northland Research, Flagstaff.

1990   *Homesteading in Arizona, 1862 to 1940: A Guide to Studying, Evaluating, and Preserving Historic Homesteads.* Arizona State Historic Preservation Office, Phoenix.

Sternberg, Robert S.
1982   *Archaeomagnetic Secular Variation of Direction and Paleointensity in the American Southwest.* Unpublished Ph.D. dissertation, Department of Geosciences, University of Arizona, Tucson.

1990   The Geophysical Basis of Archaeomagnetic Dating. In *Archaeomagnetic Dating*, edited by J. L. Eighmy and R. S. Sternberg, pp. 5–28. University of Arizona Press, Tucson.

Sternberg, Robert S., Richard C. Lange, Barbara A. Murphy, William L. Deaver, and Lynn S. Teague
1990   Archaeomagnetic Dating at Las Colinas, Arizona, USA. In *Archaeometry '90: Proceedings*

of the 27th International Symposium on Archaeometry, edited by E. Pernicka and G. A. Wagner. Birkhauser, Basel, Switzerland.

Sternberg, Robert S., and Randall H. McGuire
1990 Techniques for Constructing Secular Variation Curves and for Interpreting Archaeomagnetic Dates. In *Archaeomagnetic Dating*, edited by J. L. Eighmy and R. S. Sternberg, pp. 109–136. University of Arizona Press, Tucson.

Stevenson, Matilda Coxe
1915 Ethnobotany of the Zuni Indians. In *Thirtieth Annual Report of the Bureau of American Ethnology*, pp. 31–102. Smithsonian Institution, Washington, D.C.

Strand, Jennifer
1996 An Analysis of the Vertebrate Remains from the Gibbon Springs Site. In *Excavation of the Gibbon Springs Site, a Classic Period Village in the Northeastern Tucson Basin*, edited by M. C. Slaughter and H. Roberts, pp. 373–399. Archaeological Report No. 94-87. SWCA Environmental Consultants, Tucson.

Sullivan, Alan P., and Kenneth C. Rozen
1985 Debitage analysis and archaeological interpretation. *American Antiquity* 50:755–779.

Swartz, Deborah L.
1996 *Limited Excavations at the Eastern Margin of the Hodges Site*. Technical Report No. 96-6. Center for Desert Archaeology, Tucson.

Swartz, Deborah, L., and Jenny L. Adams
1998 *Archaeological Data Recovery at the Sunset Mesa Ruin (AZ AA:12:10 ASM)*. Technical Report No. 98-4. Desert Archaeology, Tucson.

Szuter, Christine R.
1982 The Interpretation of Rodents from Hohokam Sites. Paper presented at the 47th Annual Meeting of the Society for American Archaeology, Minneapolis.

1986 Faunal Remains. In *Archaeological Investigations at the West Branch Site: Early and Middle Rincon Occupation in the Southern Tucson Basin*, by F. W. Huntington, pp. 273–288. Anthropological Papers No. 5. Institute for American Research, Tucson.

1988a Bone Artifacts. In *The 1982–1984 Excavations at Las Colinas: Material Culture*, by D. R. Abbott, K. E. Beckwith, P. L. Crown, R. T. Euler, D. A. Gregory, J. R. London, M. B. Saul, L. A. Schwalbe, M. Bernard-Shaw, C. R. Szuter, and A. W. Vokes, pp. 385–408. Archaeological Series No. 162, Vol. 4. Arizona State Museum, University of Arizona, Tucson.

1988b Environment and Subsistence in the Tucson Basin: The Faunal Data from Hohokam Sites. In *Recent Research on Tucson Basin Prehistory: Proceedings of the Second Tucson Basin Conference*, edited by W. H. Doelle and P. R. Fish, pp. 39–45. Anthropological Papers No. 10. Institute for American Research, Tucson.

1991 *Hunting by Prehistoric Horticulturalists in the American Southwest*. Garland, New York and London.

Szuter, Christine R., and Frank Bayham
1989 Sedentism and Animal Procurement among Desert Horticulturalists of the North American Southwest. In *Farmers as Hunters: The Implications of Sedentism*, edited by S. Kent, pp. 80–95. Cambridge University Press, Cambridge.

Szuter Christine R., and Gwen Lerner Brown
1986 Faunal Remains from the Tanque Verde Wash Site. In *Archaeological Investigations at the Tanque Verde Wash Site, a Middle Rincon Settlement in the Eastern Tucson Basin*, edited by M. D. Elson, pp. 337–359. Anthropological Papers No. 7. Institute for American Research, Tucson.

Tagg, M. D.
1984 Utilitarian Ground Stone. In *Hohokam Habitation in the Northern Santa Rita Mountains*, edited by A. Ferg, K. C. Rozen, W. L. Deaver, M. D. Tagg, D. A. Phillips, Jr., and D. A. Gregory, pp. 605–664. Archaeological Series No. 147, Vol. 2, Part 2. Arizona State Museum, University of Arizona, Tucson.

Tarling, D. H.
1983 *Paleomagnetism: Principles and Applications in Geology, Geophysics, and Archaeology*. Chapman and Hall, London.

Teague, Lynn S.
1981   *Test Excavations at Painted Rock Reservoir: Sites AZ Z:1:7, AZ Z:1:8, and AZ S:16:36.* Archaeological Series No. 143. Arizona State Museum, University of Arizona, Tucson.

Thiel, J. Homer
1993   *Archaeological Investigations of Tucson Block 94: The Boarding House Residents of the Hotel Catalina Site.* Technical Report No. 93-5. Center for Desert Archaeology, Tucson.

Thiel, J. Homer, and Danielle Desruisseaux
1993   *Archaeological Test Excavations for Water Plant No. 1 Expansion, Historic Block 183, City of Tucson.* Technical Report No. 93-12. Center for Desert Archaeology, Tucson.

Thiel, J. Homer, Michael K. Faught, and James M. Bayman
1995   *Beneath the Streets: Prehistoric, Spanish, and American Period Archaeology in Downtown Tucson.* Technical Report No. 94-11. Center for Desert Archaeology, Tucson.

Tomka, S. A.
1989   Differentiating Lithic Reduction Techniques: An Experimental Approach. In *Experiments in Lithic Technology*, edited by D. Amick and R. Maudlin, pp. 137–161. British Archaeological Reports International Series No. 528. London.

Toulouse, Julian H.
1969   *Fruit Jars.* Thomas Nelson and Sons, Camden, New Jersey.

Turner, Teresa
1982   *The People of Fort Lowell.* Arizona Humanities Council, Tucson.

Tuthill, Carr
1947   *The Tres Alamos Site on the San Pedro River, Southeastern Arizona.* Publication No. 4. Amerind Foundation, Dragoon, Arizona.

Urban, Sharon F.
1981   The Las Colinas Shell Assemblage. In *The 1968 Excavations at Mound 8, Las Colinas Ruins Group, Phoenix, Arizona*, edited and assembled by L. C. Hammack and A. P. Sullivan, pp. 303–335. Archaeological Series No. 154. Arizona State Museum, University of Arizona, Tucson.

Vanderpot, Rein, Steven D. Shelley, and Su Benaron
1994   Riser Site, AZ U:8:225/1580. In *The Roosevelt Rural Sites Study,* Vol. 2: *Prehistoric Rural Settlements in the Tonto Basin*, Part 1, edited by R. S. Ciolek-Torrello, S. D. Shelley, and S. Benaron, pp. 292–329. Technical Series No. 28. Statistical Research, Tucson.

Van Devender, Thomas R., and W. Geoffrey Spaulding
1979   Development of Vegetation in the Southwestern United States. *Science* 204:701–710.

Van West, Carla R., and Jeffrey H. Altschul
1994   Agricultural Productivity and Carrying Capacity in the Tonto Basin. In *The Roosevelt Rural Sites Study,* Vol. 3: *Changing Land Use in the Tonto Basin*, edited by R. Ciolek-Torrello and J. R. Welch, pp. 361–435. Technical Series No. 28. Statistical Research, Tucson.

1998   Environmental Variability and Agricultural Economics along the Lower Verde River, A.D. 750–1450. In *Overview, Synthesis, and Conclusions,* edited by S. M. Whittlesey, R. Ciolek-Torrello, and J. H. Altschul, pp. 337–392. Vanishing River: Landscapes and Lives of the Lower Verde Valley: The Lower Verde Archaeology Project. SRI Press, Tucson.

Vestal, Paul A.
1952   *Ethnobotany of the Ramah Navajo.* Papers of the Peabody Musuem of American Archaeology and Ethnology, Vol. 40, No. 4. Harvard University, Cambridge.

Vokes, Arthur W.
1984   The Shell Assemblage of the Salt-Gila Aqueduct Project Sites. In *Hohokam Archaeology along the Salt-Gila Aqueduct, Central Arizona Project,* Vol. 8: *Material Culture,* Part 3, edited by L. S. Teague and P. L. Crown, pp. 465–574. Archaeological Series No. 150. Arizona State Museum, University of Arizona, Tucson.

1986a Shell. In *Archaeological Excavations at the West Branch Site, AZ AA:16:3 (ASM)*, by F. W. Huntington, pp. 229–250. Anthropological Papers No. 5. Institute for American Research, Tucson.

1986b The Tanque Verde Wash Shell Assemblage. In *Archaeological Investigations at the Tanque Verde Wash Site, a Middle Rincon Settlement in the Eastern Tucson Basin,* by M. D. Elson, pp. 313–324. Anthropological Papers No. 7. Institute for American Research, Tucson.

1986c The Shell Assemblage. In *The 1985 Excavations at the Hodges Site, Pima County, Arizona,* edited by R. W. Layhe, pp. 207–224. Archaeological Series No. 170. Arizona State Museum, University of Arizona, Tucson.

1988a Architecture. In *Hohokam Archaeology along Phase B of the Tucson Aqueduct, Central Arizona Project,* Vol. 2: *Excavations at Fastimes (AZ AA:12:384), a Rillito Phase Site in the Avra Valley,* edited by J. S. Czaplicki and J. C. Ravesloot, pp. 37–47. Archaeological Series No. 178. Arizona State Museum, University of Arizona, Tucson.

1988b Shell Artifacts. In *The 1982–1984 Excavations at Las Colinas: Material Culture,* by D. R. Abbott, K. E. Beckwith, P. L. Crown, R. T. Euler, D. A. Gregory, J. R. London, M. B. Saul, L. A. Schwalbe, M. Bernard-Shaw, C. R. Szuter, and A. W. Vokes, pp. 319–384. Archaeological Series No. 162, Vol. 4. Arizona State Museum, University of Arizona, Tucson.

1989 Architecture. In *Hohokam Archaeology along Phase B of the Tucson Aqueduct, Central Arizona Project,* Vol. 3: *Excavations at Water World (AZ AA:16:94), a Rillito Phase Ballcourt Village in the Avra Valley,* edited by J. S. Czaplicki and J. C. Ravesloot, pp. 45–56. Archaeological Series No. 178. Arizona State Museum, University of Arizona, Tucson.

1992 Shell Assemblage. In Organ Pipe Cactus National Monument Survey Project. Ms. on file, Western Archeological and Conservation Center, National Park Service, Tucson.

1993a Shell. In *Excavations at AZ AA:2:62 (ASM), a Colonial and Sedentary Period Hohokam Settlement near Toltec, Pinal County, Arizona,* by D. A. Gregory, pp. 55–73. Cultural Resources Report No. 80. Archaeological Consulting Services, Tempe.

1993b Shell. In *In the Shadow of South Mountain: The Pre-Classic Hohokam of la Ciudad de los Hornos, 1991–1992 Excavations,* Part 1, edited by M. L. Chenault, R. V. N. Ahlstrom, and T. N. Motsinger, pp. 359–376. Archaeological

Report No. 93-30. SWCA Environmental Consultants, Tucson.

1994 Shell Artifacts. In *Excavations at AZ BB:9:243, the Sabino Springs Site, a Rincon Phase Farmstead in the Santa Catalina Mountain Foothills,* by B. J. Roth, pp. 251–252. Technical Report. Tierra Right of Way Services, Tucson.

1995 Shell Artifacts. In *Archaeological Investigations at Los Morteros Site, a Prehistoric Settlement in the Northern Tucson Basin,* by H. D. Wallace, pp. 567–604. Anthropological Papers No. 17. Center for Desert Archaeology, Tucson.

1996a Shell Artifacts. In *A Rincon Phase Occupation at the Julian Wash Site, AZ BB:13:17 (ASM),* by J. B. Mabry, pp. 85–88. Technical Report No. 96-7. Center for Desert Archaeology, Tucson.

1996b Shell Artifacts. In *Archaeological Investigations at the SRI Locus, West Branch Site (AZ AA:16:3[ASM]), a Rincon Phase Village in the Tucson Basin.,* by J. H. Altschul, T. Bubemyre, K. M. Cairns, W. L. Deaver, A. Della Croce, S. K. Fish, L. Fratt, K. G. Harry, J. Holmlund, G. Huckleberry, C. H. Miksicek, A. W. Vokes, S. M. Whittlesey, M. N. Zedeño, and L. F. Ziady. Statistical Research, Tucson. Draft report submitted to Pima County Department of Trasnportation and Flood Control District, Tucson.

1996c The Shell Assemblage. In Vactor Ranch Project report. Ms. on file, Old Pueblo Archaeology Center, Tucson, Arizona.

1996d Shell Material from the Cook Avenue Locus. In *Archaeological Data Recovery Project at the Cook Avenue Locus of the West Branch Site, AZ AA:16:3 (ASM),* by A. Dart and D. L. Swartz, pp. 103–109. Technical Report No. 96-8. Center for Desert Archaeology, Tucson.

Vokes, Arthur W., and Frederick W. Huntington
1982 Shell. In *Archaeological Data Recovery at AZ BB:9:72 (ASM), the Fort Lowell Band Quarters Kitchen and Corral Wall at Fort Lowell, and AZ BB:9:54 (ASM), a Rincon Phase Habitation Site, Craycroft Road, Tucson, Arizona,* by F. W. Huntington, pp. 127–130. Archaeological Series No. 163. Arizona State Museum, University of Arizona, Tucson.

Wagoner, Jay J.
1970   *Arizona Territory, 1863–1912: A Political History*. University of Arizona Press, Tucson.

Wallace, Henry D.
1985   Decorated Ceramics. In *Excavations at the Valencia Site, a Preclassic Hohokam Village in the Southern Tucson Basin*, by W. H. Doelle, pp. 81–135. Anthropological Papers No. 3. Institute for American Research, Tucson.

1986a   Decorated Ceramics. In *Archaeological Investigations at the Tanque Verde Wash Site, a Middle Rincon Settlement in the Eastern Tucson Basin*, by M. D. Elson, pp. 125–180. Anthropological Papers No. 7. Institute for American Research, Tucson.

1986b   Decorated Ceramics: Introduction, Methods, and Rincon Phase Seriation. In *Archaeological Investigations at the West Branch Site: Early and Middle Rincon Occupation in the Southern Tucson Basin,* by F. W. Huntington, pp. 127–164. Anthropological Papers No. 5. Institute for American Research, Tucson.

1986c   *Rincon Phase Decorated Ceramics in the Tucson Basin*. Anthropological Papers No. 1. Institute for American Research, Tucson.

1987   Regional Context of the Prehistoric Rancho Vistoso Sites: Settlement Pattern and Socioeconomic Structure. In *Prehistoric Settlement in the Cañada del Oro Valley, Arizona: The Rancho Vistoso Survey Project*, edited by D. B. Craig and H. D. Wallace, pp. 117–167. Anthropological Papers No. 8. Institute for American Research, Tucson.

1988   Ceramic Boundaries and Interregional Interaction: New Perspectives on the Tucson Basin Hohokam. In *Recent Research on Tucson Basin Prehistory: Proceedings of the Second Tucson Basin Conference*, edited by W. H. Doelle and P. R. Fish, pp. 313–348. Anthropological Papers No. 10. Institute for American Research, Tucson.

1995   *Archaeological Investigations at Los Morteros, a Prehistoric Settlement in the Northern Tucson Basin*. Anthropological Papers No. 17. Center for Desert Archaeology, Tucson.

Wallace, Henry D., and Douglas B. Craig
1988   A Reconsideration of the Tucson Basin Hohokam Chronology. In *Recent Research on Tucson Basin Prehistory: Proceedings of the Second Tucson Basin Conference,* edited by W. H. Doelle and P. R. Fish, pp. 9–30. Anthropological Papers No. 10. Institute for American Research, Tucson.

Wallace, Henry D., and James M. Heidke
1986   Ceramic Production and Exchange. In *Archaeological Investigations at the Tanque Verde Wash Site, a Middle Rincon Settlement in the Eastern Tucson Basin*, by M. D. Elson, pp. 233–270. Anthropological Papers No. 7. Institute for American Research, Tucson.

Wallace, Henry D., James M. Heidke, and William H. Doelle
1995   Hohokam Origins. *Kiva* 60:575–618.

Wallace, Henry D., and James P. Holmlund
1984   The Classic Period in the Tucson Basin. *The Kiva* 49:167–194.

Waters, Michael R.
1985   Late Quaternary Alluvial Stratigraphy of Whitewater Draw, Arizona: Implications for Regional Correlation of Fluvial Deposits in the American Southwest. *Geology* 13:705–708.

1987   Holocene Alluvial Geology and Geoarchaeology of AZ BB:13:14 and the San Xavier Reach of the Santa Cruz River, Arizona. In *The Archaeology of the San Xavier Bridge Site (AZ BB:13:14), Tucson Basin, Southern Arizona*, edited by J. C. Ravesloot, pp. 39–60. Archaeological Series No. 171. Arizona State Museum, University of Arizona, Tucson.

1988   The Impact of Fluvial Processes and Landscape Evolution on Archaeological Sites and Settlement Patterns along the San Xavier Reach of the Santa Cruz River, Arizona. *Geoarchaeology* 3:205–219.

1989   The Influence of Quarternary Landscape Processes on Hohokam Settlement Patterning in Southern Arizona. In *Hohokam Archaeology along Phase B of the Tucson Aqueduct Project*, Vol. 1: *Syntheses and Interpretations*, edited by J. S. Czaplicki and J. C. Ravesloot, pp. 79–130. Archaeological Series No. 178. Arizona State Museum, University of Arizona, Tucson.

Weaver, Donald E., Jr.
1988   Faunal Studies. In *Hohokam Settlement along the Slopes of the Picacho Mountains, Tucson Aqueduct Project,* Vol. 5: *Environment and*

Subsistence, edited by D. E. Weaver, Jr., pp. 236–269. Research Paper No. 35. Museum of Northern Arizona, Flagstaff.

Whalen, Norman M.
1971   *Cochise Culture Sites in the Central San Pedro Drainage, Arizona.* Unpublished Ph.D. dissertation, Department of Anthropology, University of Arizona, Tucson.

Wheat, Joe Ben
1955   *Mogollon Culture Prior to A.D. 1000.* Memoir No. 10, Society for American Archaeology, and Memoir No. 82, American Anthropological Association, Menasha.

Whiting, Alfred E.
1939   *Ethnobotany of the Hopi.* Bulletin No. 15. Museum of Northern Arizona, Flagstaff.

Whittlesey, Stephanie M.
1986a   The Ceramic Assemblage. In *The 1985 Excavations at the Hodges Site, Pima County, Arizona*, edited by R. W. Layhe, pp. 61–126. Archaeological Series No. 170. Arizona State Museum, University of Arizona, Tucson.

1986b   Restorable and Partial Vessels. In *Archaeological Investigations at AZ U:14:75 (ASM), a Turn-of-the-Century Pima Homestead*, edited by R. W. Layhe, pp. 74–102. Archaeological Series No. 172. Arizona State Museum, University of Arizona, Tucson.

1987a   Ceramics from AZ BB:9:53, the Pima Canyon Site. Ms. on file, Coronado National Forest, Tucson.

1987b   Plain and Red Ware Ceramics. In *The Archaeology of the San Xavier Bridge Site (AZ BB:13:14), Tucson Basin, Southern Arizona*, Parts 1–2, edited by J. C. Ravesloot, pp. 181–204. Archaeological Series No. 171. Arizona State Museum, University of Arizona, Tucson.

1987c   Problems of Ceramic Production and Exchange: An Overview. In *The Archaeology of the San Xavier Bridge Site (AZ BB:13:14), Tucson Basin, Southern Arizona*, Parts 1–2, edited by J. C. Ravesloot, pp. 99–116. Archaeological Series No. 171. Arizona State Museum, University of Arizona, Tucson.

1987d   A Stylistic Study of Tanque Verde Red-on-Brown Pottery. In *The Archaeology of the San Xavier Bridge Site (AZ BB:13:14), Tucson*

Basin, Southern Arizona, Parts 1–2, edited by J. C. Ravesloot, pp. 117–147. Archaeological Series No. 171. Arizona State Museum, University of Arizona, Tucson.

1988   Variability in Tanque Verde Red-on-Brown. In *Recent Research on Tucson Basin Prehistory: Proceedings of the Second Tucson Basin Conference*, edited by W. H. Doelle and P. R. Fish, pp. 373–385. Anthropological Papers No. 10. Institute for American Research, Tucson.

1989   A Study of Design on Colonial Period Pottery. In *Hohokam Archaeology along Phase B of the Tucson Aqueduct Central Arizona Project*, Vol. 1: *Syntheses and Interpretations*, edited by J. S. Czaplicki and J. C. Ravesloot, pp. 375–416. Archaeological Series No. 178. Arizona State Museum, University of Arizona, Tucson.

1991   Ceramic Analysis. In *The Lower Verde Archaeological Project: Laboratory Manual*, edited by C. J. Ellick and S. M. Whittlesey, pp. 9–23. Statistical Research, Tucson. Ms. submitted to the USDI, Bureau of Reclamation, Arizona Projects Office, Phoenix, Contract No. 1425-2-CS-32-01870.

1994   Ceramics. In *The Roosevelt Rural Sites Study*, Vol. 2: *Prehistoric Settlements in the Tonto Basin*, edited by R. S. Ciolek-Torrello, S. D. Shelly, and S. Benaron, pp. 377–469. Technical Series No. 28. Statistical Research, Tucson.

1995   Mogollon, Hohokam, and O'otam: Rethinking the Early Formative Period in Southern Arizona. *Kiva* 60:465–480.

1997   Native American Ceramics. In *Pit House, Presidio, and Privy: 1,400 Years of Archaeology and History on Block 180, Tucson, Arizona*, edited by R. Ciolek-Torrello and M. T. Swanson, pp. 421–467. Technical Series No. 63. Statistical Research, Tucson.

1998a   Ceramics. In *Early Farmers of the Sonoran Desert: Archaeological Investigations at the Houghton Road Site, Tucson, Arizona*, edited by R. Ciolek-Torrello, pp. 127–167. Technical Series No. 72. Statistical Research, Tucson.

1998b   Early Formative Stage Ceramics and Cultural Affiliation. In *Early Farmers of the Sonoran Desert: Archaeological Investigations at the Houghton Road Site, Tucson, Arizona*, edited by R. Ciolek-Torrello, pp. 209–228. Technical Series No. 72. Statistical Research, Tucson.

1998c Toward a Unified Theory of Ceramic Production and Distribution: Examples from the Central Arizona Deserts. In *Overview, Synthesis, and Conclusions*, edited by S. M. Whittlesey, R. Ciolek-Torrello, and J. H. Altschul, pp. 417–446. Vanishing River: Landscapes and Lives of the Lower Verde Valley: The Lower Verde Archaeological Project. SRI Press, Tucson.

Whittlesey, Stephanie M., and Richard Ciolek-Torrello
1996 The Archaic-Formative Transition in the Tucson Basin. In *Early Formative Adaptations in the Southern Southwest*, edited by B. J. Roth, pp. 49–64. Prehistory Press, Madison.

Whittlesey, Stephanie M., Richard S. Ciolek-Torrello, and Matthew A. Sterner
1994 *Southern Arizona, the Last 12,000 Years: A Cultural-Historic Overview for the Western Army National Guard Aviation Training Site.* Technical Series No. 48. Statistical Research, Tucson.

Whittlesey, Stephanie M., and Karen G. Harry
1990 *Sabino Canyon Survey.* Statistical Research, Tucson. Report submitted to Coronado National Forest, Sabino Canyon Archaeological Plan, Contract No. 40-8197-0-0302.

Whittlesey, Stephanie M., Robert A. Heckman, William L. Deaver, Matthew A. Sterner, Matthew C. Bischoff, and Joshua Protas
1998 *The Badger Hole Ranch Site (AZ AA:12:40 [ASM]), Pima County, Arizona: Results of Additional Archaeological Testing and a Plan of Work for Data Recovery.* Technical Report No. 98-25. Statistical Research, Tucson.

Williams, Jack
1986 The Presidio of Santa Cruz de Terrenate: A Forgotten Fortress of Southern Arizona. *The Smoke Signal* 47–48:129–148.

1988 Fortress Tucson: Architecture and the Art of War (1775–1856). *The Smoke Signal* 49–50:168–188.

1991 *Architecture and Defense on the Military Frontier of Arizona, 1752–1856.* Unpublished Ph.D. dissertation, Department of Anthropology, University of Arizona, Tucson.

Wilcox, David R.
1979 The Hohokam Regional System. In *An Archaeological Test of Sites in the Gila Butte–Santan Region, South-Central Arizona*, edited by G. Rice, D. Wilcox, K. Rafferty, and J. Schoenwetter, pp. 77–116. Technical Paper No. 3, Anthropological Research Papers No. 18. Department of Anthropology, Arizona State University, Tempe.

Wilcox, David R., Thomas R. McGuire, and Charles Sternberg
1981 *Snaketown Revisited: A Partial Cultural Resource Survey, Analysis of Site Structure, and an Ethnohistoric Study of the Proposed Hohokam-Pima National Monument.* Archaeological Series No. 155. Arizona State Museum, University of Arizona, Tucson.

Wilcox, David R., and Charles Sternberg
1983 *Hohokam Ballcourts and Their Interpretation.* Archaeological Series No. 160. Arizona State Museum, University of Arizona, Tucson.

Wills, Wirt H., III
1988 *Early Prehistoric Agriculture in the American Southwest.* School of American Research Press, Santa Fe.

1992 Plant Cultivation and the Evolution of Risk-Prone Economies in the Prehistoric American Southwest. In *Transitions to Agriculture in Prehistory*, edited by A. B. Gebauer and T. D. Price, pp. 153–176. Monographs in World Archaeology No. 4. Prehistory Press, Madison.

Wilson, Eldred D., Richard T. Moore, and Robert T. O'Hare
1960 *Geologic Map of Pima and Santa Cruz Counties, Arizona.* Bureau of Mines, University of Arizona, Tucson.

Woodward, Arthur
1931 *The Grewe Site.* Occasional Papers of the Los Angeles County Museum No. 1. Museum of Natural History, Science, and Art, Los Angeles.

Wright, Barton A., and Rex E. Gerald
1950 The Zanardelli Site: Arizona BB:13:12. *The Kiva* 16(3):8–15.

Young, D., and D. B. Bamforth
1990 On the Macroscopic Identification of Used Flakes. *American Antiquity* 55:403–408.